THE DARTNELL SALES PROMOTION HANDBOOK

DARTNELL is a publisher serving the world of business with books, manuals, newsletters and bulletins, and training materials for executives, managers, supervisors, salespeople, financial officials, personnel executives, and office employees. Dartnell also produces management and sales training videos and audiocassettes, publishes many useful business forms, and many of its materials and films are available in languages other than English. Dartnell, established in 1917, serves the world's business community. For details, catalogs, and product information, write to:

THE DARTNELL CORPORATION,
4660 N Ravenswood Ave,
Chicago, IL 60640-4595, U.S.A.
or phone (800) 621-5463, in U.S. and Canada.

Dartnell Training Limited
125 High Holborn
London, England
WC1V 6QA
or phone 011-44-071-404-1585

Other Dartnell Handbooks:
Advertising Manager's Handbook
Direct Mail and Mail Order Handbook
Marketing Manager's Handbook
Office Administration Handbook
Personnel Administration Handbook
Public Relations Handbook
Sales Manager's Handbook

The Dartnell Sales Promotion Handbook

Tamara Brezen Block
William A. Robinson
Editors

Eighth Edition

FIRST EDITION—APRIL 1950
Second Printing—January 1951
SECOND EDITION—January 1953
Second Printing—January 1954
Third Printing—April 1955
Fourth Printing (Revised)—April 1957
THIRD EDITION—SEPTEMBER 1960
Second Printing—January 1962
FOURTH EDITION—MAY 1964
Second Printing—June 1965
FIFTH EDITION—OCTOBER 1966
Second Printing—March 1969
SIXTH EDITION—JANUARY 1973
SEVENTH EDITION—FEBRUARY 1979
Second Printing—July 1982
EIGHTH EDITION—APRIL 1994

3 2280 00703 9985

ISBN 0-85013-212-6

Printed in the United States of America by the Dartnell Press,
Chicago, IL, 60640-4595

CONTENTS

FOREWORD

More than 50 years have passed since Dartnell published its first comprehensive report on sales promotion. That report, which summarized most of what was known about the topic at the time, was fewer than 30 pages in length. Back then, sales promotion was in its infancy and primarily concerned with printed materials — sales letters, advertisements, posters, banners, and blotters. How times have changed!

Unknown back then, but of critical importance today, are such things as: coupons, rebates, continuity programs, contests, sweepstakes, incentives, price packs, premiums, samples, point-of-purchase advertising, events marketing — you name it! Sales promotion has come into its own, and the end isn't even in sight. To date, the sales promotion industry has spawned scores of cottage industries, created thousands of jobs, and has become one of the main elements of the marketing communications mix.

Our simple 30-page report, too, has undergone profound change and has grown to nearly 1,000 pages. From a simple beginning, the *Sales Promotion Handbook*, as it is now titled, has undergone several revisions, expanding to keep up with the ever-expanding role that sales promotion has commanded in the marketplace. It has become an important and integral member of Dartnell's series of management handbooks and is an important reference book for every marketer's shelf.

This volume constitutes the eighth revision, yet since the last edition published in 1979, sales promotion has changed probably more than it had in the previous 50 years. The roles, issues, regulations, evaluation, and understanding of sales promotion have grown dramatically. The management of sales promotion has become increasingly sophisticated and complicated. The need for a Handbook on the topic is perhaps greater than ever before for anyone involved in the planning, implementation, and analysis of sales promotion programs.

We have intended this Handbook to be a comprehensive, yet always practical, guide to what is known about sales promotion and how it's used — offering information that can guide both the experienced and the inexperienced sales promotion user. While the book cannot possibly address every question with respect to every industry, we have attempted to incorporate examples that go beyond the typical packaged-goods approach, and have included strategy chapters for durables, business-to-business, services, and even food retailing. The fact is, regardless of the many industries or audiences to which sales promotion is applied, the techniques that constitute sales promotion today are wide-ranging enough to find application in almost any situation.

Perhaps the single most differentiating factor about this new edition is that every chapter is written by an expert working in the field of sales promotion. This makes the material all the more tangible and relevant for its readers. It is what makes this Handbook more exciting than ever before and a "must-have" for every sales promotion manager or marketer. Hundreds of real examples and case histories are included throughout, often accompanied by pictures and exhibits to bring promotion to life.

We have organized the Handbook into four separate parts. **Part I. Planning** begins with a chapter that gives a complete overview of the field, followed by three important promotion planning chapters to guide in setting objectives, determining promotion budgets, and evaluating the effectiveness of a promotion. **Part II. Techniques** details the many varied techniques or areas that typically fall within the banner of sales promotion. The lines of distinction between sales promotion, direct marketing, public relations, personal selling, advertising, and marketing as a whole are becoming increasingly blurred in this new age of "integrated" communications. Therefore, chapters describing the more traditional sales promotion techniques, such as sampling and sweepstakes, are joined by chapters covering such areas as co-op advertising, event marketing, database management, and corporate sales meetings and sales training. These chapters are intended to give the reader the basics for each area, as well as insights into how to best implement the tactics. Each chapter in **Part III. Strategies** takes the perspective of a different industry, applying and relating the various techniques to the goals and strategies of that particular field. While some chapters are broader than others in their scope, it is our belief that the general principles of specific industries — the quick-service restaurant category, for example — can be applied and used by all service marketers despite the differences. Finally, included in **Part IV. Issues** of the Handbook is an assortment of chapters addressing important issues and topics not covered elsewhere, but too important to ignore. From promotion's effect on brand equity to promotion law to the impact technology is having on sales promotion, many of these topics are so important that they continue to evolve and change — even as we go to press. That is the nature of this field.

Most would probably agree that the change experienced in sales promotion over the last decade has been positive. As the field continues to ripen and mature, the future definitely promises to be bright and exciting. And, while we may not know for certain the pace and heights to which it will soar, sales promotion, in all its various forms, is here to stay and will continue to play an ever-important and ever-growing role in the marketing arena.

ACKNOWLEDGMENTS

We would like to thank and acknowledge each of the authors who contributed their time, knowledge, and experience for this book. It is rare that one finds so much expertise and talent within the pages of just one book. It is this which will make this book an indispensable addition to the promotion literature.

Thank you.

ABOUT THE EDITORS

Tamara Brezen Block is president of Block Research, Inc., a research firm providing a full range of quantitative and qualitative research services, including sales promotion analysis. She teaches graduate level research methods and sales promotion courses, among others, as a faculty member of the Medill School of Journalism's Integrated Marketing Communications Program at Northwestern University. Before joining the faculty at Northwestern, Block was an instructor in the Advertising Department at Michigan State University and a Visiting Professor at Foote, Cone, and Belding in Chicago.

In addition to coediting this Handbook, Block is coauthor of *Business-to-Business Market Research* (Probus). She has been published in several academic journals on topics related to advertising and promotion effects.

Block received a Ph.D. in Mass Media from Michigan State University. Her dissertation on the topic of sales promotion received a national award from the Council of Sales Promotion Agencies. Her Master of Arts degree and Bachelor of Arts, both in Advertising, were also completed at Michigan State.

William A. Robinson is regarded as one of the longtime leaders in sales promotion, first as the founder of the William A. Robinson Agency more than 30 years ago, and now as a principal of Robinson and Maites. Over the years, his clients have included Diner's Club, United Airlines (for which he worked on the very first frequent flyer program), and other major packaged goods companies, such as Tropicana, and business-to-business companies.

Robinson has taught graduate and undergraduate courses in sales promotion at Northwestern, Michigan State, and Florida State universities. He is currently teaching a course at the Institute of Advanced Advertising Studies for the American Association of Advertising Agencies.

Robinson is a member of the Council of Sales Promotion Agencies Hall of Fame and has been honored as Chicago's Sales Promotion Executive of the Year; is past president of the Sales Promotion Executives' Association, Chicago; serves on the board of directors for the Arthritis Foundation; is a member of the Council of Sales Promotion Agencies and the Promotion Marketing Association of America; and was nominated by *Gallagher Reports* as Outstanding Sales Promotion Agency Executive of 1988.

Robinson is a widely published author in the sales promotion industry. His columns and articles have appeared regularly in *Advertising Age, Sales Promotion Monitor, Potentials in Marketing*, and other major trade publications. His books include: *Robinson's Best Sales Promotions, 6th edition* (Crain Books); *Sales Promotion Management with Don Schultz* (Crain/NTC); *Sales Promotion Essentials with Don Schultz* (Crain/NTC); and *Promotional Marketing Ideas & Techniques for Success in Sales Promotion* (NTC).

ERRATA

The following information was omitted from this edition of the *Sales Promotion Handbook*. The Dartnell Corporation regrets these omissions.

CHAPTER 3, PAGE 30

Martin Block is a Full Professor in the Integrated Marketing Communications Division of the Medill School at Northwestern University, teaching marketing research, sales promotion, advertising, and direct marketing courses. Joining the faculty in 1985, he was previously Director of the Graduate Advertising Division within Medill. He is President of Block Telecommunications, Inc., actively engaging in marketing and research consulting for a variety of clients, such as Ameritech, Amoco, Kraft, and IBM. He specializes in sales promotion scanner analysis and telecommunications and new technology research.

Block was a Professor and Chairperson of the Department of Advertising at Michigan State University before moving to Northwestern. He has also served as Senior Market Analyst in Corporate Planning at the Goodyear Tire and Rubber Company.

Block is coauthor of Analyzing Sales Promotion, *which is now in its second edition. He has published extensively in academic research journals and trade publications, and has written several book chapters.*

He holds a Ph.D. in mass media from Michigan State University.

CHAPTER 8, PAGE 128

Don Jagoda is President and Founder of Don Jagoda Associates, Inc., which he has headed for more than 30 years. As one of the nation's foremost promotion and marketing organizations, specializing in planning and administering promotions, tie-ins, sweepstakes, games, contests, merchandise and travel incentives, and premium programs, his company may well have given away more money and prizes than any other!

PART I
PLANNING

Kerry Smith is the editor and publisher of PROMO, the International Magazine for Promotion Marketing. PROMO *circulates in 11 countries and is the only U.S. publication dedicated exclusively to coverage of the promotion industry. Prior to co-founding* PROMO *in 1987 with son Kerry J. Smith, he operated Smith Communications, Inc., a New York-based advertising and public relations agency specializing in business-to-business marketing services for a roster of clients including Abbott Laboratories, Citibank, Donnelley Marketing, and US West.*

Smith has also worked as a newspaper reporter, publicist, magazine editor, advertising agency account supervisor, media relations director, and public television executive in New York, Chicago, and Detroit.

He is a Navy veteran, a graduate of New York University, and he attended John Marshall Law School.

CHAPTER 1

INTRODUCTION AND OVERVIEW

PROMOTION COMES OF AGE

The rise of sales promotion from the minors to the major league of marketing disciplines over the past 10 years is one of the most significant business developments to have taken place since the 1950s, when advertising to mass national audiences by television and national magazines became the dominant form of consumer goods marketing in the United States.

Today, promotion marketing, as it is called, is the mainstay of a $60 billion national industry. Some 300 agencies, nearly that many service companies, and thousands of corporate marketing, brand, product, and promotion managers across the country are engaged in it full time. Promotion, which now accounts for two of every three dollars expended for the marketing of broad-based consumer products in the United States, has indeed come of age.

The explosive growth of promotion is by no means confined to English-speaking countries, either. In addition to the U.S., Canada, the United Kingdom, Australia, and New Zealand, promotion is an integral and growing part of the marketing mix for goods and services in countries as culturally and economically diverse as France, Germany, Spain, Italy, and Greece, not to mention Israel, Mexico, Brazil, India, Japan, Singapore, and even Russia.

WHAT IS A PROMOTION?

Strictly speaking, a promotion is the use of a price-off or value-added offer or incentive for the purpose of influencing purchasing behavior. Promotion marketing is the systematic use of such incentives to achieve specific sales and marketing objectives. Promotion works best in concert with, but differs from, conventional advertising in the sense that its goal is not to create a perception or polish an image, but to get the consumer to do what the marketer wants.

Promotional devices range from money-saving coupons and rebates in price-off programs to premiums, prizes, and product samples in valued-added campaigns. A promotional offer can be communicated through advertisement in conventional media, such as magazines, newspapers, radio, and TV, but it is more commonly delivered through alternative media, such as newspaper inserts, co-op and solo direct mail, point-of-purchase displays, or on the outside or inside of the package itself. Promotion differs from advertising, too, in that the promotional device — for example, a coupon or rebate — can serve as its own response mechanism and can be traced back or used to "track" actual sales.

ACTION VS. IMAGE

"Action marketing," as one agency calls promotion, has become a worldwide phenomenon, not because general advertising doesn't work but because it no longer works by itself. Gone are the days, for example, when a "roadblock" of commercials on three TV networks on a Sunday night could, as it did well into the 1980s, so pervasively deliver a brand message that retail sales would begin to rise almost immediately across the country. Today the prospect of a TV commercial doing that without some form of promotional assistance is exceedingly remote.

One reason is the continuous proliferation of brands and line extensions. Some 25,000 are introduced each year, making it difficult even for an outstanding advertisement to cut through the clutter and register an impression with consumers. Another is the high cost of making the impression often enough, and reaching audiences large enough, to have a measurable effect on sales. A prime-time network TV commercial, for example, now reaches 27 percent fewer households but costs 14 percent more to buy than it did 10 years ago (Television Advertising Bureau, July 1993).

Another reason is that consumers have come to appreciate, even to expect, promotions for many of the products they buy. If shoppers weren't so thoroughly "hooked" on using coupons to save money at supermarkets, the number of money-saving offers would not continue to set new records year after year. Likewise, the annual production volumes and expenditures would not have continued to rise these past few years for every type of incentive device available.

ACCOUNTABILITY

If promotion marketing is growing faster and commands a greater share of today's marketing dollar than general advertising, it is because of its built-in accountability as well as its appeal to bargain-conscious consumers. Compare the cost of a TV commercial during the Super Bowl, for example, to that of a newspaper-delivered insert for the same product featuring a money-saving coupon.

For about $850,000 (the average 1993 rate), the Super Bowl commercial will deliver to 37 million households a 30-second brand message which, a day or two afterward, may or may not be remembered as well as the winning play in America's most spectacular football game. It will be anyone's guess, of course, whether a post-game sales increase, should one occur, can be associated with, let alone be directly attributed to, the commercial. Why? Because there is no way of measuring, with any degree of certainty, the effect of a TV spot or a magazine or newspaper ad, on actual sales.

For roughly half that amount, however, at a page rate of $7.50 per thousand, a newspaper-delivered insert will reach 55 million households with a four-color, full-page advertisement and a coupon whose performance will certainly increase sales — those sales directly attrib-

4

utable and precisely measurable afterward in terms of coupons redeemed and cases of product sold. The degree of certainty is due to the fact that the defining characteristic of any promotion — the incentive — both motivates behavior and, through the tracking and counting of responses, enables the marketer to promote and "keep score" on the promotion at the same time.

TRADE LEVERAGE

The effectiveness of a consumer promotion is enhanced by advertising, but it is magnified when a price-off or value-added incentive is acted upon by wholesalers, distributors, and retailers who are vital links in any product's distribution chain. Neither conventional advertising nor direct marketing techniques are particularly effective at reaching these audiences, which have become extremely forceful about what will or won't happen at the retail level.

The practice of offering price allowances or "deals" to get retailers to buy, stock up on, advertise, and display featured products — an activity that can make or break a multi-million-dollar marketing effort — has undergone spectacular growth in recent years. Today half of every dollar spent on the marketing of packaged goods, according to NCH Promotional Services, goes toward the trade, with 24 cents allocated to media and 26 cents to consumer activity.

BRAND EQUITY

Those who denigrate the exchange of corporate funds for trade support as a form of bribery or an attempt to "buy" sales and market share at the expense of brand equity overlook an important point: In an overcrowded retail environment, the product that can be made to stand out physically as well as figuratively is the one the consumer will reach for. Brand presence — on the shelf, in a display, at the point of purchase — is as essential an element to the concept of brand equity today as brand image ever was.

Add the fact that two-career households leave American families with even less time for absorbing the messages bombarding them through all manner of media, and you get an idea of what mainstream advertising is up against. In short, the development and protection of brand equity has become too important for marketers to regard it as the exclusive preserve of advertising or any other single element of the marketing mix.

PROMOTION'S ROLE

The use of promotion will grow as marketers continue to realize that brand awareness and recognition by themselves are no longer enough, that effective advertising combined with incentives — for consumers to try, buy, and keep on buying, as well as for retailers to stock, advertise, and promote the sale of branded products — are what it takes to move the sales needle in the 1990s.

THE ORIGINS OF PROMOTION

As a marketing technique, promotion has been around as long as advertising. The prize at the bottom of the Cracker Jack box, for example, has sold tons of caramelized popcorn for that company's owners for more than 75 years. Donnelley Marketing was distributing Ivory Soap door-to-door for Procter & Gamble in the 1920s. Bubble gum makers have been packing trading cards with their product at the very least since World War II. And children were saving their Wheaties box tops to send in for Captain Midnight decoder rings more than half a century ago.

The difference between then and now is that we call such premium offers, trial generators, pantry loaders, and continuity programs "promotional techniques" and apply them to a vast array of products.

Until the 1970s, promotion practitioners regarded their work more as a sideline to advertising than as an industry unto itself. That was when service and supplier companies began to grow, and opportunities opened up for people who could combine consumer marketing expertise with a working knowledge of such things as product sampling, retail merchandising, point-of-purchase advertising, premium sourcing and fulfillment, direct marketing, audiovisual production, and specialty printing.

Seeing this, a number of brand, product, and promotion managers left corporate life to start their own promotion marketing agencies. Among the pioneers were Ralph A. Glendinning, founder in 1959 of Glendinning Associates, based in Westport, Connecticut. A few years later came the so-called "Chicago School" of promotion, with namesake agencies founded by Bud Frankel (Frankel & Company, 1962), William A. Robinson (now Robinson & Maites, founded in 1991), and Lee Flaherty (Flair Communications, founded in 1964).

In the 1970s a number of service companies, including Comart Aniforms (now Comart/KLP) in New York, Einson Freeman in New Jersey, and Connecticut Consulting Group/Ted Colangelo Associates (now Clarion Communications, a unit of D'Arcy, Masius, Benton & Bowles) set a trend by offering client companies strategic consultation as well as program execution.

Suddenly these and other companies that had been slide houses, display makers, direct marketers, and field service contractors found themselves acting as full-service promotion agencies. Without calling it that, of course, they were offering corporate marketers their considerable expertise in the business of behavior modification.

WHAT PROMOTION ISN'T

Despite its emergence as a marketing discipline, many different notions persist as to what promotion really is. In Hollywood, for example, the term refers to movie publicity; in broadcasting, it means on-air plugs for TV and radio programs; in the auto industry, promotion is still what they call sales literature and dealership display materials. Ad agencies continue to confuse it with the procurement of "trinkets and trash," or premiums and ad specialties. Worst of all is the Wall Street label of "promoter" as someone who profits by buying, driving up the price, and then bailing out of cheap or worthless stock before others can do the same.

WHAT PROMOTION IS

Practitioners view promotion marketing as a discipline because the offer-response-reward sequence can take place over time, and it comprises a wide variety of techniques. The essential characteristics of a promotion are (1) the creative concept or offer, (2) the vehicle or system for delivering it, and (3) the fulfillment of the reward promised in the concept or offer.

Contrasted with advertising, where the "creative" concept is the communication of an idea or image, the creative concept in promotion is the idea or proposition that gets the consumer to act. The concept of promotion as a behavioral rather than a communications medium was stated succinctly in an ad for Donnelley Marketing's co-op coupon program that ran in *Advertising Age* several years ago. "Advertising May Change Her Mind," the ad declared, "But Carol Wright Will Change Her Behavior."

The "creative" concept in a continuity program for a brand of barbecue charcoal, for example, could be the offer, over time and perhaps on a self-liquidating basis, of a cook's apron, a chef's hat, a mitt, and several outdoor cooking utensils in return for a specific number of purchases. While the theme and look of the campaign would carry through in ads, coupons, display materials, and merchandise, the "promotion creative" concept would be neither the message nor the image projected, but the proposition for participants to acquire the ensemble by behaving in a certain way, that is, buying and continuing to buy the charcoal.

A number of delivery systems — direct-mail co-op, newspaper insert, point-of-purchase display, in-store coupon, in-pack flyer — would be suitable for such a promotion. The choice would depend primarily on the availability of funds, of course, but also on the likelihood of a successful response based on what is known about the brand's usage profile, buyer demographics, market share, and the potential for meaningful trade support in the territory to be covered.

The truly effective promotion generally aims at one, sometimes two, clearly defined specific brand objectives. To name a few:

- the generation of new product trial and repurchase;
- the protection of market share in the face of a competitive threat;
- brand purchase continuity over a period of time;
- "pantry loading," or the temporary removal of users from the marketplace;
- a build-up of consumer traffic at retail;
- an increase in trade support at a critical time period or season.

Promotion marketers draw from an arsenal of devices. They include money-saving coupons and cash rebates awarded at or shortly after the purchase event, as well as *prospective* rewards in the form of cash, vacation travel, hotel accommodations, and free merchandise or premiums for participation in promotion-sponsored programs.

Promotions are communicated in various media, from television, radio, and magazine advertising to inserts delivered through co-op direct mail and newspapers; from shelf-talkers, shopping-cart ads, and live in-store demonstrations to couponing and product sampling on street corners, at state fairs, in doctors' and dentists' offices, at special events, and at commuter railroad stations.

Some devices are more appropriate than others for promoting the sales of certain products. Factory rebates are used by the auto industry, for example, to maintain corporate control over pricing as national advertising drives people into dealerships. Frequent flyer programs encourage airline passengers to stick with a few carriers rather than switch from one to another as freely as they once did. Quick-service restaurants offer premiums, sponsor children's clubs, and issue coupons to build traffic and keep customers coming back. Point-of-purchase displays are favored by alcoholic beverage marketers to encourage trade support and consumer take-away. Packaged goods manufacturers use all of these devices to sell products and influence the trade.

PACKAGED GOODS

Packaged goods manufacturers are the nation's biggest and busiest promoters, spending an estimated $60 billion a year on virtually every available type of promotion and marketing service. The makers and sellers of food, beverage, household, personal care products, and health and beauty aids are continuously engaged in a variety of activities to get consumers to choose their brands over others' brands at thousands of supermarkets, mass merchandisers, and drug, discount, and warehouse clubs across the country.

According to *Donnelley Marketing's 15th Annual Survey of Promotional Practices*, packaged goods manufacturers spent 73.1 percent of their budgets on trade and consumer promotion in 1992 and 26.9 percent on media advertising, compared with 73.4 percent in 1991 and 71.8 percent in 1990. Trade promotion expenditures accounted for 46.7 percent, and consumer promotions for 25.1 percent in 1990.

Fortune 500 manufacturers, such as Procter & Gamble, Kraft General Foods, Quaker Oats, Beatrice, Pillsbury, Ralston Purina, and others, are the biggest and busiest promoters in the marketplace because Americans spend more money on the hundreds of high-volume, fast-turn branded products they produce — $630.9 billion a year compared to $600.9 billion for shelter, $85.4 billion for automobiles, and $305.3 billion for travel and recreation — than on all other categories of consumer goods.

VALUE VS. PRICE

In packaged goods particularly, brands and line extensions have proliferated while few really "new" products have come to market in recent years. The effects of this are intense competition among the major players for "slots," or shelf space allotments in retail stores, along with a growing perception among many consumers that most products are pretty much the same. Therefore, brand names and product claims are of diminishing importance, leading many consumers to the conclusion that there's nothing much to lose by buying whatever brand is "on deal," including store brands or private label products.

The conventional solution to this problem, until a few years ago, was to get the manufacturer to "heavy up" on advertising on the premise that truly outstanding "creative," leveraged by lots of media frequency, would generate impressions strong and lasting enough to get consumers not only to recall but also to seek out and insist on the brand advertised. It's a terrific concept in an ideal world, but the fact is — except for high-tech/high-ticket items such as automobiles, boats, consumer electronics, and sports equipment — the concepts of brand image, brand equity, and brand loyalty mean less to consumers today than ever before.

There are two reasons why consumers no longer rely on logos, slogans, jingles, clever ad copy, startling photos, or catch phrases, such as "Lucky Strike Means Fine Tobacco," as symbols of quality or reflections of discriminating taste. The one reason, already discussed, is that there are too many brands, too many messages, too many media, and too little time for any advertisement to make much of a difference in peoples' purchasing behaviors. The other reason is that since most products are pretty much the same — it takes a certain level of quality just to make it to the marketplace — it therefore doesn't much matter what brand one buys as long as the price is right.

PRICE PROMOTIONS

Thus was born the price promotion, for which there are no better examples than those presented by the soft-drink industry. Consumers today are widely aware that cola drinks are pretty much alike, that if Pepsi Cola is on sale this week, Coca-Cola will very likely be discounted next week in the same stores and with the same kind of end-aisle displays. They are aware of this and they know that the manufacturers, distributors, bottlers, and retailers of the leading brands know they know it. The trade, moreover, is aware that hard-core category users wait to buy whatever is "on deal" from week to week, and that brand-loyal users routinely stock up on enough Coke or Pepsi when one or the other is on sale to tide them over to the next promotion.

If cherry-picking and forward-buying, as these practices are known, clearly run counter to the purpose of any promotion, which they do, then why do manufacturers, distributors, bottlers, and retailers continue to price-promote? The answer is that they can't afford not to, and therein lies a dilemma. Manufacturers discount their brands in a never-ending series of promotion cycles, not because the practice works for anyone but the consumer, but because nobody can afford to quit. The positive view is to consider the ongoing discount the price of maintaining brand share in a highly competitive category. But price is not the only option, as we shall see.

PRICE PROMOTION: ORIGINS

The use of price promotions as consumer purchase incentives on selected merchandise goes back to the early days of retailing. But the practice of offering manufacturer-sponsored discounts on national brands began in earnest during the years immediately following World War II and through the 1960s and early 1970s. That was when the suburbanization of America, the proliferation of supermarkets and drugstores, their consolidation into multistore chains, and the development of systems for delivering and redeeming cents-off coupons nationwide took place.

The first coupon programs were organized by retailers on an individual store basis, then later by store chains, using run-of-press, or ROP, coupons published once a week on "best food days" in local newspapers. In the early years retailers looked at the costs of advertising and couponing as burdens they had to bear in order to build store traffic. But over time they began to ask for and receive reimbursement by participating manufacturers, first for ROP newspaper ad "features" and then for coupon face values, a practice that continues to this day.

In time, however, as national brands were strengthened by mass-media advertising, manufacturers decided that they, not the retailers, should determine when, where, and how their brands would be price-promoted. Soon they were using couponing vehicles that included national magazines, Sunday supplements, and co-op inserts delivered through newspapers and direct mail. Over a 10-year period the use of these media would explode, spawning what today is a $1.5 billion-dollar industry.

Couponing, in the final analysis, has become the standard form of price promotion in the United States because in different but important ways it serves the needs of consumers, retailers, and manufacturers. As an offensive or defensive brand-marketing device, a coupon is "stealthy" in the sense that by the time the competition realizes its presence, it has already begun to do its work.

HIGH–LOW PRICING

Then, as now, the basic reason for a manufacturer to price-promote was the knowledge that a cents-off coupon could stimulate incremental sales for the product featured, and redemption rates of 15 to 20 percent were not uncommon in the mid-1970s. But as of 1974, there was an additional reason: price control. On that date, President Richard

M. Nixon, in an attempt to put a damper on runaway inflation, imposed a nationwide moratorium on wages and prices. Cents-off coupons suddenly had a dual purpose. One was to reward the consumer; the other was to protect the manufacturer.

The wage-price freeze expired in 90 days, but the packaged goods industry had learned an important lesson. Never again would it be caught with its prices down. To make sure, manufacturers would thereafter sell to retailers on the basis of one price, against which consumer and trade incentives could be applied to reduce what was actually paid. Thus, while it might be illegal during a freeze to raise or lower the price of an item, theoretically its cost could be "adjusted" legally by the simple device of a cents-off coupon or a case-off allowance to the trade.

The theory has never been legally tested, but industry observers trace to this one event the origin of so-called "high–low" pricing, as well as the many abuses that have been attributed to it, which have prevailed for the nearly two decades that have passed since it took place.

THE TRADE REVOLUTION

The 1980s marked the proliferation not only of manufacturer-sponsored couponing and rebate activities but also of a profusion of so-called "flanker" brands and line extensions whose purpose, more often than not, was as much to add to or hold onto market share by occupying retail shelf space as to increase overall sales volumes. Added to this was the need to generate short-term sales gains in order to pay off huge amounts of highly leveraged debt taken on during the many corporate consolidations that were taking place. Thus was the stage set for an enormous increase in price-promotion activity.

For the supermarket industry, it couldn't have come at a worse time. It, too, had come through a period of consolidation in the aftermath of which the survivors were up to their ears in debt and desperate for new sources of revenue to pay it off. Reacting to the abuse, whether real or perceived, of their "territory" by so many nonperforming brands as well as the heavy-handedness of manufacturer pricing and promotion practices, supermarketers began to adopt policies and practices that would put them at odds with their suppliers.

Among these policies and practices were "slotting" fees for stocking new items, the use of trade allowances and "billbacks" or off-invoice charges for ad features and merchandising support not actually given, and the forward loading and improper diversion of product offered at special prices by manufacturers in return for trade support in designated markets and time periods. By 1990 a number of supermarket chains could boast that they had in their employ a new breed of executive: one whose sole function was to forward-buy "on deal" and divert the goods to other retailers for maximum profit. More often than not, he or she was an MBA with little or no experience in grocery retailing.

TRADE PROMOTIONS

Today, so-called trade promotions or deals account for 50 cents of every dollar spent on packaged goods marketing, according to *Donnelley Marketing's 15th Annual Survey of Promotional Practices.* That amounts to some $120 billion a year.

Today the typical trade deal consists of an allowance to the retailer of, say, $3 per case, in return for which the latter agrees to purchase a certain amount of product and provide a certain amount of merchandising in the form of end-aisle displays as well as "features," or mentions in its store circulars and best-food-day newspaper ads of a predetermined size.

The problem, however, is one of verification and control. Manufacturers complain privately that because there is no really effective way of checking up on them, many merchants simply take the money and run. More than one promotion manager has wryly observed that if all the merchandising that is promised "on deals" were actually performed, there probably wouldn't be room enough in supermarkets for products, let alone product displays. Yet manufacturers are reluctant to complain because among the nonperformers are some of their "best customers."

"VALUE PRICING"

Manufacturers' own sales forces either wittingly or unwittingly become partners in the crime of retailer nonperformance for two reasons: the brand manager system, which encourages short-term sales "bumps" to show profitable performance from one quarter to the next, and the system's resultant emphasis on generating sales volume vs. profitability.

Some companies, Campbell Soup among them, have attempted to deal with the problem by decentralizing promotions and giving regional sales offices profit-loss responsibility, encouraging them to become business managers and use what are called market development funds to work with key accounts. Others — notably Procter & Gamble, originator of the brand manager system of marketing and now America's second-largest (after Kraft General Foods) packaged goods manufacturer — are moving away from promotions altogether. In late 1991, Procter & Gamble let it be known that it was moving toward a policy of "value pricing," which, with no small irony due to its retail origins, others in the packaged goods industry have dubbed Every Day Low Pricing, or EDLP.

EDLP, however, is better described as EDLC, with the *C* standing for cost. It is a program for eliminating retailer practices that manufacturers find objectionable — namely, forward-buying, product diversion, and excessive dependence on cents-off couponing. Procter & Gamble announced in November 1991 that 40 percent of its brands sold in the United States had been given over to EDLC, following reports several weeks earlier that it had cut back on couponing by some 70 percent.

Retailers at first vehemently opposed Procter's "value-pricing" concept, but several large chains (notably Kroger, but also Wakefern, Shop-Rite, and Pathmark) have since found some favor in it. The object is to offer the trade each of its products at a single low price with no allowance for advertising or merchandising support, and to eliminate couponing altogether. The idea is to treat all retailers and classes of trade alike, encouraging them to pass the savings on to consumers in the form of more competitive prices.

Retailers long accustomed to wheeling and dealing, who had over the years learned to live with "the deal," were surprised to find that the policy put them on level ground with *their* worst enemies, those "Other Classes of Trade," or mass merchandisers, discount drug and grocery chains, and the growing number of "club" stores competing for the sale of packaged goods.

THE PIPELINE

In the 1990s and beyond, having an impact on the trade as well as the consumer — that is, on supermarket managers, new-car dealers, airline travel agents, beverage bottlers and distributors, and fast-food franchisees, as well as all the people who buy from them — is what effective marketing will be all about. Why? Because the trade has something that is important to the marketer: information about and access to the retail customer base. Since manufacturers can no longer count on media leverage to "pull" customers in, they will increasingly have to rely on "pushing" products through the distribution pipeline by incentivizing those along the way.

Promotion, of all the disciplines, is uniquely suited to this task because, while advertising and direct mail aim at the consumer, promotions can be tailored to provide incentives and motivate every link in the chain, from broker to wholesaler to distributor to buyer to store manager ... right on down to the individual sales clerk.

THE BUSINESS OF INCENTIVES

That's why the incentive industry is large and growing, now at $17.7 billion a year, up 10 percent over five years. Cash and merchandise prizes, vacation trips, bonus plans, and the like constitute a multibillion-dollar industry the consumer never sees. Yet it makes promotions go.

Ironically, however, the concept has not yet fully adapted to the retail grocery trade, where the corporate bottom line rules. A peculiarity of the grocery business is that there are no real "franchisees" or dealers within a company, as there are in the auto industry. Nor are there agents, as in the airline industry. Similar to the grocery business in this respect is the fast-food industry, where buying is under central control. The challenge in these industries is to motivate the individual within the ground rules of the organization.

TARGETED PROMOTIONS

Meanwhile, there is a lot of "targeting" going on with price promotions. The growth of targeted delivery systems — co-op, direct mail, free-standing inserts (FSI), and so on — was related to the demassification and fragmentation of conventional advertising media. But until recently, even these systems were really mass media themselves.

Now, with all kinds of competition coming up — ways of targeting Carol Wright, ways of taking only sections of a national FSI and filling in with Carol Wright, Jane Tucker, or some type of more effective, more easily localized, and thus more targetable medium like Val-Pak or National Suburban Newspapers — the brand or promotion manager can target effectively on a geo-demographic basis.

Also, new systems, based on consumer surveys, such as CMT's Behavior Bank, Donnelley Marketing's Share Force, or Datacap, bring recent purchasing behavior into play. So with the combination of geo-demographic, behavioral, and lifestyle selectivity, targetability is gradually coming to nationwide price promotions.

A recent development — albeit still in a formative stage — is the prospect of promoting packaged goods using so-called database marketing techniques. What this amounts to is the manufacturer, or an outside service company, using various methods to build a file of users, nonusers, heavy users, and prospects, and with sophisticated modeling, targeting, and selective inserting techniques, reaching an individual consumer household with an offer tailored specifically to its purchasing behavior.

All of the above are price promotions. Take them away from the $60 billion total and you have value-added promotions. These are the purview of the promotion marketing agency.

THE AGENCY ROLE

A full-service, major promotion marketing agency is able to provide its clients with a variety of services that fall into three categories: consulting, execution, and sourcing.

Today there are about 350 companies calling themselves promotion agencies, of which about 50 have consulting divisions organized as profit centers. These tend to be two- to five-person shops that may or may not be connected with, or doing themselves, the executional part of the campaigns they put together.

Those that can execute are often hired on a project basis, which most full-service promotion agencies view as severely limiting their ability to serve as "partners" for achieving long-term objectives. There is a trend away from this toward retainer fees, but the majority of client companies prefer to work on a fee basis because of the short-term nature of their promotion objectives.

In promotion, as in advertising and direct response, it is the agencies that develop the concept, which is the truly creative aspect of a campaign. The promotion agency's role, however, is unlike that of an ad agency in two important ways. One is that the client often chooses to run the execution, for example, buying the free-standing insert, which is noncommissionable, or the in-store program, which is hiring and working with other outside vendors, suppliers, and services. The other is that there is no uniform or "standard" practice for charging clients — a consequence of which is, in general, a long-standing lack of mutual confidence or understanding on the part of promotion agencies and clients.

Compared with an advertising agency, where the standard form of compensation is a 15 percent commission on media purchased, a promotion agency may charge a production markup, a media commission, a retainer fee, or a combination of all three. Some even agree to be remunerated out of the results (for example, a sales increase) of their efforts — a concept unheard of, and most assuredly frowned upon, by Madison Avenue.

This is changing, however, with the diversification of small to medium-size companies calling themselves marketing communications agencies. No strangers to the concept of integrated marketing services, they offer a variety of capabilities that range from general advertising to promotion to direct-response marketing, sometimes calling themselves "behavioral marketers" for their emphasis on results.

How do direct marketing agencies fit in with this? The direct marketing industry has been on its heels these past few years due to huge increases in bulk postal rates imposed between 1988 and 1990. That and the proliferation (some call it clutter) of catalogs, flyers, and other forms of third-class mail have reduced direct mail's efficiency and its cost-effectiveness for all but the highest margin products and services in recent years.

Direct mail by itself is not a promotion system but a tool. But there is nothing new about this. Donnelley Marketing's Carol Wright division thought of itself as a direct marketing vehicle long before promotion marketing was considered a marketing discipline or strategy. The major limitation of direct marketing is that, like general advertising, it impacts the consumer but none of the other links in the distribution chain. Direct marketing techniques can be adapted for use with trade factors, of course, and there will be more of this as direct marketers master the realities and limitations of marketing high-volume, low-margin products.

The role of the full-service promotion agency will change as more middle-size general agencies get into promotion, and as more promotion agencies get into advertising. By and large, however, a major national brand will for some time continue to have its general advertising done by one major "image" agency and its promotion done by one or more smaller firms.

PROMOTION MARKETING SERVICES

Because sales promotion is so diversified, there are many promotion marketing services that are often included under this label. *PROMO's* annual spending breakdown for 1992 is shown in Table 1.1. More detailed explanations of what each of the categories shown encompasses can be found in Appendix 1.

There are also several professional and trade associations that serve this industry. For convenience, an alphabetical listing of these associations can be found in Appendix 2. Each organization is accompanied by its mission statement and current address, phone, and fax information, along with the name of the key association contact.

Finally there are several awards programs for the industry offered by various associations. Appendix 3 details these awards for anyone who is interested.

GLOBAL OUTLOOK

Those who travel to Europe are frequently impressed by the remarkable transformation of post-war Europe into a robust, free-market economy and its growing prosperity. From previously authoritarian and centralized governments with strict controls over commerce and media, European countries have embraced capitalism and deregulated to laissez-faire capitalism. As a result of this, there has been an explosion of consumer products and manufacturer brands over the past 20 years.

TABLE 1.1

PROMOTION MARKETING SERVICES	1992 EXPENDITURES
Premium Incentives	$17.7 billion
P-O-P Advertising	15.7 billion
Couponing	7.03 billion
Specialty Advertising	5.2 billion
Promotion Licensing	4.4 billion
Special Events	3.2 billion
Specialty Printing	2.4 billion
Promotion Fulfillment	2.2 billion
Promotion Agencies	950 million
Promotion Measurement	728 million
Product Sampling	176 million
In-Store Advertising	117 million
Merchandising Services	238 million
Telepromotions	435 million

Source: *PROMO™ Industry Survey*

The result has been a parallel explosion in advertising and a prolif-eration of media for carrying it: magazines, newspapers, satellite TV — not to mention the growth of advertising and promotion agencies. Indeed, there is a newfound realization on the part of European companies, including those previously behind the Iron Curtain, that they have to establish brand identities and motivate people to buy consumer products.

But because until recently audiences were never really "mass," and because media in France, Germany, and the U.K. were previously under strict government control, there never really developed a "mass" mentality on the part of European marketers or their agencies in the sense of TV commercials and media buyers dominating advertising, or price-off deals and FSIs dominating promotions.

Consequently, promotion, package design, publicity, and adver-tising developed at a more uniform pace, and in many agencies, they are more thoroughly integrated, as in the case of many small- to medi-um-size agencies in the United States.

Thus the European agency typically is more versatile and less biased in favor of one particular discipline or another, such as advertis-ing over promotion or public relations — or of one *medium* over another, such as FSIs over direct mail, or TV over print, for solving marketing problems.

For these reasons, promotion agencies and their clients overseas are inclined to use value-added vs. price-off incentives. Typically they take the form of awards or vouchers in the form of merchandise, cash, dream vacations, nights on the town, and so forth. In many ways, not only because there is less emphasis on "mass" but also because of gov-ernment restrictions on certain activities — coupons are outlawed in Germany, for example — overseas promotions tend to be more value-added and thus more "creative" than those in the United States.

PROMOTION IN THE FUTURE

Where is promotion headed? In the future, companies in the U.S. will see less emphasis on price promotions — couponing and trade deals — and more emphasis on value-added programs. Client compa-nies will demand more "creative" — that is, more value-added — solutions to their marketing problems.

Meanwhile, as the clutter of increasing coupon volume continues to reduce cost-effectiveness (coupon redemption now averages about 1.8 percent for FSIs), targeted programs will gain favor over "mass" price promotions based on price.

As a consequence, there will be more reliance on agencies — large, experienced, and versatile promotion agencies as well as medi-um-size shops — that succeed in learning not only how promotion works, but also how to make money at it. Agencies have some barriers to overcome, of course, such as battles over executive "turf" and com-pensation problems. But they can be and are being overcome in the case of many major agencies.

On the client side, the de-emphasis of retail price-related programs, such as couponing and rebates, will gradually give way to imaginative but effective promotions that are able to blend with advertising to build brand franchise and achieve short-term promotional objectives.

The major obstacle in the minds of some observers is the brand management system and the 18-month mentality that goes along with it. To make promotion decisions that tie in with the brand strategy takes someone who would rather achieve the same modest sales bump that an FSI brought last November than take a chance that something might go wrong with an otherwise potentially terrific new value-added promotion idea. The Renaissance man or woman who emerges in the future will need to be someone who knows how to orchestrate and manage the company's agencies — promotion, advertising, design, and publicity — using tools, such as direct marketing and advertising, to achieve long- and short-term brand objectives.

Joseph Flanagan is President and CEO of IMPACT, the full-service sales promotion agency he began building 17 years ago. Headquartered in Chicago, IMPACT is one of the top five sales promotion firms in the United States, with a staff of over 85 promotion professionals. In addition, Flanagan is corporate director of sales promotion services for Foote, Cone, & Belding Communications, IMPACT's parent company. In this role he is responsible for coordinating the sharing of expertise among FCB offices, acting as FCB spokesman to the sales promotion industry, and developing FCB's growth plans for sales promotion worldwide.

Flanagan was named Sales Promotion Professional of the Year in 1989 by the Council of Sales Promotion Agencies. He was president of CSPA from 1986 to 1988. Prior to joining FCB, Flanagan was Vice President and Director of Client Services for BBD&O, General Manager of the Center for Advanced Research in Design, and District Manager for TIME magazine.

He has a bachelor's degree in history from Michigan State University, where he also received an honorary degree in 1991, and an MBA from the University of Chicago.

CHAPTER 2

SETTING SALES PROMOTION OBJECTIVES

The linchpin of all promotional marketing efforts is the sales promotion objective. This chapter will examine its place in the marketing plan, what a sales promotion objective really is, what it can and cannot help to accomplish, how to prepare for developing it, and finally how to craft meaningful objectives.

Sales promotion objectives are rooted in the marketing plan. The development of sales promotion objectives and strategies is an important ingredient in a strategic marketing plan. A marketing plan is essentially a road map, guiding the way to properly achieve the volume, share, and profit goals for the product. Any marketing plan worth its salt will include the means for understanding the brand's overall marketing goals with respect to brand spending, advertising, pricing, and promotion.

Another way of looking at it is, marketing plans establish a "who, what, where, when, and how" for the brand: Who you are (and whom you serve), what you offer them, where you are today (and where you want to be tomorrow), and when and how you get from here to there. It is in the realm of the "when and how" that sales promotion plays such an important role.

After the overall goals of the marketing plan are set, both short and long term, it is time to pay attention to the specific sales promotion objectives. It is in the basic nature of marketing plans to start big and become more focused as the plans go from the general to the specific. In this sense, sales promotion objectives are the most acute of all the marketing plan elements.

Sales promotion objectives are pointed, measurable statements that guide and support specific sales velocity and frequency goals for the brand. Simply put, sales promotion objectives are the desired achievements for sales action. But before we look at how sales promotion objectives are assigned or what they say, it is important to examine what sales promotion can and cannot achieve in the first place.

WHAT CAN BE EXPECTED FROM SALES PROMOTION?

We certainly know that sales promotion has no place in Newtonian physics. For while every action has an equal and opposite reaction in the real world, the world of sales promotion is far less pat. There are just so many things promotion can do. What promotion does, it does well — but its role is very specific. Sales promotion can accomplish the following:

1. It can cause a consumer who is unfamiliar with a product to try

it. This applies whether the product is new to the consumer or the consumer is new to the product.

2. It can keep current users loyal to the product and convince them to use even more of it. Loyalty is simply any brand's biggest reward; and promotion can and does intensify it.

3. It can encourage consumers to buy more of the product. This, of course, is significant as both an offensive and defensive marketing tool.

4. It can build on, strengthen, or reinforce the advertising message. This is one of the classic uses of promotion, and today savvy promotion people are learning to get even more mileage out of merchandising the brand image.

5. It can generate trade support. Promotional activity is proof positive to the trade that a brand is going somewhere.

6. It can supercharge a sales force. There is no better way to freshen a salesperson's perspective than to give him or her a promotion to work with.

Sales promotion cannot accomplish the following:

1. It cannot overturn a negative perception of a product. It's just like the saying for advertising: a consumer will try something once, but if the product doesn't live up to its promise, it's all over.

2. It cannot turn around a product in decline. Similarly, sales promotion just can't revive a brand that's in its death throes. Nothing can.

3. It cannot create a brand image. By its very nature, sales promotion is a short-term, in–out plan of action. Image building requires a long-term plan. And that's that.

4. A single promotion cannot motivate a consumer to purchase a product over an extended period of time. It's the rare product that can thrive long term on a single burst of sales support. Go ahead. Try to think of one that has.

PREPARING THE SALES PROMOTION PLAN

The most comprehensive way in which a marketing professional might look at setting sales promotion objectives, and then strategies, is to skillfully analyze all the aspects that will affect the product's success. This may seem somewhat broad in its definition. But in today's world, sales promotion is becoming so widely used that even something as remote as the quality of the raw material used to make the product's package may control the success or failure of a sales promotion program. This is an extreme example, but it makes the point. Consider for instance, time-dated products. If better packaging materials are purchased, they may facilitate lengthening the product's end purchase date and thereby accommodate a promotion tactic that otherwise couldn't be used, such as pantry loading.

BE AWARE OF PROMOTIONAL POWER

The late 1980s and early 1990s have been times in which the world has experienced a global recession. Not all businesses have been negatively affected, but they certainly have been affected enough to result in the short-term mentality of getting sales as quickly as possible as the modus operandi. From top management to middle management, meeting sales objectives is of utmost importance. CEOs need marketing tools that generate sales fast to create jobs and sometimes to save their own.

At the next level, the chief financial officer had better not make a mistake in estimating quarterly earnings per share, or the financial community will punish the stock. The marketing director needs sales today in order to keep the distribution system healthy; and the brand manager views the fast return that sales promotion can deliver as a viable springboard for career advancement.

The quick-result nature of sales promotion feeds the corporate fire. On the flip side, the mind-set of today's consumers is "instant gratification isn't fast enough." Sales promotion fuels this appetite, too.

The point to be made is that even as the economy turns around, corporations and consumers have been so acclimatized to the benefits of sales promotion that it will never again revert to its position as a secondary marketing tool. Unless, of course, it is used that way. But the alert marketing pro will recognize the power of a promotional plan versus a single-burst promotion. In any event, sales promotion has had an addictive effect on the manufacturer, as well as on the consumer.

CONSIDER THE "BIG THREE" TARGETS

Here is another dimension to consider. Sales promotion affects not only the consumer but also the trade distribution and sales force. Generally speaking, brand-image advertising affects only the consumer, which in today's marketing world is like trying to win a triathalon with one arm tied behind your back. Attention must be paid to the trade and the sales force as well.

Each of the three big targets can also have somewhat different objectives. Traditional consumer objectives, for example, might be to (1) reach new customers, (2) hold current customers, (3) load the pantry or build consumer inventories, (4) increase product usage, (5) trade consumers up to larger sizes or more expensive lines, (6) introduce a new product, or (7) reinforce other franchise-building activity such as advertising. Traditional trade objectives might be to (1) gain distribution or shelf space, (2) build retail or store inventories, (3) secure trade support for merchandising activity such as displays and feature advertising, and (4) launch a new product. Sales force objectives might include (1) boosting morale and productivity and (2) prioritizing the sales effort.

The proper use of sales promotion to produce the desired actions by the consumer, trade, and sales force is a powerful marketing tool. If focused objectives and strategies are established up front to get these three audiences moving in the right direction, the program will be a winner. That's the good news. The bad news is that the next program will have to do better next quarter or next year. Success begets success.

FOCUS ON THE BIG PICTURE

Up to this point we have addressed the emerging importance of sales promotion as a key marketing tool and how a variety of business conditions will have an effect on its success. It is because of these issues that the proper planning of a sales promotion campaign is rooted in clearly stated and well-documented objectives and strategies.

The planning process to properly set sales promotion objectives and strategies is a line management activity centered on getting the right people, resources, and information together in order to make decisions.

Before the sales promotion planning process even begins, marketers should challenge themselves to raise their sights, to look beyond the obvious. Here are several tips for thinking about the "Big Picture":

- Question the value and need to have sales promotion as part of the marketing program. Is that where the brand is going? Is it in keeping with current momentum? Is the brand in big demand?
- Look for the largest context and audience for sales promotion. As things stand now, who is the brand reaching successfully? Who has been left out? How badly does the company want to "convert" them? How easy can it be?
- Seek contributions from other specialists who may bring new thinking to the process. What does the advertising director say that the advertising strategy doesn't? What vision does the production person have? Take the research director to lunch.
- Commit to an action orientation. Remember that advertising means image and awareness. Promotion means action. If it's going to be done, do it right.
- Center the success of a sales promotion program around end users — the consumers, the trade, and the sales force. Consider them to be like a three-legged stool. Each is pivotal to the success of the whole.
- Accept that accountability and end results will be the final judgment. Numbers don't lie, but they do educate. Whether or not a promotion is a success on paper, it will be easy to know where to go from here. And soon.

If this type of "objectivity" can be addressed up front, the planning process to reach the most rewarding company sales promotion objectives and strategies will not be filled with management bias.

GET THE KEY FACTS TOGETHER

Even though there are a number of steps in the sales promotion objectives and strategic planning process, the lines between each step are blurred. When one step is complete, the next one doesn't automatically start up. In fact, if the successive tasks were charted, they would appear to be a matrix of overlapping lines.

For this reason, the sales promotion planning process should be viewed as an ongoing one, with decision points that are deadline driven.

Here are the steps that will help get the key facts together and keep one's sights focused:

Analyze the Customer:
- This activity should include identifying the customer (consumer, trade, sales force) and how this customer audience is prioritized based on the current situation.
- This is also the point to determine how the buying decisions are made and what the customer needs are, and in what order.

Analyze the Market:
- Determine the market potential for the brand (short, mid and long term for a sense of direction) and gain an understanding of what is achievable now and later. Being realistic is important.
- Examine the structure of the market and determine what regional differences may exist. Are they exploitable? Should the focus be regional rather than national?
- Explore the breadth and scope of the market in terms of its segmentation and what differences may influence sales promotion objectives and strategies. Are buying patterns universal? Are there any demographic shifts or considerations?

Analyze the Competition:
- Identify the key competitors and understand what and why they are doing what they are doing. Look at types of promotion, time frames, and other elements. Now's the time to get the sales force to play supersleuth.
- Assess the strengths and weaknesses of the competition. How does the company's brand measure up to the competition? Be realistic. Better still, be critical.
- From this understanding planners will then be able to set objectives and strategies that attack the competition, as well as understand their cost structure.

Analyze Past Sales Promotion Programs:
- Determine the program's strengths and weaknesses. Don't forget, no promotion, no matter how flawless in design, ever meets every single expectation. If a program was 60 percent successful, it may still be viable.
- Assess the results and determine if the expectations were realistically set in the first place. Here again, give the brand the

benefit of the doubt. Even if a promotion was a dismal failure, never say never again.

Examine the Distribution System:
- Identify the priorities at the three key levels of consumer, trade, and sales force. Then try hard to meet them.

Determine if Testing Is Necessary:
- Talk to the research people. Look at test market viability for now and later. Maybe what is needed is a promotion plan that "holds its own" while the company regroups and tests bigger issues.

Determine Budget Levels to Achieve Desired Results:
- Establish realistic expectations for all three levels. Don't underestimate production and media needs. If these budgets will be small, take another look at the marketing plan.

Determine the Fit with the Overall Marketing Plan:
- Above all else, make doubly certain the plan is in sync with the overall direction of the brand. It is a lot easier to harm the brand than help it.

After this information has been prepared, organized, and understood, the sales promotion objectives can then be prepared. The sales promotion objectives also need to be considered in the context of other elements of the marketing communication mix.

SALES PROMOTION AND MARKETING COMMUNICATION

There is a variety of factors that influence the amount of relative spending on consumer promotion. There is a variety of factors that are associated with more or less spending in promotion. It is important to note that these factors represent a traditional view that sees consumer promotion as an activity that does not build the brand or the consumer franchise. This is simply not true. Much sales consumer promotion activity builds the brand and the consumer franchise. Consumer sales promotion does much more than merely stimulate short-term sales.

It is worthwhile to examine the traditional view briefly. Table 2.1 shows three categories of factors: consumer factors, brand factors, and category factors. Instances in which consumer promotion spending has been traditionally higher usually have resulted from high price sensitivity or elasticity and low brand loyalty. Promotion spending tends to be lower when there is less price sensitivity and stronger brand loyalty. Consumer promotion is also associated with products that require little information and have low perceived risk. It is interesting to note that this may be the opposite for trade promotion. Products with high risk and information needs generally require considerable trade support.

Brand factors associated with consumer promotion spending include the later stages in the product life cycle, particularly maturity and decline. Products in the growth stage are less associated with promotion spending. New products, however, require considerable

TABLE 2.1
**TRADITIONAL FACTORS GUIDING PROMOTION SPENDING
FOR A BRAND**

	Low Promotion	High Promotion
Consumer Factors		
Price sensitivity	Low	High
Brand loyalty	High	Low
Purchase planning	High	Low
Information needs	High	Low
Perceived risk	High	Low
Brand Factors		
Life-cycle stage	Growth	Maturity
Market position	Dominant	Competitive
Seasonal pattern	Uniform	Seasonal
Category Factors		
Product differentiation	Strong brands	Commodity
Private brands	Limited	Extensive

promotion support to get them established. Also, consumer promotion spending is associated with more competitive or lower share brands. Nevertheless, promotion spending is often a good way for a dominant or a high share brand to fend off competitive challenges from smaller brands.

Category factors play a role as well. Seasonal products need to use promotion to regain their position on the store shelf and in the consumer's mind when their selling season returns. Also, a category with high share private label or generic brands may require additional promotional support to maintain its position.

GETTING STARTED

Now that the planners are armed with the marketing facts, a sense of direction, and a laundry list of everyone's biases, the real fun begins — writing the promotion objectives.

Actually, writing objectives is a discipline that gets easier with practice. And like the proverbial skill of riding a bicycle, there are sure to be a few skinned knees along the way. But once a marketer learns to master the logic of it, it will only enhance the brand's performance, if not the marketer's career.

What Promotion Objectives Are. As we saw earlier, sales promotion objectives are the desired achievements for sales action. For all the drama and mystery of what they mean, they are quite simple. In fact, there are very few things the writer actually needs to remember about them.

Sales promotion objectives are simple, concise, and crystal clear. They are not a mission statement; they do not have subsets, subtexts, or sidebars. They are a bare-bones statement of what must be done.

Sales promotion objectives are action oriented. Sales promotional needs demand action. So the objective should be written that way. It should always, *always* lead to results.

Sales promotion objectives operate in a defined time frame, a very short one. Think in terms of weeks, not months. As a quick rule of thumb, a typical promotion takes from two to eight weeks from start-up to wind-down. The timetable behind the objectives should reflect this.

Here are some examples of sales promotion objectives that work:

- Generate a 5 percent increase in sales during the Jan. 1–Feb. 15 launch.
- Create awareness and trial of the new product.
- Encourage multiple purchases prior to competitive relaunch.
- Increase display and ad features by 10 percent for July 4 sales blitz.
- Motivate the sales force to attain a 24 percent sell-in.

Notice that each of these examples is short and precise; they all demand action and include a keen sense of timing and urgency. Plus there is one other unifying element. Every sales promotion objective should ultimately be measurable. If the writers start out focused on accountability, chances are they will end up with a promotion that is accountable for itself.

Tips for Writing Objective Objectives. Finally, here are some well-founded pointers for writing sales promotion objectives that are realistic yet aggressive, accountable yet flexible.

1. **Use 10 words or less.** This exercise will help the writer stay as focused as the objective should be. Plus, the fewer words used, the less chance there will be for miscommunication, misdirection, or loopholes.

2. **To get action, use action verbs.** This may be a good time to dig out that eighth-grade grammar book. Words such as *create, attain, increase, motivate,* and *generate* have a sense of direction to them. There is no mistaking their meaning.

3. **Establish a time frame.** Don't let the promotion be accountable for anything that happens before or after it is supposed to take place. And be realistic about how long it can really keep its energy and momentum.

4. **Assign one objective per target segment.** Don't get carried away. A single consumer promotion cannot possibly create awareness, generate trial, increase multiple purchase occasions, and encourage repeat purchase. The more you ask for, the less you'll get. If one main objective is written for the consumer,

one for the trade, and one for the sales force, that in itself is a tall order.

5. **Write objectives with specific results in mind.** Each objective should always answer the question: "What should be accomplished as an end result of this promotion?" That is what a promotion objective is all about. It is then up to the promotion strategy to determine how to get it accomplished.

Tamara Brezen Block is President of Block Research, Inc., a research firm providing a full range of quantitative and qualitative research services, including sales promotion analysis. She teaches graduate level research methods and sales promotion courses, among others, as a faculty member of the Medill School of Journalism's Integrated Marketing Communications Program at Northwestern University. Prior to joining the faculty at Northwestern, Block was an instructor in the Advertising Deparment at Michigan State University and a Visiting Professor at Foote, Cone, & Belding in Chicago.

In addition to co-editing this Handbook, Block is co-author of a soon-to-be-published book on Business-to-Business Research. She has been published in several academic journals on topics related to advertising and promotion effects.

Block received a Ph.D. in Mass Media from Michigan State University. Her dissertation on the topic of sales promotion received a national award from the Council of Sales Promotion Agencies. Her Master of Arts degree and Bachelor of Arts, both in Advertising, were also completed at Michigan State.

CHAPTER 3

BUDGETING FOR PROMOTION

Preparing a budget or financial plan for a sales promotion program is fundamental to its successful management. Without a budget, a sales promotion program has no reference or guidelines with which to evaluate performance. Without a budget, there most likely is no way of determining if objectives or goals have been achieved. The issue is not whether a budget is necessary, but, rather, how to prepare one.

The budgeting process can be viewed from three different points. First, there is the decision of what the total marketing budget should be for a company, product line, or brand.

Second, this total budget must then be allocated among the various marketing communications elements, including advertising; public relations; personal selling; and sales promotion, as well as other marketing variables, such as packaging. Determining the proper mix is a strategic decision as much as anything, and while this mix will vary considerably from category to category, the mix for many packaged goods is tilting in favor of promotion, with approximately three out of every four dollars spent going to promotion relative to the more traditional advertising communications vehicles.

From an integrated marketing viewpoint, the distinctions among what is and is not advertising, direct marketing, public relations, promotion, and even personal selling are blurring, and the decision of what dollars to allocate to each element of the mix is theoretically no longer as critical.

The third budgeting point occurs at the level of deciding what monies are to be allocated to any given promotion. This chapter will focus primarily on this budget decision level, but the principles and methods apply to all three budget decision points.

The selection of a budgeting method for a sales promotion program depends, to a large degree, on the culture and personality of the marketing organization. The style of leadership, managerial and personnel sophistication, and a company's accountability standards are all reflected in an organization's corporate personality. For instance, some organizations may choose to do very little planning, whereas other companies may make detailed plans for years in advance. Those that plan too little risk being unable to effectively marshall their resources to meet the competitive demands of the marketplace. Those that plan too much perhaps risk losing the flexibility sometimes necessary to meet marketplace changes. In either case, the propensity to plan is part of the organization's culture and personality and affects the budgeting process.

The traditions of the product or service category are also influential in determining a marketer's method of budgeting. It is common to hear the assertion that people who do not work in a particular product category cannot understand it. The obvious implication from this is that whatever the product or service, it is unique from others. Ways of doing business, prior use of promotion and promotional tactics, and the reliance on advertising vs. personal selling all vary considerably by category. So, too, does the budgeting method used. The influence of these traditions, founded on years of historical managerial experience, cannot be underestimated.

The avalanche of sales data, particularly in supermarket packaged goods, is a relatively new force that is revolutionizing the way sales promotion is budgeted. Scanner data, as it is most often referred to, completely changes the way these programs are understood and managed. This allows for a more precise and analytical way to allocate and evaluate promotion dollars. Similar data are becoming available in more classes of trade (such as convenience stores and drugstores), and in more product categories (such as general merchandise). Although their number is decreasing, there still are product and service categories that do not enjoy this kind of data and are, as yet, unable to take full advantage of the budgeting methods that do depend on the data.

Sales Promotion Strategy. Developing a sales promotion strategy is the first step in determining a sales promotion budget. Sales promotion strategy consists of a simple, straightforward statement of which sales promotion tactics are being applied to what market segments in order to accomplish what market objectives. A sales promotion strategy should be part of a larger marketing communication strategy and should not be developed without the benefit of the larger plan.

It is important to distinguish between strategy and tactics. Sales promotion tactics generally specify the particular sales promotion vehicles to be used, including: coupons; bonus packs; sampling; premiums; contests and sweepstakes; continuity programs; and trade allowances. Concentrating on the promotion tactics and specific executions of those tactics without regard to any overall strategy is dangerous when planning sales promotion programs and budgets. Strategic thinking requires consideration of the various target markets and the objectives for those markets in conjunction with the sales promotion tactics. Too many sales promotion programs lack a solid, underlying strategy and, as a result, have accomplished little else than reducing profit for the marketer.

Integrating Promotion Strategy. Adopting the integrated marketing communication philosophy means that a sales promotion strategy and budget should not be developed apart from other marketing communication activities, such as advertising or public relations. Sales promotion should be considered and applied in the context of all marketing communication and planned along with other marketing communication activities.

Today, it is common industry practice to treat sales promotion as a separate and distinct area. It is also true that books like this one tend to compartmentalize their subject matter. Nevertheless, other communications efforts should not be ignored in the budgeting and planning process.

Critical to the development of any strategy is the specification of a measurable objective. Normally, in marketing, the objective is expressed in terms of sales volume or share of market. In the past, it has been difficult to use sales measures to evaluate marketing communication programs because of the potential influence of other noncommunication factors — the quality and nature of the product itself; the selling price; or the availability of the product in stores. Therefore, the tendency has been to develop pseudomeasures of performance (such as the familiar communication measures of awareness, preference, and recall) and to rely on survey research techniques to document and evaluate performance. Many promotional techniques have inherent response mechanisms that can be readily used to measure performance (i.e., coupon redemption numbers, sweepstakes entries, and participation in a continuity program). With scanner sales volume data available for some categories today, it is possible to relate promotion effects back to the marketing objectives of sales and market share.

Stand-On-Its-Own Principle. Sales promotion expenditures have sometimes been justified based on the belief that some future benefit will accrue. For instance, it might be argued that consumers who are attracted to a brand because of a promotion will try it, like it, and become loyal users of the brand in the future. Thus, promotional expense can be justified as an investment toward future business and franchise building. Alternatively, an argument could be made that business obtained today through a promotion will actually hurt at least short-term future business because consumers will stockpile promoted product, deferring future purchase. Rather than being a post-promotion bonus, it has been believed that what might actually happen is a post-promotion dip in sales.

The overwhelming weight of empirical evidence from scanner panel studies suggests that neither of these scenarios is the case. Most of the time, the post-promotion sales return to the same level they were at before the promotion. This has profound implications for the budgeting of promotional dollars. If there is no future gain or loss in sales, then the promotion must stand on its own. This means that promotional expenses, including any price reductions or discounts, should not exceed the additional marginal revenue generated by the promotion. Additional or incremental marginal revenue is that revenue increase attributable to the increased sales as a result of the promotion. Simply, this means that a promotion must generate enough increased sales volume to offset its cost. *The promotion must stand on its own and be*

33

profitable by itself. To run the promotion in any other manner would result in losing money.

Certainly, there may be exceptions to this principle. No doubt, there may be both product and service categories and promotional programs that may build business in the long term, but these are exceptions, which should be documented in the sales history. To assume that a promotion will have impact beyond the promotional period for budgetary purposes requires special documentation. The conservative position is to assume the promotional program stands on its own.

Budgeting Methods. There are two major categories of budgeting methods: guideline and analytical. A third method — the subjective method — might also be used, but is not considered here. This method relies entirely on the intuition and judgment of the manager. It is the most difficult method to discuss and explain, since it depends entirely on the experience and personality of the manager. While this method is not generally recommended, it is suggested that experience and judgment should always be part of the budgeting process. The "feel" of a budget and plan should never be overlooked.

As the name implies, the guideline methods all rely on a formula approach or a way to quantitatively approximate and apply past experience with the product category and brand. Guideline methods encourage doing business in the future in much the same way as it has been done in the past because future promotions are somehow based on what was spent before.

If maintaining marketplace stability is the goal, then the guideline methods are a good choice. The best way to think of the guideline methods is "business as usual." For instance, a dominant brand needs the support it always has had to maintain its position. A reduction in promotion spending might allow competitors the opportunity to catch up. However, when breaking away from the past is the goal, then the guideline methods may not be the best choice. A competitive brand may need considerably more spending to improve its market position than the guidelines may indicate.

Current practice places guideline methods as the most popular method, although the analytical, "fact-based" methods discussed later are gaining rapidly.

There are five primary guideline methods. These include: percent of sales; competitive parity; percent change; task method; and maximum allowable. Each of these will be described in turn.

1. **Percent of Sales.** Historical records will provide a manager with information on both past sales and promotional spending for a particular brand. The same information may also be available for the product category, although it is sometimes much more difficult to obtain. A simple ratio or percentage of spending relative to sales is calculated. This percentage is then applied to a forecasted sales level for the budgeting period to

determine how much money should be allocated based on those projected sales. An advertising-to-sales ratio has traditionally been used to budget for advertising as well.

If $5 million was spent on promotion that generated $100 million in sales, then the promotion ratio would be 5 percent. If the sales for the next budgetary period are forecast to be $120 million, then the promotion budget would be 5 percent of this, or $6 million.

One advantage of this method is that it is very straightforward and easy to apply. Only two things are necessary to employ this method — the historical ratio or percentage; and a forecast of sales. This makes the method easy to communicate to others. A form of this might be applied to allocating trade promotion monies, as when an allowance is set based on case volume — such as $1 off per case; or a free case with every 10 cases purchased. This method is also easily communicated to management. Because of its simplicity, it often serves as a reasonable check or reference, even when other methods of budgeting are employed.

The obvious limitation is that too much may be budgeted in good years and too little in bad years, since the percentage applied is based entirely on historical experience, which may or may not correspond to current marketplace conditions.

2. **Competitive Parity.** This method is an extension of the percent of sales method. The point of differentiation is that the spending ratio is based on what competitors are spending rather than on a brand's own past spending. The underlying assumption is that different brands have different promotion ratios, depending on their relative market positions, and that a brand ought to be in line with other brands in similar market positions.

If conventional wisdom is correct, this would imply that the dominant national brand depends heavily on advertising support, whereas the competitive regional brand depends, relatively speaking, on promotion. A dominant national brand — one with more than 40 percent market share — should therefore have a higher-than-average advertising ratio and an average promotion ratio; whereas a competitive regional brand — one with less than 10 percent share — should have a lower-than-average advertising ratio and a higher-than-average ratio of promotion spending.

The competitive parity method is essentially the same as percent of sales, but the promotion ratio is estimated in the context of marketplace position. From that perspective, this method represents an improvement over the percent of sales method. However, copying what the competition is doing does not take other differences between the brands into consideration, and encourages a "me-too" mentality that may hurt a brand.

3. **Percent Change.** This method requires knowledge of the last period's budget and a change percentage. If the budget is to be increased, then the percentage would be positive; if it is to remain the same, then the percent change would be zero; and if the budget is to be decreased, then the percentage would be negative. This is typically the way governmental agencies and universities budget. Budgets are increased or decreased depending on an arbitrary percent change and last year's budget. The task is then to determine the appropriate percent change figure for the upcoming budgeting period.

The advantage of applying this method is that adjustments can be made in the budget to reflect changes in the business environment. For instance, increases in the costs of doing business (such as media costs), or in inflation can be built in to keep the budget in current dollars. If the economic or competitive conditions have changed, this, too, can be reflected. The percent applied can be tied directly to a company's goals (i.e., a percent increase to correspond to a planned growth strategy).

A problem with this method is that it implies a budgetary inertia with the same activity continuing from year to year, making only slight inflation adjustments. Future spending is not tied to results such as sales or profit, but, rather, to prior spending. While this method of budgeting is easy to communicate down from top management, it is not tied to objectives or performance, and prior spending may not have been appropriate or optimal.

A reaction to this method of budgeting has been "zero-based" budgeting where a budget is freshly reestablished each time based on some performance criteria. While the idea of zero-based budgeting may be a good one, it is difficult and time-consuming. These same problems are discussed with the task method. For most marketers, selection of an analytical method would be a far better choice.

4. **Task Method.** The method most often cited as one of the best guideline budgeting methods is the task method. This method begins with the promotional objectives or "tasks" to be performed for the budgetary period. The budget is determined from costing out the expenditures necessary to accomplish that task. In other words, the budget is built around the cost of the executional tactics necessary to achieve the objective.

This method is much more sensitive to the current marketplace and the needs of the brand in question. However, it fails to recognize that there are limits to what can be allocated to any one brand, given the total resources of a company. In reality, there is usually a ceiling imposed by management, often using another guideline method.

Another difficulty with this method is that there are often many ways that an objective might be achieved. Each alternative tactical plan may have different resource requirements and associated costs. If all of the possible tactical methods could be compared for their effectiveness in accomplishing the goals, and the most efficient one selected, then this method of budgeting might be a good one. However, to do so would be time-consuming and arduous. Furthermore, comparison of the different methods is typically not systematically done. Where a particular promotional program has never been run, the experience and knowledge of what it realistically will accomplish is lacking. This leads to managers proposing and adopting strategies that have been run previously and have been shown to achieve the set objectives. It is this idea of doing "business as usual" and basing future budgets on the past that ultimately classifies this method of budgeting as a guideline method.

5. **Maximum Allowable.** Another guideline approach to budgeting is the maximum allowable, typically used by direct response and catalog marketers. The maximum allowable approach works especially well for nonpackaged goods items, such as durables and fashion-oriented soft goods. These product categories typically have a relatively high margin and are often viewed as relatively high-risk or high-involvement products.

This method calculates the "maximum allowable" budget for marketing expenses. The term "maximum allowable" simply refers to the difference between the selling price and the nonmarketing costs of the item. These costs are based on historical experience in selling the product.

Maximum allowables are generally computed on an individual product basis. If a product is sold for $50, costs $10 to manufacture or purchase from a supplier, and the marketer wishes to make a 20 percent gross profit, the maximum allowable per item becomes $30. This is computed by subtracting the $10 cost of goods and the $10 profit from the $50 sales revenue.

This means that up to $30 can be spent on marketing and promoting the product. This includes all marketing expenses, such as selling costs and media advertising, as well as sales promotion. By projecting out what the expected sales will be, the total budget can be estimated; however, the budget is usually referred to on a "per item sold" basis.

A variation on the maximum allowable method is the use of lifetime value. Lifetime value is a concept borrowed from catalog marketers that assumes that once a customer is acquired, he or she will continue to make purchases and potentially expand the allowable beyond that obtainable from just the one purchase. The idea is that making a customer acquisition involves some investment that will result in future returns.

The lifetime value concept is how a catalog marketer justifies the use of a premium to attract a new customer. The use of a premium with a first purchase may boost the cost past the maximum allowable for that purchase, but the catalog marketer believes, based on historical experience, that this customer is far more likely to purchase again. Catalog marketers estimate likelihood of purchase based on past purchase history — generally on the recency, frequency, and amount of prior purchases. In this respect, the lifetime value method relies on past sales history in the same way that other guideline methods do.

Assuming that the likelihood of future purchases can be statistically associated with past and current purchasing behavior, as it generally is in catalog direct marketing, then the lifetime value concept has some application. It may work in nonpackaged goods categories and some business-to-business categories. In packaged goods, however, the empirical evidence suggests that customers do not continue to make purchases based on their acquisition purchase experience. This is especially true of those customers acquired through promotion who are especially promotion sensitive. Their purchase is in response to the next promotion, not their supposed newly established loyalty.

Earlier in the chapter, the point was emphasized that promotions must stand on their own; that most likely there is no future benefit. This view is supported by the analysis of packaged goods purchases, and may not necessarily be true for all product categories. In retailer-dependent, high-risk, and high-involvement product categories, loyalty may be easier to establish and maintain, making the lifetime value concept viable.

Guideline methods all determine budgets by applying some historical average to projected sales or sales goals. In contrast, analytical methods all derive budgets by specifying functional mathematical relationships between a given set of promotional tactics and sales response. There is a model, based either on theory or empirical data, that describes how the market operates and the interrelationships among the various marketing and communications elements, including advertising, sales promotion, and price. This allows much more sophisticated budgeting than simpler guideline methods. The actual response to a promotion can be estimated over time, and the costs associated with it directly assessed and budgeted accordingly. The key to this kind of analysis is in understanding how the response to one type of promotion varies from, and/or interacts with, that of another.

1. **Theoretical Models.** Theoretical analytical methods have long been considered "black-box" techniques that only a select few

could really understand. In the absence of actual promotion response data, these methods have had to depend on theory and assumptions of how a promotion works, utilizing statistical models and probability theory to estimate response. This theoretical complexity has made this method of budgeting seem somewhat mystical. While analytical models, such as entropy-based brand switching models and microeconomic optimization models, have had some successful applications, their use has been relatively small compared to the far simpler guideline methods described earlier.

2. **Empirical Data-Based Method.** Having actual data, rather than relying on theory and assumption, is appealing. However, before the widespread availability of scanner sales data, data could be obtained only through self-report survey research, redemption numbers, and experimentation. Each of these has inherent problems relative to today's more accessible sales data.

Traditional survey research techniques do not work very well in documenting promotion response for several reasons. Since category usage is not known in advance, identifying product category users can be a very expensive process, especially in a product category that has a low level of usage. If, for example, only 10 percent of the population uses the product, approximately 10 interviews would have to be conducted to yield one user.

Additionally, survey research methods typically rely on self-reported behavior and human memory, which are often inaccurate. People cannot always remember the details of their purchase behavior (brand purchased; quantity; size; price paid; promotion used; etc.), and sometimes confuse past events. This is especially true with frequently purchased, low-priced items. If completed properly when the purchase or usage occurs, purchase or usage diaries can serve to reduce the memory problem, but cooperation often deteriorates and, in reality, diaries are frequently not completed simultaneously with behavior. Reporting errors, combined with incomplete reports, make this kind of data extremely difficult to analyze for promotion responsiveness.

Timing can be another problem with the traditional survey research methods of data collection. Promotional events almost always occur over short periods of time. For example, the duration of a typical supermarket promotion is one week. This means that the data must be collected over a very short period of time to capture accurate response, which is possible, but difficult, for most survey research suppliers. Adding the problem of competing stores within a market — that is, some stores running a promotion while others don't, or while others run a different promotion — makes isolating the effects of a particular promotion very difficult via questionnaire.

More reliable and accurate than survey research methods is response data collected via redemptions (i.e., coupon redemption). It is easy for a manufacturer or retailer to keep counts of the number of coupons distributed and redeemed and compute a redemption rate. Comparing redemption rates then would suggest that the higher the redemption, the better or more effective the promotional program. An advantage with this kind of empirical response data is that redemption can be associated with a particular coupon promotion distribution method (i.e., newspaper or direct mail coupons). However, redemption alone has some obvious problems.

Redemption, first of all, only applies to couponing and promotions where redemption is relevant. Perhaps more important, though, is that the program cannot be understood in terms of how it impacts sales before, during, and after the promotional event. Also, how this one promotional event relates to other marketing efforts (including advertising, displays, and other price promotions), as well as to competitive promotions, is also completely unknown.

Experimentation and actual sales tests can yield useful response information for any given promotion over whatever time frame is necessary. In general, experiments allow alternative promotional strategies or budget levels to be tested in separate markets, stores, or across time, and the results to be compared to see how response differed or changed.

The use of experimentation implies stringent control over all variables that may impact on the measurable results. Consequently, these differences can be attributed only to those promotional variables being tested, and not to the extraneous effects of differing store or market characteristics and conditions.

However, when experimenting in the real marketplace — as opposed to a laboratory — tight control or manipulation of all outside factors is not possible. Therefore, usually more than one store or market is used for each test condition in an attempt to average away, or statistically account for, uncontrollable differences and single out the effects of promotion independent of other marketing variables.

Experimental designs can become quite sophisticated and complicated in order to isolate the impact of the test variable. While such empirical studies can yield good information, they can also become costly and time-consuming to conduct across very many different test conditions (i.e., different promotional strategies). Unfortunately, only through continuous experimentation with many promotion variations will a manager begin to know the impact of a given technique on actual product sales in particular circumstances.

3. **Fact-Based Analysis — The New Analytical Method.** The availability of scanner data in packaged goods categories has improved the kind of data analysis that can be accomplished, and it has led to a new concept known as "fact-based marketing." Fact-based marketing implies making marketing and promotional decisions based on analysis of continuous sales and promotional data over time, alleviating the need to depend on theoretical models or inaccurate and incomplete sales estimates.

The origins of the fact-based approach lie in the scanner technology that made continuous data collection at the point of sale possible, as well as in the concept of single-source data. The single-source concept came from the notion of obtaining all relevant data (media exposure, promotional conditions and use, individual and household demographics, etc.) from one supplier using a single sample whereby these variables could easily be related to each another analytically. Until supermarket checkout scanner technology became available, recording sales in real time at the individual store level, single-source data was not a practical possibility.

Fact-based marketing begins with a thorough time or dynamic analysis of brand sales, usually aggregating sales to a weekly level to match grocery store promotion schedules, and dividing that weekly sales volume into two components — base volume and incremental volume. The term *base volume* refers to the business that would occur without any promotion. The *incremental volume* is the extra sales gained due to the promotion (i.e., special merchandising, feature advertising, displays, or special price reductions).

The base volume for a brand is usually quite stable over time, except for seasonality cycles that occur over longer time frames. Obviously, a brand's base volume is heavily dependent on the size of the product category, the development of the brand within the category, and its physical distribution or presence in retail stores. Factors that might affect a brand's base volume include changes in list pricing, distribution, and franchise-building activity, such as advertising. Competitive product entries and the presence of heavy competitive promotions also might be reflected in base volume shifts.

The incremental volume for a brand depends more on short-term tactical efforts, such as the level of promotional support and the mix of promotional tactics employed. The amount of incremental volume relative to base volume can vary according to the fundamental characteristic promotion response of the brand. Different product categories clearly have different responsiveness to promotion, but so do different brands within product categories. A brand's unique promotion responsiveness is crucial to its potential incremental volume.

Exhibit 3.1 shows 21 weeks of sales data for a beer promotion from a store chain in combination line and bar-chart form. The lines show the nonpromoted weekly sales volume. The line that appears to move up and down slightly is the actual sales in number of six-packs for this beer brand. It seems to be fairly stable, ranging from about 40 to 80 units per week. The straight line represents the statistical average of this nonpromoted volume at about 60 units per week. This is the brand's baseline, or the best estimate of how much would be sold if no promotion were used. The bars represent four weeks of an in-store promotion. In this case, $1 off the regular $3.99 price is offered, along with a special in-store product display. The bars show dramatic volume increases to over 500 units per week during the last two weeks of the promotion.

This example translates into a tenfold increase in volume attributable to this particular promotion. The incremental volume then becomes the volume directly attributable to the promotion, or the difference between the total volume and the estimated base volume. In this case, the incremental volume would be approximately nine times the base volume.

EXHIBIT 3.1

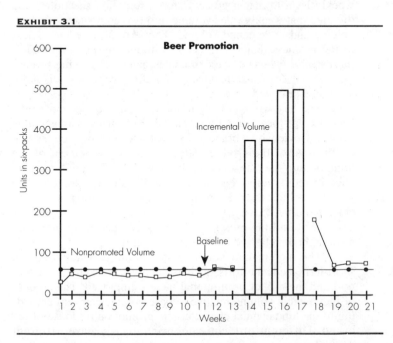

A volume increase is not the only consideration and, taken by itself, does not directly address the budget question. Converting the unit volume to margin, however, solves this problem. The central issue becomes whether the volume increase offsets the reduced margin and other promotional costs to generate as much gross profit, or total margin, as would have been obtained without the promotion.

This method of budgeting is sometimes associated by retailers with direct product profitability (DPP). In the example shown, the retailer's sales revenue is reduced on a per-unit basis from $3.99 to $2.99. The number of units sold must increase to offset the lost margin or else sales revenue will be less than what it would have been without the promotion. To be profitable, the incremental sales generated by the promotion should exceed the costs. If a trade allowance from the manufacturer was offered, this would reduce the costs associated with the lost margin and increase revenue. This is the situation in this example.

Continuing from the point of view of the retailer, the nonpromoted total dollar margin is typically about $40 per week (revenue less costs). When this promotion was run, the total dollar margin increased to over $140 per week, or 3.5 times the normal margin. Clearly, this was a very successful promotion.

This probably was a successful promotion from the point of view of the beer manufacturer, as well. The calculations work in a similar way. The increased revenue of goods sold to the retailer due to the incremental store sales volume undoubtedly offset the costs associated with whatever promotional monies were offered to the trade to generate the sales. By calculating the revenue, given normal margins at normal base-volume sales levels, and comparing this to the revenue generated by the increased demand at the appropriately reduced margin due to the trade allowance, the profitability of the promotion can be figured. Knowing approximately what the sales response for a $1 discount on the brand will be ahead of time, the revenue, cost, and profit calculations can help determine what promotions to offer and not offer by directly comparing profit. Spending promotional dollars is justified as long as the total margin or profit exceeds what would have been obtained had no promotion been run.

Strategic Response. Knowledge of a brand's base versus incremental volume over time with the fact-based marketing approach can aid in making larger marketing and promotion strategy decisions, as shown in Exhibit 3.2 and explained briefly in the following paragraphs.

EXHIBIT 3.2

	Base Volume Up	Base Volume Down
Incremental Volume Up	Sustain	Franchise-Building Program
Incremental Volume Down	Trade Promotion-Building Program	Major Overhaul

Totten/Block *Analyzing Sales Promotion.*

1. **Sustain.** The most favorable brand position in most packaged goods categories is where both base and incremental volume have been increasing. The best strategy in this situation is to continue the level of marketing and promotion programs that have led to this desirable position. Changing the mix and type of promotions and other communications efforts could affect one, or both, volume components, to the brand's detriment. However, sustaining the marketing and promotion strategy does not mean being complacent. Marketers enjoying this situation need to be especially vigilant of competitive activity.
2. **Build Franchise.** When the base volume is down and the incremental volume is up, it may mean that too much emphasis has been placed on sales promotion. In this case, it might be appropriate to shift spending in the direction of advertising or other franchise-building activity. While this may be more expensive and most certainly will require a longer time frame to yield results, a brand needs to protect and build its base franchise.
3. **Build Trade Promotion.** When the base volume is stable or increasing, but incremental volume is down, most likely it means that the longer-term, franchise-building strategies are working well, but some potential volume is being sacrificed, probably due to a lack of retailer in-store support. The remedy

is to offer trade promotions and allowances to encourage retailer support. Special in-store displays and related materials could be part of the trade promotion program.

4. **Major Overhaul.** When both base and incremental volume are showing declines, a strategy should dictate implementing a major overhaul. Neither the franchise-building activity nor the short-term promotions are working as well as they should. It might mean that there are problems with the product itself, or that there is significant new competition. This situation is the most serious for the brand and potentially the most difficult to fix. It is likely that this circumstance would lead to a reconsideration of the product itself, as well as the entire marketing strategy.

CONCLUSION

The fact-based marketing idea depends only on the sales response of the brand. If properly applied, it should always lead to the most efficient marketing strategies for a brand and should be self-correcting if any mistakes might be made. This sophisticated analysis leads to a much more profound understanding of how promotion works, and to the development of much more effective sales promotion strategies and budget plans.

John Totten is Vice President, Analytical and Technical Products, at Nielsen Marketing Research, having joined the company in 1991 after 30 years of experience with major consumer packaged goods manufacturers on both the client and research supplier sides. He serves as a liaison between Nielsen and the academic community, frequently speaking at ORSA/TIMS and other marketing conferences, lecturing in university MBA classes on the topic of sales promotion, and publishing articles on topics such as Markov analysis, sales response and consumer behavior modeling, and analysis of designed experiments using scanner data. His book Analyzing Sales Promotion (with co-author Martin Block) will be released in an updated and expanded edition in 1994. He is currently researching the ways in which Dun & Bradstreet information can be integrated into a comprehensive set of marketing mix analysis/planning models.

Before coming to Nielsen, Totten spent almost 10 years at Information Resources, Inc. (IRI). He held many positions during that time, including V.P. Research and Development, V.P. Market Response Analysis, and V.P. Product Standards and Technical Support. While at IRI, Totten developed analytical systems for measuring the impact of trade promotion on brand sales, forming the foundation for a multimillion dollar analysis/consulting business for IRI. In the almost twenty years prior to that, Totten was an internal consultant for Procter and Gamble in the areas of research and development, new product development, and market research.

Totten received his Ph.D. in Operations Research from the University of California, Berkeley in 1971.

Martin Block is a Full Professor in the Integrated Marketing Communications Division of the Medill School at Northwestern University, teaching marketing research, sales promotion, advertising, and direct marketing courses. Joining the faculty in 1985, he was previously Director of the Graduate Advertising Division within Medill. He is President of his own company, Block Telecommunications, Inc., actively engaging in marketing and research consulting for a variety of clients such as Ameritech, Amoco, Kraft, and IBM. He specializes in sales promotion scanner analysis and telecommunications and new technology research.

Block was a Professor and Chairperson of the Department of Advertising at Michigan State University before making the move to Northwestern. Prior to that, he worked as Senior Market Analyst in Corporate Planning at the Goodyear Tire and Rubber Company.

Block is co-author of Analyzing Sales Promotion, which is now in its second edition. He has published extensively in academic research journals and trade publications, and has written several book chapters.

Block received his B.A., M.A., and Ph.D. from Michigan State University.

CHAPTER 4

ANALYZING SALES PROMOTION

To really understand how sales promotion works, it is necessary to go beyond description of the techniques and observe it in operation. Sales promotion programs need to be applied to real marketing problems with the results carefully analyzed. This needs to be done over an extended period of time to be able to generalize and begin to develop some principles of sales promotion that will be usable by the marketing manager.

Until recently, sales promotion has been managed primarily on the basis of traditional and anecdotal understanding of how it works. Neither the necessary data nor the computing power has been available to do any systematic analysis. This has now completely changed, forcing complete analysis along with careful management of any sales promotion effort in order to remain competitive in the future.

ASSESSING THE IMPACT OF SALES PROMOTION

The computer revolution that has swept the business world is just now beginning to alter the traditional methods of establishing product prices, assessing the impact of price changes, and assessing the impact of promotional activity. Computer technology has made possible the collection of purchase and sales data in ways that were previously not possible, and it has greatly enhanced the ability to manipulate and analyze those data. Two factors emerge as driving forces in the move toward analysis of sales promotion. These are improved cost accounting and improved availability of data on sales performance, down to the level of individual items at an individual retail outlet.

Improved Cost Accounting. Improved accuracy of cost-accounting methods by both the manufacturer and the retailer now makes it possible to more accurately allocate both fixed and variable costs on a brand-by-brand, size-of-package basis. For example, each manufacturer can easily have dozens of different products in the same product category, commonly carrying a line of differentiated products with several package sizes in each product. Obviously, the addition of a differentiated product, such as a different flavor, or of a different package size, greatly aggravates the accounting problem simply because there are more items. However, the addition of each brand, extension, or size is justified on the basis of expanded sales volume, as the additions usually provide the additional consumer benefits of more product choice and greater convenience of product use.

The proliferation of items has led to difficulty in determining if all items are justified on the basis of their contribution to profit. However, with the ever decreasing cost of collecting and processing data by computers, historical data on profit contribution can be kept at the finest level of detail.

The retailer's cost-accounting problem might even appear to be worse than the one the manufacturer faced. A typical retail outlet in grocery, drug, or mass merchandising may handle from 15,000 to 30,000 individual items in 300 to 400 product categories. Movement of many individual items from the store may be quite small, hardly justifying individual by-hand analysis, except on an infrequent basis in making retain or drop decisions on shelf stocking. In response to the problem, retailers have adopted simple pricing formulas such as the following:

Selling Price = Purchase Price + 20%

The simple percentage markup rule is a typical method of management for many retailers. The percentage is adjusted to cover overall fixed costs, variable costs, and profit.

Markups may vary across product classes based on easily identified differential operating costs. A grocery meat department, for example, may require special processing and storage equipment and have a relatively high product loss rate due to the relatively short shelf life. Refrigerated items may require special storage and display equipment. Many produce and dairy items also have limited shelf lives. Considerations such as these may dictate differential markups on a department-by-department basis.

The use of computerized techniques enables more accurate accounting and improved cost allocation, allowing for the department-by-department approach. The largest gains in allocating costs appear to be generated through analysis of operations required from the initial order of the product through to the final sale to a consumer. Today certain systems can even estimate costs on an item-by-item basis.

Improved Data. Before the computer was employed at the grocery checkout lane, virtually no individual purchase data were available. The growth of automated checkout devices, or scanners, has been justified by most retailers on the basis of improved checkout productivity — that is, reduced labor and reduced error in entering prices. The management value of the data has been generally ignored.

A by-product of such automatic checkout device installation is an accurate recording on an outlet-by-outlet basis of the prices charged and the sales volume for each item sold during time periods as short as one week. A number of syndicated data services are currently using scanner-collected data to provide to client manufacturers detailed reporting of brand sales volume, competitive pricing, and promotional activity. Most important, the accumulation of very detailed historical information on an outlet-by-outlet basis provides a foundation for the statistical analysis of interactions among the pricing and promotional activities of competing brands. Also critically important is the ability to conduct experiments at the retail outlet level to assess the probable impact of pricing and promotional activities outside the observed range of historical conditions. Previously, such information could be obtained only by manipulating pricing and promotional activity on a much broader scale, such as the sales territory level.

The A.C. Nielsen company is a leader in using scanner data for tracking product sales and has one of the most consistent historical databases for examining the impact of pricing and promotion decisions in grocery product categories. The Nielsen data are collected using scanners in grocery, drug, and mass-merchandiser stores in selected markets around the country. The data have been collected for several years on grocery stores, providing a reasonably complete database on grocery product sales.

Two important factors limit the application of scanner data to sales promotion problems. The first factor is that no psychological variables are measured or recorded. The technology measures only the overt behavior of product purchase. Some questions, such as the long-term impact of sales promotion programs on the image of the brand, cannot be directly addressed. It can certainly be argued, however, that such questions are not particularly important given that sales are so well measured.

Historical data on some product categories are not yet available. Few durable goods, for example, are recorded in commercially available databases. To date, data suppliers have concentrated on product categories sold through grocery stores, supermarkets, and drugstores. Thus, the generalizations drawn here are based upon frequently purchased nondurable package goods only. The analysis methods described, however, apply generally to scanner-collected sales data.

Before the new data and analytic techniques can be brought to bear on any sales promotion problem, or evaluate any promotional effort, it is necessary to establish objectives for that promotion.

SETTING PROMOTION OBJECTIVES

The first step in devising a promotional program is always setting objectives. Objectives for sales promotion, like objectives for any marketing strategy, must be unambiguous and realistic. The objectives will be unambiguous if they provide for measurable outcomes. The objective of providing an "incentive to consumers," for example, is not adequate because it does not provide for an unambiguous outcome. A manager could not determine whether the promotion was a success. The objective of increasing sales by 100,000 units, however, is quite precise and measurable, assuming that the appropriate system is in place. Objectives may be stated in terms of volume sales, share of market, profitability, trial of product among previous nonusers, or changes in inventory position.

Objectives must also be realistic in terms of their potential to be fulfilled. Objectives that could never be reached should be avoided, since they make the entire process unworkable and as difficult to manage as though there were no objectives at all.

PRICING AND PROMOTION

In most analyses of sales promotion activity, it is best to separate the decision about the pricing of the product from any decision about using sales promotion. A product should have an established, normal selling price that consumers expect to pay. This price is certainly influenced by both the manufacturer's and the retailer's costs, but it is not necessarily determined by them entirely. Rational manufacturers certainly would not, as normal practice, sell any product below its variable cost of production. Retailers, however, will sometimes sell limited numbers of items below cost when they believe that such items are influential in attracting new shoppers to the store — building overall sales volume. In cases in which a product would be sold below cost, it would usually be wise to avoid incurring additional expense, such as storage costs.

There are two basic ways of determining the selling price of a particular product. The first and simplest way is to apply a simple markup rule, such as 20 percent of cost. In other words, if a mythical product costs $.80 from the manufacturer, the retailer can then apply the markup rule, in this case 20 percent, and add $.16. The selling price to the consumer is then $.96. This price would probably be psychologically adjusted to an odd-ending $.99.

The cost-plus pricing approach, in which a retailer simply applies the markup rule, has a major disadvantage: it relies on historical costs and ignores the operation of the marketplace. Often a retailer may sell a product at too low a price using this method and not maximize profits. A much better method, borrowed from microeconomics, is to use a simple demand curve.

A demand curve is the relationship between the selling price of the product and the number of units of that product that are sold. A typical demand curve would show the price-volume relationship as inverse; in other words, lower prices would yield higher unit sales, and higher prices would yield lower unit sales. While there are sometimes exceptions, such as with special products like perfume, which are sold on the basis of style or prestige, lower prices usually lead to increased unit sales.

The biggest difficulty with this pricing approach for both the manufacturer and retailer is deriving the demand curve. Traditional data, such as quarterly or annual sales, simply do not provide sufficiently precise data to do this, leaving subjective methods such as best-guess estimates from appropriate personnel or very expensive experimentation. However, today's scanner-based sales reporting can provide sufficient data to do relatively inexpensive experimentation.

Because scanning instantly records every purchase of a product, price-volume comparisons can be made on virtually a day-to-day, store-by-store basis. Products' purchase histories then can be analyzed on a daily or a weekly basis or viewed over a longer time period, such as months or years. Comparison of natural or promotion-induced price changes with their corresponding sales volumes will then provide a reasonable estimate of the fundamental demand or price-volume curve for that product. In addition, data from relatively few stores are required for experimenting with new price levels and deriving the curve's characteristics. Almost always, determining the nature of the demand or price-volume curve for the product will be the first step in analyzing any sales promotion. Exhibit 4.1 provides an example of a price-volume or demand curve.

Once the price-volume curve has been determined, costs can be directly compared. Costs usually are divided into two major components: fixed costs and variable costs. Fixed costs do not change with sales volume and are incurred even if none of the product is sold. Variable costs vary with the sale of the product and are normally directly related to the volume of the product sold. For example, gasoline requires a storage tank and pump to be sold at retail. The net expense of the pump and related equipment would constitute fixed costs. The electrical power needed to operate the pump and the maintenance expense would be directly related to the volume of gasoline sold and would therefore constitute variable costs, as would be the cost of purchasing the gasoline itself (cost of goods sold) from the refiner or area distributor.

EXHIBIT 4.1
PRICE-VOLUME CURVE

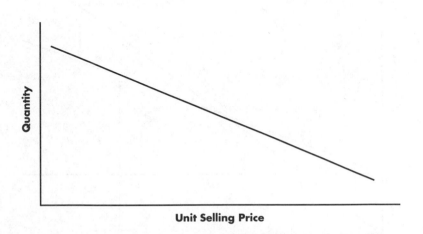

By converting the unit selling price to revenue and cost, a break-even chart can be prepared. Revenue results from multiplying the selling price by the appropriate quantity sold at that price point. Total cost is the result of multiplying the appropriate quantity by its variable costs with the addition of all fixed costs. Total revenue and total cost curves can then be plotted against the quantity sold. When the total revenue curve is above the total cost curve, profit is earned. When the total cost curve is above the total revenue curve, there is a loss. The point at which the total revenue curve and the total cost curve intersect is the break-even point. A sample break-even chart is shown in Exhibit 4.2.

From a marketing management perspective, the important variables are the price and the profit, not the quantity. A third graph or chart combines the demand curve and the break-even chart and compares the unit selling price with revenue and cost. A price-profit chart, as shown in Exhibit 4.3, is a very convenient way to assess the impact of various price levels on ultimate profit levels.

How these charts are used depends to some extent on the managerial policy of the particular organization. For example, profit can be viewed in terms of the absolute dollars or amount, or it can be viewed as a percentage or rate. One price level would often result in the highest rate of profit, and another price level would result in the greatest amount of profit. The choice, of course, would depend on how the man-

EXHIBIT 4.2
BREAK-EVEN CHART

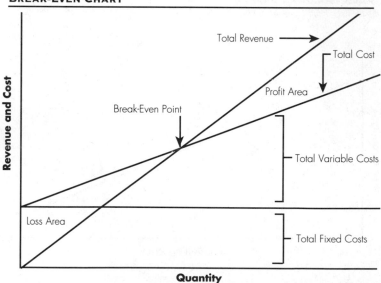

Totten/Block *Analyzing Sales Promotion*

EXHIBIT 4.3
PRICE-PROFIT CHART

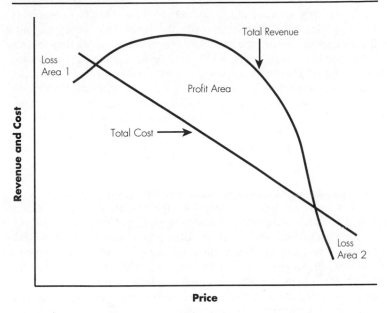

agement of the organization views profit and rate of return.

These charts provide a convenient framework for analyzing price and promotion decisions. By holding some of the variables constant, such as the normal selling price and the cost of goods sold, the impact of promotion can easily be examined. The difficult problem is understanding the impact of these variables on the sales volume; the solution normally requires research.

PRICE EVALUATION AND RESEARCH

Establishing the relationship between selling price and unit sales requires very careful study of product sales at the retail level. It is critically important that sales be studied at the retail level — where the product is ultimately sold. Examining sales at the manufacturing level can be very misleading, because the product may languish in wholesaler and retailer inventories for long periods of time before being sold to a consumer. Manufacturer's shipments reflect the aggregate effects of the way the retail trade translated the particular manufacturer's deal offerings. The manufacturer can assess with reasonable accuracy the incremental volume and profit generated by the offer, but it seldom gains insight into the way in which alternative terms might influence volume and profit. Information on competitive manufacturers' pricing and promotional activity is difficult to incorporate in an analysis of shipments. Thus, marketers must do substantially more than merely examine their own sales records.

Obtaining an accurate measure of retail sales is necessary to properly evaluate the effectiveness of sales promotion programs, and it requires a special research effort. Sales for most product categories can be measured in several ways at the retail level, though in certain situations some of the methods may be too expensive to be practical. Automobile sales may be one of the easiest to measure because the vehicle registration requirements of state governments provide a natural database describing the vehicle purchased, the purchase date, and new owner identification. Few product categories, however, have this luxury. The research required is often best performed by external specialized research organizations.

USING RESEARCH SERVICE ORGANIZATIONS

For most marketers, contracting for research services with an external research company is a common practice. Few marketers possess the specialized personnel to collect and analyze the necessary data. Also, research service companies are often in a better position than marketers to contract with retailers and wholesalers for data. It is difficult for a marketer, who is generally in a continuous bargaining position with the trade, to obtain useful information on such subjects as price discounts and competitive activity.

A marketer can contract with a research service organization in two ways: on a custom basis or on a syndicated basis. With custom research, the information is collected and analyzed for only one client. With syndicated research, the same information is collected and analyzed for more than one client. Each type has advantages and disadvantages. Custom research is known only to the client and the research service organization and is therefore secret or proprietary. Because it is custom-tailored for a client, it is also flexible in terms of scheduling and method. The primary disadvantage of custom research is that it is usually much more expensive than syndicated research since one client must pay the entire bill. A good application of custom research would be a new product test about which a marketer would not want competitors to have any knowledge.

Syndicated research, on the other hand, has the advantage of credibility when measures of competitive activity are being taken. If more than one competitor is paying for the research, there is less reason to suspect any particular bias. Syndicated research is also less expensive because the cost can be shared among more than one client. The primary disadvantage of syndicated research is a lack of flexibility; it usually requires a fixed schedule and a standardized methodology. A good application of syndicated research is the measurement of advertising-media audiences or brand-market share over time.

MEASURING PRODUCT SALES

Retail product sales can be measured in several ways. Various methods have evolved over the years for different product categories. The methods that have evolved and are described here are all commercial successes. They are all offered for sale by at least one commercial research service organization and, of course, are purchased by marketers.

Store Shelf Audits. Most grocery and package good items are sold today through supermarkets that can be relatively easily monitored. By keeping counts of the movements of products on and off the shelves, an estimate of product sales can be determined for that store. Periodically counting the store's inventory and invoices and subtracting the beginning inventory from the ending inventory, plus the goods shipped in, provides an estimate of the sales for a given period.

The A.C. Nielsen Company has provided a service based on this method for many years. Using a carefully selected sample of supermarkets throughout the country, Nielsen is able to provide a national estimate of retail market share for most products sold through supermarkets. Nielsen also audits drugstores and other retail outlets. Product sales can be easily estimated by brand and package size. In addition, Nielsen provides estimates of average retail prices, wholesale prices, average store inventory, promotional activity, and advertising. Special merchandising activity, such as premiums or bonus packs, may be noted as well. Nielsen audits the stores every 60 days.

Audit information such as this is available over extended periods of time, providing an indication of longer-run changes in brand or market position. It is generally available on a regional as well as national basis, allowing assessment of brand strengths and weaknesses by region.

There are three problems in using shelf audit data to evaluate sales promotion programs. The first and perhaps most obvious problem is that only products sold primarily through supermarkets and drugstores can be studied. If a product has a large proportion of its sales through other outlets, examining only the supermarket portion of the sales could be misleading. Products not sold at all through supermarkets, of course, could not be studied.

A second problem is the lack of any information about the consumer. This makes it difficult to study promotional influences aimed at the individual consumer or to consider any targeted impacts on different market segments. Analysis is limited to an aggregate analysis of the entire market.

The third problem is the relatively long time period between measurements. Most promotions are designed to encourage immediate response, sometimes within a single day or week. If the measurements are not taken at a frequency at least equal to the expected duration of the impact of the sales promotion program, then too many other factors can impinge on the sales of the product and dilute the effect of the specific promotion.

In the mid-1980s, Nielsen introduced a scanner-based data sales monitoring service to augment store audit information. By 1992, growth in scanner usage has allowed phaseout of audit data for projecting grocery store sales, although it still remains important for channels and markets in which scanner penetration is low.

Warehouse Withdrawals. Moving back a step in the distribution chain can simplify the monitoring process. Assuming that supermarkets obtain all their inventory from a few central warehouses, and knowing that supermarkets tend to avoid maintaining large in-store inventories, much the same information could be obtained by inventorying the warehouses instead of the supermarkets themselves.

Selling Areas Marketing Incorporated (SAMI), for instance, used a computerized method of warehouse withdrawal to gather data on sales and distribution of products sold through supermarkets. SAMI provided data nationally and in approximately 50 individual markets. The warehouse withdrawal method would have the same disadvantages as the shelf audit method but would also lack the store level information. In addition, several important classes of products are generally delivered directly to the store without intermediate warehousing. These include high-turnover items justifying shipment directly from the manufacturer in truckload lots, as well as locally produced items, often with limited shelf lives, such as bakery, dairy, or soft drink products. SAMI discontinued major portions of its business, and warehouse withdrawal information is no longer commercially available.

Mail Consumer Panels. The traditional method of collecting individual consumer-level information has been the mail consumer panel. The subjects are recruited through the mail and respond through the mail with either a purchase diary or questionnaire. The subjects generally report their purchase behavior periodically; hence, the panel design. Some of the research organizations that provide this service also offer a telephone research service as well.

There are two types of mail panel data collection instruments — the purchase diary and the questionnaire. The purchase diary is provided to the subject before purchases are made and is intended to be completed coincidentally with each purchase. The questionnaire method relies on the recall ability of the subjects, asking them to reconstruct their purchase behavior from memory for a specified period of time, such as a week or a month. The questionnaire method is currently the more popular method. Most of the mail panel research has been custom research. Mail panels have also been a very popular means of testing new products before any store placement.

Several research organizations maintain prerecruited mail panels that can easily be used to measure purchase behavior. They include National Family Opinion (NFO) and Market Facts, Incorporated.

Marketing and Research Counselors, Incorporated (M/A/R/C) offers a neighborhood panel in 25 markets that can be invited to central locations for personal interviews if necessary.

Mail panels are often questioned on the representativeness of their samples and on the quality of the data obtained. Not everyone recruited agrees to participate in mail panel research, which can be a biasing factor. Some estimates claim that as little as 10 percent of those initially contacted to participate actually do. The mail panel research organizations attempt to counter this problem with very careful balancing of their panels according to geographic areas and demographic characteristics.

Anytime people are asked questions, there is the possibility of error. When recall is used, error may occur because the memory may not be entirely accurate. Comparisons of recall of product purchase and scanner-measured purchase indicate time-compression effects. The question "What products have you used in the last three months?" may yield responses more closely reflecting product usage in the last year. Usage of private label and generic products may be under-reported. The recording of the responses may not be complete, legible, or accurate either. Therefore, the quality of the data received through a mail panel is often a problem and requires careful editing and coding.

Mail panels have an advantage, however, because they are able to collect data for virtually any product category. The product need not necessarily be sold through supermarkets or any other particular type of retail outlet. In addition, mail panels are probably still the best way to study durable goods, such as tires and major appliances.

Store Scanner Data. Perhaps the greatest technological innovation in the supermarket in recent years has been the automated checkout lane. Using the universal product bar code, a computer-controlled bar-code reader identifies the product, the appropriate price is found in a computer-maintained database, and the customer is provided a printout receipt. Each purchase is entered into a database for later analysis. An average supermarket may record approximately 150,000 individual purchases in a day.

It is interesting that supermarkets that have adopted automated checkout systems have not done so because of the value of the data they collect. Instead, the rationales for the adoption usually include the reduced clerk checkout error and increased checkout speed.

The automated checkout data include all of the package and brand characteristics, plus the exact price paid and the purchase quantity. This is considerably more information than is available from the shelf audit method. The data are precisely timed so that the date and even the time of day are known.

There are two problems with scanner data. The first is the same as with shelf audit data — they provide no information about the consumer making the purchase. In other words, analyses of consumer topologies still cannot be done. The other major problem with scanner data is that in most markets not all retail outlets are scanned. A consumer may purchase products in a store that is scanned but then go on to another store that is not. Such incomplete coverage of a market might produce very biased understanding of the market.

Several research organizations either offer scanner data or have announced projects based on scanner data. Some of the research organizations include Information Resources, Inc. (IRI), which has been using scanner data for household data collection since 1981, and Nielsen. Both offer a wide variety of scanner-based data services. Arbitron's Scan America is currently in its test phase. There is little doubt that scanner data are revolutionizing market research.

Store Scanner Panels. One solution to the consumer problem with store scanner data is the store scanner panel. By providing individuals with special cards that can be read by the bar-code reader in the store, complete recordings of all scannable purchases can be collected for a selected subset of individuals. This method combines the advantages of both the store scanner data and the mail consumer panel.

Again, the problem is coverage within the geographical market area. For the system to record all the purchases of a household, all the retail outlets in the area would have to be scanning and participating. IRI has minimized the problem by arranging nearly complete coverage of isolated markets in which few opportunities exist for consumers to shop in noncovered outlets. The expansion of many products outside their traditional supermarket channels of distribution poses a problem for data collection based on in-store methods. A.C. Nielsen solves the coverage problem by providing each household with an in-home bar-code reader to identify products purchased. Using this method, purchasing from all channels of distribution can be monitored.

The scanner panel has proven to be a viable alternative, and it is near the heart of rapidly expanding research services by IRI and Nielsen.

Single Source Data. One of the goals pursued by suppliers of scanner data is single source data. This means that data on all elements of the marketing mix would theoretically be collected from a single source or household. Retail store sales would be tracked by means of a store scanner panel, with purchases tracked in a manner that would allow matching to all stores in which a consumer shopped, and therefore, to causal data on brands available, and to pricing and promotion against the purchase data. Not only would coupon redemption be monitored, but also records would indicate which coupons were available to households. Going beyond a simple household identification, purchases would be associated with specific family members. The TV (and VCR) viewing of individual household members would be monitored, as would their radio listening. Usage of print media such as newspapers would also be captured. Exposure to point-of-sale materials such as shelf-talkers, VideoCart, ActMedia, and other in-store media would be noted. A file listing the promotional offers available to the trade would also be offered for use in assessing the reaction of retailers to different promotion terms.

All major data suppliers are working toward this ideal, though none have reached it yet. In some respects, IRI's BehaviorScan markets approach the ideal in some areas of retail food and package goods merchandising, but coverage of drug store, mass-merchandiser, and convenience store sales is less than fully complete. IRI TV monitoring captures set usage, but it does not identify which members of the household are viewing. A major criticism of IRI's approach is that the small markets dictated by the outlet coverage goals may not be representative of the larger urban markets where most marketing activity is focused.

Nielsen uses an in-home scanning system that permits capture of purchases from all outlets, but that relies on consumer diary information to capture the usage of store specials and coupons. Both Nielsen and Arbitron are experimenting with methods of capturing TV viewing that identify specific household members. A couple of coupon clearinghouses are developing information systems on coupon offers. However, no activity is currently under way to develop a database on trade promotion offers.

One thing seems certain — future databases will cover more types of outlets, a greater percentage of households, and more causal information as manufacturers and retailers seek greater understanding of the relations among the various elements of the marketing mix.

INDIVIDUAL VS. AGGREGATE MEASUREMENT

A major requirement for data used to evaluate sales promotion programs is that they be sufficiently sensitive to detect any differences in response due to promotional activity. Data that are averaged across time may not be sensitive enough because the averaging process may also be averaging away differences due to promotion.

One of the greatest difficulties in assessing promotion effects is that sales promotion is always presented to consumers in a very competitive environment. Promotions are offered to consumers so frequently that the effects of one program are almost immediately countered by those of another. In addition, the marketplace is extremely dynamic and subject to an extraordinary number of influences. Aggregated data cannot isolate or separate any of these effects.

Many studies of sales promotion programs have found that only data collected over a relatively short time period, and which corresponds to the changes in pricing and promotional activity, are precise enough to detect differences attributable to any one promotional effort. When the data are aggregated (summarized), the differences tend to disappear. Aggregate data — that is, data not collected on the individual retail outlet level on a weekly basis — generally cannot be used to evaluate sales promotion. In other words, in order to effectively evaluate sales promotion programs, the data must be collected on an individual-store-week basis, and not aggregated across time, stores, or markets.

TIME PERIOD

Data can be aggregated in time. The results need to be measured on a basis consistent with the duration of the promotional event. For a weekend-special store sale, daily measurement may be required. For a week-long event typical in many grocery, drug, and mass-merchandise stores, weekly sales are usually sufficient. Consumer coupons, sweepstakes, and similar promotional events may take several months to achieve full impact. If data are collected on a less frequent basis, the impact of an individual promotion may be entirely lost in all the competing promotions that occur later in the week or even later in the month.

The same problem of aggregation exists with data summarized over several sales outlets with differing promotional conditions. Data analysis techniques exist that attempt to estimate promotional effects from data that have been too highly aggregated, but selection of the proper level of aggregation for the base data makes promotional analysis much more straightforward.

SALES AND USAGE MEASUREMENT

Sales are traditionally presented in terms of market share in marketing plans. The term *market share* simply refers to the sales for a given product brand divided by the total sales in the product category. When one knows a product's market share, one can compare the performance of an individual brand against competing brands. This is why it is so often used as a means of expressing product sales. When used at high levels of data aggregation, such as annual U.S. sales volume, it is a good indication of relative market position.

A problem in using market share for short-run analysis is that competitive activity is included in the number. For example, if brand A runs a promotion and enjoys an increase in sales, and if brand B also runs a promotion at the same time and increases sales, brand A may have very little change in market share but significant volume sales increases. Because market share also includes competitive activity, market share loses sensitivity to a given sales promotion program. A much better measure of sales to evaluate sales promotion is sales volume.

A second problem with market share is that an accurate assessment is required regarding which brands or products are the appropriate market. Many product categories, such as sliced lunch meats, canned soups, salted snacks, cookies, and snack crackers, have a large variety of sizes, forms, and flavors. Improper specification of the items to be used as a basis for market share may materially bias analyses.

FINANCIAL ANALYSIS

The appropriate framework for evaluating sales promotion programs is the income statement, which allows direct comparison of profit levels. The income statement can provide both a most convenient planning tool and a means of evaluation.

Income Statements. The income statement is perhaps the most fundamental of all financial statements. The income statement is sometimes referred to as a profit or loss statement. It shows the relationship between sales, costs, and profits. A sales promotion program, whether offered by a manufacturer or a retailer, should have an impact on sales and costs and, of course, profits.

A simplified statement (Table 4.1) shows the relationship between the manufacturer and the retailer and the source of promotional expenses. The manufacturer incurs costs with the trade allowances and promotional expenses, while the retailer incurs promotional expenses.

As discussed previously, the expense categories each contains — fixed and variable components — need to be recognized in order to determine profit. The above model simplifies the distribution channel somewhat, in that warehouses and brokers are recognized as costs to the manufacturer. Certainly promotion can be aimed at middle agents, but most of the trade promotion in this discussion is assumed to be aimed at retailers.

TABLE 4.1
INCOME STATEMENT

Manufacturer	Retailer
Gross Sales	Gross Sales
• Discounts and adjustments	• Returns
• Trade allowances	
Net Sales	Net Sales
• Cost of goods	• Cost of goods
• Warehouse and freight	
• Brokerage fees	
Contribution to Margin	Gross Margin
• Manufacturer promotion	• Retailer promotion
• Other expenses	• Other expenses
Manufacturer Profit	Retailer Profit

Financial Forecasts. The format of the income statement can be readily applied both as a tool to evaluate a past sales promotion program and as a means to forecast the effect of a future program. Using income statements for successive time intervals, past sales promotion programs can be evaluated by comparing the intervals when the promotion was present to those intervals when the promotion was not.

The difficulty in comparing many time intervals is performing the repetitious computations that are necessary. This problem is easily solved by using a microcomputer with a spreadsheet program. A spreadsheet program makes the repetitious computations as simple as representing the relationship between rows and columns in terms of simple algebra. Almost any of the commercially available programs can be adapted to this purpose.

Once the appropriate historical data have been entered, it is then a simple matter to perform the computations. The appropriate comparisons may be made, followed by the strategic promotional decisions. The microcomputer model may also be used as a forecasting tool, allowing the asking of fanciful "what if" questions. The analyst can enter projected values for future time periods, make reasonable assumptions from the historical data, and evaluate potential sales promotion programs. Attempting such calculations manually would be time consuming and prone to error.

Forward-Buying. Many sales promotion programs involve the shifting of purchase patterns in time. Analyzing purchase timing requires that special attention be paid to the time periods before, during, and after the promotional period.

Forward-buying often occurs when a manufacturer announces a new allowance and promotional program to the trade. It may also occur because the trade may anticipate a promotional program from a manufacturer because of its previous experience with that manufacturer. Forward-buying occurs when the trade defers purchase of the product from the manufacturer until the special promotional price is available. The trade might also purchase more of the product than usual to take advantage of the special price in anticipation of future sales to consumers. Presumably after the promotional period, the trade demand for the product would diminish until the additional quantity purchased from forward-buying was sold. Not all products are suitable for forward-buying, such as perishables, seasonal items, and items that would represent high-cost inventory.

From the point of view of manufacturers, forward-buying moves quantities of the product from their inventory and may result in incremental sales volume gain. From the point of view of retailers, it affords an opportunity to obtain the product at a lower price, though this benefit needs to be carefully balanced against inventory holding costs and lowered selling prices and margins.

TIME SERIES ANALYSIS

Analyzing data across successive time periods, or a time series, is one of the best ways to generalize from the historical data. Sales data are naturally arrayed in a temporal sequence. One of the most common methods of analyzing time series data is linear regression, although several special problems need to be considered.

Linear Regression. A detailed discussion of linear regression can be found in any of several books dealing with statistics, but in general this term refers to a way of establishing a linear algebraic relationship between a criterion or dependent variable and one or more predictor or independent variables. The equation is in the form $Y = a + bX$, where Y is the criterion variable and X is the predictor variable. The criterion variable is the variable that is to be estimated, such as sales or profit. The predictor variable or variables are the variables that are presumed to influence the criterion variable, such as the presence or absence of a sales promotion program. In the equation, the a is referred to as the intercept and the b as the slope, or the relative change in X that is attributable to Y. The slope is also commonly referred to as the regression coefficient.

Linear regression, then, is an extremely useful tool for accounting for differences in a time series. The relationship, however, is limited to a straight line. If the data points in the series were plotted on a graph, they would probably not form a very good straight line. This raises the issue of fitting the best possible line through the data points. The most common method for accomplishing this is the method of least squares — that is, the regression line is the line that "fits" the best and has the smallest sum of the squared distances between the actual data points and the points along the theoretical line. Sometimes this method is referred to as ordinary least squares.

Several computer software packages are available that can perform analyses of this type. Obviously, the appropriate manual should be consulted, as well as other books on the interpretation and application of linear regression. Some special considerations in analyzing the data appropriate to the scanner-based data will be included here.

Nonlinear Regression. When the relationship between variables is not linear, then some form of data transformation or nonlinear regression should be considered. The use of a logarithmic transformation is a good example of how to make a variable that is not linear appear to be.

There are several nonlinear regression procedures available in the computer statistical analysis software packages. Algebraically, nonlinear relationships are much more difficult and generally require more mathematical sophistication to understand. In general, representing a nonlinear relationship as a linear one will understate the strength of the relationship. This means that if linear regression is used to analyze nonlinear data, the relationships will appear to be weaker than they actually are. From a statistical point of view, the error would be in the conservative direction if a linear analysis were applied. This, in part, explains why nonlinear regression has not found wider use.

Coding Variables. Linear regression has some reasonably stringent requirements for variables that can be included as either predictor variables, such as promotional condition, or a criterion variable, such as sales. Variables must be measured at least at the interval level, meaning that nominal or categorical variables are generally excluded. This means that the variable itself must be measured on a scale similar to a temperature scale, with the degrees representing equal scale intervals. Variables such as sales and price can usually be assumed to be interval variables.

Other variables, such as the presence or absence of a particular promotion, an in-store display, or an advertised price, cannot be assumed to be interval variables. The solution is to "dummy code" the categorical variable. For those time periods when the promotion is present, a predictor variable is created that is coded as a *1*. When the promotion is not present, the same variable is coded as a *0*. This same method can be applied to a whole host of predictor variables that might have some relationship to sales, such as the day of the week or the season.

Experiments. By coding the presence of a sales promotion program using dummy variables, historical data can be analyzed as though an experiment were conducted. The control condition becomes all of those times when the promotion is not present or the dummy variable is coded *0*. The nonpromotion occurrences represent the "base business" for the particular brand and are defined as the average business or sales. Particular care must be taken if one effect of promotion is to cause inventory stockpiling by retailers or consumers. In this case, baselines may be artificially depressed during periods following a promotion.

While the analysis has been described here as an experiment, it is not an experiment in the strict sense. The control and experimental conditions are not strictly parallel in time, and it is always possible that conditions during the time of the promotion were unusual in some way, making them different from the average of other times. This can be partially solved by conducting experiments in different markets at different points in time. Certainly the analyst needs to be aware of the issue.

Autoregression. A particularly difficult problem with any time series analysis is the potential for autoregression. The term *autoregression* refers to self-correlation. A variable, such as sales, is not independent across the successive time intervals. In other words, sales in this time period are influenced by sales in the prior time period because of considerations such as the size of the business, distribution, or reputation. A large retailer or manufacturer is not expected to experience dramatic, total sales fluctuations, though individual line items may have large swings. In the absence of promotional activity, item sales in any given week will be about the same as sales of the item in the previous week, with seasonal adjustments.

The problem with autoregression is that it can substantially distort the regression equation. It normally makes the relationship between the variables appear stronger than it actually is. This might give the analyst an illusion of false knowledge and lead to possible overconfidence in the estimation of the impact of a sales promotion program.

Solving the problem of autoregression is a major topic in any course in econometrics. Certainly the analyst needs to be aware of the potential of the problem. The appropriate statistical test, such as Durbin-Watson, should be run to determine whether autoregression exists. If it does exist, then a method, such as first differences, should be used to eliminate or control the autoregression. Many books on econometrics provide the necessary details, as do the manuals for statistical software packages.

INFORMATION-DENSE GRAPHICS

One headache in analyzing sales promotion data is the number of variables that need to be communicated simultaneously. Sales volume for a brand, along with its price and information in a newspaper feature or on a special in-store display, all need to be communicated across time. Obviously, visually showing this information in a graphical presentation can help communicate the interrelationships and trends across time. But loading all of this information into a single graph is tricky.

A line graph typically shows the change in sales volume over time. In this case, the y-axis represents sales volume and the x-axis delineates time, usually shown as one-week intervals. Price can be plotted on the same graph as a second line by using a second y-axis. The x-axis — that is, the one-week time intervals — remains the same. To indicate the relative importance of the sales and price, sales can be represented as a solid line, which will draw the eye, and price as a dotted or broken line. To represent the presence of a promotion, feature, display, or combination, a bar chart can be created as an overlay on the line graph. For those weeks the event is present, a bar is inserted on top of the line to indicate sales. When no bar is present, and only the line shows, no special promotional condition exists. To differentiate features and displays, bars can be filled in with different colors, patterns, or textures. This allows the user to see all the relevant variables at once and is a good example of what is termed information-dense graphics (see Exhibit 4.4).

Depending on the purpose of the analysis, the graphic representation could be easily tailored. Different organizations facing different decisions may want to alter the presentation. Varied uses of graphics are one of the areas that will continue to evolve and help solve the problem of understanding and managing sales promotion.

ANALYSIS TECHNIQUES FOR DISAGGREGATE DATA

The objective of analyzing dissaggregate data is to measure the short-term increase in sales as a result of short-term price reductions that will later be rescinded — for instance, in-store promotion, such as special display location, and local advertising (feature) of the type that is typically delivered each week in newspaper ads or advertising fliers.

The collection of scanner data provides timely and accurate information about sales of items at the brand level, by size, and by flavor, on an outlet-by-outlet basis. Typically, information is available on many different competitive brands. This wealth of information can lead to "analysis paralysis" in determining the structure of the analysis. Academic research suggests that promotion responses may vary across markets, across retail chains within a market, and across individual outlets within a chain. Responses may vary across subcategories within a main category (for example, regular vs. diet product variations), by relative price level (for example, premium, regular, or generic), and by size and flavor. This richness can lead to significant decision problems in defining the analysis. Should flavor data be added to define the brand? Should size data be included in determining total brand characteristics? Should data be added across stores to yield total chain data? Should data be aggregated across chains to give total market data? Should markets be added to give regions or total U.S. figures? Should data be combined across weeks and reduced to four-week, eight-week, or quarterly data observations?

Data Preparation. A critical first step in planning any analysis is outlining the objectives of the study: What questions are to be answered, and at what level of detail? As an example, consider the question "What is likely to happen if I take a 5 percent price hike on Brand X?" In this case, although responses to the 5 percent price hike might vary significantly from market to market, there may be many reasons why price hikes cannot be set differently on a market-by-market basis. However, because the answer is required on a national basis, this does not mean that the data should be summarized to a national level in order to perform the analysis. Typically, the data would be prepared at the store, chain, or market level; and these individual observations would be used in the analysis, even though only one average response number is to be calculated. This inclusion of observations from different collection points is called *pooling of data.* Similarly, if the price hike is contemplated on several related brands, the data might be prepared individually by brand and pooled for the analysis to give a single point estimate of the impact of the price increase.

EXHIBIT 4.4
INFORMATION-DENSE GRAPHICS

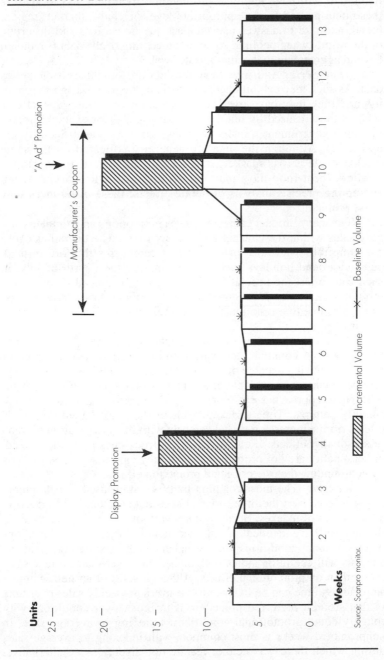

Source: Scanpro monitor.

The general rule is to aggregate within a store week all individual items that will have identical promotional treatment and to analyze these data pooled to the appropriate level of chain, market, region, brand, and size to answer management questions. To avoid distortion of the results when pooling, some preprocessing of the data is required beyond aggregating to the appropriate level.

Time Series Analysis. Scanner data are obviously time series data. As such they exhibit change over time due to trend and seasonality, and they may have overlays of irregular or semiregular effects such as those caused by holiday and pay weeks (for example, weeks in which government transfer payments such as Social Security are delivered). Although the data are generally collected on the same weekly cycle across markets, the start of the advertising cycle for retailers (best-food-day) may vary from market to market. When attempting precise analysis of subtle effects, these differences may cause problems.

For many product categories, sales promotion can stimulate category sales within the channel and can even stimulate overall category consumption. There are many product categories that are in peak demand around holidays such as Christmas or the Fourth of July. In such categories, the special holiday weeks will typically have heavy promotional activity. It becomes extremely difficult to separate increases in sales due to promotional activity from natural seasonal increases in sales.

Techniques based on time series analysis may be used to simplify the analysis. A common technique is to express the data as a ratio or index to a moving average of nearby data. The baselining methodology discussed later is an example of an analysis based on time series methods. These approaches can help to reveal overall data trends and seasonality patterns. Time series analysis of the unexplained "residual" effects from a regression model can help with the specification of trend or seasonality effects. If carryover effects from sales promotion, trend, or seasonality are not properly handled, they can mislead the analysis by confounding the true price and promotion effects.

Indexing. The most common transformation used in data preparation is to convert the time series of sales data (volume and prices) to a time series of indexes. Because stores vary in size, unless all stores in the analysis have identical promotional conditions, some combinations of promotional conditions will be unbalanced on store size, and the analysis will cue in on stores with higher- or lower-than-average sales rather than on promotional effects. Although sales of an item within a store across time can be indexed to the average weekly sales over time in that store, a preferred procedure is to index over conditions with roughly equal promotional conditions. Indexing to average sales in nonpromoted weeks is most common, with indexing to average sales during which there was neither feature nor display as an alternative.

For price data, prices may be indexed to the average nonpromoted price, recent nonpromoted prices, the average price across all stores in the city, or other price series, such as the price of a major competitor.

Indexing also aids in the interpretation of analysis results. Regression coefficients become more directly interpretable, representing the index point change in sales per point change in the independent variable. Analyses run across different chains or different cities using the same analysis procedure become directly comparable instead of generating results that report "a Memphis feature adds 437 cases to city sales while a Los Angeles feature adds 14,885 cases." Results can instead report that "a Memphis feature increases sales by 87 percent of the average sales in a nonpromoted week in Memphis, while a Los Angeles feature increases sales by 54 percent of the average sales in a nonpromoted week in Los Angeles." The latter conveys information in a more suitable form for making comparisons.

Price Representation. One of the striking findings from the study of scanner data is the diversity of prices and price environments that exists. Prices vary within a store across time. Within a chain in one city, there may be several price zones across which prices vary as a reflection of very local competitive conditions. In one market some chains may have prices that reflect a policy of every day low pricing, while other chains may have significantly higher prices. Promotional policies with respect to price may range from frequent promotions with small price reductions to infrequent promotions having deep price discounts. The amount of pass-through of manufacturers' incentives into price discounts on a given brand may vary widely from chain to chain.

As a result of this diversity, the actual price charged for a product is generally not usable directly in an analysis of pricing and promotion, unless the objective is to study per capita consumption as related to the price charged. Even then, it is probable that transformations will have to be made to reflect market-to-market differences in economic factors such as household income. As a result, most price-promotion analyses focus on the impact of changes in price over time within a store (time series response), and transform the data to minimize the impact of price differences across stores (cross-sectional response).

The most common transformations are to consider price differences relative to competitive prices in the store or to index prices to some base or average condition for the product in a store. Differencing against a competitor is seldom used unless there is one and only one major competitor per store. If there is more than one competitor, constructing an adequate price difference function becomes quite difficult. Even if the difference series can be constructed, price differences may be quite wrapped up with promotional activity.

In the previous section, several alternatives were mentioned for constructing price index series. The exact choice will depend very specifically upon the objective of the analysis. If one of the goals is to assess the impact on sales of long-run price changes, then both price and sales variables for a store should be indexed to bases that change only slowly over time. For analyses covering a relatively short period of time (18 months or less), prices might be indexed to the average nonpromoted price over the time period. For longer periods of time, it might be necessary to construct a price series that accounts for price inflation over the analysis period.

When the focus of the study is to analyze the impact of short-run price reductions on sales, the prices may be indexed against an average of recent prices charged by the store. A problem arises when the recent past contains other promotional prices. This may complicate the meaning of a particular price index against the base. A preferred transformation is to remove previous promotional prices and index versus recent regular price, or base price. This choice of transformation may still cause problems when pooling across an every-day-low-price set of stores and a set of regular-price stores in a market. In this case, the same advertised price might represent little if any discount in the every-day-low-price store, but it might represent significant price reduction in the higher-priced store. Thus, a highly composite price series might be in order where the base is constructed from recent history within a store if unadvertised but constructed from market average advertised prices when advertised.

Deflating Series. When a study is conducted that covers a long period of time, pricing variables may have to be adjusted to account for the pattern of general consumer price inflation that has prevailed in the United States since the early 1960s. The typical procedure for grocery store prices entails first indexing a monthly consumer price index to its average over the analysis period and then dividing store prices by this index. After completing this price deflation, the analysis can proceed in the same manner as an analysis using undeflated prices. Similarly, sales volumes for a long-run analysis might have to be placed on a per capita basis or otherwise adjusted for changes over time in the population being served by the store.

For shorter-run analyses, the most common type of series deflation is a seasonality adjustment. If a product has significant changes in sales level within a year on a regular and predictable basis, promotion usually occurs during periods of high seasonality rather than during low seasonality periods. In this case, a comparison of average weekly sales during nonpromoted weeks against average sales during promoted weeks could be significantly biased by seasonality effects.

Another problem that can cause the need for series adjustment is the presence of a time-trend component that the impact of pricing and promotional activity by the brand and its competitors cannot explain. If the category sales are relatively stable and smooth across time, then many of the problems associated with seasonal changes and category growth or decline trends can be eliminated by analyzing share instead of volume. However, a more robust and generally applicable procedure is to construct a moving average of total category sales by store, convert each of the series to an index series, and use that index series as a deflator that removes category trend and seasonality from a brand sales series.

Complications may arise if the specific brand (or size) set being modeled has a trend component or seasonality pattern that is different from that of the overall category. For example, diet products often are not as strongly seasonal as other products in the category. Where possible, the category definition should be based on the notion of similarity of seasonal pattern as well as strength of competition. In the extreme, analysis methods should be used that allow construction of a seasonal series based on data for a single brand (and size).

Baselining. The need to separate promotional impacts from normal sales when analyzing manufacturer shipments, and later, scanner data, led to the development of time-series-based analysis methods modified to cope with the special problems associated with sales promotion. These methods are variations on the ratio-to-average methods of time series and attempt to separate weekly sales into two components: (1) base sales, which refer to the level of sales expected, including trend and seasonality but excluding the impact of sales promotion (including short-term carryover or loss), and (2) incremental volume, that extra amount of sales attributable to retail sales promotion activity. Variations of this methodology are used by SPAR, IRI, and Nielsen Marketing Research in the analysis of promotional activity.

Once the separation has been made into base and incremental volumes, analysis of many questions relating to volume sales is also simplified. Short-term promotional effects of price reduction, ad featuring, and in-store display can be analyzed by using only promoted observations and studying the relation of total sales to base sales. Long-run effects such as the impact of changes in the base price, the introduction of new competitors, the impact of TV or print advertising, and the general pattern of trend and seasonality can be studied using the base volume, without confounding by short-term promotional activities.

Baselining is a heuristic procedure and depends upon many assumptions. One of the first assumptions occurs in the flagging of observations as promoted or not. In the generally inflationary environment that has existed in the United States since the mid-1960s, most consumers have been conditioned to accept upward changes in price as permanent and to view downward changes in price as temporary. With this in mind, weeks with price increases are generally not flagged and are removed from the baselining procedure. Weeks of reduced prices are flagged as promotion weeks (temporary price reduction). Occasionally, examination of the time series of prices will reveal that a price reduction was permanent.

Due to the general consumer conditioning, it seems likely that the initial weeks of the reduced price will be responded to as though they were temporary, but as time passes, the reduced price will become accepted as the new base price. The length of time for this to occur probably varies from product category to product category (and is probably related to the length of the average purchase cycle). Analysis methods such as SCAN*PRO require that each week be marked as promoted or not prior to calculating the baseline, so the length of time that a reduced price is considered to be a promoted price, as opposed to a base price, often becomes an input assumption rather than an analytically derived output.

A significant problem encountered in baselining scanner data occurs when several different UPC codes are logically related. For example, bath soap may be sold routinely as single bars and two-bar packs. From time to time, a four-bar pack might appear with the label "Buy three, get one free" (bonus pack), or a specially printed two-bar pack may have the legend "10 cents off" (price pack). The presence of the temporary special packs will obviously affect the sales of the regular packs, and there is no special requirement that the trade maintain consistent per-volume pricing on different packs of the bar soap. In this case, an aggregate data series and an aggregate price series may have to be prepared, and the presence of the special packs in sufficient quantity may in itself constitute a type of promotion.

The strongest competitors to a brand size are often other sizes of the same brand, because loyal brand buyers may shift sizes to obtain promotional discounts. This may make the combining of individual brand baselines and base volumes up to the brand level a nontrivial task.

Finally, in extreme cases such as the heavily promoted carbonated beverage categories, virtually all the observations may be marked as promoted, leaving few, if any, observations on which to establish a baseline value.

Despite the problems noted above, the positive attributes of baselining methods for use in evaluating short-term promotion impacts have led it to be the basis for promotion analysis on scanner-based sales-tracking data. Significant research is being conducted to address the issues noted, and the properties of baselining should become increasingly well known as this research progresses.

Multiperiod Effects. A second class of variables arises when an activity has an impact over several time periods. In this case, a continuous variable might be used to model the impact over time. As mentioned above, a number of analyses using dummy variables to model the effect might first be run in order to then establish a template variable that captures the average time relationship. Examples of such activity might be the dropping of a manufacturer's coupon. The impact might be greatest in the first week of the drop and decline thereafter at a rate related to such factors as the coupon value and the repurchase cycle for the category. One way to statistically represent this is to construct a continuous variable that is the number of weeks since the last coupon drop. If there is a template that shows the average percentage of a total coupon effect that is realized in each week, then this template can be used to estimate the effects given the number of weeks that have passed. There are several typical time-path effects that can be studied.

Weekly change in response to price reduction is a typical time-path effect. It seems reasonable to assume that response to price reduction would be greatest in the first week of the reduction and would gradually decline as people become accustomed to the new price. If one were attempting to determine the optimum length of time to maintain a temporary price reduction, the time path of response could become an important subject of study.

Time path of response to continued in-store display is another typical effect to be studied. Often, in-store displays may be left in place for several weeks. Studies often show little fall-off in display response from the first week to the second and even from the second week to the third, but response may show rapid fall-off after the third successive week.

Seasonal effects are another typical path. The log model estimates the average promotional response as a function of the price discount and promotional condition, and it estimates this response as a ratio to nonpromoted sales. This ratio might, however, vary from peak season to sales trough. Constructing a variable that is equal to the seasonality index, or the log of the seasonality index when the brand is on promotion, and zero otherwise, will allow testing to determine if the effects vary as a function of the season of the year.

Effects that vary by brand share are yet another typical path to study. The construction of a share index variable by dividing a brand's long-run share in a store by its long-run share in the market or total U.S. could be used to test the hypothesis that the brand's response to its own pricing and promotion activities, as well as its response to the pricing and promotional activities of competitors, is related to its share level. A similar set of variables could be constructed to test the hypothesis that a brand's pricing and promotional response will vary as a function of its brand or category development level (sales per million category buyers, or category sales per million households in a marketing area).

FORECASTING VS. STATISTICAL ANALYSIS MODELS

One distinction should be clearly made as part of the initial specification of a model. Is the model analysis to serve as a basis for management decision-making, or is the model to be used as a basis for preparing a forecast of future brand performance? The answer will usually materially alter the form of the analysis in the rich environment of scanner data. When the purpose of the analysis is to prepare a forecast of future sales, one must forecast all the independent variables. If the model were to contain a term such as *feature exclusivity*, then one of the inputs required in preparing a forecast of future sales would be an assessment of the probable split of future features into exclusive features and nonexclusive features. If no effort is going to be made in the future to control feature exclusivity, the base model should not include a feature exclusivity term. Without this term, the feature impact estimated is the average feature impact based on the historical relative frequencies of exclusive and nonexclusive features.

In contrast, if the model is not to be used for forecasting, then ANOVA (analysis of variance) methods may offer some powerful shortcuts in the construction of models designed to compare the relative impact on sales of alternative actions. For example, if the focus of the investigation is to determine the relative impacts of feature exclusivity against nonexclusivity, the principles of analysis of covariance might be used to include variables that are powerful adjusters for changes in marketing conditions not explicitly included in the model. For example, provided that the focus of the study does not include questions about trend, seasonality, and major competitive effects, one might include category volume in a store as a covariate. This would summarize all the effects of trend, seasonality, and competitive marketing actions, considerably simplifying the model. To use the resulting model for forecasting brand sales, however, would require first preparing a forecast of category sales (including the sales of the analysis brand), in order to forecast sales of the analysis brand.

In the course of a total analysis, both types of models might be used. The first phase of the analysis might be based on variables appropriate for statistical analysis. As a result of this analysis, one might make decisions either to alter marketing actions in the future or to continue current practices. The result of the feature exclusivity analysis might show, for example, that 40 percent of all features are nonexclusive, and that total sales on nonexclusive features are reduced by 10 percent. In the second phase of the analysis, a base-case forecast might be prepared using the "average effect" simple model, with alternative scenarios based on the degree of success in eliminating nonexclusive features. The most common cases occur with the use of precise disaggregate models to estimate response curves for various factors in the statistical analysis phase, and with the use of simple robust models on aggregate data to prepare base-case forecasts of the expected levels of next year's sales under the assumption of "business next year much the same as this year."

ANALYSIS TECHNIQUES FOR AGGREGATE DATA

Precise explanatory analysis cannot be conducted once data are aggregated and summarized beyond the level of retail outlet by week. However, often a highly precise, time-consuming, and expensive analysis is not desired — only a ballpark estimate of an effect. For example, management might make the following exploratory request: "Last year we ran two trade deals. What was the average increase in our business for each deal?" A simple tabulation of average U.S. weekly sales during the deal periods against average U.S. sales during nondeal periods might suffice to answer management's question. Alternatively, the question "Should we revise our discount structure for this year's two trade deals?" might require extensive and precise analysis of promotional responses against price. When significant questions have been identified that occur repetitively, an aggregate data analysis can be defined that highlights the answers to the core questions identified while averaging over all other effects.

Seasonality. Proper calculation of seasonal indexes is difficult. Weekly seasonality indexes are generally not provided as measures, because proper generation might require a different seasonality index series for each major brand (size) included in the database. For analyses at an aggregate level, seasonality estimates are usually provided from external sources, particularly at the regional and total U.S. levels. For simple analyses at the aggregate level, moving averages of the total sales of a brand or group of related brands are usually used in constructing seasonality series. Where more precise measures of seasonality are required, an analysis of aggregated data may be used to provide a more precise series for weekly seasonal effects.

Many retail products exhibit short-term changes in sales levels that are repetitive and predictable from year to year. Often these changes are related to the weather, but there are many other factors, such as social custom and traditions, that also lead to cyclical fluctuations in product sales over the months of the year. Until the advent of large quantities of scanner data in the mid-1980s, most seasonality analyses for consumer products were conducted on highly aggregated data series such as Nielsen bimonthly sales audit data, monthly SAMI estimates of warehouse withdrawal, or monthly shipment data by plant, sales region, or nation. The typical analysis method was based on univariate time series methods and generated a seasonality index by month.

Aggregate Data Sources. Traditional methods of data reporting and analysis have been primarily based on aggregate data with simple models. Comparison of the results of a time period and the same period a year ago is commonly used for bimonthly, quarterly, or annual data. Causal data have been limited to measures of average price and to gross promotional measures, such as the number of feature ads run per account or the percentage of volume sold with promotion.

The advent of weekly scanner-based tracking data makes weekly data available at the key account level for many accounts, as well as on the market, regional, and national levels on a week-by-week basis. The need to support many types of analyses for product brand management, product sales management, retail category promotional management, retailer stocking, shelf management, pricing decisions, and broker accounting has led to a proliferation of data measures that prepare the data precisely to support both traditional and emerging types of analyses. From 20 to 50 specific data series on a weekly basis might be required to support commonly performed analyses. The growing capacity of personal computers allows an analyst to keep such weekly aggregate series on a large variety of geographical levels. Because the data are available, it becomes tempting to perform an analysis with data series that are close to the desired series, often with puzzling results.

Typical measures available at the aggregate level include the following:

1. **Volume measures** such as total sales volume, base sales volume, incremental sales volume, and sales volume per million dollars of retail sales (actual cash value). Transformations of volume might be brand share, base share, and incremental share. Volumes are typically equalized across items.

2. **Pricing measures** such as average price per volume, average base price per volume, average promoted price per volume, average nonpromoted price per volume, average penny price reduction per volume when on price reduction, average percentage price reduction per volume when on price reduction. These measures are usually available on either a price per sale unit or a price per equalized volume basis. These measures are generally available for each of the most common retail promotion types — feature/display combination, feature without display (feature only), display without feature (display only), and price reduction only (price reduction without feature or display). Depending on the predominant forms of promotion, composite measures might also be provided based on the following conditions — any feature, any display, or any promotion.

3. **Compositional measures** show the level of volume activity by promotional type. Examples include the percentage of volume sold with feature and display, with feature only, with display only, with price reduction only, with any feature, with any display, or with any promotion. Another class of compositional measures shows the brand performance based on the ACV of stores performing some activity. Examples are percentage ACV of stores carrying the product (ACV distribution), percentage ACV of stores with feature and display, feature only, and so on.

4. **Performance measures** show the estimated response to promotional activity. Usually based on a model (such as PromotionScan), examples include the average percentage increase on feature and display, on feature only, and so on. An alternative is to report performance measures in terms of incremental weeks. For example, a promotion that generates 1.5 incremental weeks in the store in which it is run generates a 150

percent increase in weekly sales. If the stores that carried the promotion accounted for 15 percent of the brand sales, the promotion would generate .225 incremental weeks for the market.

In summary, analysis of disaggregate data is preferable, where possible, in order to understand the response at the point where the marketing action is applied. However, confounding effects such as cross-store or cross-size cannibalization may require analysis of aggregate data in order to fully capture the net effect of a retail marketing action on manufacturer sales. Disaggregate data may not be available, or they may represent an amount of data too large to accommodate in the analysis. In addition, analysts can construct data series that minimize aggregation bias by avoiding the volume weighting of results of marketing actions that have clearly different sales responses.

ANALYSIS STRATEGIES

A number of questions can be answered through the analysis of scanner-based promotion data. Perhaps the most obvious application is the evaluation of the promotional events themselves. The promotional event can be analyzed both in terms of sales volume and in terms of profitability.

Beyond the analysis of promotional events, the character of a brand itself can be analyzed. Sales volume can be divided into base and incremental components. This kind of brand analysis can lead to market simulations — that is, asking "what if" questions about varying levels of marketing and promotional support along with differing promotional mixes. What would happen, for example, if an additional promotion were run? What would happen if television advertising were increased?

For the manufacturer, fact-based marketing, as this kind of analysis is called, considerably enhances the ability to gain distribution, gain promotional support, and determine the right mix of promotional activity for the brand. For the retailer, fact-based marketing helps make decisions about the reallocation of promotional resources provided by manufacturers, helps review marketing strategies, and aids in evaluating manufacturers' proposals and promotional programs.

PRINCIPLES OF PROMOTION ANALYSIS

Based on the discussion and the analysis of numerous sales promotion programs, a number of sales promotion principles and issues can be summarized. (For a more detailed discussion please refer to Totten and Block [1993].) These principles and issues should serve well as guidelines for those who are managing sales promotion programs. The summary is divided into two sections: (1) fundamental principles, and (2) the role of sales promotion analysis.

Fundamental Principles. Ten fundamental principles of sales promotion have resulted from the ongoing analysis of scanner-based data. These fundamental principles are as follows:

1. **Store-level data are critically important.** Aggregate market-level data simply are not sufficiently sensitive to detect the true sales impacts of promotional programs. Data must be measured at the individual store level and analyzed on at least a weekly basis to understand the dynamics of sales promotion. Even when the analysis is for a single chain in a single market, analysis should be at the individual store level. Promotions, particularly in-store displays or shelf-price reductions, may not be equally effective across stores, offering opportunity for profit optimization. Detailed results may be aggregated and summarized after the analysis is complete. Where analysis must be conducted on aggregate data, the method of analysis should be cross-validated with store level detail data.

2. **Sales volume is the key measure.** While market share as a measure of sales performance has a strong tradition, competitive activity and other factors make it insufficiently sensitive to measure the short-term impact of sales promotion. The promoted brand's sales volume is by far the best measure of the performance of a sales promotion program.

3. **Trade promotions should generate incremental profit.** One of the most important findings from the analysis of scanner-based data is the consistent return to the base level of business for a brand after a promotional period (for established products). In other words, future sales do not seem to increase as a result of the promotion. The promotion generally stimulates sales only during the promotional period. This clearly means that to be justified, the promotion itself should generate incremental profit. Use of trade promotion for objectives other than profit, such as volume/share maintenance or obtaining retailer goodwill, should be clearly identified and should have the trade-promotion costs identified and tied back to the activity.

4. **Package size is important.** Not all consumers favor the same package size, despite their interest in the product. It is critically important to promote the package size that matches the appropriate market for the promotion to be a success.

5. **The demand curve is kinked.** For the first time, marketing managers can begin with a realistic, empirically estimated demand curve. Both pricing and promotion decisions can be made on the basis of the fundamental understanding of the relationship of price and sales volume for the product category and brand. In many product categories, that demand curve is clearly kinked, meaning that lowering the price in certain ranges will not necessarily result in increasing the sales volume, or that raising the price would not necessarily result in decreased sales volume. Obviously, knowledge of any existing kinks greatly

improves the efficiency of the revenue potential for the brand.

6. **Competitive effects are minimal, except smong switchers.** Despite common sense expectation, promoting one brand in a product category has very little impact on loyal purchasers of other brands. In other words, a sales promotion program does not necessarily cut into the competing brand's business. Promotion clearly has the greatest impact on brand switchers. Promotion is most likely to influence the switchers, with additional volume potential available from infrequent category buyers.

7. **Price sensitivity and promotion responsiveness are different.** Not all brands will respond in the same way to price. Some products may behave entirely on the basis of price, while impulse-driven items may respond primarily to promotion elements, such as an in-store display. Responses depend on the loyalty characteristics of the brand.

8. **Retail trade performance is essential.** Even the most successful consumer promotions can be substantially enhanced by the trade. The cooperation of the trade with in-store displays, ad features, and its own promotional programs creates a special synergy that can result in sales that far exceed what either the manufacturer or retailer could do alone.

9. **Reduction of promotion results in loss of volume.** Generally, every time a promotion program ends, the sales volume substantially declines. Clearly, there is a strong relationship between the promotion and the sales volume for the brand. However, the loss of sales volume does not necessarily mean that profit is lost. The revenue lost due to lower prices and the cost of the promotion itself may· mean lower profit during the promotion.

10. **Analysis of real data maximizes profit.** The most important point of this discussion is that promotional programs should be analyzed in terms of the incremental sales generated and the additional costs incurred. Local competitive conditions and volume response differences can lead to dramatically different profitability from region to region, or even from store to store, in a market for apparently similar promotional activity. The profitability of the promotional program should be the ultimate criterion for the management of promotional programs.

The Role of Sales Promotion Analysis. Beyond the fundamental principles of sales promotion is the evolving role of analysis in managing an integrated marketing communications program. The special role of sales promotion analysis can be summarized in the following seven ideas:

1. **Competitive promotion.** Not only should a brand's own sales promotion programs be analyzed, but also competitive promotions should be analyzed. This additional analysis not only aids in understanding the competition, it provides insight into the

product category.

2. **Head-to-head promotion with competition.** In those instances when two promotions are in direct competition, the sales results of the brand, the direct competitor, and the product category need to be understood. Analyzing scanner-based sales data is the only way to understand the impact of the head-to-head competition.

3. **Display wear-out.** While displays generally are the most effective way to build short-term sales volume, the effectiveness diminishes over time. Assessing the effectiveness of displays requires a special store level analysis over time.

4. **Holiday promotion effects.** Understanding any special synergy that may exist from holiday or other event-related promotions is very important in stretching a limited promotional budget. Analyzing holidays requires special attention to temporal detail.

5. **Coupon drops and other direct promotions.** Understanding the sales results from coupon drops and other direct promotions in the contexts of the marketplace and category is very important. Expanding the analysis beyond the in-store displays and feature advertising to include other consumer promotions is vital to managing an integrated marketing communications program.

6. **Short-term TV advertising.** Advertising analyses are also critical to managing integrated marketing communications programs. Special attention needs to be given to the role of competitive advertising and its long-term effects.

7. **Temporal response for price reduction.** How long should a special price reduction be maintained? Such questions can be answered directly through analysis. The impact of a price reduction is related to both its magnitude and its duration.

The solution for both the manufacturer and the retailer is fact-based marketing based on scanner data analysis. Marketing and selling strategies for both retailers and manufacturers should be based on a thorough understanding of both base and incremental sales volume and the impact of marketing communications programs. This will put the success of any marketing program in the hands of the consumer, where it belongs.

Suggested Readings

Blattberg, Robert C., and Scott A. Neslin. *Sales Promotion: Concepts, Methods, and Strategies*. Englewood Cliffs, NJ: Prentice Hall, 1990.

Totten, John C., and Martin P. Block. *Analyzing Sales Promotion*. Second Edition. Chicago: Dartnell, 1993.

PART II
TECHNIQUES

Dan Ailloni-Charas is Chairman and CEO of Stratmar Systems, Inc., a marketing services company providing sampling, couponing, fulfillment, and other in-store and out-of-store support programs. Prior to his 25 years as CEO of Stratmar, Ailloni-Charas was Marketing Research Manager, New Products Manager, and Manager of International Marketing Services for Cheseborough-Pond's. He also was Director of Consumer and Communications Research at Forbes magazine.

He has been an active member of the Promotion Marketing Association of America since 1978, serving on the Board of Directors as Chairman of the Education Committee and Premium Shows Subcommittee, and, for the last five years, has served as Vice President and a member of the Executive Committee. He is past National Vice President of the American Marketing Association (AMA) and past President of the New York AMA chapter. In addition, Ailloni-Charas has served as Editor of Marketing Review and has been on the Board of Editors for The Journal of Consumer Marketing since 1982. He is the author of Promotion: A Guide to Effective Promotional Planning, Strategies & Executions, published by John Wiley & Sons (1984).

Ailloni-Charas has taught marketing as an adjunct or visiting professor at several universities, including Pace University and New York University. He received a Ph.D. from the Graduate School of Business Administration at New York University. He received bachelor's and master's degrees from the University of California.

CHAPTER 5

SAMPLING

SAMPLING AS TRIAL: ACCELERATING THE ADOPTION OF A NEW PRODUCT

It has been said that the fastest way to kill a bad new product is to sample it to potential consumers. Indeed, since sampling is designed to accelerate the adoption process, the quicker consumers know that a new product will not meet their expectations of satisfaction, the quicker its demise.

Consider the following: Trial, or first use, is critical to the adoption of a new product. It is a necessary step the consumer must take before a product can be deemed acceptable for consumption and repeated buying.

Initial purchases of a new product can be brought about through persuasive communications of one sort or another. However, initial purchases all require a potential consumer to "risk" the purchase price, since a new product may or may not live up to its performance promise. Because consumers, under the barrage of an unending stream of new product communications, are slow to take such risks with their money, the nonrisk proposition of sampling serves to accelerate the introduction process.

The introduction of new products has always been an "iffy" proposition. Few products advance from the test-marketing stage to broad-scale commercialization, and, among those that do, many eventually fail. Often, this may be due to a lack of sufficient support over the time frame that is needed for consumers to become aware of a new product, knowledgeable about it, and, finally, interested enough to make that first trial purchase. By then, it may be too late, since the product may have lost its distribution at the retail level.

As manufacturers spend large sums of money to develop and introduce new products and line extensions, R&D costs — coupled with manufacturing, packaging, and front-end loaded advertising and distribution costs — add up quickly. Distribution is critical; unless a product is on the shelf where customers can find it, all is for naught. In recent years, the trade has been exacting increasing levies from manufacturers before accepting their products for distribution at retail. Slotting charges — payments the manufacturer is required to make before the product is accepted by an account for distribution in its stores — further increase the investment required in the launching of a new product.

Today, manufacturers are allowed about three months to prove to the trade that a new product can "make it" in the marketplace. Success is determined by moving an acceptable number of cases of product every week. Should that movement level be achieved, the new product may be allotted a permanent home on the shelf. Should it fail to make it, out it goes, and with it, the sizable investment made to that point. Given more time, that new product might have been successful — but translating "sales in the mind" made through advertising requires time to build up to sufficient levels. Time, however, is a scarce commodity in today's retailing reality; hence, a new product may be delisted before it can make it, and once it is no longer carried by an account, it is virtually impossible, and very costly, to get it back on the shelf.

Enter sampling. By short-circuiting the process through nonrisk trial, we will have accelerated the adoption of the new product — should it meet performance expectations — and enhanced the likelihood of its obtaining a permanent home on the retail shelf. By doing so, sampling helps safeguard the sizable investment made in the new product launch and, most likely, at a fraction of that initial investment.

THE GROWTH OF SAMPLING

Over the years, the sampling "industry" has continued to grow, through good times and bad, and for all the good reasons outlined previously. While no exact figure can be determined regarding the aggregate corporate expenditures spent on sampling, including both costs of product and distribution, it would be safe to assume that hundreds of millions of dollars are spent today by manufacturers throughout the U.S. to jump-start the adoption process.

Since the essence of sampling is the placement of a trial size of a product in the hands of a potential user, there is a continuous proliferation of methods designed to achieve this purpose, from sampling on airplanes, to state and county fairs, to in-home parties. The number of alternative sampling vehicles are many, and new ideas abound. For our purpose, the remainder of this chapter will spotlight the major sampling venues with a clear understanding that the number of potential alternatives is limited only by the creativity and imagination of those active in this area.

SAMPLING AS INSURANCE:
SECURING A TRADE FRANCHISE

Sampling as an insurance policy, representing, in effect, a defensive strategy, is a relatively new idea. For years, offensive objectives were targeted by sampling. The goal was primarily directed to conversions to regular usage (purchases), leading to quicker payouts of total launch investments. While the offensive criteria are still inherent in the accelerating action of sampling, the emphasis today is on faster consumer takeout at retail, which is conducive to regular listing. This, parenthetically, accounts for the literal explosion of in-store sampling activities over the last 10 years or so.

A national study recently published by the National Association of Demonstration Companies (NADC) reports on the growth of this mode of sampling in recent years, as well as anticipated growth through the year 2000. Here are some findings of the survey, which was conducted in mid-1992:

- 70.7 percent of product manufacturers and 100 percent of retailers indicate they are going to increase the use of in-store sampling between now and the year 2000.
- 79.3 percent of shoppers say they will buy a sampled product if they like it and if it is one they need and want.
- Demonstration is the promotional technique shoppers remember the longest, when compared with in-store coupons, end-of-the-aisle displays, or signage on a shelf.
- Shoppers also like sampling because it is "hassle free," that is, they can choose whether or not to participate — and they also like the fact that there is often an "instant discount" associated with the demonstration.

Having reviewed the role of sampling as a trial vehicle conducive to following up full-revenue purchases, we can classify such efforts by positioning them to generate immediate consumer takeout vs. efforts that bring about purchases of the product or services at a later time.

The dividing line here rests with the point of purchase. Sampling a product on the retail floor can be tied to promotional efforts resulting in price featuring, display activities, and incremental pipelining to retail. In effect, we signal to the shopper who samples a product in-store that if the product "experience" was satisfactory, he or she can make a first, full-sized purchase at a promotionally advantaged price. Easing a new user into regular usage of a new product through trial, followed by a discounted first purchase, will usually accelerate the building up of both consumer and trade franchises.

However, it is important to note that not all products can be actually experienced at the actual point of purchase. One can try out a new scent from a tester on a department store counter, taste a few sips of a new beverage, or put a few drops of a new lotion on the back of one's hand to test its level of greasiness. But few people will sample an antacid or laxative while in the store before they decide whether to purchase the product.

A more extreme case is represented by pet foods, which are judged first by their palatability to the pet, their compatibility with the pet's digestive system, and, finally, by their nutritional claims. This trial-and-evaluation process obviously cannot take place at point of purchase.

Additionally, one must also realize that some purchases are made in-store by an adult in his or her role as a purchasing agent, and not by the ultimate consumer who will have the final say regarding the suitability of the sampled product for regular purchase.

SAMPLING AT OR NEAR THE POINT OF PURCHASE

Sampling can be carried out in, near, or away from, the actual point of purchase. This distinction may seem simple, yet it is important. Products that can be "experienced on the spot," at the point of purchase, can be immediately converted into a revenue sale. This allows the sampling effort to be executed as a total "event," fully involving the distribution channel in the process of quickly building up both trade and consumer franchises.

Sampling conducted away from the point of purchase is more akin to the "sale in the mind" effect attributed to advertising. The more time that elapses after sampling the product before the actual opportunity of buying the product in the store presents itself, the more likely the occurrence of "interference" — ranging from competitive efforts to simple forgetfulness — which will negatively impact the initial intent of buying the product sampled.

Further, when an account implements a sampling program in its stores, it is safe to assume that the product is in distribution (in at least the account's stores) facilitating the conversion of customers sampled to actual users/purchasers. This may not be the case when the product is sampled away from the point of purchase where gaps in distribution may have a further negative impact on the customer's intent to buy.

For goods, sampling at the point of purchase, as indicated, is preferable in many ways that can lead to an immediate purchase. However, several caveats must be observed:

1. The product must be in distribution with sufficient stock at retail to satisfy immediate conversion needs. Running out of stock during a sampling period represents a clear case of lost opportunity. It is customary that product is "plussed out" by an account's warehouse in conjunction with a promotional period. Given the number of parallel promotions running every week, one would be remiss in anticipating that sufficient merchandise will automatically be sent out from warehouses to stores. Both quantities and timing must be negotiated and monitored by the manufacturer's sales organization.

2. While trade support of the product through advertised price featuring will help accelerate consumer takeout, manufacturers are advised not to offer label price-off deals on their products during an introductory stage. This would prevent them from establishing a firm value/price reference point for such products in consumers' minds. Price features offered by the trade are acceptable, and even expected. The fact that such price features are based on increased allowances given by manufacturers to the trade so that products may flow through to consumers does not necessarily affect consumers' perceptions of product value.

3. Generally speaking, retail floor displays increase consumer takeout of any product, new or old. Since displays are associat-

ed in consumers' minds with special deals, takeout increases significantly when a product is displayed in one form or another. Given the limited floor space available for displays in the context of the number of items carried by a retail store, manufacturers usually "buy" space for their displays through special allowances. At this point, the retailer must decide how much of this allowance to pass on to his or her shoppers.

Retailers set up their displays at the beginning of the week — usually on Sundays when most of the their advertising is circulated, while sampling is executed Fridays through Sundays, which are considered the best in-store-traffic days. Manufacturers' displays start selling through as soon as they are set up, thus significantly adding to the consumer takeout during the sampling week. In that sense, some of the sampling will take place in the home — after the product is purchased. It is important to note that the placement of a display on the retail floor as part of a sampling event further ensures against potential out-of-stock crises.

4. Securing a spot on an account's promotional calendar is critical and should be accomplished early enough to enable the sampling program to be optimally executed. The program should take into consideration not only the availability of sampling stations on the retail floor (to guard against the possibility of postponement, due to limited floor space), but also potential tie-ins with product advertising schedules, as well as consumer and trade promotions that are planned for later follow-up periods.

One must keep in mind, however, that the complexion of in-store sampling programs has changed radically since the mid-1980s. Pressed for finding new revenue sources to shore up their weakening financial bases, most retailers identified in-store programs as yet another potential profit center.

Under the guise of insisting that they must retain control over activities in their stores, many retailers have set up their own sampling/demonstration units. Alternatively, some retailers have signed exclusive access agreements with one local service or another whose sampling fees often include hefty payments to the trade for such agreements. Where manufacturers are allowed less fettered access to the retail floor through in-store services of their choice, the trade may nevertheless demand significant payments on the premise that giving a manufacturer in-store access to their customer base is valuable and, thus, chargeable. Either way, the costs of in-store sampling have skyrocketed. Nevertheless, sampling as a promotional technique has increased many times over in the last few years, attesting to the growing importance of the point of purchase in manufacturers' marketing plans.

To the trade, individual brands are no longer as important as they once were. Having recognized the commoditization of many of the product classes sold in their stores and consequently noticing the lack of product loyalty and the ease with which consumers switch from brand to brand — retailers have abandoned their commitment to full assortments, concentrating instead on overall product categories. Concerns for specific brands are now left to those manufacturing them. Given that brands cannot survive in the marketplace without adequate distribution at retail, the trade has been able to increase its "take" from manufacturers in many ways — overrides on in-store sampling programs being one.

Still, the key problem is not one of payments, which, however reluctantly, may be disbursed from and calculated in overall marketing plans as part of the cost of doing business. The real problem is one of accountability.

Based on current practices, there can be no doubt that increasing numbers of retailers are using their growing clout over manufacturers to demand more and more money from them as part of their continuing business relationship. At the same time, they are becoming less and less accountable for the performance the money is supposed to buy.

This is certainly true with in-store sampling programs, in which more stringent auditing on the part of manufacturers has helped uncover some of the more glaring performance problems that, lacking proper monitoring, are often papered over.

The pursuit of accountability, then, demands attention to the following:

1. Are all samplers/demonstrators showing up in-store as scheduled? If, for whatever reason, a sampler/demonstrator does not show up at the appointed time, is the sampling service he or she works for alerted to the situation immediately? Does the service have a backup procedure? Will it take immediate action on it?

2. Does the sampling service adhere to the schedules set up by manufacturers to coincide with other promotional and advertising efforts, or does it take it upon itself to change and adjust these schedules to conform to its own considerations and deployment of resources?

3. Are the samplers/demonstrators handling the program assigned to them by strictly one manufacturer, or are they handling additional items at the same time while fees are collected separately from each principal?

4. Are the samplers/demonstrators properly trained, and are they sufficiently knowledgeable about the product, its superiority claims, and its proper preparation — in the case of an actual demonstration — to be able to present it persuasively to shoppers?

5. Often sampling programs require both equipment and supplies. Are these being handled properly and in a timely fashion?

6. More often than not, sampling programs include coupons designed to accelerate immediate purchases, and, in most cases, they are handled separately from the samples themselves. How are they secured? Since coupons are "cash," mishandling of them can be quite costly — potentially exceeding the cost of the sampling effort itself.

7. Is the sampling service ready and willing to conduct program prechecks to ensure that the stores involved are properly alerted to the program and have sufficient stock on hand to meet the ensuing incremental consumer takeout? As previously mentioned, running out of stock during a sampling/demonstration program can seriously hamper the success of such an effort.

8. Will the service provide readings of merchandise sold during the sampling/demonstration period and verification of the number of coupons and samples handed out, as well as information on pricing, display activities, and consumer reactions? Such information is both descriptive (allowing one to judge performance in terms of conversion levels and units moved) and prescriptive (enabling one to fine-tune future efforts using the database accumulated in this and other programs).

9. Does the service carry all applicable liability insurance coverage? Insurance claims follow those with the "deepest pockets," and that may turn out to be the manufacturer whose product is being sampled.

10. Is the service responsive to manufacturers' needs and questions, or is it holding them at arm's length under the premise that its allegiance is to the retailer it is associated with, and not to the manufacturer who is paying the bills?

11. Is the service willing and able to fully document all expenses incurred — particularly the cost of the sampled product, which is often purchased in the store — as it bills for such expenses?

Often, manufacturers (primarily, their local sales organizations) will insist on fielding and managing the execution of in-store sampling programs in their sales areas through services that are available locally. Given the hodgepodge of services operating in each market, and the fact that different accounts or stores will allow access to different services, one can end up using 20 or more in-store sampling companies in one single market.

This makes for the rather formidable task of calling on each local sales office to recruit, train, assign, monitor, and process reports on the work done on each sampling program fielded. Further, one must order supplies and equipment; arrange for their timely delivery and transshipment, where needed; and determine whether the product used in sampling is to be warehoused and delivered to stores, according to schedule, or purchased in-store. The local sales offices also must store and distribute coupons, when they are used, to the individual demonstrators under secure conditions and, finally, provide a paymaster function, carefully evaluating all documentation submitted on both time and expenditures.

Since most in-store sampling programs are still executed locally under the conditions described above, one must query the logic of continuing these practices, given the costs involved. Many argue, with obvious justification, that, in today's competitive environment, salespeople have their hands full properly servicing their own accounts. Diverting their efforts and attention to the handling of sampling programs — a task which, if it is to be done well, is highly time-intensive — is neither desirable nor cost-efficient.

The alternative, assigning in-store sampling programs to national companies that provide top-to-bottom management and performance accountability across the board, is becoming increasingly prevalent. The reasons for this growing shift are many:

1. Employment of national companies frees local sales organizations from responsibilities that, however time-consuming, have no direct bearing on the key account management function with which salespeople are charged. It enables salespeople to target those areas that are, indeed, critical to the success of an in-store sampling program by securing the type of trade support needed to enhance overall performance.

2. Using a national company ensures that the same performance standards will prevail across all markets included in the coverage plan. Allowing each local service in each market to conduct the in-store sampling program according to its own individual procedures can fragment a program to such an extent that no coherent data collection may be possible, thus preventing needed accountability and analytical evaluation.

3. One argument advanced for contracting in-store sampling efforts locally is based on cost. Local assignments cost less money. True, national management has a price. However, studies conducted by some manufacturers have enabled them to conclude that the incremental value inherent in the national management of an in-store sampling program significantly exceeds its cost.

PERSONAL SAMPLING AWAY FROM THE POINT-OF-PURCHASE

Sampling potential users away from the point of purchase can take many forms. These sampling techniques are all commonly designed to accelerate the trial of new products, and the mode chosen to distribute samples hinges on both the nature of the product sampled and its distribution pattern.

Products in high-penetration categories in wide distribution benefit from intensive sampling, reaching large numbers of people as cost-efficiently as possible. Conversely, niche products directed to targeted consumer segments require tailored sampling approaches that are specifically relevant to both usage and purchase of these products.

High-traffic sampling that depends on reaching large numbers of potential consumers over short periods of time is indicated when the product sampled fits in broadly based usage categories, thus minimizing the potential waste inherent in handing out samples to people who are not likely to use them.

Sampling in high-cluster areas (such as shopping centers and commuter stations), and at special events (such as county and state fairs) enables companies to generate immediate, large-scale trial. In years past, cigarette companies used to sample heavily on street corners in downtown locations. Given their shrinking user base, this is less prevalent today. However, companies that manufacture food products (such as candy, beverages, and those that do not require special preparation or storing conditions) continue to include high-traffic sampling in their plans.

The following criteria should be reviewed when high-traffic sampling is being considered:

1. Will the program reach people within the marketing area sampled — thus affecting local takeout patterns at the retail level — or will it target people in the market for short periods of time (such as tourists)? Sampling in San Francisco's Union Square, for example, may be the wrong approach if a product is only being test-marketed in that metropolitan area. Remember that for a sampling program to be successful, it must be translated into actual, full-revenue purchases at retail.

2. Local ordinances and rulings must be reviewed before locking in a sampling plan downtown and in other public locations. While licenses are not usually required, since sampling is not generally viewed as solicitation — no transfer of money is involved — some jurisdictions limit it to certain areas (particularly when public events are scheduled).

3. Litter is of major concern when executing a high-traffic sampling program. This is particularly critical in cases where the sampling effort generates instant discards, such as candy wrappers or cups used in sampling a beverage. Care should be taken to keep the sampling area and its vicinity as litter free as possible by strategically placing garbage cans around the area's perimeter.

4. In order to achieve optimal distribution levels, it is important that sampling be limited to one sample per person. Monitoring this in high-traffic locations is difficult. However, duplication can be significantly reduced if sampling crews in downtown areas or other high-traffic locations are properly spread out to discourage people from walking a little farther or crossing the

street a few times in order to obtain additional samples.

5. The high-traffic sampling plan should allow for the timely resupplying of all sampling stations to prevent "out-of-stock" conditions. Not all samples can (or should) be stacked up in unopened cases next to the sampling station. Some products, such as food samples in need of refrigeration, limit the number that can be handled by samplers at any one time. Also, those products that can be handled in greater numbers are subject to pilferage — one case at a time. Thus, one must build into the plan a good delivery system that is fully cognizant of traffic patterns, particularly when they are affected by the specific event that provided the context for the sampling effort in the first place.

6. Fees may be required, and they usually vary from event to event. While no fees may be levied for sampling in downtown traffic, access to shopping malls, special events, and fairs may require payments based on the number of samplers used and the number of days involved. In the case of fairs, it may require further commitments to staff a booth during the full duration of the fair.

Up to this point, we have talked about in-hand, person-to-person sampling efforts. This form of sampling allows for several levels of selectivity:

- *Locational selectivity* — Sampling is executed selectively in areas that meet the specific potential user profiles, whether classified by area of the country, urban vs. suburban locations, ethnic clusters, and so forth.
- *Visual selectivity* — This allows samplers to visually identify the people who are to be offered the specific samples. (Samplers can visually separate males from females; the young from the old; or bald people from people with hair.)
- *Verbal selectivity* — The ultimate selectivity level in which people can be queried about their likelihood of using the sampled product; that is, their having a dishwasher in their home or owning a dog or cat.

SAMPLING BY MAIL

A great deal of sampling is conducted today by mail. Its ease of execution, coupled with its potential reach of every single dwelling across the country, makes it attractive, although not necessarily economical, particularly in a marketing environment that mandates increasingly narrow targeting.

Much of the sampling by mail goes third class. This is primarily "occupant" mailing that delivers samples to current residents in dwellings in the geographical areas included in the distribution plan. There are no time imperatives to the delivery of samples sent by third-class mail. While first-class mail has overall priority, samples sent third class may linger for a long time in local post offices. When they add up to a lot of undelivered units, the local post office may decide to "lighten the mail" and donate them to a local county hospital, for example, for distribution to its needier patients. That, of course, may not have been the intent of the company whose samples they were.

First-class mailings are often used in preference to third-class mailings when specific recipients have been identified and addressed. By law, the post office must return to the sender mail that cannot be delivered, or forward it if the addressee has moved away and filed a forwarding address. While this is deemed positive, some companies continue to use third class, as they find that the additional benefits inherent in first class do not justify the additional costs involved. These include the incremental cost of buying and processing specific target mailing lists available from various compilers who specialize in this field.

Here are some of the issues that must be considered when mailing samples:

1. How extensive should the sampling program be? Assuming a given conversion level from trial to regular purchases — as indicated by the manufacturer's market research department through earlier product placement and other research efforts — the size of the sampling program should be sufficient to help the new product reach a calculated consumer franchise level. For example, this may call for a 20 percent penetration of households in a specific market. Sampling at twice that level may not be necessary.

2. How good are the mailing lists used? The mobility of households in the U.S. is well documented. "Old" lists — lists that have not been updated for six months or more — will result in a considerable amount of waste. Not only are delivery costs at stake here, but also costs of wasted product add up, as well.

3. How inclusive are the lists used? Do they include single-parent households, a small but growing segment of the market? Do they include buildings with multiple dwellings? High-rises are noted for the way samples, particularly those mailed third class, are left in bulk on tables in mailroom areas to be taken by whoever passes. Do they include ethnic areas, particularly those in midcity?

4. Can the samples be sent out by unsolicited mail? In many states, the mailing of unsolicited samples of health products, for example, is not allowed. This is due partially to the fear that they may be delivered and then consumed by nonadults who may not be sufficiently qualified to understand and follow the cautionary label indications before using these products.

5. As a follow-up to the above point, is the packaging used to mail the samples sufficiently sturdy — not only to protect the

integrity of the product in transit — but also to prevent potential tampering?

To sum up, sampling by mail is widely used and can be quite effective. It must be planned with care and with due consideration of all elements in the process that can optimize its effectiveness, while at the same time avoiding the pitfalls that may, at worst, cause it to fail altogether rather than being just cost-inefficient.

IN-HOME SAMPLING

While mail samples are delivered by the U.S. Postal Service, in-home sampling (often referred to as "door-to-door" sampling) is carried out by special crews who work out of delivery vans.

At one time, door-to-door sampling was quite prevalent, particularly when heavier samples were distributed. In recent years, this form of sampling has declined significantly; only a few companies continue to use it to any substantial degree.

While it enables one to pinpoint distribution to specific clusters of homes, and does not impose the same size limitations that one must keep in mind when sampling by mail, door-to-door sampling raises questions of its own:

1. How is the sample delivered? The "ring-and-leave" approach in which the sample is left — usually in a polybag hung on the doorknob — after the deliverer rings the bell to alert those inside the dwelling, is the way most sampling takes place. It is the least expensive method because the sampling crew can move quickly from house to house. It is also the most prone to mischief, since the samples are left unattended. Remember that in-home deliverers cannot use the mailboxes since legally they are considered to be federal property.

    Conversely, one may choose to "ring, wait, and give." In this case, controls increase considerably because the sample is given by hand to a person actually living in the specific home. Productivity, however, is only a fraction of what it is with the "ring and leave" approach, and, therefore, for the most part, is unaffordable.

2. The safety concerns when samples are distributed by the "ring-and-leave" approach increase significantly, since samples left unattended can be pilfered, tampered with, and misused by minors. Safety requires extra strong and safe packaging be used, and the corresponding costs can be high.

3. The same questions regarding the inclusiveness of the sampling plan, when sampling by mail, apply here, as well. Most door-to-door sampling programs avoid coverage in high-rise areas and limit their reach to single-home dwellings. Given continuing urbanization trends in both city and suburban areas, this method of sampling is quickly losing ground.

SUMMARY

Following is a brief summary of the points and caveats reviewed in this chapter:

1. Sampling is a powerful trial device designed to accelerate the adoption of new products by allowing customers to experience them at no risk.

2. Since the availability of new products at point of purchase is critical to the adoption of the new product (at least for consumer package goods), sampling at or near the stores carrying them, when translated to full revenue purchases, will further ensure the securing of a permanent home at retail.

3. Conducting sampling programs in-store has become increasingly complex as retailers, keen on identifying new income sources to shore up their generally shaky finances, have been exacting increasing fees for giving manufacturers "access" to customers in their stores. Even while paying these fees, manufacturers must insist on full accountability of the moneys spent.

4. Sampling a product that fails to meet a reasonable level of anticipated consumer satisfaction is going to accelerate its demise.

5. Sampling programs should not be executed in a vacuum. They must be supported before, during, and after by other components in the marketing plan. As such, sampling programs should be carefully planned as an integral part of one's marketing strategy.

Tamara Brezen Block is President of Block Research, Inc., a research firm providing a full range of quantitative and qualitative research services, including sales promotion analysis. She teaches graduate level research methods and sales promotion courses, among others, as a faculty member of the Medill School of Journalism's Integrated Marketing Communications Program at Northwestern University. Prior to joining the faculty at Northwestern, Block was an instructor in the Advertising Deparment at Michigan State University and a Visiting Professor at Foote, Cone, & Belding in Chicago.

In addition to co-editing this Handbook, Block is co-author of a soon-to-be-published book on Business-to-Business Research. She has been published in several academic journals on topics related to advertising and promotion effects.

Block received a Ph.D. in Mass Media from Michigan State University. Her dissertation on the topic of sales promotion received a national award from the Council of Sales Promotion Agencies. Her Master of Arts degree and Bachelor of Arts, both in Advertising, were also completed at Michigan State.

Larry Tucker has been prominent in the promotion and direct marketing fields for more than 20 years and is a recognized authority on target marketing, list analysis, promotion, and direct mail. For the past 16 years, his firm, Larry Tucker, Inc., has sponsored the nation's largest targeted co-op mailing program, "Jane Tucker's Supermarket of Savings" — now mailing almost 150 million co-op envelopes annually to growing families, older active adults (50+), and black and Hispanic or Latino families.

An active member of the Direct Marketing Association, the Promotion Marketing Association of America, and many other industry groups, he contributes frequently to industry publications and regularly addresses meetings of marketing executives.

CHAPTER 6

COUPONING

Couponing in the nineties, like other promotional techniques, has begun to reach its mature stage. While the 1980s were boom years for couponing, especially 1982 through 1984, couponing has been increasing at a more modest rate since then. This is due, in part, to the fact that there are very few major product categories that have yet to enter the couponing field. While couponing remains a primary sales promotional tool of grocery and drug manufacturers, its use has extended far beyond the package goods domain. Coupons are used for almost every other kind of product from apparel to toys to airline transportation.

The best sources of coupon information differ on current coupon growth trends, but they do agree on the fact that couponing is still on the rise. Nielsen Clearing House (NCH) estimated that in 1991 manufacturers distriubuted approximately 292 billion coupons, which represented a 4.5 percent growth over 1990. Carolina Manufacturers Service (CMS) reported even larger numbers with 314 billion coupons distributed in 1991, representing a 12 percent increase in numbers of coupons distributed, claiming the state of the American economy in 1991–1992 contributed to the increase in coupon activity.

The two main sources for coupons are manufacturers and retailers. Most manufacturers are generally happy with "direct to the consumer" couponing results but are exploring new avenues and added-value ideas. Retailers are still looking to see how they can make the most of coupons, and are increasing their own in-ad couponing as well.

As couponing matures, manufacturers and couponing service firms alike are viewing this as a time to make the tool more efficient and to generally improve the state of the couponing art.

DEFINITION AND STRATEGIC USE

Coupons, simply stated, are certificates that offer the consumer a stated value, for instance, cents-off or free product, when presented to the appropriate vendor accompanying the appropriate purchase. It is easy to see why coupons, with their obvious immediate value and savings, are the one promotional technique that has dominated the last two decades.

Coupons have many advantages. First, couponing to consumers helps ensure that savings are passed directly to the consumers. Trade allowances paid to the retailer, often to encourage price discounting, may or may not ever filter down into savings to the user. Second, while the consumer receives the benefit of a cost savings, this is perceived as a temporary special offer rather than a price reduction, which would have greater ramifications if removed. Third, coupons can create traffic for retailers, especially when retailers capitalize on this promotional device by doubling or tripling the coupon redemption value at their own expense.

Couponing is not, of course, without problems. Foremost, couponing has become so popular and widespread that the enormous number of coupons in circulation create "coupon clutter," resulting in falling coupon redemption rates. This coupon clutter also increases the potential for misuse and abuse through coupon fraud and misredemption. Furthermore, some allege that couponing is often used as a life support mechanism for weaker brands, while redemption for established brands occurs primarily from loyal users and thus rarely generates incremental business from new users, as it was intended.

Because coupons can be distributed via many different avenues, from mass distribution with free-standing inserts (FSIs) in newspapers or magazine advertising to more targeted delivery via the package itself or through direct mailings to the home, coupons offer flexibility in accomplishing a variety of common promotional goals. The most common objectives for using couponing follow.

Couponing for Trial and Awareness. Coupons are particularly efficient at generating trial of new products or line extensions of current brands. By offering significant savings on a first purchase, coupons reduce the risk to the consumer of trying something new. Alternatively, coupons can be exchanged for free product, almost as a sampling device, to completely eliminate any risk to the consumer at all. In these cases, the free product is often a special "trial size" package, just large enough to give the consumer sufficient trial to entice repeat purchase.

Almost any of the delivery methods mentioned earlier (and detailed more thoroughly later in this chapter) could be used to encourage trial if targeted at potential users. Print advertising, whether in magazines, Sunday magazines, newspaper FSIs, or runs of press (ROPs), can announce the benefits of the product with an accompanying coupon. In-store delivery, whether it's on the pack, on the shelf, on a display, or with a product demonstration, can alert the consumer to the new product in the store. Cross-item trial can also be generated by including a coupon for the new product in or on the package of another product bought by a similar user base.

Because coupons are typically delivered with accompanying sell copy as in an advertising environment, regardless of whether the coupon is redeemed, they can create awareness among the delivered audience of the new or improved brand.

Couponing for Repeat Purchase. While trial is often a first goal of couponing, converting trial users to regular users is also a key couponing task. When a consumer is faced with the decision of which brand to buy, a cents-off discount on an acceptable or superior brand may tilt the balance toward the couponed brand. That is why in-pack samples are almost always accompanied with a cents-off coupon and why in- or on-pack couponing is quite effective. In fact, in-pack or on-pack couponing is a way to cost-effectively reward existing users and encourage repeat purchase or loyal use.

Couponing to Trade Consumers Up. The specific terms of a coupon deal can be designed to manipulate users into buying larger quantities of a product or particular brand flavors, sizes, or forms if that is the goal. For instance, rather than offering cents-off on one unit of the product, the coupon terms might dictate that multiple units must be purchased for redemption, with the possible effect of increasing consumption. This is often the case with quickly consumed items having a short purchase cycle, such as cat food. In the same way, a coupon might be offered for a larger, and usually more expensive, package (for example, cents-off a 32-ounce container of catsup) or a different or more "deluxe" form of a brand (for example, brownie mix with nuts vs. the same mix without nuts). In these examples, the coupon promotion is specifically geared to trade consumers "up" in their purchasing behavior.

Couponing for Competitive Pressure. Couponing can be used with respect to the competition as either a defensive tactic or as an offensive move. By discounting one brand to users of competing brands, coupons entice those competitive users to buy the couponed brand instead. The obvious goal is to encourage continued patronage. But this kind of "switching" behavior can result in increased sales and profits in the short term, even if those consumers switch only for the sake of the temporary deal.

As a defensive price/value tactic, couponing can defend a brand against competition in the same way. By offering current users coupons toward continued purchase or "loading" current users up with product through a cents-off promotion for multiple brand purchases, coupons keep current users using and ward off competitive switching.

Couponing to Encourage Retail Distribution and Support. Couponing, as with any promotion, demonstrates support for a brand. However, if coupons are distributed locally through newspapers or direct mail, this shows local support and impact for retailers. Since manufacturers' coupons are paid for and distributed by the manufacturer in most cases and must be redeemed within a retail store, couponing benefits the retailer with very little out-of-pocket cost. This can help to gain trade support and secure product distribution. Manufacturers can win extra in-store support through increased brand shelf facings or off-shelf displays with the promise of a coupon drop which will further leverage the promotion for both parties. In fact, many retailers will dovetail their own promotion with that of the manufacturer by doubling or tripling the face value for consumers who redeem in their stores, boosting store traffic along with redemptions. Co-op couponing arrangements between the manufacturer and retailer are another way of gaining that ever-so-important retail support.

Couponing to Move Out-of-Balance Inventories. Discounting a brand through couponing can increase sales considerably, thereby moving product out of the store relatively quickly and within a certain time frame. When inventories are at higher-than-desired levels, by either manufacturer or retailer terms, couponing can act as a catalyst to trigger interest and pull the product through the distribution channels. This is especially effective for seasonal products or products with strong seasonal cycles, such as cold remedies or suntan lotions. This can also be a solution when a manufacturer is preparing to introduce a newer version of the brand and wants to clear out the inventory of the old brand in order to maximize profit and minimize cannibalization.

Couponing to Target Different Markets. Coupons can be strategically placed within particular media aimed at key audiences or targeted directly to particular consumers on a list. When there is little overlap between the various delivery mechanisms, effectively different deals can be offered to different consumers. For instance, with a knowledge of who the current users, competitive users, or nonusers are, greater incentives can be targeted to the competitive or nonusers to rally them to switch (or buy), while somewhat smaller savings can be offered as a reward to current consumers who might likely buy anyway.

The same strategy works when differentiating between markets. For example, greater incentives might be needed in a market where the promoted brand has a small market share than in markets where the brand dominates the category.

Couponing to Cushion Price Increases. Price increases are a fact of business but can deter sales in the short term if consumers become aware of the price change. Coupons offering enough of a discount to offset the increase in price can temporarily cushion the sting of the higher price until the time when consumers become accustomed to the higher price levels.

Couponing as an Add-On to Other Promotional Efforts. In a world where both the trade and consumers expect and demand promotion, using more than one promotional technique can leverage the results further by creating more awareness of the brand/promotion and greater sales synergies. Often, couponing will be used in conjunction with refunds or sweepstakes to increase participation (and purchase). As an example, coupons might encourage multiple and continued purchases of baby food, while the product labels and/or sales receipts can be exchanged for additional savings in the form of a refund. A coupon can serve a double purpose if a consumer writes in his or her name and address on the coupon when redeeming so that the coupon then becomes a means of entry into a sweepstakes promotion.

Sometimes coupons can be designed to work with in-store elements to encourage trade support and consumer involvement. An instance of this might be where the face value of the coupon can only be deciphered if brought into the store and held up to a special display or to the product package itself.

TACTICAL VARIATIONS OF A COUPON DEAL

A coupon promotion can be designed to offer deals or savings in many different forms. In reality, most coupon offers exhibit a combination of the following characteristics and can become quite complex and thereby difficult to classify.

1. **Cents-Off.** The product to be purchased is offered at a certain cents or dollar amount off the regular price for a specified time frame. This is probably the most common notion of couponing.

2. **Free.** A free product is given upon redemption. This is essentially an efficient means of sampling interested consumers since it avoids the waste and expense of sampling everyone.

3. **Buy One, Get One Free (BOGO).** With the purchase of a product at the regular price, a second is given free. This encourages multiple purchases and is a good way of rewarding regular users. As with everything else in an inflationary economy, today's BOGO is often inflated to where it is necessary to buy three or five to get one free!

4. **Time Release.** Several cents-off coupons are positioned together with different expiration dates. The objective is obviously to encourage repeat usage over time, aligning the expiration dates with typical usage/purchase cycles. Another variation on this might be when a manufacturer or service distributes coupons via a calendar, where a different deal is available each month.

5. **Multiple Purchase.** The coupon offer applies only when more than one unit of the product is purchased. The goal here is to load up the consumers with product, taking them out of the market for a period of time or with the hope of increasing consumption in the short term.

6. **Self-Destruct.** Two or more coupons are printed over each other in an overlap manner so that in order to redeem one, the other is destroyed. This is a way of offering different deals, perhaps to different types of consumers, without the clutter of multiple deals. Often, a self-destruct coupon is used in combination with time release, whereby greater savings are offered if it is redeemed sooner as opposed to later in an attempt to encourage quick redemption. It is common to see self-destructs used for the purpose of trading consumers up by offering the better deal on the larger size or deluxe form of the brand.

7. **Personalized.** The coupon is personalized by geographic location or store and is redeemable accordingly. This can be effective when used as a sales tool to elicit trade support.

8. **Cross-Ruff.** A coupon for one product is obtained with the purchase of another, unrelated product. When the user base of one

product overlaps substantially with the users of another product, it makes sense to coupon one to the other. Usually cross-ruffs are delivered via the package of a carrier brand.

9. **Related Sale.** A coupon received from the purchase of one product applies to another product, which is related in some way to the purchased product. This is a variation on the notion of a cross-ruff, wherein the couponed brand is connected in some way to the carrier brand, such as when hotdog and mustard coupons are delivered in hotdog bun packaging. The intent is often to encourage consumers to buy add-on items from the same manufacturer, but it can also be coordinated as a co-op between two manufacturers.

10. **Sweepstakes Entry.** The redeemed coupon becomes an entry into a sweepstakes promotion. Overlays of contests or sweepstakes may improve the impact and redemption rates of coupon promotions.

COUPON DISTRIBUTION METHODS

FSI couponing accounted for 77 percent of all coupons distributed in 1991, while all other distribution channels combined account for less than one in four coupons delivered. Given the sheer absolute numbers of coupons, every distribution channel contributes substantially to couponing's success and some, like targeted direct mail couponing, are becoming more popular.

The diverse distribution vehicles can be categorized into five basic distribution modes. That there are so many ways to deliver a coupon obviously adds to the flexibility of this promotional tactic. Each delivery mode has its own distinct advantages depending on the goals, target audience, and budget of the user. This section will briefly discuss each distribution method in detail.

Direct Mail. Direct mail distribution uses the U.S. Postal Service to deliver coupons to mailboxes of consumers. The coupons can be selectively delivered to households by name or more broadly targeted to the "resident" or "occupant" of a dwelling. In this latter case, the desire might be to distribute coupons to all households in a given zip code area.

Direct mail couponing achieves the highest redemption rates of any media or mailed couponing, primarily due to its more targeted distribution. It can offer many options for the user. Through careful selection of lists and demographic breaks, it offers the most selectivity. Through zip code saturation, it also potentially offers the highest coverage. As a result, direct mail is often used by retailers. Compared to other media delivery methods, mailing directly to consumers results in less misredemption. However, compared to most print media delivery methods, it is more expensive.

Couponing that is mailed can be either solo or co-op. A solo coupon promotion would consist of coupon(s) for a single company or brand. Solo mailings usually receive higher redemptions because of the exclusive selling environment for the brand or company. In fact, in combination with a sample, solo mail coupons can be used very effectively for new product introductions.

A co-op coupon promotion includes coupons for a combination of brands usually from different companies. Clearly the co-op route is more efficient and cost effective but there are some limitations to co-ops in terms of their potential pinpoint delivery to very specific list criteria or competitive users. Generally the most used co-ops are either mass broad-reach mailings to 30 million households or more, or demographically selective co-ops to specific target audiences such as households with babies, preschoolers, senior citizens, or specific ethnic groups. Because of the nonexclusive nature of a co-op promotion, there is less opportunity for selling any one brand; therefore, this mode is less desirable for new products.

In-Store or Central Location. Coupons are often distributed in the store where the items can be purchased or in high-traffic locations such as malls, shopping centers, and street corners. Coupons can be handed out personally in combination with or separate from a product demonstration, available for dispensing in a kiosk or display somewhere in the store, or automatically dispensed via a battery or electronic device usually placed near the product itself. Recently, several methods of automatically dispensed and electronic in-store couponing have been developed or are currently in the testing stage.

One such recently introduced distribution device is a battery-controlled coupon dispenser positioned at the point-of-sale on the shelf where the product is stocked. Another notable unique in-store distribution method involves dispensing coupons at the checkout counter, triggered by the scanning of a purchased product's UPC code. This kind of checkout, computer-controlled delivery method allows a brand to strategically target nonusers or competitive users, for example, by distributing coupons for Brand A coffee to those who purchase Brand B coffee.

In cases in which retail participation is a key objective, in-store couponing can be very effective. Additionally, in-store, mall, or shopping center couponing might be especially appropriate if it is part of some other promotional event.

In-store or central location handout couponing gives you some valuable flexibility and options. For instance, product samples and/or demonstrations of the product's use can accompany coupon handouts. Handout couponing also allows for a certain amount of selectivity regarding to whom the coupons are distributed. The people who are sampling or demonstrating or simply handing out coupon packages can screen consumers by asking if they have a dog or cat at home and then handing out the appropriate pet food coupon.

There are some disadvantages to in-store couponing, such as the logistics involved when distributing coupons across a large number of stores. If a number of different outlets in a geographic area are couponing, it is also possible for waste to occur because multiple coupons may be dispensed to the same consumer.

Print Media Delivered Coupons. Print media represent the dominant method of coupon delivery today. Advertising in newspapers with run-of-press (ROP) coupons or free-standing inserts (FSIs) and including coupons in magazine advertising constitute the primary print media used for delivery. Also in this category are print ads that offer consumers coupons if they send in their name and address or call an 800 or 900 number. In this case, the offer is delivered in the print medium and the coupon is delivered by mail.

FSIs comprise over three-fourths of all coupons distributed because of their good color reproduction and ability to efficiently reach a large circulation (50 million) in one day. They are printed in four color on high-quality paper stock and mechanically inserted into the newspaper, usually Sunday newspapers. They have the flexibility to provide special printing options such as rub-offs or scratch-and-sniff coupons.

Although traditional black and white ROP couponing is used much less today, it still has the advantage of very short closing dates, usually less than those for FSIs even, in cases where there is some need to react quickly to a marketing problem or opportunity. Color in ROPs is generally not used because of its poor quality color reproduction. Newspaper delivery shows local support for a brand and can be a sales tool for the trade.

Magazines are used less as a delivery mode for coupons today primarily because of their high costs, lower redemptions, and general inefficiency with respect to targeting. However, depending on the product and how narrowly defined the target market is, some magazine coupons may be a good idea. For instance, in the case of cosmetics or beauty products targeted toward young women, *Seventeen* might effectively deliver coupons to teenagers and *Cosmopolitan* might be appropriate for young working women.

Magazine delivery is of two forms: on-page and tip-in coupons. On-page coupons are usually integrated into a magagzine advertisement that provides both advertising and promotion value for a brand. The quality color reproduction and ad copy provide a good promotional environment, while the presence of a coupon can often increase readership of the advertisement. The ad space is purchased in full-page, half-page, or two-page spread increments, as with any other print advertising. Tip-in or pop-up coupons are typically printed on a heavier weight card stock and are bound in the magazine alongside a brand advertisement. When the magazine is opened, the coupons "pop up." Tip-ins cost more to deliver but almost always redeem at a higher rate than on-page coupons because of their ease in removing (no cutting is required) without destroying the magazine. A variation of the tip-in is the gatefold insert coupon whereby the coupons are printed as an extension of the advertisement and folded over the ad to provide a pop-up effect. Most magazine vehicles allow only a limited number of gatefolds per issue. While this method is more expensive, co-op opportunities can offer a savings.

In-Pack and On-Pack Coupons. In-pack coupons are preprinted and packed inside the product or another product's package. In the case of in-pack coupons, the carrier package inevitably features additional package graphics or copy, for example, a caption that announces "25¢ coupon inside." On-pack coupons are printed on a product's packaging or product label. Instant coupons, another form of on-pack couponing, are affixed to the outside of the package for easy removal and immediate redemption.

In- or on-pack couponing is an ideal strategy for encouraging repeat purchase of a given brand and holding current users. It is a relatively inexpensive distribution method in comparison to other methods, without the same misredemption potential of media delivered coupons. Even though in- and on-pack couponing may not have the same broad coverage of mail or media delivery, and it often delays redemption until the product is gone, redemptions tend to be high. Instant couponing offers the consumer immediate in-store access and redemption for the current purchase of a product and, as a result, receives the highest redemption of this genre and of all couponing delivery methods.

Cross-ruff couponing (in which coupons for one product are carried in or on another product) can be effective for generating trial of a related product in a brand line. This kind of cross-ruff couponing offers a dual benefit: the couponing brings trial for the couponing brand as well as visual point-of-purchase impact and added value for the carrier brand. Selecting the right cross-ruff partner can avoid the waste of mass nonselective couponing, for example, a coupon for cat food can be strategically placed in cat litter. In many instances, co-op cross-ruffs can generate greater consumer interest because of the greater promotion value.

Retailer In-Ad Coupons. In-ad coupons are manufacturers' coupons that are distributed via retailers' advertising and/or mailings. Recently, their use has increased greatly. In fact, according to CMS, in-ad coupon distribution increased from 7 billion coupons in 1990 to more than 23 billion in 1991, a 231 percent increase! Some manufacturers are already seeking ways to reduce their use. Yet, they do gain prominent space and attention in a retailer's ads and/or circulars, and they represent a form of quality "featuring" for a brand name that is hard to resist.

In-ad coupons can be for a single or multiple purchase. They are generally very limited in time, with typical expiration dates of one or two weeks. The average face value for in-ads also tends to be much higher than that for other coupon methods. In-ad coupons are, in a way, another form of trade promotion because they stimulate product sales for a specific retail account. In most cases both the face value and handling charges are paid by the manufacturer, while the media or mailing costs are borne by the retailer. In some cases, manufacturers have agreed to a trade allowance that compensates retailers for inclusion of their brand in in-ad coupons, and those coupons are thereby destroyed by the retailers and not sent to the clearinghouse for reimbursement by the manufacturer in the normal way.

COUPON REDEMPTION RATES

Through the later half of the 1980s and into the 1990s, redemption rates have declined and flattened. This is probably due in part to the clutter of more coupons across more product categories, along with the increasing saturation of competitive couponing within a given product category.

Redemption rates vary depending on a number of product and coupon characteristics, including face value, product category and competitive activity within the category, area of the country, coupon delivery method, audience characteristics such as brand loyalty, and the design and appeal of the coupon advertising itself. Listed in Table 6.1 are average redemption rates in 1990 and 1991 for the overall grocery category by delivery method, provided through NCH Promotion Services.

As discussed in the previous section, the highest redemption rates occur for in- and on-pack delivery methods in which coupons are selectively targeted to users of the product in conjunction with purchase or use of the product. In-store handout couponing and direct mail delivery offer relatively high redemptions as well. The lowest redemptions occur for print media delivery, which usually requires more effort on the part of consumers to cut or clip the coupon.

TABLE 6.1
AVERAGE COUPON REDEMPTION RATES

Delivery Method	1990	1991
Instant on-pack	35.0%	32.5%
In-pack	12.5	12.3
On-pack	10.8	9.2
Cross-ruff on-pack	4.1	4.9
Cross-ruff in-pack	3.1	3.4
Handout couponing	4.1	4.9
Direct mail	4.7	4.3
FSI	2.5	2.4
Sunday magazine supplements	1.5	1.6
Newspaper ROP	1.5	1.5
Magazine tip-in	1.5	1.3
Magazine on-page	1.2	1.2

COUPON FACE VALUE

Traditionally, the face value of a coupon has been set at about 15 percent of the product's retail price. Therefore, average face value varies across product category and is a relative variable. It should be noted that for new products the face value is usually higher to entice first-time purchase and trial.

In general, redemption rates increase as face value increases but not proportionately over the whole range. At some level, redemption rates begin to plateau, and higher face values bring in less or no incremental redemption. Some research has shown that redemptions for regular or frequent buyers are typically higher on average across all face values, while higher-valued coupons are more effective in soliciting redemption among infrequent or nonbuyers of a brand.

Based on when coupons are submitted for reimbursement at the clearinghouse, an average profile of the financial liability for a manufacturer develops over time. This pattern does vary by coupon distribution method to some degree. As might be expected, redemptions for FSI coupons, direct mail, and newspaper-delivered coupons tend to peak more quickly and drop off rather quickly in comparison to magazine-delivered coupons. In- or on-pack couponing redeems the most slowly of all because it is tied to the usage of the product. A timing chart such as this can assist in managing, budgeting, and evaluating coupon promotions.

THE COUPONING PROCESS

Coupon redemption can be a complex process because it involves handling by many different individuals across several stages. The entire cycle is usually completed in approximately 60 to 90 days.

The couponing process begins, of course, when a manufacturer decides to run a coupon promotion. The promotion is planned and coupons are printed and sent to the appropriate distribution points for dissemination to the public. A consumer then redeems the coupon at the store and receives the given cents-off on the appropriate product. Depending on the size and type of the retail operation, a store may forward its coupons to the chain headquarters. From there, the store or chain will send the coupons to one of three places: a retailers' clearinghouse, a redemption agency, or directly to the manufacturer. Because there are so many manufacturers, most retailers use clearinghouses.

Clearinghouses work for and are paid by the retailers. A clearinghouse is responsible for sorting the redeemed coupons and invoicing the manufacturer or the manufacturer's redemption agency. The manufacturer's redemption agency will sort any coupons sent to it and send an invoice and a report to the manufacturer. Payments are then made to retailers to reimburse the total face value of the redemptions plus a handling fee per coupon. The retailer then pays the clearinghouse for handling the process.

The preceding process applies only to manufacturer-originated coupon programs. There are also retailer or store coupons for which the retailer would have the responsibility for printing and distribution, as well as any financial liability. Sometimes a cooperative agreement may be in force between the manufacturer and retailer in which the manufacturer pays either directly for some part of the cost of the promotion or indirectly through trade promotional allowances.

Basic Couponing Costs. The basic costs to the manufacturer for couponing can be summarized as follows:

- Media costs for distribution
- Printing costs (if separate from media costs, for example FSIs)
- Face value of the redeemed coupons
- Handling charge for the retailers, currently $.08 per redemption
- Redemption house or in-house clearing and reporting costs
- Creative/art/photography/production costs

THE COUPON PAYOFF

There are many ways to plan and evaluate the effectiveness and "payout" of a couponing program. However, establishing the effectiveness criteria in advance, along with a preplanned program to evaluate the payout, is essential in any coupon promotion. For example, payout could be measured as (1) increased trial among new users, (2) the best efficiency as measured by the lowest cost per coupon redeemed, (3) incremental volume during a given promotion period, or even (4) increased market share.

Table 6.2 shows figures for calculating the cost and efficiency of

TABLE 6.2
SAMPLE COUPON COST-EFFICIENCY TABLE

($.25 COUPON*/1991 COSTS & RATES)	FSI	Direct Mail	Magazines
Distribution	50 million	30 million	20 million
Cost/M (incl. print)	$7.00	$18.00	$17.00
Cost/media ($000)	$350	$540	$340
Redemption rate	2.4%	4.3%	1.2%
Total redeemers	1,200,000	1,290,000	240,000
Misredemption estimate	25%	—	—
Total valid redeemers	900,000	1,290,000	240,000
Redemption costs ($000)	$420	$451	$84
Grand total costs	$770	$991	$424
Costs per valid redemption	$.85	$.77	$1.76

* $.25 face value plus $.08 handling plus $.02 redemption costs equals $.35
Source: NCH 1991

a coupon promotion. This analysis includes a factor for misredemption. Given a 25 percent misredemption, for example, for FSIs distributed to 50 million consumers as shown in the first column below, only 900,000 coupons would be considered "valid." Consequently, the cost per valid redeemed coupon for FSIs would be approximately $.85.

DESIGNING THE COUPON

While coupons vary widely in the specifics of their "deal," their design, and their placement or distribution method, all coupons look essentially similar.

The following are some guidelines to use in designing the coupon:

- A coupon should look like a coupon — funny shaped coupons are logistically impractical. Consumers expect them to be squares or rectangles, which are easier to clip and store, and the retailers need to fit them in cash register drawers.
- The face value and expiration date should be prominently displayed where they are plainly visible.
- Both the UPC code and manufacturer's coupon code should be included.
- The use of a package shot is preferable if the design allows. This can aid consumers in redemption and cut down on misredemption at the checkout. If it is a multiple-purchase coupon — for example, 10¢ off on two boxes of tissue — showing two packages on the coupon can deter misredemption.
- Burying coupons in complicated graphics within an ad or mailing is discouraged.
- Grocery Manufacturers of America (GMA) standards for coupon size and other specifications should be followed.

COUPON MISREDEMPTION AND COUPON FRAUD

Misredemption is a term used to describe the misuse of a coupon or the redemption of coupons without proper purchase of the specified product. The actual extent of misredemption is unknown, but most manufacturers plan for it and factor it in as a cost of doing business.

Often innocent consumer misredemption occurs when a coupon is redeemed (1) after its expiration date, (2) without the proper brand specifications (the proper quantity or size restrictions), or (3) when the product is not purchased at all. In out-of-stock situations, consumers will knowingly substitute other brands for the unavailable couponed brand. By informing retailers of a coupon promotion in advance or by couponing only brands with sufficient retail distribution, much of this deliberate consumer misuse can be avoided. Furthermore, printing expiration dates so that they are easily noticed and printing a picture of the brand itself in the quantity required for redemption on the coupon front can alleviate problems.

Misredemption that occurs outside the normal customer-retailer in-store transaction constitutes fraud. Most coupon fraud would be difficult without some level of retailer involvement because manufacturers only reimburse coupon submissions received from supposedly legitimate retailers. Therefore, fraud is often committed by "rings" of retailers cooperating and participating with coupon criminals for some of the profit or by criminals who organize phony storefronts or clearinghouses, which mass-clip coupons for submission. This kind of trade misuse is much more serious than consumer misredemption. Criminal redemption can result in massive losses. While estimates vary, NCH has estimated that coupon fraud costs manufacturers at least $250 million annually. Some estimates are as high as $700 million per year.

The situation for trade misredemption is complicated in that abuse can happen at any stage in the coupon process — printing and production, distribution, or redemption. For instance, during the production phase, coupons can be fraudulently printed in deliberate overruns, or the printing plate can be stolen and used to reprint coupons strictly for fraudulent redemption. When coupons are shipped to distribution points, as is the case with FSIs for example, theft can occur even before distributors retrieve them. It is generally accepted that FSIs experience a higher level of misredemption than direct mail or magazine-delivered coupons simply because of this ease of theft and the efficiency with which they can be collected and clipped in mass. Typically in this situation, coupon criminals organize people to cut, clip, and sort the coupons for a percentage of the actual face value. Coupons are then submitted for the full face value. Cashiers, store owners, and managers and retailer clearinghouses may commit fraud to a lesser degree by "salting" coupon submissions (adding fraudulent coupons to the legitimate claims).

Over the years, there have been several cases of mass misredemption that have been brought to trial resulting in criminal convictions. Because coupons are usually redeemed through the mail, or the redemption check is mailed back through the postal system, coupon fraud falls under federal jurisdiction through the U.S. postal codes. The federal government is becoming more actively involved in the surveillance and prosecution of criminal coupon fraud.

Manufacturers can protect themselves from coupon fraud to some extent by selecting the coupon delivery system carefully, with an understanding of the potential for misredemption. In fact, in some cases coupons can be sequentially numbered or specially coded so that mass submissions are more easily detected. This is possible with FSIs, direct mail, and magazine tip-in coupons. Today, many manufacturers and clearinghouses routinely inspect coupon redemption patterns in order to detect suspicious submissions. New coupon scanning equipment is being tested in stores that electronically reads the UPC codes on coupons and verifies redemption at the point-of-sale. This is also expected to assist in cutting costly misredemption.

The following are some suggestions on how to avoid or detect excessive misredemption:

- Excessively high face values should be avoided because higher values are more likely to attract misredemption.
- The number of coupons amassed in one vehicle should be limited. Large groupings of coupons not only result in higher total coupon value but also in more efficient mass clipping for misredemption purposes. Therefore, multiple coupons per magazine page or per mailing are to be discouraged. Again, FSIs, because of their coupon masses, attract misredemption more than other delivery modes. Where appropriate, self-destruct or overlapping coupons could be used in order to limit the actual number of usable coupons.
- Designating a fixed face value per coupon rather than offering free product (shelf value coupons) is preferable to alleviate the temptation to the trade to artificially inflate shelf values for increased reimbursement.
- Coupon expiration dates should be coordinated with product purchase cycles to minimize the time period for redemption. Also, a trade reimbursement policy should be established that allows payment to retailers only within a specified time period after the coupon expires, such as 60 days following the coupon expiration date.
- Retaining a reliable printing firm is an important step toward reducing fraud. Print overruns should be eliminated, and printing plates should be destroyed or retrieved back from the printer after printing.
- One should monitor, or at least be aware of, possible misuse through the distribution channels: for instance, (1) the number of deliverable mail coupons can be estimated based on the mailing lists used, (2) returns on any undeliverable direct mail coupons can be specified in advance, and (3) policies for newsstand returns of magazines and newspapers should always be known.
- A record should be kept of those retailers who do not stock the product being couponed so that illegitimate coupon submissions for the product can be detected.
- Establishing and enforcing a strict policy on coupon misredemption is a must if one is to reduce coupon misuse. For instance, in markets where misredemption is very high or among retailers for which misredemption has been previously detected at high levels, couponing should be avoided.

COUPONING INTERNATIONALLY

Other than Canada and the United Kingdom, most countries represent a relatively small factor in the world of couponing. Couponing in South America has been limited by the fact that newspapers do not have the coverage they do in the United States or Canada and because of the poor mailing systems in those countries. There is also limited distribution of coupons in Australia, Italy, France, Belgium, Spain, and other countries. Recently, however, the Japanese Trade Commission reversed a previous policy, allowing couponing in that country. Japanese couponing has been tested in small booklets distributed by mail and in both newspaper ROPs and FSIs.

Table 6.3 shows distribution numbers (in millions) for 1990 and 1991 in four countries tracked by NCH internationally. As can be seen by these numbers, couponing is substantially more prevalent in the U.S., given that 292 billion coupons were distributed in the states in 1991.

TABLE 6.3
COUPON DISTRIBUTION IN FOUR COUNTRIES

	Distribution (in millions)	
	1990	1991
Canada	23,400	26,000
United Kingdom	5,000	8,000
Italy	421	582
Spain	171	141

COUPONING TRENDS

While trends come and go, there are several current trends in couponing that are worth mentioning. The first is that coupons are increasingly being used as a way to selectively target specific consumer groups. Coupon programs that deliver particular demographic audiences have become increasingly popular because of their efficiency and effectiveness compared to other promotions.

More group promotions are appearing that combine several products or brands in one coupon display, often with related products or a family of brands. Along the same lines, promotions combining couponing with other promotional tactics are on the rise. In other words, couponing is increasingly becoming just one component of a multifaceted promotional program. Also increasing is the use of couponing overlaps or tie-ins, especially with sports and charities.

Today more than in the past, more attention is being paid to the creative element in a coupon promotion deal in an effort to increase the appeal and efficiency of the technique. To further leverage coupon effectiveness, more attention is also being given to designing coupon promotions with an eye to how the retailer is benefited. Since the front line of the battle field is in the retail outlet, developing better retailer relationships is of critical importance to manufacturers.

A final trend in couponing is that promoters are more aware of the problem of misredemption and the impact coupon fraud has on the bottom line. Better controls are being implemented across the board to reduce this threat.

Don Roux is President and CEO for Roux Marketing Services, Inc., which provides consulting services to packaged goods manufacturers on promotion concepts, services, fulfillment, and chance and skill promotion handling and judging. Roux has spent the last 30 years in the promotion marketing industry and is one of the leading authorities on promotion fulfillment, collateral material warehousing and distribution, and sweepstakes and contest program handling, judging, seeding, and fulfillment. He has won many awards, including two Reggies and the Association of Incentive Marketing's CIP Man of the Year.

Previously Roux was President and CEO of the Carlson Marketing Division of Carlson Marketing Group, Inc; President and CEO of Spotts International, Inc., one of the nation's largest fulfillment services; and Vice President of the Western Division at Revere Copper and Brass, Inc., working with promotions and product sales.

He is Director and former Chairman of the Board for the Promotion Marketing Association of America. He is also a former director and past president of the Association of Incentive Marketing (AIM) and a founding member and past president of the Minnesota Incentive Organization. He is a frequent speaker and author on marketing and sales promotion subjects.

CHAPTER 7

PREMIUMS, REFUNDS, AND PROMOTION FULFILLMENT

PREMIUMS AND MERCHANDISE INCENTIVES

The usage of merchandise incentives (premiums) dates back to the mid-1800s when B. T. Babbitt began using lithographed prints as an inducement to consumers to purchase Babbitt's soap products and promoted the offer by using the Barnum Bandwagon, which traveled throughout the country.

In recent years, the words *premium* and *merchandise incentives* in sales promotion have become interchangeable. Merchandise incentives are used in numerous promotional techniques. Account openers, business gifts, container packs, continuity and coupon plans, dealer and sales rewards, on-packs and in-packs, free-in-the-mail, frequent user plans, and self-liquidation offers are some of the more common usages for merchandise incentives.

The most concise definition of the term *incentive marketing* appeared in *Incentives in Marketing* written by George Meredith and Robert P. Fried and published by the Association of Incentive Marketing (formerly National Premium Sales Executives, Inc.). Fried and Meredith describe incentive marketing as "a promotional device that induces purchase or performance on the part of a consumer, salesperson, or dealer through the offer of tangible reward in the form of merchandise or travel." The only addition to this definition in today's marketplace would be to include "employees" to the list of those induced.

Incentive, one of the industry's leading publications, reported that consumer promotion sales totaled $59.4 billion in 1991, with $6.5 billion spent on consumer premiums. Another $115.3 billion was spent on trade promotions with $2.03 billion allocated to dealer incentives. Sales incentives totaled $17 billion, which included $4.4 billion for merchandise incentives, for a total estimated merchandise incentive sales volume of almost $13 billion in 1991.

Premiums and merchandise incentives are used for the following objectives:

Consumer incentives:
- Attract attention at the point-of-sale
- Sample new users
- Boost repeat sales
- Enhance consumer goodwill
- Obtain higher advertising readership
- Provide sales with a talking point
- Encourage store display usage
- Increase overall sales volume

Trade and sales incentives:
- Introduce new or improved products
- Pull slow-moving or line extensions through the system
- Increase the customer base
- Reinforce consumer promotions
- Offset competitive promotions/introductions
- Boost sale/dealer morale
- Obtain sales display
- Increase productivity
- Increase overall sales volume/market share

Premium/merchandise incentives cannot make up for a product that is inferior in quality or does not do what it has been advertised to do. Nor can these incentives substitute for inadequate advertising or a poorly trained or inferior sales staff, or change negative consumer attitudes. Consumers can be motivated to buy and try a new product or service or to retry an improved version of the product or service, but if that product does not perform as advertised or the "new, improved" version is not really improved, no amount of incentive promotion will induce consumers to continued purchases.

Each type of merchandise incentive promotion has its advantages and disadvantages. When planning promotions involving merchandise, the advantages and disadvantages must be weighed carefully. For planning purposes, the following is a recap of these plus/minus elements for the major incentive promotion types.

Mail-in Premiums — Self-Liquidators, Partial Self-Liquidators, and Free-in-the-Mail Offers. Oftentimes, premiums are acquired through the mail. The premium may be offered free to the consumer responding to the promotion, or it may be purchased by the consumer — usually at less than the expected retail price. A self-liquidating premium is one for which any direct cost associated with the premium, including mailing or handling charges, is paid up front by the respondent. For instance, the incentive to the consumer consists of receiving a desirable premium item at the same low wholesale price at which the promoter can buy it. Therefore, the consumer receives a good value at very little cost to the promoter. A partial self-liquidator, then, is a promotion for which at least some of the cost is paid by the respondent.

Advantages of mail-in premiums:
- Can be easily targeted to the promoted product or to a specific advertising theme
- Can be selected to encourage future use of the promoted product or group of products
- Attract brand switchers
- Increase product consumption
- Are relatively inexpensive
- Encourage on- and off-shelf display

- Create consumer goodwill
- Leave a long-lasting recall of the product or service

Disadvantages of mail-in premiums:

- Difficult to measure true sales results
- Require long lead times and require a dedicated product resource
- Product liability insurance coverage and a legal contract with supplier must be implemented
- It is always difficult to forecast merchandise needs, and this could lead to the added expense of sending "delay notices" or selling excess inventories at a loss.

Frequent Buyer/User and Continuity Plans. Frequent user programs have been in existence for many years and fall into a number of categories. A differentiating factor here is that, in order to encourage continuity of use/purchase, customers must save up to acquire a premium. By redeeming product proofs of purchase, game pieces, or savings stamps the consumer can "buy" a premium, often selecting from a variety of options offered at different price levels.

One of the longest-running programs has been the Brown and Williamson Tobacco Companies' Raleigh-Belaire coupon program. Coupons are packed in each individual pack of Raleigh and Belaire cigarettes and are redeemable for a wide array of merchandise that is presented in a beautiful four-color catalog. The catalog is redone regularly to keep up with new merchandise trends and prices.

Savings stamps that were widely used by the petroleum retailers and supermarkets in the 1950s, 1960s, and 1970s suffered serious setbacks in the United States during the recession and inflationary times of the late 1970s. This rapid decline in the popularity of trading stamps was the result of the grocery industry's attempt to reduce or maintain price levels by reducing costs. In reality, while prices were reduced by as much as the 2 percent that grocery chains claimed the stamps were costing, prices soon returned to original prices and the cost savings went to the bottom line. Today, services such as hotel chains and airlines, consumable products manufacturers of frequently purchased items, or multiple-line manufacturers use this type of frequency promotion most often.

Another type of frequency program is the "save-a-tape" programs run by supermarkets. These plans ask the consumer to save a predetermined dollar value of cash register tapes that are redeemable for merchandise (usually encyclopedias, cookware, flatware, or dinnerware). These programs usually require a cash payment in addition to the tapes, which makes the program self-liquidating.

Advantages of frequency programs:

- Gain good retailer support
- Attractive to consumers
- Create heavy user involvement

- Encourage continuity of purchase habit
- Keep customers from taking advantage of competitors' short-term promotion/couponing efforts
- Can be easily targeted
- May promote slippage

Disadvantages of frequency programs:
- Expensive to promote
- Require a long-term commitment
- Can require substantial back-up inventories
- Requires dedicated suppliers
- Difficult to cut off

Direct Premiums — In-Pack, On-Pack, and Near-Packs. Direct premiums are those directly received by the consumer upon purchase of a product by virtue of being packaged or sold with the premium. In-pack and on-pack incentives are either packaged in or on the product being promoted. The most widely recognized in-pack offer is the one that has been used to promote the sale of Cracker Jacks for more than 50 years. Cereal companies are major users of in-pack offers.

A near-pack incentive is usually shipped separately from the product being promoted and is displayed directly adjacent to the product. Fast-food restaurants also use this type of promotion to promote add-on sales — for example, buy a burger and a carbonated beverage and get a special, decorated glass free. These promotions usually have a number of differently designed glasses to encourage continuity of purchase.

While the previously described incentive programs require mailing in for the premium or saving toward a premium, direct premium offers provide instant gratification and create a "warm, fuzzy" feeling with consumers. Users can repeat such programs in a predetermined time slot year after year to further the continuity of the offer.

Advantages of direct premiums:
- Promote off-shelf display in grocery outlets
- Generate trial
- Encourage continuity of purchase
- Provide instant gratification
- Can tie directly to the promoted product or service
- Eliminate the need to pack and mail to consumers
- Cost per premium used can be closely controlled
- Differentiates the promoted product from the clutter
- Can be used in conjunction with a tie-in partner to help control promotion cost

Disadvantages of direct premiums:
- Heavy breakage of fragile merchandise
- High employee pilferage rate
- On-packs may require special packaging
- Retailers may refuse to purchase/display on-packs and near-

packs because of the additional space required
- Pretesting is expensive and alerts the competition
- Not appropriate for all products or services

Container Pack Incentives. Specialty container packs have been used for many years. One of the most successful container pack promotions was offered by General Foods on their Maxwell House coffee brand. Maxwell House packed its coffee in a decorated glass coffee carafe, which was given to consumers at no additional cost. This program generated tremendous sales increases in Maxwell House coffee and provided consumers with an ongoing reminder of the brand. Glassware incentives have also been used for years on jam and jelly products.

Advantages of container packs:
- Encourage future consumption of sponsor's product
- Can be inexpensive when normal container cost is deducted
- Provide instant gratification to consumers

Disadvantages of container packs:
- May be refused by retailers if a new stock keeping unit (SKU) is required or special container takes too much shelf space
- Cost to produce, package, or distribute may be prohibitive

Account Openers. Account openers have been used by many companies to encourage their current and new consumers to purchase an item on time or, in the case of financial institutions, to open a new type of account or to secure a loan or certificate of deposit. The direct mail industry utilizes these incentives to encourage consumers to purchase or try an item of merchandise of much greater value. In the event the consumer wishes to return the trial item for credit or refund, the incentive item may be retained as a reward for the trial.

Advantages of account openers:
- Encourage trial of service or product
- Control rewarding current users
- Costs can easily be controlled
- Instant gratification

Disadvantages of account openers:
- Some consumers partake of an offer for the incentive only with no intent to try or purchase the item or service
- Can encourage account switching just to take advantage of the incentive

Business Gifts. Business gifts are rewards given to stockholders, customers, business friends, and employees as an expression of appreciation for performance, loyalty, or friendship. The federal government limits the dollar amount that can be paid for such rewards. While there are some minor advantages and disadvantages to this type of incentive, the major purpose is a gesture of friendship.

Employee Awards. Incentives used to reward employees for safety, quality control, attendance, productivity performance, longevity, or suggestions fall into the employee awards category. Most employers use one or more of the motivational techniques to reward employees for predetermined performance levels. There have been substantiated reports of employee lost-time accidents being reduced by more than 50 percent as a result of safety award programs. It is a normal practice to present these incentive awards at special luncheons and dinners to honor those who have achieved the level of excellence required to earn an award. This recognition can also encourage teamwork and is an employee morale builder.

Advantages of employee award programs:

- Loyalty builders
- Create employee goodwill
- Are very cost-effective
- Easy to implement
- Result in higher profits
- Can reduce total employees because of absentee reduction

Disadvantages of employee award programs:

- Require long-term management commitment
- Management training is required at all levels

Dealer Incentives. Dealer incentive merchandise sales accounted for more than $2 billion of the almost $13 billion of incentive sales in 1991. Dealer or trade incentive programs are structured to reward these customers for purchasing, displaying, and selling products and services. The program can be a "short-term" offer built around a single item — for example, purchase a predetermined quantity of product, put up a display detailing the consumer offer, and keep the consumer incentive item affixed to the display when the program is completed. Alternatively, these programs could be very detailed "long-term" offers promoting continuity of purchase and requiring accumulation of points redeemable for high-cost merchandise and/or travel displayed in very high-quality, four-color, comprehensive catalogs with custom-designed covers and promotional literature. There are also "step" catalogs offering a variety of items at various point levels that are used for this type of incentive, as well as offering executive gifts.

Advantages of dealer incentive programs:

- Costs can be structured to fit even the most austere budget
- Encourage display
- Increase off-shelf display
- "Load" merchandise into customers, keeping the competition out
- Recall of incentive source is very high

Disadvantages of dealer incentive programs:

- Load dealers with merchandise that can cause sales dip following promotion
- If used in standard cycles, can result in dealers delaying purchases while awaiting the incentive offer
- Delays in fulfilling dealer incentive awards can cause negative reactions

Sales Incentives. Sales incentives provide a reward for achievement performance of a predetermined sales goal during a defined time period. The length of the program varies from very short-term events, often referred to as "spurt" programs, to programs that last the entire year. These programs can be designed to motivate a salesperson to sell a particular product or service, a product line, or multiple lines or services.

Many believe that a salary or commission should be sufficient motivation to perform to the utmost ability, but the use of sales incentives has proven that sales forces can be motivated to achieve sales goals far in excess of forecasted levels. The drive to make the extra sales call or push the promoted line or service to "win" the sales contest or award has resulted in sales increases of more than 100 percent of the projected goal.

Cash, merchandise, and travel are the most popular awards. Some sales incentive programs offer a wide selection of gifts, and this merchandise is pictured in a catalog from which winners may select awards based on the points or credits they have earned as a result of their sales efforts. Other programs offer exotic travel destinations for all winners who have achieved or surpassed their sales goal. Successful sales incentive programs are structured so that even the top goals are within reach of all participants. If goals are set at levels that are not achievable, a negative reaction could result.

Advantages of sales incentives:
- Motivate the sales force to achieve sales levels beyond budgeted levels
- Reward sales personnel for "going that extra mile"
- "Load" customers to take competition out of the market
- Move a slower-selling product or service
- Can be structured to fit any reasonable budget

Disadvantages of sales incentive programs:
- Can reward the sales staff for doing the job they are being paid to do
- Sales support staff personnel can become disgruntled if they do not have some type of incentive program to reward them for their added workload
- Sales following the program may decline because of inventory buildup resulting from the extra sales effort during the program
- Long-range programs require continual updates and progress reports

FULFILLMENT

The incentive promotion is not completed until all awards, incentives, and premiums have been delivered to the recipient in perfect condition. Failure to complete the fulfillment process on time, properly packaged, and in good condition can turn a successful program into a disaster. The fulfillment process must be carefully planned to assure that this critical delivery cycle is handled efficiently.

Fulfillment of consumer incentives and rebate offers, because of the high volume of response and control, is usually handled by professionals who specialize in the high-volume, low-cost, fast turnaround of incoming mail responses. These fulfillment houses have the electronic data processing software programs that are capable of eliminating duplicate requests, producing zip sorting labels, and making checks to take advantage of the best postal and United Parcel Service (UPS) rates. They also have database management systems and specialized packaging equipment to provide low-cost, safe packaging to assure that merchandise and materials arrive in good condition.

The cost for this service is based upon volume of mail that is processed and the amount and quality of service that is provided. The companies offering fulfillment services must also have the capability of providing on-line consumer service to assure that any consumer inquiry is handled quickly and efficiently to avoid any dissatisfaction.

To provide marketing data, each medium used to promote the offer to consumers is usually provided a separate post office box or specific media code so that responses to the different media can be carefully evaluated for future advertising consideration.

When an incentive merchandise order has been processed, shipment of the merchandise can be made directly from the fulfillment house, or labels can be forwarded to the incentive supplier or their designate for drop-shipment. The processing of orders through the mail is closely regulated by the Federal Trade Commission (FTC) and must be shipped to the respondent within the time specified in the offer, or a delay notice must be sent to respondents advising them of the delay and offering them an opportunity to cancel their request and receive a full refund if they elect not to accept the delay.

Dealer and sales incentive merchandise or travel award mailings are usually handled by professional incentive merchandise suppliers who keep running totals of how each participant is progressing toward his or her goal. They also send updates on this progress to the participants and motivate them to work harder to assure they qualify for their desired award. Mailings are also made to the participants' spouses asking for their help in motivating their spouse to achieve the goal.

In some instances, large, multiple-line consumer product companies have their own fulfillment centers. These companies must have sufficient mail volume to be cost effective. For instance, General Foods Corporation, R. J. Reynolds, and Scott Paper Company have set up their own fulfillment operations.

One of the most damaging occurrences in any incentive program is the lack of merchandise necessary to fulfill requests in a timely manner. This normally is the result of poor planning/forecasting or unanticipated response levels. It is imperative that a contingency plan be incorporated into every promotion plan to assure that merchandise of equal or better value is available should requests surpass projections.

REFUNDS/REBATES

Cash and coupon refunds are the second leading promotional incentive behind manufacturers' store-redeemable coupons. Refunds/rebates are very easily implemented and can be set up to combat a competitive promotional effort in a very short period of time.

Unlike merchandise incentives, cash refunds require no inventories and can be advertised to consumers at point-of-sale, in best-food-day advertisements, on a regional or specific market basis, nationally in FSIs, magazines, or Sunday supplements without a great deal of time required to put the promotional effort together.

Refunds/rebates may be paid in cash or in store-redeemable coupons. Consumers are required to purchase the product or service and submit a specified "proof-of-purchase" by mail to receive their refund. Most often, refund programs set specific limits on the total number of rebates a single consumer may obtain, and strict legal copy explains precisely what these limits are.

To prevent rules violations, computer programs are set up to eliminate duplicate responses or requests for refunds that exceed the specified dollar amount allowable. To request, receive, and cash a duplicate refund check or to redeem a coupon in excess of the limits of the offer constitutes a violation of the United States mail fraud statutes (18 USC sections 1341 and 1342). This crime is punishable by a fine of as much as $1,000 and imprisonment for as long as five years.

Prior to the mid-1970s, most refund offers were fulfilled with cash because the cost to key respondents' names and addresses on checks was prohibitive. In the mid to late 1970s, the advent of mini-computers and microcomputers and laser scanning technology made it possible to send impact-printed check refunds, usually containing a personalized "thank you" note. Check stock had to be ordered in advance and could be expensive if a special check was required on a lower-volume promotion. Check and coupon stock had to be stored in high-security storage areas or vaults because checks were preprinted with the dollar amount and were signed. Preprinted coupons could be easily redeemed for merchandise or sold illegally to retailers who could redeem them for cash.

The introduction of high-speed laser printing technology has advanced refunding to the 21st century. The requirement of having large quantities of blank, presigned checks in stock, which creates a major security problem, is no longer a necessity. Today, check or coupon stock, printed with only a pantograph background, is all that is required to laser-produce checks. Company or brand name logos and check authorization signatures can be electronically digitized and laser printed on the check along with the payee's name, dollar amount, the required OCR (Optical Character Recognition) numbers, and any personalized message. Messages may be changed and dollar amounts varied to correspond with the item the consumer purchased or the quantity of proofs-of-purchase submitted.

Coupon refunds can also be laser printed and personalized to a particular consumer, retailer, or both. The personalization of coupons helps to reduce consumer fraud and misredemption. It also eliminates the possibility of theft of preprinted coupons. The flexibility of laser printing on high-speed equipment has revolutionized the cash and coupon refund business. Cash and coupon refunds are structured in many ways:

- **Buy one, get one free.** Consumers purchase the promoted product, mail in the required proof-of-purchase, and receive a coupon good for free product.
- **Multiple-purchase coupon refunds.** These are structured similarly to the "buy one, get one free" offer, except that multiple purchases are required (for example, consumers purchase two products and get two free, or make four purchases to receive three free).
- **Refund and coupon combination offers.** These are used in tandem to provide greater incentive value to consumers (for example, purchase a product, submit the required proof-of-purchase, and receive a $1.00 rebate plus a coupon good for $.50 off the next purchase of the same product or, if desired, off a related product, whichever the manufacturer prefers).

The combinations of possible refund scenarios are endless, and "tie-in" promotions with other noncompetitive companies are often set up to add value to the offer and reduce the cost to both companies because they can share the mail processing and mailing costs.

Advantages of refunds/rebates:
- Easy to implement
- No inventories required, except of preprinted store-redeemable coupons
- Encourage trial
- Encourage multiple purchase
- Can be used to counter competitive product introductions and other incentive offers
- Easily used with tie-in partner to share fulfillment costs
- Easy to control budgets

Disadvantages of refunds/rebates:
- Easily countered by the competition
- May delay purchase if used too often; Consumers will delay purchase awaiting another refund offer
- Misredemption or duplicate refunds to same consumer
- Reward regular users

• Mail delays and losses may cause consumer dissatisfaction

It is estimated that more than 75 percent of all households in the U.S. take advantage of at least one refund annually. There are numerous refund publications available for a very low subscription price that list all refunds, rules, expiration dates, and required qualifiers.

Over the years, Don Jagoda Associates has worked with almost all of the top Fortune 500 companies, including Lever Brothers, General Foods, Coca-Cola, Philip Morris, Showtime Networks, and hundreds of other major corporations that have all used his innovative concepts to promote products.

Jagoda is on the Board of Directors of the Promotion Marketing Association of America, Association of Incentive Marketing, Incentive Federation, and Marketing Communications Executives International. He is a member of the Premium Merchandising Club and the Long Island Advertising Club.

CHAPTER 8

SWEEPSTAKES, GAMES, AND CONTESTS

Sweepstakes, games, and contests are among the hottest sales promotion techniques today. There are several reasons for this popularity. Certainly, one of the best is that a lot of people, in a lot of fields, have learned how to use them effectively.

Let's put this into numbers: Back in 1980, according to industry publication studies, $650 million was spent on sweepstakes. By 1983, this total rose to $732 million. By 1990, the billion-dollar mark was passed, with total sweepstakes spending estimated at $1,135,327,148 — a 74 percent increase in just 10 years.

Sweepstakes are no longer confined simply to packaged products with carefully built-up identities and images. Today, we are seeing sweepstakes utilized by a host of new industries that never before ran any promotions other than basic trade incentives and allowances.

Recent sweepstakes promotions have included instant-winner games for combination locks; a programmed-learning sweepstakes for design engineers with questions on the applications of urethane foams; a sweepstakes for paint contractors requiring pickup of entries at paint stores; a sweepstakes designed to create frame-by-frame involvement with a hot rock-video release; an instant winner game with preselected lucky numbers designed to get farmers into agricultural equipment dealerships in the United States and Canada; a programmed-learning program for cattle ranchers, focusing on a pest insecticide; an instant winner game for beauty salon operators designed to get them into cash-and-carry wholesale locations, supporting a major hair care marketer's professional products; and a qualified-entry sweepstakes designed to encourage bookstore browsing — and purchase — of a line of paperback romances.

Clearly, sweepstakes are growing and are very much in the forefront of people's minds. By "people," we mean marketers, wholesalers, retailers, and, most important, consumers.

It's really ironic, because 30 years ago, when Don Jagoda Associates started in this business, the sweepstakes was often considered a last-gasp promotion. It was something that was used when all else failed and a brand was dying.

Today, sweepstakes have done a complete about-face. Along with games and contests, they've been repositioned as a hard-hitting, sales-generating promotion technique, transformed from a passive promotional technique into an aggressive marketing tool.

It is change that has engineered this 180° turnaround and has made sweepstakes a state-of-the-art promotion. Specifically, change has occurred in four significant areas.

1. **Change in legality**. There's been a definite trend toward easing of federal and state restrictions on lotteries and sweepstakes. And, while this type of program still calls for significant legal as well as promotional expertise, it's not as handcuffed as it used to be. Today, you can run a sweepstakes in all 50 states.

2. **Change in consumer acceptance.** Today, more than half the states are conducting their own lotteries. Every state lottery ad or commercial helps build simultaneous acceptance for sweepstakes and games of all types. This, combined with a general liberalization of consumer attitudes, has been a tremendous help in removing the stigma that used to be attached to sweepstakes.

3. **Change in economic conditions.** The inflation and recession of the 1970s and early 1980s became a one-two punch that devastated a large part of the populace. Today, with the economy mired in recession, anything offering the consumer a chance to become Cinderella or the hope of a better life or something for nothing is warmly welcomed. As a result, cents-off coupons, refunds and rebates, sweepstakes, games, and contests have blossomed.

4. **Change in entry mechanics.** This is the most visible area of change. It has added the whole new dimension of greater involvement — that is, getting the consumer to do more than just write down a name and address. Ways have been developed to make participating more interesting, literally by forcing consumers to study an ad, handle a product, and, yes, even buy a product.

BASIC DEFINITIONS

It is important to understand the terms sweepstakes, games, and contests. A sweepstakes is a prize promotion in which winners are selected by chance. These promotions are regulated primarily by federal and state lottery laws, which declare that a lottery is an illegal promotion. A lottery is any promotion that contains these three elements: prize, chance, and consideration (purchase).

So, how can the states run lotteries? They pass legislation authorizing their own lotteries.

Private-sector marketers avoid the lottery restriction by eliminating the element of consideration. Authorities have agreed to allow sponsors to request proof-of-purchase with sweepstakes entries, as long as consumers are given the alternative of not submitting proof-of-purchase. In most cases, the acceptable alternative is a plain 3" x 5" piece of paper with the brand name handwritten on it.

All forms of sweepstakes, including the instant winner games that utilize some form of concealment device, fall under the same laws and guidelines. All these programs, no matter how complex or how steep the odds, are random-chance events.

A contest, like a sweepstakes or lottery, is a prize promotion. However, in a contest, prizes are awarded not on random chance but on the basis of a test of skill or personal talent. A contest can require a recipe, a photograph, a jingle, or an essay as a test of skill. The winners in such a program are not picked randomly. All contest entries must be opened and screened, and the judging proceeds according to a weighted set of criteria that are made known to all entrants as part of the contest rules.

Because the element of chance is not present in contests, they are not subject to the same restrictions that govern sweepstakes. In a contest, consideration, or purchase of a product, may be required for entry in many categories. Because skill is involved, contests logically generate far fewer entries than sweepstakes. In fact, in terms of entries, industry observers say sweepstakes will generate anywhere from four to 10 times more entries than contests. Because a contest will generate only a fraction of the entries generated by a sweepstakes, many marketers waive any purchase requirement in a contest, even though such a requirement is legal. The idea is to present as few obstacles to entry as possible.

ADVANTAGES OF SWEEPSTAKES, GAMES, AND CONTESTS

Why should marketers use sweepstakes, games, or contests? We see five key advantages.

1. **Fixed budget.** The sweepstakes, game, or contest is one of the few promotions in which you can determine your costs in advance. Because it is not open-ended, like a coupon offer, the sponsor can establish the budget and tightly control expenditures. Regardless of how many entries are received, the sponsor's liability is limited to the budget established in advance.

2. **Excitement.** The sweepstakes carries its own built-in excitement. The basic appeal is to acquisitiveness and the fact that it's human nature that everybody wants something for nothing. There is also something of the thrill of gambling. However, the consumer is really safe because little, if anything, is being risked. The big promise — The Grand Prize, such as a car, a trip, cash, or a variation on these — is always a surefire attention getter. When executed properly, the inherent excitement of the sweepstakes, game, or contest literally magnifies the promotion, making it look much bigger than it actually is.

3. **A sales tool.** Frequently, we'll tell a client his sweepstakes will be a success or failure before the first ad ever appears. Why? Because the primary reason for many prize promotions is simply to give salespeople a selling tool, more ammunition, to enable them to offer the buyer a whole promotion, an event that meets the buyer's need, not merely another price deal.

4. **Generating displays and features.** In packaged products, increased sales invariably occur when a product is featured in an on-or off-shelf display treatment. The inherent drama and excitement of a sweepstakes (which translates into more eye-catching displays) and its potential for increasing store traffic are two of the reasons why many buyers will approve the store displays and support a sweepstakes event.

5. **Greater ad readership.** The magic lure of free prizes draws people into reading sweepstakes, game, and contest ads. Certainly, their readership scores, as shown in the next section, are higher than average. By carefully integrating the brand copy platform into the sweepstakes' theme or mechanics, you can further extend the reach of your advertising and therefore your advertising dollars.

ESTIMATING RESULTS

Two concerns of marketers who are considering using sweepstakes are their appropriateness for the particular target audience and the question of what a sweepstakes can actually do.

It is difficult to gauge the impact of a sweepstakes. The number of entries received bears little or no relationship to sales, since product purchase cannot be required. A sweepstakes that is heavily advertised will naturally generate awareness and recall. Today's generation of instant winner games, matching games, programmed-learning sweepstakes, telemarketing promotions, and the like can increase store traffic; and this will impact on sales, but in a way that cannot be predicted with certainty. Many sweepstakes today are, in fact, geared to development of a database of users or, at least, of aware consumers.

It is probably best to think of a sweepstakes as a dramatic element of a brand's advertising strategy, since a good sweepstakes will have a theme and a prize structure in keeping with the product and its advertising. The advertising will impact on the trade and the consumer. A sweepstakes may or may not be advertised in consumer media. But it must get visibility at the point-of-purchase, even if only on the product package itself.

To the trade, utilizing sweepstakes at the point-of-purchase helps create in-store excitement. Increasingly, trade sweepstakes are held in parallel consumer programs.

The rule of thumb is that sweepstakes should generate entries on the order of 1 to 2 percent of total circulation of the program, including advertising and point-of-purchase materials. As an example, a sweepstakes featured in a national FSI ad (circulation 50MM) and generating a response of 1 percent of the circulation yields 750,000 entries. The real power of sweepstakes advertising lies in the attention paid to it by consumers. The figures in Table 8.1 show readership scores for a recent food product sweepstakes appearing in a major women's magazine.

TABLE 8.1

SWEEPSTAKES READERSHIP SCORES

	Noted	Read Most
Sweepstakes ad	49%	17%
Norm for all food product ads	46	9
Sweepstakes ad index	107	189

While the sweepstakes ad was noted by 3 percent more readers than other food product ads in the same issue of the magazine, the dramatic difference is the extent of intensive readership. The sweepstakes ad's rate of "read most" attention on the part of the readership sample was nearly double that of other food ads in the same issue. The lure of big cash, travel, or merchandise prizes will get people reading and keep them reading.

WHO ENTERS SWEEPSTAKES?
Nearly half of the respondents in a study of 2,000 consumers by a major polling organization reported that they had entered a sweepstakes at least once in their lives, and nearly one-third reported that they had purchased products featured in a sweepstakes ad (see Table 8.2).

Sex, age, working status of female heads of households, and marital status are apparently not major determining factors in sweepstakes entry. What seems to matter most is the existence of children under 18 in the household, the size of the household itself, and family income, along with the region of the country in which the family lives.

Larger households with young children, families with larger incomes, and people living in the West seem to constitute the most active sweepstakes-entering groups. Younger and larger households with higher incomes tend to buy the featured brand more, as part of the overall sweepstakes program.

By and large, the greatest response to a sweepstakes promotion comes from the same audience that is more involved with consumer promotions of all types, consisting of larger, relatively affluent families.

SWEEPSTAKES PROMOTION FORMATS
Few marketers are aware of the many types of sweepstakes, games, and contests. There are no fewer than five sweepstakes formats plus three types of games.

First is the *Standard Sweepstakes* (see Exhibit 8.1), in which a consumer receives an entry in some print media or at the point-of-sale and is instructed to mail it in to a specific post office box or deposit it in a handy ballot box. The drawing to select winners is conducted at some specified later date.

TABLE 8.2
PARTICIPATION IN SWEEPSTAKES

	Percent of each group who purchased products along with sweepstakes offer	Percent of each group who "ever entered a sweepstakes"
Total Sample	48.2%	28.4%
Sex:		
Men	44.0	28.4
Women	49.1	28.4
Age:		
18 to 34	51.5	32.3
35 to 49	53.3	31.2
50 and over	42.7	23.6
Female head of household:		
Working	50.9	28.6
Not working	47.8	27.2
Marital status:		
Married	51.2	29.0
Single	46.4	33.8
Children under 18 in household:		
One or more	53.3	32.4
None	44.5	25.4
Household size:		
One to two persons	41.8	24.0
Three or more persons	53.9	32.4
Annual income:		
Under $10,000	42.0	23.1
$10,000 to $14,999	50.5	29.3
$15,000 to $24,999	54.1	34.6
$25,000 and over	54.6	34.8
Geography:		
East	42.6	24.6
Midwest	50.3	31.0
South	46.5	27.0
West	55.7	32.1

Yes, this is the old workhorse program we've all known since sweepstakes began. But, given the right product, the right prize structure, and the right advertising support, this type of program can grab attention and deliver readers. It is why so many more marketers are using sweepstakes today.

Second is the *Multiple-Entry Sweepstakes* (see Exhibit 8.2), in which each prize is literally a separate sweepstakes by itself. So, in order to be eligible to win any of the prizes in this type of program, a separate entry is required for each prize. This type of format greatly multiplies consumer involvement in the advertising and, not incidentally, mushrooms the number of entries received.

The multiple-entry sweepstakes is clearly an ideal way to focus on or enhance the importance of a specific number. For Benson & Hedges 100s, which used the format for many years, that number is obviously 100 — 100 individual sweepstakes, supporting a top 100mm brand.

The *Programmed-Learning Sweepstakes* (Exhibit 8.3) uses a technique that's popular in elementary education. It's like an exercise in conditioning. As a prerequisite to entering, we require the consumer to read the ad and give us back key copy points or information.

The *Qualified-Entry Sweepstakes* is similar to programmed learning except that the information needed to qualify the entry is not presented in the advertising: The consumer must guess the answer from clues or solve a puzzle, for example. Involvement here is at a maximum. Increasingly, marketers are using toll-free or 900-number telephone systems to provide clues or information to qualify entries.

One of the hottest sweepstakes techniques today is the *Automatic-Entry* format (Exhibit 8.4), where a store coupon in an ad doubles as a sweepstakes entry. When the consumer redeems the coupon with the name and address information filled in, he or she is automatically entered in the sweepstakes without the need for mailing in the entry or adding extra postage. The result? Incremental entries. In fact, we estimate that automatic-entry coupons will hype coupon redemption rates by as much as 25 percent.

Interactive telephone programs also offer an automatic-entry mechanism for consumers. By calling an 800 or 900 telephone number featured in advertising, consumers may also enter a sweepstakes.

THREE TYPES OF GAMES

Games represent the most powerful sweepstakes formats to create traffic and sales. The *Matching Instant Winner Game* (see Exhibit 8.5) literally steers consumers into stores. That's because one key element of a matching game is an ad that contains a matching symbol the consumer has to take to the store to find out if and what he or she has won. In fact, the headline often says, "You May Have Already Won — ."

EXHIBIT 8.1
STANDARD SWEEPSTAKES FORMAT

EXHIBIT 8.2
MULTIPLE-ENTRY SWEEPSTAKES FORMAT

EXHIBIT 8.3
PROGRAMMED-LEARNING SWEEPSTAKES FORMAT

EXHIBIT 8.4
AUTOMATIC-ENTRY SWEEPSTAKES FORMAT

For a major paint retailer, which at the time was an official NFL licensee, a matching game was developed in which consumers took scrambled color game symbols to participating stores across the country and unscrambled them by placing the symbols behind special acetate screens to reveal the hidden matching symbol. All of the motivating terminology of football, from touchdown to reverse, and exciting football graphics were used to excite the primarily male target audience. The delivery medium was a special eight-page color Sunday tabloid insert, with the sweepstakes getting front-page treatment.

In matching games, where it is difficult to set up displays, the UPC number, which is on every package, may be used as the matching element.

Collect-and-Win Games (see Exhibit 8.6) are often used in conjunction with instant winner games, but they can stand alone, as well. In this format, consumers get a game piece or symbol that represents a piece of a picture or part of a name or phrase. By getting enough game pieces to spell the name or complete the picture, the consumer can win a prize. Generally, one or more of the individual collect-and-win phrases or symbols is a rare game piece, limited to the total number of prizes available.

Instant Winner Games (see Exhibit 8.7) are self-contained and self-judging random-chance promotions. Consumers receive a game card requiring one or more scratch-offs or peel-offs to reveal a prize message, or instructions to enter a "second-chance" random drawing, or to save for a collect-and-win prize. New technologies include interactive games in which cards are scanned by readers with a voice message announcing a win or "Sorry, Try Again" message, or even devices that heat or cool the cards to reveal a hidden message.

CONTESTS FALL INTO BASIC TYPES

A contest requires a demonstration of skill or personal trait on the part of the entrant, who mails the entry to a post office box or deposits it in an on-premise container. The contest, therefore, has remained a basically static type of promotional program. Regardless of the theme, the specific test of skill required, or the prize structure, contest programs, when stripped to the bare essentials, are all pretty much alike (see Exhibit 8.8).

This does not mean that there is no purpose for contest programs. In recipe contests, marketers are trying to appeal to heavy users and tap the creative genius of the American homemaker. Winning recipes may appear on product labels, in printed ads, in TV commercials, or in recipe booklets. In photo contests, winning entries may provide visual elements for a continuing series of advertisements. An essay contest winner may be recruited as a corporate spokesperson for the brand or service.

EXHIBIT 8.5
MATCHING INSTANT WINNER GAME FORMAT

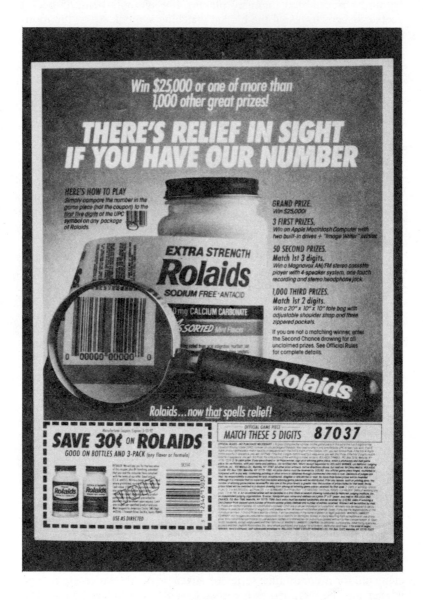

EXHIBIT 8.6
COLLECT-AND-WIN GAME FORMAT

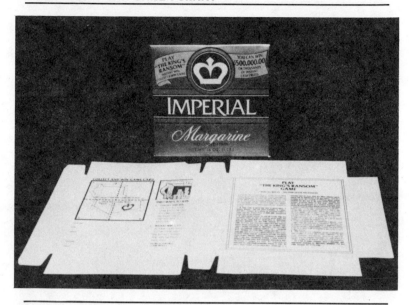

EXHIBIT 8.7
INSTANT WINNER GAME FORMAT

EXHIBIT 8.8
CONTEST FORMAT

Marketers who equate promotion success with sales may select contests over sweepstakes simply because proof-of-purchase can be required. However, contests will generate only a fraction of the entries generated by a sweepstakes. If a sweepstakes entry blank asks for either an actual or a facsimile proof-of-purchase, the number of actual proofs-of-purchase will probably far exceed the number generated by a contest identically exposed and advertised to the target audience, simply because the sweepstakes generates so many more total entries.

PLANNING FOR SWEEPSTAKES, GAMES, AND CONTESTS

1. **Determine the objectives**. Before you can know whether a sweepstakes, game, or contest will do the job, you must analyze the reasons for the promotion and determine what you expect it to achieve. For example, you must decide whether the problem is sales or distribution and whether the promotion is to cover a single product or the full line.

2. **Establish the markets.** The next step is to determine whether the promotion is to be national or regional and to establish the audience at which the sweepstakes will be aimed. Both these factors will affect the ad media and the prizes.

3. **Assign responsibilities**. Decide who will be responsible for each facet of the promotion and who will do the planning and create the sweepstakes idea and mechanics. Specify what your ad agency will be responsible for and who will handle the sweepstakes and post-sweepstakes details. Decide whether to use the services of a sweepstakes planning organization. Sweepstakes specialists can create sweepstakes ideas; develop the mechanics; draft the rules; receive, process, and store entries; judge the winners; arrange for the prizes; and handle all details and correspondence in connection with the prizes, including supervising their delivery. The important thing is to use every available source of assistance to carefully plan and administer the promotion.

4. **Develop the theme**. The sweepstakes idea or theme must be integrated with your objectives so that your product will not suffer from being subordinated to the sweepstakes itself.

   Another approach is to spotlight a specific product feature or benefit and build the sweepstakes theme around it. As noted, Benson & Hedges 100s cigarettes focused on the length of the product in its sweepstakes.

   Another effective way of integrating a sweepstakes and the product is to make the product an integral part of the grand prize, as Sunkist did recently with a "Win a Carload of Oranges" sweepstakes.

5. **Determine the entry mechanics**. Should the promotion be a sweepstakes or a skill contest? If getting a lot of entries is

important, then a sweepstakes is best. On the other hand, if you want to be able to require a proof-of-purchase with every entry, you'll have to go with a skill contest. As we've seen, that doesn't mean you're limited to the old "25-words-or-less" format. There are jingle-writing contests, photography contests, and the ever-popular recipe contests. Bear in mind, too, that a clever entry device can sometimes greatly enhance the promotion.

The entry mechanics should spell out the duration of the promotion and the conditions covering participation and judging. In a skill contest, it's especially important to make certain that you establish measurable, judgeable criteria. Most important, keep the sweepstakes and the rules as simple as possible.

6. **Check the regulations.** Although there's some confusion in this area, sweepstakes are perfectly legal. It's lotteries that are illegal for use in connection with consumer goods and services. There are federal, state, and local lottery laws, as well as Federal Trade Commission regulations, that must be adhered to. And several states now require that sweepstakes be registered and reported. Just make sure that you, your attorney, or your sweepstakes planning firm is up on the latest statutes governing games of chance.

7. **Select the prizes.** The prizes are the heart of any sweepstakes, contest, or game. They should be appropriate for the audience and the time of the year, and they should tie in with the theme. Offer as many prizes as possible so that people will feel they have a better chance of winning. For the supplementary prizes, a variety of merchandise is preferable to cash. Merchandise is more interesting and significant than a small cash award.

8. **Estimate the costs.** Early in the planning stage, firm up estimates of the cost of advertising, production, sales promotion and display materials, prizes, handling, and judging.

9. **Plan the advertising.** If you're going to have a promotion, promote it. Be prepared to devote both print space and airtime to the sweepstakes. Use the same media you have used all along. Keep the layouts simple and feature the prizes prominently; they are the carrots you are dangling before your audience.

10. **Get the sales force fired up.** Whether you have your own sales force or you sell through brokers, jobbers, distributors, or dealers, the task is still the same: to convince them that the sweepstakes is a sales tool designed to make their jobs easier and help them write more business. The sweepstakes gives them a change of pace, another reason for asking for a display or an order.

11. **Sell the trade.** Dealer cooperation is essential. Sometimes it's the reason for the whole promotion. Get dealers excited about

the impact the promotion will have on consumers and the traffic it will pull into their stores. Set up a trade sweepstakes to run simultaneously with the consumer sweepstakes; this will give dealers an added incentive to cooperate.

12. **Plan the publicity**. Back up the advertising with publicity. Frequently, the sweepstakes idea or the fact that you are running a sweepstakes is news. Send trade publications a publicity story spelling out the details. When it's over, send releases to every prizewinner's hometown paper. Then follow up with "how-we-did-it" articles.

13. **Arrange for judging the winners**. Whether you're running a sweepstakes or a skill contest, the safest thing is to have the judging done by a professional organization. You want to make certain that the winners are selected fairly and impartially; so leave the judging to the experts.

14. **Check the major winners**. Conduct a background check on the major prize winners to ascertain that the entries are their own work and that there is no question about their entries or their eligibility as winners. The judging agency usually will handle this for you.

15. **Announce the winners.** Once the sweepstakes is over, see that the judging is done as quickly as possible and that the winners are announced promptly. You must also send a list of winners to anyone who requests it.

16. **Deliver the prizes.** Nothing creates more ill will than a disappointed prize winner. Delivery of the prizes should therefore be handled quickly and smoothly.

17. **Analyze the results.** The most important criteria are as follows: Did the sweepstakes achieve its objectives? How did the sweepstakes affect sales? Did it succeed in getting all the displays you wanted? What did the sales force think of the promotion?

BUDGETING FOR SWEEPSTAKES, GAMES, AND CONTESTS

As has been noted, a critical benefit of a prize promotion is the fixed-cost nature of the event. The fact that there are no major open-ended liabilities in a sweepstakes or contest makes this type of promotion affordable to marketers for whom an elaborate program of coupons, samples, or refund offers may be too costly. At the other end of the spectrum, a sweepstakes may be ideal for brands in product categories with such high volume and purchase frequency that a coupon drop or refund offer will result in a redemption rate so high that the promotion becomes a victim of its own success, blowing budgets through the roof.

Many sweepstakes and contest programs are overlaid with coupon offers for the sponsoring brand. This has the function of encouraging purchase of the product in association with the sweepstakes and of utilizing media delivery of a sweepstakes or contest ad to provide a direct price incentive to the consumer. In such combination programs, the cost of the add-on promotion device must be budgeted separately from the sweepstakes or contest event itself, and the marketer must use all the data available in planning for the coupon response.

The costs of the sweepstakes or contest event can be grouped as follows:

1. Advertising and point-of-purchase production and media costs,
2. Prize costs, and
3. Administration and judging costs.

Advertising and point-of-purchase costs in a prize promotion are no different from those in any other type of promotion, and the result of a greater expenditure on media advertising is also the same. Strong, extensive national advertising and a major drive to get the store materials up will result in a much stronger program, whether it's a coupon drop or a sweepstakes. Television and radio support will also increase awareness of the program and add somewhat to the entry rate, but at an increased cost.

Prizes in a sweepstakes or contest are the great variable. We have long since crossed the $1 million threshold in private-sector prize promotions. The various state lotteries have yielded cash prize jackpots of $50–$60 million or more, and this has had an impact on prize promotion planning.

Depending on the product, the theme of the sweepstakes, and the regionality and nationality of the event, a prize budget as low as $25,000 can still produce an exciting, results-getting promotion.

While cash prizes may be the most universally accepted and desired, they raise a number of problems and questions for the marketer.

1. There is no disputing the impact of a large grand prize of, say, $1,000,000. However, smaller cash prizes may be unexciting, depending on the amounts, the nature of the target audience, and the relevance of a cash prize to the featured product and to the theme of the event. In the case of a sweepstakes aimed at children, for example, cash prizes would be meaningless. Children want to win trips, bicycles, games, and electronic gadgets. A $1,000 cash prize means less to a child than a $500 video game plus game cartridges.

2. A cash prize cannot be discounted or bartered. A $100,000 cash prize costs the marketer $100,000. The same $100,000 expressed as retail value of merchandise prizes may cost the marketer far less. In fact, when advertising exposure to a potential prize supplier is significant — for example, when there is extensive national print advertising, point-of-purchase advertising, or even a special 30-second TV commercial — prizes may

be obtained at little or no cost in exchange for this valuable exposure. It becomes an advertising bargain for the prize supplier and a trade-off for the sponsoring marketer.

3. The tax implications to winners of cash prizes may be considerable. Prizes over $600 must be declared as income. In fact, professional sweepstakes administration and judging organizations report this income directly to the IRS. A cash prize thus may involve a greater tax liability than a merchandise prize.

Administration and judging costs depend on such factors as the complexity of the program mechanics, special printing involved in concealed-device instant winner games, the need to visit printing or packaging plants to supervise the production and distribution of instant winner game cards and packages, prize fulfillment, and special tabular analyses of entrants. For planning purposes, marketers may estimate that the administrative cost of a typical prize promotion, exclusive of any special printing, will range from $7,000 to $25,000.

The total prize promotion package, including administration, judging, prizes, and media and point-of-purchase advertising, could range from $100,000 to $500,000 for a national event.

In budgeting for a prize promotion, the utilization of a professional administration, implementation, and judging organization is probably the least costly element, but it could be the most important one, since independence and objectivity are vital in the proper handling of these programs; a professional service can anticipate problems before they arise, thus helping the marketer avoid them.

For most marketers, a do-it-yourself sweepstakes is entirely possible. But, putting clerical people and legal retainers who are relatively inexperienced in this area to work on the event can prove far more costly and cumbersome than letting the professionals do it in the first place, not to mention creating a potential legal nightmare.

James Feldman is president of several motivation companies, including James Feldman Associates, a full-service marketing services agency; Incentive Travelers Cheque International, Inc., which offers individual travel incentives; Incentive Travel Corporation, providing group incentive travel; and Fulfillment Awards, Ltd., a data-processing and fulfillment house. His companies have provided merchandise, advertising specialties, data processing and fulfillment, and sweepstakes to clients that include Toyota Motor Sales USA, Apple Computer, Helene Curtis, Frito Lay, MGM/USA, Volkswagen USA, and Clairol, among others.

Feldman is a featured international speaker, trainer, author, and advocate for incentive usage. He has been an active member of the Association of Incentive Marketing (AIM) since 1979 and currently serves on the Board of Directors and as Seminar Director for AIM. He has been a speaker at almost every AIM seminar since 1980. He also has been an active member, board member, and committee chairman for the Society of Incentive Travel Executives (SITE) and a contributor to In-Site, *their quarterly magazine. He has been a member of the Promotion Marketing Association of America since 1981.*

CHAPTER 9

CONTINUITY PROMOTIONS

The excitement and challenge of sales promotion revolves around the fact that motivation is always changing in application — but the central concept seldom changes. This is a people business. The application of motivation planning to tangible products or services is universal whether you represent a small company or a giant corporation.

Sales motivation program results are measured by the company's maintaining or increasing its share of the potential market, as well as improving the overall sales effort within its marketing organization. The selling organization might consist of highly controlled, company-directed, salaried people. In addition, it might include uncontrolled, independent distributors, jobbers, and retailers and their sales employees. In all cases, there is a common element — the end consumer, the person who is the final purchaser, the ultimate user of the product or service. And it is that individual who is the target.

No matter how good the product or service, it must be consumed to keep the system moving. If it remains on the shelf, if the plane seat is empty, or if the hotel room is vacant, the loss of revenue causes a backup in the system. Fewer pilots are needed; fewer and smaller planes are built; there are no new construction of hotels, no refurbishing of existing properties, and no new stores; fewer employees are needed to manage, sell, or service; and the economy becomes sluggish.

Frequency or continuity programs are one of several basic sales promotion techniques that form an integral part of the marketing arsenal available to use in today's marketing mix. These are promotions whereby customers are rewarded in some manner for repeated or frequent purchase or use of a product or service. The parameters of the promotion may vary, but the intent is the same — to encourage purchase loyalty, continuity, and frequency. Today, all indications appear to point to frequent "buyer" programs as one of the most important promotion forms available to consumer marketing.

All three programs — continuity, frequency, and stamps — are considered in this discussion, but for the purposes of simplification, they will all be called frequency programs. The term *frequency marketing* is an arbitrary name for a new but now familiar promotional strategy. It has become a more familiar term through its use in the travel industry in the form of frequent flier, frequent guest, and frequent renter programs.

To continue from a solid conceptual foundation, a definition is needed:

To identify, maintain, and increase yield from the best customers through a long-term, interactive, value-added relationship that encourages our target audience to continually utilize or purchase the services and products we offer.

Millions of business travelers have been conditioned over the past decade to trade brand loyalty for miles and points, for trips, prizes, and special treatment. It has worked so well that major packaged goods manufacturers are energetically launching national frequent shopper programs in the grocery business.

The benefits of frequency programs include the ability to break through the clutter of a crowded marketplace and bring customers in to shop at a store, fly on a particular airline, stay at a given hotel, rent cars, or purchase a branded product or service. Once a customer has purchased a product or service, the programs can also be an effective method of ensuring that the customer stays loyal and that he or she comes back week after week. Perhaps most important, frequency programs can be a powerful defensive strategy to counteract competitive activities — a key benefit in an age of product parity, intensified competition, and eroding brand equities. Frequency programs can go a long way toward building a wall around customers to keep the competition out and customers in.

Exhibit 9.1 is a simplification of how adults learn. In the case of frequency programs, one can easily see that the key target audience falls into an area between 70 percent and 90 percent. By having one's customer make frequent purchases of the product or service, a pattern of buying is created that causes trial, continuity, and reward. It is much the same principle of having a child learn by repetition. Once adults get into a buying pattern, they are often likely to continue that pattern.

Frequency programs all ask the customer to "purchase today, get a reward later." Exhibit 9.2 shows the entire universe of potential prospects.

As one moves up the triangle, notice that prospects may also be former customers who switched brands for a number of reasons. Frequency programs or any other promotion may have the effect of returning them to the promoted brand. While the prospects are not first-time customers, they may have forgotten the brand, the product differentiation, or its positioning in the marketplace. They often are very fickle customers because they switch from brand to brand, depending on the promotion. Therefore, the instant gratification portion of any promotion will have great appeal to this segment of the target audience.

Frequency programs require repeat purchases. Repeat purchases require establishing a buying pattern as shown in Exhibit 9.1 and makes them repeat customers as shown in Exhibit 9.2. This repetition of buying habits is one of the main benefits of any frequency program.

EXHIBIT 9.1

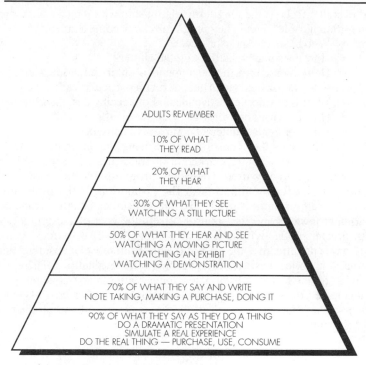

ADULTS REMEMBER

10% OF WHAT
THEY READ

20% OF WHAT
THEY HEAR

30% OF WHAT THEY SEE
WATCHING A STILL PICTURE

50% OF WHAT THEY HEAR AND SEE
WATCHING A MOVING PICTURE
WATCHING AN EXHIBIT
WATCHING A DEMONSTRATION

70% OF WHAT THEY SAY AND WRITE
NOTE TAKING, MAKING A PURCHASE, DOING IT

90% OF WHAT THEY SAY AS THEY DO A THING
DO A DRAMATIC PRESENTATION
SIMULATE A REAL EXPERIENCE
DO THE REAL THING — PURCHASE, USE, CONSUME

EXHIBIT 9.2

BEST CUSTOMERS

REPEAT CUSTOMERS

FIRST-TIME CUSTOMERS

FORMER CUSTOMERS

PROSPECTS

In all cases there are economic issues, implementation problems, and overall effects on the long-term relationship with the consumer and trade (if applicable). Frequency programs can become a curse:

- Who bears the sponsor's cost?
- How does one break through the clutter?
- How does one bring customers to enter the store, stay at a hotel, fly on a given airline, or rent a particular car?
- What is the most effective method of keeping customer loyalty?
- How are customers brought back, week after week?
- How does one counteract competitive activities?

So who bears the sponsor's cost of using this promotional technique? As is well known, marketers operate in a very competitive environment. Properly used, frequency programs increase sales and require loyalty for the duration of the promotion. If the promotion increases sales volume sufficiently, the consumer benefits from the additional rewards and the sponsor offsets the cost of the promotion with greater productivity and greater utilization of resources. If the program is not effective, the cost of the program must be absorbed and used as a historical basis for future promotional evaluations. There has been no research that substantiates some claims that frequency programs raise prices. However, any promotion becomes a cost of doing business that must be covered in the gross margin of the product or service being sold.

TYPES OF FREQUENCY PROGRAMS

The particulars of a frequency program and how it can be structured vary. A brief discussion of continuity, frequency, and stamp programs, and what distinguishes one from the other, follows.

Continuity Programs. A continuity program is a self-liquidating or profit-making plan, most often used by supermarkets, in which a set of related items is offered. For instance, the consumer could get a different item each week for a given time in return for purchase or use. Supermarkets may offer dishes, flatware, cutlery, glasses, or encyclopedias. Today, these types of programs are used by quick-service restaurant establishments as well, where a continuing line of toys is offered each week to be collected. The programs encourage regular repeat visits. Most often the store purchases a completely packaged program, tailored to the specific needs of the sponsor, with a guarantee that the supplier will take back all unsold merchandise. Generally they are not directed to a specific product, but a specific dollar purchase for each visit.

Frequency Programs. A frequency program is a tracking program of purchases by a given consumer of a particular product, with a reward, usually free goods or services of the same nature as what was tracked or purchased. These programs are customized by the sponsor. Frequency programs are most often used by airlines, hotels, and name-brand products, such as canned goods.

The airlines pioneered this concept when industry leaders fought back against regional carriers that were taking away their customers. Frequent flier programs gave customers added value for choosing a specific airline when making reservations. As the airlines attracted new customers and generated passenger loyalty, they enhanced their programs with newsletters that offered additional values and monthly point statements that maintained interest.

The hospitality industry rewarded loyal customers with special amenities and low- or no-cost upgrades in services. Quick service restaurants spawned a flood of games, premiums, and incentives. Alert marketers in every field learned that if there is a way to monitor customers' purchases, it is possible to analyze and act on that information.

The very nature of this huge database tracking system has led to many companies selling their services and/or data to other firms. Examples can be found with airlines such as United's Mileage Plus and American's AAdvantage; hotels such as Hyatt's Gold Passport, Marriott's Honored Guest, and Fairmont's President's Club; and charge cards including Diners Club Premier Rewards and Citibank Dollars. And now a packaged goods program that tracks, through proof-of-purchase, more than 100 brands. The participant clips and saves the proofs-of-purchase and mails them to the processing center. Using preprinted personalized bar code stickers, the travel credits build a bank of air miles to be used for future travel.

Trading Stamp Program. Stamp programs were created long before the term *frequency program* was developed or implemented. In this instance, stamps are collected in conjunction with use or purchase and redeemed for merchandise. Stamp programs were most often used by gas stations and supermarkets because they built strong loyalty for an individual store, bringing the customer back repeatedly. Trading stamp popularity spread usage from store to store until the stamps lost their power to set apart any individual store. Now, due to the popularity of frequency programs in general, trading stamps are enjoying renewed interest as a continuity vehicle.

Trading stamps afford guilt-free shopping for discretionary items. The awards-merchandise for the family, for gifts, or for the home or garden has lasting value. Families enjoy pasting the stamps into books, spending the books, and planning for their free purchases.

Sweepstakes Continuity. This kind of continuity program works by collecting the parts to build a slogan, picture, or other device. Much like a jigsaw puzzle, each game ticket is obtained by making a visit or purchase or writing to the sponsor. Several game tickets are needed to complete the picture that will allow either a winner or an entry into a random-draw sweepstakes. (See Chapter 8 for a detailed explanation.) The premise is the same — buy now and get the reward later. However, in these programs there are often instant winners. These are prizes that keep up the interest of the participants. Upon opening the game ticket, a winning prize is revealed that may be instantly obtained from the sponsor.

For example, an instant prize, as well as the collectible feature, was used by Apple Computer. The top portion can be rubbed off to reveal an instant prize. If the participants wanted to obtain that prize, they could not rub off the bottom section. If they did rub off the bottom section, they forfeited the instant prize. Once the bottom section was revealed, they collected the "points" revealed on each card. If more than one section of the bottom was revealed, the card was void.

The Purpose of Frequency Programs. The differences in the reward structure define the type of frequency program, and it does not matter whether trade channels or consumers are the target. Yet frequency programs all have the same purpose and have one ultimate goal: to get the targeted purchaser to build brand loyalty. This loyalty pattern may mean continued spending, a repeat of using the service, staying at the same hotel chain, flying the same airline, charging on the same credit card, or using the same detergent or cereal. In exchange for that loyalty, the sponsor of the program will provide some form of reward to the purchasers.

ADVANTAGES OF FREQUENCY PROGRAMS

The advantages of using a frequency-type promotion are many. Frequency programs can achieve some or all of the following:

- Increase frequency of purchases of goods or services
- Increase frequency of store visits, where applicable
- Create a purchase habit that continues after the promotion period is over
- Provide a database of participant buying behavior
- Are easy to measure and track effectiveness

One of the side benefits of creating a promotion to induce short-term continuity of purchase is that these programs can also create a purchase habit that continues after the promotion has ended. (See Exhibits 9.1 and 9.2.) Frequency marketing is extremely effective in focusing the loyal customer's attention on the brand over the long term.

A very important advantage of most frequency programs is the extraordinary database that can be obtained. Properly maintained, it contains the buying or usage habits of consumers over time. Information gained from the program can actually become an additional source of revenue through the sale of mailing lists, information, purchasing habits, interests, and other data to providers of noncompetitive services. In many cases they also provide data that can be used to target new products and offer a reason for both former customers, as well as new prospects, to purchase.

As an example, United Airlines rented its list of frequent fliers who had made more than one trip per month to Los Angeles. The local Hyatt in Los Angeles sent a mailing to those fliers in the hope that they could encourage them to stay at a Hyatt instead of some other chain. Hyatt paid United for the list, United customers earned frequent flier points if they stayed at the Hyatt, and United frequent customers were given upgrade certificates for suites if they presented their "Mileage Plus" cards upon check-in. Then Hyatt gave United information about the frequency that each member stayed at Hyatt, and the duration of each stay. United could then check to see if that customer flew into and out of Los Angeles on a United flight. This kind of data exchange can be invaluable to program sponsors in furthering their business among customers and prospects.

One of the most important blessings is that it's relatively easy to measure a frequency program's effectiveness. Consumers' involvement in the program is obvious — if they are collecting their reward, they are participating.

DISADVANTAGES OF FREQUENCY PROGRAMS

The disadvantages of frequency programs are as follows:

- May have a limited appeal
- May have difficulty in getting trade support due to the long-term nature of programs
- Opportunities exist for misredemption, barter, or reselling
- May create an IOU for the sponsor that can have detrimental effects on total dollar allocations (reserves) needed to address the building of obligation to participants
- May be difficult to alter
- May be difficult to terminate
- May be more costly to administer than estimated
- May be easy for competitors to duplicate and improve
- Possible rewards may be given to customers who did not alter their purchase habits, but were rewarded anyway
- Customers may anticipate program and collect proofs-of-purchase before announcement, to hold for later redemption. This is especially effective in label savings' programs such as school computers, for which high levels of collectibility are required.

A frequency program can suffer from limited appeal if the consumer doesn't perceive that the added value of the reward is high enough. It can also be difficult to obtain trade support because, by their nature, frequency programs are long term and there can be a substantial difference between a sponsor's interest and the retailer's. It could be a major mistake to assume that retailers or distributors will participate in the program unless their needs were considered in its development.

Frequency programs can also, unfortunately, have a high potential for abuse. The opportunities for misredemption, bartering, and reselling can be significant. Airline frequent flier programs have found this to be an especially difficult problem to overcome.

The contingent liability of a frequency program is another potential problem. In essence, the program creates an IOU for the sponsor that can have a detrimental effect on the total dollar allocation needed to address the building obligation to participants. In addition, for this reason, frequency programs may be difficult to terminate. It's critical that the sponsor plan an exit strategy to minimize any negative impact on program participants. Just as the program may be difficult to terminate, it may also be difficult to alter. Changing the rules of the game midway through a promotion is likely to create customer relations headaches, not to mention possible legal problems.

When American and United tried to change the points needed for travel redemption, there were groups that threatened to file legal claims against the carriers. To make a smoother transition, both carriers agreed to carry on the old mileage points for several years and for the same travel point redemption requirements. New mileage points could not be used to purchase the old awards, but the old awards could be used to purchase the new travel prizes.

Careful administrative planning is essential to the successful frequency marketing program. Costs can get out of hand if the program grows more quickly than anticipated and there's a poorly designed system in place to handle it.

A FREQUENCY MARKETING EXAMPLE

Most recently a company called Air Miles became a frequency partner with many companies who could not deliver these programs on their own. Products such as charcoal, potato chips, condiments, and other less expensive products all joined with Air Miles to create a collectible program that rewards participants with air miles on certain carriers.

At the same time, American Express created a similar program so that each dollar charged on its credit card would allow the points to be converted to several of the existing airline frequency programs. To experienced participants, this meant that they could earn points for charging on their credit card, earn points for flying on that same airline, and earn additional points by staying at certain hotels, and charging on their credit card. Table 9.1 shows an example of a business trip and the points that could be earned.

Currently a round-trip, coach-class United Airlines ticket is 20,000 points. In Table 9.1, it can be seen that a short trip with normal activities obtained about one-third of the points needed for a coach round-trip ticket and two of the 10 nights for a free weekend stay, and it probably was written off as a business expense. In addition, the cost of the ticket was coach, but the participant flew first class, stayed at the hotel for the corporate rate but obtained an upgrade to a suite, and drove

TABLE 9.1
FLIGHT FROM CHICAGO TO LOS ANGELES

Charge the United flight tickets on Diners Club, earn 2 points for each dollar spent ($1,000.00).	2,000 pts.
Mileage Plus gives me 1,850 miles. If an Executive member, it is doubled and upgraded to first class using flight coupons.	3,700 pts.
Rent a Hertz Rental Car,	500 pts.
charge on Diners $50-double points. Upgraded to luxury sedan using coupons from United.	100 pts.
Stay at the Hyatt LAX one night ($170), Gold Passport Bonus point plan—double points.	2 nights
If Diamond member, upgraded to suite. Charge the room on Diners — double points.	240 pts.
Took a client to lunch $100, charged to Diners.	200 pts.
Took client to dinner, charged to Diners. Took client to theater. Had brief meeting, cocktails after theater. Total for above = $350.	700 pts.
Purchased a gift for my children and wife.	150 pts.
TOTAL POINTS EARNED	7,590 pts.

a luxury car for the price of the economy size. Instant rewards were given, as well as long-term point accumulation for future vacation travel.

PLANNING A FREQUENCY PROGRAM

To be effective, frequency programs should address the following marketing issues. Answers to these questions can be used as a template for creating a frequency program.

1. What is the measurable goal of the frequency program? In almost all cases, increasing the frequency by which the participant continues to purchase the product or service is the main goal. Frequency programs want to establish loyalty in the purchase cycle of a product or service.

In order to measure and reward continued purchase and use, behavior must be individually tracked. Since the collection of proof-of-purchase seals or points for each purchase or each stay is the method of earning the reward, the targeted participants want the points to be tracked and participate willingly in the process. They present their account number, collect the proof-of-purchase seals, and fulfill other requirements. In all cases the accumulation of these data is needed to determine the type of reward that participants can earn.

In a 1991 Promotion Marketing Association of America (PMAA) survey of its members, respondents were asked what criteria they used to measure success for their continuity programs. Sales increases, use of displays, redemptions, and market share gains were all cited. The survey showed that:

- 86 percent indicated that an increase in sales was the measure.
- 59 percent indicated an increase in displays.
- 55 percent used redemptions as their criteria.
- 41 percent increased their market share.

2. *When is it appropriate to use a frequency program?* When the objective is to increase sales, frequency marketing is an obvious choice. In fact, this is the number one reason for any frequency program.

Brand loyalty, however, is important for maintaining sales. Today many products exist that have the same characteristics, price, and awareness. To keep customers from trying other brands, frequency programs offer a reason for the customers to remain loyal. Frequency marketing is very often used, therefore, to maintain sales.

Logistically, it is difficult to turn on and turn off a frequency program; these programs require long-term commitments. For this reason, it is more difficult to use this type of promotion with seasonal items. Likewise, short-term frequency programs do not work with any product that is not consumed or repurchased within a week's time. Most often quick service restaurant operators use short-term frequency programs, and even then they run for several months at a time.

As Table 9.2 shows, there are certain conditions that favor frequency marketing and those that are less favorable. If there is little differentiation between the sponsor's product or service and the competition's, frequency marketing can be beneficial. On the other hand, if the sponsor's product has the best prices in the market, frequency marketing may be a costly strategy with little potential for market share gains.

When the sponsor can absorb extra sales with little extra operating costs, frequency programs can also be useful. If the sponsor is already operating at near capacity, however, the incremental sales generated may not translate into added profits. Sponsors should have the room to make substantial market share gains among the target purchasers before setting up the program. Furthermore, if the sponsor has little competition and already dominates the market, frequency programs aren't likely to increase business.

It's also critical that the prospective customer perceives significant rewards for loyalty to the brand, so that switching to the brand will be worth breaking old purchase habits.

Finally, the customer needs to be able to switch brand loyalty at will and without hindrance. If it's inconvenient for the customer to switch, the frequency program is not likely to help.

TABLE 9.2
FREQUENCY MARKETING

Favorable Conditions	Unfavorable Conditions
Little product differentiation	Distinctive product
Little price differentiation	Best prices in market
Sponsor can absorb extra sales with little extra cost	Operating near capacity
Sponsor can experience substantial gains among target	Little competition dominates market
Prospective customer recognizes significant rewards for loyalty	No incentive to switch; rewards are not incentive
Customer can switch loyalty at will without hindrance	Pricing, proximity, etc.; switching prohibited

3. Determining the proper audience. Some consideration must be given to the audience of the promotional program early on in the planning stages. Who is the purchaser? Can the purchaser buy more as a result of the frequency program? Will purchasers continue to repurchase as a result of the program? Will they willingly do what is necessary to participate by collecting pieces or tracking usage? A program must be structured with the intended audience in mind.

4. Financing and budgeting for a frequency program. Budgeting for a frequency program is similar to budgeting for any promotional program. The key questions are what monies should be allocated to the program and where should these monies come from? A fixed percentage method is often used whereby a certain amount of money from previous product sales or value of services rendered is set aside for developing a frequency marketing program. Decisions such as which department(s) should fund the program are important in the initial planning stages. In many cases, variable allocation is used across several sponsoring brands or services, depending on the profitability of the particular product or service purchased by participant. How this is done depends on the situation, for example:

- Tape plan for grocery stores
- Mileage for airlines
- Per night allocation for hotels
- Percentage of merchandise cost for credit card companies or merchandise retailers

5. How should the frequency program be structured? There are several basic decisions that need to be made that determine the scope and structure of a frequency program. For instance, if the program encourages purchase of, say, a packaged goods product, what purchases qualify for accumulation in the promotion? The product(s) to be honored need to be specified — what brands, what sizes, and the like. Whether a certain number of purchases will constitute "winning," or whether a dollar volume instead will be the determinator, needs to be decided.

Once this basic parameter is set, a key question to ask is what will be used as the "proof-of-purchase"? Often, packaged goods products have the convenience and opportunity to use package labels or the UPC codes from the label, box, or bag as the proof-of-purchase. Where labels are not easily removed or collectible, or where other specifications — such as time of purchase or dollar amount — require more than a label can provide, grocery store receipts are an acceptable alternative. These can be saved and presented as purchase proof, especially when an identifier is printed on the receipt as with grocery store scanners. Sometimes both the receipt and a label are necessary to claim that a purchase was made, and this should be clearly stated for the consumer.

Where the product is a service, some "unit" of use needs to be determined for the frequency program. With airline travel, specifics regarding what constitutes a ticket must be decided in advance. Either the distance flown or the dollar value of a ticket could be used in accumulating toward a reward, but most airlines today use the miles. For hotels, there is sometimes a minimum room rate in place or a minimum number of nights required for qualification in a frequency program. If dollars spent at a hotel (as an indication of length of stay) are to be used as the unit, some rules need to be set regarding whether other room charges will count toward the reward. Everything must be anticipated and written into the program in order for it to run smoothly and successfully.

A last structural detail for frequency programs is the amount of time to be allocated for the program. This is especially important when determining the program liability. Some programs are meant to increase or at least sustain purchase or use within a certain time frame, such as a month or a season or a period in association with a holiday or an event, and as such have clear start and stop dates to delineate the time parameter. Any purchases or accumulation before or after those particular dates are then no longer redeemable or no longer qualify for a reward.

Other programs are more long term, perhaps ongoing over an indefinite period. In this case, to limit liability, purchases, usage, or points accumulated expire after a certain length of time. In other words, there is a moving window of eligibility. In this respect, miles flown on an airline, for instance, cannot be counted toward free trips after a certain number of years. The old miles drop off and the new miles continue to accumulate. This encourages consumers to redeem their miles in a regular and timely manner.

6. *How should rewards be defined?* What is the best way to reward participants in the program — with merchandise, travel, or cash? In each case, of course, the exact nature of the merchandise or travel, and the cash amounts, need to be determined. Sometimes participants can be allowed to self-select their own award from a variety of alternatives.

There is always the alternative of giving away more of the product or service that was sold in the first place. One needs to ask whether doing so will have a positive or negative effect on business. If future business is negatively affected by awarding more product, this may not be desirable. However, where the product or service is perishable, this may be a good way to go. An airline sells seats on an airplane; a hotel sells rooms; a cruise ship sells cabins. In all cases, if those seats/rooms/cabins are empty on a given flight/day/cruise, the profits from them are lost. In this case, it makes economic sense for the marketer to fill those vacancies with program winners at no extra cost. In many cases, the seats awarded are in addition to normal traveling requirements and do not diminish future sales.

7. *Should a multilevel awards program be created?* It is possible to create a multilevel program where what the participants are awarded or are eligible to win is scaled to fit the level of use or purchase. Participants may be inclined to purchase more or use a service more often over a competitor's if the increased benefits of attaining and maintaining higher levels of participation within the program are valuable to them. Programs such as Hyatt's Gold Passport Program — with its Gold Passport, Platinum Passport, and Diamond Passport tiers — have successfully applied this concept to reward different levels of usage and loyalty to visitors staying at the hotel chain. While many applications of multitiered programs have developed within the services categories, a multilevel structure can also be used by packaged goods companies to create special incentives and increase frequency.

Of course, if multilevel awards are developed within the general structure of a frequency program, the criteria for maintenance at a particular level need to be decided. Once participants have achieved a certain level within a program, can they be bumped down a tier if they do not continue to maintain high levels of participation? Criteria regarding how strictly to adhere to the rules established in this regard should also be developed. This can be a sticky problem in a service-oriented category in which frequency programs are attempting to generate participant loyalty and goodwill, as well as their increased usage.

8. *The frequency program database.* As mentioned earlier, one of the side benefits of using a frequency marketing program is the ability to build a list of current users that can be leveraged for future promotions and/or tracked in terms of future sales. If capturing a database of participants is a goal, however, what information should be gathered and maintained for the frequency program database? While a listing of

names and addresses can be convenient for targeted mailings of promotions in the future, much more has probably been learned about these customers, which should also be kept. Not only the level of usage, but also the specifics of what, when, and how might be important information to retain.

9. Forecasting response. In any promotion, some thought must be given to what the demands of the promotion will be so that a sponsor can be ready to fulfill those demands. Anticipating response and participation levels is an important step in determining how much product to have on hand during the promotion period, or how to handle the increased traffic and loads in a service-oriented industry. Where suppliers are involved, contracts may need special provisions to accommodate promotion demands. In some cases, most likely in service areas, safety provisions need to be considered.

If rewards are to be given, forecasting these demands is also critical. Poor word-of-mouth can result when rewards remain unfulfilled as promised. Lead times and delivery issues are a constraint to be reckoned with. If a company is purchasing merchandise instead of rewarding participants with its own products, the goal is to properly plan for maximum sales with minimum leftover merchandise.

Estimating program participation and resulting needs is obviously integral to creating a budget and pro forma statement for the program.

10. Integration of frequency programs with advertising and public relations. How can a frequency program be integrated into an advertising or public relations program? Frequency programs often become an advertising tool that overshadows normal advertising messages. The goal is to integrate and best use the natural strengths of both to attain the objectives set for the brand or sponsor.

Many frequency programs have come under attack because the realization of the reward is not anticipated, creating public relations problems. For instance, upgrades for car rentals, hotel rooms (to suites), or airline tickets (to first class) may not be readily available for redemption by participants. Another problem situation that results when a loyal consumer becomes a winner, based on consumption or usage, is that service seems to be less effective than when the participant was in the purchase cycle.

What can be done to correct this condition? Most companies should remember that they encouraged purchase of their product or services. Once winners want to redeem, they are still purchasers and should not be treated in less than a "first-class" manner. Many participants have been treated so badly once they redeemed their prize, they switched to other suppliers in the hopes that they would be treated better. This obviously negates the progress toward the objective set in the first place — to encourage loyalty and continued purchasing.

DIFFICULTIES IN IMPLEMENTING FREQUENCY PROGRAMS

One of the key reasons for using frequency programs is to attract incremental sales. However, it is not always easy to fine-tune the promotion strategy so that it has the desired effect of building business. Sometimes, customers who don't alter their purchase habits are also rewarded. Additionally, most industries have seasonal shifts in usage that can have an impact on program response patterns. The trick is in finding a way to reduce nonrevenue participation during peak selling seasons and drive redemption to off seasons — not an easy task.

The other problem that has not been discussed is the customer who anticipates the program and collects proofs-of-purchase to be redeemed before the program has been announced. Salem brand cigarettes once offered free Hyatt weekend stays for proofs-of-purchase from their cigarettes. Hundreds of redemptions took place within days of the initial announcement of the event. This kind of redemption would have required a consumer participating in the program to have "smoked" hundreds of packs of cigarettes — not possible within the time frame for the promotion. This example is only one of many problems encountered by both packaged goods companies, as well as those with proofs-of-purchase that are easy to remove or collect. This can be a particular problem where high levels of collectibility are required such as the Apples for Students program or the Campbell Soup program in which labels were used as points for purchase of computers or athletic equipment for schools.

A last thing to consider when implementing a frequency promotion is whether consumers view frequency programs as adding "additional cost" or creating additional benefits. What is the consumer's attitude toward these programs? Anticipating trade response, too, is advisable. In most cases, the trade likes frequency programs because they encourage more purchasing.

In general, the primary roadblock to implementing a successful frequency program is managing the program over its duration and understanding the investment required to support and sustain the program. The right mix of support must be available to field a successful program.

CONCLUSIONS

In the 1991 PMAA survey mentioned earlier, association members were asked about their experiences with continuity programs. The survey found that, of those responding:

- 51 percent indicated that they conducted a continuity program in the last year
- Nearly four programs (an average of 3.8) were run by those members surveyed
- The average duration of the continuity program was 16 weeks
- The average cost of these programs was $147,800 — although

the range was from $28,000 to $31 million
- 100 percent stated that the program was successful

The fact that no one claimed his or her program to be a failure is noteworthy. Either frequency programs are creating much success, or marketers were in the process of justifying their budgets for next year when the survey was taken! In many instances, respondents reported overlaying other types of promotional techniques with the frequency programs. For instance, 58 percent used rebates and 58 percent used coupons with purchase.

Given all the positives, it appears that frequency programs are here to stay. They offer increases in sales, displays, and brand loyalty. Frequency programs are a way of gaining the attention of the purchaser when basic services or goods are quite similar in the eyes of customers and whenever there is excess capacity. In industries such as airlines, hotels, or canned goods, the product may have a unique life cycle or buying pattern. The differentiating power of frequency programs is that the reward can be unique to the purchaser. Free hotel rooms, airline tickets, and upgrades have a perceived value that is significantly higher than the actual cost to the supplier. Further, with these rewards, the customer is once again retained in the exclusive franchise and prohibited from discovering the competition.

To the sponsor, frequency programs give more information about their customers' habits than ever before available. Airlines know when and where customers fly, they know how far in advance tickets are purchased, in what seats they reserve, and what special meals are ordered. This marketing information alone could make the frequency program cost-effective.

Clearly, under many conditions, frequency programs will be a blessing. Whenever a product or service is similar, the value of the frequency program is evident. Frequent customer buying increases turnover in inventory, assists in research information, and allows the sponsor to target promotions more effectively.

Douglas B. Leeds joined Thomson-Leeds, a leading New York point-of-purchase advertising agency, as account executive in 1977 and became its president in 1988. His agency has won more awards for creativity and innovation than any other company in the industry, creating displays for a broad range of clients, including AT&T, Bausch & Lomb, CBS Records, Ford, Kellogg's, Lever Brothers, Nike, Philip Morris, and Sony.

A frequent speaker at industry conferences in the U.S. and abroad, Leeds is currently on the Board of Directors of the Point-of-Purchase Advertising Institute (POPAI) and was formerly chairman of POPAI's Educational Relations Committee and POPAI's Annual Industry Conference and Marketplace Show. Leeds is a trustee of the Whitney Museum of American Art, a director of The American Theatre Wing, The Checkerboard (film) Foundation, and Ronald McDonald House Associates. During the last six years, he has produced two Broadway shows.

Leeds is a graduate and past trustee of Babson College in Wellesley, Massachusetts.

Chapter 10
POINT-OF-PURCHASE

If dollars spent is the measure, marketing's battleground clearly has moved from the TV set to the retail store. A research study by Veronis, Suhler & Associates, published in *P-O-P Times*, an industry trade publication, reported that spending on promotional advertising media outweighed that of measured media (television, radio, magazines, newspapers) by $108 billion to $80 billion in 1990, the end of a five-year reporting period. Promotional spending was further projected to lead measured spending by up to $46 billion a year over the next five years, reaching $153 billion to measured media's $108 billion by 1995.

The Veronis, Suhler study measured expenditures on point-of-purchase (P-O-P) advertising, meanwhile, at nearly $20 billion in 1990, making P-O-P the fastest growing segment of all promotional advertising categories. Allocations to point-of-purchase advertising and displays, the study predicted, will reach $30.2 billion by 1995 and account for 19.8 percent of all promotional outlays. In short, promotional media budgets continue to outpace those of measured media advertising, and P-O-P leads the promotional advertising pack in spending growth.

What is Point-of-Purchasing Advertising?
How does one define point-of-purchase advertising? As the name itself suggests, point-of-purchase is advertising where the sales transactions occur. Point-of-purchase advertising dominates the moment at which all the elements of a sale converge — namely, the buyer, the seller, the money, and the product. Point-of-purchase advertising assumes countless forms and employs myriad materials, but it always is directed toward one very important objective: to communicate sales and marketing messages at the moment purchasing decisions are being made.

Why Is P-O-P Growing in Importance?
Point-of-purchase advertising is and always has been a highly efficient and effective way to influence consumer behavior at the moment buying decisions are being made. P-O-P's long-held and well-documented ability to target, inform, persuade, enhance, and sell have lately positioned the medium as a more pivotal element of the marketing mix. Following are 10 reasons point-of-purchase advertising has grown to become so important:
1. **Retail support is declining**. The level of sales personnel at retail has declined steadily, creating a selling environment in which products must speak for themselves. The reasons for sales personnel reduction are many, ranging from cost-cutting

measures to changes in store formats. P-O-P has stepped in to fill this salesclerk void, providing product information and a measure of persuasion to help consumers make purchasing decisions.

2. **Consumers respond to self-service.** Long gone are the days in which shoppers were attended upon by aproned clerks behind counters. With the advent of the supermarket came a strong consumer preference for helping oneself. The importance of having point-of-purchase materials rose accordingly, particularly for product categories such as pharmaceuticals, food and beverage, do-it-yourself products, and electronics.

3. **Consumers make unplanned purchases.** Often quoted is the statistic that two-thirds of all purchasing decisions are made at the point-of-sale. Few are aware, however, that this phenomenon was first measured in a 1945 study by duPont deNemours & Company, which conducted the research because of its product packaging business. That 1945 study showed that 51.8 percent of all purchasing decisions were made in-store. By 1949, however, the percentage of in-store purchasing decisions had grown to 66.6 percent; and by 1954, duPont found that the figure had ballooned to 70.8 percent!

   Today, the Point-of-Purchase Advertising Institute reports in-store consumer purchasing decisions at the two-thirds figure, which is generally accepted and supported by scanner data. This now-famous statistic has helped confer enhanced status on point-of-purchase advertising, now regarded as a critical element in prompting both unplanned purchases and last-minute brand-switching.

4. **Retailers appreciate P-O-P's value.** Retailers view P-O-P as a way to increase sales and profits, affording manufacturers an opportunity to build mutually beneficial relationships with retailers through strategic P-O-P programs. Retailers welcome with open aisles in-store marketing concepts that will make their profit margins grow, concepts that manufacturers are eminently well qualified to deliver.

5. **The local marketing trend increases.** The shift in attention from a single national marketplace to multiple local markets today often takes yet another step down to specific neighborhoods and individual stores, where P-O-P can pinpoint specific consumer segments. Linked to databases detailing demographics, psychographics, brand preference, and purchasing patterns of shoppers in a particular store's trading area, P-O-P programming can easily be tailored to suit both local marketing conditions and class of trade.

6. **Excitement for mature product categories grows.** Most consumers regard shopping as a form of entertainment, and P-O-P can add fun to the experience. This presents special opportuni-

ties for mature product categories, since P-O-P can draw attention and excitement to products, such as frozen foods, that otherwise would be considered uninteresting and therefore largely ignored.

7. **Comparative CPMs are favorable.** Point-of-purchase advertising is not only a highly effective medium able to target purchase-ready consumers, but it is also relatively inexpensive. The cost-per-thousand of reaching a consumer by P-O-P usually does not exceed 50 cents and is often far less. By comparison, the cost-per-thousand to reach a consumer via a network television commercial ranges to as much as seven or eight dollars.

8. **P-O-P focuses money on consumers, not the trade.** Point-of-purchase advertising has emerged as a key means of bridging retailer and brand objectives. P-O-P serves the retailer's interest in earning healthy profits while meeting the manufacturer's objective of building brand equity. By providing retailers with profit-building displays, manufacturers have an opportunity to reallocate dead-end trade funds to brand-building consumer programs. Such funds otherwise would have gone directly to the trade's bottom line (in the form of off-invoice discounts, slotting fees, etc.), with little or no pass-through to the consumer.

9. **Performance is easy to measure.** Whether the marketing discipline is advertising, promotion, or point-of-purchase, accountability is a central concern. Advertisers need to know that the marketing activity has had a tangible effect on sales. P-O-P has grown in popularity in tandem with the installation of checkout scanners, which can provide up-to-the-minute reporting on the effectiveness of an in-store advertising program.

10. **Brand images are reflected and built.** Point-of-purchase advertising often shares the look of an image advertising campaign, sometimes even bringing to life product mascots such as Kellogg's Tony the Tiger. P-O-P is capable of reinforcing a brand's image while promoting the product's sales. With consumer loyalty to brands reportedly declining, the importance of conveying product personality in-store cannot be underestimated. As an advertising medium, point-of-purchase is uniquely qualified to remind shoppers why they prefer one brand over another, blunting growing perceptions among consumers that all products essentially are the same.

TYPES OF POINT-OF-PURCHASE

Attempts to categorize point-of-purchase advertising can be difficult, because standard P-O-P concepts frequently cross-pollinate to produce new ideas. P-O-P advertising can be as small as a window decal or as large as a self-contained boutique. It can be permanent or temporary and can be used indoors or out. It can hang on a ceiling, sit on a floor, or perch on a counter or cash register. P-O-P can be any and all of the above, combined and recombined to suit specific brand and retailer objectives. The array of display types and how they function truly is infinite.

Perhaps even more important, a virtually unlimited array of potential materials applicable to P-O-P affords the medium an extraordinary capacity to continuously reinvent itself. Because of this executional flexibility, one can easily make the case that no other advertising medium offers as much nonstop creativity as P-O-P.

No other advertising medium can use all materials known to humankind. Point-of-purchase advertising is not confined to a printed page or taped images and sounds, though it can incorporate both. P-O-P can use light, motion, sound, smell, or texture. It can be flat or dimensional. You can touch it. It often uses ostensibly mundane materials such as paper products, plastic, wood, and wire. But it can also employ unlikely elements such as water, rock, or sand, and even the latest in laser or interactive technologies. Such possibilities give P-O-P an unmatched opportunity to communicate brand benefits and sell products.

Timely knowledge of the infinite variety of materials is pivotal to effective development of P-O-P programs. The P-O-P executive who is resourceful and digs deeply into production materials and methods invariably creates more effective and distinctive point-of-purchase advertising.

To develop a manageable working understanding of P-O-P displays, it is useful to categorize them by (1) length of time they are to be used, (2) location in which they are to be used, and (3) their marketing function.

1. **Time.** A P-O-P program is considered permanent if its materials are durable and its intended period of use is six months or longer. Anything less is considered a temporary or semipermanent display. These guidelines were established by the Point-of-Purchase Advertising Institute, which administers an annual awards contest for both permanent and semipermanent displays. Obviously, the type of material used and method of manufacture greatly affects a program's potential for permanence. So development of a P-O-P program requires the planner to determine first the desired length of use.

    A study by Nielsen Marketing Research, reported in *P-O-P Times*, provided an affirmative answer to the question: Are semipermanent displays worth the extra expense? Nielsen conducted research on behalf of a packaged drink manufacturer that supported the argument that higher-quality displays generally are worth the extra associated costs. While both types of displays are of comparable effectiveness, the semipermanents have a bottom-line edge because more retailers accept them and they stay up longer.

2. **Location.** Every square inch of a retail environment represents an opportunity for P-O-P advertising. Just where the advertising ought to be positioned for maximum result is a central issue when planning P-O-P programs, because location tremendously influences performance. Designing P-O-P to fit a specific location can increase its effectiveness. Another Nielsen study, reported by *P-O-P Times*, showed that displays for a snack product located in the front, rear, and lobby of a store generated up to twice the volume of displays in other locations. The manufacturer also discovered that "substantial differences in responsiveness" to specific display locations differed brand by brand and region to region (see Exhibit 10.1).

The ability of marketers to make informed recommendations to retailers concerning the strongest sales-building display locations for their brands is greatly enhanced by scanner data generated at the checkout counter. Applying such information is

EXHIBIT 10.1
POTENTIAL DISPLAY LOCATIONS

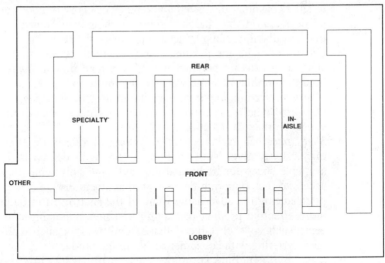

Potential display locations are: (1) **LOBBY** — the area between the front of the checkout counters and the front walls as you enter the store; (2) **FRONT** — the front of the store between check-out counters and the front end-caps; (3) **IN-AISLE** — any of the areas between the two ends of the primary shelving units, i.e., the main shopping aisles of the store; (4) **REAR** — the rear of the store, between the end-caps and the back wall; (5) **SPECIALTY** — any area in the main traffic flow devoted to a specific product, i.e., cheese, wine, flowers, etc., that appears to be a store-within-a-store; (6) **OTHER** — any place out of the main traffic flow that does not fall into one of the other five areas although there may be shelving units and additional displays.

crucial for marketers in today's retail environment, where the trade is increasingly tightfisted about how nationally advertised brands are presented at the point-of-purchase. Marketers must be prepared to prove that a retailer's category-wide profits will improve if their brand is given special exposure in a prime retail location. Some retailers, aware of the ability of displays to increase sales, now design their stores to maximize the potential of display space. Such was not the case 10 or 20 years ago.

3. **Function.** What P-O-P advertising can accomplish at retail falls into a variety of broad categories:

- *Merchandisers* generally are designed to hold the product being advertised and are meant to create a specific "home" for the product apart from standard store shelving. Examples include permanent racks that hold candy, overhead racks for cigarettes typically found at the checkout counter, and pallet displays. Temporary units known as prepacks consist of the shipping cartons themselves, turned inside-out to become a display unit.

- *Signage* reinforces a product, company name, or an advertised theme. It can also simply inform the consumer of various product benefits. For example, an outdoor sign might be used to tell a consumer that a certain brand or category of goods or services is available. Indoors, signs can help alert consumers to the availability of a product and influence the sale.

- *Glorifiers* make the product stand out to the consumer in stark contrast to other products. Glorifiers almost always hold the product in some way, by placing it on a pedestal or otherwise surrounding it with an attention-getting device.

- *Organizers* help the retailer control inventory or help the consumer make a selection more easily.

- *Shelf space* has itself become something of a de facto point-of-purchase advertising medium. Faced with decreasingly available space for traditional displays (and only temporary access to such opportunities), many manufacturers are cleverly enhancing the advertising value of the shelf itself through more effective product packaging and merchandising concepts, such as "shelf-talkers" that extend from the shelf without interfering with consumer access to the products.

- *New media* include shopping-cart "billboards," in-store sound systems, digital signage, interactive video kiosks, and even television sets at checkout lanes.

P-O-P INTEGRATION

"Integrated marketing programs" became a popular concept in the advertising community in the late 1980s and early 1990s. A number of advertising and promotion marketing companies responded by packaging together various promotion and retail marketing groups in hopes of offering advertisers a cohesive resource capable of creating a unified message.

In fact, the idea of making the various marketing disciplines work more effectively together is nothing new. *Advertising at the Point-of-Purchase*, an out-of-print volume edited and compiled by the Point-of-Purchase Advertising Institute (POPAI) and the Association of National Advertisers (McGraw-Hill Book Company, Inc. 1957), devoted an entire chapter to the concept of integrated marketing; within it appeared this prescient passage:

> Because point-of-purchase is present at the place and time goods are bought, it has the opportunity to supply the final nudge — the stimulus or impulse that creates the actual transaction. In doing this job, it ties all advertising together, probably more than any other single medium, by restating the selling theme at the point-of-sale. This tying together is known as "integration."

And later:

> [I]t is important to note that integration includes a good deal more than repeating the campaign theme in copy and pictures. It also takes into consideration timing, geographical considerations as to seasons and regional markets, distribution, publicity, trade advertising, and promotion literature. ... At a POPAI panel discussion, one member advocated that salesmen have some voice in planning since they are in the field and know what material is wanted.

Integrating P-O-P advertising with a brand's image advertising campaign and coordinating the program with both the advertiser's sales supports and the retailer makes fundamental good sense. A recent study by Information Resource, Inc. showed that when P-O-P reinforces an advertising message, sales increase for that product 128.2 percent over P-O-P that does not underscore the ad (see Exhibit 10.2).

Integration, however, should not be considered the end-all and be-all of marketing into the 21st century. Another study, this one by Nielsen Marketing Research conducted exclusively for *P-O-P Times*, showed that displays generated significant sales increases by themselves, without any accompanying promotional or advertising support. The research study analyzed scanner data across 26 product categories in 323 markets over a two-year period, and found that display-only promotions consistently improved sales in every instance. The average percentage increase in sales for stand-alone P-O-P advertisements ranged from 12 percent in Tampa to 108 percent in Milwaukee, and from 10 percent for salad dressing to 117 percent for dishwasher liquid (see Exhibit 10.3). .

EXHIBIT 10.2

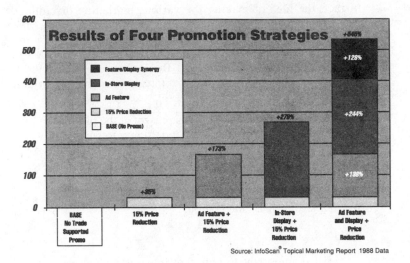

Source: InfoScan® Topical Marketing Report 1988 Data

Although the power of P-O-P is uniformly evident in this research, it is also clear that P-O-P effectiveness can vary by product category and region. This underlines the imperative for marketers today to fully understand the dynamics of P-O-P advertising relative to the specific, market-by-market conditions that affect the fortunes of brands. When developing a P-O-P program, one must also consider the manner of distribution. Will the program be installed by the advertiser's sales force, by independent reps, or by the retailer's own staff? Such considerations must be factored in when designing the program.

The decline of small, "mom and pop" retailers and the consolidation of retail chains throughout the country has given the retailer a strong voice in the in-store marketing environment. P-O-P advertisers must consider whether the retailer will accept a particular P-O-P program — even before thinking about whether a consumer will respond to it. Many retailers today have their own facility planners who dictate the type of display material they will allow in their stores. Displays may be required to conform to customized gondolas and may be restricted in terms of color, height, size, or location.

MANAGING THE P-O-P FUNCTION

The P-O-P industry is comprised of a diverse group of individuals and organizations that design, manufacture, or subcontract P-O-P advertising materials.

EXHIBIT 10.3

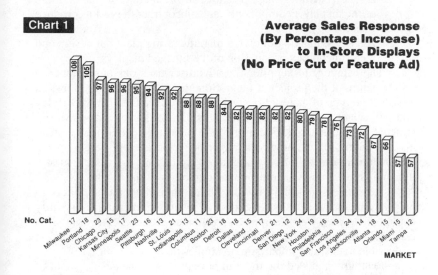

Chart 1

**Average Sales Response
(By Percentage Increase)
to In-Store Displays
(No Price Cut or Feature Ad)**

No. Cat.

MARKET

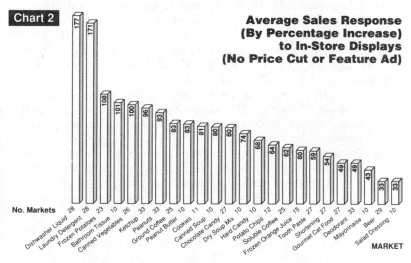

Chart 2

**Average Sales Response
(By Percentage Increase)
to In-Store Displays
(No Price Cut or Feature Ad)**

No. Markets

MARKET

Advertisers typically see the industry as comprised of three types of suppliers:

1. Factories that specialize only in production of a specific type of display, such as wire or corrugated;
2. Agency/Factories that specialize in production of one or more of the display's components and subcontract the rest to produce finished displays; and
3. Agencies, that do not own a manufacturing plant but design and then subcontract production of the finished displays.

The category of supplier the advertiser uses obviously depends on the nature of the project at hand. Sometimes an advertiser knows in advance the type of material best suited to produce the planned display and will select a supplier based on its ability to deliver a display constructed of that material. Because of the rapid advance of new materials and technologies, however, advertisers increasingly are keeping options open because a new material or production process might significantly reduce costs or improve the durability of the display.

Advertisers generally review about three potential suppliers to help ensure that a healthy selection of available alternatives is fully explored. Because P-O-P suppliers fall under different categories, it is extremely important that the advertiser provides as much information as possible to ensure comparison of "apples to apples."

Planning is indeed the most important step in the development of a point-of-purchase advertising program. Initial planning will deliver the best possible return on the merchandising investment. Preparing information regarding the following points will help provide the information the advertiser should give its supplier. Again, the more information the advertiser provides, the better the job the supplier can deliver. This point cannot be stressed strongly enough.

- *Objective.* The very first step is to define the display's purpose — for example, introduce a new product, highlight new features, motivate impulse purchases, promote deals, announce special promotions, or link to other products.
- *Brand image.* Integration requires a design consistent with the product's image. The supplier should be given copies of any advertising that expresses the product's advertised image.
- *Other media.* Integration also requires consideration of other media to be used in connection with the display. If the display is to be activated during a television, print, or radio campaign, the supplier should be aware of the intention to integrate.
- *Type of display.*
  — Function. Determine whether the display is intended as a merchandiser, information-provider, product image-maker, or signage.
  — Packaging. Consider the number of packages to be displayed, the size, weight, and variety. Think about the total

weight of the merchandise and whether it is compatible with the type of display you envision. If new package designs are to be incorporated, they should be made available to the supplier at the outset.

— Structure. Establish the type of material you prefer and whether you wish to incorporate motion, light, or other special effects. Decide whether you require a display for the shelf, wall, floor, counter, ceiling, or gondola and if that display will be indoor or outdoor.

- *Competitive research.* As with any marketing program, it is critical that the competition is shadowed, that you identify competitive merchandising efforts, and that your display program factors in your marketplace position relative to that of other brands in the category. Advertisers frequently rely on their P-O-P suppliers to provide original research in this regard, including performance analysis of previously used displays in the category.
- *Quantity.* It is essential that desired production quantities are achievable given the intended delivery schedule.
- *Distribution.* Is this a regional or national program? Are there any warehouse limitations regarding size? Do you intend to ship the displays by truck or air? Is it to be a drop shipment or bulk?
- *Permanency.* The supplier must know whether the display is for short- or long-term use to select appropriate materials and display designs.
- *Placement.* Determine *where* your display is to be set up. This must be considered both in terms of class of trade (drug, food, mass market, service station, hardware) and in-store location (counter, floor, wall). Identify any dimensional limitations for each retail environment, as well as any trade practice limitations.
- *Sell-in.* Winning trade acceptance is mostly a matter of understanding retailer needs as precisely as possible. Retailer objectives vary from chain to chain and even store to store. The advertiser should make suppliers aware of any account-specific element of the display program, which may mean the display should be designed for flexibility in terms of size, style, construction, and function.

    The supplier should know if the display is to be used as a sell-in incentive, with its availability linked to purchase quantities. If so, it should be designed for and constructed of especially high-quality materials. Suppliers should also be aware of any intention to develop sell-in materials — such as sales sheets, brochures, special presentations, or videos — and any role they may be assigned in the development of such materials.

    Suppliers should also be made aware of the profile of your sales force to ensure it is equipped to implement the proposed display program. The supplier should be told the size of the force and be apprised of its executional capabilities. If brokers are to be used, the supplier should know this so that the display is designed (1) to win brokers' undivided attention and (2) to not burden brokers with complex assembly requirements.

Advertisers should also take care to ensure that the sales force is adequately compensated with bonus incentives for display placement.

- *Presentation.* Specify the type of presentation you will need to select your supplier, and pinpoint a deadline. Establish whether you require sketches, models, prototypes, or units for testing prior to final production.

- *Budget.* Both advertiser and supplier should be up front about costs. A good supplier knows how to design and produce programs that meet an advertiser's budget. If advertisers cannot identify a budget, they do a disservice to both themselves and the supplier because they are likely to get wildly different solutions, some of which they may not be able to afford.

With a specific budget, smart suppliers will make several options available to an advertiser. Often, suggestions are made that are lower, on target, and slightly higher, so that an advertiser has a full range of choices. The skill of a good supplier is to give the advertiser the absolute best program for the budget. By having a specific budget, it is also easier to judge the creativity of one supplier against another.

It is important to understand that the value of a display to the advertiser does not consist exclusively of the cost of its components. It is the display's ability to attract consumers to the advertiser's product and to motivate a sale. Therefore, its value cannot be equated to the cost of materials only.

Advertisers should also be aware that their suppliers incur costs from the moment a project starts in the creative phase. Expenses continue through all phases of design, production, and shipping of the finished displays. This process often covers many months, requiring considerable expenditures. For this reason, it is absolutely imperative that the advertiser select a supplier that is financially stable.

- *Production control.* Producing a complex job often requires multiple materials processed in multiple plant operations so that the finished display meets the advertiser's needs. This typically requires the skills of experienced project managers, whose job is to oversee all phases of the work in progress. Often this requires daily in-plant inspection to maintain promised delivery dates as well as quality.

The project management function sometimes requires the involvement of several people with expertise in various fields, such as printing, injection molding, or assembly.

Managing the P-O-P function for both agency and supplier is a complex process. The following points summarize the key elements that advertisers should look for and suppliers should provide when planning point-of-purchase advertising:

- *Experience.* a seasoned account team that knows the advertiser's dealers and its product;
- *Creativity.* a wide selection of creative ideas, incorporating the specialized expertise of point-of-purchase, and not stifled by any particular class of material or production process;
- *Cost-effectiveness.* display proposals developed to fit an established budge, and guaranteed for delivery at the promised per-unit price; and
- *Reliability.* a full-time staff of experts prepared to follow up on all phases of production and delivery of the display program.

CREATIVITY AND P-O-P

Creativity in point-of-purchase advertising is *not* a pretty picture. P-O-P creativity is not merely a question of clever design — the truth is, you can be equally effective with cardboard and magic marker as with microchips and cathode-ray tubes. Creativity in point-of-purchase advertising, first and foremost, is about building brands, sales, and *profits.* To reverse William Benton's famous quote, "If it isn't creative, it doesn't sell." Creativity in point-of-purchase advertising first requires a complete understanding of the exceedingly busy retail environment in which the product is being sold. Designers should go out and visit the store, as should product managers. The challenges for P-O-P advertising are immediately evident. Package facings and competitive displays vie for attention. Digital selling messages pulse overhead and laser beams trigger news of product specials as shoppers wheel their carts down the supermarket aisles. Commercials crackle over a public address system; television sets continue the pitch while consumers wait to check out.

"Cutting through the visual clutter" is an overused phrase in point-of-purchase, but it holds true; the job of a creative P-O-P is indeed to cut through that visual clutter and stand out.

The two key design principles of point-of-purchase advertising are especially challenging, but if followed, they help the creative process:

1. Keep the design simple, using symbols and not words wherever possible; and
2. Make the product the "star," not the display. David Ogilvy said it very well: "Make the product itself the hero of your advertising." Never lose sight of the fact that it is the *product* you are selling, not the display.

And, as in any creative endeavor, distance yourself from what you think you know to be true. One of the most common, creativity-stunting misconceptions is that point-of-purchase displays are a few steps short of a commodity. Nothing could be further from the truth. Creativity in point-of-purchase advertising first demands an understanding that effective P-O-P amid the cluttered retail environment requires *ownable* ideas. Generic, off-the-rack solutions are nearly always inadequate and are unnecessary given the wide choice of materials with which to work, as detailed in this chapter's section on "Types of P-O-P."

Following are four open-ended "rules" for opening the door to creativity in point-of-purchase advertising, including some examples of especially creative P-O-P programs.

1. **Be visual.** Anyone who walks into a supermarket and sees a floor display shaped like a giant Dixie Cup knows immediately what is being sold (see Exhibit 10.4). Putting freezer tape in a freezer makes the same statement, as does displaying champagne in an outsized champagne bottle replica.

   - Nikon wanted to show how sophisticated their least expensive camera was. The creative solution: laser cut the camera in half and enclose it in a case. The unit was placed on the counter where sales personnel could explain the product's benefits to customers. It was a very successful display — and one that did not feature a single word. Not even Nikon's name was on the box (see Exhibit 10.5).
   - Keds introduced a new line of children's washable sneakers with a tiny washer/dryer that churned and tumbled miniature images of the footwear (see Exhibit 10.6). This in-store advertisement sold product benefits with real soapsuds and water but without words.

2. **Involve the consumer.** As discussed, store help today is scarce to nonexistent. Every time you can involve the consumer, therefore, you are closer to closing a sale.

   - Teledyne actually helped customers understand what their new shower massage felt like, without taking a shower. The display featured a rubber membrane that the customer could touch. A pump created the sensation of the shower massage. It was an extremely effective merchandiser that won POPAI's "Display of the Year" (see Exhibit 10.7).
   - Revlon created an interactive display that was also a mechanical accomplishment because it used no electricity. The display used a combination of weights and levers to help customers learn their skin types so they could select the proper makeup (see Exhibit 10.8). An accompanying brochure brought the consumer closer to a sale.

3. **Provide information.** While big, bold images are great for capturing attention, the job of good P-O-P sometimes is simply to

EXHIBIT 10.4

EXHIBIT 10.5

merchandise information in a new and better way.

- Ford Motor Company wanted its service customers to hear about a new lifetime guarantee. Service center walls are typically packed with selling messages, so developing a poster or the like was not the best solution. Asking service managers to wear buttons reading "Ask me about the lifetime service guarantee" and embroidering the message on their uniforms were not practical options.

  But between the service adviser and the consumer was a clipboard on which the service manager wrote the customer's name and service requirements. The clipboard was redesigned so the customer could easily see the selling message (see Exhibit 10.9). In addition to accomplishing the merchandising objective, the clipboard proved to be better than the one previously used by dealers and has become a standard throughout the Ford Motor Company.

- Sony Corporation had 23 different television sets, and needed to place information about each model and its features at the point-of-sale. Because the sets are often sold in department stores and high-end retailers, however, signage was met with resistance. This situation spawned a merchandising device called Y.E.S., which stands for "Your Extra Salesperson."

  The Y.E.S. unit consists of a retractable panel printed

EXHIBIT 10.6

EXHIBIT 10.7

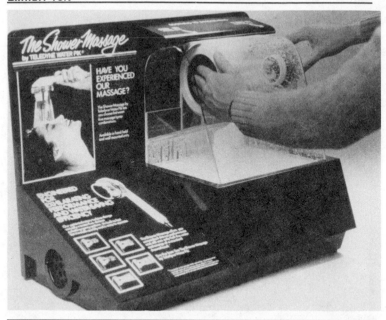

EXHIBIT 10.8

EXHIBIT 10.9

EXHIBIT 10.10

with product information that pulls out and scrolls back like a small window shade (see Exhibit 10.10). This breakthrough in-store advertising medium attached flat and discreetly — above, below, or beside the product — without disrupting store decor.

4. **Enhance the brand.** Building a brand's image does not necessarily mean translating its advertising campaign into an in-store setting. Displays that project moods, taste, prestige, glamour, and excitement are also ably communicated at the point-of-purchase.

- Holly Farms, the chicken marketer, had a different problem: Raw chicken is probably the least attractive product in a supermarket. To overcome this, an illuminated billboard system featuring appetizing prepared chicken dishes was developed to fit over the poultry section in the meat department (see Exhibit 10.11). The graphics were changed monthly and free recipe cards were made available to the consumer.
- Ray-Ban used a counter display that put the consumer in the mood for the glasses by using strong, lifestyle-reinforcing graphics (see Exhibit 10.12).
- Sperry Top Sider combined various display components to create the ambiance of a yacht club. This boating environment set just the right tone for the brand's target audience (see Exhibit 10.13).

Creativity in point-of-purchase advertising takes many forms and can make a giant difference. A profit-driven creative approach can reduce the cost of producing or shipping P-O-P displays or programs. Creative construction can make it easier for a retailer to set up and, thereby, increase usage. Creative design can more effectively communicate to the consumer in the retail environment.

If it isn't creative, it doesn't sell. To bring out the best creative effort, both the buyer and creator of P-O-P must join together and get to know each other and each other's business. Then, within their respective organizations, others must be allowed to *dare* to approach point-of-purchase advertising in a fresh, new way. There is always a better way to do something, but we must be challenged to find it. And when that fresh, new approach is found, we must have the courage of our convictions to do what we believe will work.

Of course, all this is risky. You may strike out, but you will also hit some home runs rather than a few safe singles. So take risks. And above all, have fun. Without fun, creativity at point-of-purchase is only an academic exercise.

EXHIBIT 10.11

EXHIBIT 10.12

EXHIBIT 10.13

Larry Tucker has been prominent in the promotion and direct marketing fields for more than 20 years and is a recognized authority on target marketing, list analysis, promotion, and direct mail. For the past 16 years, his firm, Larry Tucker, Inc., has sponsored the nation's largest targeted co-op mailing program, "Jane Tucker's Supermarket of Savings" — now mailing almost 150 million co-op envelopes annually to growing families, older active adults (50+), and black and Hispanic or Latino families.

An active member of the Direct Marketing Association, the Promotion Marketing Association of America, and many other industry groups, he contributes frequently to industry publications and regularly addresses meetings of marketing executives.

CHAPTER 11

DIRECT RESPONSE

GENERATING COST-EFFECTIVE RESPONSE OR COUPON REDEMPTION WITH INSERTS, RIDE-ALONGS, AND CO-OP MAILINGS

Many marketers are responding to the escalating costs of "solo" mail by cutting down on new-customer acquisition programs. Not only are costs up substantially, they point out, but also the failure of these relatively expensive "outreach" mailing programs to break even on the bottom line has been very disappointing.

But cutting back on mail marketing is a shortsighted policy. Approximately 20 percent of your current customers move each year, and your third-class mail won't follow them. Other direct marketers and newly aggressive local retailers are constantly chipping away at your current customer base. It's now more important than ever before to keep a steady, reliable stream of new business flowing in.

Some companies have turned to television advertising, magazine ads, or catalog-request sections and other alternative media. But the most logical and potentially most profitable medium is *direct mail itself.*

Lots of Options. There are hundreds of alternatives to expensive "solo" mail. Co-op, statement-stuffer, ride-along, and package-insert programs are available at reasonable cost, ready to bring your selling proposition to millions of interested, qualified, ready-to-respond prospects at only a few pennies per insert. And there is now enough experience with these programs to be able to predict with confidence your probable success.

You can print your offers on insert sheets and place these in co-op mailing programs, which *share the costs* of postage, lists, envelopes, addressing, and inserting among a number of *noncompeting marketers.* Some programs will even design and print the insert for you. Or your insert can "ride along" in (or on) the packages of products being sent out to known recent buyers. There are also many "statement-stuffer" and invoice enclosure programs, from those reaching catalog buyers of specific products to magazine subscription billings, or even cable TV monthly mailings.

There are so many of these programs that the *Standard Rate & Data* directories have dedicated a separate section to listing them. Finding the ones that will work for you — and then utilizing these programs productively — can take quite a bit of research, testing, time, and money. But proper use of one or more of these wide-ranging programs can open up a significant and continuing source of profitable new customers.

During more than two decades in the direct-response field, I've seen hundreds of companies succeed in this area — and hundreds of others fail. Success hinges on the interplay of a number of factors: strategy, offer, pricing, timing, graphics, headline, copy, and even color, paper stock, and format.

Look to Your Past Successful Efforts. In starting up an insert campaign, one of the first things to bear in mind is that these programs can build naturally on your established strengths. Oftentimes, you can feature a proven product or offer that's been popular in your ads or in your solo or catalog mailings (or something similar). You'll want to start out with the time-tested price points, product features, offers, and promotional approaches that have drawn responses in the past.

Determining the Best Offer for Each Audience. Before you decide to *adapt* one of your standard or "control" offers or try to create a new offer out of the blue, you'll want to study the audience reached by the medium in which you'll be placing your inserts. Find out from the sponsor, manager, or broker as much as possible about these consumers: their ages, interests, income, lifestyles, and past purchasing habits. If the distribution is to catalog buyers, get a copy of a recent catalog. If lists of magazine subscribers are part of the distribution mix, get current copies of the publications, as well as advertising media kits and circulation statements, and examine them carefully (look particularly at the mail order ads, if any, in these publications). Data cards on lists are particularly useful, along with information on who rented the lists and for what offer.

Our company conducts continuing, extensive research on our own co-op recipients through surveys, focus groups, and other methods in order to help our participants and prospective clients learn more about our audience (including their purchase and usage of product or service categories). And we compare this data with information on response to other offers in the past for similar products or services.

Of course, you'll want to choose a medium that reaches *households with consumers who resemble your present profitable customer base.* A number of programs offer you a "profile" that's a good match to the majority or a distinct segment of your current buyers. Several programs have a strong skew toward families with young children, for example. Sports enthusiasts or outdoorsmen make up other distinct markets. Small-business owners are clearly identified in many programs. Working women are yet another identifiable group. Then there are pre-retirees over 50, the fast-aging "baby boomers" who represent the fastest-growing group in the nation. And the 65+ generation is also still expanding and is very responsive to its mail.

When you can reach many millions of potential customers with shared characteristics in one mailing (such as a targeted co-op), you have a real opportunity to improve the "pulling power" of your printed inserts very efficiently and with only a little cost and effort.

An Inexpensive Experiment. Almost any company can afford to prove for itself whether an insert program will work cost-effectively. Production charges can be held to a minimum — especially if you have photos or even color separations on hand. We regularly help our clients to position their offers and even to design attractive and eye-catching insert presentations.

You don't need very large quantities to start. To get a valid reading on response and to properly evaluate both the media and the insert itself, you can test as few as 10,000 pieces in the typical package-insert program. However, in a widely circulated program with several million recipients, it's wiser and more practical to schedule tests of 100,000+ pieces to get a reliable reading. Coupon testing generally requires a base of 100,000+, restricted to one or just a few markets.

Aiming for Long-Term Profitability. Although there are definitely marketers who consistently make money on the initial order, a number of the most successful users of insert programs don't aim to "break even" on their prospecting programs. They make their profit down the line with repeat orders, bounce-backs, subscriptions, or continuity programs. Their paramount concern is simply to bring in as many qualified responses as is reasonably possible.

Once you determine a format, price point, headline, copy, and graphics that bring in satisfactory (or better) response levels, you'll find that you can utilize insert programs year-round to keep new business flowing in. This can serve to "even out" the peaks and valleys from your established cycles of solo mail. And you may also be able to get the jump on your competition by using these regular, continuing programs to test new products, approaches, or strategies.

Customizing Your Graphics, Offers, and Copy. While many of the early ventures into this area utilized standardized inserts for inclusion in dozens of different programs, it has been proven over and over again that creating and designing inserts specifically for individual (or several similar) insert programs can bring much better results.

Smart marketers will "customize" *graphics, offers,* and *copy* on inserts going into targeted programs to attract the consumer's attention, using *language* that speaks to these identifiable prospects directly and forcefully. Our colleagues in general advertising follow a similar path as they practice "media mapping": a technique whereby packaged goods advertisers and others promote the same brands in a different manner to different audiences.

Not only are the models in the ads appropriate to the audience targeted by the publication or TV show, but also the *language* of the ad, the *style* of speaking or writing, the *offer,* and the *graphics* are fine-tuned to appeal directly to a "niche" audience, whether college students, young parents, senior citizens, Latinos, or blacks. For example, Dial soap is promoted as a "nose guard" in *Sports Illustrated,* as a "stress management tool" in *Fortune,* and as a "self-esteem boost" in

Parents. The copy and photos are designed to win the empathy of each group.

Your insert can feature self-identifying label words or buzzwords common to the specific group, such as "uh-huh" for Pepsi and "Mom" or "Grandma" or "Working Mothers" or "Fishermen" in headlines and body copy, along with appropriate photographs. You should speak directly and exclusively to the individual as part of this specific audience and keep generalities to a minimum. Be especially careful if you're addressing anything other than your own age group. This approach, if carried off well, will definitely make your offer seem more relevant and personally appealing to each person in your target audience.

Making Money at a Response Rate of 1 to 10 per 1,000. Typical response rates for an insert placed by mail marketers in a package or a co-op environment range from 1 to 10 per 1,000. But because the entire cost of participation (including printing) runs about 10 percent of the cost of solo mail, the cost-per-response figures balance out. The larger circulation programs let you reach millions of households in a very efficient manner, helping you to uncover new markets or to discover new "hot spots" quickly.

"Cents-off" coupons distributed to targeted audiences by mail, for packaged goods or health and beauty products, generate between 5 percent and 10 percent redemption (depending, of course, on factors such as the money value of the coupon, the product, and the applicability to the specific audience reached). That's two to three times the redemption generated by Sunday newspaper FSIs, and substantially more than is generated by "neighborhood/resident" mailings to every house on the block.

Any offer, copy, graphic, or format that can raise this response rate a fraction of a percentage point will pay off handsomely! At these low response levels, a very small improvement in response or redemption can make a big difference to the bottom line of a program — especially when you get up into the millions (or tens of millions) or total circulation spread out over a year or more.

The time, effort, and up-front expense involved in creating a "custom" insert will almost always pay off over the long run. You can sell the same thing to different people in dozens of ways — each most appropriate for the specific audience you're appealing to.

Look for Demographic and Lifestyle Indicators. We have found that millions of consumers in a given age group share a number of common interests, and they can often be motivated to respond by an approach that takes these interests into account. Older consumers, for example, are almost always interested in convenience, quality, or security; and they respond well to both endorsements and guarantees.

When you're advertising or promoting in a medium targeted largely to older consumers, you'll want your offer to appeal to their particular point of view. Remember that, by and large, these are experienced shoppers who are not easily swayed by exaggerated promises and definitely not willing to put up with shoddy products or poor fulfillment performance. Ply them with testimonials from authorities or from people their age who have a similar lifestyle. Let your graphics show vital and vigorous older people in the act of enjoying or using your product. Studies consistently show that older people envision themselves as five to 10 years younger than their actual chronological age, so bear that in mind as you select or create graphics and photos. Also include grandchildren, if appropriate.

Guarantees should be featured prominently and in no-nonsense language, with the signature of a company principal (or founder). Pictures of this individual in the office or in a buying location, and even of the factory or warehouse, can be placed within or near the guarantee box or "certificate" to give added credibility and assurance.

Remember to keep your type a bit larger to compensate for poorer eyesight. Conservative type styles, colors, and layout work best. Keep tones under type to a minimum. And, in general, avoid type reverses.

You'll want to *stress benefits* that show the older consumers exactly how your product or service can make their lives easier, more rewarding, or more enriching. Picture your product in actual use. Diagrams can be utilized to explain how something works or charts can be used to compare products or drive home a point. Older consumers are real readers; the more information you give them, the better.

Many senior consumers grew up in an era when the Sears and Montgomery Ward catalogs were staple sources of products they simply couldn't buy at the local stores. They're lifelong mail order shoppers. And now, with a bit more disposable income, credit cards, and a large extended family, shopping by mail can be a pleasurable and convenient experience for them. They may even become your very best continuing customers.

Shift Gears as the Audience Changes. Younger adults should be approached in a very different fashion, with emphasis on the new, the stylish, and quick gratification of their desires. Graphics should be brighter and more contemporary. These are impulsive, impatient, on-the-go people who are generally very active socially.

If you offer premiums to younger adults as an ordering incentive, you'll want to select items tuned in to their tastes. Audiotapes or videotapes, novelty telephones or radios, or stylish accessories seem to appeal strongly to this group.

Copy addressed to people under 25 should be brief and catchy. They won't sit still for long sentences or detailed explanations. Use photos or diagrams to explain a complex idea. Subscription terms should be kept short, and payment terms should be stretched out. Be sure to structure your offers and order form to avoid poor payout and bad credit as much as possible.

But there's definitely another shift once these young people settle down, get married, and have children. Responsibility (for the family unit, their credit rating, and the welfare of the children) become their paramount concerns. With the mini baby boom now going on, this is a vibrant and growing audience — one that is very profitable if it's approached properly. Offers aimed at young parents or working mothers can feature strong appeals to maternal concerns, stressing activities that can be shared with the children. Settings should be in a warm home environment or in shared family leisure activities. This is a terrific continuity audience, which can be developed to buy from you for years to come!

For busy parents, you'll want to emphasize time-saving or convenient features, product durability and safety, and good value. Information is a dominant need here, so reprints, booklets, manuals, or instructional videotapes are excellent premiums. Members of this audience will send away for product samples, and they are among the strongest requesters of catalogs, "soft" offers, "free" issues, and introductory deals. The overwhelming majority of these women work outside the home, and so convenience is something that they are willing and able to pay for.

Try to feature photos of a child of the approximate age of those in the majority of the households reached by the medium your insert will be carried in — babies, toddlers, preschoolers, school children, or teenagers. If two or more child age groups are involved, look for or create graphics that show a multichild family. You want the reader to identify as much as possible with your piece.

If a particular sport, recreational activity, or hobby is common to a significant number of the recipients of an insert-carrier program, by all means include a reference to this in your graphic and perhaps in your copy as well. Even a fishing hat on the table or a golf club casually propped by the door can help win over an audience of enthusiasts, without alienating or even alerting the others.

People representative of your target audience who are doing things that your audience does (or would like to be doing) can combine in a strong emotional appeal. Show grandparents with grandchildren and pet lovers with dogs, cats, birds, fish — whatever is most appropriate.

Although the creation and customization of these "individualized" inserts may cost from a few hundred to several thousand dollars initially, the additional "lift" they will bring should pay off your investment in a matter of months.

SELECTING AND FEATURING PRODUCTS FOR CO-OP OR PACKAGE-INSERT PROGRAMS

The range of products and services that can be profitably marketed in a co-op or package-insert environment is very broad, but effective use of this medium requires the application of *proven techniques* that can make the difference between success and disappointment.

Over the past 15 years of sponsoring widely circulated consumer co-op mailings, we've worked closely with major direct-response marketers in selecting, presenting, and promoting their products — consistently bringing them substantial new business from previously untapped sources, cost-effectively.

The product you offer doesn't need to be new or even novel. But it *does* have to be representative of your general line, and it should be perceived as an *outstanding value* by the type of person who will be asked to order it. Once your offer, headline, and graphics gain his or her attention and interest, the perception of a bargain price (or tempting terms) can convert prospect interest into customer action.

Remember that you've got to come up with a *combination* of an attractive (even novel) product and low price. That's what drives so many direct marketers to the novelty and premium shows and to frequent shopping trips to Europe and the Far East.

Creating a Unique Price/Feature Combination. You'll note the language: the "perception" of a bargain. That's a very important point, and one that's better reserved for the section on pricing. In general, successful offers to first-time buyers feature a one-time price under $20, including all charges. But price alone is rarely the most important key to a successful insert program. The audience you are trying to woo probably has never been properly introduced to you; they know very little about your company, so you'll have to make it easy and agreeable for them to do business with you for the first time by creating the assurances of a "risk-free" environment.

Many successful mail marketers create a special "loss leader" for a product offer — something that they have particular and sometimes unique success in manufacturing or importing. The product should be as universally appealing to the specific audience as possible (wallet, pocketbook, scarf, baby clothing, knife set, cookware, or collectibles, for example) and should carry a price that would seem to be less than that of a comparable item found in a retail store. If no comparable item is available in stores, so much the better!

Marketers of cosmetics, lotions, perfumes, and costume jewelry can offer terrific "bargains" up front because of the ratio of product cost to the perceived value. If you're also marketing a related product, you may want to offer one of these bargains as part of a "bargain package."

Try Adding the Personal Touch. The most ordinary belt or blouse or robe can be given additional value and attractiveness with personalization: the initialed belt buckle or the monogrammed initial have great appeal. Recipe books or family bibles with a family's name on the cover or binding may work very well. A family crest can easily be obtained for the 100 most common surnames. Even wine with personalized labels could be sold this way. Brainstorm how you can personalize your own products. Don't forget the continuing popularity of Zodiac signs as well.

Audience-Specific Products. If the co-op mailing your insert is included in (or the package or ride-along) is going to a *demographically definable* group of households, then your work may be made a bit easier. Special personalized mugs, plates, bibs, or spoons for babies are a perennial favorite among young mothers, along with anything that will increase household safety for the toddler or give the mother more free time by cutting her workload.

For new movers or newlyweds, other possibilities present themselves; stationery, embossed towels, or personalized doormats are just the tip of the iceberg. Change-of-address files from established catalog companies should be especially fertile ground.

For older consumers, items to make them more comfortable or safe in the home or car are long-established winners — everything from devices for safety and convenience in the bathtub to shoe inserts and foot massagers. Many retired people are frequent travelers (as are business executives), and you may want to offer them items as varied as magnifiers for map reading, auto compasses, or special security money carriers.

Coming in the Back Door. You may want to present your product with another approach. Instead of selling shoes or jewelry or cosmetics, you can recruit new "dealers" or sales representatives — all of whom get a special discount price, even on limited quantities. Or you can offer membership in a special "club" or "plan" to sell a wide variety of products. This requires a complex back-end, but you can reap benefits for years from your respondents.

Package Your Offer with Add-Ons. It's almost always a good idea to present your product along with a *built-in bonus,* especially if you're selling something intangible, such as life insurance. A detailed booklet on health-promoting diet habits and easy-to-do exercises may bring in many more inquiries, and it helps the insurance company in its long-term mission of cutting the mortality rate. A travel atlas will boost inquiries about an auto club, cruise line, travel agency, or moving service. A lawn-and-garden checklist can bring in leads for a lawn maintenance service. Printed materials are inexpensive to produce, yet they are perceived as being worth several dollars by the public.

If you're selling magazine subscriptions, it's been proven that reprints of published articles are excellent incentives. Or you may create a special annual or seasonal issue (or a directory or guide), and offer it free to all new paying subscribers, no matter when they begin.

With the decrease in cost for producing audiotapes and even videotapes, a number of magazine marketers are trying these as attractive incentives for the paid-up new subscriber. From sports highlights or training/instruction tapes for *Sports Illustrated* to home repair tapes for the fix-it publications and lure-tying tapes for the fishing books, your options are limited only by your imagination. And how about a model Ferrari or Lamborghini for the sports car magazine subscriber? Or a custom gearshift knob with the buyer's initial?

A few marketers are experimenting with offering two related items as their "product," with one being a promotional "loss leader." If two items go naturally together, and one of them is quickly perishable, you have a natural fit — for example, razor blades given away with a razor.

A general rule of thumb is that the closer the add-on is related to your basic product, the better quality of response you'll generate and the longer you'll keep the customer. When you combine relevance with "desirability," you've got a winner!

Making the Bargain Seem Even Better. You'll want your package to look like a terrific bargain. Adding a 10¢ carrying case to a $3 order for personalized pencils or a $3 cigar cutter or carrying case to a $30 order for a box of cigars is just good marketing strategy. Watch those TV ads: "But that's not all … ." One more incentive may tip the balance from interest to action.

Once you select a product or package of products, you should try to create a *unique positioning* for it. Your product may actually have one-of-a-kind features (a knife that never needs sharpening or pantyhose that never wear out). But more often, you'll want to create or point out singular benefits that your products offer — selling the "sizzle" instead of just the steak. The promise may be as important as the product, and the two should be sold as one dynamic marketing idea.

No Competition in Most Co-op Mailings. Most co-op mailings will guarantee you a competition-free environment — an "exclusive" on your own product or service category. Make sure that you spell these terms out carefully and completely as you look at different carrier programs. If you're selling women's clothing, for example, there may well be someone else in the mailing package who is selling men's clothing or women's handbags, shoes, or perfumes.

But what about scarves? Are you protected? Maybe you'll want to offer a free or reduced-price scarf with each order, or you'll want to use the back of your insert to showcase your own line of scarves. Try to corral as much as possible of the consumer's purchasing power in your own broad category. Discuss this frankly with the program sponsor, and get your parameters set down in a written and signed agreement.

Pricing Strategies to Increase Response. When you're planning to test various offers, pricing strategy is an important factor. Whether you're selling a $99 figurine or a $3.98 continuity item, your pricing must be perceived as a bargain by the audience perusing the insert.

If the normal perceived retail value of a category of products is relatively high (even though product cost may be relatively inexpensive), you have a lot of room to maneuver. With products such as perfume, beauty cream, jewelry, or decorative items, it's easy to give liberal partial-payment terms, extra bonuses, free samples, half-off prices, or "bill-me-later" options. We'll look at each of these approaches in just a moment.

However books, periodicals, and records/tapes/CDs represent a different challenge. Profit on the initial order may not be that great; as a matter of fact, the majority of companies in these fields expect to "buy" a new customer by *losing* money at the outset. Their overall, long-term profitability is dependent on generating multiple shipments to a paying customer (or a continuing paid subscription) extending over a number of months or years. With profitability spread out over time, a company with continuity programs can make compelling offers such as "6 Records for only 1¢" or "3 Books for 3 Bucks — No Commitment — No Kidding!"

In periodical publishing, where the need to maintain a substantial number of readers or a "rate base" for advertisers is a very important consideration, circulation directors may use a bag of tricks to bring in the initial orders. Requesting cash-with-order has become rare, and "Examine your first issue FREE at our risk" has become the benchmark offer. Even this liberal policy may not be tempting enough to draw the large number of responses that are needed, and premiums or special pricing and terms may be combined with this "no-risk" offer.

General auditing regulations require that your final price offered be no less than half the normal subscription-term rate. But since cover prices are generally higher, you can often offer $1 off a $1.50 cover-price magazine and stay within the guidelines.

Selling Merchandise with Minimum Risk. For items such as clothing, gifts, and knickknacks, the aim of companies prospecting for catalog buyers or long-term customers is often to break even on the first order, so that the cost of bringing in the new customer can be minimized. The other basic approach offers a free catalog or may ask for a nominal amount for the catalog (taking that or a larger sum off the first merchandise purchase).

Obviously, in programs dedicated to increasing catalog circulation, the total costs to the vendor of the entire operation (soliciting the order for the catalog, data entry, printing and mailing the catalog, and direct mail or telephone follow-up) must be factored into the final break-even figure. Some companies can manage to sell "loss leaders" at attractive prices to generate the first actual order. But all of them are "buying a new customer," banking on the projected "lifetime value" of the newly acquired customer. Catalog companies regularly rate their new customers after 18 or 24 months to determine "lifetime value." Future solicitation is then based on this evaluation.

Getting consumers to ask for a catalog and then getting them to buy from the catalog (or one of your subsequent solo mail offerings directed to them) becomes a more complex, "two-step" marketing task.

We'll deal with this in detail later on. In general, bringing in qualified leads can be a sound business practice when the ultimate sale is complicated or if it involves a big-ticket or long-term commitment.

For low-ticket or impulse items, insert programs can generate orders profitably if the right price point can be found. But this can change from one moment to another as other vendors rush to market with similar items. Sufficient response must obviously be generated to make these pay out, and this is one area where the combination of pricing and offer is critical.

Inserts can do a thorough, cost-effective job in each of these categories, bringing in hundreds of thousands of purchases (or millions of inquiries, sample requests, or catalog orders). Determining the right price point *and* pricing policy depends largely on your goal: to break even, make a profit, or "buy" a new customer at an acceptable price.

Higher Profit Margin Allows Higher Risk. Many items successfully marketed by mail are manufactured or obtained at a fraction of their normal selling price. Particularly for trendy, style-oriented products, cosmetics/scents, new high-tech items, or "collectibles," pricing may be "blind" — that is, the consumer has very little reference against which to judge it. Markups of 300 percent or more are not uncommon in these cases. And even in the field of books and audio or videotapes, the incremental manufacturing cost is only a small portion of the price asked.

In these cases, the marketer can take more risk up front in formulating tactics to bring in the initial order. "Send No Money Now: Examine in Your Own Home for 10 Days at Our Risk" is a financially sound offer for these products because it takes into account the substantial no-payments and the returned merchandise that will probably ensue. The added initial response gleaned from the majority who will pay (and stay), coupled with the substantial built-in profit margin, makes this type of offer profitable.

Spread Out the Payment Schedule. Of course, many marketers now allow consumers to make their credit card payments in several installments. "Only $9.95 a month for four months" may be a lot easier to swallow than a flat $39.80 as a price point. Some larger marketers even offer their own credit payment systems to holders of Visa, MasterCard, or Discover cards.

You can keep your pricing in the bargain range by breaking up the billed payments into two or three parts — a two-step program with billing for the first installment going out *after* the initial "send no money" order is received by the vendor and *before* shipment of the product. The first payment can completely cover the cost of the product and shipping. Those who pay the remaining one or two invoices amortize the media costs and provide the profit margin.

Satisfied customers will often respond to bounce-back advertising or subsequent solicitations as they pay the installments, and they provide a substantial profit bonus! And each billing cycle provides you with an opportunity to sell other items or add-ons.

Smaller Sizes, Samples, and Initial-Order Premiums. Another way to make your price more palatable is to offer a smaller size, the first piece in a series or set, or a reduced number of items in a grouping. This gives you a chance to add a premium (for example, a chess board with your first chess piece, a display cabinet with your first collectible figurine, a bookcase with your first classic book or encyclopedia volume).

Several food marketers offer "samples" of cheese or smoked meats or canned goods at greatly reduced prices. You can offer prospective long-term customers a choice between the "10-day supply" of vitamins or cosmetics at $3.98, while the "30-day supply" may be only $5.98. And don't be surprised if a number of $5.98 orders come streaming in!

Cash up front, "bill me," offering smaller quantities or starter sets — all of these are propositions that bear testing. You may well find that one approach works well in several related media but that other media produce better results with a totally different strategy. Only testing will reveal whether asking for a check (or credit card number) to accompany the order is better over the long run than offering another, more liberal option. My long-term experience has been that the easier you make it to place the order and get the initial commitment quickly, the more orders will flow in.

Connie Kennedy is Vice President of Targetbase Marketing, an M/A/R/C Group Company based in Dallas, Texas. With more than 18 years experience on both the client and supplier sides, Kennedy provides marketing consulting and full-service database marketing for clients such as Southwest Airlines, Frito-Lay, and Warner-Lambert.

Prior to joining Targetbase Marketing, Kennedy worked in product management at General Mills, was Director of Marketing at Mattel Electronics, Director of New Products at Taco Bell, and Vice President of Advertising at 800-Flowers. Her broad base of experience includes working with new products, sales promotion frequency and cross-sell programs, lead-generation programs, and extensive work in developing and testing database programs.

Kennedy is a member of the Direct Marketing Association (DMA) Council and the North Texas chapter of the DMA. She has a B.A. in Marketing from University of Arizona, an MBA from Arizona State University, and she is a graduate of the DMA Collegiate Institute.

CHAPTER 12

DATABASE MARKETING

DATABASE MARKETING DEFINED

Database marketing has become a buzzword. Many view it as a panacea for what ails marketing today. Some have already moved on to relationship marketing or integrated marketing. But database marketing is at the root of it all.

What is all the hype about? What is this new marketing technique called database marketing? Is it right for every business?

Database marketing has evolved from the recent dramatic changes in our world. Consumers face unprecedented choices. Table 12.1 shows the explosive growth in media vehicles and new products in the last 20 years.

TABLE 12.1
ACCELERATED CHOICE

	1970	1980	1990
Average no. TV channels	7	9	33
No. consumer magazines	1,075	1,490	2,265
No. products in average supermarket	12,400	14,145	25,855

The service economy rules where the manufacturing economy once prospered: 67 percent of the gross national product and seven out of 10 American workers are part of the service sector. Add to these changes the clutter and the decline in efficiency of the traditional mass media, and you have a very dynamic market, one that is not as easily forecasted as the one of old.

Contrary to popular opinion, loyalty is not dead. Businesses are simply not delivering what is required to foster loyalty. The differences between product A and product B are fewer and fewer. Customers are searching for companies that understand their needs and tailor their products and services to those needs. Only by building a strong relationship that recognizes those needs do you foster long-term loyalty.

These changes demand that marketing and sales promotion experts alike stay in tune with an ever-changing marketplace. To stay in tune, one must know who is shaping the change. Quite simply, the customer is. Essential to success today is understanding and meeting the needs of the customer. Because the needs that must be met are no longer needs shared by the masses, the new challenge is to market to the individual. A company must be driven by the characteristics, needs, desires, and preferences of the individual consumer. A relationship must be fostered customer by customer.

Database marketing is, in reality, a return to the very basics of marketing: know your customer and serve your customer through technology. The marketer of the 1990s can utilize the individual-based selling techniques of old. Once again, the proprietor knows his or her customers by name and the products they purchase. A new method of understanding and communicating with the customer is required. This new method is database marketing. The new medium is the database.

The advances of computer technology have made it possible to practice individualized marketing on a very large scale. The cost of storing vast quantities of information has dropped dramatically over the last 20 years, facilitating the development of marketing databases. Thus, keeping track of your customer's product preferences and purchase history is affordable. The database becomes the platform to market to individual customers based on their needs and desires.

One of our clients feels so strongly about the importance of customers and their relationship that the client capitalizes the first letter of customer wherever it appears. The capital *C* alerts all employees to who the real boss is. Our client is profitable in an industry in which the major players are losing money. You cannot underestimate the importance of the customer. And, you can no longer treat all customers the same.

Simply stated, database marketing is the promotion of products or services customer by customer, by means of an information source. The information source is the database. The database provides the information necessary to customize the communication to meet the needs and desires of the individual customer. Currently, the communication vehicles used in database marketing are the mail, interactive point-of-sale, and interactive telecommunication services.

DATABASE MARKETING APPLICATIONS

As with all business endeavors, the purpose of a marketing database is to positively impact the financial performance of a company. There are three fundamental strategies to achieve this. The first is the acquisition of new customers. The second is the retention of current customers. And the third is the maximization of the contribution of current customers. No matter what the business-building objective is, one of these three strategies would be employed in its pursuit.

Acquisition of New Customers. New customers come in two types. The first is a customer that is new to your product or category. Given the penetration of most products and services these days, this target may only be a marketing opportunity for truly new categories of products and services. The second group, the competitor's customers, is an opportunity for a much larger group of companies.

Both types of new customers can be part of a database. The decision about who to include on the database is made during the planning stage of the database, which will be discussed later in the chapter.

Highly targeted acquisition programs can be designed utilizing the individual level information that the database provides. Imagine, if you will, a database of your competitors' best customers and the ability to tailor your marketing programs to their needs, putting your company's best foot forward.

The automobile industry is a perfect example of this strategy. In any direct communication, success is predicated on addressing the right people at the right time with the right offer. Through the information derived from the licensing of motor vehicles, the automobile makers can populate a database with owners of competitors' automobiles. Through customer research, they have determined which competitive car owners are most likely to purchase next their make and model. For instance, a Thunderbird owner, when trading in the car, might consider a Cadillac, a Lincoln Town Car, or a Mercedes for the next purchase. Armed with this information, Cadillac knows which group of potential buyers to target.

The automobile industry, through an extensive analysis of car buying, has determined that the most likely time for people to trade in their car is four and a half years. The identification of these potential switching patterns is valuable, but what makes it powerful is the knowledge of approximately when someone will purchase a new car. By building a relationship just prior to the next purchase, the manufacturer ensures that his make and model will be included in the set of automobiles that will be considered. Thus, he has begun the sales process. The initial goal is to capture the next purchase occasion. The long-term goal is to create a relationship that lasts beyond one purchase and results in repeat purchases within his line of cars.

Retention of Current Customers. The airlines' frequent flier and hotels' frequent stayer programs are excellent examples of proactive retention programs. Using a database of all the flights and visits, the travel industry is able to fashion programs based on past behavior. For example, if a traveler normally takes a flight to Kansas City every month, an early warning system might alert the marketing and promotion team when two months go by without a trip. The airline or hotel has the ability to send a personalized message to the individuals offering a special perk on the next trip if she returns a satisfaction survey for previous trips. The program identifies if there is a problem and also provides an incentive to make sure the valued traveler is not flying on a competitive airline.

Another example of retention programs is reactive programs. The Tylenol product tampering scare of several years ago was dealt with very effectively by McNeil Consumer Products. The damage control plan would have been even stronger if a database of Tylenol users had been available. Imagine a letter sent within a matter of days to loyal Tylenol consumers explaining the extent of the product tampering, describing the steps the company was taking, and delivering a coupon to ensure the loyalty of this important group. A private, direct channel of communication to customers without a news media filter through a database would be invaluable.

All reactive programs do not involve product tampering or product liability. Many times marketers are faced with a direct assault on their most valued customers by a competitor. American Airlines recently was under attack in its home market of Dallas by Delta Airlines. Delta offered membership in its most-valued customer program, the Medallion level, to Dallas fliers. The offer did not require the Dallas-based fliers to comply with the normal Delta program requirements.

As a Platinum member of the American Advantage frequent flier program, I received a letter from Mr. Michael Gunn, Senior Vice President of Marketing, reinforcing how important my business was to American and contrasting my benefits as a member of the Platinum program against those of the Delta Medallion program (see Exhibit 12.1). The letter was received within days of Delta's announcing its offer in the mass media. This counterattack by American Airlines minimized the impact of the Delta offer.

Maximization of Customer Contribution. Imagine being able to tailor a promotion based on past behavior in your product or service category. A continuity program could be designed that would cause even the heaviest customer to make an incremental purchase. The information on the database can provide the foundation for programs to promote cross-selling of other products, trading up to a more expensive line, and increasing your share of purchases from a customer. An industry that employs a customer maximization strategy is financial services. These programs leverage the information available at an individual level to ensure your company receives the maximum purchases possible. The only way to truly maximize the volume and profits of a company is customer by customer, matching programs and incentives to individual customer behavior and potential.

An excellent example of a maximization program is the Weight Watchers' Winners! program. The program realizes an excellent cross-selling opportunity for both the weight-loss centers and the 250 portion-controlled food products that are sold through grocery stores. The Winners! program leverages the Weight Watchers' brand name across to different retail channels. The objectives are to foster continued membership in Weight Watchers and to generate incremental volume for the food products.

Membership solicitation utilizes both channels of distribution. New enrollees in the Weight Watchers weight-loss plan were automatically entered in the Winners! program. Shoppers were intercepted in the grocery store and given a chance to enroll. The enrollment kit included information on Weight Watchers meetings and the weight-loss program. The program consists of accumulating points for atten-

EXHIBIT 12.1

October 1, 1992

Ms. Connie Kennedy
614 Meadowview Ln   AAdvantage #B341786
Coppell, TX 75019-5746

Dear Ms. Kennedy,

Because you are one of our most frequent customers, we would like to take this
opportunity to thank you for your continued loyalty to American Airlines.
We hope that you are enjoying AAdvantage Platinum status, and we would like to
reinforce our commitment to providing you with the most innovative frequent
flyer program in the industry.

The AAdvantage Platinum program offers many benefits which some other
frequent flyer programs do not. For instance, on American you earn free
upgrades for *every* 10,000 miles you fly. As a Platinum member you *always*
earn bonus miles each and every time you fly on American or American Eagle. You
may upgrade from any fare--not just the full Coach fare. And AAdvantage Platinum
members may upgrade in advance of all other members of our frequent flyer program.

Finally, as an AAdvantage member, it's important to you that we provide the most
daily flights to more destinations than any other carrier at DFW including the
most international service and the most nonstop flights to Europe. The
frequency and the variety of our flight schedule give you far more choices to
fit your busy schedule and far greater opportunity to earn miles faster.

As you read in the September/October newsletter, we are making it even
easier to earn free trips this fall. When you fly either eight segments
or 12,000 miles on American Airlines or American Eagle with purchased
tickets, you'll earn a certificate for a free round-trip Main Cabin ticket
which may be used for travel within the contiguous 48 United States,
Canada, Mexico or the Caribbean. Two certificates are redeemable for one
free round-trip Main Cabin ticket to Hawaii, Europe, Latin America or
Japan. This offer is valid on flights September 8 through December 18, 1992,
so you may already be on the way to earning a free trip!

Your loyalty to American Airlines is very important to us, and we want to
continue to provide the best frequent flyer program in the Dallas/Fort Worth
area. We look forward to serving you again in the near future.

Sincerely,

Michael W. Gunn
Senior Vice President-Marketing
American Airlines

American Airlines® AAdvantage Platinum
MD 5200, P.O. Box 619281, Dallas/Fort Worth Airport, TX 75261-9281

dance at Weight Watchers meetings and the purchase of Weight Watchers food products. The points are redeemed for various gifts.

Additional mailings, coinciding with potential weight-loss plan dropout times, provided further encouragement to stay in the program through incentives and product information.

THE DATABASE MARKETING ALTERNATIVE

Database marketing is a viable alternative to other available sales methods for two key reasons — effectiveness and efficiency. The targeting ability of database marketing eliminates waste, thus increasing efficiency and effectiveness. Unlike mass media vehicles such as broadcast and print media, you only communicate with known customers of your products and services. A more relevant message is delivered because you know the individual characteristics, needs, desires, and preferences of each customer with whom you are communicating.

Table 12.2 outlines the cost per effective impression for various mass media vehicles and database marketing. An effective impression incorporates the cost to reach each customer and the impact of that impression (recall).

TABLE 12.2
COMPARISON OF DATABASE MARKETING TO MASS MEDIA

Media	Total Impressions (MM)	Category Incidence	Recall Rate	Effective Impressions* (MM)	Advertising Cost Effectiveness (CPI)
Mass (TV, Radio, Print)**	2,100	39%	24%	197	$0.15
FSI	50.7	39%	13%	2.6	$1.12
Database	15.0	95%	81%	11.5	$0.26

* Effective Impressions = Impressions x Category Incidence x Recall Rate.
** Budgets = Mass: $30.0MM, FSI: $3.0MM, Database: $3.0MM.

Should Everyone Have a Marketing Database? Eventually, everyone will. With continued improvements in data collection, computer processing, and data storage, the cost of building and maintaining a database will be affordable to all relevant companies. Today, not everyone who could benefit from a database can afford one.

To determine if you should develop a database, a cost/benefit analysis should be undertaken. On the cost side, you need to estimate how much it will cost to acquire and maintain the appropriate information on the database and deliver programs to the database. Exhibit 12.2 details itemized costs that should be considered.

EXHIBIT 12.2
COST CHECKLIST

Acquisition — Cost of the names, addresses, and pertinent information

Database design

Preparation of data for the database

- Merge/purge
- NCOA
- List clean
- Address standardization
- Normalization

Query system

Maintenance of database

- Updates
- NCOA
- Additions

Database marketing program costs

- Printing
- Postage
- Creative development
- Data entry
- List pull
- Incentive

As shown in this exhibit, there are two main categories of costs — database related and program related. The cost of building the base is directly related to the availability of the information. For instance, a video store has the name, address, and all transactions for each customer; whereas a consumer packaged goods company only knows the name, address, and sales associated with the intermediary — the retail outlet. The cost to develop a marketing database for the video store will be much less than for the consumer packaged goods company because the data are already available. The consumer packaged goods company will incur the additional cost of acquiring the data. If the database costs are fairly significant, you should consider whether to amortize that cost over a longer period of time than one year. The information has value beyond a year; therefore, a two- or three-year time frame should be considered.

The costs should be compared to the benefits that can be derived from a database. A simple way to do the comparison is to estimate the lifetime values (LTVs) of your customers and compare them to the database costs. To determine the LTV, one must first assume a time frame for a customer's "lifetime." Few products or services can assume a customer will buy from them during the entire time they are in the market for their product. Given the battle for share of market and customers' growing propensity for brand switching, a year may be the longest you can assume they would be in your franchise.

Your customer base does not have one lifetime value. There are as many lifetime values as there are customers. In the calculation of lifetime values, a value should be calculated for several pertinent groups. A database does not have to reflect your entire customer or prospect base. The database can be populated by subgroups such as heavy, medium, and light customers. The database could house only competitive or franchise customers. Any combination of the above subgroups is also possible.

When determining for which of the groups you should compute an LTV, you should consider that competitive customers represent 100 percent incremental volume. Heavy customers by definition will be worth more than medium or light customers, but you already have their purchases, right? Wrong, at least not in the majority of products and services today. Your heavy customers are not giving you 100 percent of their purchases in your category. Everyone knows that it is much easier to keep and increase share of purchases with current customers than to convert a competitive customer. The appropriate audience for the database could be *both* current and competitive customers.

Competitive conversion in these days means increasing the share of purchases customer by customer, not gaining 100 percent of their purchases. To obtain 50 percent of the purchases of a competitive heavy customer would be significant. The profit per purchase will aid in determining whether you include only heavy customers or consider including the next level of customers.

For the initial evaluation, an LTV should be calculated for all relevant customer groups. Exhibit 12.3 outlines the lifetime calculation for several audiences.

EXHIBIT 12.3
LIFETIME VALUE (LTV) CALCULATIONS

Formula:	LTV = Annual Purchases x Profit/Purchase
Average Customer:	LTV = 6 purchases/year x $6 profit/purchase
	LTV = $36
Heavy Customer:	LTV = 12 purchases/year x $6 profit/purchase
	LTV = $72

Now that you have the costs associated with database marketing and the LTV of your customer groups, you can determine the additional volume necessary to cover the cost. For example, if the cost of acquiring the pertinent information amortized over two years is $1 and the cost of the annual program is $9, the total annual costs would be $10. Based on the heavy customer example from Exhibit 12.3, only two incremental purchases per year are needed to cover the costs of the program and generate incremental profit.

To determine how likely the benefits of a database will outweigh the costs, you must consider how much of an impact the unique characteristics of this medium would have on your business. Table 12.2 showed how highly targeted, knowledge-based marketing can affect a business. In that example, the database was at a 3 to 1 cost disadvantage to the FSI but proved to be more effective and more efficient. You should search for case histories in relevant categories to determine what database marketing has been able to achieve. In this search, you will find response rates and incremental volume rates that will surprise you — as the cost per effective impression did.

BUILDING A MARKETING DATABASE

As with any successful endeavor, you plan before you build. The process of building a database is comprised of seven phases. The phases are detailed in Exhibit 12.4.

EXHIBIT 12.4
DATABASE BUILDING PROCESS

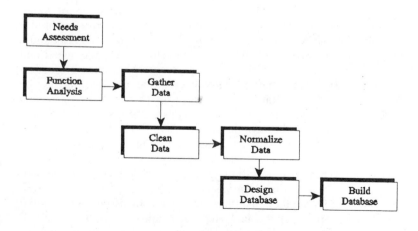

Needs Assessment. The first phase is the needs assessment. In this phase, you determine the objectives for the database. Thorough planning with an eye to the future is required when establishing the objectives for the database. Key areas that the objectives should cover are audience or target, expectations for the database (financial and marketing), who will be using the database, and the degree of interaction required. The objectives drive who will populate your database, what data structure you will use, how much it will cost, and who can access it.

For example, assume the objectives are (1) to convert competitive customers, (2) to deliver significant incremental volume in the first year, and (3) to provide an analytical tool for nontechnical staff. These objectives would result in a database that is made up of customers of your competition, is of a size sufficient to generate incremental volume in its first year, and has a user interface that a nontechnical person can master.

By identifying competitive customers as the target, you will not be populating your database with your own customers. If, in the future, you would like to begin communicating with your customers by means of the database, you will need to acquire the information and add it to the database. The database structure will need to be adapted, and a new data collection effort will have to be undertaken. Had the future need for current customer information been identified in the initial planning, the database would have been designed to carry the additional information, and the initial data collection could have included current customers, thus saving time and money.

The total cost of building a database is greatly affected by the size and the speed with which a database is built. Unless you have a captive audience and a system that traps all the information you need to market effectively (frequency of purchase, items purchased, brand, or source), it will probably take multiple screening efforts to build a database that has a high penetration in your target audience. To build a database of any size cost-effectively, one should balance speed and cost. The shorter the timeline, the more costly the data collection efforts are. Significant incremental volume in the first year may not be in the best interest of the long-term plan for that database. You may find that a lower incremental volume goal in the first year will lead to a higher cumulative profit from the database over several years.

If nontechnical personnel will be accessing the database, special design considerations come into play. What information will they access and what functions will they want to perform? For instance, will they want to print out mailing labels once they selected a group from the database? Or are they just interested in how many customers might qualify for a specific program? The first requires access to name and address and formatting for labels. The second requires access to purchase and demographic characteristics. These demands require very different access capabilities. Your plan will need to include a training component for those individuals utilizing the database.

Even though the cost of storing information has been drastically reduced, it is still very important to maintain only the characteristics of a customer that facilitate better targeting and improved communication. Maintaining extraneous information can negatively affect the performance of database processing, cause you to take your eye off the really important variables, and incur unnecessary costs to keep nonpertinent information current. Customer research can be very helpful in determining the key variables to place on the database. Segmentation studies and research that describes your customers, their attitudes, and their purchase behaviors will aid in identifying the information. Past research can be used or you may have to field a new research study. Validity and relevancy of the information are the key.

Therefore, as a part of the needs assessment, you must determine what information is required to meet the objectives you have set for the database. The checklist in Exhibit 12.5 lists the types of information that could be key for targeting and influencing purchase behavior through a database.

Function Analysis. This phase of the database building process focuses on what the database has to do from a technical standpoint to meet your objectives. The answers to the questions during this phase will aid in determining which software and hardware are required.

EXHIBIT 12.5
DATABASE CUSTOMER INFORMATION

Required:
Name and address (business or home, depending on your industry)

Potential:
Brand preferences

Brand purchased most often

Frequency of purchase

Units purchased per occasion

Demographics

Lifestyle indicators

Phone number

If you are able to track every transaction, you can add the following:

Total lifetime sales

Total annual sales

Recency

Sales by product purchased

Combination of products purchased

EXHIBIT 12.6
FUNCTION ANALYSIS CHECKLIST

- ❏ Is 24-hour on-line access required?
- ❏ How many customers will be housed on the database?
- ❏ What type of response time is required for certain processes?
- ❏ How often will the information be updated?
- ❏ How much customer information will be stored?
- ❏ How many new customers are anticipated in the next one to three years?
- ❏ What provisions should be made for additional customer information?

Sample questions from this phase are listed in Exhibit 12.6, but a technical person well versed in marketing databases is an essential part of this process.

Internal vs. External. Once the needs assessment and function analysis are completed, the question of where and how to house the data must be answered. First, you must determine if the database can be built and maintained internally.

A marketing database is very different from a financial or inventory system. Typically, financial and inventory systems are not concerned with individual customer-level data, which are primary focuses of the marketing database. Financial and inventory systems are focused on current orders or weekly, monthly, quarterly, or annual sales. A marketing database must be able to relate data from a marketing perspective, not a financial or operational view. The architecture for the data is built around this perspective and will not resemble the structure of operational systems currently in use. The output of a marketing database includes customized promotional lists, opportunity identification, scoring, early warning systems, and reporting on past programs. Only some types of reporting will resemble functions that the current operations systems perform. There are off-the-shelf or licensed products that could meet part or all of your needs, and personnel could be trained in these systems. Your company's current in-house resources may or may not be able to adapt to the requirements of a marketing database.

When making the decision, it is important to consider both options. Housing the base internally will require additional head count, training, software, and potentially hardware. If the marketing department will have access to the database, you will also need a group to support these users. Any and all additional costs associated with housing the database internally should be compared to outsourcing the database.

Outsourcing the database provides several benefits. First, you will be able to access the knowledge of people who have years of experience in this area. Second, you will be a number-one priority even at month's close. Third, you will be able to choose a company that can provide one or all of the services required to implement database marketing. Building and maintaining the database is only one of the components of database marketing. A diagram of the components of database marketing is shown in Exhibit 12.7.

There are companies that provide all of these services, specialize in a few, or offer only one of the components. If an external source is the answer, you will be able to tap the service's experience in all the areas necessary. Finally, you own the data and, depending on your agreement, the software. The database could always be brought in-house at a future date, allowing you to develop the necessary resources over a period of time.

Database Architecture. The architecture or software in which your data are stored should be chosen based on functionality. Many people will tell you that you do not have a marketing database if you are utilizing a flat file format. The format is merely a record with the name and address and a string of information following it as shown in Exhibit 12.8.

EXHIBIT 12.7
DATABASE MARKETING COMPONENTS

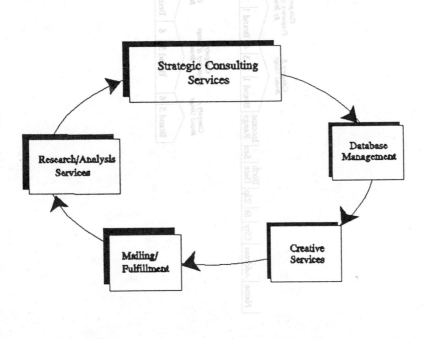

EXHIBIT 12.8
FLAT FILE DATABASE FORMAT

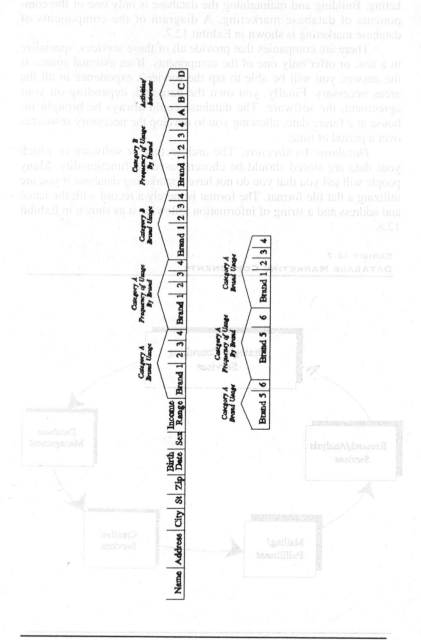

Many feel that you have to be in a table-driven or relational format to be a true database. The table-driven format links customer information by means of a set of tables. A diagram of a table-driven format is shown in Exhibit 12.9.

This format operates more efficiently than a flat file because you do not have to pass every record in the database each time you process. You search the tables to determine who should be included in the process, and then only access those that meet your specifications.

There are variations on these two formats. The flat file format can be linked by a series of indices to make it more efficient. A table-driven format can have direct on-line access. Both can reside on mainframe, mini, or personal computers.

The important criterion for deciding which software and hardware to employ is cost-effectiveness. Your objective is to be able to mine the gold from your database. To do that, you need to be able to direct the data from many different perspectives. Cost should not keep you from evaluating a potential opportunity.

Gather Data. Now that you have determined the information that should be included in the database, the source(s) of the data should be identified. Internal sources should be evaluated first due to their cost-effectiveness. The sources that are usually maintained internally are billing and inventory systems, customer service, panel or advisory boards, and mailing lists. The external sources are outlined in Exhibit 12.10.

EXHIBIT 12.9
TABLE-DRIVEN DATABASE FORMAT

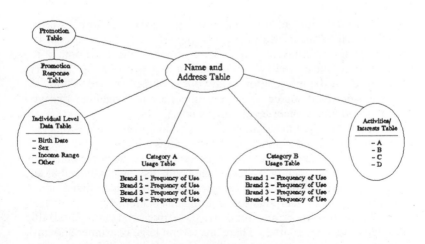

EXHIBIT 12.10
EXTERNAL SOURCES OF DATA

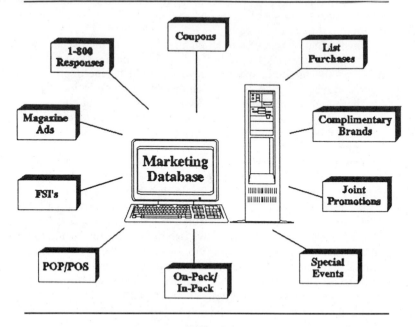

Information from promotions such as those listed above, is sometimes saved. This past information should be evaluated before inclusion. The key is the time that has passed since the promotion. During that time, the respondents may have moved, changed brands, or entered a new stage of life.

The goal is to gather the information as cost-effectively as possible. You will want to evaluate each source on the basis of cost per screened name, validity, and the time required to collect it. Some of the sources may not have all the information that you require. You may have to solicit the information from your customer or overlay the data from a syndicated source. It is very important to remember that you need individual customer-level information.

You can solicit the additional information from your customers at the time of their next purchase through a questionnaire in-pack, on-pack, or administered by a sales representative. A separate screening effort through the mail or by telephone could also be conducted at any time. The information that is gathered should be standardized across sources for ease of interpretation and implementation.

Demographics and some lifestyle information is available through syndicated sources. There are several large consumer and business databases that you can match to your database and then overlay the appropriate information on your customers' records. Some of the demographics are based on census information. In these instances, the information is carried down to the household level from either a zip code, census tract, or block group. The data assumes that the residents of a zip code, census tract, or block group are identical. Inferred data, such as census data, are not as powerful a targeting tool as actual behavior or respondent data.

Some of the most common sources of syndicated demographic or lifestyle consumer data are as follows:

- Acxiom Corporation
- Donnelley Marketing Services
- NDL
- R. L. Polk
- Database America
- Equifax

Business syndicated sources provide such information as Standard Industrial Classification (SIC) codes, total company sales, number and location of branches, and total sales. Dunn & Bradstreet has offered this type of information for many years.

Obviously, competitive customer information cannot be gathered in the same manner as information on your current customers. You will need to rely more on external sources — list purchase, mail or telephone screening, or promotions geared to bring in competitive customer information. Once again, the same information should be collected in the same format as it is with your current customers, and an overlay of syndicated data should be considered.

Clean Data. The information for your database will come most likely from multiple sources. Prior to loading the information into the database, several steps are required to "clean" the data. The first step is to place the data from the multiple sources in the same format. The name and address will be placed in the same fields, and the additional data will be given the same specific locations in each customer record.

Next, the customer names and addresses will be sent through a piece of software that standardizes the addresses according to U.S. Postal Service guidelines and corrects or adds zip codes and zip-plus-four. These changes increase the deliverability of any mailings from the database.

The next step is to eliminate duplicates. Duplicates can occur during data entry or are the result of a customer responding to more than one stimuli. When an exact duplicate has been identified, one of the records is deleted.

The final step in cleaning the data is the updating of the addresses. With more than 20 percent of all households moving every year, some of your customers will no longer be at the address contained in your information. By using the National Change of Address (NCOA), a service of the U.S. Postal Service, the addresses can be updated electronically. The source of NCOA is the change of address card you fill out to notify your mail carrier of your move.

Database Design. The first five phases provide the input for this phase. The architecture, hardware, functions, and information requirements shape the design of the database. In this phase, the actual detailed database design is completed. The design may encompass the writing of a customized database architecture or merely the customization of a licensed or off-the-shelf software package.

Tests of all functions occur during this phase. Modifications are made as necessary to meet the processing and marketing objectives.

Database Building. During this phase the information is loaded into the database. Final tests are conducted prior to the system's being released. Any further modifications are made during this time.

Care and Feeding of the Database. The value of a database is determined by two factors — the information contained on the database and the accessibility of the information. Information and accessibility are of equal importance. Imagine the right information but only a costly and tedious method of access. The converse, the wrong information but easy, affordable access, is equally as worthless. These areas were addressed in the needs assessment, function analysis, and design phases of the database building process, but they cannot be evaluated once and forgotten. Technology is in a state of constant change. Today's business environment is in an ever-increasing state of evolution. Your database will require changes over time to meet your processing and marketing objectives. Periodically, advances in pertinent technology should be reviewed. The marketing information contained on the database should be in constant review. After every program, the value of the information should be assessed. Market research should be employed on an ongoing basis to aid in this assessment. The types of market research and their purpose will be discussed in a later section.

For the information to be truly valuable, it must reflect the current environment. To maintain current information, the ongoing database marketing plan should include two methods for updating information. The first involves two of the processes described in the data cleaning phase of the database build. Addresses should be updated at a minimum on an annual basis. To supplement NCOA, you should consider requesting address corrections on all mailings. The cost of address corrections should be evaluated against the benefit. Addresses will need to be updated to meet changes in postal areas, such as zip codes and carrier routes.

The population of your database is not static. You will be adding and deleting members. Information will be updated through response to programs. The second area of maintenance accomplishes this through what are most commonly called adds and updates. An add is the process of adding new customers to the database. An update is the process of updating some part of an already existing customer record.

In an add, all steps of the cleaning process should be undertaken.

This process is similar to preparing the original names, addresses, and information for the database. You will need to make sure the "new" customer is not already on the database, a duplicate, and the data will need to be normalized to fit the database structure.

In an update, you are adding some information to an already existing customer record. The first step is to prepare the information for insertion in the database. If it is an address change, the address will need to be standardized to meet postal standards. If the information is sales, demographic, or lifestyle, the codes will need to be reviewed to determine if they match those already on the database. The second step is to locate the current record on the database and append or change the appropriate information.

Another type of update is aging. This update involves information based on time. For example, if age is a critical factor in your targeting, you would want to update a customer's age annually. Another example is recency, the time since a past purchase. To be able to update your customer information, you need a source for that information. The sales information can be captured through coupon response, rebates, refunds, or sales transactions. The competitive set, demographic, and lifestyle data may require what is called a rescreen. A rescreen involves a questionnaire or screener that is completed by the customer answering such questions as brands purchased on a regular basis, brands used most often, frequency of purchase, and demographics/pyschographics. The timing of the rescreens is dictated by how dynamic your business environment is and how critical these variables are to the performance of the database.

SHOULD TESTING BE PART OF THE PLAN?

Testing should always be part of the plan. The real question is which one of the two types of testing that should be considered. The first is the overall evaluation of the database marketing. Many times, your cost/benefit comparison will leave you in a gray area. The level of performance required from a database marketing program is the likes of which you have never seen before. At the same time, your intestinal judgment tells you there is something there. Remember that this is a new medium with pinpoint accuracy that can deliver sales results at unprecedented levels. A test can be constructed to confirm or deny your intestinal judgment. The key to constructing this test is to evaluate several alternatives for each of the key components of the program — namely target audience, list, creative, and offer. As with any effective media plan, frequency is part of the equation for success. You should test the effect of building a relationship and consider more than one mailing. A sample test matrix is shown in Table 12.3.

TABLE 12.3
TEST MATRIX

Target Audience	List Source	Creative	Offer
A	1	Newsletter	High
	2		Medium
	3	Brochure	Low
B	1	Newsletter	High
	2		Medium
	3	Brochure	Low

To determine the impact of the test, three measures should be included. Behavior is the most important variable to be measured. Response by test cell will provide the immediate reaction to the program. An estimate of incremental volume generated by the program measures the true effect of the initial reaction and can capture additional purchases tied to the program. The final measure is that of the attitudinal impact. Attitudes precede behavior. If in the attitudinal measure you find that your product or service is now favorably viewed by a group that was not predisposed to it prior to the mailing, you can anticipate that with continued communication they will try your products or service. All of these measures should be factored into the success of the program. Two questions need to be answered: Does database marketing make sense for your product or service? If so, what components were the most successful and should continue?

The second type of testing is ongoing. Direct mail organizations include a test cell in every mailing to see if they can improve on what they are currently doing. They will vary either the list, the offer, or the creative to see if they can surpass the response rate on their benchmark (most successful execution). If they do, the new execution becomes the benchmark, and the quest for an even more effective program continues. This constant testing is second nature in a medium that is as accountable as direct mail. Database marketing has this same accountability. With this medium, you can be continually fine-tuning your efforts. This does not mean that you are constantly in test mode. You are merely carving out a small portion of a large-scale program to evaluate an alternative.

How Do I Effectively Use My Marketing Database?

The first step is to develop a database marketing plan for each product or service that will utilize the database. You will want to consider long- and short-term objectives. Strategies to achieve those objectives should then be drafted. Many of the same types of strategies that are used in the mass media are appropriate for database marketing. You must keep in mind, however, the differences in the medium. These differences are not handicaps. They are opportunities.

For example, a marketing objective could be a 10 percent increase in customer loyalty. The strategy could be a continuity program covering a number of purchases. In a mass medium, you would deliver an offer in-pack, in print, or on broadcast media. For example, the offer could be to send in six proofs-of-purchase and receive a poster, seven and receive a baseball cap, and so on. All participants would receive the same offer. Typically, there would be no follow-up communication regarding the program.

In a continuity program delivered through database marketing, the alternatives are almost limitless. You can select any appropriate subgroup of your database for participation in the program. If you have been tracking loyalty, you could target a group that has been slipping or one that shows high potential for increasing its share of purchases with your company.

You are able to customize the offer based on the behavior of the target audience. You can target only customers who have recently reduced their number of purchases, as opposed to all customers who receive your mass communications. For example, one group may have purchased from you 10 times a quarter, but has now slipped to only eight purchases in a quarter. A second may have gone from eight to six purchases in a quarter. Through database marketing, you can customize a program for the first group to return to its prior purchase rate of 10 and then structure a stretch incentive to push it to 12. The second group would receive a program based on its past purchase rate of eight and a stretch objective of 10.

A series of follow-up communications can be used to support the program. In the beginning, they would elicit participation in the program. Then, the mailings could encourage meeting the various levels of the program. If, for example, the program is half over and a group of the participants is one purchase short of the first goal, the mailing could be tailored to encourage hitting the higher goal. The mailing could be personalized to include how many purchases have been made and how many more are needed to reach the higher level incentive.

The key to developing a database marketing plan is to take off the blinders of mass media. Think about your customers as individuals, not as "Women 18–34." Design plans that treat your customers the way you would if you knew them all by name.

Resources Required. If you had no prior experience, you would never develop a television commercial just because you have in-house creative capabilities. The same holds true for building a marketing database or designing and executing a database marketing program. You will need to develop the expertise in-house or form a relationship with an experienced database marketing supplier.

If the decision is to develop the expertise in-house, you must determine whether to hire experienced individuals, to train current employees, or to combine hiring and training. A combination of hiring and training is probably the best. As it was with direct marketing several years ago, there is no degree in database marketing. Colleges are not turning out trained professionals in this discipline. The training that has occurred has been in the trenches. Individuals have learned by experience — their own and those of their colleagues.

The Direct Marketing Association (DMA) and the National Center for Database Marketing do provide several single and multi-day seminars on the subject. Numerous books have been written on the discipline that can aid in training. Several of them are listed in the "Resources" section at the end of this chapter.

Even if the decision has been made to develop expertise in-house, you will probably need some outside help in executing your database marketing programs. There are two types of suppliers. The first is a full-service database marketing agency that supplies all the necessary components of database marketing, as outlined in Exhibit 12.11.

Similar to general advertising agencies, many full-service database marketing agencies will manage outside vendors to supply some of the components, such as printing and fulfillment. Generally, a full-service agency will maintain the database and provide the analytical services and the strategic consulting because the information is so important.

EXHIBIT 12.11
FULL-SERVICE DATABASE AGENCY

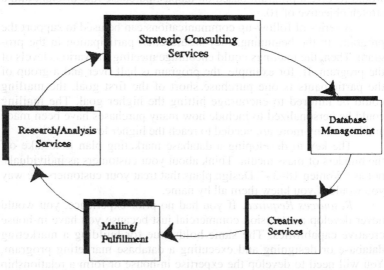

Information and the proper interpretation of that information are key to the success of a database marketing program. If correctly managed, the information will help drive your database activities. New volume opportunities will identify themselves through analysis of buying trends. Groups whose loyalty is eroding will raise their hands. In general, the database allows you to analyze your market and develop programs at the individual level. General advertising agencies that have branched into database marketing often employ a computer service bureau to maintain the database and utilize another source for analytical services.

The second type of supplier is one who specializes in one or two of the components. There are numerous consultants who specialize in database marketing. The consultants specialize in providing direction for the development of a database system and/or database marketing programs. Normally, they stop short of the execution of the plans; however, they can screen and recommend suppliers for the execution. Database marketing consultants can be very helpful in the early exploration of the medium.

Another type of specialist is a service bureau. A service bureau focuses on the systems and the data processing component. In working with these specialists, you should have a good working knowledge of your marketing and basic systems requirements.

There are numerous production suppliers that have experience in direct mail. Guided by a knowledgeable, on-staff database expert, you can use the services of a creative boutique to develop your creative product. Printers and fulfillment suppliers also provide some components of database marketing.

If multiple suppliers are your choice, a strong internal manager who has experience in database marketing will prove very valuable. Coordinating multiple suppliers will require someone who knows your company's database marketing vision and knows how to translate that vision across several entities. Database marketing is a process. Every program will provide learning that can be used to improve the next one. To maximize the value of your database marketing plan, continuity and involvement by someone from your organization at every level is key.

The checklist in Exhibit 12.12 can help you to determine which supplier is the best for you.

The Role of Research and Analysis. As stated above, the foundation of database marketing is information. For database marketing to be successful, research and analysis play a very important role. The database is rich with information that can guide you in marketing to the important group of customers that resides on it. The database tracks behavior. From time to time, it may need to be supplemented with customized research among specific groups. The customized research can help provide the reason behind the behavior. The reasons and the

EXHIBIT 12.12
SUPPLIER CHECKLIST

1. **Who will manage the database marketing effort?**

   What are their database marketing strengths?

   What are their database marketing weaknesses?

2. **What role do you want the supplier to play?**

   ❑ Turnkey supplier

   ❑ Systems supplier

   ❑ Marketing consultant

   ❑ Systems consultant

   ❑ Consultant to select suppliers

   ❑ Strategic consulting

   ❑ Creative supplier

   ❑ Fulfillment supplier

   ❑ Research supplier

   ❑ Analytical supplier

3. **What is the experience of the suppliers in your industry and in the role you would like them to play?**

4. **If the suppliers are turnkey suppliers that utilize outside resources for some of the components:**

   What are those components?

   What are the qualifications of those outside suppliers?

   How critical is an intimate understanding of those components to the success of your database marketing plan?

   Does the turnaround time for programs match your needs?

   Are the suppliers committed to database marketing or is it an add-on service?

---

associated attitudes help in the development of offers, creative, and program ideas. Custom research can help you understand if the purchases of your product were truly incremental or why an incentive did or did not work. Customer market research can even help you understand if an incentive is necessary. This information leads to more effective and efficient programs. As with any marketing program it is important to talk with your customers to better understand how to meet their needs.

Analysis of the database information plays a key role in two areas. The information on the database is the meat for a very actionable customer segmentation analysis. Traditionally, a segmentation analysis is conducted on a sample drawn from your total customers. At the conclusion of a traditional segmentation analysis, you know there are different subgroups among your entire customer base and how they differ.

You do not know where they live, and you do not have a direct line of communication with them. When the segmentation analysis is completed on your database, you do know where they live and can reach them through your database marketing communications. You can then track their reaction to your programs over time and continually refine the segments.

The second area in which analysis plays a key role is in the combining of customized research information and the information on the database. A sample of the database will be involved in a customized research study, but that information can be inferred from key characteristics and applied to a much larger population. Thus, you can enrich the database with attitudinal information to increase your understanding of all the members of your marketing database.

To be truly successful with database marketing, a strong research and analytical plot should be included in the overall plan. The research and analysis is not just a requirement during the first year. To understand your diverse and ever changing customer base, ongoing research and analysis will be required.

Common Mistakes. Probably the most common mistake is that of not capturing response to the programs at the individual level. Many times elaborate targeting up front will be negated because the response will be captured by a group code on the response vehicle. The group code is similar to the way your response vehicles now receive different codes based on the media vehicle. For example, if the database program included franchise and competitive customers, this method would result in an F1 code for the franchise group — *F* for "Franchise" and *1* for the program. This type of coding will only allow you to analyze the respondents by the predetermined groups. You will not be able to examine differences between nonrespondents and respondents. Nor will you be able to break the franchise group into subgroups, such as "bought in the last three months" or "haven't purchased in six months." Individual results are stressed because these lead to the most meaningful groups for future mailings. The individual-level results free you of the preconceived customer groups you are accustomed to and allow new customer groups to emerge.

Another common mistake when you begin using database marketing is to forget the back-end. The back-end is the pulling together of all the results of each program at the individual level. Even when the response information has been captured by individual, it can be hard to fight the old tendencies of analyzing preconceived groups and evaluating them at the individual level.

The tendency in the beginning is to view the marketing effort as a highly targeted program and evaluate response results in total to determine if the effort was a success. There will not be one response rate; there will be many different response rates. They are generated by the different target audiences and even subgroups of these different target audiences that were included in the program. In any program, there are winners and losers. For example, if your program included competitive and franchise customers, there is a response rate associated with competitive customers and another with franchise customers. Table 12.4 shows various subgroups that could be analyzed by their response rates.

TABLE 12.4

BACK-END ANALYSIS

Group	Subgroup
Franchise	Loyal franchise customers
	Franchise customers who use one other product or service (Dual)
	Franchise customers who use multiple products or services (3+)
	Competitive loyal competitive customers
	Dual competitive customers
	3+ competitive customers

Many times there is more than one way for a customer to respond. There may be multiple coupons, a coupon and a rebate offer, or a cumulative point program involving multiple purchases. A back-end analysis evaluates the breadth (total number of respondents) and depth (responding to multiple devices) of response for various groups and subgroups.

Because you have response at the individual customer level, you know who responded and who did not. Another level of analysis in the back-end work is this comparison of nonrespondents to respondents. The comparison helps you understand why a program was not appealing to the nonrespondents but was to the respondents. Differences between the two groups can be used in selection of future participants. The next program could exclude those who resemble the nonrespondents or a different, more appealing program could be offered to them.

New opportunities are discovered during the back-end analysis. The analysis of these individual results leads to revisions or discontinuance of programs. The costs of the program are compared to the value of the incremental volume generated by the program. This constant review with the ability to learn from previous efforts provides the ever increasing efficiency of database marketing.

A final common mistake is satisfaction with the status quo. Early gains in database marketing may prove so rewarding that the hunger to market "smarter" diminishes. You overlook how fast your customers are changing.

The marketing database can keep pace with these changes, but it must constantly be evaluated and questioned. Does the database have the right information? Is the information as current as it should be? Are you letting the data talk to you? Do you have the right customers on the database? Is there another way to reduce costs? The list of questions is as endless as the quest for maximizing the value of database marketing. Truly knowing your customers provides the power to constantly improve on past performance.

THE FUTURE

Database marketing has been well served by recent advances in computer technology. Mini computers and microcomputers are handling the tasks that were once reserved for mainframes. Processing time has decreased. Many more of us marketing types are getting knee-deep in our data because of less technical interfaces, such as Apple and Microsoft Windows.

Technology will continue to shape the future of database marketing. Computer technology will continue to make strides in the data storage and processing area. These improvements will come in the form of multitask work stations, parallel processing, and wider usage of disk array. The move will continue to smaller platforms or machines. A key benefit of the movement to microcomputers (souped-up PCs) is the software that is already available and the number of companies that write software for these machines.

To move ahead, database marketing will require software that puts the marketers closer to their customers. The software will need to facilitate access and interpretation of the data by nontechnical people. The more marketers learn about their customers, the more they will want to know. The microcomputer environment has numerous packages to help the nontechnical person take advantage of the computer age. As more databases move to this platform, software will be developed to facilitate the two-way communication between marketers and customers by means of the marketing database.

Technology will affect database marketing in other arenas. The first is printing. Great strides have been made in developing truly personalized packages in cost-efficient, on-line systems. Addresses can trigger the imaging of a map showing the retail location closest to a customer. Coupon values can be varied from one customer to another based on purchase behavior. Copy can be adjusted to address the benefits that are key to one household against another.

Imaging technology will continue to improve. What if the logos, illustrations, and photos could be imaged package by package? A completely variable package might be achieved through four-color imaging. No longer would you need multiple press runs to customize a package for a certain audience. The marketing database would drive the development for a package customized to each customer's needs.

In the future, unlimited selective insertion will result in mass production of mail packages that have as many variations as your customer has needs. For example, if a large consumer packaged goods company wanted to do a mailing across its brands of pet food, diapers, and detergents, only a household that had a dog or a cat or a child in diapers would receive all three coupons. If there was a household with a dog and no child in the diaper-wearing ages, only a detergent and dog food promotional piece would be included.

This production capability will benefit more than just cooperative programs. Imagine a business-to-business, large-scale mailing that requires specification sheets and brochures for a number of products. On-line production of this piece could accommodate the information requirements of all your customers. To meet those requirements today, collation and insertion by hand or sending everyone every specification sheet and brochure is required. Mailings will be more effective and more affordable because they will contain only relevant information and will be produced in a mass production environment.

The final area of database marketing that will benefit from technology is that of communications. Currently, the message is primarily carried to the customer through the mail. Some database marketing applications use 800 numbers and interactive telecommunications to capture customer information to be added to the database. In the future, new communications channels will be available to database marketers. One of these is interactive television.

A company by the name of TV Answer is developing a two-way communications tool that works through your television. The technology is similar to a cellular telephone network. Radio waves transmit signals between users' home units and central cell sites. The information can then be transmitted via satellites to TV Answer's headquarters and other designated destinations.

A customer will be able to request product information, check bank balances, and transfer funds. TV Answer will even have a direct link for ordering different products, such as catalog items, delivered food, flowers, and distilled spirits. The service will introduce interactive programming. The viewers will play along with sporting events and voice their opinions on news and talk-show programs.

In the beginning, direct communication by marketers to only certain customers will not be available. Marketers will be able to gather more information for their databases through the customers' requests through TV Answer. Imagine a prime-time network television commercial for Jeep Cherokee. Every household can view the commercial, but only TV Answer households can react to it instantaneously. Their screen will have a menu of actions from which to choose. Viewers could request that a salesperson give them a call or that a brochure be sent out. This information is communicated to Chrysler, and a sales lead for a new Jeep Cherokee has been generated.

Another use of the service is the capturing of new members for your marketing database. Questions regarding brand and service preferences can be answered, and the information can be added to the database. As the technology progresses, marketers may be able to communicate selectively with households in the interactive program.

Privacy issues can have a positive or negative effect on the future of database marketing. If direct and database marketers continue to respect the customer's right to privacy and only use information to better serve, the impact will be positive. The Direct Marketing Association (DMA) and its members are active in self-regulation regarding the use of sensitive information. The DMA has a service called Mail Preference Service. You can request that your name be taken off all mailing lists. Members of the DMA then use this list to delete individuals who are not interested in receiving direct mail.

Database marketing will continue to evolve as changes in technology bring marketers closer to their customers. Information will become easier to obtain, and the methods of interpreting it will become even more sophisticated. Developments in communication will facilitate the direct communication and relationship-building of old.

RESOURCES

Organizations:
Direct Marketing Association (DMA)
11 West 42nd Street
New York, NY 10036-8096
(212) 768-7277

National Center for Database Marketing
109 58th Avenue
St. Petersburg Beach, FL 33706
(813) 367-5629

Books:
Maximarketing
Stan Rapp and Tom Collins
McGraw-Hill Book Company, New York, 1987

The Great Marketing Revolution
Stan Rapp and Tom Collins
McGraw-Hill Book Company, New York, 1990

Relationship Marketing
Regis McKenna
Addison-Wesley Publishing Co., Inc.; Reading, MA; 1991

Integrated Direct Marketing
Ernan Roman
McGraw-Hill Book Company, New York, 1988

Publications:
Target Marketing
North American Publishing Co.
401 N. Broad St.
Philadelphia, PA 19108

Direct
Cowles Business Media, Inc.
911 Hope Street
Six River Bend Center
Box 4949
Stamford, CT 06907-0949

DM News
Mill Hollow Corp.
19 W. 21st St.
New York, NY 10010

Neil L. Fraser's experience with co-op advertising goes back over 30 years to his work with a distributor of General Electric and Sunbeam appliances. While with the distributor, Fraser helped develop pioneering distributor/dealer co-op advertising programs. Fraser left that post to join an Atlanta advertising agency as an account executive. He became the firm's Vice President before organizing Fraser Advertising, Inc., in 1963.

As an advertising agency executive, Fraser has worked on many different types of co-op advertising. He developed and administered distributor/dealer programs on local and national levels for brand name products such as Carrier Air Conditioning, RCA Television, Whirlpool Appliances, Westinghouse Appliances, and Magnavox Television. His industrial co-op experience includes programs for distributors of Caterpillar Tractors and International Construction Equipment. He developed and is current administrator of the Network Services Authorized Sales Representative co-op programs for Southern Bell and South Central Bell. In addition to conventional vertical co-op programs, Fraser has set up horizontal co-op advertising campaigns for several clients.

Fraser has written on the subject of co-op advertising for many different trade publications. A Glossary of Cooperative Advertising was developed by Fraser and published in 1984 by Commerce Communications. He has been a speaker on co-op at meetings around the country and abroad. His educational work in this specialized area was recognized in 1988 when he was named one of the six original members of the Co-op Hall of Fame.

CHAPTER 13

CO-OP ADVERTISING

COOPERATIVE ADVERTISING'S PLACE IN MARKETING

Cooperative or co-op advertising is the sharing of advertising costs between mutually interested businesses, usually retailers and their suppliers. The basis for co-op goes back to 1903, when the Warner Brothers Company, makers of Warners Rust Proof Corsets, issued the first known co-op plan. Today's marketers will find Warner's words to be familiar:

> One of our chief helps in promoting the sale of our corsets is to assist you locally in bringing the particular styles you carry to the eye of your customer through local means.

In an advertising brochure dated 1907, Warner told its retailers that cooperation is:

> ... a word that has become inseparably associated with our selling plans. It means that we work with you and for you in enlarging your corset business if you work with us and for us. This cooperative advertising that you and we do together naturally advertises our corsets as well as your shop.

As Warner so accurately stated at the beginning of the century, cooperative advertising serves the mutual needs of manufacturers and retailers for local advertising. Why is this local advertising needed? Because it is a valuable force in moving merchandise and meeting competition. Without the advertising that co-op helps to provide, most merchants are at a disadvantage in the retail arena, with resulting lost sales and lost profits.

Since the turn of the century, co-op has earned a secure place in the marketing of goods and services. Today, the use of this advertising and promotional technique is increasing, and its role in marketing is becoming more important.

While there are no reliable statistics on the amount of money spent each year on co-op advertising, estimates suggest that in retailing, co-op funding supports more than 20 percent of all advertising expenditures. Co-op also is used to advertise and promote the sale of industrial products and in the marketing of services. Across a wide range of industries, shared advertising cost is vital to the success of both large and small businesses in almost every segment of our economy.

To understand co-op's role in advertising and its importance in the sale of goods and services, you must examine those elements that make up a co-op advertising program and the motivation behind them, beginning with the manufacturer-retailer relationship. Most co-op dollars are spent within this vertical chain of production, distribution, and sales. The vertical co-op chain starts when a manufacturer establishes a program, either at the retail or wholesale level, to support local advertising and sales promotion by offering to pay part, or even all, of the cost. As part of this support, the manufacturer also may provide material for use in the retailer's advertising or sales promotion programs. The co-op support is not unconditional. There are usually extensive rules with the co-op offer to be sure that the retailer or wholesaler actually advertises or promotes the manufacturer's products.

A manufacturer's conventional advertising is a responsibility of its advertising department. Media used, timing, and content are under complete control. The manufacturer's co-op advertising is under the control of a customer, the retailer, who usually decides on timing, media used, and advertising content, within the restrictions of the manufacturer's co-op policy. In addition, the retailer's advertising will usually have a feature lacking in the manufacturer's advertising: price and where to buy.

Manufacturers who run conventional advertising campaigns in the mass media (television, radio, newspapers, magazines) are pre-selling to create demand. Their intent is to make customers go to retail stores to look for the advertised products. Such advertising does not identify specific places where the products are sold and gives pricing only in the familiar "suggested retail" form. Manufacturers' advertising may also be intended to create consumer demand so retailers will want to sell the advertised products.

Since co-op advertising runs at the level where products are being sold, its intent is to attract customers into specific stores by identifying products with prices and a retail location. Those products have already been purchased by the retail store, and may or may not have been "presold" by the manufacturers' advertising.

Co-op and the Law. When a manufacturer offers co-op funds or assistance to a retailer, our unique antitrust laws become involved. Those laws started with the Sherman Act of 1890, a move to break up the cartels and trusts that controlled the economy of that period. There were loopholes in the Sherman Act that were closed by the Clayton Act of 1914. But the Clayton Act overlooked one very large loophole: advertising and promotional allowances. During the 1920s big retailers used that loophole to gain price advantages from their suppliers and stifle competition from smaller stores. The worst offenders in this area were the grocery chains, with the A&P being the most aggressive and visible offender. In 1936 the Robinson-Patman Act passed, specifically prohibiting discriminatory practices when using promotional allowances in the sale of commodities in interstate commerce. The laws do not apply to intrastate commerce or to the sale of anything but commodities. Those three pieces of legislation are known as our "antitrust laws." They are intended to prevent discriminatory pricing and price fixing and to maintain open and competitive free trade. Since the provision of co-op money for advertising and promotion reduces advertising and promotion expense, it affects the price at which a product sells at retail. That is why the antitrust laws regulate co-op advertising and all promotional allowances.

In 1969, a landmark ruling by the U.S. Supreme Court ordered the Federal Trade Commission to lay down guidelines for the use of advertising and promotional allowances. Those guidelines, known as the "Meyer Guides," define the rules of co-op advertising. Anyone involved in the use of co-op and promotional allowances should have a copy of these guides, which can be obtained from the Federal Trade Commission.

As a result of the antitrust laws and the court decision, co-op advertising and promotional allowances are almost universal in our marketing system. The laws have helped in assuring that co-op funds are available to all retail outlets that sell products whose manufacturers offer co-op and in making that co-op proportionally equal to the co-op given to other competing retail customers. In other free market economies, where there are no such laws, co-op is still offered on an arbitrary and unfair basis.

Co-op's Basic Conflict. A basic conflict of interest in the co-op system is revealed on examination of the motives behind manufacturer and retailer advertising programs. Manufacturers want advertising to boost sales of the products they make, regardless of where those products are sold. Retailers run advertising to bring people into their stores to buy whatever they sell, not necessarily the items shown in advertising.

When manufacturers fund retail advertising through co-op programs, bringing traffic into a store, the retailer may sell another manufacturer's products. Taking that chance is part of the co-op picture. The two conflicting sales goals have successfully coexisted for many years, even if they have been a source of friction between the co-op parties.

Internal Co-op Conflict. Budgeting advertising funds for co-op can produce internal conflict at the manufacturer's level, with a tug-of-war over allocation of dollars between national and local advertising programs. While co-op sometimes wins the money, national advertising has all the glamor and usually gets all the creative efforts. Co-op, on the other hand, is frequently produced by in-house advertising departments working with sales personnel and receiving little management attention. Co-op is, nevertheless, a real marketing workhorse, and its importance cannot be overemphasized.

Co-op's Influence on the Sale of Various Products. The types of products or services sold influence the value of co-op and determine its application. The sale of basic products — basic products available everywhere, such as razor blades, soap, and toothpaste — are less likely to depend on co-op funds for promotion or advertising. The sale of these products, where prices are too low for sustained local advertising by individual retailers, usually depends on manufacturer advertising in mass media, packaging, or point-of-purchase displays. Retailers of higher-cost merchandise, such as appliances, clothes, or home furnishings, are more likely to use co-op.

Selling higher-priced products also is more dependent on the ability of retail outlets to identify with brand names through local advertising and to feature the prices and locations at which those are sold. The importance of co-op in the marketing mix can be roughly divided between product categories as shown in Table 13.1.

There are, of course, exceptions to these examples. Co-op is used in the marketing of many low unit-cost products sold in groceries and drugstores, where it is frequently provided in the form of point-of-purchase material instead of advertising dollars. Co-op also is an important element in the local advertising of hardware stores, automotive parts stores, and in the retail advertising of brand name food products run by grocery chains. Co-op advertising for low unit-cost items usually appears in so-called "omnibus" ads containing a variety of products. Newspapers are filled with such advertising by chains. Much of that advertising is by their suppliers.

How Co-op Is Provided. Most co-op programs assign funds for local advertising based on the amount of their customers' purchases. The most commonly used system is that of the percentage accrual, in which a percentage factor assigned to retailer purchases accrues in a co-op account and is available for use in co-op advertising.

TABLE 13.1

Co-Op Is Less Important	Co-Op Plays a Significant Role
Convenience goods	Items shopped for, such as clothing
Mass-merchandised packaged goods	Infrequent purchases
Impulse purchase items	Appliances and home entertainment
Self-selling products	Furniture and durable goods
Utilitarian products	High brand-loyalty products
Easily understood products	Technical products
Low-cost items	Specialty products or services
Everyday items	Hobby or recreational products
High-cost items	Ego-enhancing goods

Another form of co-op funding is the promotion or unit allowance, extensively used in the marketing of packaged goods, groceries, pharmaceuticals, and products for the automotive aftermarket. This type of co-op funding automatically allocates promotional money on cases, dozens, pounds, or any other unit factor, at the time of the product's purchase.

The promotional or unit allowance and accrual co-op are parallel marketing tools, but the marketing motivation behind each one's use may be quite different. Accrual co-op, tied directly to the dollar value of a retailer's past or most recent purchases, is an after-sale device intended to help the retailer move the supplier's products out of the store. A specific co-op advertising commitment by the retailer is part of the accrual plan. Unit allowances are generally presale marketing tools intended to get merchandise into a retail establishment. Making an advertising commitment on the retailer's part is not always required to get the allowance, which is available as soon as the purchase is completed.

The least complicated of all co-op funding is the "open-ended" system. Here the supplier matches the retailer's expenditures without limits as long as the advertising or promotion helps the sale of its products. Most co-op suppliers fear the lack of control that an open-ended policy implies. Yet a carefully structured policy of this kind can be the most effective way of applying co-op.

Manufacturers' Use of Co-op. A general insight into exactly why manufacturers use co-op is demonstrated by the following list of the reasons they give when asked about the purpose of their co-op programs:

- Building sales for the most profitable product line
- Supporting the most profitable product line
- Building sales for a weaker product line
- Introducing a new product
- Meeting competitors' efforts
- Leveling out peaks and valleys of demand by timing of program,
- Acceding to requests of retailers, wholesalers, distributors, and others
- Building sales in a particular region
- Heightening brand awareness
- Controlling local ad content
- Stretching advertising budgets

Most suppliers offering co-op do so for one or more of these specific reasons. On the average, however, fewer than half have systems in place with which to measure the effectiveness of their co-op programs in accomplishing their stated goals.

MANUFACTURERS' GOALS IN CO-OP ADVERTISING

By taking the responses given by manufacturers as their reasons for having co-op programs, each area of co-op motivation can be analyzed.

Building Sales. Increasing sales is an easily recognized basis for any advertising or promotion program. The statement is modified to include "our most profitable product line." Co-op is not so limiting, and may be offered to support a manufacturer's complete line of products, sometimes with the intention of making an unprofitable line into a profitable one.

Exactly how does co-op act to build sales? The movement of products at the retail level is influenced by the support of co-op programs that supply both advertising money and promotional assistance. A manufacturer may advertise and promote products at the national level, but unless customers know where and at what price they can buy those products, the national advertising will have little effect. To bridge that gap, manufacturers offer co-op to their retailers.

Co-op also has extended effects that increase its selling potential. Co-op advertising at the local level serves to identify a retailer with a product line and a brand name. That retailer becomes recognized as a source of a manufacturer's products, and this recognition has a durability that goes beyond individual ads. In addition, many co-op programs seek to further solidify local ties. They do so through sharing in the cost of signs, Yellow Pages listings, uniforms, truck painting, in-store displays, and other ways of linking retailers to manufacturers and brand names. A retailer's investment in brand identification makes it more difficult to buy competing brands and builds repeat orders for the co-op supplier.

Another way in which co-op builds sales is through its influence over other retailers in the same market area. Stores check the advertising of their competitors very closely. A strong co-op advertising program, visible to competing stores, can open the door to a manufacturer's rep and help in securing new sales outlets. Co-op advertising run by strong retailers also can serve as an "umbrella" for smaller retailers. Customers seeing ads run by large stores may look for the same products at retailers in their neighborhoods. A co-op campaign run by major department stores featuring a brand name product will frequently produce traffic for smaller stores selling the same product.

Supporting Most Profitable Products. The qualification of "most profitable product line" is another important aspect of co-op. Many suppliers give this factor as a sole justification for offering co-op support. Many manufacturers feel that most of their profits come from specific segments of their product line and that all advertising and marketing efforts should promote these products. The remaining products may be less profitable but still necessary as part of the mixture required by the marketplace. An example of such a situation would be a manufacturer who produces four different models of an appliance simply to meet the overall need of the market and be recognized as a full-line supplier, knowing that 75 percent of sales and profits is going to come from only two of those models. The manufacturer might well limit a co-op program to the two models accounting for 75 percent of sales because the other two models, with perhaps specialized applications, do not warrant co-op support.

Boosting a Weak Product Line. Co-op can be very useful in strengthening a weak product line. When research or field reports indicate a line should have a greater market share based on product features and consumer demand, special co-op programs help improve the picture. Channeling funds into advertising and promotional support for the weak line can produce the extra local exposure needed to increase sales and make the product line more appealing to retailers. Such co-op support might take various forms, including increased cost sharing, reduction of restrictions on local ads, or even paying all the retailers' advertising costs. Because of its flexibility as a marketing tool, co-op is a problem solver in this and many other marketing situations.

Introducing New Products. Co-op is used to launch new products in much the same way it is used to boost weak product lines. The promotion of new products is a far more common application of the co-op concept than is the practice of strengthening weak products. An enhanced co-op program is almost a necessity when placing new items on the retail market. In some cases product introduction turns out to be a manufacturer's first venture into co-op after finding that wholesalers and retailers will not accept the new line without a supporting promotional program.

Meeting the Competition. Having a co-op program that equals or surpasses one that is offered by the competition should be an important part of any sales strategy. A strong and well-organized scheme of advertising support can be as important as the features of the product line itself when retailer buyers are deciding which lines to carry and promote. On the other hand, the inadequacy of a co-op program can turn retailers toward competing suppliers who are willing to provide the kind of help needed in the marketplace.

Unfortunately, many co-op programs rest entirely on the "we do it because the competition does" principle. Simply having a co-op program because it is an industry practice is like wearing a suit because everyone else wears one, without considering fashion, color, cut, and all the other ways clothing can improve appearance and make a good impression on others.

Leveling Sales by Timing. One of co-op's tangible advantages is the supplier's ability to time advertising emphasis to take advantage of seasonal demands or to compensate for off-season slumps. Examples of seasonal advertising efforts can be seen in the traditional emphasis placed by the toy industry on pre-Christmas promotions. As a result, this industry has suffered from off-season inventory costs and cash flow problems. Toy manufacturers now try to increase promotional activity at other times of the year to level out sales. The home comfort industry places co-op emphasis on the preseason advertising of air conditioning and heating equipment. Co-op also is used for seasonal emphasis in the marketing of sporting goods and recreational products. Whenever timing is a factor in selling, co-op programs can be adjusted to meet marketing requirements.

Meeting the Requests of Retailers and Wholesalers. Since co-op has become an integral part of our marketing system, wholesalers and retailers ask for and sometimes demand co-op from their suppliers. Buyers habitually pressure sales representatives for co-op before purchasing their goods. When those salespeople represent companies that do not offer co-op and find that they are losing sales, they apply pressure on management to provide the needed assistance. It is at this point that many co-op programs are born.

Building Sales by Region. Co-op has the additional advantage of being the type of advertising that can be used selectively by region as a market-strengthening device.

Co-op plans may vary to meet the demands of different markets. If a supplier has a low level of sales in a particular area, extra co-op funds can be channeled into that area as a way to increase sales promotion activity. The same co-op program enhancements used to launch new products or to strengthen weak product lines can apply when trying to improve regional sales. In these cases, many co-op programs go beyond "sweetening the co-op pot" by tailoring campaigns and advertising messages to offset specific weaknesses in given areas and by supplementing advertising with displays, sales incentive programs, or signs. In addition, market-building programs often employ extra advertising run entirely by the manufacturer or distributor that is tied directly to an increased level of retailer advertising — that is, if retailers agree to run a certain amount of advertising based on normal co-op, the supplier agrees to run additional advertising at no cost to the retailers. Co-op policies can be adjusted to allow for factors such as the higher rates paid for advertising in metropolitan markets by underwriting some of the additional costs.

Heightening Brand Awareness. While few manufacturers give brand awareness as a reason for offering co-op, this may be because the idea is completely accepted and is no longer a prime consideration.

When looking only at numbers, national and mass media advertising can give a manufacturer both product and brand name exposure at very low cost. Yet seeing the manufacturer's products and brand name in a local newspaper or hearing them advertised on a local radio or TV station in direct connection with a local merchant is important to the overall impression made on the consuming public. Local ads not only tell the customer where to buy and at what price, but they give the significant extra impact of bringing a selling message close to home, increasing consumer confidence in both the manufacturer and the product. Even when no substantial sales result directly from the local advertising, consistent efforts will leave a lasting impression on the market area.

Control of Advertising. Co-op has always produced a struggle between the parties involved over control of the advertising funded under the terms of the co-op agreement. When supporting local advertising, suppliers want to exercise some degree of control over spending and over the content of the advertising. The majority of manufacturers offering co-op place limitations on the media used, and many carefully watch the content of retail level ads as well. Industry trends currently show that suppliers are continually increasing their control over co-op usage.

Considering the large sums of money involved, co-op controls are justified. But restrictions in a co-op policy can be carried too far, making a co-op plan so inflexible that it becomes useless in practical application. Providing market flexibility while retaining necessary control is a primary goal in good co-op planning.

The struggle over who controls co-op, manufacturers or retailers, will always be an underlying element of discord in all co-op advertising, whether or not the policies are flexible. Retailers feel that they know their markets and should be able to decide which advertising is best for their stores. Manufacturers feel that they should direct their co-op so that local advertising conforms to the goals of overall marketing strategies. The conflict is a basic one: retailers trying to use co-op to promote a place of business and suppliers using co-op to sell a brand name or product line. Which party comes out ahead in the power struggle usually depends on who can exert the most financial leverage. Large retailers and chains usually get their way unless dealing with suppliers who are strong enough to resist, while smaller retailers have to live within the limits imposed by co-op policies.

The small retailer, in fact, sometimes stands to benefit from controlled co-op. Many advertising programs pool dealer funds for greater impact on a market. Some wholesalers, for instance, manage entire programs by establishing a fund from available retailer co-op to be used for advertising throughout that wholesaler's territory, benefitting all sales outlets in that territory.

Many manufacturer- and wholesaler-controlled programs bill participating retailers only for their share of the cost, thus avoiding paperwork and the traditional co-op paradox of having customers send bills to suppliers. There are other controlled co-op systems in which advertising itself, in the form of packages of radio or television spots, newspaper space, or billboards, is offered to retailers instead of co-op funding. Such programs are directed by suppliers with minimum input from the retailers involved.

The development of so-called "vendor support" advertising gives co-op a new twist. This type of co-op program is produced by retail chains putting together entire promotional packages, then enlisting (or demanding) the support of their suppliers.

Co-op interests large retailing organizations primarily for the money it provides to pay for their advertising, and they resist any sort of co-op policy restrictions. It is not unusual to see products in department store ads identified with their manufacturers only in the body copy. This occurs even when those manufacturers' co-op policies say that brand names and logos must be prominent for the advertising to qualify for co-op.

Another method now used by large retailers and chains to gain control of co-op money is that of turning their catalogs into advertising media in which space is "sold" to vendors. In this fashion, stores can often get around a co-op policy's funding requirements based on allowances or accruals on purchases. Partially because catalogs supply extra money from the manufacturers, the use of this advertising medium currently ranks second only to the use of newspapers.

Two more parties are active participants in the struggle for co-op funds at the retail level: the media and advertising agencies. Newspapers, the traditional co-op media, are losing ground to catalogs and flyers and to broadcast media. Advertising agencies, which once stayed away from retail advertising, are becoming increasingly involved in co-op and in both regional and national co-op programs for their clients. In addition, strong retailing chains, frequently aided by advertising agencies, are pushing hard to get more "vendor support" to supplement their advertising programs. Broadcast sales management is also aware of the extra advertising dollars co-op can bring in. Many TV and radio stations have co-op coordinators on their staffs to work on developing retail advertising and helping local merchants to get extra co-op funds.

Finally, there is the growth of cable television together with the changes it brings to retail marketing through specialized programming and the ability to localize coverage. As technology changes and laws against cable monopolies take effect, new ways to advertise and sell at retail are around the corner. These will include interactive systems for in-home shopping and electronic "Yellow Pages." Vendor co-op support will be a part of this new advertising field.

Stretching Advertising Budgets. The importance of cost-efficiency is far down the line in any survey of manufacturer motivation for using co-op. Yet co-op is an advertising bargain. When advertising in newspapers, for example, manufacturers have only to look at the difference in the rates they pay, the so-called national rates, and the local rates paid by retailers, to realize that space bought under co-op agreements can increase advertising levels. Local broadcast time, too, is often a more economical buy at the local level than at the national level. When retailer participation becomes part of the program, advertising dollars are stretched even farther.

There are exceptions to this principle. Some manufacturers will pay their retailers 100 percent of a national newspaper rate just to get local advertising, preferring to have the advertising run over a retailer's name even with no cost advantage. In the packaged goods industry, advertising allowances are provided merely for having products featured in an ad, with the allowance bearing no relation to the cost of the ad space. Since there are sound marketing considerations in each case, co-op still serves its basic purpose.

Co-op programs can also be "tuned" for cost-efficiency. With the computer data now available on advertising rates, co-op can change market by market, with sharing based on actual advertising costs in each location. Manufacturers and service bureaus are becoming increasingly sophisticated in the techniques of cost-efficient co-op administration.

Summary. To be successful in the marketplace, co-op advertising has to meet the goals of both manufacturers and retailers by creating demand for a product and bringing buyers into the stores where it is being sold. Manufacturers want to sell their products; retailers want traffic coming into their store to buy any product sold there.

From the manufacturers' standpoint, co-op can perform all the many marketing tasks mentioned: boosting weak products, launching new products, strengthening weak markets, timing promotional emphasis, meeting the advertising demands of wholesalers and retailers, establishing control over local advertising, and extending advertising budgets. In accomplishing these goals, co-op can go far beyond the funding of local advertising programs for retailers. Co-op can share the cost of many other promotional expenses such as in-store demonstrations, audiovisual aids, displays, packaging, coupons, contests and prizes, premiums, bonuses, and sales incentives. The range of co-op application is almost unlimited, extending to such exotic retail promotion devices as inflatables, laser skywriting, rolling billboards, or any other conceivable method of tying a product name and a retail source together.

Co-op is now used in more ways than ever before and is increasingly important to both manufacturers and retailers. The amount of money spent for local retail advertising, much of it funded by co-op, continues to grow each year. However, with the rising cost of advertising, the amount of additional exposure gained is not proportionate to the increase in expenditures. This fast-rising cost factor makes it necessary that co-op programs be even more effective and efficient, placing future emphasis on co-op's value in the marketing of both consumer and industrial products.

RETAILER GOALS IN CO-OP ADVERTISING

Here are some statements often made by retailers when asked how they feel about co-op advertising:

> *Co-op is too much trouble. I wouldn't use it if it weren't for the money.*

> *I love it!*

> *Co-op is a curse; stores are too dependent on the money, advertising only the merchandise that comes with the largest number of co-op dollars.*

Viewpoints as divergent as these are not uncommon when talking about co-op to anyone in retailing. The first opinion, however, reflects the essence of co-op at the retailer level — money to fund advertising. The use of that money may be as variable as the world of retailing itself, but it forms part of the two basic reasons why most retailers want co-op: getting money to fund advertising and to extend store promotion budgets and getting help with the creation and expansion of store advertising programs. Within those two frameworks — funding and promotional assistance — co-op must fit the basic needs of retail advertising. These common goals include the following:

1. Creative and timely advertising programs that will enhance the image of the stores involved and bring customer traffic into those stores.
2. Advertising of products that are needed and wanted in the store's market area at prices that are competitive and attractive to consumers.
3. Linking of stores to brand name products, frequently through advertising and promotional programs that coincide with national or regional promotions on the part of the vendors.

Except to exclusive dealerships, brand recognition is least important to the retailer. Good retail advertising is structured on offering merchandise that people want to buy, not on co-op dollars. Retailers who carry a variety of merchandise may find it impossible to use all the co-op available from their many suppliers, choosing to advertise only products they feel will produce traffic in their stores.

Co-op as a Money Source. Estimates on how much of the co-op money made available by manufacturers, distributors, and other vendors is spent are varied and unreliable. Media organizations like to talk about the huge sums of co-op dollars that are left "on the table," with concurrent scrambling to get at those elusive dollars.

Current estimates of co-op funding place the amount available in the broad range of $12 to $20 billion annually, which gives an idea of the vast importance co-op holds as a source of advertising funds.

Unquestionably, poor communication between suppliers and customers, combined with ignorance about co-op application, means that fewer co-op dollars are spent than are technically available. But co-op is not a handout nor an open bank account; it is a practical marketing device that is valuable under certain conditions.

As the parties to co-op arrangements (vendors, retailers, and wholesalers) work out better and more effective methods of co-op application, the amount of co-op money spent will increase in relation to the amount that is technically available but never used.

Who spends most of the available co-op funds is a better documented area of marketing information. The large retailing organizations spend most of the co-op money available from their suppliers. Approximately 200 retailers account for some 65 percent of all retail advertising dollars and a correspondingly high percentage of available co-op money.

Co-op and the Big Retailers. To the large organizations who dominate retailing, co-op is primarily a money source. These stores seldom buy merchandise solely on the basis of co-op, but among vendors competing for the business of these large retailers, those having the best or the most flexible co-op programs will be favored.

It is not unusual for a major retailing organization to have an advertising budget that runs into hundreds of millions of dollars annually. Nor is it unlikely that 25 percent of that budget will come from co-op suppliers.

Manufacturers dealing with such retailing giants as Woolworth's, JC Penney, Kmart, Wal Mart, and others must set up co-op programs that fit in with the planning and logistics involved in major promotional efforts. Woolworth's, for instance, includes co-op in the planning and preparation of more than 50 tabloids each year, each with a circulation of more than 15 million, produced in 26 different printing plants across the country.

Handling the major production tasks of programs such as Woolworth's tabloids requires making advertising plans far in advance of actual ad dates. To do their planning, retailers such as Woolworth's expect to have the financial and material commitment of their suppliers from six to eight months ahead of time. Co-op programs unable to make this kind of commitment run the risk of having the products they sell omitted from the advertising programs of large retailing firms.

Collecting co-op money becomes another major task when it assumes the scale found in large organizations. Large retailers can carry millions of dollars in co-op receivables on their books, with many of them 90 to 120 days old. The failure of manufacturers to promptly process retailer claims for co-op can lead to the failure of their co-op programs and negate much of the efforts made by their sales forces. It also can lead to the very common problem of off-invoice deductions for co-op funds without proper claims and documentation, an administrative nightmare.

Large retailers look to their vendors for the same co-op terms: policies that allow products to be featured within the stores' advertising formats, commitments for funding and support far in advance of actual advertising dates, and prompt payment of co-op claims with a minimum of paperwork.

Co-op's Benefits for Smaller Retailers. A good example of what a small retailer can do with co-op money from suppliers can be found in the example of a small clothing store in Cape Cod, Massachusetts. In 1974, the store had an advertising budget of $15,000. Co-op was a minor part of that budget, with only about $2,000 coming from suppliers. The decision was made to adopt a more aggressive advertising program and to seek out co-op funds that might be available by querying all the store's suppliers. The result was the expansion of a $15,000 ad budget to $28,000 using funds from more than 100 different co-op plans.

Another example is an air-conditioning contractor in Augusta, Georgia, who launched his business with advertising that made him, within five years, the largest contractor in the area just by aggressive use of co-op funding from his primary brand name supplier. The contractor, realizing that his competitors were not advertising, even though they had available co-op money, mounted a concentrated television, newspaper, and billboard program that quickly established the name of his business and linked it firmly with the well-known name of the manufacturer he represented, producing a rush of business. Without the strong co-op support this contractor received, his company could not have grown so quickly in so short a time.

Extra Market Effects from Co-op. The air-conditioning contractor's success story has a secondary twist that illustrates the influence co-op can have on an entire market. The contractor's highly visible advertising program spurred his formerly dormant competitors into mounting vigorous advertising efforts using co-op from their suppliers. The result was a tremendous increase in the sale of air-conditioning equipment in the Augusta area. Consumers benefitted from more competitive pricing, and the media were the beneficiaries of many extra advertising dollars.

This air-conditioning contractor's initial co-op advertising efforts and later joint advertising programs involving a group of dealers selling the same brand of equipment did not come about just from co-op funding. The planning and coordination of the advertising were largely the work of the manufacturer's distributor sales force. The sales staff made the dealers aware of what could be done with co-op and worked with them every step of the way. This brings up another important element in good co-op programs: the partnership that develops between the supplier and the retailer in achieving their common goals of increased sales. Like any good business partnership, the successful co-op arrangement takes effort by all concerned.

Co-op Limitations on Retailers. Success stories, such as those of the clothing store and the air-conditioning contractor, abound in the examination of co-op's application in marketing. Co-op is, however, sometimes as capable of limiting a retailer's advertising as it is of expanding it. The majority of co-op programs in use today run contrary to a basic rule of marketing — namely, that advertising and sales promotion should generate sales. Instead, with the accrual system, the programs use the level of a retailer's purchases to determine co-op funding. It is a convenient accounting device used in some form by more than 70 percent of all the U.S. manufacturers who offer co-op to their customers. It is also a device that retailers do not like for the very reason stated: advertising plans are tied to current or past purchases and not to potential sales. The accrual system not only inhibits retail advertising planning, but also frequently puts co-op money where it is not required and starves developing market areas of needed promotional funds. Building flexibility into the co-op accrual system can help avoid these problems. Money can be assigned before purchases are made based on previous purchasing levels. In new markets, or for new dealers, initial funding can be introduced based on anticipated sales, with accruals allowed to catch up as the retailer's business develops.

Co-op and Grocery Retailing. Even in this introductory examination of co-op, it is worth separating grocery retailing from other types of retailing. Once again those unreliable but ubiquitous estimates say that the grocery trade spends 60 percent of all co-op money. Grocery retailing has undergone significant changes, with today's supermarkets carrying a tremendous variety of nongrocery items. This product mix brings more co-op plans into their marketing pictures. At the same time, the grocery industry is faced with intense competition and marginal profits. The industry has tried to increase the cost-effectiveness of advertising and promotion as a partial answer to its problems; consequently, there is more extensive use of co-op.

Grocery retailers are now employing co-op in new and different ways and are aggressively seeking additional funds from their suppliers. Many suppliers have, in turn, altered co-op plans to make those plans more useful to the grocery trade and have developed special co-op programs just for grocery marketing. Packaged goods manufacturers have, for instance, reduced a customary dependence on national advertising for demand effect and have turned toward providing their grocery customers with co-op programs that will provide more localized advertising. Part of this shift has involved the increasing use of television in grocery store advertising. Sales messages similar to those in nationally run television ads can be used at the local level. On the other hand, the traditional grocery store newspaper ad contained little more than product name and price. A "donut" is a prerecorded commercial with a "hole" in the middle to insert current information. For example, a supermarket that advertises frequently will produce a donut spot to highlight its products on sale each week. The commercial is standard except for the inserted message. Donut commercials save money by eliminating the need to produce a new commercial for each new product offering or sale announcement. More extensive use of donut commercials also lends itself to co-op advertising; these commercials carry standard opening and closing messages identifying the store but may feature several different products and prices in the center section. Grocery stores also rely on point-of-purchase sales tools, including videos and in-store "broadcasting" over their public address systems. Some chains are experimenting with the sale of spot advertising on their in-store audio systems to community merchants, so manufacturers are now having to adjust their co-op policies to include this new "medium."

Intense competition among suppliers to the grocery industry has brought about a phenomenon directly affecting promotional budgets. Because product movement in grocery stores is dependent on visibility, shelf space has become the measure of sales success. This has produced the "slotting allowance," which is a charge paid by a manufacturer to get products onto the shelves of a grocery chain, with no related advertising or promotion activity.

Extra Retailer Benefits. When using the air-conditioning contractor as an example of a small retailer's successful use of co-op funds, it was noted that the vendor's sales representative in the territory was due much of the credit. Perhaps the real drama of the co-op marketing technique is seen in a situation such as this one and not in the allocation of megadollar budgets. Co-op works hardest when it is a retailer's basic source of advertising assistance, as well as financial support. To many small retailers, who often know very little about advertising, the co-op arrangement plays a vital part in the survival and growth of their businesses. Help received from knowledgeable manufacturer or media sales representatives in planning promotions, advertising copy, and materials supplied by vendors, and opportunities to participate in joint advertising programs using pooled co-op money, are all tremendously important to retailers who lack the ability and the staff needed to handle their own advertising and promotion programs.

In addition to assistance in the use of conventional advertising media such as newspapers, radio, and television, small retailers also benefit from all the extras included in most well-planned co-op programs, such as signs, point-of-purchase material, Yellow Pages listings, product catalogs and literature, and even uniforms for service personnel.

Summary. The function of co-op is more limited at the retailers' level than it is at the manufacturers' level because retailers' goals are more immediate in nature. Retailers want to run advertising that will bring traffic into their stores and only secondarily to link their establishments with national brand name products. Most retailers, particularly large ones, can be very selective about which products to advertise, and they will not use co-op simply because it is available to them. Smaller retailers are far more dependent on co-op to enhance their advertising budgets and for the additional advertising help and material that comes with many manufacturer co-op programs.

Retailers and manufacturers share the common advertising and promotional goal of selling merchandise to the public, but retailers are also selling their places of business. In pursuing this latter aim, retailers use co-op and try to exercise as much control as possible over its application. The struggle for control of funds produces one of the basic conflicts of the co-op system. Co-op itself, however, provides sound benefits to both parties. The manufacturers who offer co-op encourage promotion and sales of their products by retailers, get local exposure, and reduce advertising costs. The retailers benefit from the co-op funding by the availability of more professionally prepared advertising material and by being linked to a nationally recognized brand name. These joint benefits have given co-op a secure place in our marketing system.

THE WHOLESALER'S PLACE IN THE CO-OP CHAIN

In the vertical chain of co-op advertising that links the manufacturer to the retailer, there is quite frequently a middleman: the wholesaler or distributor. The presence of the wholesaler can have varying degrees of influence on the co-op arrangement, depending on the way in which a manufacturer establishes a co-op program.

Wholesalers and distributors, when handling a particular product line, may have exclusive sales territories. Some manufacturers may also sell their products directly to larger retailers within their distributors' sales territories. In other cases, the types of products sold may not lend themselves to exclusive distributorships and are available to the market through several wholesalers with overlapping sales territories. These different methods of distribution influence how co-op advertising reaches the retailer by way of a wholesaler.

Types of Wholesaler Co-op Plans. Manufacturers who sell through exclusive distributorships set up co-op plans in which the distributor is the customer. Under these plans no direct payments are made to retailers; all co-op funds go to the distributor. The manufacturer's policy is, however, tied to retail-level advertising with the requirement that proof of such advertising be available for audit. The distributor is expected to have a co-op policy with rules that conform to the manufacturer's co-op specifications. The distributor may also share advertising costs with the manufacturer, becoming a co-op provider in the process. The manufacturer is expected to be sure that distributors provide co-op to competing retailers on a proportionately equal basis. This can be a source of problems, because it is difficult for a manufacturer to determine how much product each retailer has purchased from the distributor. Distributors and wholesalers may be required, when using manufacturer co-op money, to furnish records of retailer purchases to verify their eligibility.

In other types of policies, wholesalers may be no more than conduits for co-op information and materials. Retailers make their claims for reimbursement directly to the manufacturer or service organization, providing wholesaler invoices as proofs of their purchases.

Combination Retailer and Wholesaler Plans. When a manufacturer sells directly to some retailers in one market and through wholesalers to others, co-op policies may differ for each category of customer. While the policies may vary, each must result in providing competing retailers with proportionately equal benefits. Combination programs have to base co-op funding on two different price structures — the one paid by the direct purchasing retailer and the one paid by the wholesaler. To provide comparable benefits for those retailers buying from the wholesaler sometimes requires the addition of the wholesaler's money to the co-op funding. It is still the manufacturer's responsibility to be sure that the proportionately equal doctrine is adhered to at the retailer level.

Wholesaler Co-op Objectives. When using co-op, wholesalers share the goals of both the manufacturers they represent and the retailers who are their customers. Most wholesaler advertising and promotional programs contain the following two basic objectives:

1. **Building market share.** Increasing market penetration for product lines handled is a distributor or wholesaler's main promotional aim. To expand sales, distributors usually try to involve as many retail customers as possible in organized advertising efforts built on specific products and brand names. Such wholesaler organized and directed advertising may pool available dealer co-op money to mount joint advertising that covers an entire sales territory. When conducting this type of promotional program, the wholesaler's goals closely parallel those of the manufacturer, with emphasis given to product, brand name, and features. The difference is in the ability of the wholesaler to adapt to small markets with advertising that includes both pricing and localized promotional offers and is centered on individual retailers. This is something that manufacturers can seldom do except when selling directly through large retailers and chains.

2. **Building the wholesale organization.** Wholesalers can use co-op as a device to build up their businesses by increasing sales to retail customers and helping to get new customers. Most wholesalers are keenly aware of how important retail advertising is to their success, and they aim at keeping continuous promotional activity going in which their retailers can participate, which makes them better sources than competing

wholesalers. To fund various promotion programs, wholesalers will use whatever co-op money is available.

Multiproduct wholesalers are interested in obtaining co-op help and money from a number of suppliers, pooling the money to fund various advertising programs. Examples of this type of wholesaler advertising are the circulars and newspaper inserts of hardware stores and automotive parts stores, which are usually produced by their wholesalers using co-op funds. The advertising is intended to generate sales by increasing store traffic, which is the motive for the retailer's use of co-op.

How Manufacturers Gain from Wholesaler Co-op Efforts. Because many national co-op programs are too broad in scope to fit individual market needs, there are real advantages in channeling those programs through wholesalers. Being one step closer to the retail firing line, wholesalers can adapt co-op to regional or local market needs and are very often innovative in doing this. Many manufacturers have taken successful distributor programs and built them into national co-op programs. Other manufacturers make it a point to share information on successful advertising among their distributors.

From a practical standpoint, using or adapting good wholesaler co-op programs is a way to get field-tested advertising into a national co-op offering. This also makes a good case for closer coordination between national and distributor sales promotion personnel and the structuring of such organizations as distributor advertising councils to discuss common marketing goals.

Wholesaler Contribution to Co-op. When manufacturers distribute their products through wholesalers, the intermediary firm plays an important role in the application of co-op, a role often overlooked or minimized in outside studies of co-op marketing techniques. The salesperson in the field, usually the wholesaler's representative, is charged with persuading retailers to advertise and to use their co-op funding. The local sales representative must also work with groups of retailers in his or her territory, showing them how to use co-op material and helping them to set up joint co-op advertising. In addition to selling products to these retailers, the wholesaler's representative has to function as a sales promotion adviser.

Wholesaler management also must be familiar with the use of co-op and structure co-op advertising programs that cover entire sales territories, handling all the administrative problems that go with those programs. Necessity has made wholesalers particularly adept at using co-op, and manufacturers can normally count on them to take all available co-op money. These organizations deserve more credit and recognition than they are given when co-op is written about or discussed.

INGREDIENT PRODUCER CO-OP PLANS

In addition to manufacturers, retailers, and wholesalers, another party sometimes enters the co-op picture — a producer of the ingredients contained in a finished product. The makers of synthetic fibers, for example, are interested in the sale of carpets; cotton growers, in the sale of clothing; orange growers, in the sale of orange juices; and coffee growers, in the sale of coffee. Fabrics have been leaders in this field, but many other basic ingredient manufacturers promote end products at retail through ingredient co-op plans.

Ingredient producer co-op plans differ from conventional co-op because there is no direct buyer-seller relationship, so the offer of co-op is not a pricing factor. Ingredient producers can choose where and how they feel their money can be best used.

Most ingredient producer co-op money is connected with promotions of higher-priced merchandise. The programs are set up through powerful retailers who can influence a market. Ingredient co-op policies want the ingredient to be prominently identified either by brand name or through a logo or promotional name used by a trade association in its own advertising. The aim of these programs is to sell the consumer on the desirability of the ingredient, to help establish the ingredient as a selling advantage to the retailer, and to encourage use of the ingredient by manufacturers.

Because the retailer may be several steps removed from the supplier of ingredient co-op, there is no practical way of relating money to sales. Ingredient plans usually designate advertising dollars by market, by retailer, and by medium; then they tie these limits to specific types of products advertised within given time periods. The lack of a buyer-seller relationship has been held to exclude ingredient co-op plans from the Robinson-Patman Act's restrictions that require proportionately equal co-op offerings to competing retailers.

The use of ingredient co-op funds produces the problem of a retailer taking money from two sources and making claims against both. Manufacturer co-op plans must be written to require that extra funding be deducted from a claim before the manufacturer's share is calculated.

INDUSTRIAL CO-OP ADVERTISING

Shared advertising cost in the form of programs similar to those offered for consumer products is also a part of marketing for a number of industrial products. This is an area where the use of co-op is rapidly increasing.

The basic concepts of industrial co-op are the same as those found in consumer goods co-op, but the style is different because the industrial co-op advertiser is speaking to other businesses. The industrial advertiser who uses co-op is rarely trying to attract floor traffic but instead is trying to establish a business as a source for sales and service on a particular product line and to open doors for salespeople. Industrial co-op plans are usually smaller and more limited than their consumer co-op equivalents, so they are likely to be less formal and restricted. Many business-to-business co-op programs do not have written policies, making funds available on demand or through arrangements set up by supplier sales reps.

Many consumer goods manufacturers also make industrial products and so offer co-op in both areas. There is also an overlap of consumer and industrial markets for any number of products such as automobiles, appliances, and electronics.

In business-to-business advertising, manufacturers find many of the co-op advantages known to their counterparts in retail advertising, for example, closer association with sales outlets, lower regional advertising costs, or better adaptation of advertising to market needs. Unlike retail outlets, however, most industrial product sales outlets are tied closely to their suppliers, so their local co-op–funded advertising can be a more accurate reflection of the manufacturers' national programs.

CO-OP IN SERVICE INDUSTRIES

The U.S. economy has become one that derives most of its income from the sale of services instead of manufactured products. As it has in the marketing of manufactured products, co-op has found a place in the marketing of services.

Co-op is usually applied in the promotion of services only where there is a vertical relationship similar to the one found in the manufacturer-retailer chain. In the sale of services, there is no product and only an after-the-fact income based on charges to the consumer. Expenses do not involve inventories or large capital investments in manufacturing plants and materials, only direct overhead plus labor costs. Because there is no product or "commodity" involved in the sale of services, the restrictions of the Robinson-Patman Act and the FTC guidelines do not apply to co-op programs in this field of marketing.

The techniques of mass marketing are as applicable to services as they are to consumer products. Individual real estate firms, quick copy shops, personnel agencies, wedding photographers, income tax preparers, karate studios, auto rental agencies, and many of the thousands of service organizations that now serve the consuming public can more effectively promote under a recognizable brand name backed up with national advertising. The marketing device used for cohesive promotion of services is often the license-to-sell authorization or the franchise agreement, which can give even the smallest shops a national identity and framework for advertising — a vertical relationship selling a name instead of a product.

Advertising and promotion plans are part of most franchising and licensing agreements, but co-op is not always present. Without merchandise to sell and with income derived from franchise fees or service charges, it is difficult to set a basis for co-op funding.

In franchise organizations, there is a reluctance on the part of franchise management to become involved in sharing advertising costs with franchise holders, who are independent businesses operating under a common framework. But franchise service businesses are encouraged to advertise by the franchiser through the offer of limited co-op — with participation based on factors such as the number of franchises in a trade area — by making fixed amounts of co-op money available each year or by establishing co-op as a percentage of the franchise's sales. In addition, the franchiser will supply various types of local advertising and promotion material and lay out promotional plans for the franchise holder.

Co-op for services is part of the promotion planning of many different types of manufacturers when the services are vital to the sale of their products. In the automobile industry, co-op advertising is provided for service because the sale of cars is dependent on service availability. In areas such as heating and air conditioning or home appliances, co-op for service advertising is important because a large volume of new product sales comes from replacement of the old or defective equipment found during service calls. Appliance manufacturers have also discovered and are promoting a new source of revenue: the extended service contract. In the aircraft industry, manufacturers provide co-op to flight schools that use their aircraft, with the knowledge that training pilots is necessary to the continued sale of airplanes. Regional telephone companies, so long restricted by regulations, now market a variety of business and consumer services through independent sales organizations and retailers. Co-op is playing an important role in the expansion of these services. A good example can be found in the cellular telephone market, where co-op and sales incentive funds provided by the service suppliers support advertising, sales commissions, and even the cost of the telephone equipment itself.

HORIZONTAL CO-OP ADVERTISING

Advertising among franchise shops, while sometimes backed with co-op from the franchiser, is more often a joint agreement among all the franchises in a trade area to pool resources for advertising. This is an example of how co-op becomes horizontal instead of vertical, because the cost sharing is all at the same marketing level.

Horizontal co-op also figures in many vertical co-op programs, because the pooling of retailer funds is a common method used to increase advertising levels in various markets. In such cases, vertical co-op from a manufacturer or wholesaler and horizontal co-op from groups of retailers are pooled to fund a regional or area-wide advertising campaign. Since this type of joint effort may include competing retailers, the advertising and the co-op arrangement has to stay clear of preferential treatment or specific pricing.

Even where there is no vertical participation, horizontal co-op is a common marketing device. Groups of automobile dealers pool funds to increase brand awareness without factory participation, as do retailer groups selling many other consumer products.

There are hundreds of other examples of common business interests producing jointly funded advertising. Industrial advertising also sees a great deal of this type of promotional effort, sometimes under the auspices of trade associations, sometimes as a result of promotion-minded groups within an industry that band together to achieve more advertising impact.

MUTUAL-INTEREST HORIZONTAL CO-OP

Horizontal co-op can be found in advertising done by different businesses that get customers from each other's services. Airlines may offer co-op to travel agencies. Credit card companies may offer co-op advertising to businesses such as hotels, car rental outlets, and major department stores that honor their cards.

Wherever one form of business can scratch another's back, there is the potential for mutual-interest horizontal co-op advertising. A substantial amount of co-op falls into this category, and it is sometimes part of a vertical co-op arrangement in the same way as ingredient co-op. In the days of cheap energy, for instance, power companies would augment co-op funds available from manufacturers of electric appliances as a way of increasing the demand for electricity. Today they offer similar advertising incentives to retailers for selling energy-efficient appliances. That funding goes to retailers who also may receive manufacturer co-op, thus substantially expanding their advertising budgets.

WHEN SHARING IS A POSITIVE FORCE

Wherever co-op appears in our marketing-oriented economy, it is a positive force that aids in the efficient movement of all types of products and in the sale of many different services. Approximately half of the retail advertising in newspapers is co-op funded. A large amount of broadcast advertising revenue is derived from co-op, and an increasing amount of magazine advertising is now coming from this marketing device. It would be fair to say that not just advertising, but co-op advertising, is the financial underpinning of our society's major communications systems and of our free press.

Co-op is often misunderstood, frequently cumbersome, and has many drawbacks and disadvantages; but it has withstood the test of time in our marketing system and continues to gain in importance and become more widespread in application each year. Knowing how to use co-op and what it involves is important to anyone in the field of retail marketing.

COMPONENTS OF A CO-OP POLICY

All co-op policies should be written documents that clearly spell out the terms under which co-op funds are offered by a vendor to a retailer. Those terms involve the following:

1. Funding. Above all, co-op is a financial arrangement, money paid out for services rendered. The amount of funding is very basic to any co-op policy. The vendor must decide how to accrue or assign money to customers in the form of co-op or other promotional allowances. That financial decision rests on the various aims of the co-op program — for example, product line profitability, market needs, or competitive conditions. Once the method of funding is decided, then a system must be set up to make the assignments and to track the funding as it accrues to retailers. In writing the co-op policy, the conditions for funding must be made very clear to the retailer or wholesaler. Because funding is so very basic to co-op, it is also a major source of problems. Retailers consider accrued co-op money as if it were in a reserve for their use. Co-op, however, is neither a handout nor a bank account. To get the co-op money, a retailer must fulfill the requirements of the co-op policy for advertising or promoting a product.

Manufacturers do not accrue the amount of money based on customer purchases that is stated in their co-op policies. Instead, they use their own or their industry's experience on co-op usage and accrue only the amount they think will be used.

2. Advertising conditions. The co-op policy must define exactly what the retailer must do in the form of advertising or promotion to get co-op reimbursement. These conditions fall into five general categories:

Amount of reimbursement. The policy must show how much of the advertising cost the supplier will pay. In most co-op policies the cost sharing is equal, or 50-50. But there are many variations, with some that pay 100 percent or more of the retailer's advertising cost. Market and industry factors enter in to how much a supplier pays in co-op.

Approved media. Here is where a supplier can direct the use of co-op funds to the areas most helpful to the sale of its products. Certain media, for example, can be emphasized by setting co-op at a level higher than the amount paid for other media.

Advertising content. These rules tell the retailer how the supplier's products must appear and be described in local advertising, how logos must be used, what trademark and tradename restrictions apply, and where pre-approval is required.

Timing of advertising. This condition specifies the period in which the co-op policy is in effect, usually a calendar or fiscal year, and whether there are any seasonal limitations on advertised products and funding.

Reimbursement procedures. This rule spells out what the retailer must do to get co-op reimbursement from the supplier. This includes how and when to file a co-op claim and what proof of advertising is required in the form of media invoices, tearsheets, or scripts.

Making these co-op specifications and requirements should be done in simple, readable terms. The conditions themselves should not be difficult to fulfill, and they should fit in with both the supplier's and the retailer's capabilities and objectives. Many co-op policies are too complicated, with resulting loss in advertising and promotion effort at the retail level — exactly the opposite of what co-op is intended to accomplish for the supplier.

Karen Raugust has been Editor of The Licensing Letter, *a monthly newsletter published by EPM Communications, since 1991. In addition to writing and editing TLL, Raugust writes EPM's other licensing-related publications, including the* Licensing Business Profit and Opportunity Outlook *and the* Licensing Business Databook. *She also serves as Editor of the* EPM Licensing Business Sourcebook *and contributes to EPM's* Entertainment Marketing Letter. *Raugust acts as a consultant to the licensing community through EPM's 60-Minutes Consultant service, and she is frequently quoted in the business and consumer press.*

Raugust has a B.A. from Carleton College and an MBA from Columbia University.

CHAPTER 14

PRODUCT LICENSING AND TIE-INS

Both retail licensing (the purchase of the rights to a legally protected name, logo, design, or likeness for use on an item to be sold for
profit) and promotional tie-ins (licensing agreements for an advertising
or promotional use) have grown exponentially over the last decade.
Retail sales of licensed products in North America, for example, have
tripled from a total of $20.6 billion in 1982 to $62.2 billion in 1992,
according to figures compiled by *The Licensing Letter*. Since 1990,
growth has leveled off; the market for licensed products has matured
after close to 15 years of enormous growth. In addition, a recession
adversely affected retailing in the early 1990s.

Still, a $60 billion-plus business is significant, and product
licensing has become recognized as an effective way for an owner of a
legally protected name, graphic, or likeness (a property) to earn significant revenue. A manufacturer who associates with a particular property
(the licensee) stands to increase awareness of its products without having to build a brand from scratch. Simply being linked with a licensed
property is not in itself enough to guarantee increased sales, of course.
But licensing, as part of a total marketing strategy, can be a successful
sales tool if the fit between product and property is a logical one.

The potential of a licensed property to drive product sales has
been proven by such examples as the Teenage Mutant Ninja Turtles
and *Star Wars*. According to the companies that handle these licensing
programs, merchandise based on the Turtles surpassed $5 billion at
retail in six years beginning in 1987, while products based on the *Star
Wars* movie trilogy rang up more than $2.5 billion over six years start-
ing in 1977. In the sports area, retail sales of both Major League
Baseball and National Football League merchandise surpass $2 billion
annually.

While these examples illustrate the *potential* of a large licensing
program, it is not accurate to say that such blockbusters are the only
way to make money through licensing. Smaller, more targeted programs also can be lucrative for the property owner (the licensor) and
effective marketing tools for the manufacturers permitted to make
property-based merchandise. For example, the television show
Northern Exposure spawned a licensing program focusing on cold-
weather wear and a limited number of collectible items, marketed to its
core audience primarily through direct response.

It is also important to realize when thinking about licensing that
there are two types of programs: those based on classic, evergreen
properties (Mickey Mouse, Looney Tunes, or Peanuts, for example),
and those based on short-term, "hot" properties (such as 1989's

Batman movie, which tallied worldwide retail sales of $1.3 billion, or 1990's *The Simpsons*, which sold over $2.1 billion worth of products worldwide, mostly in the space of a year and a half). A short-term property, if well managed, allows the licensor and licensees to garner significant revenues over a short period by selling merchandise in several — even hundreds — of product categories. The classic property, on the other hand, brings in less revenue in a given year than a "hot" property might at its peak, but it will be a steady business for its licensor and associated manufacturers over many years. This scenario assumes that the program is managed so that it does not oversaturate the market with products, thus causing the property's demise. Licensors and licensees who use licensing as a primary focus of their business strategy generally prefer to combine a selection of short-term properties with some steady, evergreen ones.

As in product licensing, promotional tie-ins can also utilize both evergreen and short-term properties. A tie-in is a form of licensing agreement whereby a company pays a fee for the right to use a property in conjunction with an advertising or promotional campaign (that is, for nonretail product uses). It is difficult to come up with a figure for the value of tie-ins, in part because much of the "payment" comes in the form of trade-outs (that is, the donation of something of value to the promotion in return for something else of value without cash changing hands). *Entertainment Marketing Letter,* an industry publication, estimated the value of tie-ins involving video releases alone at $110 million in 1991; that figure was higher in 1992. (The $110 million incorporates the total value of measurable media time and space, tradeout exposure, premiums, cash payments, and the value of on-cassette advertising by all promotional partners for all of the video promotions done that year.)

On the high end of the spectrum, a single multipartner tie-in can be valued as high as $50 to $60 million. Examples include a tie-in surrounding the video release of Walt Disney's *Beauty & the Beast* in 1992, or the CBS television network's promotion supporting its fall 1992 schedule, which involved Nabisco and Kmart as primary promotional partners.

While tie-ins can have a high monetary value attached to them in terms of what is brought to the table by the various partners, they can also be lucrative sales tools. As in the case of product licensing, however, the fit between the partners, the property, and the promotional elements must be sound.

While huge corporations with deep pockets, such as Coca-Cola and Pepsi, McDonald's and Burger King, and Nabisco, play a major role in tie-ins, there is also room for smaller companies to engage in creative promotions. A small marketer can participate as one of many partners (which spreads the costs over several players). Or, it can develop a targeted tie-in, such as with a special-interest videocassette.

For example, in 1992 Nutrasweet tied in successfully with an exercise video starring the actress Cher. It can also link itself with past hits, such as classic films, or with less-than-hit characters that are popular with its target audience.

PRODUCT LICENSING

The main players of any licensing agreement are the *licensor* (the property owner) and the *licensee* (the purchaser of the rights to the property). The *property* is the trademarked or copyrighted entity, be it a character, design, name, logo, sports league or team, event, or likeness. In some cases, a *licensing agent* will also be involved. The agent acts on behalf of the licensor in seeking appropriate licensees, negotiating contracts, and overseeing the licensing program. *Manufacturers' representatives* sometimes act on behalf of licensees in seeking appropriate licensed properties for their products.

The types of properties licensed out for other products fall into 10 major categories:

- **Art**, which includes copyrighted designs and fine art for use on a wide range of products;
- **Celebrities and estates**, which include the likenesses and names of famous people such as James Dean, Marilyn Monroe, Laurel & Hardy, and many others;
- **Designer names**, particularly in fashion and home furnishings, such as Gloria Vanderbilt, Ralph Lauren, Donna Karan, and Bob Timberlake;
- **Entertainment and character properties**, which comprise films, television, classic cartoon characters, and comic book superheroes;
- **Music and musical artists**, including Elvis Presley, New Kids On The Block, and the Grateful Dead;
- **Nonprofit organizations**, such as the World Wildlife Fund and other environmental groups, relief organizations including CARE, medical research and money-raising organizations;
- **Publishing**, which includes book characters such as Waldo from the *Where's Waldo?* series, or Babar the elephant, as well as magazines (*Playboy, Cosmopolitan*) and book titles (*The Baby-Sitter's Club*);
- **Sports**, incorporating all four major leagues and colleges, as well as other sports entities such as the Olympics, NASCAR auto racing, soccer, wrestling, and so forth;
- **Trademarks and corporate brands**, from all areas, especially apparel brands (J.G. Hook), footwear (Converse), automotive trademarks (Jeep, Harley-Davidson), and food and beverage brands (Betty Crocker, Coca-Cola, Budweiser); and
- **Toys and games**, that license out into other products, such as

Barbie, LEGO, G.I. Joe, Transformers, Hot Wheels, and videogame characters such as Super Mario Brothers and Sonic the Hedgehog.

Table 14.1 shows the relative importance of each of these segments in terms of the amount of retail sales attributable to them in 1992. Trademark licensing ranks as the largest segment, followed by characters/entertainment and sports licensing.

Each of these types of properties is licensed out for innumerable product categories. In fact, almost every type of product you can imagine has been associated at one time or another with some kind of license — hot dogs, milk caps, condoms, you name it. The major categories, however, are listed in Table 14.2, along with their relative retail sales for 1992.

Many manufacturing companies find that both licensing in (that is, purchasing rights to a property for one of their products) and licensing out (selling the rights to their own properties) fit into their strategy; thus, they act as licensors and licensees. For example, the toy manufacturer Mattel oversees licensing programs based on its own properties, Barbie and Hot Wheels, extending to apparel, accessories, and many other products. Meanwhile, they also manufacture toys under license from other companies, such as plush toys based on Walt Disney animated films, fashion dolls based on the television show *Beverly Hills 90210,* and Nickelodeon brand games and activity toys.

The Licensor's Role. From the licensor's point of view, licensing is lucrative monetarily. In fact, for some films, the advances from licensing agreements help pay for the production of the film itself; the film's existence is predicated upon expected future licensing income. In addition, licensing increases awareness of a new property. For example, consumers will be exposed to their local sports teams not only through print and broadcast advertising and sportscasts, but also by the logoed products in nearly every department of the stores where they shop.

Property owners also use licensing to extend a franchise into new product categories in which the company does not have expertise, and new distribution channels where the brand does not currently exist. For example, Marvel Entertainment manufactures comic books. But in order to extend its "X-Men" and "Superheroes" brands into new product categories (such as toys), it opts to license its brands to other manufacturers because its own expertise is in publishing. Licensing also minimizes the financial risk of developing new products from the licensor's point of view, because the research and development costs generally lie with the licensee.

On the other hand, the licensor does face some challenges. These include the possibility of diluting the property's value if licensees produce poor-quality products, and the probability of shortening a property's life span if the market becomes oversaturated with products. The

TABLE 14.1

1992 Shares of Licensed Product Retail Sales by Property Type
(Dollar Figures in Billions)

Property Type	1992 Retail Sales	Pct. All Sales
Art	$4.4	7.1%
Celebrity/Estate	$2.4	3.9%
Designer Names	$5.0	8.0%
Entertainment/Character	$14.1	22.7%
Music	$0.9	1.4%
Non-Profit	$0.6	1.0%
Publishing	$1.4	2.3%
Sports	$12.1	19.5%
Trademarks/Brands	$18.6	29.9%
Toys/Games	$2.5	4.0%
Other	$0.2	0.3%
TOTAL	$62.2	100.0%

Source: The Licensing Letter

© *Copyright 1993 EPM Communications*

TABLE 14.2

1992 Shares of Licensed Product Retail Sales by Product Category
(Dollar Figures in Billions)

Product Category	1992 Retail Sales	Pct. All Sales
Accessories	$5.9	9.5%
Apparel	$10.7	17.2%
Domestics	$4.0	6.4%
Electronics	$1.0	1.6%
Food/Beverage	$5.0	8.0%
Footwear	$1.9	3.1%
Furniture/Home Furnishings	$0.7	1.1%
Gifts/Novelties	$5.5	8.8%
Health/Beauty	$3.5	5.6%
Housewares	$2.0	3.2%
Infant Products	$2.0	3.2%
Music/Video	$1.1	1.8%
Publishing	$4.1	6.6%
Sporting Goods	$2.1	3.4%
Stationery/Paper	$2.9	4.7%
Toys/Games	$6.6	10.6%
Videogames/Software	$3.0	4.8%
Other	$0.2	0.3%
TOTAL	$62.2	100.0%

Source: The Licensing Letter

© *Copyright 1993 EPM Communications*

property's brand image can also be hurt if branded products end up in the wrong distribution channel — that is, if a product based on an upscale brand, perceived by consumers to be of high quality, ends up in a mass market chain, the brand itself and all associated licensed products will risk being hurt.

To minimize the effect of these challenges and to help ensure the success of the program, the licensor's responsibilities include the following:

- Adequately protecting the copyrights and trademarks involved for all properties in all geographic areas where licensing will be undertaken and for all appropriate product categories;
- Maintaining the quality and value inherent in the property itself through specifying appropriate art and logos for licensees' use and instituting a rigorous product approval process;
- Selecting quality licensees, keeping a rein on the number of manufacturers and product categories to avoid market oversaturation;
- Supporting licensees and retailers by creating and maintaining the property's awareness through point-of-sale materials and other in-store signage, by arranging tie-ins and publicity, by encouraging licensees to work together in cross-promotions, and by convincing retailers of the benefit of displaying all licensed products together in one area of the store; and
- Extending the franchise and keeping it fresh through line extensions (for example, focusing on the Baby Bart and Maggie characters of *The Simpsons* appeals to new mothers), sub-brands (Walt Disney's Princess Collection as a sub-brand for girls, incorporating princesses from various Disney films), sequels (the Ninja Turtles' three films over six years), and new media (such as *Batman: The Animated Series* to extend the *Batman* film property).

A licensing program offering all of these elements would be an ideal scenario; however, many licensors do not provide the whole package. This situation is slowly beginning to change as the market for licensed properties matures. Licensors are beginning to realize that the long-term success of their programs requires them to take responsibility for more than just trademarking and copyrighting their properties and arranging for licensees. And manufacturers and retailers are starting to demand all of the elements listed above before signing on to a property.

The Licensee's Contribution. For the manufacturer that pays for the right to use a property in association with its products, licensing provides the immediate awareness that is attached to a known entity, thus providing brand awareness without having to build a brand from scratch. The property itself generates awareness in the minds of consumers, with little need for additional advertising by the manufacturer to create that awareness. The various licensed products based on the same property also serve to advertise each other throughout the store and across various distribution channels.

An association with a licensed property can also create an entry into a new distribution channel to which a manufacturer does not currently sell. For example, a particular apparel manufacturer may not be selling to Wal Mart. But an exclusive association with a hot character license may be a significant incentive for Wal Mart to try the firm as a new resource; if the relationship is successful, the retailer may continue to work with the vendor on some of its other, nonlicensed brands.

In addition, a license can give a product an immediate image of quality with its consumers, who may not be familiar with the manufacturer's own name or brands. The food brand Betty Crocker, for example, is perceived by consumers as a high-quality, valued food brand. Consumers translate that same perception of quality to Betty Crocker-licensed housewares products. This image automatically provides a distinct competitive advantage to the bakeware or appliance manufacturer who holds such a license (see Exhibit 14.1).

Licensing can also exhibit a down side for the manufacturer. Any new, unproven property — especially films or television shows — may flop, in which case consumers might hold unfavorable opinions

EXHIBIT 14.1

about merchandise associated with it; perhaps they may not even have heard of the property at all. Second, for all types of properties, a portion of the payment — sometimes a large amount of money — is usually paid up front as an advance and is nonrefundable. Thus, if the property fails or if the fit between property and product is not right, the manufacturer loses the advance money, as well as any development and manufacturing costs.

Timing is another important issue. A short window of opportunity exists for peak sales on entertainment-based merchandise (about six weeks for the average stand-alone film), which means that any delay in production or delivery can cause a significant chunk of potential sales to be lost.

Licensees are responsible for product development and manufacturing of the product (subject to the specifications of and product approvals by the licensor), as well as selling to their own distribution channels. (Manufacturers that bring a large range of distribution channels to the party often have the advantage over other companies in terms of being selected as a licensee.) Potential licensees are sometimes expected to provide advertising to trade and consumer channels, as well.

Evaluation of Potential Partners. Negotiations can be initiated by either the licensor or the potential licensee. Both sides need to carefully evaluate each other as potential partners — the personal relationship between licensee and licensor is among the most important elements of the agreement. While licensing agreements can be terminated at the end of the contract period if either side fails to perform up to expectations, both partners would prefer to select a company that they can trust to keep up its end of the bargain.

A licensor looks for the following information from potential licensees in order to evaluate their requests for a license:

- Product quality (in the form of samples, current catalogs, promotional materials, or price lists);
- Distribution channels, including largest retail accounts and contact names of buyers at those outlets (The fit of distribution channels — upscale or mass market — with the property's image is as important as the number of outlets);
- Annual gross sales and volume for recent years;
- Annual advertising and promotion budgets for several prior years;
- Credit information;
- Proposed merchandise that the licensee plans to manufacture under license and samples of those products;
- Proposed timing — that is, when the various products will be introduced at retail; and
- Projected sales for the potential licensed merchandise.

In turn, prospective licensees must also evaluate the licensors —

simply owning a popular property is not enough to provide the basis for an agreement. Licensees need to evaluate whether the property is short-term or evergreen and which type better fits their strategic goals. Is the target customer for the property the same as the licensee's target audience? Does the property itself — animated series, film, live-action series, sports event, personality, design, trademarked brand — provide excitement or value and promise to maintain its current image? What types of support does the licensor provide to licensees and retailers in terms of promotion and advertising? How does the licensor plan to maintain the longevity of the property and keep it fresh? What other licensees are involved in the program? Manufacturers should feel free to ask for a licensee list and contact references.

Agents and Manufacturers' Representatives. Some licensors assign their properties to licensing agents, who represent that property — often exclusively — in various geographic territories or for selected product categories. Agents have contacts throughout the industry and are able to help with the licensee selection process, oversee royalty payments, expedite product approvals, and assist in identifying appropriate product categories for a licensor to fill. With their expertise, agents can be beneficial to new licensors because they will significantly shorten the learning curve. Many agents focus on one segment of licensing, be it trademarks, entertainment licenses, designers, or sports properties. Agencies range from one-person operations representing only one or a few properties to relatively large entities representing a long list of clients. In return for their expertise, agents are paid a percentage — usually between 25 percent and 50 percent — of royalty income.

Licensees, on the other hand, occasionally retain manufacturers' representatives or consultants to help them identify appropriate licensed properties for their products. They, too, have extensive contacts within the industry and are able to help manufacturers launch and maintain their licensing efforts.

Trademark and Copyright. Since licensing centers around the use of various rights to a protected trademark, logo, design, or likeness, adequately protecting the copyrights and/or trademarks in question is an essential part of the licensor's role. The following brief definitions do not even begin to skim the surface of the legal intricacies involved in trademark and copyright protection; they are meant as a simple launching point.

Copyright is legal protection for intellectual works including artistic and literary endeavors, among others, whether published or unpublished. Art and graphics to be licensed must be copyrighted. Titles, short phrases, names, and type cannot be copyrighted. In general, copyrights last until 50 years after the author's or artist's death (for works created after January 1, 1978).

Words, names, symbols, and combinations of these must be

trademarked. Logos and short phrases associated with brands ("Diet Pepsi, Uh-Huh") are also trademarked. Company names (trade names) cannot be trademarked, but brands must be, in order to be legally protected.

For information on copyright definitions, procedures, duration, and costs, contact the Copyright Office of the Library of Congress, in Washington, D.C. Trademarks are under the jurisdiction of the U.S. Patent and Trademark Office, also in Washington, D.C.

Because the licensing business really hinges on the existence of a legally protected entity — all of the information in this chapter is moot if the property is not adequately protected in every area where licensing will be undertaken — the lawyer you select should preferably specialize in the licensing business. Several such attorneys exist, now that licensing has become such a widespread activity among many diverse types of companies.

Payment. The royalty is the main component of payment for the right to use a property in conjunction with a retail product. Royalties are paid as a percentage of the wholesale price of all products sold. They are negotiable on a case-by-case basis — there is no business-wide standard royalty — and they vary greatly, from a low of 2–3 percent for some agreements to as high as 18–20 percent for others. Royalties average just over 7 percent across all property types and product categories.

A number of factors play a role in determining the specific royalty rate. The popularity of the property affects the rate; the more people who want a particular property, the higher its price will be. Short-term entertainment properties that are unique in some way, for example, generally command a higher rate than a corporate trademark or art property where hundreds of fairly similar properties compete. A film that is expected to be the star performer of the year in terms of sales of licensed merchandise can command 10 percent to 12 percent (even as high as 16 percent on occasion), while an artist's design may result in a range of 3 percent to 6 percent.

The product category affects royalty rates as well. Products with lower profit margins end up with lower royalty rates; low margins only allow for a certain royalty percentage before licensing becomes non-cost-effective. Food product manufacturers, for instance, generally pay low royalties of 2 percent to 3 percent, while a fine-art poster producer may pay 10 percent for the rights to the same property. Children's apparel firms fall in the middle, at 4–8 percent (see Table 14.3).

Some manufacturer expenses are subtracted from the royalty payment (although this, too, is negotiable). Cash discounts, freight charges, and returns are often deductible, while advertising costs are not. A cap of 2 percent to 5 percent of royalty income is usually placed on the allowable deductions.

TABLE 14.3

Average Royalty by Product Category, 1992

Product Category	Average Royalty	Range
Accessories	7.5%	3-15%
Apparel	7.5%	4-12%
Domestics	6.0%	3-10%
Electronics (non-game)	7.5%	5-10%
Food & Beverage	3.0%	1-5%
Footwear	6.0%	4-11%
Furniture/Home Furnishings	6.0%	2-10%
Gifts/Novelties	8.5%	3-12%
Health/Beauty	7.0%	3-10%
Housewares	6.0%	3-10%
Infant Products	6.5%	5-10%
Music/Video	8.5%	5-20%
Premiums	7.0%	4-10%
Publishing	7.5%	4-12%
Sporting Goods	6.0%	3-10%
Stationery/Paper Goods	8.5%	4-12%
Toys/Games	8.0%	4-12%
Videogames/Software	8.5%	5-20%
OVERALL AVERAGE	7.1%	

Source: The Licensing Letter

© Copyright 1993 EPM Communications

After a royalty rate is negotiated, the partners agree on an annual guarantee. The guarantee is typically a percentage of the royalties expected to be generated each year by the licensed products. It is non-refundable and is paid, usually quarterly, whether or not the product line generates sales high enough to warrant that amount of royalties for that period. The purpose of the guarantee is to protect the licensor in case sales of the product line do not meet expectations due to a lack of effort by the licensee.

Guarantees are paid "against royalties." That is, royalties are accrued — but not paid — up to the level of the guarantee. After sales generate royalties equal to the guarantee amount, additional royalties are paid to the licensor as further sales warrant.

Like royalties, guarantee amounts vary widely; for example, they can be as small as $3,000 for low-priced stationery items or as much as $750,000 or higher for some items. Separate guarantees may be required for different products manufactured by a single licensee or for different geographic areas for which a single licensee has rights, to make sure that an equitable level of attention is paid to each product and each region.

Part of the guarantee (typically from 25 percent to 50 percent, but this varies) is usually paid up front as an advance at the time of contract signing. The periodic guarantee payments are then adjusted accordingly to reflect the amount paid up front. If a guarantee is particularly small, the entire guarantee may be paid as an advance.

Contracts. Contracts vary depending on the individual agreement and, as mentioned in the section on trademarks and copyrights, it is advisable to retain an attorney who is specifically versed in the licensing business. While each agreement is different, the following elements are among those that will be included in virtually all contracts:

- The contract should identify the parties entering into the agreement.
- It should specify the length of the agreement. The average duration of most contracts is two or three years with an option to renew, but this may vary. A first agreement with a firm may be only a year in duration, while a contract with a known, successful licensee may be long term, even up to 10 years.
- The contract should list the specific merchandise being produced under license, including a description of the products and any traits that distinguish them from other similar merchandise (for example, a particular design or the specific materials used in manufacturing).
- The agreement should outline the specific geographic territory or territories covered by the agreement.
- It should summarize the specific distribution outlets covered by the contract (for example, department and specialty stores, mass market outlets, specific locations, or direct mail outlets).
- The agreement should clarify who owns what rights, such as rights to new entities created by the licensee based on the property.
- The contract should outline conditions for the agreement's termination and put in writing the sell-off procedures that will occur after termination.
- It should specify what happens in case of infringement by a third party — who can bring suit, who pays legal costs, and who keeps the monetary results of the suit, if any.

PROMOTIONAL TIE-INS

A promotional tie-in is typically a licensing agreement for the use of a property that is promotional in nature (as opposed to permitting the creation of a product for sale). Consequently, since there is no sales figure upon which to base a royalty, the core element of payment is a flat fee, with other additional costs added on as applicable. The cost structures of certain tie-ins can become quite complicated, depending on the nature of the promotion, and in many cases the amount of the flat fee itself is hidden among all the other elements of payment.

A tie-in can be as simple as the use of a character in a print ad. On the other hand, it can be as complicated as a multi-tier, multi-partner promotion involving premiums, advertising in various channels, rebates, packaged goods promotions, sweepstakes and contests involving mail-ins, and interactive phone technology — all targeting both consumers and the trade (retailers or distributors) Tie-ins can involve sports personalities and events, nonprofit entities, or entertainment properties. Timing is variable as well; a film tie-in, for example, can coincide with theatrical release, video release, or subsequent broadcast and cable airings.

Tie-in Participants. For licensors, tie-ins serve the purpose of generating awareness for their properties, thus advertising the event or entity itself (as well as related products made by licensees, if any). Tie-ins also enable the property to become known in channels where it would normally not be advertised. Filmgoers traditionally become aware of new films through print or broadcast advertising or through in-theater trailers, for example, but a tie-in allows the message to get to the consumer in other outlets, such as grocery stores and fast food restaurants. Last, but certainly not least, tie-ins are lucrative for licensors. The income earned through tie-ins can be as important a factor for them as the marketing benefits, depending on the property.

Entertainment companies (besides the licensor, if the property is in the entertainment area) also can be involved in tie-ins. Theater chains, home video distributors, music companies, film studios, and cable and broadcast networks are all frequent tie-in partners. Product licensees can also be involved in tie-ins, either through the provision of premiums or through participation in cross-promotions as part of the tie-in. Comic books, trading cards, plastic cups, squeeze bottles, plush figures, plastic figurines, and small toys are particularly popular for premiums, as well as to cross-package with other licensed merchandise. The provision of premiums can be a relatively risk-free way for authorized manufacturers to sell large quantities of licensed products.

Retailers are often involved in tie-ins, too. They benefit from their participation by attracting increased store traffic during the time period of the tie-in and by generating additional sales for licensed products based on the entity being promoted. (Other products may also see greater sales during the tie-in period due to the increased store traffic.) Retailer partners can also raise awareness of their company name by associating with a high-profile property. Tie-ins can be expensive for the retailer, however, and can be risky, especially for short-term entertainment properties. If a film flops, most of the potential benefits of the tie-in will not occur, but the money paid up front cannot be recouped. Among the types of retail outlets frequently involved in tie-ins are fast food restaurants, mass market chains, department and independent stores, grocery stores, video retailers, and toy stores, among others.

Tie-ins often include other product manufacturers, in addition to licensees. Their involvement usually incorporates changes in their product packaging to promote the tie-in; it can also include other elements, such as cents-off coupons or cross-promotions with licensed products or with other manufacturers involved in the same tie-in. The manufacturers hope their participation will lead to increased sales because of the excitement of their association with the property. They usually receive increased advertising exposure through being mentioned in ads by other partners, above and beyond their own promotional efforts. Much of their contribution to the promotion is in the form of packaging, hangtags, and other promotional exposure, rather than cash payments. Food and beverage companies; apparel, accessory, and footwear manufacturers; and health and beauty firms are among the most frequent participants, but many others are involved as well.

Finally, various media partners are also involved in tie-ins. They can include radio stations in local markets, local television stations and national networks, and print media — magazines nationally and newspapers locally. Their participation allows the other partners further opportunity to promote the tie-in at less cost, since the media partners usually donate space or time, thus saving significantly on advertising costs. In return, the media partner benefits from the cachet of being associated with a highly visible property.

Most tie-in promotions in the 1990s involve multiple partners, with the exception of straightforward advertising uses or some long-term associations with classic characters. Bringing in several companies spreads the cost of the tie-in over more players, thus making it more cost-effective for each partner. In addition, the participation of more partners maximizes consumers' exposure to the tie-in in as many outlets as possible. On the other hand, the more partners there are, the more problems are likely to arise. Coordination among partners becomes more difficult, as does the timing of the tie-in, with lead times (required time periods between signing the contract and implementing the promotion) varying from partner to partner. Flexibility, trust, and communication among the players are all essential ingredients in order for a multi-partner promotion to work.

Techniques. Virtually any sales promotion technique can be used in a tie-in with a nonprofit, sports, or entertainment entity. The main element of the tie-in is the licensed property, so the promotion will focus on that. A major use for the property itself is using its likeness or logo in advertising — for example, television, print, newspaper inserts — or on packaging. In addition, personal appearances by a film or sports star or a costumed character at retail outlets, local promotional events, press functions, and so forth, are also often included as tie-in components. And contest prizes can involve meeting key personalities associated with the property, seeing behind-the-scenes action such as a locker room or film set, or attending an event such as a film opening, a concert, or a sports event.

The other elements of a tie-in — components that support the use of the property itself — are common to any cross-promotion. Since

PRODUCT LICENSING AND TIE-INS

most are discussed in depth elsewhere in this book, the following is a brief rundown of possibilities that are commonly considered for entertainment, sports, or nonprofit tie-ins:

- **Use of premiums.** These can be give-aways or self-liquidators, offered on-site or via direct response. In general, the premiums will be directly related to the property. They are either purchased from the retail licensee, or licensed separately as unique products for the tie-in only. Sometimes premiums are purchased specifically for the tie-in from a contracted manufacturer rather than as a licensing arrangement. The main concern regarding use of premiums, from the manufacturer's point of view, is that the premium items do not cut into sales of similar products made by retail licensees.

- **Rebates and cents-off coupons,** including bounce-back arrangements in which several promotional partners become involved. Rebates and coupons can be included on-pack, in free-standing inserts, and in newspaper or other print advertising.

- **Contests and sweepstakes,** fulfilled through mail-in mechanisms or interactive phone technology. These techniques can be targeted toward the trade or to consumers, or both in many cases.

- **Advertising on videocassettes.** Advertisers are unconvinced of the effectiveness of this technique, due to concerns that viewers fast-forward through the commercials and start viewing at the beginning of the film, or at the trailers. In addition, it is difficult to measure the effectiveness of such ads, and an accurate cost per thousand, upon which advertising agents base pricing, does not exist. Still, some tie-ins — especially those involving nonprofit groups and theatrical-film or special-interest videocasette releases — do include ads on cassette, sometimes simply to promote the nonprofit group's activities and sometimes with an 800 or 900 number that encourages donations or allows viewers to participate in a contest or sweepstakes.

- **Media support.** Media support usually includes a tag for the promotion in print and on-air advertising (often part of existing media schedules) by the various partners. It can also include involvement by magazines or networks that are themselves partners in the promotion and that donate advertising space or editorial coverage in return for being associated with the tie-in. This is often the case when one of the partners is a nonprofit entity, since the media partners feel that the association with a cause is a good public relations effort in the eyes of their constituents.

Incidentally, the use of nonprofit overlays to sports or entertainment promotions is on the rise. Bringing in a nonprofit partner along with the retailers, packaged goods companies, and property owners adds an additional element to the promotion in terms of goodwill for the partners. Conversely, the added excitement of the sports or entertainment tie-in can benefit the nonprofit group by increasing awareness and donations.

Case Studies. As noted, tie-ins can be simple, or they can be complex, multipartner arrangements. The following examples demonstrate the wide breadth of techniques and combinations of elements that can occur. Tie-ins arose out of the need for marketers to distinguish themselves from their competitors (to help them break out of the clutter with a "unique" promotion). But as the number of tie-ins increases, the promotion alone is not enough to provide that distinction. Increasingly more creativity is needed to make a tie-in truly unique.

An example of a straightforward use of a classic character for broadcast advertising occurred in early 1993, when Taco Bell licensed the characters Rocky and Bullwinkle for a series of animated ads. The fast food restaurant wanted to distinguish its menu from what it termed "boring burgers" offered by other chains, and it used original animation featuring the offbeat characters to get its message across. The selection of classic characters meant that the company would appeal both to older consumers, who were familiar with Rocky and Bullwinkle from their youth, as well as to younger consumers, who have been introduced to the characters since 1991. The campaign was supplemented by in-restaurant posters, tray liners, and carry-out bags and cups; Taco Bell employees wore Rocky and Bullwinkle T-shirts as well.

An early 1993 Tropicana tie-in with Hemdale Home Video illustrates single-partner promotion of a videocassette release. Tropicana chose to tie in with the video release of *Little Nemo*, an animated children's theatrical film, to promote its Tropicana Triplets boxed juices. Tropicana offered a $5.00 rebate on each videocassette of the film purchased, and it promoted the rebate on packages of Tropicana Triplets in 25,000 stores and in its national advertising. Tropicana also offered a free premium — a *Little Nemo* activity set produced by licensee Colorforms. Hemdale cross-promoted Tropicana in its advertising and promotional displays, as well as placing a Tropicana message on the videocassette.

In the sports area, the National Basketball Association tied in with McDonald's in March of 1993 with a national promotion called McDonald's NBA Fantasy Packs (see Exhibit 14.2). The tie-in involved prizes from several NBA sponsors, including Norwegian Cruise Lines, Bausch & Lomb, American Airlines, ITT Sheraton, and Dollar Rent A Car. Items from several NBA licensees were also offered as prizes, such as fantasy salaries from Sports Fantasy Contracts, uniforms from Champion, jackets from Starter, and apparel and basketballs from Spalding. Licensee Upper Deck created a set of trading cards especially for the promotion. In addition, NBA players

EXHIBIT 14.2

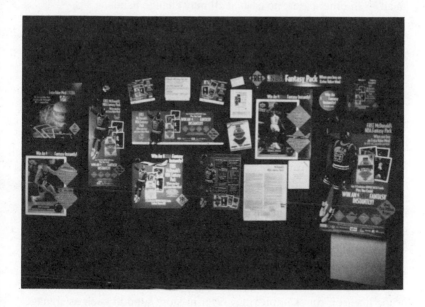

were involved (a one-on-one game with Michael Jordan), and some winners earned the opportunity to participate in NBA events or win tickets to games.

Nickelodeon launched a new block of programming in late summer of 1992 with a $20 million multi-partner promotion. It included an on-air sweepstakes sponsored by Sega, Kraft Handi-Snacks, and Pizza Hut; trading card premiums packaged with Capri-Sun Fruit Drinks; tune-in messages on packages of Kraft Handi-Snacks, which also advertised Nickelodeon merchandise available with proofs-of-purchase of Handi-Snacks; tune-in messages on Sega videogame cassettes; a Nickelodeon spread in *Sega Visions* magazine; sponsorship of Sega's mall tour by Nickelodeon; and tune-in messages on grocery bags in Kroger and Shop-Rite stores.

Payment. "Payment" is difficult to quantify when discussing tie-ins. Much of the payment comes in the form of trade-outs, so no cash actually changes hands. In fact, the licensing fee itself is often not even quantified; rather, the elements that each partner has to offer are negotiated through give-and-take until all partners are satisfied that what they will get out of the promotion — in terms of increased sales, increased awareness, goodwill, or whatever their goals may be — exceeds what they are putting into it, whether it be cash, added impressions for the other partners, or other components of value to the tie-in. While the licensor may sometimes receive cash for the right to use its property —

especially for a relatively simple tie-in such as the use of a character in an ad — in other cases, no cash at all may change hands.

In lieu of cash, the promotional partners may contribute other added value. For example, one partner may be responsible for providing premiums. Another partner may offer some type of advertising, perhaps in the form of a tag on existing print advertising. A partner's contribution may involve promoting the tie-in on-air during time already reserved for its ongoing ad campaign. This incremental media is considered part of the value of the promotion, even though the advertiser is not paying anything more than what it normally would pay — it is just putting it toward the tie-in instead of toward other uses.

In the case of a media partner, the contribution may involve the provision of free airtime or print space devoted to the tie-in. Similarly, a video marketer could offer free space for advertising on a cassette, or a manufacturer may provide space to promote the tie-in on its packaging or on hangtags. Again, this cost is an incremental one because the company would need to print packaging or hangtags for the products anyway; the additional costs are mainly in the form of creative input, as well as slightly higher printing costs that may arise as a result of shorter print runs.

There are other ways partners can contribute to a tie-in. A retailer or the licensor, for example, may offer in-store support such as signage or point-of-sale materials, countertop cards, or in-store flyers devoted to the tie-in. Another partner may contribute the operational costs of overseeing contests and sweepstakes, including fulfillment of premiums and prizes.

Measurement of Results. It is difficult to quantify many of the benefits of a tie-in, such as increased awareness, much less to trace which results are attributable to which part of the promotion. In addition, one of the major difficulties in terms of measuring the success of a tie-in is to try to ascertain which results, if any, are traceable to the use of the property itself, rather than being attributable to other elements of the promotion.

Some of the measurable elements include, of course, the number of coupon redemptions, the number of contest entries, the number of calls generated by interactive phone lines, and the number of premiums sold or given away. The elements that are measurable but not necessarily traceable include the following: increased attendance at films over previous comparable films, which may have been affected as much as or more by the quality of the film as by the tie-ins surrounding it; increased sales over nonpromotional periods or over other similar tie-ins with different properties; increased traffic at retail outlets over other time periods; and awareness of the property and of the tie-in partners' brands, as measured through recall studies at periodic intervals during and after the tie-in.

Of course, some elements of the tie-in cannot be measured at all, including goodwill generated by a tie-in toward a product, brand, or company, or the "excitement" associated with a product due to its connection with an entertainment or sports property. These attributes, while not measurable, are ironically among the major reasons for involvement in a licensed tie-in.

Issues and Challenges. Entertainment, sports, and nonprofit tie-ins — while they can be wildly successful — are not without their challenges. For example, lead times may vary between property owners and other tie-in partners. A film studio may be working on a lead time of as long as 24 months for a particularly hot film, while a packaged goods company may prefer a lead time of nine to 12 months. Both may be able to work with as narrow a lead time as four months, however, if the deal is important enough to them and the cost is right. Flexibility by both partners is required to minimize lead-time differences.

Another timing problem can occur, particularly with film tie-ins, due to the fact that release dates are changeable. A film's theatrical or video release may be moved up a week, for example, forcing tie-in partners to have all promotional elements in place a week earlier, with little advance notice. Or, a film may be delayed by six months if production is not running smoothly or if preview audiences pan the film, thus forcing last-minute changes. A packaged goods or retail company, whose promotional schedule is set a year or more in advance, will suffer; the promotion will most likely be canceled, and the sunk costs associated with it forfeited.

In the case of licensed or property-specific premiums being used in a tie-in, care must be taken that the premiums do not hurt retail sales of similar products. This risk can be minimized by making all affected parties aware of the premium use from the beginning — while there is still time to make changes.

Another timing issue is that of potential repeatability — or lack thereof — associated with various properties. A sports tie-in may be optimal if a company wants the opportunity to repeat a successful promotion year after year during the same selling period, thus facilitating planning and coordination with sales forces, wholesalers, and retailers. A successful Super Bowl promotion, with slight annual variations and improvements, may occur year after year. On the other hand, there is no guarantee that a successful film promotion may be repeated. The chance that a sequel of a hit film will be made is good, and getting better, but there is no telling when that sequel will occur — in what selling season or in what year.

If the tie-in partner's goal is to have an ongoing, long-term promotional arrangement with a property, then a classic character or a well-known nonprofit may serve the purpose best. Sports tie-ins can also work to some extent but, even if the tie-in doesn't involve an annual event like the World Series or Super Bowl, there is still an inherent seasonality to sports properties because their respective seasons do not last year-round. A long-term tie-in does not bring with it the "excitement" and high profile of a tie-in with a (what is hoped to be) hot film or a major sports event, but it does provide a point of difference between the tie-in partner and its competitors, and is usually less risky.

Aside from the challenges involving timing, tie-ins also carry with them certain risks inherent to the properties themselves. Entertainment properties may not be a hit, for example. People won't be attracted to a tie-in if its central element is unknown or if potential customers actively dislike it. One way to guard against this risk is to maximize the impact of the tie-in by scheduling it in the months or weeks *before* a film opens or a television series premieres. That way, although the tie-in partners do not receive the same benefit they would have if the property had been popular, at least they received enough value ahead of time, while excitement was building, to rationalize the costs involved.

In the case of films, more and more tie-in partners are choosing to associate their brands with videocassette rather than theatrical releases. That way, the property has a track record and is thus perceived as less risky. In addition, videos — particularly those for children, which are more often sold than rented — offer the added benefit of repeat viewing. Children like to see the film over and over, thus maximizing the awareness of the property itself and products associated with it through licensing or tie-ins.

Both entertainment and sports properties carry with them the risk of controversy. Athletes can be injured or be indicted for drug use or gambling or some other activity with which a tie-in partner does not want to be associated and over which it has no control. Entertainment personalities can be controversial as well, and films rated PG-13 or older can contain themes that unexpectedly offend a tie-in partner's target audience. These occurrences not only negate any benefits of the tie-in but also can actually hurt sales (or attract negative perceptions by consumers toward the partners). Tie-ins with cartoon characters, G-rated films, sports leagues rather than individual athletes, and estates of deceased celebrities are common ways to avoid this risk.

Finally, another challenge inherent in entertainment promotions in particular is the risk that key personalities will not want to participate in a commercial venture such as a tie-in. If the use of the star or the star's likeness is crucial to the structure of a partner's tie-in, it is essential that likeness approvals are acquired up front. Promises by the studios that likeness approvals are no problem should be double-checked by talking directly to the talent or the talent's agency representatives. On the other hand, successful promotions can be built around films or television programs without the use of the stars. If the promotion does focus on the star, however, the partner should be sure that the star is agreeable before it's too late and the tie-in has to be redone at the last minute, at the sacrifice of dollars and perhaps quality.

CONCLUSIONS

Simply associating with a popular property is not enough to effectively differentiate a product or brand from its competitors; thought and creativity need to go into tie-ins and product licensing relationships in order to make them successful. Rather than an automatic way to sell merchandise, licensing and tie-ins are now recognized as effective marketing tools, used in conjunction with the rest of a company's marketing strategy.

As a result, not only "hit" properties are used for tie-ins and licensing. The fit between the property and its licensees and tie-in partners is more important than the overall popularity of the property. There are times when companies will successfully tie in with the high-profile "hits" — they still generate excitement and widespread, short-term awareness. But different companies have different marketing needs, and there are many properties out there that can fit the bill, depending on a marketer's specific goals.

Licensing and tie-ins should be part of a company's overall marketing strategy, not the only facet of that strategy. Risks should be minimized as much as possible (although marketers should be aware that most licensing and tie-in deals are inherently risky). And all properties should be considered — not just the obvious hot entertainment properties, but smaller properties, long-term classics, trademarks, nonprofits, sports outside of the major sports leagues, and so forth.

Flexibility and trust among the partners are key to a successful relationship. Those two elements — as well as open communication among all players — will help allow the creation of a unique tie-in, will minimize risks, and will enable the partners to adapt to unforeseen contingencies.

Paul Stanley is President and Creative Director of PS Productions, Inc., Chicago, which he established in 1974. PS is the largest entertainment event marketing agency in the country. Previously, Stanley was President/Creative Director of the SR&B Advertising Agency in Detroit, Michigan, for 12 years. He also managed a record company, founded the Royal Oak Music Theater and Castle Farms outdoor venue in Charlevoix, Michigan, and was a concert promoter throughout Michigan for 14 years, promoting more than 2,000 concerts and events. Stanley produced, wrote, and hosted his own television show out of Detroit called Takin It to the Street.*

Stanley designed the first corporate sponsorship of a rock/music tour and created and trademarked the entertainment event concepts of Sponsownership™, Multiple Tiered/Modular Programs™, and Trade Learning Customization™. His PS Productions agency creates and executes corporate sponsorships for clients that include Procter & Gamble, Philip Morris, Kraft, Frito Lay, Borden, the Dial Corporation, Chrysler, Alberto-Culver, and many more. He is also founding judge of Adweek Magazine*'s Annual Event of the Year Awards.*

Stanley will soon complete a master's degree in advertising from Michigan State University with an eye to teaching event marketing at the college level.

CHAPTER 15

EVENT MARKETING — IT'S NOT THE
EVENT THAT MATTERS

Event marketing is one of the most powerful marketing tools in existence today. The results, measured against the initial objectives of the sponsor, continually exceed marketer's expectations. In fact, marketer's reactions to the event medium have gone from caution, skepticism, and downright aversion to "We haven't seen this type of retail support and record sales in years." The sophistication of the event marketing medium has continued to increase to the point where the industry is projected to top $5 billion in 1993!

The first real event marketing music sponsorship program, "Ford Motor Company Presents The Rockets" (a rock and roll band big in the Midwest in the late 1970s), was created to reach college students and "talk" to them "on their own turf." A four-college market tour was scheduled with the primary objective of gaining "a warm feeling" from the college target and moving the attitude needle toward Ford in a positive manner. Ford implemented consumer research to evaluate this program, and the results baffled Ford's own research people. The needle didn't just move, it soared off the page! From "do you think Ford makes a good product" to "would you buy a Ford," the response was extremely positive.

One year later, "Jovan Cologne Presents the Rolling Stones" came to life, and an industry was on its way. Event marketing got everyone's attention.

When dealing with event marketing, it's not the event that matters most. Without grasping that basic premise, the power and essence of this very innovative marketing tool cannot be understood. The measure of an event marketing program's success is in how you *leverage* the event, not the event itself. By looking at the individual players and figuring out what the objectives of each are and then working to satisfy those individual objectives, the whole event program returns results that are much more than the sum of its parts.

Most of what is done in event marketing is common sense. Still, when properly used, event marketing is the most powerful results-oriented and "fail-safe" means of achieving marketing objectives today.

WHAT IS AN EVENT?

The fundamental notion behind an event sponsorship is that a sponsor/marketer associates with an event property — entertainers, sports, Olympics, Superbowl, etc. — and "trades off" on the popularity of that event to fulfill its marketing objectives. Sponsownership™, a concept trademarked in the early 1980s, is a sponsorship that is owned by the sponsor. This ownership not only allows sponsors/marketers to utilize and leverage the event to achieve their marketing objectives, it also allows them to take in revenues generated by the event itself (ticket sales, merchandise sales). It allows marketers to build and control their own events for years to come, thus building equity and longevity into their own marketing programs. Because of their effectiveness and profitability, sponsownerships are sure to become the marketing avenue of choice for sponsors over the next few years.

To understand better what event marketing is, several examples of successful event sponsorships and sponsownerships are briefly described in this section. While most of these concentrate particularly on entertainment events for packaged goods marketers, the basic principles remain the same for all events. An event can be created and utiltized to support, sell, or market any product or service, from the automotive industry to electronics. The event can focus on entertainment, sports, or some other theme created especially for a brand's image. The same principles also apply whether your need is of a national scope or a one-market execution. Despite the fact that each event is ultimately quite different from the others in its theme, scope, and audience, keep in mind: "It's not the event, it's how you leverage the event."

- **"AT&T College Comedy Tour."** A sponsownership program designed for AT&T featuring leading comedians on 20 college campuses. The tour was also taped for an MTV special. It required securing all talent, booking college campuses, and producing the tour and TV special. The program was tied to AT&T service sign-up and image enhancement.
- **"Sparkle Crest Presents The ABC Family Fun Fair."** A multicharacter mall tour (20 weeks) for ABC Television, sponsored by Procter & Gamble. It became the number one mall tour in audience attraction (40,000+ per market) and mall satisfaction. The Sparkle Crest objective was to launch a new product, to gain retail support, and to enhance image. Retailers could not keep the product in stock. ABC's objective was to promote its Saturday morning lineup, and it went from third to first in ratings.
- **"Procter & Gamble Presents Barry Manilow."** A test program developed to meet the exact marketing objectives (displays, incremental cases) of P&G's Era and Ivory Liquid brands. The promotion it achieved was so successful, it was expanded to 20 markets. Another similar event followed, consisting of a 20-city, multiple-brand extension of the test program, leveraging Manilow's Broadway show with media and trade support to obtain incremental case sales and to enhance trade relations.
- **"The Wrangler Country Showdown."** The world's largest talent contest: tie-ins with 400 radio stations, 2,000+ Dodge

dealers, local tie-ins with 500+ Wrangler retailers, talent competitions at 52 state fairs, and a national talent contest showdown finish at The Grand Ole Opry in Nashville. The event leveraged $13.5 million in free media coverage.

- **"Chivas Regal Presents Frank Sinatra's Diamond Jubilee."** Chivas and Sinatra, two legends, teamed up to produce one of the most outstanding music marketing tours ever staged. The national tour tied in with consumer sweepstakes, trade hospitality, POP displays, a CD/cassette offer, and a 900 line. It was designed to produce high visibility and an awareness for the brand, retail support, display, and consumer sales.
- **"Borden Snacks Presents The Beach Boys."** The concert tour promoted 16 brands in 75 markets. The event was designed to increase display and feature support incentives and span three generations of consumers. Strong consumer takeaway/sell-through was built into the promotional program. Unique venues (baseball parks and a charity tie-in to the Better Homes Foundation) added even more power to the promotion. It was the biggest and most successful promotion in Borden Snacks' history (see Exhibit 15.1).
- **"Alberto VO5 Presents The Moody Blues."** This was an industry first in the health and beauty aids category. It was designed to gain increased display and feature support, incremental consumer takeaway, and expanded distribution within the top 50 ADIs. Results surpassed even the most optimistic of the company's projections (see Exhibit 15.2).
- **"Swift-Eckrich Presents Meet The Greats of Baseball."** This event was a 27-market mall tour, featuring Major League Baseball alumni. It was designed to increase trade support, stimulate incremental takeaway, and raise awareness of all deli products during the key summer season. Events included a one-of-a-kind photo exhibit, baseball clinics, and photo sessions and autograph signing by former baseball stars. Tie-ins with local deli counters included free photos and autographs and chances to win tickets to 1993 spring training exhibition games with proofs-of-purchase. The promotion achieved more than 90 percent total trade participation on initial sell-in.

A HISTORICAL PERSPECTIVE

Event marketing is not really a new idea. Rather, it is the updated use of very sound marketing and promotional disciplines that have been molded to fit today's marketplace. To really understand why events have become such a successful promotional tool, consider what they offer:

- An exciting, memorable, often entertaining environment, exclusively available to the sponsor and free from competitive

EXHIBIT 15.1

EXHIBIT 15.2

clutter and distractions;

- A completely captive and receptive audience, who is often quite demographically homogeneous and thus desirable from a targeting point of view;
- An opportunity to satisfy all the key players in the marketing arena, including the consumer, the trade, and the media, simply by capitalizing on and leveraging the event's popularity; and
- A tool that can enhance a brand's image and shift some marketing clout and power back into the hands of the manufacturer once again.

Events offer what no other medium today can, and in many respects, events offer the best of what radio, television, and advertising used to offer, only in today's marketplace. Consider history.

In the early days of brand advertising, marketers set out to create a brand image. With the invention of radio, advertisers found that by creating programming they, in fact, created an "event" that consumers tuned in to hear religiously every week. This captive audience was in a relaxed and receptive mode — a perfect disposition for creating and selling a brand image. By building this brand image, marketers could realize trial and sales objectives, putting *power in the brand*, a brand that Ms./Mr. Consumer would actually ask for. This brand power allowed manufacturers to dictate the retailers and receive more shelf space, line extensions, display support, and, later, feature pricing and trade advertising. They could also use that brand power to generate support for their new and lesser known brands.

As consumers bought into brand imaging primarily through radio events, a new, more powerful medium came upon the scene. The power of television would become unsurpassed in its reach and effectiveness for decades. With television came the need for new and different programming that would attract the desired demographics, hold the consumers' attention, and open their minds to advertisers' messages. Television was new, entertaining, exciting, innovative, and *live*. The shows themselves were events. Milton Berle, Jack Parr, Steve Allen, and Ed Sullivan became events that flowed into America's living rooms. Procter & Gamble created the soap opera, hooking millions of consumers who were a captive audience to their messages. Commercials were live, often starring the celebrities themselves as endorsers, adding a new dimension of credibility. Even the commercials were entertaining and captivating. Television brought even more power to the manufacturer/advertiser over the trade.

Fast-forward to the 1990s. Today, there is a whole new ball game, and brand power is almost gone, at least in terms of the retail trade. The number of competitive brands is at an all-time high. Couponing and discounting are a way of life. Retail deals and dollars have never before been spent at such a pace. Marketers have come to learn that the best way to sell products is through retail trade support, off-shelf displays, feature ads, and feature pricing. Manufacturers created their own monster by initially paying for this support, and now they cannot find a way out. Kraft General Foods, as an example, spent over $1.5 billion on "trade deals" in 1992. What is worse, the company is not really sure where all the money went!

The trade has never been more powerful than it is today. A majority of retailers don't even make their money selling products anymore; they make it on trade deals, case allowances, slotting allowances, diverting, forward-buying, co-oping, and many other ways that marketers, not long ago, had never even heard of. If one manufacturer isn't willing to pay, there are plenty of other manufacturers in line that will. Further, price seems to be playing a continued major role in consumer purchases, which results in a continuing decline in brand profits and equity. If that weren't enough to make it downright tough to sell products, look what has happened to the advertising world.

Never before have there been more media vying for consumer attention than there are today. Gone are the days of a few television networks, radio stations, and print vehicles. Cable television alone provides more than 100 channels. With the coming of skylink (a very affordable home satellite dish), the choices will be staggering. Couple that with a very mobile society, more women in the workplace, and an overall squeeze on consumer time, you now have a consumer who is almost impossible to reach through traditional marketing vehicles.

Marketers have at last realized that a national marketing strategy can no longer work, and they need local market strategies. Local promotions allow a marketer to adapt to a market from consumer, trade, and media perspectives. However, the question remains, "How do we implement that strategy?"

Unfortunately, to date, the primary strategy has basically been to "pay off the trade" while dumping millions of coupons on the consumer. That strategy, however, is no longer as effective because everybody's doing it, and manufacturers have created a merry-go-round they cannot seem to stop.

Enter event marketing. Event marketing can deliver everyone's objectives simultaneously. Events create a "win-win-win" scenario. No other medium can make that claim. For instance, if you're going to take money away from the trade, then you'd better have something else to offer in its place. And to do this, you must think about the objectives and needs of the trade. Understanding and unlocking those goals and needs are the key.

Event marketing is not about the numbers of people who show up at a concert or tennis match. It's also not about hanging a banner at the event. Promotional success shouldn't be about ticket sales, either. It is all about leveraging the event to meet everyone's objectives in that market. Unfortunately, early on, too many people based their whole promotion on the success of the event itself, and to some extent, they still do. In reality, the main focus should be on the three to four weeks prior to and following the event. This period is the key to successful event marketing.

MAKING EVENTS WORK FOR YOU

The following information on event marketing will deal with the nuts and bolts of creating, executing, and measuring the success of an event marketing promotion. Please remember that the basics are the same, whether you utilize sports or entertainment or you create your own event (Sponsownerships™). It is also wise to have an experienced event marketing firm with a proven track record to handle most of the event execution workload and to provide daily assistance if necessary.

It all starts with the marketer's/sponsor's objectives. Because event marketing is multidimensional, it can simultaneously deliver multiple objectives. Therefore, all objectives must be identified. For example, what objectives might event marketing accomplish for a laundry detergent?

- Trial and incremental sales
- Trade support, displays, features, promotional pricing, incremental case orders
- Reaching women ages 25 to 49
- Key selling or competitive timing
- Brand image and awareness

- Publicity
- Easy sell-in for the sales force
- Sales force enthusiasm
- Trade relations building
- Cost-effectiveness
- Easy/turnkey execution

Once marketers/sponsors have carefully identified all the objectives they wish to achieve, the criteria by which the success of the program are measured must be determined. While some may question whether event marketing results are, in fact, measurable, the reality is that events provide more measurable results than most other advertising media and promotion techniques.

The key and "soul" to successful event marketing is to remember the following: *Marketers achieve their objectives through event marketing by achieving the objectives of others. Marketers' success depends on influencing the trade, the consumer, their sales force, and the media to do their bidding.* No other medium has the direct ability to allow all who are important to a marketer's goals to achieve those goals simultaneously. Therefore, after identifying the objectives (manufacturer/sponsor), you must look at the objectives of the other players who will be affected by the event promotion.

This diagram may also be expanded to include other "players" (depending on the manufacturer/sponsor) such as franchisees, bottlers, promoters, and brokers.

These players' objectives, and how those objectives can be met through an event program, will be discussed in the following sections.

THE TRADE

Traffic and sales are primary objectives of the trade. Today, when manufacturers run an advertising campaign, theoretically, they are creating demand for their product, which should create traffic to retail and, of course, sales for both retailers and manufacturers. Why, then, are manufacturers spending billions of dollars a year "paying off the trade" if trade objectives are being met through manufacturers' advertising?

What if manufacturers could, in fact, meet the trade's objectives while meeting their own? To do this through an event marketing program, the trade's objectives must first be identified and built into the program. Obviously, the trade wants traffic and sales as stated earlier. But what else do retailers desire?

Retailers want to be a part of something big in their community or, at the very least, to not be left out of something big! They like to be a part of localized media. They need to turn sales quickly. They like to reward their own employees in special ways. They like new profit centers that earn a healthy markup, especially when those profit centers require no cash outlay against those profits. They want to reward their customers for their shopping loyalty. They like to be a part of something that is not the everyday "ho-hum" that has become the way of doing business. And one last thing that members of the trade enjoy is something that can include their own families — a work, yet family, experience.

Accomplishing all of this may seem like a big challenge, but the reality is that an event marketing program can, in fact, be designed to deliver *all* of these objectives and desires to the trade in exchange for the trade's achieving a marketer's/sponsor's objectives. Competition among retail trades is fierce. That fact can be used to a manufacturer's advantage.

Here is a summary of retailers' objectives: traffic, sales and quick turns, new profit centers, local media, staying competitive, rewarding their customers and employees, something new and innovative, community involvement potential, and something that is family-oriented for themselves.

Members of the trade are, of course, key to any manufacturer, but they are only part of the equation in achieving sponsor/marketing objectives today. Other players will also help achieve the trade's objectives.

THE FIELD/SALES FORCE

The field, of course, is the sales force of a manufacturer and the direct link between the retailer and the manufacturer. The field may be directly employed by the manufacturer or may include independent brokers or direct delivery systems (for example, truck or route drivers). The field is, of course, critical to any manufacturer, and an event program can be designed to achieve the objectives of the field as well.

Whether they are direct salespeople or brokers, today's field pretty much faces the same obstacles, problems, and frustrations. With all of the megamergers of the 1980s, the field is overloaded and inundated with brands, demands, and quotas. Personnel in the field have sales quotas to meet on multiple brands; they have to introduce new products and line extensions. They usually deal from a position of weakness with the trade and, of course, the competition has never been greater or more fierce. In addition, they are usually responsible for putting up point-of-sale and special displays, and their duties do not end there.

What this means is the field does not want or need any extra workload — period.

And it is wise to recognize that the field personnel can make or break any event promotion or, at the very least, hinder it. One key benefit of event marketing for the sponsor brand is in focusing the full attention of the sales force on the sponsoring brand.

What else can event marketing do for the field and its objectives? Let's look at some of these objectives. The field needs to increase sales. Salespeoples' bonuses are most likely tied to sales performance.

To do this, they know they must:

- Gain as many retail displays, extended displays, and end aisles as possible;
- Gain trade features and support pricing;
- Have promotional overlays to drive consumer takeaway; and
- Beat their competition.

Event marketing can achieve all of these objectives and more. How? An untold benefit of event marketing is its ability to boost field morale. This is a major plus. When people are happier and more excited, they sell better.

Event marketing gives the field something to bring to the "Lion's Den" (aka "the trade buyer") — something new, exciting, and most important, built for the trade's own objectives and with no competitive equal.

Event marketing allows field personnel to be big shots in their own markets because they are "hosting" the event and, therefore, are in control of prime tickets, special merchandise, special media, and most often, powerful backstage or private party passes. These items can be highly leveraged.

Think about this. If the field from brand A offers the trade this comprehensive, integrated event program with all of its perks, what does the field from competitive brand B counter with? Another case deal? More coupons? The fact remains, event marketing has no apples-to-apples comparison. This noncomparison factor packs one big cannon for the field. Therefore, the sponsoring brand can *finally* regain some much-needed and long-lost power.

It is important to teach field personnel that with all they are bringing to the trade — the event, the media, the customization, the traffic and sales builders, to name a few — they owe their customers *nothing* more. Consequently, for once, they can get up and walk away from an uncooperative retailer. That retailer is only hurting itself; nine times out of 10, the other retailers will not only "pick up the slack" but also will actually support the promotion beyond normal levels. Event marketing works, and smart retailers will not want to be left out.

The concept of the field walking away from the table or not throwing cash at the retailers is a refreshing change for the field. The only problem is that some field personnel are so "shell-shocked" or trade brainwashed that they actually need to be retrained. It is vital to train and communicate with the field exactly what the event program is about, how it works, and how it works for the other players. Field personnel are the direct link to the market and the trade. Supply them with field training films and other helpful collateral materials. More important, explain how the trade can use that power to achieve its own objectives.

Furthermore, it is important to equip the field with trade sell-in videos which can explain to retailers the event promotion and its power overall. These tools can even be customized for each individual trade and/or buyer. These selling tools can be created with a little touch of fun, as well, because it's all right to have some fun for a change.

The field is key. Yet, the field is also very busy. So remember those two points when executing an event promotion, and design the promotion for easy field execution. Make sure the program is initially very well communicated to field personnel with a chance for them to ask questions. Weekly sell-in success stories can be exchanged between different field personnel in different markets, as can funny stories, tips, and experiences. Encourage the field to "get creative with the promotion" if it chooses and to have some fun, or, as the field force for the "Borden Snacks Presents The Beach Boys" event promotion would come to say, "Have some fun, fun, fun!"

Today, field personnel utilizing an event in this way are gaining *multiple* display periods and multiple feature ads from the trade, in addition to the mandatory displays directly tied to the event marketing promotion time frame. First-quarter event promotions can and have been leveraged by the field for not only first-quarter support but also for Labor Day displays as well! New product distributions and line extensions have also been successfully leveraged with the trade against the event promotion.

THE MEDIA

The media, on both national and local levels, are just as competitive as any other business today. They are also a powerful partner in an event promotion. They can be utilized to create consumer awareness, call the consumers to action, provide further leverage with the trade, and contribute a host of additional benefits to the brand, sponsor, or event.

Start with the media at the same starting place as with all "players" in an event promotion – with their own objectives. Whether dealing with a television network or a local affiliate, a radio network or a local station, a cable network or a local cable system, a local newspaper, *USA Today*, or a magazine, they *all* want increased viewers or listeners or readers. They want to be able to offer exclusives/rewards to their audiences, and they also want to make money.

Can an event promotion offer a media partner or partners the ability to achieve those objectives? You bet!

By offering a station a multifaceted package, it is possible to meet and surpass not only the station's objectives but also those of the sponsors as well. A typical package would include the following:

- Exclusive tangibles (front row tickets, backstage passes, new artist releases);
- Exclusive intangibles (presenting station, exclusive on-stage welcomes);
- Value-added sales opportunities (ancillary media tie-ins that

media partner can sell off);
- Special programming (also a media sales opportunity); and
- Cash spot buys.

The biggest surprise to most sponsors is that the event promotion can actually allow the media partner(s) to sell parts of the program to noncompeting companies/brands without detracting from the promotion or the sponsors' presence/objectives. On the contrary, the more the media partner(s) sell, the more the promotion, brand image, and special offers are promoted! These are "value-added" sales opportunities for the station and an extended promotion for the sponsor. The media can even approach the sponsoring trades and put together other ancillary media tie-ins that further benefit the sponsor and the trade.

The key with the media is the word *leveraging*. Typically, an event will generate, on purchased media, ratios that range from $4.00 in promotion for every dollar spent to $30.00 in promotion for every dollar spent. That's a lot of media in every local market that is not only promoting the event, brand, and special consumer offers, but which is also choking out competitors. What is the competition going to do? Buy more straight brand-image advertising? The event sponsor should only hope so, since it will be purely wasted cash that the competition cannot use elsewhere.

One hundred thousand dollars was spent overall in event media buys across 75 markets on the "Borden Snacks Presents The Beach Boys" event promotion. More than $2 million in *measured* media was received in return, in support of the brands, the promotion, and the consumer offers. The majority of this media power was focused on trade and sponsoring brand displays. This created a lot of trade traffic and sales, which fulfilled two big trade objectives. This kind of synergy among the "players" can be leveraged by the sponsoring brand for its own objectives. How do you beat that? You don't.

How can a high level of media support be achieved? Look for ways to build exclusive benefits into a program based on the media's objectives. That can include, as stated, ways that the media can sell promotional parts of an event to noncompetitors, ways the media can attract listeners or viewers while tying to the sponsoring brand's displays and products, exclusive perks such as live remotes from the event site, exclusive access to interviews with entertainment or sports celebrities who are sponsored, and exclusive event merchandise.

Creating special programming for radio and/or television that can be bartered with the local stations is an effective ancillary to an event program. Media hypes customize the programming locally with their stations or news personalities and sell off time in the program. The program is, of course, tied to the sponsored event, artist, or sports celebrity, and the time reserved for the sponsor or special broadcast program provider may be utilized by the sponsor to further promote its brands, events, or consumer offers, and as leverage with the trade.

These are but a few ideas. Depending on the event, be creative and remember to keep the media's objectives in mind. Believe me, they will hear you loud and clear.

PUBLICITY

This is a good time to mention the endless publicity opportunities that exist with event promotions. Publicity is not paid media; it's news stories, articles, and interviews that primarily promote sponsor or brand image and awareness on both a national and local market-by-market basis.

If an event includes an entertainer, sports celebrity, movie star, politician, or other high-profile personality, there is a walking spokesperson who can interact with every medium in every market and on a national level, as well. After all, that's what shows such as *Good Morning America, David Letterman, The Tonight Show, Donahue, Oprah,* and others are all about and need! Take advantage of the publicity they can give! Local radio disc jockeys love guests or phone-in interviews; newspapers need stories; *People* is about exactly that — people and events.

Publicity opportunities are a big bonus to event marketing and to sponsors. Not only does the sponsor or brand reap all the benefits, but also, what can the brand's competitors do to match this? Even with celebrity advertising endorsers, competitors will never reach the audience that an event's publicity will reach. They would have to pay a celebrity endorser as much as it would cost to pay for an entire event marketing program, spokespeople included.

An event promotion may also include a cause, charity, or fundraising tie-in. This gives the sponsor other avenues to gain image, awareness, and a "good citizen" aura. The event itself can actually raise much needed money for charity at the same time. "Live Aid," "Hands Across America," and "Farm Aid" were events that raised millions of dollars for great causes while they also furthered their sponsors' objectives.

Event promotions are also *very* flexible and allow for quick reaction to situations. During the 1989 event "Procter & Gamble Presents Barry Manilow," Hurricane Hugo hit the South. Manilow and Procter & Gamble both wanted to help — and quickly. The tour was diverted to a building (that was still standing) in Columbia, South Carolina, and raised more than $100,000 dollars plus tons of food and clothing donations. Not only was it a nice thing to do, but also the public relations benefit was endless, and everyone came out smelling like a rose.

An event promotion allows sponsors to reach out and "shake hands" with their customers/consumers and public. It's said that the strongest form of advertising is "word of mouth," so let an event speak out!

There are several different ways to position each project, but there are also a few things that should be done for publicity's sake that are common to all projects:

1. Start with a national "kickoff" campaign.
2. Initiate a well-thought-out promotional plan aimed at the consumer audience in general, targeting the particular demographics for the event.
3. Work with local media outlets to augment their promotional objectives in individual markets.
4. Use phone interviews, live interviews, press releases, and feature stories. Use your event property in a way traditional media cannot equal.

EVENT PROMOTERS

Events have promoters. Every concert, play, or tennis tournament that comes to town has someone, somehow putting up money to be a part of that event in exchange for sharing in revenues (ticket sales, merchandise, concessions).

If revenues do not exceed the total cost of staging that event, a promoter loses money. Whether it's an individual company, a charity trying to raise money, or the local nightclub highlighting local talent, these entities are risking their money and time to make money. In a sense, event promoters make a living by rolling the dice every day, gambling that an event will be a success. Most people do not understand what it takes to bring a major show or event to town. Promoters do this without any guarantee of earning a profit but with the risk of losing a lot of money.

The important thing to remember is the money that brought the event to town and that advertised it is the promoter's. In the early days of music events, sponsors would contract directly with the artist to perform on their tours, and they paid the artist directly for that right. The promoters didn't see a dime, yet promoters were asked to give tickets to some sponsor's friend (tickets the promoter was counting on selling), hang banners, and advertise for nothing! Very often, sponsors and their representatives were met with resistance and received little cooperation from promoters.

Although promoters still do not directly share in sponsorship dollars per se, they are most cooperative when they, too, are included in an overall sponsorship.

How can a sponsor include them? Again, begin by considering their objectives. A promoter's number one objective is to sell tickets as quickly as possible (in order to cut advertising expenditures as quickly as possible). To do this, a promoter must let as many people as possible know that the event is coming, while also building some "hype" around the promotion. A sponsor's marketing plan and marketing power can help achieve the promoter's main objective.

The sponsor and promoter have some common ground — awareness. Awareness for the event is critical for ticket sales. Start there.

The sponsor needs to build its promotional and advertising plans and execution to include a means for the local promoter to also promote its shows. Whether you "tag" sponsor media or point-of-sale materials, remember the other common ground between sponsor and promoter — both want the event to succeed.

Keeping a promoter happy is something that helps ensure that the things a sponsor needs to achieve at the event will go smoothly — from getting the right number of tickets in the right locations at the right times, to inclusion in the promoter's advertising, event signage, and sampling, to the hospitality parties at the event's conclusion.

Always think of promoters from the start when putting sponsorships together. That way it won't be a "gamble" when dealing with them.

THE EVENT PROPERTY

Event marketing obviously deals with an event of some sort. Whether utilizing entertainers or sports celebrities, there is always an event "property."

In the early days of event marketing, especially in the entertainment and sports arenas, sponsors usually showered sponsor cash on the event property. This practice, however, can be detrimental to the event industry as a whole. The use of any medium must deliver a "payback" to the user, which is generally measured in overall sales. Ultimately, all sponsors are, of course, going to measure the success of their sponsorship by comparing overall sales results with total costs. In other words, did the promotion pay out? It is therefore important to keep event property fees in check, both for the success of the given event promotion and for the event industry as a whole.

Remember, early on in event marketing, many in the marketing business, especially advertising agencies who were starting to lose some of their advertising revenues to promotional events, were taking potshots at this new medium. Comparing effectiveness to cost is always an easy place to start looking for problems.

Event agencies that represent a corporate sponsor are responsible for protecting that sponsor and advocating that client's interests. The interest is obviously not in making the event property — those entertainers and celebrities pivotal to an event's success — any wealthier than necessary. Event agencies that represent the event property, as well as the corporate sponsor, face potential conflicting interests. A representative for an event property is interested in getting as much money out of a corporation as possible, and if he or she is also representing the corporation, the sponsor may not receive the best deal possible. Unfortunately, this goes on all the time.

If not excessive cash, is there something else that a sponsor can offer an event property to ensure cooperation? What are the event property's objectives? Usually, they are almost identical to the promoter's — ticket sales, ticket sales, ticket sales, plus merchandise sales — and all achieved at as little advertising and promotional costs as possible.

Unlike the promoter's objectives, an event property may also want to sell something else. Entertainers want to sell records. Sports celebrities may want to sell clothing, instructional videos, or autographs. Cultural events may want to raise additional charitable dollars or sell subscriptions to something. The key is to know the event properties well enough to find their "hot" buttons. These then represent a negotiating or leveraging position from which to deal.

While it is a lot easier to simply pay an event property's asking price, in the long run, it is far better to avoid this because an event promotion will be more profitable in the end.

What happens after identifying the event property's interests? It's time to get creative again. This time, let's do it by example.

When Procter & Gamble sponsored an event with Dolly Parton and Kenny Rogers ("Downy Presents Kenny Rogers/Dolly Parton," 1988), it was a fourth-quarter promotion, and both Kenny and Dolly were coming out with holiday record albums. This presented the perfect opportunity for using the event's clout to help achieve objectives mutually beneficial for the sponsor and the event property. In this case, the reach and marketing power of Downy was used to help sell records. In addition to making Kenny and Dolly offers that included marketing their concerts (ticket sales), there was also an offer to help them sell their new records. Every bottle of Downy carried a "hangtag" alerting the consumer that if they bought a certain size of Downy fabric softener *and* Kenny and/or Dolly's album, Downy would send them a two-dollar rebate. On all of the Downy in-store point-of-sale materials and displays that supported the in-market event (Kenny and Dolly's concert), the new albums were featured, furthering consumer awareness of Kenny and Dolly's new products. Conversely, inside all of Kenny's and Dolly's new albums was the information on how to receive the rebate. Furthermore, each album was flagged on the outside telling consumers they could buy this album and receive the rebate. This created a win-win situation. Kenny and Dolly received a lot of nontraditional advertising and awareness for their new albums, and Downy was featured in nontraditional marketing avenues as well — record stores and in and on the albums.

While Downy picked up the tab for the $2.00 redemptions, it was a better use of money than paying direct cash to Kenny and Dolly for the event sponsorship. Money that is thrown at an event property is "dead" money in that it is money that cannot be used to achieve the sponsor's objectives. The creative use of rebating in this case helped Kenny and Dolly gain cash through higher album sales, yet Downy also achieved its objectives simultaneously.

Scratching someone else's back will always get a positive

response. Creativity here can go a long way toward making an event more profitable all around. The saying that "Cash is king" is still true. However, when negotiating with event properties, it is better to think "Direct cash is not always king." Accomplishing other objectives for them can achieve royalty as well, or, in the record business, royalties!

THE CONSUMER

The almighty consumer. That's what marketing and promotion are all about, is it not? The goal is to get the consumer to buy or try a given product or service by creating brand image and brand loyalty which, along with a good product, will keep the consumer buying the product.

However, the majority of purchases today are impulse purchases, and that's the hard fact. In addition, consumers very often can be swayed from one brand to another through certain promotional inducements, such as coupons, rewards, and exclusives. These avenues are often strictly price-oriented and typically have no connection to brand imaging and awareness.

Event marketing allows marketers to reach consumers through multiple traditional and nontraditional means and to induce or reward them to buy or try products while simultaneously building brand image and awareness.

The importance of the trade in supporting and displaying a brand in the store has already been discussed. Trade support is especially important for impulse purchasing. Once trade support is forthcoming, including "loading up" on product stock, higher levels of consumer takeaway (sales) are possible than are accomplished through traditional trade support of displays, features, feature pricing, and other methods. Research has shown that consumers would buy or try a product to get a discount on tickets for an event or concert that they were interested in attending. Consumers claim also to buy or try a product if it allows for other special rewards or exclusives — for example, on-pack offers for exclusive tour merchandise, audiocassettes, or other event- or entertainment-oriented tie-ins or specials.

Several consumer and product purchase offers and rewards were tested in conjunction with Kellogg's 1991 "Kenmei Cereal Presents Barry Manilow in Concert" event. These included (1) a $7.50 discount off each Manilow concert ticket with two proofs-of-purchase for Kellogg's Kenmei cereal, (2) a free audiocassette of Barry Manilow with two proofs of Kellogg's Kenmei cereal redeemable right in the grocery store (instant gratification), (3) discounts on tour merchandise, and, of course, (4) special rewards of front row concert seats and backstage passes. The brand experienced a share increase of seven times its then-current position! Kellogg was also able to achieve an approximate share of four times its initial share position in the months following the promotion/event, meaning that consumers were repurchasing the brand in order to exchange product purchases for rewards (see Exhibit 15.3).

EXHIBIT 15.3

In addition to rewarding consumers for their purchases, event marketing also allows a marketer to build instant brand imaging and awareness through the close association with the event property (artist, sports figure) and its own inherent image. People, by and large, are very image-conscious and like to be associated with things that "tell" them or reinforce to them that they are, in fact, "cool."

The "Chivas Regal Presents Frank Sinatra's Diamond Jubilee" tour/event for the House of Seagram's premium scotch created an association which in itself said something instantly to the consumer and the trade. Sinatra is as premium as one gets in the entertainment industry and to consumer demographics that fit Chivas Regal targets. If Sinatra represents "the best," Chivas Regal must too.

However, do not make the mistake that lots of failed event marketing programs have. Remember it's not the event; it's how the event is leveraged to accomplish multiple goals! The Chivas Regal/Frank Sinatra program included retail display tie-ins, retail hospitality, media tie-ins and public relations, a special customized Chivas Regal audio-cassette of Frank Sinatra's greatest hits that was featured on-pack, plus more tie-ins to make sure the brand received trade support, media support, and, of course, consumer takeaway. The program was hailed as one of the most successful programs Seagram's has ever had and "raised the bar" for future House of Seagram promotions.

Consumers spend over $700 million a day on entertainment and recreation. Event marketing can uniquely reward both the consumer and the sponsor company by allowing all parties involved to get a little closer to something they already revere and enjoy. It definitely surpasses most sponsors' competitive promotions!

EXECUTING AN EVENT

Execution is the most important element in event marketing and probably in every other marketing venture. A big idea is just that, an idea. To bring it to life and to make it work takes flawless execution and implementation.

This following story typifies the problem of executing major event programs:

> A grandmother was walking her little grandson down a Miami beach one day, when all of a sudden a giant wave came out of the sea, grabbed the little boy, and took him away. Horrified, the elderly woman looked up to the sky and said, "I've never asked you for anything in my life! I've lived a decent, moral, and righteous life and I just do not deserve this." And so she said, "I'm asking now, please return my grandson to me, please!" With that, a giant wave appeared from the sea again, this time gently placing the little boy next to his grandmother, unharmed. The woman looked down to her beloved grandson, then she looked up to the sky and said, "HE HAD A HAT!"

To properly execute a successful event marketing program takes a lot of experience, much planning, proven systems for implementation, and the realization that it's not the obvious things that will get in the way of success. Rather, the small, almost unknown or unseen elements will cause an event to falter — like the hat in the story.

Consider a 70-city musical tour/event for a major sponsor. Everything is humming along — free media support, retail support, and sales surpassing the prior year's sales by 180 percent in a bad economy! The president of the sponsor company shows up totally unannounced with his teenage daughter and her friend, in a city where he has no ties. He did not bother to get concert tickets, nor did he show up to the event on time. Needless to say, there was some trouble accessing the talent backstage to impress his daughter and friend, and the star had already left by the time they did go backstage. Product sales were through the roof — but so was he. It didn't matter that his company was seeing sales results it hadn't seen in decades, or the fact that this was the most economical marketing program ever done. In his eyes, the program wasn't a success.

To be a successful event marketer, agency, or sponsor takes a talent for execution that cannot be taught anywhere. Successful execution takes experience, an unbelievable amount of diplomacy, and an ability to respond quickly to unforeseen problems when they occur. All the planning and focus on detail are critical, but so is the ability to react and to react quickly.

In the previous situation, a private rendezvous with the event's star for the president and his daughter was arranged by having the local sheriff stop the star's motorcade to explain the situation. Now local dealers and the president have agreed that this was an enormously successful event/promotion.

So, careful planning, realistic time and action tables, and being prepared to expect the unexpected are essential to an event's success. Face any problem or situation Honestly, and find the needed Answer in a very Timely manner. An event involves so many people, so many egos, so many elements. Always remember the H.A.T.!

MEASUREMENT

Not only can an event's success be measured, but also the results can be measured better and more accurately than with almost any other medium today. Since the exact promotional periods of the event promotion are known, event success can be directly measured:

By Account:
- Case sales
- Display penetration
- Shipments
- Features
- Price reductions
- Post-event surveys

By Intangibles:
- Image/awareness
- Product positioning
- Trade relationship building
- Field enthusiasm

By Media:
- PR (conversion)
- Leveraged (affidavits)

By Consumer:
- Scanner detail
- Redemption
- Nielsen (market share)
- Exit polls/intercepts

There also exist "bonuses" to event marketing that are harder to measure directly but are certainly part of its success. These bonuses/elements include:
- **Trade relationship building** — especially after a successful program with a fun personal backstage party visit
- **Sales force morale** — giving them the upper hand for once and making them feel good about their jobs
- **Brand imaging and awareness** — through the multitudes of media and promotions and the association with the event or star

One event can deliver all of the above; it is doubtful that a television commercial could do the same.

SUMMARY — IT'S NOT THE EVENT
By now it should be obvious how potentially powerful this medium of event marketing can be. Marketers have only just begun to experience the *surface* of what it can offer. It works because it addresses everyone's needs in today's marketplace. It is one of the most flexible means of marketing today because it permits adaptation not only to every individual market but also to every individual retailer, local medium, and consumer need.

The sales increases that event programs have generated are staggering, especially in today's economic climate. Event programs can gain four to eight weeks of retail and media support and obtain big consumer takeaway directly tied to special proof-of-purchase offers. Seldom do well-conceived events garner less than 85 percent retail support in any given market. In fact, cooperation is usually closer to 100 percent and lasts for extended weeks — without trade incentive dollars! Product sales typically range anywhere from 45 percent more than the prior year to 200–300 percent more than the prior year. And all of these event programs can, and should, be based on total payout, that is, the programs can and do pay for themselves while generating these levels of sales and profits. Does event marketing work? You bet!

The future of event marketing has only just begun. Event marketing is an innovative promotional technique and one that works very well. But the key to successful events is to remember that it's not the event itself, it's how you leverage it, add to it, evolve it, and use it that matters.

Richard G. Ebel is Director of Marketing Communications at Promotional Products Association International (PPAI), an Irving, Texas-based trade association representing manufacturers and distributors of ad specialties, premiums, business gifts, and awards. Affiliated with PPAI since 1969, he currently supervises the association's public relations, advertising, and marketing research activities.

Prior to joining PPAI, Ebel was on the editorial staff of The National Underwriter, *a leading insurance newspaper, and subsequently served as editor of membership publications for the National Association of Retail Druggists and the National Moving and Storage Association. He is a frequent contributor to advertising and marketing publications.*

Ebel is a graduate of the Medill School of Journalism at Northwestern University, and has an M.A. degree with a public relations emphasis from Northern Illinois University.

CHAPTER 16

SPECIALTY PROMOTIONS

Advertising specialties or specialty promotions is one of the oldest forms of producing a sale or advocating a cause, yet nobody seems to really understand it. In the United States, ad specialties have been around for a spell. In its extensive exhibit of antiques at its Irving, Texas, headquarters, Promotional Products Association International displays a *Farmers' Almanac* promoting a chemist (drugstore) in 1830. And that is not among the earliest of the promotional almanacs.

When Ohio newspaper publisher Jasper Meek found in 1880 that revenues from printing ads on schoolbook bags and horse blankets were enough to successfully operate a stand-alone business, he drew numerous imitators and, in effect, launched what has since become a $5.5 billion industry.

In the early days, the ad-imprinted merchandise — usually made of cloth, paper, wood, glass, or leather — was thought of as "reminder" or "goodwill" advertising. Those functions are still important. However, the inventory of applications has proliferated enormously.

This versatility is reflected in the diversity of users: manufacturers promoting to dealers, retailers trying to draw store traffic, trade associations and labor unions recruiting members, churches attempting to boost attendance, fund-raisers soliciting donors, and politicians chasing votes.

PROMOTIONAL PRODUCTS: COMPONENTS AND DISTINCTIONS

Under the "promotional products" umbrella we find ad specialties, business gifts, premiums, awards, prizes, and commemoratives. The fact that an item, such as a desk paperweight, can be used as any of these promotional products, tempts one to ignore some significant distinctions.

Ad specialties are always imprinted with an advertiser's identification or message, and they are given free.

Business gifts are also given free. They cost more than some ad specialties, and normally they don't carry an imprint. Nowadays, however, there seem to be more business gifts with the donor's logo subtly inscribed.

Premiums are the true incentives because the receiver needs to do something to get them. Sometimes imprinted, but usually not, premiums are distinguished from ad specialties by the fact that they are earned by making a purchase, a deposit (in a bank), or a financial contribution.

Awards, too, are earned by performance or simply by hanging onto the job long enough to be honored for retiring gracefully.

The point is, the items can be the same in all cases, and the only difference may be in their functions. Yet it is a difference that goes beyond mere hairsplitting.

TYPES OF PRODUCTS: WHEN TO USE WHICH PRODUCTS

Someone with apparently nothing better to do once added up the different types of merchandise used as ad specialties and calculated that number to be about 15,000. When one takes a type — for example, writing instruments — and multiplies it by model — ink pens, ballpoints, rollerballs — and by brands, figure on tens of thousands more.

In 1980, Jim Lindheim, then with the old Yankelovich, Skelly & White social research firm, told an audience of ad specialty practitioners that the desire of younger Americans for self-expression on the things they wore would have a considerable impact on the promotional products industry. His prophecy was right on the money. Today, one out of every five dollars spent on ad specialties goes for T-shirts, baseball caps, and other wearables.

Other top-five product categories are writing instruments, desk/office accessories, ceramics/glassware, and calendars.

For the most part, these are useful, conventional, everyday products. Where, then, are the unique, the novel, the one-of-a-kind? They serve a purpose, and thus they are out there, too.

If the objective is to be remembered and appreciated, a promotional product that the intended audience will want to keep is important — for example, an attractive, quality, personalized ballpoint or ink pen. On the other hand, if the objective is attention — not retention — and what is really wanted is a tangible exclamation point, a ballpoint that is contorted into a shape, from a heart to an outline of the state of Texas, may be more suitable.

The industry caters to differences in objectives and sizes of budgets. These differences include items that are kept and maybe even revered, as well as items that are thrown away after the objective has been accomplished.

STRENGTHS AND WEAKNESSES

Ad specialties are a perfect way to keep a company's name in front of its prospects, provided, of course, that an item has been selected that is useful to the prospect and is likely to be retained. The ability to give a company a continuous presence with buyers is an important attribute of ad specialties, but there are other advantages as well, such as the following:

- **Long-lasting exposure** that produces high recall.
- **Targetability.** Like some other forms of promotion, ad specialties can deliver impressions to narrowly defined audiences.
- **Budget flexibility.** With prices ranging from a few cents apiece to tens of dollars, there is a good choice of items for

even the leanest budget.

- **Goodwill.** People like to receive something for nothing. Their appreciation builds points for the giver.
- **Unobtrusiveness.** Impressions can be conveyed without becoming a nuisance — no doorbells to answer, no phone calls to disrupt dinner, no frequent commercial breaks to interrupt entertainment.
- **Compatibility with other media.** Promotional products work well with other forms of promotion and enhance their effectiveness. They boost response rates and increase traffic counts.

The following are some caveats to consider:

- **Small copy area.** Given the size of many promotional products, long messages are often out of the question. Sometimes space will accommodate only the corporate logo. Marketers who need to say more can surmount this problem by using advertising curls, tags, and other printed appendages.
- **Long lead times.** Lead times may be longer than what some marketers are accustomed to. Don't place an order and expect to get delivery next week. Figure on three to five weeks as a norm (or be prepared to pay rush charges) on catalog products. Custom work will take even longer.
- **Duplication.** Suppose an item is chosen and the recipient already has 10 of them. The gift may be ignored and pitched. The wastebasket can be avoided if the item is more attractive, more useful, more distinctive than similar promotional products the recipient might have. Or, why not personalize the item by imprinting the recipient's name or initials? People tend not to discard gifts with their names on them.
- **Sporadic accountability.** In many uses of ad specialties, it's difficult to say just what effect the items had on the promotion. As with some other forms of advertising and promotion they may be using, marketers may believe the imprinted "gifts" are having an impact but not really know if they are or not. Fortunately, the promotional products industry is developing measurement systems, generally associated with pre-test/post-test methodologies, and some are now available.

This brings up some options to ponder. Should one buy out of a specialty catalog or does one go to the expense of customizing the item given? Should one look for durability in a specialty product, or is there an advantage to wear-out? By supplying a company's sales force with desk note trays to give their prospects, as the notepaper is used up, salespeople will be particularly welcomed on subsequent visits when they bring refills.

If the goal is to thank or reward customers, but the budget prevents going top-of-the-line, then resort to stratified selection. The "A" customers or prospects — for instance, the heavy users — get first-quality items, while the "B" customers appropriately receive more modest gifts.

TYPICAL APPLICATIONS

As noted earlier, there is a multitude of objectives that can be successfully addressed with promotional products.

Creating Awareness. Creating awareness was the objective of IBM when it scheduled demonstrations of its PCs on campuses of three private universities in Texas. On one campus, the company announced the demonstration in the school newspaper. At the second school, imprinted combination ballpoint/highlighters were distributed in engineering and computer science classroom buildings. At the third campus, IBM split its promotion budget between the school newspaper and ad specialties. Surveys of the demonstration audiences showed that twice as many persons attributed their attendance and exposure to the demonstrations to the ad specialty than to the newspaper. In fact, exposure to the ad specialty alone was also more effective than the ad specialty-newspaper combination.

The point to be made here is that, like direct mail, promotional products represent a targeted form of promotion that is particularly effective among selective rather than mass audiences.

Generating Leads. When it comes to lead generation, direct mail often bogs down because of mailbox clutter. Promotional products, however, can make a difference in response rates.

A good illustration is furnished by Premier Bank, one of the largest in Louisiana. The Shreveport branch targeted 1,500 difficult-to-reach prospects — many of them doctors, attorneys, and accountants — with the intention of securing appointments for the bank's calling officers. A sales letter to one group drew a 1.8 percent response. Aided by inclusion of an inexpensive ad specialty (a digital clock), the mailing to the second group produced a 2.7 percent response. Even more effective was the offer to the third group of an incentive to return the enclosed business reply card. The incentive offer — a more expensive digital clock — produced a 7.3 percent response. It also achieved a per-appointment cost of $34.76 compared with the $100.24 cost of the sales letter alone.

Dimensional items are particularly effective in neutralizing gatekeepers such as secretaries and mailroom policies that shield executives from third-class mail. A bright-yellow package with the likeness of Einstein and the copy "Positively Brilliant" was mailed to 500 ad agencies and photo labs. The inference was that the mailer, Color Corporation of America, was capable of brilliant work. Inside the package was a pair of imprinted sunglasses for the recipient and vivid graphics on the interior depicting the famed genius wearing similar sunglasses (see Exhibit 16.1). An 80 percent response rate suggested that penetration was accomplished.

EXHIBIT 16.1

Obtaining Referrals and Recommendations. Referrals and recommendations from satisfied customers and influencers are coveted by almost every sales manager, but sometimes it takes more than just asking for them. A California insurance agency, Dodge, Warren & Peters, augmented its appeals to clients with an imprinted pocket telephone index. Then, when they referred a prospect, clients received an imprinted pocketknife, and later a desk diary.

To induce veterinary receptionists to recommend its brand of canine vitamins, the Upjohn Company mailed samples along with a mug for coffee breaks. Enclosed with the mugs and samples were a cassette tape and stickers for a sales log. Each sale was worth points, and receptionists could redeem their completed logs for prizes.

Building Traffic. Like premiums, ad specialties can be effective traffic builders. In a controlled field experiment involving trade show attendees, Hoechst Celanese Corporation found that mailing an ad specialty to advance registrants drew three times more traffic to its booth at the National Plastics Exposition than an invitation without a gift. Hoechst also experimented in a preshow mailing of an ad specialty coupled with an offer of an additional gift that could be picked up at the booth. The response, in terms of bringing the invitation coupon to the booth for redemption, was nearly twice as great (11.6% vs. 6.7%) when the preshow gift and the at-the-booth gift were companion items, in this case an imprinted coffee mug that went with the ceramic coaster that was mailed before the show.

As a traffic builder, promotional products work for retailers, too. Merchants at Burtonsville Crossing Shopping Center in Maryland banded together to draw commuters to the mall. On the second Tuesday of every month, hostesses at a bus stop greeted park-and-ride commuters with coffee, rolls, and coupons. After work, the commuters could redeem their coupons for ad specialty gifts, such as pocket flashlights and coffee mugs, at the store shown on the coupon. Redemption rates were impressive, ranging from 72 percent to 83 percent.

Introducing New Products or Services. Ad specialties are often used in introducing new products, services, and facilities and in reinforcing awareness of existing ones. As physical objects, ad specialties constitute a promotion form capable of being touched and inspected as well as being seen. That makes them ideal demonstration devices.

An Alabama distributor, Wholesale Wood Products, took advantage of this attribute when it introduced a new synthetic wood to lumber yards, builders, and architects. The item selected was a desk pencil caddy. But not just any pencil caddy. This one was fashioned from a block of the synthetic wood being promoted (see Exhibit 16.2).

Motivating Salespeople and Other Employees. A customary tactic for motivating salespeople and other employees is to stage a contest.

EXHIBIT 16.2

That is good thinking, but contests work so much better with promotional products, used either as a reward for performance or as a means of maintaining interest and excitement in pursuing the reward. Since enthusiasm tends to flag during a long-term contest, reinforcement with promotional products is advisable.

When Sparkletts Water Systems discovered that supermarket stockers were lax in replenishing shelves with the company's bottled water, marketing management was aghast at the sales being lost. The solution, the managers decided, was to get the broker salespeople to do the stocking. To announce the change, salespeople were mailed a brass dart and a walnut desk holder engraved "Stick it to the competition" (see Exhibit 16.3). Theme-imprinted decals were affixed inside the bottle cartons. Salespeople could redeem the decals for two cents each. To get them, of course, they'd have to unpack the cartons and stock the shelves. The salespeople were to bring their darts to the monthly sales meetings. Those who collected the most decals were eligible to fling the darts at a board on which were listed cash bonuses in various amounts. In this way, Sparkletts reduced out-of-stock averages by 30 percent.

Typical contests feature a start, sprints, and a finish. At its annual sales meeting, Sysco Frozen Foods launched a two-month contest. Doffing an Indiana Jones-style hat, the marketing vice president distributed foil-wrapped chocolate coins from a treasure chest. Salespeople

EXHIBIT 16.3

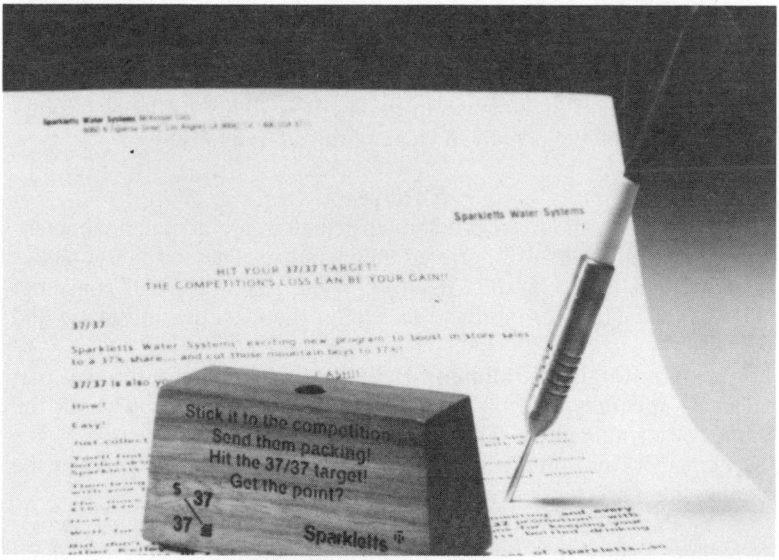

also received an ice scraper (copy: "Scrape up sales this winter. Relax in Bermuda this spring.") and a corked bottle containing half a treasure map. To sustain interest, midway through the contest period, pocket puzzles were mailed to the sales force. The first person to unscramble the puzzle was treated to a dinner for two. Once in Bermuda, members of sales teams making their goals were handed cardboard treasure chests. Inside was the other half of the treasure map that revealed a gift certificate which could be found when the goalbusters checked into their hotel rooms.

Creating Goodwill. The role of goodwill in marketing tends to be underemphasized, totally ignored, or relegated to the public relations department. Goodwill certainly isn't a concern of sales promotion. This is an attitude in need of adjusting, particularly as marketers contend with declining brand loyalty and recognize the economics of customer retention.

Beginning in the late 1980s, the marketing faculty at Baylor University executed a series of studies on the impact of specialty advertising on customer goodwill. The results of goodwill, researchers determined, are (a) customer loyalty, (b) willingness to make repeat purchases, and (c) willingness to recommend the company/brand to others.

In field experiments involving the Houghton-Mifflin Publishing Company and a Texas-based regional wholesale florist, researchers found the following:

- By using ad specialties as opposed to a thank you letter only, you can enhance your goodwill standing with customers significantly.
- By using ad specialties, you can increase your goodwill standing over competitors.
- The level of increase in goodwill is likely to depend somewhat on the perceived value of the ad specialty.

TACTICS

Skillful promotional products distributors are as much tacticians as they are purveyors of imprinted merchandise. They often use tactics related either to the product itself or to the psychology of consumer behavior. Designed to motivate or excite, these tactics are many and varied.

- **Contingent fulfillment.** Here the target audience receives part of an ad specialty — maybe a pair of sunglass lenses without the frames or a single glove. They get the other part — the one that makes the item work or completes a pair — only when they respond in the manner the marketer desires (see Exhibit 16.4).
- **Peer approval.** A helmet adorned with performance decals does more than give a football lineman an opportunity to crow about the number of running backs he's leveled. Such symbols motivate

EXHIBIT 16.4

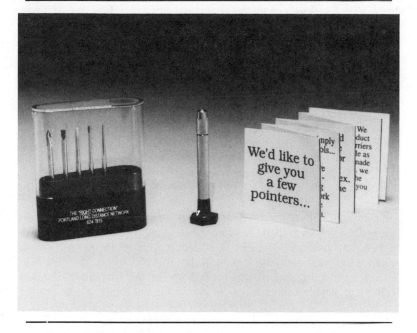

teammates to earn their own insignia that infer they belong in the company of star performers. So, too, awards and other recognition devices drive salespeople to either show them who's best or at least justify their position on the payroll.

*   **Status conferral.** A riverfront restaurant in Virginia offers ID cards to its best customers, making them feel special, which they are. Flashing the cards to the maitre d', they get preferred seating and don't have to bother with long waiting lines. They also receive T-shirts, sunglasses, and other ad specialties from waiters serving their tables. Club privileges are much sweeter when they create envy.

*   **Curiosity arousal.** Arousing curiosity goes beyond mere teasing. The target audience needs to ask, "What is it?," and be willing to find out. For instance, a bank in Spokane, Washington, scheduled a grand opening for a new branch. Prospective depositors were mailed an unrecognizable plastic disk and were told they could find out what it was — and get the part that made it a useful appliance — by attending the open house. Several hundred did, and they found out that the mailed enticement was the top to a tape dispenser.

*   **Collector appeal.** From antiques to baseball cards, the pervasiveness of collector mania is evident in the number of newspaper columns, magazines, and trading shows devoted to this special interest. There is a marketing parallel, too. One National Basketball Association

team provides an example. As an attendance builder, a set of coins was struck with likenesses of the team players. For many fans, the first one they were given was sufficient bait to draw them to the next dozen or so home games to acquire the complete set.

• **Influencing the influencers.** Perhaps no group influences purchase decisions more than children, a perception that led to placing the first premium in a cereal box. Promotional products formed the enticement of the "Kids Go HoJo Fan Club" campaign in which children, ages 3 to 12, of guests at any Howard Johnson property received free "fun packs." The contents included imprinted crayons, coloring/activity books, decals, and postcards. And tactics that work with children can also work with adults.

• **Authentication.** In this case, the specially crafted promotional product becomes attention-getting memorabilia because it is actually a piece of the real thing. For its "Dodger Diamond Dust" campaign tying into the 25th anniversary of Dodger Stadium, a cable TV service scooped up dirt from the L.A. team's infield and it authenticated, polybagged, and packaged the dirt in collectible cans. An accompanying romance curl described the inaugural day in 1962 when "the dust of a freshly groomed diamond was kicked up for the first time." To add excitement, genuine diamonds were inserted in randomly selected cans.

SOURCES AND SERVICE PROVIDERS

The 15,000 types of imprinted promotional products mentioned earlier are provided by 2,500 or so companies. They are called suppliers rather than manufacturers because many — assemblers, converters, or importers — don't manufacture anything. What they have in common, however, is an imprinting capability, which could be letterpress, silk screening, hot stamping, photo etching, laser engraving, embroidering, and a number of other processes. Since suppliers have no sales forces, they market their products through independent distributors. Some suppliers will sell directly to end users. But most, eager to avoid competing with their distributors, prefer not to. In that respect, promotional products differ little from other packaged goods industries.

The 12,000 distributors in the United States offer some diversity in services. Some are basically product sellers. Their customers are agencies and companies who rely on their own creative departments to provide what creativity, if any, is called for in integrating the promotional products into the campaign. At the other end of the scale are distributors — more aptly called promotion planners — that do it all. In addition to supplying the items, they do the creative and the execution, sometimes in conjunction with the clients' agencies.

Regardless of the services distributor firms may offer, what makes them indispensable to end users is the familiarity they have with their business environment. Their personnel are expected to know not only what products are available but also what suppliers are reliable in terms of quality production and imprinting and in making delivery schedules. Neglecting these considerations can result in a very stressful promotion experience.

ELEMENTS OF PROMOTION DEVELOPMENT

Promotions obviously differ from distribution, which can amount to no more than setting out a box of imprinted matchbooks on the cashier's counter. The architecture of promotions involving imprinted products has many of the same plinths and columns found in other types of campaigns. The planning elements to be dealt with are as follows:

- **Objective.** What is expected to be accomplished with the promotion?
- **Target audience.** With whom will the promotional products be communicating?
- **Budget.** How much can be spent on the promotion?
- **Distribution.** What is the most effective way of delivering the promotional products to the target audience? By direct mail? On sales calls? Through a related third party?
- **Theme.** Often no more than clichés on their billionth go-around, themes nevertheless give the promotion an identity and coherence that ties everything together.
- **Item selection.** Of those 15,000 imprintable items that exist, which will do the job best?
- **Evaluation.** Evaluation is often ignored, but without some sort of auditing, whether the promotion worked is unknown.

When laying out a plan, one of the first things to notice is how some elements will dictate others — budgets, for example. If there isn't enough money to reach an audience with anything but a very cheap item, it may be difficult to accomplish a particular goal. If the budget can't be increased, sending a more expensive and attractive incentive only to respondents may fit the bill better than sending a less attractive, less expensive item to the entire mailing list.

There are many trade-offs to be made, and the trick is to adjust and compromise without reducing the voltage.

James Kunze has 14 years of experience in providing marketing planning, advertising, and sales promotion services to clients, including his responsibilities at J. Brown Associates, a Grey Advertising subsidiary, where he currently is Executive Vice President and General Manager. He has worked with a wide range of clients, including AT&T, Procter & Gamble, United Airlines, Polaroid, Texaco, Philip Morris, R.J. Reynolds, and others.

Prior to joining J. Brown Associates in Chicago, Kunze was Executive Vice President for William A. Robinson, directing that agency's business development and strategic planning functions, in addition to managing clients. Also in his career he has worked in sales management at Procter & Gamble; directed consumer promotion and brand management activities at Warner-Lambert; and was responsible for advertising and sales promotion at Estech.

He is a graduate of the Krannert School of Management at Purdue University and attended law school at Indiana University.

CHAPTER 17

TRADE PROMOTION

OVERVIEW

The practice of offering rewards in order to induce specific kinds of actions by the distribution channel for a packaged goods product is generally known as trade marketing or trade promotion. The practice has evolved over the past quarter-century into an extremely important class of marketing tool. Most sources today agree that trade marketing expenditures are the largest segment of marketing spending, representing more than 40 percent of total marketing expenditures. A comparison of expenditures for major categories of marketing between now and 20 years ago shows the shift (see Table 17.1).

TABLE 17.1
PERCENT OF TOTAL MARKETING BUDGET

Spending Category	1971	1991
Consumer advertising	60	35
Consumer promotion	15	25
Trade promotion	25	40

What has fueled this growth? Basically, several factors have contributed:

1. **Initial success.** When marketers shift funds to reward retailers for the performance of specific objectives, such as extra display or new distribution, the result is usually very good initially. Display commitments happen, new sizes go into distribution, and extra sales result because an important distribution channel variable has been altered.

2. **Recessions.** When marketers have faced recession in the last 20 years, the response has been to emphasize price reduction through special allowances and price-oriented consumer inducements, such as rebates. Having placed so much emphasis on price in tough times, most marketers find that the road back to a more balanced marketing approach is exceedingly difficult, if not entirely impossible, without absorbing a large volume reduction in the short term.

3. **Shift in power.** An explosion in the number of new products, new forms, new sizes, and new flavors has resulted in higher demand for retailer services by marketers. The demand has enabled retailers to reap the benefits of ever higher trade spending.

If your responsibilities are in sales planning, sales promotion, or brand management, you'll want to know how to employ trade marketing for maximum effectiveness in both the short and long term. Your success will probably depend upon it. Because trade marketing has become such a large portion of most marketers' budgets, the amount of time spent planning, discussing, and defining trade marketing programs has mushroomed.

Today, in fact, most brand marketers find that it is extremely difficult to achieve management approval for brand advertising and/or consumer promotion plans, because every discussion of these subjects converts into a discussion about how the trade support necessary for volume achievement will be obtained and where the funding for the advertising and/or consumer promotion will fit into the overall budget, since trade promotion must be funded first.

You'll want to know the techniques of trade marketing and the objectives each is intended to accomplish. The next segment of this chapter will provide a review of these areas. Then, you'll want to know about the long-term implications for your overall marketing plan of employing trade marketing techniques. This discussion will follow the techniques review.

Finally, you'll be introduced to a trade marketing approach that is new and very promising and that illustrates the need to do effective trade marketing planning within the context of overall brand building, rather than within the short-term volume perspective exclusively.

THE TECHNIQUES OF TRADE MARKETING:
PURCHASE INCENTIVES

There are two primary classes of trade marketing techniques: purchase incentives and performance allowances.

Purchase incentives are all of the forms of payment offered to the distributors of packaged goods products, which are designed to cause initial purchase, restocking, or increased inventory of the product. Within this class of trade marketing techniques, we'll look at the following:

1. Slotting allowances
2. Off-invoice purchase allowances
3. Dating
4. Free goods

This class of techniques has seen explosive growth in recent years. It's this class in which the shift in power from marketer to retailer has been so strongly reflected. Retailers collectively have been extremely successful in obtaining ever growing amounts and forms of purchase incentives.

To illustrate the dramatic shift, one of America's largest and most successful food marketers has seen an overall net shift in marketing spending from 30 percent trade/70 percent consumer focus 20 years ago, to 70 percent trade/30 percent consumer focus currently.

Technique at a glance

Type: Slotting/shelving

How it works: Usually expressed as a percent-of-invoice price of product, that is, 5–15 percent of nonpromotional invoice cost of merchandise.

Objective of the technique: To induce buyers to place the product into distribution and assign it warehouse, computer, and store shelf space.

Discussion: Slotting/shelving allowances are a relatively recent form of purchase incentive. The term has come into broad-scale use during the past 10–15 years. It is the result of a tidal wave of new products, sizes, flavors, and forms offered by product marketers to retailers in recent years. For example, the average supermarket today carries more than 16,000 items, which is 40 percent more than just six years ago.

Slotting allowances have come about for two main reasons: first, to fulfill a need for distributors to recoup their true costs of adding all of the new items on a constant basis and second, to recognize an opportunity to extract additional funds from marketers because of the increased demand for store and warehouse space. For many packaged goods marketers, slotting allowances have become a major barrier to the successful introduction of new items. The level of slotting allowance required frequently is greater than the budget for advertising the product to the consumer. *An example:* An entirely new beverage product was introduced by a mid-sized beverage marketer in the mid-1980s. The product had strong taste and health benefits to sell to the consumer. The product was positioned to an upscale audience and was premium priced. The product was successfully tested and the sales target for year one nationally was set at $100 million. This is the kind of product that performs best with high levels of consumer awareness, which requires significant advertising levels, perhaps in the $10–20 million range. However, since the brand was forced to introduce with an introductory plan that was top-heavy with slotting and promotion allowances, less than $6 million was left for advertising. The brand achieved year one sales goals on the strength of the strong trade merchandising support, but it could not sustain this volume longer term, since overall levels of consumer awareness were too low. The brand has now shrunk to less than $50 million annual volume.

Some marketers have resisted paying slotting by emphasizing the importance to the retailer of the new item and the high level of support that will be placed behind the item by the marketer. Generally, only a few of the largest and strongest consumer marketers have been able to make this approach work.

The good news: Slotting fees usually result in successful initial placement of a new item.

The bad news: Slotting fees frequently reduce the budget available for making the new item a success with consumers, thus contributing to the high failure rate of new items.

Technique at a glance

Type: Off-invoice

How it works: An amount, usually 5–25 percent of the nonpromotional case price of the product, is subtracted on the invoice, leaving a discounted case cost to the distributor for a specified time period or limited number of orders, usually one or two.·

Objective of the technique: To induce purchase of inventory, which is significantly in excess of needs based on normal rate of sale.

Discussion: Off-invoice allowances represent the largest class of purchase inducement. The technique is direct, easy to understand, and effective in inducing the distribution channel to buy additional inventory. Off-invoice allowances have replaced many forms of performance allowances, which are paid only after performance has been confirmed. This has occurred because of retailers' objections to billback offers and their appreciation for direct off-invoice offers.

The technique is most effective when employed concurrently with an extra advertising or consumer promotion effort designed to sell through the additional product inventory to the consumer. Too often, however, the technique is used to stimulate a short-term increase in shipments without any accompanying consumer effort. The result is a period of significantly increased shipments followed by a period of significantly decreased shipments because the distributors' inventory is excessive. The off-invoice purchase inducement in this case has produced forward-buying and has done so at a major cost, primarily, the amount of the discount. Further, some distributors aggressively forward-buy when a product is offered at a large off-invoice discount, then reship the product to other distributors after the deal period ends and the manufacturer is then offering the product at normal price. This practice, called diverting, is very disruptive for the marketer. The sales force's local quota/shipment goals may be significantly distorted, leading a marketer to think that the product is enjoying a major growth pattern in a certain market when it is not, or that a product in a market where diverted merchandise is flowing in has a major decline occurring when no such problem exists.

Diverting can significantly alter promotion analysis and can be very difficult to control, and the level of difficulty increases as the level of off-invoice allowances increases. In some distributors, an off-invoice allowance will result in a temporary reduction in resale price to the consumer, with a resulting increase in rate of sale.

The good news: Off-invoice allowances are easy to execute, and they are a form of allowance that many distributors strongly favor.

The bad news: Off-invoices are a very tempting short-term "fix" for volume problems, which can result in forward-buying and little else.

Technique at a glance

Type: Dating

How it works: The extending of payment terms to the distributor which are lengthier than the marketer's normal invoice payment terms — usually expressed as a cash discount if paid within a stipulated number of days, for example 2 percent 10/net 61 days, which means 2 percent discount if paid in full within 10 days; full amount due within 61 days.

Objective of the technique: To induce distributors to buy sooner or to induce the purchase of extra inventory.

Discussion: The use of extended dating terms as a promotional tool is intended to enable the distributor to commit early to a new product or to a promotional or seasonal buying program. In all of the cases, the product may not have any significant rate of sale established until new-product advertising begins or until the season starts. In these situations, some distributors prefer to delay ordering until demand is established. Since this reduces availability of the product to the consumer, the marketer may utilize a tool such as dating to induce earlier distributor purchase.

Dating is usually effective in achieving the noted objectives, because it effectively allows the retailer to sell the product before having to pay for it. The true cost of this trade marketing tool is the cost of financing the order amount for the extended time period. In some cases, the opportunity cost for the funds is considered as well when attempting to assign a cost. Many corporate controllers are reluctant to permit the use of dating because of the effects on cash flow and the cost of the tool.

Another factor to be carefully considered before offering special dating terms is the precedent-setting nature of this offer. Future programs will be much tougher to sell without extended terms, once the practice has been utilized.

The good news: Retailers like it. Dating is simple and effective against limited objectives.

The bad news: It can be extremely expensive when precedents are considered. Dating can result in undesirable competitive reaction and in unwanted repetition.

Technique at a glance

Type: Free goods

How it works: Distributors receive additional cases of product at no cost, at a predetermined ratio to cases purchased, for example, one case free with 12 purchased.

Objective of the technique: To increase inventories of product in the distribution channel.

Discussion: Free goods are used in lieu of off-invoice allowances by some product marketers to induce purchase of additional inventory by distributors. Proponents argue that offers of free goods result in greater inventory increases than from comparable off-invoice offers. Their reasoning is that, in an example account, the sales representative with a 10 percent off-invoice allowance may suggest a promotional order of 1,000 cases to an account that normally sells 500 cases per month. The sales representative with a matching free goods offer, one case free with 10, will do likewise. But after selling the distributor on 1,000 cases, the additional "free" 100 cases will be added to the order, making the total order 1,100 cases.

Detractors say that free goods offers are more confusing to explain, and they don't really result in more inventory. This form of inducement is less frequently used in packaged goods than in some other industries, such as apparel. *The good news:* Offer of free goods may result in additional inventories when compared to off-invoice offers. *The bad news:* The offer does not provide for a temporary case price reduction by the distributor to the retail outlets and therefore may not provide any retail stimulus.

Purchase Incentives Wrap-Up.

The good news: The most frequently used type of trade marketing tools, purchase incentives are favored by retailers because they directly reduce the cost of goods, and they don't require any other special activity. Some sales managers like them because distributors will buy additional inventory and because sales presentations are simple and straightforward.

Marketers who rely heavily on this form of promotion cite lower training costs and higher sales calls per day as advantages. Purchase incentives generally are effective in achieving short-term tactical objectives.

The bad news: Purchase incentives are relatively less efficient in generating incremental sales to the consumer than performance allowances, which require distributors to perform consumer-influencing activities to earn. The use of purchase incentives on a regular basis has developed an inefficient distribution pattern for many marketers in which retailers forward-buy to capture an allowance then sell product at the regular rate, thus reducing orders for a following period.

The additional negative is that large purchase allowances result in the practice of diverting, further distorting the distribution picture. The marketer then has a shipment pattern that contains significant "peaks and valleys," causing plant inefficiency, shipping problems, and forecasting problems.

Most important, the too-heavy use of purchase allowances reduces funds available for consumer-influencing activities and consequently has an important negative effect on long-term brand vitality.

PERFORMANCE ALLOWANCES

Performance allowances are all of the forms of payment offered to distributors of a product, which are designed to induce an action by the distributor that increases the rate of sale of the product to the final consumer. Key activities that occur in the distribution channel and positively affect the rate of sale of a product to the consumer include the following:

1. Temporary price reduction
2. Second location or off-shelf display
3. Expanded shelf space
4. Demonstrating or sampling product in store
5. Advertising the product under the store's name to the consumer

Marketers typically offer performance allowances to induce some or all of these activities on their products. The next section will review these specific types of performance allowances:

1. Price reduction allowance
2. Display/merchandising allowance
3. Advertising allowance
4. Count/recount allowance

A marketer wishing to use performance allowances has many hurdles to overcome. First and foremost, retailers generally resist bill-back offers because too much administrative time is used qualifying and collecting and because they want additional flexibility. Second, retailers have the benefit of the balance of power to use to enforce more favorable terms, and that enables the request for less restrictive kinds of offers to have more clout. Third, the marketer's own sales force resists performance allowances because of the extra time it takes to administer the contracts and because of the retailer resistance, which limits their success.

The fact that marketers still do use performance allowance offers indicates how much value comes from giving them, in spite of all these difficulties. A general rule today is that the program for which performance allowances are offered should be an exceptionally strong one with obvious retailer benefits to offset the negatives of the offer.

Technique at a glance

Type: Price reduction allowance

How it works: An allowance per unit is paid to the retailer for a corresponding price reduction for a specified time period. The allowance may be an offer for purchases during a particular time period or an annual accrual on all case purchases.

Objective of the technique: To induce the retailer to reduce the price to the consumer for a product during a specified time period.

Discussion: This type of performance allowance is a major category of brand promotion spending. Many products today have a price reduction allowance that is accrued on an annual basis and that represents 10–15 percent of brand sales volume. The allowance may have any of several different names, including Brand Development Fund, Special Marketing Fund, Key Market Fund, or Customer Marketing Fund. An indication of the importance of this category of trade spending today is that, for many brands, price reduction allowances are the largest item on the brand marketing budget, larger than total advertising expenditures, for example. The use of periodic price reduction allowances continues but with less usage than that of the annual-fund type of price reduction format.

The good news: Price reduction allowances are very effective in generating strong trade promotion for a brand. This type of retailer effort on behalf of a brand generally is successful in producing incremental consumer sales for the brand.

The bad news: Price reduction allowances have grown to be the largest category of marketing spending on many brands, reducing the amount of consumer effort the brands can afford. This trend is therefore shifting the balance of brand consumer communication strongly toward "buy because it's cheap" and away from "buy because it's better."

Technique at a glance

Type: Display/merchandising allowance

How it works: An allowance is paid to the retailer in exchange for a specific kind of in-store merchandising performance, usually either a second location display or an enhancement to normal shelf space or position.

Objective of the technique: To obtain a visibility advantage for the product in-store or to secure year-round shelf space advantage.

Discussion: Merchandising/display allowances represent another form of allowance offered to packaged goods retailers. These allowances are aimed at a key sales-inducing variable: retail visibility. Since extra display and/or shelf space has been shown to be a major sales increase factor, it is not surprising that marketers seek to induce retailers to provide this advantage for their product.

A quick look at some typical results of studies of retail visibility variables shows the following:

1. Off-shelf, second location display of a product at the everyday price increased the sales of a beverage product by 104 percent.
2. A study of shelf space dynamics showed that sales increased by 32 percent for a product whose shelf space was increased by 50 percent.
3. A product whose shelf position was changed from a standard on-aisle location to a higher-traffic location near the front end of the stores saw sales increase by 57 percent.

Allowances offered for the achievement of a specific retail visibility variable may or may not be successful. Success factors include the effectiveness of the sales force in enforcing display requirements prior to the retailer's receiving payment, the appeal of the product to the trade as either a traffic-builder or a profit opportunity, and competitive reaction.

An additional factor in making the offering of display allowances less successful is a trend to pay display allowances off-invoice in exchange for intended performance. As a result, in recent years many marketers have moved away from offering display allowances in favor of price reduction allowances, with the hope that good sales force follow-through coupled with a retailer price feature will result in extra display.

The good news: Extra display for a brand at retail can be a major sales booster.

The bad news: Display allowances are tough to enforce and more difficult to administer if they are paid after performance via billback.

Technique at a glance

Type: Advertising allowance

How it works: An allowance is paid to the retailer for advertising the product in the retailer's ad.

Objective of the technique: To induce the retailer to advertise the product to the retailer's customers.

Discussion: Advertising by the retailer can increase the sales of a packaged goods product by as much as 50 percent for a weekly promotional period. Advertising by a retailer also frequently is the prerequisite for achieving extra merchandising or special pricing; so most marketers include some kind of advertising inducement in their retailer offers, along with a merchandising allowance, a price reduction allowance, or a special consumer offer to induce good retailer participation.

Advertising allowances from marketers represent an important revenue source to retailers. These moneys are frequently used to defray some or even all of the costs of the retailer's advertising program and department. The type of advertising generally achieved is brand name, package visual, and price, with size or length of ad being influenced by the requirements in the allowance agreement.

In most offerings of advertising allowances, retailers are given broad discretion to create any ad they choose, using perhaps a required package shot and allotting a prescribed amount of space or time to the product. Much less frequently, advertising allowances are accompanied by specially developed creative from the marketer that the retailer must utilize in order to collect the allowance. This is a particularly important area for future development, and one which will be discussed at the end of this chapter.

The good news: Advertising allowances usually are effective in achieving the goal of retailer advertising of the marketer's product.

The bad news: Significant administrative follow-up is frequently required. An ad allowance doesn't work well without also offering purchase or price reduction allowances.

Technique at a glance

Type: Count/recount allowance

How it works: Qualifying warehouse accounts receive a payment for each case of product shipped to retail stores during the promotional period.

Objective of the technique: To increase retail inventories.

Discussion: The count/recount allowance is so named because it requires the determination of warehouse inventory at the beginning and at the end of a promotional period. The difference, plus inbound shipments received during the period, determines the number of cases of product on which the count/recount allowance is paid. This form of allowance is less prevalent today than in years past, having been replaced by slotting and price reduction allowances in many cases.

The good news: The performance called for is measurable.

The bad news: The allowance frequently represents a second payment for the same product, after the slotting or initial purchase allowance, and it still doesn't require any activity that will increase the rate of sale to the consumer.

Performance Allowance Wrap-Up. Performance allowances generally are effective in achieving target objectives if the following can be achieved:

1. The trade resistance to being given a conditional offer can be overcome by a resourceful sales force.
2. A competitor's heavy use of off-invoice purchase allowances hasn't made a performance approach unattractive.
3. The marketer hasn't so overused nonperformance allowances that the offering of performance allowances is ineffective.

Because performance is required, the marketer must judiciously choose requirements that are measurable and that the marketer's sales force is capable and willing to enforce. In spite of the difficulties, a trade marketing plan that includes performance requirements generally produces a greater return for the marketer for each dollar invested.

The good news: Performance allowances enable marketers to focus on specific objectives that best suit their overall marketing efforts, resulting in better program payout.

The bad news: More selling time is required to explain, enforce, and follow up on performance allowance offers. The retailer does not like conditional offers and will resist their use.

THE DILEMMA

Here is the dilemma you will face if you're considering what type of trade marketing effort to propose for your products. Carefully constructed trade marketing efforts, which are executed with precision and discipline, usually meet or exceed objectives. That's good, right? Initially yes, but the dilemma is how to meet or exceed those results in the next quarter or annual period.

This dilemma exists and becomes increasingly bigger over time because of the following rationale. Since trade marketing by itself primarily attracts consumers by means of the positive effects of extra in-store merchandising and sale pricing, most marketers find it is impossible to meet or exceed the sales volume of the first trade marketing program without repeating the trade marketing offer that fueled the earlier success.

In fact, since most trade marketing efforts of equal value do slightly less well the second time around, the temptation is to enrich the program to achieve sales goals. At this point, the marketer is well along on a path to marketing that is increasingly weighted toward trade marketing. This is the exact path that most packaged goods marketers have followed over the past 15 years.

This continued growth in trade marketing expenditures has caused a major reduction in funding for consumer marketing initiatives. Reduced consumer marketing efforts produce less consumer demand for the product. To maintain sales volume, the marketer must increase trade inducements, thus repeating the cycle and further reducing consumer demand for the product.

Today, many packaged goods products do not have adequate funding to achieve high levels of consumer awareness and attention based on the benefits of the product. Marketers know that inflated trade marketing costs are the problem, but they don't know how to reduce those costs without a disastrous reduction in sales volume. Is there a better way? The answer is a qualified yes.

THE BETTER WAY

The better way is to utilize trade marketing as part of a balanced overall program of marketing, with sufficient funding for brand franchise-building activities — for example, brand-equity-focused advertising, trial-generating consumer promotion, product innovation. This is easy to say, but it's very hard to do, especially if you're already spending heavily on trade marketing.

A number of leading packaged goods marketers today are embarking on an effort to alter the balance to a more favorable consumer-to- trade ratio by significantly reducing the overall level of allowances and at the same time reducing the everyday cost of the product to the retailer and the consumer.

This effort has acquired a name: EDLP (everyday low pricing) or value-pricing. This effort has quickly drawn much media attention and significant retailer resistance. Retailers are very concerned about seeing a major revenue source reduced, and trade marketing funds are a major revenue source. In fact, the trade marketing expenditures of the top two packaged goods marketers, Kraft General Foods and Procter & Gamble, last year exceeded the total profits of the 40 largest food chains.

What will it take to make the reinvestment in brand-building consumer marketing — that marketers need — and at the same time, address the retailers' need for building customer loyalty and traffic and for maintaining high levels and advertising awareness of their stores? It will take a concerted effort by marketers to create and implement programs that:

1. Reach consumers with brand-building messages,
2. Identify individual retailers and their special merchandising,
3. Do both at the same time.

The best news is that this type of approach has been tried with major success by a few leading marketers. This is how it's been done.

First, the marketer decides how best to attract the consumer to his product with positioning and consumer benefits, traditional advertising tools. Then, the marketer creates and runs the advertising for the consumer to see. But rather than creating the advertising and then placing it in the traditional manner, the marketer goes to the retailer, shows the advertising and shows how it will look with each retailer integrated into the advertising. The marketer obtains the retailer's commitment to specially merchandise the product at a time of the retailer's choosing, and then the marketer schedules advertising to run that tells the consumer both about the product and about the retailer's special merchandising in the same ad.

The marketer does this for each retailer on a proportionately equal basis. The net result is a total amount of advertising that is effective in achieving share of voice for the product. In addition, all of the advertising directs the consumer to a specific retailer who has special merchandising on the product at that time; consequently advertising and merchandising work together to generate incremental results for both the marketer and the retailer.

Since the advertising is brand-benefit based, it attracts consumers who are interested in the product because of its benefits, not because it is cheap. Since the advertising is also retailer-specific, it attracts the consumer to a store with strong brand visibility for the product. So the retailer who provides special merchandising gets extra sales with less emphasis on deep-cut pricing.

For the marketer, the best news is that dollars previously deployed for wasteful levels of couponing and/or too-frequent trade deals can now be rechanneled to reward both the retailer and the marketer with significantly higher sales and better long-term prospects.

A major additional benefit is that marketers can create and implement brand-reinforcing consumer promotion programs, which will provide big sales volume increases at the same time. This is possible because the program is advertised with effective message, reach, and frequency to the target audience, and with the news of which specific retailer has special merchandising of the event.

Benefits scorecard

Benefits for the retailer:
1. Meaningful equity-building advertising for the store
2. Extra sales from each merchandising effort
3. Relief from deep-cut price total emphasis

Benefits for the marketer:
1. Significant incremental sales with brand equity focus
2. A net increase in consumer spending and strong retailer support at the same time
3. For the first time, a way to communicate value-added news and reward the retailer who merchandises it well

A few facts from some of the early uses of the program illustrate the potential:
1. Incremental sales of 182 percent against display without the advertising.
2. More than 400 retail accounts participated in the program, representing more than 70 percent ACV.
3. An average of 400 Gross Rating Points nationally on TV during the month of the program, totally funded by nonmedia funds.

Implementation of this program has limitations:
1. The program requires a specialized resource expert in the nuances of the program who is executionally equipped to handle 400–500 individual media buys and commercial customizations, in quick turnaround fashion, with 100 percent accuracy.
2. The approach works well only if the marketer has a meaningful investment in brand equity to leverage.
3. The program must be turnkey for retailers. That is, their participation must be no harder than buying and merchandising the product.
4. The program must work for all sizes and types of retailers. To do so, the program needs media choices and flexibility designed in.

This approach to trade marketing, reaching the consumer with brand-building programs that also leverage each individual retailer, is particularly well-suited to helping marketers restore long-term brand health in an uncertain economic environment. This approach also permits the marketer to reevaluate the elements of the overall marketing plan in order to be consistent with long-term brand building and shorter-term volume requirements at the same time.

TRADE MARKETING KEYS

For the person with trade marketing responsibilities, the following short list of keys is recommended to guide your efforts:
1. Use trade marketing wisely and carefully to achieve important

distribution channel objectives.
2. Fight to limit use. It's really tough to cut back.
3. Use it to support a consumer marketing approach/program rather than as a stand-alone effort.
4. Build an effective long-term trade marketing program by providing tools that help retailers and the brand at the same time.

Norman Abelson is an advertising/marketing/trade show consultant for hundreds of industry and government projects. He is the author of Trade Shows: Successful Sales Techniques, *a complete training program for both professional and novice exhibit managers. He has also written articles on trade shows and marketing for a number of publications.*

Abelson's career spans over 30 years during which time he was general manager of a fabricating facility in New York and exhibits manager for Tektronix, Inc. He did exposition work for the New York World's Fair and was fabrication consultant and coordinator for Expo '67 in Montreal. In addition, he was an account supervisor at a major New York City advertising agency.

Abelson is a graduate of Rochester Institute of Technology and the University of Buffalo, holding degrees in both engineering and business administration.

Richard Hagle is Editor, Business Books, for NTC Publishing Group in Lincolnwood, Illinois. He is former Editor/Publisher of the Sales Promotion Monitor *and former Executive Editor, Dartnell Books.*

CHAPTER 18

THE ABCs OF TRADE SHOWS

For as long as there have been business and commerce there have been places where buyers and sellers met to exchange goods and services. Several thousand years ago it might have been a few stands at the intersection of two roads. Its contemporary counterpart might be a local "farmers market" or a few roadside stands along a country road, but it could just as well be a high-tech exhibition with a thousand exhibitors using a combination of audio and video displays and 30-minute product demonstrations. Regardless, they share a common, centuries-old marketing tradition: a place where buyers come to buy and sellers come to sell.

BIG BUSINESS

Trade shows have been, and continue to be, an important way of doing business. In the United States more than 77 million individuals annually attend more than 8,000 trade shows, where more than 150,000 companies display their wares. These individuals — exhibitors *and* visitors — spend more than $8.7 billion on their direct participation and an additional $7 billion on related goods and services, such as meals, lodging, transportation, and pre- and postshow activities. Table 18.1 shows just some of the related expenditures. And, despite innovations in communications, the importance of trade shows as the one place where buyers and sellers can meet to see, touch, hear, and even taste and smell products will not diminish in the future. If anything, the increased globalization of business is likely to accelerate the importance of trade shows in the marketing mix.

TABLE 18.1
U.S. TRADE SHOW ESTIMATED ANNUAL EXPENDITURES

Attendance (in millions)

Show Attendees	77.0
Exhibitor Personnel	2.4
Auxiliary Personnel	4.6

Total Exhibitor Expenditures

Category	Amount in U.S. Dollars (Millions)
Airline Travel	$1,200.0
Hotel, etc.	2,284.8
Show Services	681.8
Space Rental	4,236.9
Display	221.0
Total	$8,624.5

Source: Trade Show Bureau, Denver, CO, 1993.

KINDS OF TRADE SHOWS

Trade shows can be classified by audience/product and by geography. Consumer-oriented shows are open to the general public, while attendance at business-to-business shows is restricted to industry specialities. (This article will concentrate on business-to-business shows, although similar principles apply to consumer-oriented shows.) Shows also can be regional or national in scope. Some industries use trade shows more than others. Table 18.2 shows attendance of trade shows by industry.

TABLE 18.2
TRADE SHOW PARTICIPATION BY INDUSTRY

Classification	Percentage
Manufacturing	86.9
Transportation, Communications, etc.	81.2
Wholesale Trade	75.8
Retail Trade	36.9
Finance/Financial Services	41.2
Other Services	66.8
Advertising/Promotion	29.6

Source: Trade Show Bureau, Denver, CO, 1993.

ADVANTAGES

Trade shows have several distinct advantages over every other marketing communications vehicle.

Self-Selection. By attending the show attendees have already demonstrated their potential interest in your product or, at least, product category. One of the cardinal rules of marketing and sales is to get a prospect to demonstrate interest. Trade shows meet this rule to the maximum. The figures in Table 18.3, which show the results of a survey of people who attended trade shows, confirms this: More than 75 percent visited a show to see existing or new products. Attendees are there to see *you* and *your products*. In addition, they have spent the time and expense of traveling to the show site, whether across the country or even halfway around the world. Even if the show is located in the attendees' hometown, they had to invest the time and money to travel across town and pay the entrance fee. Traditional direct marketers are happy to get a prospect to open an envelope or return a postcard to inquire about a product!

Sales Opportunity, Focus, and Efficiency. Sales time can be used more efficiently at a trade show because it is more compressed. It also provides the chance for buyers and sellers to meet face-to-face, where products can be demonstrated and handled. Unlike a typical sales call,

TABLE 18.4
NUMBER OF CALLS REQUIRED TO CLOSE A TRADE SHOW LEAD

Number of Calls Required to Close	Percent
None	54
1	16
2	10
2 or more	20

Source: Trade Show Bureau, Denver, CO, 1993.

EXHIBIT 18.1
COMPARATIVE COSTS OF CLOSING A SALE

Field Sale		Trade Show Sale	
Cost of Contacting a Prospect in the Field	$292	Cost of Contact Phone Call or Letter	$292 x .8 $234
Average Number of Calls to Close	x 3.7	Cost Per Show Visitor Reached	+185
Total	$1,080	Total	$419

Source: Adapted from Trade Show Bureau Report SM17A; Cahners Advertising Research Report No. 542.1H and 542.5A; and Exhibit Surveys, Inc.

egory. Your presence tells people that you and your products are worthy of serious consideration.

Because virtually all potential buyers, including those who are unreachable or unknown to sales reps, are present, attendance can give reps a great opportunity to expand markets and become known to potential new buyers. A Trade Show Bureau report indicated that 83 percent of the contacts at a specific exhibit had not been previously contacted by a sales rep (see Table 18.5 and Exhibit 18.2).

TRADE SHOWS: MARKETING STRATEGIES AND TACTICS

Later in this article a long list of possible objectives for attending trade shows will be provided, but the two major objectives of attending any trade show are to get immediate orders and sales at the show and to generate leads that can be translated into future sales. Strategies and tactics can be based on these two kinds of key objectives and on the basic kinds of trade shows.

Basic Strategies. As mentioned above, strategies can be based on the two basic objectives for attending trade shows (generating leads and generating sales) and related to the kinds of shows: timing (as related to the organization's year-round marketing activity) and location/geography.

TABLE 18.5
REASONS FOR TRADE SHOW ATTENDANCE

	Regional Shows (%)		National Shows	
	Average	Range	Average	Range
To See New Products and Developments	52	29-77	56	31-88
General Interest	10	2-20	8	6-16
Specific Product or Company	23	3-77	11	3-41
Technical/Educational Sessions	6	2-25	15	2-66
Technical/Product Information	13	3-88	10	2-48
Other	18	1-19	33	1-54

Source: Trade Show Bureau Report, Denver, CO, 1993.

EXHIBIT 18.2
QUALIFIED PROSPECTS NOT VISITED BY A SALES REP

Overall
83% — Not Visited   17% — Visited

Type of Exhibitor
Components and Materials — Not Visited: 89%
Capital Equipment Under $5,000 — Not Visited: 82%
Capital Equipment Over $5,000 — Not Visited: 79%
Consumable Products — Not Visited: 54%

Source: Trade Show Bureau, Denver, CO, 1993.

Timing. Most organizations understand the importance of generating leads and sales from their trade show attendance. The problem is timing and coordination with other marketing activity. Shows can be the focus of sales activity, but they cannot be a replacement for marketing. Shortsighted managers see the sales spikes created by trade shows and incorrectly conclude that other marketing activity isn't needed. The results are usually a short-term loss of sales because of inadequate preparation and long-term decline in sales because attendance will lose its effectiveness because lead generation will decline.

On the other hand, if trade show attendance is coordinated with year-round marketing activity, attendance can be the focus of both marketing and sales activity. Before attendance at the first show, prospects can be identified and qualified. These individuals can be met and sold at the show. At that show additional leads can be generated for follow-up by sales or marketing and sold at the next show. Over an extended period of time, this approach can be used to enable sales reps to provide better service with longer-term customers and to generate more new customers. For example, Customer A (a long-term customer) can be contacted before a show and, either through a sales rep or through information provided by marketing, his or her needs identified so that a sale can be closed at the show. Customer B (a prospect who has not purchased in the past) might be contacted in a general way before the show and qualified more completely at the show. A follow-up contact, either by sales or marketing, can set the stage for closing a sale at the next show. Exhibit 18.3 illustrates how this strategy might be developed.

The specific sequencing and implementation of this strategy can differ with the needs of the specific organization — the experience and the nature of the organization's industry — but the principle is the same: Use the show as the focus of sales activity, and all marketing and sales activity should be directed toward that end.

Location/Geography. Depending on the organization's experience, the nature of the product category, and the nature of the market (especially location of customers), shows can be attended by their location. This kind of strategy can be especially effective for newer or inexperienced companies that need sales, but especially need to identify potential customers and generate leads — and do so on limited start-up budgets. The following is a possible sequence: The first year could concentrate on local/regional shows and the second year might include successful first-year local shows and a national show. The sequence could continue to roll out, combining the most effective shows on all levels (see Table 18.6).

Basic Tactics. The two most common promotional tactics used at trade shows are special price-driven promotions and new product announcements and introductions. Both are time-tested, but they require require careful planning to ensure successful implementation.

"Ten Percent Discount with Purchase at the Show" or "Free Installation with Order at the Show" are typical price-driven show offers. This tactic can stimulate sales activity, but it can also create "price junkies" — customers who only buy on deal. Also, price- or special offer-driven promotions can create artificial sales spikes. As mentioned previously, shortsighted managers who see these spikes on a sales chart can draw incorrect conclusions about the effectiveness of a particular show and about other year-round sales activity. On the other hand, if ongoing, year-round marketing activity is coordinated with trade show attendance, then the trade shows can be used as the focal point of sales.

Many companies attempt to time new product introductions to coincide with major trade shows. In addition to stimulating interest — and, hopefully, sales — this approach can support other objectives, such as projecting an image as an innovator. This can be a powerful

EXHIBIT 18.3
SAMPLE TIMING STRATEGY

Preshow — Show 1
Show 1— Generate (Close) Orders/Sales From Preshow Contacts
    — Generate Leads
Follow-up: Sales Contacts: Close

Preshow 2 — Existing Customers
    Contacts From Show 1 and Preshow Marketing
Show 2— Close Sales — Long-term customers
    — Contact Leads from Show 1
    — Generate New Leads

TABLE 18.6
SAMPLE GEOGRAPHIC SCHEDULE

Year 1	4 Local/Regional Shows
Year 2	2 Local/Regional Shows (2 dropped from Year 1)
	2 National Shows
Year 3	3 Regional Shows (2 previous best and 1 new show)
	2 National Shows (best from year 1 and 1 new show)
	1 International Show

approach, but some companies overuse it or simply use it incorrectly. For example, many computer electronics companies have been accused of "new product announcements" that referred to products that were six months or more away from release to the market. In some instances, these "products" were nowhere near introduction. The result of such misuse of this tactic is to create skepticism in the market. Buyers don't believe it until they see it and begin to have doubts about the company's claims in general. Thus, to maximize the effectiveness of this approach, the company should be certain to coordinate marketing, show, and new product activities and to really have something important to say.

Implementation. In general, strategy can be implemented by a combination of three tactics: direct marketing, the trade show itself, and direct sales call.

Direct marketing. Approximately one to two months before the show, prospects should be contacted by mail. If the company has attended the show in the past or has customers who have said they will be attending, this is the logical place to start. If not — if, for whatever reason, the company does not have the names of attendees — a list can be developed by contacting the show's management, who can provide a list of past attendees and registrants of the upcoming show.

The direct mail piece can be as simple as a brief note or as complex as a multiple-item, four-color mailing piece. This is the time to announce the company's attendance at the show and to announce any special offers or special reasons an attendee should visit the exhibit. If product presentations are to be made at specific times, the schedule should be included. In any case, the piece should reflect the basic principles of any direct mail piece: State the benefit clearly; state the offer clearly; state how the prospect can capitalize on both; and give the prospect the chance to respond.

One week to two weeks before the show, as many relevant attendees as possible should be contacted by phone. Obviously, the first people to contact are those who have expressed interest — either by responding to the direct mail piece or to the sales force. If possible, an appointment should be set up with the telemarketing rep, or the contact should be sent to show staff for scheduling. In either case, preliminary screening and qualifying can be done at this point. The prospect's needs, interests, problems, and so forth can be determined, and the information can be forwarded to the appropriate individual.

At the show: Sales and lead generation. The show is the focus of sales activity. Presentations should be made to prequalified prospects; sales closed or at least confirmed; and additional leads generated. Most important is to get all relevant information with respect to the prospect or customer. Specifics on presentation are included later in this article.

Direct sales follow-up. Information on all contacts should be available to the sales force as soon as possible after the show. In any event, leads should be closed or prepared for disposition no more than a month after the show. In some instances, this process can be started by a follow-up mailing piece or phone call.

THE IMPORTANCE OF PLANNING

The potential benefits of trade show attendance are obvious, but the cost, in terms of money for travel and time, means that the stakes are extremely high. This means that proper planning is critical to success. Exhibit 18.4 is a typical planning form that can be used to avoid mistakes and heighten the chances for success. It follows the same general process for any marketing plan. Following is a discussion of the basic processes needed to plan successfully for any trade show.

Analyze Markets. Who are your customers? Who are your potential customers? The reason for asking the first question is obvious. If your customers don't attend trade shows, then you won't meet them there. The second question might also be obvious, but it has other implications. Trade shows provide the opportunity to demonstrate your product to potential customers who might also want your product. But it also can be an information-gathering opportunity. You might have

EXHIBIT 18.4
SAMPLE TRADE SHOW PLANNING CHART

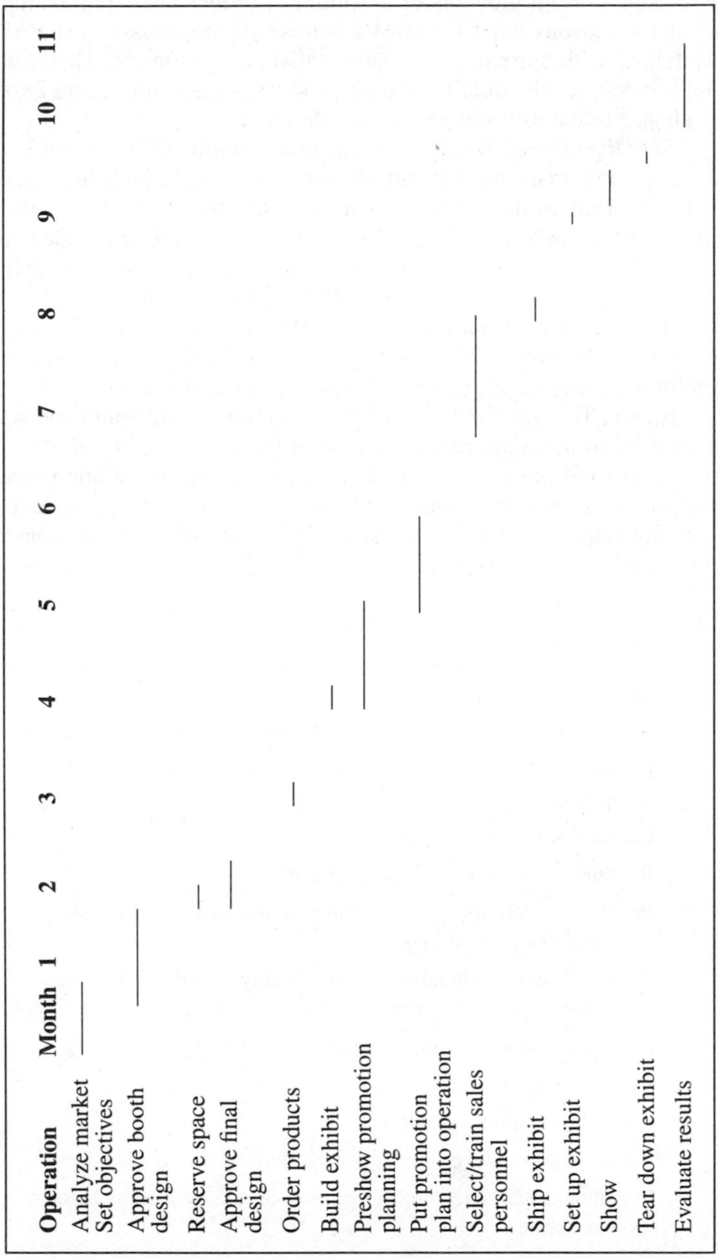

Operation	Month 1	2	3	4	5	6	7	8	9	10	11
Analyze market	▬										
Set objectives											
Approve booth design	▬										
Reserve space		▬									
Approve final design		▬									
Order products			▬								
Build exhibit				▬							
Preshow promotion planning				▬							
Put promotion plan into operation					▬						
Select/train sales personnel							▬				
Ship exhibit								▬			
Set up exhibit									▬		
Show									▬		
Tear down exhibit										▬	
Evaluate results										▬	

the chance to show your product to people who don't like it. Feedback from such an encounter could be an important source of information for revising current products or expanding product lines. For example, one of the reasons cited for IBM's demise in the market is that they only talked with current, presumably satisfied, customers. They failed to talk to people who didn't use their products — and missed an important chance to identify shifting market demands.

Set Objectives. "What do I want to accomplish?" is probably the most important question you can answer. You need to be able to define what you want to do before you decide whether you should do it. Exhibit 18.5 gives a typical list of objectives for attending a trade show.

Budgeting. The magic question, of course, is "How much will it cost?" Exhibit 18.6 is a sample budgeting form. It includes at least most of the cost considerations you will have. If the show is new to you, you might want to consult with show management or past attendees for a "reality check." The following is a brief discussion.

Space. This should be sufficient to accommodate booth and staff. If you need to accommodate more than a basic 8' by 8' or 10' by 10' space, make the proper allowances for alternate demonstration space, space for meeting with clients, and other needs. Also check on the cost of renting tables, display racks, and additional chairs for demonstrations, meetings, and presentations.

EXHIBIT 18.5
POSSIBLE OBJECTIVES

- To make sales
- To maintain image and continuing contact with current customers
- To create an image and initiate contact with potential customers and qualified buyers
- To introduce a new product
- To demonstrate nonportable equipment
- To offer an opportunity for customers to bring their technical problems and get solutions
- To identify new applications for an existing or projected product by getting feedback from booth visitors
- To build the morale of local sales force and dealers
- To relate to the competition
- To conduct market research
- To recruit personnel or attract new dealers
- To demonstrate interest in, and support of, the sponsoring association or industry

EXHIBIT 18.6
SAMPLE BUDGETING FORM

Budgeting Checklist

	Due Date	Date Mailed/ Ordered	Estimated Actual Costs
Space Rental			
Hotel			
Air Travel			
Land Travel			
Car Rental			
Hospitality			
Waitress			
Bartender			
Liquor			
Soft Drinks			
Coffee, etc.			
Food			
Hostesses			
Seminar/Presentation			
Room Rental			
A/V			
Invitations, etc.			
Literature			
Presenters			
Literature			
Invitations			
Type			
Printing			
Shipping/Drayage			
Booth			
Literature			
Premiums/Giveaways			
Catalogs			
Promotion			

Hotel. Most meetings get special room rates for attendees and exhibitors. Be sure to have arrangements made by the necessary dates.

Travel. Some shows are also able to get special discounts for air-fares. Check on availability and restrictions. In addition, airports can be a long way away from the show. Take local transportation needs into account. Will attendees be carrying exhibits or a considerable amount of extra baggage. Again, this may require special local transportation arrangements. Allow for additional costs.

Hospitality. Do you plan to have a hospitality suite? Will it be on-site or at another location, such as at your hotel? Quotes for some include all refreshments and personnel; others don't. Be sure to get an itemized estimate.

Seminars. Be certain that space for special presentations is convenient to the booth site. Also, all items to be included should be itemized. Who will provide the speakers? Any equipment? Who will run it?

Literature and premiums. All costs for support materials should be included.

Catalog entries and other promotion. Most shows have booklets including lists of exhibitors and attendees and space for ads. What other promotion activity will be used? Will you send special preshow mailings to attendees or make a special offer to people who stop by your booth?

Design: Define Image/Create Concept. A trade show is the time to put your best foot forward with clients and potential customers. What image do you want to project? This should reflect the character of your company as a leader; an innovator; a low-price, high-quality alternative to name brands — whatever your company's identity is. What is the size of your booth and booth space? The following are a few guidelines.

Your product and your competition. Although you may have several specific objectives for attending a show, there is only one real focus and reason for attending: your product — promoting and selling it. Your booth display should present your product and its benefits to the best possible advantage. Within budget limitations, your display should take into account the need for physical demonstration; audio/video presentation; places for potential buyers to ask questions and examine the product in detail; and space to accommodate support literature and other materials.

What do your competitors do? What is your market position relative to them? You might want to "meet the competition" in terms of the kinds of displays and presentations you make, or you might want to present a completely different image. Regardless, you should consider how you want to present your company and its product(s). Build your booth around your product.

Graphics. All the principles of point-of-purchase apply. Graphics — especially colors and lettering — should be eye-catching and easy to read. While a show is a great place to get attention from potential customers, remember that all other exhibitors have the same intentions. Thus, your booth should attract the attention of people who are being inundated by impressions of other exhibitors who are also trying to get their attention. It should state your company case clearly and succinctly — and give the right people a reason to want to stop and talk with you.

Traffic flow. Once you have attracted attention, you want your booth to be accessible. Booth space and configuration should enable prospects to approach your booth, examine materials, and talk with staff with a minimum of difficulty. If you have a simple booth, organization should be fairly straightforward and simple. If your booth is large — for example, to accommodate a printing press — the space should be organized to allow a staff member and a prospect to walk easily through the display and provide space for more extended discussions.

Use. Is the booth for one-time use, or do you plan to use it many times? Will it need to incorporate heavy equipment or audio and video presentations? Whether it is a simple, portable 10-foot booth that fits in a carrying case, or a multicomponent display comprised of 10 display elements that covers 2,000 square feet and is shipped in five or six crates, components should be durable and easy to assemble.

The more your booth travels, the more likely it is to get abused. Sturdy materials, or special containers for fragile materials, can save a lot of money.

Simplicity of assembly can save a lot of time, money, and aggravation. Even if your booth is large and has many components, small pieces that require multiple connectors should be kept to a minimum. It will help hold down the cost of assembly at the show by professional builders. If your staff puts the booth together at a show, the fewest number of screws, nuts, and bolts, the better. It's a good way to minimize the number of last-minute panic calls from a convention floor. Also, the simpler the assembly, the less the need for a "designated booth builder" for every show.

PROMOTION

What is your primary promotion objective? How important is show attendance in accomplishing overall company objectives? Do you want to generate immediate sales? Generate leads for new business? Maintain company image by "showing the flag"? Gather information for new competitive thrusts or for possible new products? Your answers to these and related questions will determine preshow promotion, personnel selection and training/preparation, and promotion activity at the show.

Preshow promotion. Again, what are your objectives? What do you wish to accomplish? Do you have a special story to tell? The answers to these questions will determine your tactics. Following are the basic information sources you will need to consult:

- Company records: past performance. Did your company attend the show last year? If so, consult records and talk with personnel who attended. Exhibit 18.7 is a sample of a show report evaluation.
- Industry sources. If you don't have experience with the show, you need information from other places. The trade press can be a good source of information about the kind of activity and performance of trade shows. Obviously, look for articles that are analytical rather than straight reportage or based on press releases by show management. Another obvious, but often-overlooked, source is competitors, customers, and the like who have experience with the show you are considering.

Similarly, show management can be helpful. On one hand, they are trying to sell space and attendance to you, so they might be inclined to paint an excessively rosy picture. On the other hand, if the show truly isn't for you, they probably will be candid with you. They live on their reputations, and smart managers realize that they don't need a dissatisfied exhibitor, especially one who felt he or she was misled.

These sources can give you insights on the most effective kinds of preshow promotion. Below are several approaches.

Direct marketing. Show management usually can provide a list of attendees with names and addresses. Mail a special invitation to these people. Whether a simple note or an expensive brochure, the mailing should include your booth location and number. Of course, include any special information about your company and its products. Are you introducing a new product — or a product that is likely to be new to show attendees? Be sure to present it prominently in its best light within the limitations of your mailing.

Your knowledge of likely attendees will determine the size of the mailing. For instance, your list should include customers, as well as other likely prospects, who will be attending. Examine the list of attendees for other likely candidates for your message. Some companies use telemarketing for qualifying and prospecting before mailing. This approach enables you to target your mailing and thus limit mailing costs. It also enables you to identify key buying influences at the show — sometimes people have changed positions since the prior show. In addition, sometimes a company decides not to attend a show. Contact by phone allows you to get your message to a prospect and make a nonshow contact or sale.

Advertising. Shows provide several opportunities to advertise.

Show programs. Shows give all attendees and exhibitors a program of events. Sometimes these are quite simple listings; sometimes they are quite elaborate publications that include advertising space, even in four-color, or "sponsorships" for the program. Sometimes exhibitors are given a special rate.

EXHIBIT 18.7
EXHIBIT RESULTS & CRITIQUE

Total trade show attendance: _____

Sales quality of attendance : _____

Total estimated booth attendance: _____

Number of inquiries/literature requests: _____

Orders/prime leads developed: _____

Reactions to display, general interest level, etc.:

_____

Booth location: __Excellent   __Good   __Fair   __Poor

    Comments:_____

Competitors' exhibits (notes, etc.): _____

Show management evaluation:

    Preshow planning_____

    Services/labor available _____

    Exhibit/meeting time _____

    Security _____

Exhibit hall evaluation: _____

    Lighting _____

    Heat/air conditioning _____

    Traffic flow _____

    Fire safety _____

    Transportation _____

Cost summary:_____

    Exhibit space/services _____

    Prorate booth cost _____

    Other display costs_____

    Model fees _____

    Setup and breakdown labor _____

    Shipping/drayage costs _____

    Entertainment/suite _____

    Hotel/transportation_____

    Miscellaneous _____

               TOTAL _____

Overall critique:_____

_____

_____

Recommendations for future participation:_____

_____

By: _____   Date: _____

Similarly, if the show provides attendees with an elaborate package, you can get your information included in the show package. Is one of your executives on the show program? Are you making a special presentation at the show? Are you introducing a new product? These are some of the considerations.

Depending on the degree to which they are tied to an industry, publications devote editions to a show. These editions can be a good place to advertise. As mentioned above, with respect to direct mail, be sure to focus on industry concerns and your special message — and don't forget your booth number and location.

Publicity. Unlike advertising, publicity is free media exposure. That doesn't mean that it doesn't cost money or require planning. Regardless of whether you plan to send out a simple press release, place an article, or get coverage at an elaborate press party, the first thing to remember about getting publicity is the old saying in the newspaper business: "We publish 'news,' not 'olds.'"

More press releases and publicity wind up in the trash because they don't provide any new information. From a reporter's or editor's perspective, they are a waste of time — and to the company they are a waste of money. If you don't have something new to say about your product or company, don't expect much.

You need to develop a good list of publications and editors, and then you need to talk to them. What do they consider "newsworthy"? What are they looking for? Most editors will be responsive and give you the kinds of guidelines you will need to get maximum exposure and coverage. In the case of an article, expect the editor to assign a reporter to cover your company and its products.

Some show-oriented publications — put out either by the show management or by an industry publisher — are published exclusively for distribution at the show. If you can get an article included for free, fine. Some of them, however, require the purchase of an ad — in which case you are getting "paid publicity," i.e., advertising. If that meets your needs and objectives (and your budget), fine. But understand what you are getting.

Preshow contacts. All of the activity described above has one purpose: to get as many appointments with solid prospects and customers as possible. The two most important — and frustrating — problems are qualifying and scheduling.

Qualifying is a basic skill, and we will assume that you know the basics. One exception: A trade show is different because time is compressed. You don't have a second to waste. Exhibit 18.8 is a helpful "hit list" for identifying the absolute best prospects.

Scheduling can be especially problematic. Missed flights and commuting time to, from, and within the show are just a few of the problems. In addition, does your product require a complex presentation? How many staff people need to be involved? What will the customer be focusing on? How much time will all this take? These are just a few questions you need to consider. Whatever your estimate is, add about 50 percent.

Exhibit 18.8 should be helpful in scheduling your time, but one idea to keep in mind: In general (with some obvious exceptions) you should spend as much of your time at the booth meeting potential prospects. Thus, except for presentations, you probably will want to schedule meetings with especially hot prospects during nonexhibition hours or at breakfast or dinner meetings.

At The Show. Although your specific, immediate objective for attending a trade show might be to generate leads, match the competition, present a new product, or enhance your image, there is only one *real* reason to attend any trade show: to sell more product. If you have done all the proper preparation, your booth should be in good condition, showing your product well. And you should be ready for appointments you have already made with hot prospects. Now what?

A DIFFERENT SELL: YOUR EXPANDED ROLE AT TRADE SHOWS

The shrinking personal contact between supplier and customer and the desire on the part of the customer for greater personal communication means that the salesperson becomes one of the most important elements of the communications medium (at a trade show, the other is the product).

You and the product: Those are the first things a prospect sees. And you probably should be first because you should be out front and visible. More potential prospects get turned off by sales reps apparently loafing on the job than anything else. *Apparently* is the operative word here because you can never change a first impression. Make that first impression the best possible.

EXHIBIT 18.8
PRETRADE SHOW QUALIFYING FORM

Name:

Title:

Company:

Street:

City/State:

Phone/FAX:

Product Interest:

Needs/Special Problems:

Preferred Time:

Dress for your audience. The obvious: Hair should be neat, shoes should be shined, and clothes should be clean and pressed. Research has indicated that there are two factors to consider: geography and occupation.

Geography:

- Eastern audiences generally respond better to conservative dress: a white or muted-color shirt and regimental striped or club tie.
- Midwestern audiences respond to a little more relaxation in dress: jackets, coordinated outfits, or suits in muted colors and quiet plaids.
- In the West (Texas, and Florida) informality can seem hospitable and can foster the rapport-building process between the attendee and salesperson. For example, open-neck sports shirts or skirt-and-blouse outfits may be acceptable.

Occupation:

- Professional audiences (medical, banking, business) respond better to dress formality in any part of the country.
- Service-oriented audiences (maintenance, trades, hourly rate personnel) can be put off by a "corporate" look.
- Uniform: Many companies distinguish their exhibiting sales personnel with special jackets, suits, or lab coats. This helps attendees recognize who to approach. The name badge, high on the right lapel, is proper.

As with dress, your attitude should be "tailored" to your audience. A prospect approaches your exhibit or responds positively to your initial contact because he or she is interested in one or more of your products. Be prepared. Be warm, open, and accommodating without being aggressive. Eagerness to help is difficult to resist, and it should be easy for you to move from open, easy dialogue to a convincing presentation.

Making the Sale. In the field, the sales process starts with a brief introduction; then identification of the potential customer's needs and interests; then product presentation and discussion; then a detailed discussion of the product's benefits and features; and then, hopefully, a sale. At the show, the sales process starts with the product, and then moves on to qualification of the prospect as soon as possible.

Asking the right question. How do you know whether a prospect is qualified? Ask! That much is always true, but at the show it is critical to ask the right question because if you don't, you've lost the possibility of the sale — probably for good.

What's the right question? Not: "May I help you?" Most of the time it elicits an automatic "no." Ask an open-ended question that will open a dialogue between you and the attendee. Referring to the product, you ask: "Do you understand how the spring releases the capsule?"; Or "Can you see the difference in the graphite absorption of these two markers?" The point of these kinds of questions is to encourage or lead the prospect into giving more than just a "yes" or "no" answer.

The prospect still might give a one-word answer, but probably not. And even if he or she does, you still have the basis for continuing the conversation by responding: "Well, maybe you should look at it from this angle"; or a simple, "Well, let me show you." Also, if the prospect gives a signal, verbally or physically, that absorption isn't important, then you can ask another question, such as, "Is absorption important to you, or is color quality more important?" The conversation can go in a number of directions, but the most important point is that it can go somewhere because you are getting the prospect to qualify him- or herself in terms of needs for the product and interest with respect to current problems and potential uses. It also enables you to identify individuals who aren't appropriate.

Assuming that your prospect is initially qualified, and you have focused his or her attention on your product, you can further qualify him or her in terms of buying influence, resources, and purchase time frame. Budget five to seven minutes (10 at the most) for qualifying, and another interim period of one to two minutes for approaching the next prospect. This should allow you time for approximately six contacts per hour. This guideline is dependent on your product and, of course, show traffic.

Investigate and assess. At this stage, the most important word you can hear from your prospect is "no," and, yet, it's the one many sales reps fear most. And they really shouldn't, because a "no" response at this stage usually helps you move the sale. Will blue match the prospect's office decor? No? Well, then, what about green — or red — or black or ...? In short, a negative response helps you determine the prospect's needs more precisely, gets him or her involved in confirming the sale, and thus makes the final close that much easier.

Demonstrate the product, highlighting the benefits and features that the prospect has indicated are important, and show how your product's features meet his or her needs.

The Close. Unless you can write the order on the spot, closing at a trade show means recording detailed information that will permit your sales manager and the field rep follow-up to write up the sale in the quickest and most expedient way. Such information includes:

- Contact's name
- Contact's position
- Product interest
- Product application
- Special appeals — features of most interest
- Others involved in the buying decision
- Date for follow-up call
- Date for intended purchase

• Company, division, and address for each buying influence

So, you have closed on the product. Do any other products meet your customer's needs? Explore other possible needs. One of the most important reasons for your attendance is to generate leads. This is the time.

Appraisal/Evaluation. Trade shows can be evaluated on two bases. First, of course, is the ultimate criterion: the hard numbers; the quantitative dimension. However, a trade show can also be evaluated on "softer," qualitative criteria. The importance of the hard numbers is obvious, while the soft numbers can be more difficult to assess and justify. Nevertheless, they can be equally important, especially if the position of the company and the product line is considered — and just as useful if information is handled properly. Exhibit 18.7 is a sample show sales report. Note that it incorporates both dimensions. Exhibit 18.9 is a form for individual contacts.

GOING GLOBAL

Does your product or service have sales potential on the international level? Given the global nature of most business, your answer probably could be "yes" — or at least it is a possibility worth exploring.

The Seven "Deadly Sins" of International Trade Shows and How to Avoid Them. On one hand, attending an international trade show (or trade fair) isn't that different from a U.S. show. On the other hand, the differences are enormous. In the words of the old adage: "It's simpler than it looks and more complicated than you can imagine." Preparation and information gathering are key, and it is wise to plan to the point that you feel is overplanning rather than leave anything to chance. The following outlines the seven most common mistakes and offers suggestions on how to avoid them.

Mistake 1: Underestimating potential. There is no single, comparable expenditure of time and money likely to match the effectiveness of exhibiting at an international fair. Exhibiting can bring your product into contact with the greatest number of possible buyers and potential sales representatives. Many of the attendees — professional buyers — are in a position and can be motivated to make big orders on the spot.

Information, of course, is the most important currency. The first thing to do is contact the U. S. Department of Commerce. Look up the district office (there are offices in nearly every state) and talk with one of the trade specialists about your plans. The first question to ask is which fair(s) are most appropriate. While some fairs cover several product categories, most are highly specialized. In addition, it is probably best to start with the most highly targeted fair possible.

The next step is to contact the relevant fair authorities, most of which have representatives in the United States. If the participation of U.S. companies is government-sponsored, this step won't be necessary. However, for all others, this step is a must. Exhibit 18.10 is a sample

EXHIBIT 18.9
CONTACT EVALUATION FORM

Customer Name _____

Title _____

Company _____

Address_____

City _____Phone_____

Special Handling/Instructions _____

inquiry letter regarding attendance. The information kit, which will be sent in response to your inquiry, will cover most of the issues you will be concerned about for a domestic show — with, of course, special considerations.

The fair authority will respond within two to three weeks with an information kit including application forms plus other relevant information. The following list includes some of the basic cost issues:

- Stand Rental
- Construction and Setup of Stand/Display
- Utilities
- Round-trip Tavel Costs
- Lodging
- Shipping Exhibits and Equipment (including insurance)
- Printing/Translating/Advertising
- Public Relations
- Local Support Personnel (interpreters, extra security, etc.)

Mistake 2: Blurring the distinctions between domestic and international fairs. All trade fairs are fairly similar with respect to structure, but they are not carbon copies. With some exceptions, an international fair is everything its American counterpart is — only more so. While all fair exhibitors attend shows to demonstrate their products, international attendees expect to make significant purchases. There is less emphasis on simply renewing contacts and friendships. Exhibitors expect to do more than just generate leads and make contacts — they expect to make sales. Underestimating this seriousness of purpose can mean significant lost opportunity. Planning is of the utmost importance.

Mistake 3: Thinking negatively. For the businessperson who has ever sold on an international scale, the initial obstacles can appear overwhelming, even insurmountable. However, there is a lot of help available from the U.S. Department of Commerce, the U.S. and Foreign Commercial Services, and the trade authorities. On the international scene, trade fairs are viewed as a very important way of doing business, and assistance in overcoming language and cultural barriers is everywhere.

EXHIBIT 18.10
SAMPLE LETTER OF INQUIRY TO A GERMAN TRADE ORGANIZATION

Cologne Trade Fairs and
Exhibitions, Limited   or
(Messe- und Ausstellungs-
Gesellschaft mbH Koeln)
Postfach 210760
D-5000 Koeln 21
Germany

Mr. Hans J. Teetz
Manager
Trade Fairs Department
German American Chamber
of Commerce
666 Fifth Ave.
New York, N.Y. 1013

Dear Sir or Madam: (or dear Mr. Teetz:)

My firm is considering exhibiting our decorative panels in the May 10–14, 1993, INTERZUM Fair in Cologne. Since this is the first time we would be exhibiting in a German (European) trade fair, I would be pleased to have any suggestions or advice you care to offer.

Our preliminary estimate is that we will require roughly 160 square feet (4 x 4 meters) of exhibit space. However, any suggestions you may have about both the size and ideal location of a booth, as well as advice on other relevant matters, would be welcomed.

Specifically, I would appreciate your advice on the following:

1. Could you please provide me with a plan that indicates which hall and precisely where in that hall our exhibition space would be located?

2. Can you provide prefabricated shell exhibit stands?

3. Could you please supply me with the names of private, local contractors who are capable of constructing an exhibit booth for my firm?

4. Could you also send me the names of firms from whom I can rent chairs, furniture, or other equipment I might need in my booth, including audiovisual equipment?

5. My firm will have to hire an interpreter. Could you please supply me with lists of qualified interpreters, well in advance of the fair, so that I may provide the interpreter selected with background materials? Also, please indicate the current fee per day paid to interpreters working at the fair.

6. It will be necessary for us to have our promotional brochures translated into German and French. Can you please supply me with a list of firms qualified to perform this service and also indicate the charge normally assessed for such servcies?

7. Is there a local freight forwarder whom you especially recommend?

8. I understand that it is extremely difficult to obtain hotel accommodations for the duration of the fair. Can your office help us with hotel reservations or, perhaps, supply me with a list of hotels in the area, along with their phone numbers?

Finally, please let me know the name of the officer in your organization who would be my contact with respect to possible participation at your fair. I would be grateful if that person would kindly provide me with any available background material on the fair, including the results of previous fairs and a general indication of what steps your office takes in order to ensure that qualified buyers or potential agents for our products will be present at the event.

Thank you very much for your cooperation and assistance. I look forward to hearing from you.

Sincerely,

Name

Title

Mailing Address, Telephone, Fax

Mistake 4: Procrastinating. Once the decision to attend a show has been made, it is necessary to move quickly and methodically. The first step should be to visit the nearest U.S. Department of Commerce and the appropriate international desk at the Department. If the U. S. government is sponsoring or endorsing an official American pavilion at the event, many of the logistical headaches can be eliminated. The Department will be especially interested to see a sponsored or endorsed event succeed and is very helpful to participating companies and organizations.

If there will not be an official U.S. pavilion, two steps are necessary. First, a freight forwarder should be contacted immediately to determine costs. Second, a marketing strategy should be sketched out. By this time, this second step should be at least near completion. The decision to attend should have been based on assessment of market potential, which should include at least a general strategy stating how the show would be used to develop a new market, expand market share, and so forth.

In both respects, the sooner these issues are addressed, the better. Exhibit 18.11 lists all the steps that should be taken prior to attending an international fair.

Mistake 5: Aimlessness during the fair. Much of this can be avoided by careful marketing planning.

Nevertheless, the week prior to the show can be critical. It is preferable to arrive two or three days before the opening of the show to allow the exhibitor to arrange meetings with the stand assistant/interpreter before the opening of the fair and to conduct a final briefing just before the fair's opening.

During the main days of the fair, it is important to keep focused on the "market" — attendees. What booths are they visiting? What appears to be their interests? If you initially misread the interests of attendees, or if their interests have shifted, this is the time to adjust. The exhibitor might want to change the focus of presentations and/or product mix. Walking around the fair and examining competitive activities can provide clues.

Toward the end of the fair, it is good to take an initial assessment. If the conclusion is positive, the exhibitor should make arrangements for the next year. Many fairs assign booth space and position by tenure of attendees. Thus, booking space right away can ensure a better position next time. Similarly, for the booth assistant, hotel accommodations, and logistical considerations, the sooner these can be arranged, the greater the savings in time and money. The most convenient way to make these arrangements is locally — on the spot — rather than by long distance.

Mistake 6: Not following up after the fair. The primary purposes of attending any trade show are to make sales on the spot and to generate leads for future sales. The greatest single failure that exhibitors

A. Phone or Write the U.S. Department of Commerce.

   1. Ask for background on the local/regional economy and on "your" fair.

   2. Determine whether there will be an official or certified U.S. pavilion at the fair.

   3. If you want to appoint a local representative, initiate the Agent/Distributor Service (ADS) through the nearest U.S. Department of Commerce District Office.

B. Contact the Fair Authority.

   4. Write 12 to 18 months before the show's opening.

   5. Try for good space.

   6. Identify, in advance, potential interpreters to work in the booth.

   7. Reserve hotel/lodging.

   8. Contact a public relations firm, if needed.

   9. Arrange advertising, if needed.

C. Develop Your Game Plan for the Fair.

   10. Identify your concrete goal or goals:

      a. On-the-spot sales? How much?

      b. How much in sales are expected in the year(s) after the fair?

      c. Agent/distributor?

      d. Price/style/technology/trend information?

   11. Does my budget fit my goals?

D. Look Into Standards.

   12. Determine whether your product must meet local/regional safety or performance standards.

   13. Identify and work with an authorized local/regional testing organization.

   14. Become familiar with local standards for currency, electrical voltage, and measurements.

E. Miscellaneous.

   15. Contact a U.S. or regional bank with strong commercial ties and arrange for transfer of funds, a letter of credit, etc.

   16. Have your product literature translated into the language of the country in which you are exhibiting (and possibly other languages, depending on the event and your goals).

   17. Line up an experienced U.S.-based freight forwarder.

make is not following up on every lead or following up after the lead has gotten cold. Failure to follow up on any lead should be considered a serious mistake, but failure to do so after having spent a lot of money and time to travel several thousand miles to attend an international fair is unforgivable — and potentially disastrous. The exhibitor should have a system for evaluating and communicating the needs and requests of every visitor and an assessment of their potential. In addition, there should be a system for communicating this information to all levels of sales and marketing.

Mistake 7: Ignoring cultural differences. Cultural differences are real and should be honored. For example, some cultures are extremely time-conscious, and lack of punctuality is nearly unforgivable. In some cultures, business contact is initiated with a high degree (from an American perspective) of formality, beginning with a ritual-like exchange of business cards. In some cultures, joviality is expected. In others, it is considered a sign of disrespect and is to be avoided. All appropriate sources of information — from general publications to U.S. Department of Commerce personnel to fair officials, to past exhibitors — should be consulted for tips on meeting and greeting booth visitors.

SUMMARY: THE ABCs OF TRADE SHOWS

Entire books have been written on the subjects of managing trade shows and using them in a marketing mix. Thus, the idea that one article could cover the subject comprehensively is little more than absurd. We have tried, rather, to be suggestive and representative in our coverage and to just "touch all the bases." This effort can be summarized as "the ABCs of trade shows:"

- Attendance
- Booth
- Contacts

With the hundreds of shows available for any organization, regardless of industry, the preeminent question to address is: "What show(s) should I attend?" The answer to that question, as it is to all marketing and sales questions, is found in knowing your customers and markets. With target markets and potential customers identified, the next step is to plan the staff duties and most effective kinds of activities that will maximize sales potential. In addition to market analysis, this includes budgeting and organizing.

As mentioned several times in this article, the overriding purpose of attending any trade show is to make sales. The main focus of that activity is the booth, where you project your organization's image, present its products, meet customers, find prospects, and, of course, generate leads and make sales. Design and composition are important, of course, as are organization for traffic flow, presentations, and accommodation of booth visitors.

The key to making sales is first to make contacts. The proper planning will enable the exhibitor to identify and prequalify the maximum number of prospects. Dynamic presentations will ensure the maximum number of sales and quality leads, and proper record keeping will enable the sales and marketing departments to follow up prime leads.

These three elements — attendance, booth, and contacts — provide a handy shorthand way of maximizing trade show success.

Robert S. Byer is a Senior Vice President at Wells Rich Greene BDDP in New York. He is responsible for sales promotion and collateral for the IBM account as well as IBM PC Company, a wholly owned subsidiary of IBM. In all, he has 17 years of experience doing sales promotion and collateral. In 1987, he received a Clio for the "Best National Consumer Promotion" for the fifth anniversary celebration of the IBM Personal Computer.

Byer received a Marketing degree from Florida State University.

CHAPTER 19

SALES AND COLLATERAL MATERIALS

WHAT IS COLLATERAL?

Simply stated, collateral is sales literature that companies use to promote their goods and services. It is different from other sales promotion materials because collateral is used primarily to promote the sale of considered purchases — automobiles, computers, washing machines — to both consumers and businesses.

Collateral can come in many different formats, depending on the available budget, expected shelf life, and a host of other considerations. There is a type of collateral for every need.

Regardless of usage or design, the purpose of collateral is always the same — to motivate prospects toward making a purchase by providing detailed information not necessarily employed by other marketing media. In order to do this, collateral must overcome apprehension, reluctance, doubt, concern, or any other inhibiting emotion a potential customer may have.

The task is not simple. Marketers must understand the complex decisions that take place in a prospect's mind before cash is laid down. Research must be undertaken to determine the features and attributes most important to the customer in the category in which the product competes. A comparative analysis should follow to single out those aspects of the product that would most interest and excite the customer. Only then can an effective collateral be created.

THE ROLE OF COLLATERAL IN MARKETING AND SALES

To understand the role of collateral in marketing and sales, it is helpful to understand what collateral is not. The best way to discover what collateral is not is to look in the dictionary. The dictionary defines the word *collateral* as "associated but of secondary importance." It is a definition, which in terms of marketing communication materials, is misleading.

It is wrong because in many marketing situations collateral is the primary vehicle for driving sales. In fact, collateral often plays a more significant role in supporting sales than advertising, direct mail, or any other communications medium.

Collateral is used most often by a salesperson during a sales call or during a selling scenario such as a trade show. The salesperson may use it as a sales aid to walk a customer through features, benefits, and competitive strengths. The brochure stays with the customers as a "leave behind" so they can mull it over and share it with their buying group — whether that is their family or boss. Because the collateral piece is the virtual presentation of the product or service, it has the most power to persuade than any other communications medium.

If collateral is critical to the success of sales, then how can marketers — when developing a marketing plan — ascertain its role in conjunction with other communications media? The answer lies in a new definition: Collateral is a marketing communications tool whose role is defined by the nature of the product and the level of difficulty in reaching the "heart and pocketbook" of the customer.

Whereas the task of advertising in all its shapes and forms (TV, radio, magazine, billboards, newspaper) is to stimulate an emotional response through imagery, the more daunting challenge confronting collateral is to stimulate a purchase through facts that support the selling proposition. Collateral must convert an interested prospect into a cash-paying customer.

That is not to say effective collateral does not evoke emotion. On the contrary, collateral should always seek an emotional response. However, collateral is different from advertising in the sense that the emotions that stem from collateral are the underpinnings of a sale. The emotions that stem from advertising are the underpinnings of perception. Advertising stirs interest, but collateral closes the deal.

Collateral accomplishes this through a logical presentation of facts that dispels apprehension, builds confidence, and ultimately generates a purchase. Of course, it can be argued that salespeople are the last and most important step in the sales process. Many salespeople, however, develop their sales presentations around the propositions described in their companies' collateral materials. In effect, if the collateral does not present the product well, the sales pitch will not.

Worse yet, salespeople who feel that their product collateral is ineffectual (or absent) will develop their own homegrown product pieces, possibly diluting or misdirecting product and corporate strategy. Especially for the smaller company that must be on the mark every time, this is a certain disaster. For the sales team, accurate, persuasive product collateral is fundamental to their success. They have a real world vision of what the piece must accomplish and are invaluable sources of input.

In addition to direct selling, other uses of collateral include distribution at trade shows, inclusion in publicity kits, and fulfillment of information requests fueled by direct mail, broadcast, or coupon advertising.

TYPES OF COLLATERAL

Collateral can be grouped into several general categories, as described below.

Brochures/Booklets. Brochures, booklets, and pamphlets are the quintessence of collateral pieces. Because brochures are seen as a traditional piece, they are usually well regarded by prospects. They (and the sales force) may also perceive them as a necessity for evaluating a product. The good news is that brochures offer a flexibility in design, size, and production options, allowing the creative team a good deal of freedom to proclaim a product's message — while staying within budget. Brochures are used during sales calls as sales aids and leave-behinds. They are good tools to send to "hot" prospects who need immediate attention or to geographically disbursed buying committees.

Miscellaneous Single Sheets/Flyers/Bulletins. Single-sheet collateral pieces fulfill myriad collateral needs. They can be used for specific promotions such as summer sales. They serve as price sheets, product specifications, product overviews, and buying guides. Single-sheet pieces are often cost-effective solutions for information that has a short shelf life, because they don't require the production expense associated with brochures. This makes them excellent for use during a trade show or as a fulfillment piece to inquiries from "old" or "warm" prospects. Gang-printing single sheets along with a brochure creates a unified collateral look and provides a ready-made shell for quick, in-house updates.

Reference Materials. Reference materials can take the form of charts, pocket guides, or more comprehensive bound materials. They are important for product or services that have large lists of options or features. Reference materials are ideal for outlining product families and comparisons against competitive products. If a product or service is technical or requires purchasers to perform specific steps, it may benefit from collateral that provides reference materials.

Multimedia. A growing technological sophistication among consumers and businesses has spawned greater use of multimedia collateral. Whether it is a computer diskette, a videotape, or an audiocassette, multimedia collateral offers an opportunity to relay a product or service message in a compelling format. Multimedia can be especially useful for cutting through the competitive clutter, making a particular piece stand out. Rapid advances in technology have improved quality and have made multimedia more affordable. In some vertical markets, particularly health care and high technology, a multimedia collateral piece is almost necessary.

Testimonials/Success Stories. No other form of collateral is as powerful as a customer testimonial. Although testimonials or success stories can be created in almost any collateral format (brochure, single sheet, multimedia), they are important enough to review singularly. Testimonials carry more credence because they come from the mouth of a customer, not a marketing department. They allow prospects to try on a product through other customers' experiences, allowing them to see how it would work for them. A good testimonial can even reveal aspects of a product or service that have great appeal to your prospects but have not received a great deal of marketing emphasis. If the task is to sell an intangible, such as quality, reliability, or service, adding testimonials to the collateral inventory is worthwhile and recommended.

INTEGRATING COLLATERAL WITH OTHER MARKETING COMMUNICATIONS

All marketing communications disciplines work together as integral steps in an educational process which, over the course of time, convinces prospects to make a purchase. The sales process may take a day, a week, or a year depending on the importance of the product to the customer.

The process is not linear. The time when advertising is launched and direct mail is mailed may not coincide with the time a prospective client is in need of a product. However, in an ideal situation, advertising begins the process by broadcasting a favorable message to a wide audience of potential consumers. Direct mail personalizes the message to a narrowly defined group of potential customers. Collateral is the last phase.

Consequently, what is relevant is not when or in what form the prospect is exposed to the sales message but the content of the message. There must be a compelling reason that moves him or her along the path from casual interest to serious intent to purchase.

Developing effective collateral is an art, as well as a science. Years of experience provide the insight and intuition an astute marketer needs to create sales literature that motivates the reader and fosters a sale. Marketers must be many things — strategists, psychologists, behaviorists, analysts, technicians, and creative thinkers. The task is not as difficult as it sounds. If we divide the process into three stages, it is much easier to appreciate: (1) strategic planning, (2) concept and creative development, and (3) production. The collateral development process is shown in Exhibit 19.1.

Strategic Planning: How to Develop a Strategy That Works. The first step is to develop a strategy that correctly positions the product or service within its competitive environment. This means articulating a selling proposition that effectively motivates the target audience (the potential customer). Next, decide how different communication vehicles, including collateral, can best support the proposition and associated marketing goals.

EXHIBIT 19.1
THE COLLATERAL PROCESS

1. Product Input
2. Competitive Research
3. Creative Strategy Statement
4. Concept Development
5. Costs and Timetable
6. Execution (copy and art)
7. Production

To appreciate the mind-set of the target prospect, one must become that person, shedding all personal beliefs, attitudes, and affectations about the product or service that is to be to promoted. One must empathize with the target market and understand its attitudes and beliefs.

A fast and easy way to relate to the prospect's lifestyle or business, depending on the type of product being promoted, is to read magazines the prospect would read, visit stores the prospect would shop in, and do things (within reason) the prospect would do. Magazines and stores that appeal to a target are successful because they understand how to address these people in a credible fashion. Details such as the tone and attitude employed by these vehicles, or the colloquial expressions or unusual vernacular used in these environments, will provide clues that will enable one to express a strategy in a context appealing to the target.

Studying the competition is also important. Obtain competitors' promotional materials. Examine their advertising. See if they do anything extraordinary to market their product. Define their selling proposition.

After the product's marketing environment has been analyzed, study the product and all current and former communication materials used to promote it. Learn everything there is to learn about it, including its weaknesses as well as its strengths. Obtain whatever background material there is. Consult trade magazines that have reviewed the product to understand the trade's perspective. Call or visit stores that have sold the product. Most important of all, speak to people who have purchased the product.

After the research has been carefully done, a selling proposition that is convincing and compelling can be formulated. The strategy should be succinct. It should clearly state what position the product or service occupies in the market and what characteristic will make people want to buy it. Do not be vague and use words that may equally describe other products. Develop a point of view that no other product can claim.

If possible, summarize the strategy in one word. The sharper and clearer the strategy is, the easier it is for the creative team to think of fresh ideas to promote the product. For example, "IBM RISC System/6000s are the best computers in their category" is vague. "IBM RISC System/6000s are the most robust workstations available for number crunching applications" is sharp. In one word, power.

Enhance the strategy with a definition of the target audience. "IBM RISC System/6000s are ideal for anyone who works with numeric-intensive data such as engineers, scientists, and financial professionals." Last, describe the tone most appropriate for addressing potential customers "benefit-driven and technical."

Creative Concept Development and Execution. Once the team

has developed a strategy, the creative people go to work on creative concept and execution. "Creative concept" is the fundamental creative idea used as a vehicle for the client's message. Another way of looking at it is as a two- or three-word summary of the positioning/strategy statement, in which the persuasive power of the statement flows more from the implied image than the actual words themselves.

Thus, good concepts, almost by definition, can be stated succinctly. For example, a brochure for computer networking solutions in which the communications strategy is to emphasize the vital need for unimpeded data flow throughout different but related networks might use the close-up image of a leaf showing its veins and topology as the key visual. The creative concept is then "The Leaf."

"Creative execution" is how the idea is fleshed out in the pages of the brochure. This means the actual writing of the headlines and copy, layout of the pages, selection of stock photography, planning and shooting of new photography, and making sure the whole effort appears as a cohesive whole.

Background.

To ensure that the creative work reflects the strategy and accurately presents the product, the creative people will require a certain amount of background information to do their jobs. Exhibit 19.2 outlines this information.

EXHIBIT 19.2

   I. A complete understanding of the product
     A. What it does
       1. Problem(s) it solves
       2. How it works
     B. Benefits
  II. A general understanding of the marketing environment
     A. Competitive products
     B. Similar products
     C. Alternatives to using the product to solve the problem
     D. Other problems competing for the prospect's attention and dollars
     E. Position
       1. Share and share growth
       2. Market segment and market segment growth
     F. Competitive marketing communications
       1. Ads, direct response, and collateral used by the competition
       2. Production values and sophistication levels expected by prospects
 III. A general idea of the budget for the project
 IV. An absolute knowledge of the schedule, with particular emphasis on due dates

---

Since much of this information is the same as the information used in developing the strategy in the first place, one might conclude that it's easier and more efficient to simply include the creative personnel in all client briefings, meetings, and input sessions from the very start. Many very successful agencies have reached the same conclusion and do indeed work in this way. There are two situations in which this can be a problem.

First, management may feel the need to withhold information from the creative team as a means of "controlling" the account internally. This unprofessional attitude benefits no one. The creative people are hamstrung, and the manager in charge ultimately produces inferior work. Second, the creative people may feel they do not have the time to attend meetings. This, too, is generally unprofessional. A valid concept requires total understanding — and so does good, in-depth copy.

Certainly there are aspects of account management that aren't the business of the creative team, and which can be said correctly to waste their time. These include discussions with the client about accounting, estimates, and spin control when things go wrong. At the same time, attending product and market briefings is absolutely necessary for the creative people. If they refuse, one should start looking for team members who will commit their professional energies more appropriately. Thus, part of the job is to maintain an environment of respect for everyone's professional needs. For example, try not to schedule a small creative presentation for the same meeting with a two-hour discussion of back bills.

The Schedule.

Do not overlook the importance of creating a realistic production schedule and sticking to it. Begin with the delivery date and work backward through the steps in production. Selecting a delivery date may be part of the strategic consideration. Are you shooting for a trade show? Is this collateral intended for use as fulfillment for a direct response ad? When does that ad break? Is the need for the product seasonal? When does the selling cycle begin? Who is printing the piece, and how long will it take to get all the copies from that location to the show, the field offices, the depository, or other required site? How long will the run require to print and dry?

Ask these questions and all others implied by the production process for the collateral piece being worked on. Find out the normal times and the expedited times, and how much special expediting services, such as overtime, could cost. Then make a schedule based on normal response times with as much time allowed for concept and creative development as possible. The reason that so much time is needed for concept and creative development is that this is generally the part of the process that's most likely to encounter problems, even when done correctly.

The creative component is where pictures and writing and the client's business all come together. These are topics with which everyone is familiar and about which, therefore, everyone has strong opinions — and not all of them entirely rational. Don't worry about this, it's just human nature, and there's nothing you can do to change it. But one can build enough time into the schedule to deal with it.

What kind of time? A winning concept can take anywhere from a week to six weeks. Three weeks is a good, comfortable amount of time in most cases. Always remember, it's easier to deliver the final project sooner than it is to get an extension.

The Concept.

Recognizing a great creative concept is easy, provided you've got one on the table. A great creative concept for a brochure illustrates the problem and the solution in one fell swoop in the cover art and headline, and it does so in a way that is at once crystal clear and totally unexpected. What's more, the visual theme or analogy on the cover is readily explored throughout the brochure in a way that aids the prospect in quickly understanding the client's product and essential points of difference or benefit. It has been said that a really good brochure can communicate its essential message in headlines and pictures alone — the copy is there to provide details to the prospect whose immediate needs might be met by the product.

While most people will usually recognize a truly great creative concept, most of the time concepts range from "pretty good" to "excellent." Unfortunately, even excellence is not obvious to most people. The more people in the room when a concept is presented, the more likely it is that even an excellent idea will die. There will be too many opinions and passions for the rational assessment required to answer the only relevant question: "Does this idea serve as a clear, compelling vehicle for the product?"

This kind of conflict is another example of human nature that can't be changed. But once again, it can be worked around. Part of the job in managing the process is to ensure that the work is reviewed by the smallest number of people possible. Strive for access to the decision maker and get a decision.

Do not be surprised or discouraged if making several presentations is required before a creative concept is accepted by all parties involved. This is the hardest part of everybody's job. It's hard for the client to take the risk that's built into making a commitment to a single creative idea. It's hard to keep everyone focused on just the relevant issues. It's hard for the creative team to keep coming up with sound ideas.

So by the time a concept is sold, everyone will be spiritually drained to some extent. Repeated disappointments may have eroded relationships with the clients and at the agency. Because so much is at stake in the course of this ordeal, it is of the utmost importance that the project manager never drop the ball in any part of production. One is straining the relationship when selling a concept. One must demonstrate worthiness of that trust, over and over again.

The Execution.

Creative execution, on the other hand, should be relatively straightforward. If the concept is approved, all that remains is designing the pages and writing the copy. If the strategy and product are adequately and correctly understood by the creative team, and the concept has been fully accepted and understood by the marketing client, the project should move forward without further strain. The copy will be accepted with few, if any, revisions, and the layouts will be clearly appreciated. Nevertheless, the following snags are likely to occur:

1. **Deadlines are missed.** Either the creative team fails to deliver the work on time, or the client sits on approvals. Either way, the schedule and the relationship are compromised.

2. **The scope of the project/strategy/product changes.** There's nothing like seeing words on paper in black and white to get people thinking about what they really want to say. It often happens that marketing people change their minds as they review the copy and layouts. The best response in such situations is to start over, working against the "true" objectives. One is more often forced by deadlines and budgets and other considerations to have the creative people adapt the work to reflect the new direction.

3. **The creative team gets it wrong.** It often happens that the input wasn't fully understood, and this isn't really apparent until all the details of execution are explored. This sort of problem, whether caused by the incompetence of the creative team, failure to provide adequate background, or the marketing client's inadequate input, strains the relationship.

In any of these scenarios, the clock suddenly seems to start ticking faster and louder. Once again, therefore, leaving enough time in the creative concept and execution phases of the schedule to compensate — and knowing exactly where you can expedite down the line — are of paramount importance.

Production. The final step in the process of developing outstanding collateral is the execution of the ideas — the transfer of conceptual thinking into a printed piece. Production is as important as strategy and concept development. If a great idea is not executed well, the purpose of the effort — to communicate effectively — can be compromised. Achieving high production values is not simply submitting materials to a printer and expecting the finished piece to look exceptional when it is off the press. A great deal of planning or "pre-pro" should precede.

Under ideal circumstances where budgets are large enough to allow for a team of professionals to work on a collateral project, it is the responsibility of the art director to prepare materials for the printer, and it is the responsibility of the production manager to supervise printing. However, in many situations where budgets are constrained, people have to double up. Managers may perform as writers, writers may perform as art directors, and art directors may accept the responsibility of production managers. Regardless of who does what, there are certain basic rules of thumb everyone should follow when producing collateral.

To begin with, go back to the original concept and ask how it can be executed. In other words, determine what components — photography, stock photography, illustration, computer graphics — are necessary to achieve the desired creative effect. Involve all creative personnel at this stage, including and especially the printer. Ask the printer's advice. If the desired creative effect is a soft, slightly out-of-focus close-up of a woman's face, for example, then the printer may suggest a special printing technique that can enhance the mood. On the contrary, if the desired creative effect is a sharp, freeze-frame action shot of a soccer player then suggested printing techniques will be entirely different.

The manager must make sure that the entire creative team is in unison. The art director, the photographer or graphics artist, and the printer must be working toward the same objectives. If the photographer does not light the subject properly or does not include enough of the subject in the composition to accommodate the layout, the printer may not be able to make adjustments to compensate for these oversights.

To avoid costly and embarrassing errors in production, ask the printer to provide, in advance, samples of the paper stock the art director has specified. Also ask if the printer can provide printed samples of collateral done for other clients using the same stock and printing process. This will assure beforehand that the desired creative effect is easily achievable.

The selection of stock is largely determined by format. Depending on size and design, brochures, flyers, pocket guides, pamphlets, binders, mailers, and the like may require stock with different weights, textures, and finishes. Some stocks send subliminal messages that should be considered. Slick, glossy paper says high tech and modern. Subtly textured and colored papers seem conservative and may be appropriate for certain products.

There are really no hard and fast rules. It is very subjective and often a matter of what feels and works best to execute the creative goals. However, there are some conventions that should be kept in mind.

Covers are usually printed on heavier stock than text, brochures and flyers are usually printed on coated stock, and letters are usually printed on noncoated stock.

Paper companies have different names and different methods of describing stock. Get stock sample books from several paper companies to compare quality, texture, color, and price. If a certain stock is wanted, then request enough large sheets to construct a working model. If it is something that is intended to be mailed, then bring it to the post office to find out how much it will cost to mail. One may want to select a stock that is slightly lighter but considerably more affordable.

Aside from stock, there are other factors that must be considered before printing takes place — inks, varnishes, and printing methods. Again, these are factors best handled by experienced professionals, but there are a few basic rules everyone involved should know.

Printers use inks called process colors — cyan, yellow, magenta, and black. Process colors blend together in the printing process to produce "full" color. Process color printing is perfectly acceptable when color is not critical to your selling message. However, if one is promoting cosmetics or fashions, consider an alternative technique that makes use of inks called PMS inks. When process colors are used to create a particular hue — for example, turquoise or mauve — they tend to be "muddy." PMS inks are mixed prior to printing and are loaded into individual wells on press. Consequently, they produce color that is cleaner and considerably closer to the color of the product.

Varnishes determine the luster or lack of luster on the collateral piece. Printers can "spot varnish," which means they control the area in which the varnish is laid down. If the layout features photographs interspersed with text, then varnish the photographs to accentuate the color and protect the photographs from fingerprints. On the other hand, if a glossy stock is used, lay down a dull varnish to reduce glare in the areas that feature photographs.

CONCLUSION

As a professional, create collateral that not only is strategically correct but is of high production value. Make certain that every creative element that goes into the collateral piece is flawless. Everyone involved with the project should be encouraged to inspect each phase from typesetting to the preparation of art and mechanicals to printing. Each step should be thoroughly reviewed in an effort to eliminate all errors. If the project includes the production of several printed pieces that must all fit together, then working models should be constructed beforehand. During production, therefore, each piece can be examined both as a free-standing unit and as part of the overall package.

Printing and production possibilities are endless. It is an area that requires the collective judgment of seasoned professionals. Exercise good judgment, plan well in advance, and make certain that all creative and production personnel communicate. The final piece will be exemplary and worthy of display to prospective clients.

Jim Rapp is founder and president of The Rapp Group, Inc., an organization in Alexandria, Virginia, that writes for business publications, corporations, and associations. With a background in sales, marketing, sales training, and meeting management, he was previously sales manager for General Foods Corporation and Director of Education for the National Office Products Association.

Rapp has written numerous books and self-instruction materials for Addison-Wesley, Prentice-Hall, Bill Publications, and The National Society of Sales Training Executives. He is the author of Dartnell's Successful Sales Meetings Manual.

CHAPTER 20

CORPORATE SALES MEETINGS

Sales meetings are held for many reasons, but there are very few in which product and sales promotion do not play an active part. In fact, most corporate sales meetings are held for the primary purpose of introducing or promoting a product or service.

Unfortunately, some sales meetings get so bogged down with topics that should not be discussed at such a gathering that new products or exciting promotions tend to get lost in the shuffle. Too bad! Sales meetings provide one great opportunity to inform and enthuse — to get the sales force really charged up.

A company's sales, marketing, advertising, and sales promotion people should never assume that their salespeople will leave the meeting full of enthusiasm for the work they've just been asked to do. The salespeople have to be sold, in the same way that they have to sell each of their customers. This means that corporate sales meetings must be well planned and carried out with excitement, encouragement, and rewards.

Corporations hold more regional and local sales meetings these days, some shunning the big national meetings altogether. However, just because a meeting is smaller doesn't mean it has to be less exciting. In fact, smaller meetings can achieve more at less cost if they are properly planned and carried out.

This chapter serves as a guide to the specifics of planning and conducting successful corporate sales meetings.

THE MEETING AGENDA

A sales meeting should have set, specific objectives. A meeting without objectives is a meeting to cancel. It is a wise boss who asks right off, "What do we hope to accomplish by the meeting?" The answer had better be specific and to the point. In other words, *action objectives* are critical. For instance, suppose that a firm is a major factor in the decorative fabrics market and, mid-season, one of its mills has come up with a new weaving technique that allows for a more attractive product at a lower cost. The sales force must know this fast. It is time for a meeting — and an *action objective*, that is, acquiring 400 new accounts before the competition catches on, which it is bound to do.

What are the benefits to be gained from the meeting in this example rather than from a long sales bulletin with swatches of the new fabric attached? Well, how about those familiar words *impel* and *incite* and the action objective of getting more accounts in a hurry?

The agenda for any meeting should *always* be as simple as possible, which is just another way of saying that it must be focused. One can't cover the waterfront in a single sales meeting; even if it could be done, the attention of about half the sales force would be lost by the end of the meeting. Therefore, the agenda must be focused and have an action objective as its centerpiece.

When the agenda has been set, it's time to move on to the next consideration — accommodations for the meeting. These will depend, of course, on the size of the meeting planned, the hurry-up nature of the gathering, and the proximity of the sales force. It is important not to procrastinate on nailing down accommodations as soon as all signals are "go" for the meeting! Securing and reserving accommodations can be, and usually is, a time-consuming and frequently frustrating part of the entire sales meeting plan.

This brings up another question: Why use a manual in preparation for a sales meeting? After all, isn't it a relatively simple matter to get the salespeople together in some hotel meeting room, feed them, bunk them down, then impel and incite them? Those who have tried this off-the-cuff approach to sales meetings know the answer to this is *no*, it is not possible. *Organization* is the key factor here. Organizing, together with using checklists to keep track of the myriad details involved in any sales meeting, is the only guarantee of achieving goals and of justifying the costs involved. Even with the best planning, no one can guarantee that a meeting will draw plaudits from salespeople and boss alike, but without organization and detailed planning, it's a safe bet the meeting will be a shambles.

PLANNING THE MEETING

When people find themselves in the position of planning a meeting as just one part of their job (and this is the case in the majority of firms), there may be times when they wonder how they ever got involved in such a time-consuming, detail-laden operation in the first place. Thus, there is a temptation — a real one — to wing it for the next sales meeting. Odds are overwhelming, however, that if they adopt a casual approach to what is probably costing the company a bundle of money and time, they will be held responsible.

The best meetings — those that accomplish something on schedule — are meetings that appear to be effortless as they play out, with no gaffes in either meeting flow or arrangements. This doesn't happen by chance. Good meetings require professional planning. The aim is to make everything appear to be effortless. The people who are involved in the planning may be the only ones who know what effort and planning it took; but then, a great actor doesn't remind the audience after each performance how much time he or she has spent planning every move on stage. It's called professionalism.

In planning the meeting, here are the key guideposts:

1. First, what is to be accomplished with the meeting? In other words, what are the goals? Probably the most common goal at meetings boils down to education. Any firm these days, large or small, feeds and grows on constant change and improvement in product or manufacturing technique. No business today stands still. It's a constant push for new and better products. In most businesses the advent of a new line is a natural (and necessary) launching pad for a meeting. The aim, of course, is to educate the sales force in the new product and achieve sales dominance within the product category.

Assuming the primary goal of the meeting is education — for example, the introduction of a new product that requires the prominent display of promotional material in each territory — is it enough just to say the display is key to the successful kickoff of the new product? Or to suggest jokingly that the promotional materials will do no good in the trunk of the salesperson's car?

The action objective for each rep is to name his or her key accounts, the ones where, at a minimum, the materials must be on display. After each rep names the key accounts in his or her territory, the number should be noted or recorded. When it's all over, the number of key accounts can be totaled and the minimum number of display stations for the new product can be announced. That's an action objective and not just some feigned enthusiasm when the mock-up is shown with a suggestion of how much it will help. The salespeople must commit themselves verbally so later on they'll take action.

2. The next consideration is the meeting context, or agenda. Without fail, the most effective meeting is the one that has an established agenda that has been communicated in advance. The agenda should tie the meeting to company goals and provide precise direction during the meeting itself.

It's also a good idea to solicit ideas or suggestions for the agenda from as many people as possible within the organization. At first glance, this may sound like a formidable, if not messy, undertaking. However, most times the response is surprising and helpful. Most people will zero in on common concerns within the organization. There will, of course, be the odd agenda request, but the majority of your responses will be similar, even if phrased differently. When these responses have been received — and this should be done well in advance of the actual meeting — it is a relatively simple matter to read them carefully to determine the patterns of concern and/or interest among managers and other personnel. This is a far more efficient method of setting an agenda than having informal chats in hallways or encouraging long memos from respondents.

Further, this technique is invaluable in giving everyone a sense of participation in the meeting *before* it convenes. It brings the team approach into planning the meeting at its earliest stages, which in turn gives a head start on making the meeting a success.

What emerges from the study of suggested topics for the agenda will be the preliminary or general format of the meeting. This can be a simple general list of what will be going on and in what order. For example, the preliminary list for a one-day meeting might read as follows:

1. Welcome and orientation
2. Guest speaker
3. Break
4. Workshops
5. Lunch
6. Tour of plant
7. Coffee break
8. Panel discussion and workshops
9. Question and answer period
10. Summary
11. Announcements
12. Banquet

The final agenda should include specific times for each agenda item, and every attempt should be made to enforce these times. Normally, the tendency is to crowd too much into an agenda. Because of this, even slightly exceeding the time limits can find the meeting far behind by late afternoon, and audience interest will lag. It needs to be made clear to all concerned that it is essential to stay within time allotments.

3. In addition to setting up and following a pertinent agenda for the meeting, the next most important step in the planning process is selecting a location and appropriate accommodations for the meeting. As anyone who has planned meetings can attest, this process is sometimes a minefield of broken promises, inefficient service, and one snarl after another. It thus behooves anyone responsible for a meeting, large or small, to pay strict attention to the details of *when* and *where* and, not least, *how much*?

In site selection there is no substitute for a personal, far-in-advance inspection of the premises. This inspection should encompass a number of subjective considerations one might not think would have much to do with a sales meeting. Alas, they do.

For instance, much grief can be avoided by the briefest of look-sees at the average convention establishment. A lot can be learned by just peeking into a set-up meeting room. Having lunch in the establishment's dining room or coffee shop is also telling. Is the help efficient? Courteous? Well groomed? Is the food barely edible, average, or prepared with obvious professionalism? These are all judgments made in nonprofessional capacities every day, and they are considerations that carry over into group dining. It's not hard to spot surly service, inefficiency, or unsanitary conditions. Nor is it hard for a stranger to sense the tone of any hotel or meeting center. A meeting planner should ask to see an average bedroom as well. The manager will be delighted to show one if there's nothing to conceal.

4. The meeting should be announced far in advance. The more advance notice that is given on the exact time and place of the sales meeting, the better. Those who call hurry-up sales meetings are likely to be considered suspect by the very people they are attempting to motivate. Moreover, there are frequently very good reasons why a rep shouldn't drop everything and rush to a meeting. His or her territory may be undergoing some important buyer changes, for example, and the rep's on-scene monitoring of the situation may be critical in meeting sales objectives.

There is probably never a perfect time for everyone to come to a sales meeting, but one thing is certain. There will be less flak about timing if everyone is informed as far in advance as possible. Smart sales managers start planning the next sales meeting the day after everyone heads home, at least in terms of where it will be and on what dates. As soon as the dates are finalized, a sales bulletin should be sent out with the news. This is a bulletin that should be brief and should stand on its own. The date should not be buried among routine announcements. The announcement shown in Exhibit 20.1, or one as simple, should go out *at least three months in advance of the meeting*, earlier if the dates can be nailed down.

EXHIBIT 20.1

SALES BULLETIN

Mark your calendar now. Our next sales meeting will take place (date) at company headquarters in Minneapolis starting at 9:30 a.m. The meeting will run two full days.

To build up interest, it is a good idea to fill in the details in future sales bulletins as actual details of the meeting are assembled. The exact time, date, and place of the meeting should always be repeated. These advance teasers of the meeting should include more details as the process moves along and as plans for the meeting become increasingly organized. However, if there is some surprise for the meeting, that ought to be saved for the meeting itself. One shouldn't give away a second-act climax before the meeting — particularly not in a sales bulletin.

Naturally, as the date of the meeting approaches, meeting planners will be in daily contact with many of the regional people, either on the phone or by memos. It is a good idea to talk up the sales meeting occasionally in these informal encounters and answer questions as they arise. Although the questions will be many and varied, answering them all is a good way to create a climate of interest and involvement in the forthcoming meeting.

BUDGETING

There are two basic budgeting considerations involved in planning a sales gathering. First, there are the up-front costs, which include all the obvious expenses such as travel, hotel rooms, food, entertainment, and speakers. These are relatively easy to calculate, if difficult to justify. Second, there are the hidden costs, such as the downtime of the sales force while at and en route to and from the meeting. These costs are not nearly as easy to calculate as the up-front variety. They can be subjective, with many variables. In preparing these costs, the best advice is to err on the side of being generous.

Obviously, a final budget cannot be calculated until other segments of the meeting planning, particularly negotiations with hotel and meeting site personnel, have concluded. A ballpark figure on such costs can be estimated — and it's good to have one as a guide — but certain key costs can't be nailed down until there are signed hotel contracts, airline and rental car commitments, and other commitments. All the more reason why planning for a meeting or convention must be a long-range process. It is difficult to work within tight budget restrictions for spur-of-the-moment gatherings. The hospitality industry just doesn't work that way.

After pulling together the logistics of the meeting, with commitments from all suppliers, it is time to prepare a detailed budget, including up-front and hidden costs. It may be interesting to know that many experienced meeting planners build in a 10 percent contingency factor in order to finish at or under budget.

As much as possible, the budget should be easy to understand and submitted on simple forms. Budgeting proposals should be submitted to management far in advance of the meeting because instant action on proposals isn't likely. Except in rare circumstances, corporate decisions of this magnitude aren't made overnight. Anyone with experience in following meeting budgets through to their successful conclusion — that is, planning and executing a successful meeting — knows how frustrating the approval process can be.

It is wise to avoid some of the more obvious financial objections by considering carefully *where to spend*. This cannot be stressed strongly enough! Many otherwise solid budgets for meetings have become instantly suspect because of some quirky enthusiasm of the budget-writer. For instance, the salespeople can get along without a banquet appearance by some expensive TV luminary.

Is it necessary to hold the meeting in season at a famous resort, when if held a couple months later, it would be possible to get the same service and accommodations at half price? No matter how lavish a meeting may be, it is always best to put money where it is likely to count: meeting the objectives for the session. No one will cry poor-mouth when it comes to housing and entertaining the meeting participants, but there is a big financial difference between luxury and perfectly adequate accommodations.

The same thinking applies to good services at a meeting or convention. There is a big difference between the cost of specialty foods (and drinks) and the cost of menu items commonly available and served as part of the hotel's traditional fare. This is not to suggest that everyone should go to McDonald's at lunch break but merely that the atmosphere and food should not obscure the point of the gathering, which is the accomplishment of preset objectives, clearly articulated to management in the budget proposals.

If there is the budget to splurge for a meeting, the spare change would be best spent on educational materials, effective speakers and workshop leaders, and pertinent audiovisual materials.

The following are some areas in most meeting budgets that usually can be trimmed, or at least, which might benefit from a second look:

1. **Travel.** This is a sales meeting expense that can get out of hand rapidly. Airlines themselves are often confused these days about fares and even their own so-called supersaver programs. If possible, a meeting planner should work with a reliable travel agency as far in advance of the meeting as possible. If a meeting can be scheduled during off-peak seasons and off-peak days of the week, the savings in this area can be substantial. Also, booking in group lots and avoiding individual fares where possible will save money. Therefore, it is smart to avoid the everyone-is-on-his-or-her-own concept in getting people to and from the meeting. The same applies to ground transportation. There is usually economy in numbers. *Get a reliable travel agent involved*, and do it early.

2. **Hotels.** Shopping around in the hospitality industry always pays off in planning a meeting. What are the local competitive factors? What are the off-season, off-day periods? Local convention bureaus are a good starting point, moving on to specific locations for comparative pricing later. Some fine hotels have been built in recent years in pretty strange locations. Favorable tax laws have spurred such development and, to get established, these hotels frequently offer outstanding bargains to meeting planners.

3. **Meals.** It pays to study this segment of a meeting plan with care. If the sales force is national, chances are some of the trendy (and expensive) ideas that have crept into hotel cuisine in recent years will not appeal to the staff. It is possible to go basic in this category without being dull and, thereby, please the majority of the people attending. Most hotel food service departments offer a price per person, and there is a wide variation in per-person cost depending on simple menu offerings.

In budgeting for a meeting, there are certain areas where it really does not pay to skimp:

1. **Speakers.** Nowhere is it more true than in this category that people get what they pay for! The best advice again is to shop around. Many top-notch universities and colleges maintain speaker bureaus. Educators with knowledge of a given industry and/or its problems probably are available nearby and are more than eager to speak at gatherings. These college bureaus can provide resumes for perusal, along with fee schedules, usually much lower than the famous "names" on the lecture circuit.

2. **Workshop and seminar leaders.** These people don't come cheap. This is no place to skimp, either, for bombastic or ill-informed trainers can undercut an entire meeting. Workshop and seminar leaders should always be carefully chosen and checked in advance.

3. **Audiovisual aids.** While there admittedly is a lot of technical razzmatazz in this field today, this is not a place to pinch pennies. The key is to concentrate on what is pertinent to the meeting, not on what is trendy or merely amusing. If, for example, a film is really the best way to assist in a new product presentation, the film should be done by professionals. The same goes for training aids. There are many good sales training films available, but the best cost money. When it comes to films or tapes, it is best not to settle for second best. This, of course, means that a meeting planner must become something of a film critic or rely on the word of an associate or friend.

The overriding consideration in budgeting for a sales meeting is to make the budget realistic, and not only because it stands a better chance of approval. A meeting planner must be sure that the cost is balanced by the accomplishment of objectives. When there is uncertainty, a good rule of thumb in budgeting is to consider whether the boss would take a chance on a particular item. If the answer is no, the budget needs refinement.

SALES MEETINGS TO INTRODUCE NEW PRODUCTS

Due to increasing competition, even the most hidebound industries are introducing new products when they are ready to go and not waiting until the annual or semiannual sales gatherings.

In a sense, these meetings are the easiest and sometimes most rewarding to organize and bring off. They are relatively easy because the meeting has a direct focus: a new product or service, and they are rewarding because newness — if it really is new — is intrinsically exciting to everyone, particularly a sales force.

The task is to *sell* the new product or service to the company's people. It may be a product that competes directly with one of the firm's established favorites, or it may be a product with consumer appeal but which is bulky or difficult to show. Sometimes a new product may even pose a threat to the salespeople, who are comfortable with what they are selling at the moment.

One of the best techniques to use in selling a new product to a sales force is to step aside and turn the platform over to the people who came up with and implemented the idea. These people — stylists, packaging experts, or inventors — frequently speak with great sincerity (after all, it's their baby!), even if they may not visualize the product's sales potential. Experts should be allowed to be questioned at whatever length and allowed to outline in their own words the product's advantages. While this technique may not convince every salesperson in the room, it is almost certain to gain allies from the most skilled salespeople. Another advantage in letting the experts speak is that a perceptive salesperson invariably will pick up sales pointers from such a presentation — pointers he or she later can translate into benefits for a buyer.

MEETINGS FOR CONTEST WINNERS

This type of meeting has taken a needlessly bad rap in recent days, probably because there's a bit of jealousy involved among the nonwinners or some resentment involved among the winners in having to attend a meeting as "penance" for being a winner. Neither position is justified if such a meeting is structured to do what it is supposed to do: improve on excellence.

If the meeting is no more than an extended trip to a spa, with little but socializing involved, it probably will create jealousy. If it's a long haul over familiar territory, it will induce boredom. What is the happy medium at a meeting of contest winners?

In coming to grips with this dilemma, it is a good idea to keep foremost in mind that the reason these people have been assembled is because they are good — and people who are good generally want to be even better. That's an oversimplification, but thinking it through, people get to be good because they are always learning. It follows, then, that a meeting of contest winners should focus on shared experiences and should function as an enlarged rap session dealing with sales techniques. Setting aside time to praise and to hand out awards is imperative.

What should be avoided at these meetings are nuts and bolts reviews of company policy and any references to the possible shortcomings of colleagues not fortunate enough to have won a contest.

MEETINGS THAT PROVIDE EDUCATION

The schoolroom approach to education and training won't work at a sales meeting. There will be an audience, but the built-in resentments of "back in school again" are likely to overpower the educational content.

The best technique, and there are a variety of ways to achieve it, is to make the training as painless as possible, meaning as nonacademic as possible. Training ideally should be one of the fun segments of the meeting; in other words, the meeting planners will have to resist the temptation to get the training over with as fast as possible by the excessive use of chalkboards and pointers.

Why is education such an essential ingredient of any sales gathering? The most likely answer is that the need for training is the very reason the sales meeting was scheduled in the first place. Most sales meetings focus on line introductions, scientific breakthroughs, or some facet of a product line that is genuinely new and, therefore, unknown to the sales personnel in terms of what it is and how to sell it.

In order for management to capitalize on the potential of a new product — the development of which likely cost a bundle — they must further invest in seeing that the salespeople know what they're talking about when they go before the customers. Not only must reps be trained in the new product, they must also be trained in how to present the new product most effectively. This is the basic challenge of virtually all sales meetings.

The needs of the salespeople are centered on product education and on how best to present the product. The needs of management are centered on how to make the product a success. The lubricant in this mix-match of needs is training, best carried out at a sales meeting. All the sales bulletins in the world are no substitute for a hands-on training session at a sales meeting.

Considering the time limitations of most sales meetings, by necessity, much of a meeting will be structured around training, which needn't be as dull as it sounds.

First, most salespeople are in the top bracket of the general population when it comes to alertness. They are fully aware, even subconsciously, of the twist on the old saying, "The more things change, the more they change." To stand still on old products and concepts in today's marketplace is to lose ground. All sales personnel know that; they are eager for a new, freshened product and are receptive to any ideas that will help them sell the product. Because of this, the job of structuring the sales meeting around education is a lot easier than it seems at first glance. But it is still important to avoid the pedantic approach to sales training; preaching and exhortation may have their place elsewhere, but not at a sales meeting.

The very word *lecture* has negative connotations, so its use should be avoided in circulating the meeting agenda. Whatever it is called, a talk to any group of people to impart information is by definition a lecture. There's nothing wrong with a lecture, assuming it is prepared (and delivered) by someone who knows what he or she is talking about. A lecture is not a speech, even if the two can at times overlap in content and purpose. It can be said that a lecture is a speech by an expert and, as such, should be as devoid of gimmickry and obtrusive witticisms as possible.

Frequently a lecture is an effective way to impress on the salespeople the importance of a new product and the amount of time and effort that went into its development.

The lecture as a training device is most effectively used in conjunction with other training techniques. The lecture should (1) impress, (2) inform, and (3) illuminate. It should not bore. Here again, the chances of boring the salespeople with a preliminary lecture on the details of a product from whose sales they will be making their livings is remote. Moreover, if the lecturer is regarded as an in-house expert, the attention quotient for this segment will most likely be high indeed.

It is best when using an opening lecture format to follow the lecture immediately with a question and answer period, while ideas are fresh in everyone's mind. It is a good idea, too, to record the question and answer session for later circulation to the sales force. Most experts — if they truly are expert at something — tend, unfortunately, to think everyone knows almost as much as they do. It can be similar to coming in on the second act of a play: one knows how it all turns out, but how did it start? That is why a lively question and answer session at the end of a lecture is all important. These sessions can be training at its best.

Following the lecture (and the brief question-answer period) with a *workshop or seminar* is another good way to deal in practical terms with the new material while its technical aspects are still fresh in everyone's mind.

Workshops and/or seminars frequently suffer from two common failures: (1) the groups are too large and (2) the goals are not limited and defined. Workshop breakout groups should not exceed six or seven persons and, preferably, should be limited to five. This will increase the likelihood of each individual's participation. Large groups tend to inhibit the members of the group who are the least aggressive in terms of expressing themselves before their peers. These individuals are sometimes the most thoughtfully incisive thinkers. If possible, then, the workshop group should be kept down to five, with random selection of group participants. It is usually best to discourage participants from buddying up at the sessions in order to avoid predictable results.

Any new product, new policy, or switch in company direction is complicated and can lend itself to endless examination. It's the job of the meeting planner to narrow down the discussion possibilities in a workshop to, at most, two key points. Any more than this will lead to diffuse, unfocused rap sessions rather than result-producing workshop conclusions.

Often a new product may have both positive and negative consequences in the minds of the salespeople, and these consequences should be dealt with. For example, the introduction of an entirely new packaging idea for one of a company's best-selling food products for which the package is slightly larger than the current package, but the price of the unit remains the same. This is an oversimplification, of course, but this brief summary of what's new might already have set up two thoughts. More for less? The customers will like that. Bigger package? The customers won't like that.

In this example, it probably would be a good idea to focus the workshops on how to overcome buyer objections to the change in size. Considerations such as the appearance of the new package, use of colors, and type of container should be set aside. These will all arise in the discussion groups, but they should be secondary to thrashing out the focus question. It is up to each workshop leader, named by each group, to keep the group on track and, within a limited time, to present a summary of the group's recommendation on how to overcome the obvious buyer objection to a larger package. The goal might be for each group to brainstorm five briefly stated methods of overcoming this objection and, to ensure that they are stated concisely, to have the workshop leader fill out a form at the end of the time allowed for discussion.

When these workshop responses are in hand and have been reviewed, there will likely be a pattern of agreement in how best to approach the difficulties inherent in the merchandising of any new product development. What's more, the solutions will have been provided by the people who are most immediately concerned, the salespeople. Workshop findings should be summarized and announced as soon as possible. If time permits, it is best to do this immediately following the workshop sessions and, in effect, to set an informal sales policy concerning the presentation of the new development.

EDUCATIONAL TOOLS

Many sales managers are reluctant to use **television** at sales meetings, relying instead on the more traditional forms of equipment, such as slides, overhead transparencies, and 16mm projectors. For members of several generations brought up with television, these traditional forms can be a bit dull.

One shouldn't be afraid of TV. It's easy to hook up and is more trouble-free than most equipment. Consider the advantages:

1. Television can be motivational.
2. Television can stimulate discussion.
3. Television can impart knowledge.
4. Television can teach sequential activities.
5. Television can present information in a variety of ways not possible with any other media.
6. Video technology can allow users to magnify and "freeze" any image.
7. Television, unlike films or slides, does not require the meeting room to be darkened.
8. Television can take the learner anywhere.
9. Television has the advantage of being able to integrate most

other audiovisual materials.

10. Videotape playback is much easier than rewinding a film. It can be played back in a variety of ways to enhance learning.

11. Vocabulary problems may be overcome by saying and showing at the same time.

12. Television can be used for immediate feedback when the television camera is in use, such as with role-playing.

13. With televised instruction, meeting leaders or trainers can substantially reduce their preparation time.

14. Nonverbal information can be presented best through the television medium — the audience sees facial expressions close up, as they do in the real-life session in the buyer's office.

15. No description by a meeting leader of what a salesperson did or said can come close to that action being replayed on the video screen. The camera makes the judgment, not the leader or instructor. The instructor becomes a facilitator, not a judge.

16. The cost of producing a videotape is far less than that of producing a film. This is particularly advantageous when the presentation will be used only once or for a limited time. Additionally, time of preparation is far less for a video production.

17. *Sesame Street* is proof positive that small children can learn new words faster and with more accuracy through television than with any other teaching process. Why? Because the learner receives simultaneous signals through more than one sensory organ. The learner sees something and hears a voice talking about it, with a word or words superimposed on the bottom of the screen at the same time. In a classroom setting, the learning is further enhanced and reinforced by the meeting leader's words and more particularly by the discussion of the topic by the students themselves. This combination for learning is impossible to beat, and it makes one wonder why schoolteachers continue to concentrate on reading and lecture, the two least effective ways for the majority of schoolchildren to learn.

18. Television allows the sales manager to bring subject matter experts and highly respected individuals to the sales meeting at a very small cost. These individuals, such as the company president, leading educators, and other well-known people, can talk to your sales force on a seemingly one-to-one basis.

19. Properly used, videotaped role-playing can be one of the most valuable tools for any sales manager or sales trainer. By working in small peer groups, with no threat of embarrassment, the television camera can teach a salesperson more than a dozen trips in the field. Take the time to learn how to use and not misuse this powerful teaching tool.

20. Television can present content in many forms, such as demon-

stration, group discussions, lecture, interviews, narration, voice-over, dramatic action, cartoons, and graphics. By using different forms in a single presentation, each student is provided with one or more forms that appeal to him or her, that the student can identify with and is comfortable with. This point may be the most important thing to remember when developing a television program for a sales meeting — use more than one form!

Training films can be the lazy man's or woman's way out in building training into sales meetings. Simply put, there are films and then there are films. It's time-wasting and even counterproductive to use film in training unless what is being shown is pertinent to the product or to the firm. It may well be that a picture is worth a thousand words, but not if the picture has nothing to do, except in a remote way, with what is being explained.

Far too many sales meetings have utilized a generalized "sales techniques" film, supposedly to stir enthusiasm. The market abounds in such films and, at this very moment, doubtless many more are in production and many are being played to hapless assemblages of salespeople.

If a company is fortunate enough to have the resources to produce its own specific training film or video, it possesses a potent training tool. If not, all generalized market offerings should be prescreened before booking them for a sales meeting. This is about the only method to use that will ensure the training film won't be a clinker or that it's one that has little or no informative value for your group.

Role-playing sets up mini-dramas that are pertinent to a sales situation and then asks salespeople to enact the various roles in the drama. No one needs to be an actor to participate — better if no one is — but each person in the mini-drama should take his or her role seriously. The idea is to keep role-playing on as serious a level as possible and also to make sure the "plot" is germane to the sales situation involved. Outlandish situations or ones that might produce humor but little substance are to be avoided. Keeping the "cast" in these mini-dramas down to a minimum number is also wise.

To set the scene for role-playing, it is necessary to make some hard choices about the structure of the plot of the mini-drama. The key is to *be specific*. There shouldn't be room for rambling observations in the spontaneous dialogue. Mini-dramas should focus on one single issue. The plots to be played out by the salespeople have one aim: training by example. They should be realistic, representing something any of the staff would be likely to encounter in his or her daily rounds.

If a firm is undergoing a radical change in packaging, complete with new logo, one possible scenario would be to have a sales rep explaining why the change will be of benefit to his customer, a role assigned to another salesperson. They might just happen to be sitting with the buyer's boss, a tough merchandising manager. That's the bare bones of a "plot," and the "actors" can take it from there within a set time frame.

The best way to proceed is to allow the actors to play their roles with no interruptions, followed by an open critique of how the objections were met, how the change was explained as an advantage to the buyer and consumer, and how the buyer's objections were framed. This critique session is a valuable part of the role-playing process because invariably the audience was thinking of a number of points to make while the mini-drama was unfolding. This is the time when all these points will come forth.

In role-playing it is essential, too, to avoid any embarrassment to anyone. Some people think faster on their feet, while others are more reflective. Listening to role-playing and participating in the critique that follows can be particularly valuable to those on a staff who tend to be more introverted than others. It is therefore important to call on as many reps as possible during the critique session following the dramatic presentation.

Small group discussion can be a valuable tool to use in assessing meeting effectiveness. This can be either structured or free-flowing. The valuable part of this technique becomes apparent if one remembers playing that old parlor game in which each person turns to the person on the right and whispers a story to him or her. That person repeats the story to the next person and so on, with the last person in the ring telling the story aloud. The story usually will turn out to be radically different from the one first told. Discussion of a situation by small groups tends to cut down on future misunderstandings. In effect, it cuts down the risk factor inherent in the truism that people tend to hear what they want to hear.

In small group discussions, it is important that all who are involved in the training program be on hand to clear up anything that may arise out of these sessions. Following the small group discussions, it is a good idea to review the major points made during the training session. Learning, particularly if the subject is difficult or off-routine, is accomplished by repeated review or practice with the facts.

Not too much time should be devoted to these small group discussions, however. If they drag on, the tendency is for them to become exercises in futility. They should be kept brief. During the group discussions, someone should circulate as much as possible to see that the discussions stay on track, and more important, to pick up where the problem areas may be.

A more serious type of special meeting is the one involving the use of **case studies**. These are highly productive if — and it's a big if — the studies are well documented and have a beginning, a middle, and an end. These are narratives of a specific sales encounter, including what happened and why it happened. They can be either success stories or admitted failures. That's not important. What is important is that they provide guidelines for use by other members of the staff.

Plenty of time should be allowed for preparation when case studies are used, and general formats for preparing a case study should be given. It is important in this type of meeting to allow enough time for presentation of a case study but not too much time for introspection on the part of its author. It should be told as it was. This can be followed by a fixed time for questions and comments. There should never be more than five or six participants per break-off group in a case study meeting, preferably with each group consisting of those with similar sales problems or territories.

PROVIDING A THEME

The so-called "theme" meeting has long been popular with sales managers and salespeople alike, and for good reason. Use of a theme provides instant focus to any sales gathering.

The only problem with relying too much on the theme technique for a meeting is that it may, if abused, go against the grain of some of the younger people on a sales force. There is a fine line between the intelligent use of a meeting theme and its overuse. In other words, the medium can too easily become the message. Many of the tried-and-always-thought-true theme meeting techniques of the past are, to put it bluntly, out of date. This is not to claim that the theme meeting is in any way passé. Far from it. The trick is to hold down the heavy doses of hokey stuff when theme meetings are called for.

What this amounts to is a truth all sales managers are facing these days: the young people entering sales are, generally, better educated than those of a generation ago and, yes, far more sophisticated. This requires far more subtlety in conducting theme meetings than was necessary even a couple years ago.

Before theme meetings are consigned to the trash bin as outmoded (or too difficult to handle in a subtle manner), their major advantages should first be considered and perhaps restructured in terms of today's sales realities.

First, what are the virtues of a theme meeting?

1. An appropriate, viable theme for a sales meeting can act as the core of the gathering. Everything else is built around this core concept. This makes planning the meeting far easier, because the theme unifies the entire proceeding, thereby reducing the chances of straying off the topic throughout the meeting. In sum, a theme meeting stands a good chance of staying both on course and on time — no small considerations in any meeting.

2. Done correctly, the theme meeting can provide solid advance interest by the sales force. A good theme can start salespeople planning what to say and do prior to coming through the doors for the first session of the meeting.

3. A theme meeting can and should tackle a major problem or

development within the firm head-on and deal with it at length. The editing process that takes up so much time at an unthemed meeting is done in advance. The theme announces right off: "Here's what is going to be discussed and thrashed out."

Care needs to be taken in selecting a theme. If the choice is too restrictive, it may not even be germane to what's actually going on within the company. If it's too broad in concept, there's no use in bothering with a theme at all. Most important, a theme should never be injected into a sales meeting merely to fit it around some clever presentation technique or some new item of electronic gadgetry that's just come on the market. The theme, to be effective, must come from the dynamics of a given firm, either a problem that needs addressing or a product that needs a major introduction — even a major policy that's being changed or abandoned. The theme also should be of the variety that lends itself to expansion as the meeting assumes its own dynamics. One that is too restrictive will, again, have to fall back on gimmickry to stay alive for the course of a meeting. A thread of common and shared interest in the theme should exist, one broad and pervasive enough to allow for give and take during the entire meeting.

One of the most workable themes in today's business climate is overcoming competitive factors from foreign markets. Virtually every industry in the land faces direct or indirect threats from foreign competition. It is a theme, too, that's discussed informally in living rooms every night on network news. Everyone has an opinion in general terms on how to overcome this competition, but few zero in on how their own company can cope.

Most themes, including the one above, are universal and can be built around the concepts discussed herein.

Once a theme has been chosen for a meeting, the problem is how to boil the concept down to easily understood terms on which to hang the main ideas that are necessary to get across. In sum, the theme needs illustration. Even though the idea itself may be relatively complex, a few words that get the idea across can be used as a zingy handle.

If, for example, the theme centers on the need to fill expanded quotas in a line, the phrase "Over the Top" might be chosen as a theme focus. This allows for various illustrated materials, slogans, and graphs to set the tone for discussion of the theme as people enter the meeting room for the first time. The "Over the Top" theme can also serve as a starting point for a variety of other visual techniques, such as the use of huge thermometers on the stage. The most important thing to remember in bringing off a theme meeting is knowing when to lay off the gimmicks and when to dwell on the facts that tumble forth from the stimulation of the gimmicks.

Other possible themes include:
- Enthusiasm
- Warming up cold calls

- Teamwork
- A salute to our customers
- Knowing our competitors
- Merchandising
- Look good, feel good, be confident
- Selling service
- Problem solving
- Christmas in July (or some other month)
- Hawaiian holiday
- Back to the basics
- Being creative
- Return to the fifties
- Breaking new ground (getting new customers)
- Time (importance of, time to think, time control, time is money)
- Quality counts
- Sale themes (old-fashioned sale, holiday sale, anniversary sale)
- Slogans as themes (Let's be No. 1, Sell the Sizzle, Go for the Gold)
- Movie titles (*Gone With the Wind, The Orient Express, Casablanca*)
- Break the bank
- Game show titles (*Jeopardy, Wheel of Fortune, Hollywood Squares*)
- Let's go fishing (for new accounts)

The theme meeting, almost by definition, requires a skilled organizer and a person running things who doesn't get carried away by the props or the game itself.

Regardless of the theme, remember that a feeling of involvement and participation by every salesperson is the key to the successful use of a meeting theme.

How to Use Showmanship

Balance, a sage once wrote, is the most desirable goal of the human condition.

The same might be said of balance as a goal — a tough one to achieve — when it comes to the use of showmanship in meetings. When too little showmanship is tucked into the serious material, the meeting runs the risk of inattention and boredom; with too much showmanship, it risks overwhelming the serious aspects inherent in any business gathering.

When it comes to showmanship in a sales meeting, the organizer is cast in the unlikely role of a theatrical producer. He or she must hold the audience and give the people something to go home with other than smiles on their faces.

Again, the word is *balance*. There has been a tendency in recent years, particularly during the past five years or so, for sales meetings to go the sobersides route: "We're here for business, not fun." This can be attributed to the mean-and-lean quest of top management, itself an outgrowth of the merger-takeover mania. Management never wants to appear frivolous in the eyes of stockholders. Gala sales meetings, complete with star comedians and ice shows at the final banquet, are much too costly and are out these days. However, eliminating the more showy aspects of showmanship doesn't mean that a certain lightheartedness is not appropriate in these lean-and-mean days. In fact, the contrary is true. Showmanship is an essential ingredient in the sales meeting mix.

Why is showmanship so vital when running a sales meeting? Basically because it is easier to catch flies with honey than with vinegar. Study after study in psychology labs at major universities have shown that memory retention increases markedly in most people when a fact is presented (1) in its context and (2) amusingly or dramatically. The latter is nothing more or less than showmanship. Take a lesson from the TV commercials.

If a sales meeting must be more than a social get-together of people who just happen to work for the same firm, it is essential that the sales reps go back to their territories with a huge number of facts firmly implanted in their memories. Viewed in this light, showmanship is a necessary technique in a sales meeting to ensure memory retention.

Showmanship itself too frequently gets confused with just one of its elements: humor. Showmanship includes humor, but it is much more than that; it is the stage setting, the props, the lighting, the sound amplification, and whatever else goes into mounting a production, which in actuality is what a sales meeting amounts to.

There was once a sales manager whose experience with little theater groups had made him an expert in lighting. At that time, he worked for a large manufacturer of ready-made draperies, curtains, and bedspreads. The tradition in this industry is to hold two sales meetings a year, essentially to introduce the new line to the sales force. The meetings, coming as they did like clockwork every six months, tended to be dull. The line innovations and introductions were not all that breathtaking. The problem was how to get some pizazz into the line presentation, the heart of this particular sales meeting. This manager wisely opted to make use of his stage lighting skills to inject some showmanship into the line presentation. It worked beautifully. Fabrics and designs that looked sort of ho-hum when just laid on a table and described as a "new cotton-polyester blend" suddenly came to life when backlighted. Fabric designs highlighted by a pin spot in a darkened room took on their own identity. Instead of droning on under house lights about this or that fabric and its virtues, this sales manager put on a show and created a note of glamor the fabrics otherwise lacked.

The sales force was *impressed*, one of the main purposes showmanship at sales meetings can and should accomplish. Better still, this bit of showmanship fired up the salespeople to imitate the boss on their customers' display floors. This in turn created a healthy increase in consumer interest and in sales.

Another reason to use showmanship at a sales meeting is to make some point or product *memorable*. In the example above, few members of the sales force were likely to forget a couple of the patterns so artfully lighted at the line presentation. The same showmanship technique can, of course, take many forms, but the key is to accentuate the positive. This can be accomplished by humor, stunts, or any other unusual (but in context) technique of showmanship.

Last, but certainly not least, showmanship is important as a technique because, done properly, it *entertains*. By definition it implies something out of the ordinary, a departure from the routine. It can individualize a product or premise in anyone's mind. And having a product that is *unique* is bound to make any salesperson happy.

Basically, the goal is not merely to entertain but to teach. Both can be accomplished at the same time. Some of the best teachers in high school or college exemplify the point of how teaching can go hand in hand with entertainment.

Showmanship, however, can be totally out of place when overused or used at the wrong time. Whatever else it is, a sales meeting should never become a vaudeville show; to repeat, the key in the use of showmanship is *balance*.

Special forms of humor, perhaps appreciated only by a few, should be avoided, as well as overly subtle stunts, ones that are done more for their shock value than for emphasizing an important point that needs impressing on the minds of the sales force.

How to Get Participation

Thankfully, sales meetings have advanced from the days when they were run in an autocratic manner, with participation from the floor not only unwelcome but actively discouraged. It wasn't too long ago, in fact, that any sales manager who tolerated participation was suspect.

The new trend, however, is toward openness in meetings, in which sales rep participation is not only solicited but also sometimes required. The main reason for this is that generally society is much more open than a decade or so ago. Young people are trained these days to question, to get in their two cents' worth. The flip side of this coin is, or should be, that once people get in their two cents' worth, they are responsible for carrying through on any program adopted from their wisdom.

Why is participation needed? First, participation all along the line makes achievement of company objectives easier and thus makes the meeting more effective. If the objective is a 12 percent increase in sales in the coming year in one specific product line, the sales manager may feel this can best be accomplished by the simple (on paper) expedient of setting a 12 percent quota increase on each salesperson.

But is it that easy? Of course not, even if sales managers in the old days tended to think it was. Rather than receiving a dictate from on high — and getting on with the meeting — this is the time for participation from the sales force. Several of the people may already have saturation or near-saturation distribution of the product in question. The problem, then, is not opening new accounts but is any or all of the following: poor advertising and promotion support, delivery problems, quality problems, bad packaging, unrealistic pricing, or poor distribution. Participants should be allowed to expound on any or all of these possible deterrents to the objective. As the salespeople sound off, notes should be taken — allowing for certain exaggerations and even fingerpointing. Through it all, the necessity to meet the 12 percent goal should continue to be stressed.

When this winds down, it is possible (even probable) every reason in the book will have been voiced about what needs to be done to meet the goal. But is that bad? Certainly not. In the first place, the areas where corrections are necessary have been determined. Most of all, each person in the room will have actively become involved in meeting that 12 percent sales increase. In other words, the meeting has actively promoted enthusiasm and interest in the objective by allowing all ideas on the subject. These people now are *involved*, not just passive participants in some mysterious company goal.

Granted, this technique of achieving participation creates a lot more work than the old no-democracy-here method, but it stands a far better chance of focusing on and achieving objectives.

The trick, as mentioned earlier, is to achieve participation without inciting anarchy. Aside from a few born dissidents in any organization, most salespeople are possessed of good manners and a sense of fairness to one another and to management. Those who haven't tried full-hearted and sincere participation may be in for a surprise at how reasonable (and understanding) sales reps can be. When the meeting is open to participation, the most vociferous dissidents are disarmed.

In achieving constructive participation, it is necessary to plan for it well in advance. It is necessary to have one primary goal in the meeting. A meeting planner courts chaos by pressing too many objectives at any one meeting. A primary goal should be selected carefully for full-scale participation: how best to market a new product; how best to reinvigorate an old, reliable, and dull product; how best to overcome a competitive threat.

Once the primary goal for participation has been settled upon, it is essential that the meeting be publicized as far in advance as possible, listing what will be under discussion and at which points participation will be requested. This will give all involved an opportunity to think over the problem before getting on their feet to sound off at the meeting. Participants, in effect, will thus do their own editing, saving a lot of time.

To avoid the pitfall of sounding autocratic, it is a good idea to involve salespeople in the planning of the meeting, particularly in what they would like to focus on at the meeting. Do this before the meeting agenda is cast in concrete. A simple form mailed to each salesperson well in advance of the meeting is an orderly way of keeping tabs of what's on the minds of a sales force. While it may not be possible to bring up many of the suggestions received, chances are that a common thread of either concern or information in these responses will be discovered, one that perhaps hadn't been thought of previously.

Furthermore, it is a good idea to involve the sales force as much as possible in site selection, distance to get to the meeting, and days of the week most convenient to be away from the territory. The more salespeople are involved in every phase of the meeting, the more successful the meeting likely will be. The trick, again, is to maintain control and efficient planning while at the same time making each person who will be attending feel that he or she is very much a cog in the wheel.

How meeting planners handle making the meeting assignments depends on how well they know their people. If they know someone well, a simple personal note saying, "I'd appreciate it if you'd give me a hand by making sure the audiovisual equipment is in place and functional at the meeting" will get the job done. Even during the actual meeting, when unexpected situations arise, a meeting planner can do a lot to ensure participation by calling on someone in the sales force to handle the situation. This is an effective way of not only talking participation, but in getting it. Another truth, of course, is that most people want to be needed.

Hal Fahner is currently Vice President of Corporate Marketing for Blue Cross and Blue Shield of Florida, Inc. He has been Vice President of Sales and Marketing for three major corporations and has extensive experience in management, sales, and sales training.

Fahner is the author of three books on sales and sales management, published by Prentice-Hall. He has also authored regular articles in Sales and Marketing Management Magazine, *as well as several other corporate publications. He has conducted seminars throughout the U.S. and Canada and has served as a member of the faculty of the Sales Management Institute, sponsored by Sales and Marketing Executives International.*

Christen P. Heide is the Executive Editor for sales and marketing publications at Dartnell, Chicago, and has been on staff at Dartnell for 17 years. Heide edits several Dartnell publications, including "Overcoming Objections," "Sales and Marketing Executive Report," and "Marketing Times," the official publication of Sales and Marketing Executives International. In addition, he is the author of Dartnell's 27th Sales Force Compensation Survey.

Heide's articles have appeared in Advertising Age *and* Marketing News. *He is a frequent speaker on sales and management issues and is quoted frequently in the business press as a sales and marketing authority.*

Heide holds a bachelor's degree in Philosophy from the University of Wisconsin-Madison.

CHAPTER 21

SALES TRAINING

The most creative and well-thought-out promotional effort will not succeed if it isn't delivered to the distributor, dealer, retailer, or end user. Unfortunately, all too often the sales force — the primary delivery system — does not understand its part in using promotion.

Defining the role of the sales force in the total promotional campaign should be a basic step in developing a promotion. The success of any program will depend, to a very large degree, on how well the salespeople are informed, trained, and sold on the program's benefits, so they can carry out their part in the effort.

SALES TRAINING BEGINS WITH NEEDS ANALYSIS

One of the least understood and appreciated functions in marketing and sales is sales training. The power of sales training to maximize the advertising and promotion efforts is substantial. In addition, sales training will increase the effectiveness of the face-to-face sales force, as well as the distributor, dealer, and retailer when multilevel distribution is utilized.

The principle is very simple. It goes back to the beginning of the industrial revolution and the days of Frederick W. Taylor, who was a proponent of what was then known as scientific management. The idea was simply to analyze the job, identify the components necessary to produce the desired end result of production, and then provide the most effective and efficient tools and train the workers in their use.

National Cash Register (now known as NCR Corporation), under the direction of founder John H. Patterson, was the first company to apply the same principles to the training of the sales force specifically. In fact it was Patterson who, in the late 1800s, developed what is now known as the "canned sales pitch." Under his auspices, sales training at his company became systematized, resulting in publication of one of the earliest sales training manuals in history. Known as "The National Cash Register Primer," it was distributed to each of the company's sales offices. To say that Patterson was committed to sales training would be an understatement. He so thoroughly believed in the power of prepared sales presentations that he was known to personally pay surprise visits on his salesmen and give them an on-the-spot quiz on the contents of the primer. Those who failed the test were immediately fired.

As the post-World War II sales boom wound down in the 1950s and 1960s, sales training received renewed prominence in many companies as they searched for a means of increasing sales force productivity and the volume and profit of the entire enterprise. The starting point of sales training is generally known as needs analysis. A written check-off form, such as the one illustrated in Table 21.1, is generally utilized to help in thoroughly analyzing the steps to be completed, the methods used, and the tools to be used to do the entire sales job.

TABLE 21.1

Learning or belief needed by customer	Who will provide	Methods, tools, sales aids available	Observable indication of success in customer behavior/attitude change	Target date for completion

Sometimes a more general checklist format is used by sales training managers:

1. What is needed?
2. Who must do?
3. How can it be achieved?
4. By what date?

An analysis of the task, beginning really by working backward from the end result desired and identifying the steps necessary to reach that desired end result, enables one to be assured that the required communication steps are completed. An added benefit is that following this procedure sometimes helps to identify and even invent additional sales tools or communication aids to help the sales force in successfully completing a communication step. In other words, one side of good sales training is also the invention of additional sales tools. When salespeople are observed attempting to communicate, the attempt to correct any communication difficulties provides the opportunity for changing and improving the methods and processes, as well as to invent new, easier-to-use communication devices, tools, and sales aids.

It helps to observe the use of training in the area of production. In production basic indicators such as production records, cost analysis, quality control reports, personnel turnover statistics, grievance data, and customer complaints are inspected. Production managers look at training as a tool to correct gaps between acceptable production and current levels, in that it reveals the basic processes, methods, and tools used as well. The principle is the same in the sales process.

THE JOB OUTLINE

A logical starting point is to observe the way the job is being done now. This means the obvious major steps are simply outlined and written down. The preceding checklists help as reminders to identify the tools used (or the opportunity to introduce tools) and to simply recognize the separate steps that must be accomplished. The observation of the current way of doing the job and the subsequent analysis may lead to additional steps being added to the process, steps being eliminated, or an entirely new and different process being invented to replace the old. The discipline of analyzing the total task will certainly make thorough training possible and may result in the use of improved methods and tools as well.

Sales promotion itself is generally a sales tool. It has been said that sales promotion educates and creates enthusiasm in salespeople, distributors, dealers, retailers, and consumers. In the total marketing scheme, advertising, promotion, and personal selling are generally looked upon as closely related tools that must coordinate together to move the buyer through the buying process successfully. Since promotion is usually very focused and aimed at well-defined market segments, the additional effectiveness that training the sales force can provide is obvious.

TRAINING METHODS

Sales training involves a sort of closed system within which the behavior required for the successful completion of the task or production of the end result can be identified. If the capabilities already possessed by the trainees before they begin training are then subtracted, it is easy to identify the gap that must be covered by the training. Finally, the effectiveness of the training must be evaluated through observation or testing against the standard of producing the end results required by the company. This is a closed system because we are now back to the observation and identification of the training problem and adjustment of the training to provide the additional skills and/or knowledge required to produce the necessary end result. In other words, the following questions are always asked:

1. Is there a training need?
2. What specific training is required?
3. What training methods should be used?
4. Evaluate-observe performance vs. results required.

Learning takes place within the learner rather than being completely controlled by the trainer. Adult learning can be described as shown in Exhibit 21.1.

That is, an adult learner must first see the need for change in order to be motivated to learn or change. Once an adult learner is motivated to learn, he or she will be receptive to the trainer, self-learning material, or other learning-training methods.

Stimulus is then applied in the form of learning materials. For example, this might be as simple as a videotape showing the failure of the incorrect use of demonstration methods using new promotional materials and then a demonstration on the same tape showing the correct method and the success it provides.

EXHIBIT 21.1

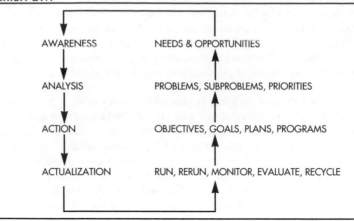

AWARENESS   NEEDS & OPPORTUNITIES

ANALYSIS   PROBLEMS, SUBPROBLEMS, PRIORITIES

ACTION   OBJECTIVES, GOALS, PLANS, PROGRAMS

ACTUALIZATION   RUN, RERUN, MONITOR, EVALUATE, RECYCLE

Response is the next step in the adult learning model. In the above example, this would be the opportunity for the learner to practice doing the demonstration following the correct-way model. The learner may practice in a role-playing situation with fellow salespeople at a sales meeting or immediately begin using the recommended method in live sales situations.

Confirmation is the term sometimes applied to the feedback, reinforcement, or reward step of the learning process. The reinforcement or reward (or confirmation) can take place in the form of feedback from fellow salespeople and manager in a role-playing situation in a sales meeting or from the observation of the sales manager on a live sales call. Salespeople *do* receive feedback on an ongoing basis from prospects as they achieve their goals with prospects or fail to get the response they desire from a prospect.

Some training methods that might be used include lecture, show-and-tell in a sales meeting situation, or one-on-one in the office. Sales training kits or self-learning modules that may be written or used with closed circuit television are other possibilities, as are personal computer programs supplemented with informational training or coaching on the job by the manager. Role-playing or practice-selling to develop skills can tie these efforts together.

Generally, the delivery of promotions will require some communication skills. When the learner must merely know something, listening to a lecture or reading material on the subject will generally provide knowledge. However, when a skill is involved, knowledge is only half of the requirement. When a skill is involved, practice is generally required — that is, role-playing or live sales call practice with some provision for feedback on specifically what is going right and what needs improvement.

COACHING FOLLOW-UP

Due to the increased communication that is generally needed in relation to any given promotion and the need to communicate this information to distributors, dealers, retailers, and end users, on-the-job follow-up by the sales manager will most likely be a requirement. On-the-job coaching is at the heart of the sales management function. Making coaching calls with each salesperson on a regular basis is a basic part of sales management. On a coaching call, the sales manager is neither a salesperson nor a technical expert. The sales manager is an observer on a coaching call. It is the sales manager's function to see how the salesperson can be helped to be more effective on future sales calls. Coaching can take place on any kind of sales call — first call, sales interview, sales presentation, a cost of profit presentation, calls on current customers, and so on. On every sales call there is an objective that the salesperson wants to achieve. The sales manager/coach is looking for those things the salesperson does or fails to do that interfere with achieving that objective. When time is short for the introduction of a new sales promotion, coaching may become the primary method of training the salespeople to use the newest backup and tools from headquarters.

The entire coaching process is summarized in Exhibit 21.2.

MORE COACHING TIPS

Sales coaches should not hesitate to make notes during a call, but they should take very short notes and be subtle about it. For instance, if the salesperson and prospect are checking a date for some reason and both have their pocket calendars out, it is an excellent opportunity for observers to take theirs out, too, and make the desired notes. The salesperson should be told ahead of time that some notes may be taken during the call to help recollection after the call. Coaches should try to capture key phrases that will recall an entire segment of the call for the salesperson.

Every salesperson should be coached at least one day per month. It is important to remember that if salespeople are not coached from the positive side, when they're "hot," they will resist coaching when they're in a slump.

Coaching should not have the negative atmosphere of the sales manager being on the sales call for the sole purpose of acting as judge — to see how good or bad the salesperson is. Rather, good coaching should produce a bond of respect between the salesperson and the sales manager that is similar to the bond that exists between Olympic coaches and their rapidly developing charges. Good coaching produces an atmosphere of growth and progress. The sales manager must have a sincere respect for the salesperson who works hard at self-development. The salesperson respects the manager who works hard at helping salespeople become the best they can be but who never tries to take credit for their accomplishments. The sales manager's aim at the end of every coaching day should be to leave the salesperson feeling that the job can be done. The salesperson should feel that he or she grew some more today. The sales manager should make the salespeople feel successful.

EXHIBIT 21.2
STEPS TO EFFECTIVE COACHING

Before the call, the sales manager/coach should always discuss what the salesperson knows about the prospect, the objectives of the call, and the sales tools to be used.

WHAT TO DO	HOW TO DO IT
Step 1	
Analyze the salesperson's performance.	• Observe the call. • Determine a specific need.
Step 2	
Indicate areas for improvement.	• Ask for the salesperson's feelings about the call. • Give a sincere compliment. • Indicate a specific improvement area. • Probe for underlying causes. • Tell the results of the present method. • Explain the recommended method.
Step 3	
Demonstrate the desired method.	• Show how. • Discuss what you did and why.
Step 4	
Have the salesperson perform the desired method.	• Observe the call. • Determine areas of need.
Step 5	
Repeat Steps 1 through 4.	• Until they reach a satisfactory level.

ADDITIONAL TRAINING GUIDELINES

Developing an atmosphere in which it is easy for the salespeople to ask questions is important. If they don't get it at the beginning, they may be afraid to ask later because they feel they should know all those basic things. The job of training cannot be delegated to service personnel or senior salespeople without first training them to do what needs to be done the way the sales manager would do it. Whenever training concerns a new sales promotion, the sales manager should always strive to stay in direct contact and communication with the developers of the sales promotion. The more completely field sales managers understand the entire strategy and concept, the more comprehensive and effective their training of the sales force will be.

The sales manager should provide for a practice and feedback session in a nonthreatening environment whenever possible in preparation for "live" practice in actual sales situations.

ONE SALES MANAGER'S ADVICE

Frank Ladwig was National Sales Manager of Culligan, U.S.A. for years — until he opened his own Culligan dealership in Jackson, Michigan. He has seen the training of salespeople from both the "trenches" and from the home office.

The home office program prepares salespeople well and can have them full of confidence and enthusiasm. But if they don't get the support in day-to-day practical information and answers they need at the local level, they'll be flat on the floor in no time. You've got to continue to work with salespeople. In direct selling, every day is like starting a new job over again. You can't rest on your laurels. The turndowns in this business can be personal blows to the ego. You've got to start with a motivated individual who has a sales personality, who likes people, and go from there.

You know from the national point of view, it's one thing to tell others how to do it, and another to do it yourself. The dealer and the sales manager need to take that same basic training and to refresh themselves in the basics regularly. The salesperson is dependent on the sales manager, to a large degree, for knowledge, methods, and sales tools. You can't let them down. You've got to keep supporting, helping. Everything should be kept positive with the salespeople. They are exposed to so many negatives, so many turndowns for every sale. We need to keep their contact with the company positive. I'm always striving to keep the salespeople learning, selling better, until they are the best.

EXHIBIT 21.3 — FIELD CHECK GUIDE

Date:
Name of company/division:
Territory/location:
Sales manager:

A. Personal history

- Name of salesperson
- Age
- Education
- Title
- Years of selling experience
- Years with present company
- Prior selling experience (if any)

B. Territory assignment size

- Characteristics (urban/rural)
- Extent of trade or metropolitan areas
- Business/economic conditions
- Coverage frequency
- Routing problems
- Length of time in territory

C. Accounts contacted

- Total number of accounts in territory
- Types of accounts called on with greatest frequency
- Frequency of contact
- Major wants, needs, requirements
- Primary problems
- Assistance and services expected by customers
- Call schedule maintained (how many calls per day)
- Extent of prospecting and lead development activities

D. Competitors

- Number of competitors in territory
- Activities of competitors affecting sales
- Acceptance of competitors by customers and prospects
- Strengths and weaknesses of competitors
- Means used by salesperson to offset strengths and capitalize on weaknesses
- Aggressiveness of competitors
- Number of salespeople competitors have in territory

E. Selling assignment

- Basic requirements of the job from the salesperson's view point (what the person thinks he or she must be able to do to be productive)
- Specific activities for which the salesperson is responsible
- Types of budgets/quotas/objectives received from supervisors
- Records/reports maintained (what use does the salesperson make of them?)
- Sales tools provided by company (as well as those designed for personal use)

- Extent of supervision received (when, by whom, under what circum
  stances)
- Frequency of contact with supervisors

F. Selling activity
- Basic selling skills salesperson believes are required in
  order to perform effectively
- The methods, procedures, techniques used most successfully by the
  salesperson in terms of:
  - Planning (time, daily work, long-range)
  - Basic selling strategy
    - The approach (to uncover customer needs,problems — how the
      salesperson determines the right people to see)
    - Building the case (how the salesperson sells strengths
      and capabilities of product or service — how he or she relates these
      to needs of the buyer)
    - Selling benefits (how the salesperson sells benefits of
      product or service — relating them to problems of accounts or
      prospects)
    - Proving (how the salesperson presents evidence of the
      company's ability to solve the buyer's problems and meet the
      buyer's needs)
    - Closing (how the salesperson keeps the door open dur
      ing presentation — how he or she tests for a close, what the sales
      person does if turned down)
    - Handling objections (typical kinds received — how he or she han-
      dles them)
    - Overcoming resistance (how the salesperson converts
      resistance to build confidence and create a favorable impression of
      his or her company)
    - Secondary-level selling (how the salesperson sells to decision makers)

G. Accounts contacted with salesperson
- The sales manager should call on a mix of both new customers
  and existing accounts, trying to make at least three to four calls
  while with the salesperson, and noting:

  Name
  Location
  Type or classifications
  Prior history
  Objectives for call
  Personnel seen — and why (titles, authority)
  Results achieved during call
  Follow-up after call

H. Reminders
- If the salesperson is unable to provide specific items of information
  (that may be available), he or she should be requested to send them after
  the field-check interview. The feedback provided to the salesperson
  should be in the form of constructive guidance.

FIELD-CHECK GUIDE FOR DIRECT SALESPEOPLE

The guide in Exhibit 21.3 can be adapted for use when working with salespeople in the field. Kept up to date, this guide will provide an accurate assessment of each salesperson's strengths and weaknesses — areas in which assistance would be most beneficial.

A LOOK AT CURRENT SALES TRAINING PRACTICES

It's often helpful to take a look at what other companies are doing in their management practices. This can help one get a handle on a sometimes difficult subject and suggest ideas that can be adopted or adapted for one's own use. The following tables and figures have been excerpted from *Dartnell's 27th Sales Force Compensation Survey* (1992) and are, at the time of this printing, the latest data available. To check on the availability of updated figures, contact the customer service department at the Dartnell Corporation, (800) 621-5463.

Training Methods. Companies rely heavily on individual instruction and on-the-job training to meet their sales training needs. In-house training classes and external seminars are used by more than half of the companies responding to the Dartnell survey; home assignments are the least popular method of training and are used by less than 20 percent of survey respondents. A look at Table 21.2 tells the complete story.

In reviewing a company's sales training practices, it helps to bear in mind that the more variety that is injected into a sales training format, the better chance there is of reaching salespeople "on their own wavelength."

Training New Hires. Table 21.3 takes a look at the total cost and length of training period for new hires. An interesting trend is that smaller companies, those under $5 million in total annual sales, are spending more on sales training than they did in years past. These companies are also increasing the length of time they spend on the training of new hires.

Training Experienced Reps. Table 21.4, again from *Dartnell's 27th Sales Force Compensation Survey*, examines how much training experienced salespeople receive throughout the year and the approximate cost of this training on a per person basis. Overall figures indicate that experienced salespeople are, at the time of this printing, being given just over 30 hours a year of ongoing training. This is up slightly over the 27 hours reported in a previous survey and reflects a continuing commitment on the part of management to provide ongoing learning opportunities for their senior salespeople.

It's interesting to note that companies divide training time about equally between product training and training in selling skills. A 1992 Dartnell study found that the selling skills sales managers thought were most important were precall planning, time management, overcoming objections, approach and involvement, closing, and qualifying. Skills that sales managers ranked lower in terms of importance included

TABLE 21.2

	Individual Instruction	Home Assignments	In-House Class	On The Job	External Seminars	Other
Company Size						
Under $5 Million	74.7%	18.4%	50.6%	82.8%	71.3%	2.3%
$5MM-$25MM	72.9	15.3	55.9	81.4	64.4	5.1
$25MM-$100MM	66.7	18.8	66.7	83.3	75.0	10.4
$100MM-$250MM	60.0	20.0	60.0	90.0	70.0	0.0
Over $250MM	85.0	25.0	85.0	95.0	60.0	10.0
Product or Service						
Consumer Products	79.6	13.0	68.5	79.6	68.5	1.9
Consumer Services	73.1	23.1	65.4	90.4	71.2	7.7
Industrial Products	74.5	17.3	60.9	80.9	70.9	4.5
Industrial Services	67.9	16.0	66.7	85.2	75.3	2.5
Office Products	82.4	17.6	55.9	88.2	67.6	5.9
Office Services	80.8	26.9	59.6	90.4	75.0	7.7
Type of Buyer						
Consumers	70.1	24.7	63.6	84.4	68.8	6.5
Distributors	73.6	17.6	53.8	76.9	71.4	2.2
Industry	69.6	22.0	59.5	85.1	71.4	6.0
Retailers	69.3	20.0	56.0	81.3	69.3	5.3
Industry						
Business Services	80.0	25.0	50.0	87.5	62.5	7.5
Chemicals	83.3	0.0	50.0	83.3	50.0	0.0
Communications	62.5	25.0	87.5	100.0	100.0	12.5
Educational Services	60.0	40.0	60.0	80.0	40.0	0.0
Electronics	70.0	10.0	50.0	100.0	70.0	0.0
Fabricated Metals	66.7	22.2	66.7	77.8	77.8	11.1
Health Services	75.0	25.0	100.0	100.0	75.0	0.0
Hotels & Other Lodging Places	50.0	0.0	66.7	66.7	83.3	0.0
Instruments	80.0	0.0	80.0	100.0	80.0	0.0
Insurance	84.6	23.1	53.8	100.0	76.9	15.4
Machinery	60.0	30.0	50.0	70.0	60.0	0.0
Manufacturing	80.0	10.0	60.0	80.0	60.0	10.0
Office Equipment	75.0	0.0	75.0	100.0	50.0	0.0
Paper and Allied Products	100.0	33.3	50.0	83.3	66.7	0.0
Printing and Publishing	85.7	21.4	57.1	92.9	92.9	0.0
Retail	87.5	12.5	62.5	62.5	75.0	0.0
Trucking and Warehousing	33.3	0.0	33.3	66.7	33.3	33.3
Wholesale (Consumer Goods)	63.6	27.3	45.5	54.5	72.7	0.0
Wholesale (Industrial Goods)	84.6	30.8	61.5	92.3	76.9	15.4
Overall	**72.8%**	**18.3%**	**58.9%**	**83.9%**	**69.2%**	**5.4%**

TABLE 21.3

	Training Period for New Hires (Months)	Cost
Company Size		
Under $5 Million	3.9	$ 5530.0
$5MM-$25MM	3.7	6227.3
$25MM-$100MM	3.9	8083.3
$100MM-$250MM	3.0	3750.0
Over $250MM	4.7	6587.5
Product or Service		
Consumer Products	3.3	4995.0
Consumer Services	3.6	4130.0
Industrial Products	4.2	9763.2
Industrial Services	3.8	6610.7
Office Products	3.1	3408.3
Office Services	3.2	4005.0
Type of Buyer		
Consumers	3.5	4253.6
Distributors	3.5	7334.3
Industry	3.9	6570.7
Retailers	3.4	4546.2
Industry		
Business Services	3.0	5478.6
Chemicals	4.5	15000.0
Communications	5.2	3125.0
Educational Services	3.0	3500.0
Electronics	5.0	11500.0
Fabricated Metals	5.0	10625.0
Health Services	2.0	3250.0
Hotels & Other Lodging Places	3.0	5000.0
Instruments	5.0	22500.0
Insurance	5.6	7083.3
Machinery	4.2	6125.0
Manufacturing	3.3	6125.0
Paper and Allied Products	2.2	6500.0
Printing and Publishing	2.7	5566.7
Retail	4.8	2875.0
Wholesale (Consumer Goods)	5.0	9166.7
Wholesale (Industrial Goods)	5.9	9333.3
Overall	3.9	$ 6225.6

TABLE 21.4

	TYPE OF TRAINING		
	Hours Per Year of Ongoing Training	Selling Skills(%)	Product(%)	Cost
Company Size				
Under $5 Million	28.4	45.2%	50.9%	$ 2395
$5MM-$25MM	36.5	44.9	49.4	3919
$25MM-$100MM	28.3	42.1	51.8	2895
$100MM-$250MM	19.0	64.0	30.0	1525
Over $250MM	31.5	36.2	51.8	3977
Product or Service				
Consumer Products	30.5	44.7	51.4	2806
Consumer Services	30.8	50.1	45.6	3039
Industrial Products	30.2	39.3	52.9	3262
Industrial Services	32.0	48.7	47.0	2966
Office Products	30.0	41.3	50.5	1962
Office Services	34.6	49.5	45.0	2733
Type of Buyer				
Consumers	30.6	44.7	51.0	2607
Distributors	29.3	45.8	45.1	3443
Industry	29.5	46.6	49.7	3078
Retailers	29.0	48.3	45.0	1767
Industry				
Business Services	33.1	52.4	40.6	2529
Chemicals	18.3	56.8	44.6	4500
Communications	45.0	50.6	45.0	4700
Educational Services	41.7	57.5	30.0	1125
Electronics	34.4	29.4	66.0	5483
Fabricated Metals	37.5	37.9	47.1	2900
Health Services	41.0	22.5	56.2	2000
Hotels & Other Lodging Places	25.3	63.8	20.0	1400
Instruments	60.0	29.0	45.0	11875
Insurance	31.4	46.8	42.1	4750
Machinery	26.4	23.9	65.0	2257
Manufacturing	18.4	43.1	61.7	1917
Office Equipment	27.5	40.0	60.0	2000
Paper and Allied Products	34.5	45.0	48.3	2300
Printing and Publishing	15.7	33.3	56.1	1510
Retail	38.8	26.4	71.4	1220
Trucking and Warehousing	0.0	100.0	0.0	2000
Wholesale (Consumer Goods)	49.8	62.2	42.0	1067
Wholesale (Industrial Goods)	45.3	40.0	63.1	2494
Overall	**30.2**	**44.7%**	**49.8%**	**$2991**

using the telephone, demonstrating, and managing paperwork. Based on this study, it's safe to conclude that the skill training that is given to experienced salespeople is focused on those skills sales managers deem most important, specifically, precall planning, time management, overcoming objections, approach and involvement, closing, and qualifying. Following are details from that study.

DARTNELL'S SELLING SKILLS SURVEY

Of all the skills salespeople use daily, which are the most important to their long-term success? Overcoming objections? Closing the sale? Qualifying prospects? Prospecting? All of the above? None of the above?

While all the fundamental selling skills have their place, and vary in importance from industry to industry, some are so critical that virtually nothing can be accomplished without them. But which ones are they? To find out, Dartnell asked sales managers and sales reps alike to select from a prepared list the fundamental selling skills that they, in their opinion, thought were the most important to a successful career in sales.

To simplify tabulation of responses, Dartnell compiled a list of 14 fundamental selling skills that are generally thought to be the building blocks of a good sales training program. Dartnell then asked respondents to rank these skills in order of importance (listed here in alphabetical order):

Approach/involvement
Closing
Demonstrating
Handling problems
Making presentations
Managing paperwork
Managing time
Negotiating
Overcoming objections
Post-call follow-up
Pre-call planning
Prospecting/cold-calling
Qualifying
Using the telephone

Additionally, the questionnaire asked respondents to list and rank any additional skills not on the prepared list to make sure a vital ingredient of sales success was not overlooked.

Six skills consistently ranked in the top categories for both sales managers and reps. Put another way, six skills were judged so important that they consistently tied for the top positions. In fact, a good number of respondents indicated they couldn't decide which one of the top skills was most important because they were all equally important.

These are the top skills in the order they were ranked:
1. Pre-call planning
2. Managing time
3. Overcoming objections
4. Approach and involvement
5. Closing
6. Qualifying

While salespeople and sales managers ranked these skills in slightly different orders, both groups of respondents agreed that these six skills were the most critical to sales success. This is not to say, of course, that the remaining skills are not important in selling.

Although sales training has never strayed far from the basics, the results of the Dartnell survey seem to indicate that if salespeople concentrate on excelling in these six areas, they can achieve maximum success.

Both managers and salespeople placed the next group of skills, ranked seven to 11, right in the middle of the pack. These skills included making presentations, negotiating, handling problems, prospecting/cold-calling, and post-call follow-up. These skills represent activities that may be more important to particular types of sales. For example, negotiating may not apply to some kinds of businesses. Or, the skill may be perceived as simply part of overcoming objections. Similarly, managers and salespeople may have ranked making presentations as a secondary skill, because it's hard to separate it from the basic skills of approach and involvement or closing.

The three skills of using the telephone, demonstrating, and managing paperwork brought up the rear. This may reflect a basic assumption among businesspeople that using the phone is a minimum competency skill that requires little training. Demonstrating may be considered by respondents as a subskill of making presentations, and it's likely that many companies don't rely on old-fashioned smoke-and-mirrors-style demonstrations. Managing paperwork, while important to personal and corporate organization, ranked dead last among reps and managers.

As mentioned, the survey asked respondents to name additional skills that didn't appear on the list of preselected skills, and they gave the following variations:
- Listening
- Enthusiasm and dedication
- Self-discipline
- Product and market knowledge
- Persistence and perseverance
- Appearance, image, and manners
- Building relationships
- Building credibility
- Understanding the customer
- Confidence

The skills most frequently mentioned by survey respondents

were listening to the customer and identifying the customer's needs.

Each industry and each market has different requirements for sales success. Some companies may require excellent demonstration skills; others may place special emphasis on cold-calling. But every salesperson must master a short list of skills before moving on and up to narrower techniques.

CASE STUDY

The following case study illustrates how the principles and guidelines outlined in this chapter can be successfully applied to "real-life situations."

Ross Roy Communications/Customer One Case Study. While the need for and commitment to training for outstanding customer service is nothing new to the retail automotive market or to Chrysler Corporation, it has only recently become the priority. Many businesses try to differentiate their products by improving the customers' satisfaction with their buying experience. It is in such a "customer satisfaction" environment that Ross Roy Communications, Bloomfield Hills, Michigan, designed the Customer One Education Initiative for the Chrysler Corporation.

An aggressive new product development plan was initiated at Chrysler Corporation, aimed at rejuvenating its aging product line to make it more competitive in the world market. Millions of dollars and countless hours were spent to ensure these new vehicles would "exceed" consumer expectations. The resulting vehicles, the "LH platform" cars with the new cab-forward design (Chrysler Concorde, Dodge Intrepid, and Eagle Vision), received rave reviews from the automotive press.

However, Chrysler dealers' lack of recent experience with the expected audience for these cars cast doubt on whether the dealer body would be able to properly handle the potential customers for these vehicles. These "new" customers attracted by the exciting LH vehicles would be coming into the showrooms with a much higher expectation level than Chrysler's previous customer base. Unfortunately, customer satisfaction with Chrysler dealership experience was significantly lower than that of Ford, General Motors, and many import dealers, as industry customer satisfaction and sales satisfaction scores showed. Would the excellent quality of the new product line be enough to overcome these obstacles? With so much invested in the successful launch of the LH line, Chrysler and Ross Roy, its sales promotion agency, felt it imperative to increase the level of dealership performance to match the exceptional quality of the products.

Ross Roy's strategy would be to emphasize this new priority in three ways: to stress the importance of a satisfied customer, to initiate a major cultural shift (attitude building rather than skills training), and to stress to the general public the change in attitude. The solution was

Customer One Education Initiative, a major training effort aimed at reviewing performance standards and facilitating cultural change at all levels of the corporation, with specific follow-up and research to measure the effectiveness of the program.

In order to lay a proper foundation for the Customer One Education Initiative, Ross Roy researched the customer service techniques of other companies with exceptional reputations in the area of customer service, including Saturn, Infiniti, and the Walt Disney Company. These businesses provided the benchmarks by which Chrysler would rate its own efforts. Extensive consumer research was also conducted to identify the consumer values that directly affect customer satisfaction. The end result was a definitive model of exceptional customer service that could be easily implemented by Chrysler dealerships. This model, and the entire Customer One rationale, are based on the following points:

- Today's consumers are more knowledgeable and have higher expectations than previously assumed.
- Today's consumers expect professionalism and honesty.
- Today's consumers judge a business every time contact is made with one of its employees.
- First impressions are usually the strongest and, if poor, the hardest to overcome.
- Consumers want to establish a long-term relationship with a business and its representative.

These points became the foundation for the Chrysler/Ross Roy development of a new set of individual job function performance standards and the entire program philosophy and design.

Instructor-led field training modules were designed to cover the basics of customer satisfaction, including people-handling skills, teamwork, and listening and communication techniques. These modules were scripted in a meeting leader-guide format, with emphasis varying according to audience. Corresponding student guides were produced to reinforce training and provide participants with a take-home reference. Virtually all forms of available media were used — classroom activities and instruction, videodisc, satellite broadcasts, print pieces, off-site hands-on activities, and computer-based training. Rather than following a typical training format of presentations and written exercises, peer discussions and experiential activities were used to provide the most concrete, interactive, hands-on experience possible in order to maximize learning and retention. All aspects of the training initiative underwent considerable testing and validation with pilot audiences before implementation.

Implementation of Phase I began in June 1992. Since that time, more than 100,000 Chrysler Corporation retail personnel have participated in the Phase I activity, held at 131 locations nationwide. The sessions were conducted by 220 specially trained professional facilitators, hand-picked from among the best in the nation based on their previous customer service training experience and other criteria. Two-day sessions targeted different dealership audiences, from dealers and managers to sales, service, and parts personnel. While the first day of each two-day session was the same for all sessions, the second day covered material that was similar in content but focused on specific populations. Chrysler Corporation's top 200 executives also attended this phase of training. Consolidated one-day sessions were held for support staff and corporate personnel. Even most Ross Roy employees have participated in the Customer One seminars.

Although the "process" is ongoing, the results from this training effort to date are impressive. Significant improvement has already been seen in Chrysler index scores measuring customer satisfaction for salesperson and dealership performance. Since the Customer One training began in June 1992, the Chrysler Sales Satisfaction Index (SSI) has increased by .06 points to 3.47 (on a four-point scale) and continues to rise. This indicates significant improvement coinciding with the initial stages of Customer One training. To put this in perspective, the entire year of 1991 (first year of the SSI program) showed very little fluctuation, with an average score of 3.4 and only a .02 variance throughout the entire year. The second half of 1992, when Customer One training made an impact, saw an average increase of .06 points compared to the same six-month time period in 1991. These figures were determined from recent shopper surveys used by Chrysler and Ross Roy to monitor the effectiveness of the ongoing training.

The Phase I sessions were followed by Phase II, a "learn-and-drive" event giving dealership personnel hands-on product knowledge training on the new LH product line. With more than 20,000 participants in 14 weeks, this event was the first opportunity Chrysler personnel had to drive the new vehicles and compare them to the competition. The Phase II learn-and-drive format will be continued with future new product launches.

Customer One Phase I training will continue on a quarterly basis to reinforce the new corporate philosophy and to train new employees. Satellite broadcasts have been planned to reemphasize the training to widespread audiences. As a follow-up to the Phase I training, an Action Adviser Program has been instituted, providing two-day in-dealership follow-up interventions to help dealership personnel successfully implement Customer One techniques.

While it is still fairly early to realize the extent of the training effectiveness, all preliminary feedback indicates a successfully launched culture change. At Chrysler, it's just the first step of a long-term commitment to customer service in the retail automotive industry. The hands-on activities and peer interaction format of the Chrysler Customer One Education Initiative, implemented by Ross Roy, is just one example of how effective an integrated approach to training can be.

PART III
STRATEGIES

Joel Weiner was Senior Vice President, Corporate Marketing, at Kraft USA, Kraft General Foods. In prior years at Kraft, he was General Manager (President) of the Retail Venture Division. Before joining Kraft, Weiner was Executive Vice President, Marketing for Seagram Distillers Company, and he spent much of his early career at Bristol-Myers. Weiner has over 25 years of brand management, product management, and general management experience across a wide range of categories, including health and beauty aids, household products, beverages and spirits, and food. His entire career has been spent in consumer packaged goods marketing.

Weiner is often quoted in the business press and has served on the boards of The Ad Council, The Kraft General Foods Foundation, The Museum of Broadcast Communications, the Council of Independent Colleges, and the Joint Council for Economic Education.

A graduate of Northwestern University, Weiner currently resides in Kenilworth, Illinois.

CHAPTER 22

CONSUMER PACKAGED GOODS SALES PROMOTION

Dating back to the advent of couponing in the 1890s for Post Cereals and the use of Wrigley gum in the early 1900s as a premium incentive, consumer packaged goods has been differentiated by consistent innovation of promotional techniques. In the late 1920s and 1930s, Procter & Gamble introduced and refined the brand manager system, which further set into motion the empirical quantification of marketing and sales promotion techniques and tactics. Consumer packaged goods, therefore, helped pioneer many of the standard techniques used today across all product categories. This occurred as packaged goods-brand trained managers left the industry and brought the techniques and training that were quickly applied to other industries. This happened rapidly in the 1950s and 1960s as former packaged goods-trained managers were lured away by consumer banking, retailing, beverages, transportation, hard goods, and a host of other industries.

In trying to determine why consumer packaged goods led the way, it is difficult to pin down any one answer. Nevertheless, there are numerous commonalities. First, the frequent repurchase cycle allowed market research methods to be refined over and over. This enabled research to play a significant role in tracking sales and sales promotion techniques and resulted in the most sophisticated market research techniques in all categories of business. This included retail store audits, warehouse withdrawal studies, awareness and tracking studies, in-store market projection models, and a host of qualitative and quantitative tools that had their origin in consumer packaged goods.

Second, the intensive interface with advertising agencies attracted innovative, entrepreneurial managers who became partners in the creative process and were rewarded for innovation. This contrasted with the structure of many industrial companies whose managers were rooted in operations, engineering, or finance and utilized a central advertising department to manage media, sales promotion, and collateral material. So instead of numerous brand managers competing to develop new marketing techniques, one central department managed the process.

Third, the major inroads of UPC scanning in food supermarkets and the data explosion were made possible by outside suppliers, knowing it was often easier to sell test markets to consumer product brand managers than have an industrial manager "risk" national folly if the idea didn't work. Clearly, retailers could test in a limited number of stores, so often the tests became partnerships between the retailer and manufacturer. While changing and fine-tuning products is always lengthy and time consuming, it's harder in industrial products where long-term tooling and engineering are necessary for virtually any change.

Last, consumer managers were accustomed to spending more money on obtaining data. Not only were advertising to sales ratios higher, trade deals were often higher, as were market research budgets. These budgets drove outside suppliers to "invent" techniques that other industries were often not willing to fund in their start-up cycle.

While consumer packaged goods clearly led the way in the evolution of marketing techniques, most other industries have caught up today, and it is now more of a two-way street. For the first time, the consumer packaged goods industries are now picking up ideas from other industries, and the new pragmatic philosophy is "if it works, it's right."

BACKGROUND

Historically, companies sold the majority of their products for full price, called "open stock." Usually the only discounts were for prompt payment, and these generally did not exceed 2 percent. So-called "deals" or trade promotions then began to be run two to four times a year. In some industries with seasonal merchandise there was only a deal during the pre-holiday period. Often these had to be coupled with guaranteed sales wherein unsold merchandise after the season could be returned for credit.

By the 1950s and 1960s trade dealing was rampant. Whereas at one time a deal was a special occasional opportunity, it evolved into an almost universal way of doing business. Originally companies that moved to four deals a year still only ran them for 30 or 45 days. Soon the deal duration began to run to 60 days or even longer. Then deals began to run back to back with other deals, rather than having a deal with a 30- to 60-day period of open stock between deals. Deals were often closely allocated and capped, which meant that once the inventory or dollar objective was achieved, no further sales would occur unless a senior executive authorized it.

During the 1960s the industry crossed over the 50 percent deal/50 percent open stock threshold. By the early 1970s most consumer packaged goods companies were selling more than 75 percent of their annual volume on deal. Today many companies sell virtually all their annual volume on some sort of deal. This has resulted in trade deal and promotion budgets that often exceed total traditional advertising media spending as dealing becomes a necessary cost of doing business so that retailers can feature deep-discount pricing.

DEAL COORDINATION

At one time the chain of command and authority in developing deals were clear. In most companies, brand management kept the funds, evolved the (usually) four key deals a year, and sold them to sales management with sales management's input. Today as the retailer trade has consolidated, key accounts have taken on more clout, and warehouse and discount stores have become significant. Classical brand management has had a more difficult time dealing with a less homogeneous marketplace. It is, therefore, important that consumer sales promotion, sales management, and brand management all work together in coordinating a completely integrated sales promotion and deal strategy and operating plan for each brand. More and more truckload sale promotions and critical mass multibrand line promotions deliver the clout that both manufacturers and retailers need to create impact with the overwhelmed consumer. It is increasingly the role of the sales promotion department to prepare an annual plan for brand and sales management, to strategically think through glue-ons or overlays to enhance the straight-deal underlay price incentives.

Brands should be careful not to be reduced simply to price featuring. Unless a company has manufacturing or other efficiencies that allow it to be the ultimate low-cost producer, in which case it can have a low-price deal strategy, incessant deep-discount dealing without a clear deal strategy built into the overall marketing plan can be inconsistent with yielding the correct profit margins necessary to build a healthy brand and company. So while dealing is a necessary "fact of life" tool, it is a good news/bad news situation, because for value-added brands and famous brand names, low cost is an incentive only as long as the value-added image remains intact.

WHAT DO PACKAGED GOODS SALES PROMOTION DEPARTMENTS DO?

Unlike media departments in advertising agencies or brand management departments in consumer packaged goods manufacturing companies, sales promotion departments and promotion managers' duties vary significantly from company to company. Listed here are some of the more common functions of a sales promotion department:

- Development of multibrand promotions, corporate sales, solo, or brand-specific promotions.
- Advising on the selection and hiring of outside sales promotion agencies. Qualification of outside vendors in concert with the purchasing department.
- Solicitation and recommendation of companion merchandising and tie-in partners. Idea generation of companion merchandising events.
- Preparing the annual sales promotion strategy and planning specifics along with budget and allocations.
- Preparing recommendations and monitoring compliance with couponing, sampling, direct mail, sweepstakes, and contest vendors. Selection of fulfillment houses for self-liquidators and contests.
- Preparation of "deal" sheets and sales promotion collateral

material along with "sell" sheets that outline the sales argument to be used.

- Testing and evaluation of split runs, innovative techniques, and identification and trial of new systems and ideas for test-marketing.
- Development of electronic interactive media, outside sampling services, and in-store fixed point-of-sale media.
- Development of floor displays, dump bins, header cards, catalogs, shelf-talkers, window banners, dealer loaders, premiums, and myriad point-of-sale (POS) materials utilized by the field sales force to sell in trade deals and programs.

The sales promotion department is best utilized as a sort of internal sales promotion agency that recommends programs to the assigned brand (marketing) groups. Sales promotion must also work closely with and monitor field sales results to ensure that sales promotion programs work and are easy to sell-in. In essence, sales promotion recommends, gets marketing's approval, and supervises the logistics of implementation of the consumer programs while monitoring the trade programs with field sales management.

One of the classic debates in the industry is whether sales promotion should be (1) centralized as a corporate function, (2) centralized within an operating division, (3) decentralized with sales promotion account executives assigned to brand marketing groups, or (4) dissolved completely with brand assistants performing the function utilizing a trafficking coordinator for sales and collateral material.

There is no right answer to this dilemma, and the structure varies from company to company. As a general overview, small companies or companies with lean brand/product manager departments often gravitate to the brand manager devising the sales promotion either with or without outside agencies. Medium and large companies currently are trending toward separate centralized departments for each separate division as opposed to one corporate department that services all divisions. It is important, however, to communicate clearly the in-place procedures and rules of the road if total decentralization takes place. This usually then falls to senior management and legal counsel.

THE ANNUAL PLAN

Sales promotion plans should be written in concert with the annual marketing plan cycle. If this cannot be done because of insufficient lead time, the sales promotion plan should be written prior to the final annual brand marketing plan. Dependent on the custom of the company and class of trade, it is not uncommon for companies to plan sales promotion calendars forward 12 to 24 months. From 14 to 18 months is the most common objective, while six or nine to 12 months is in the minority in today's environment. These longer lead times are often necessary so that combined programs can be set up to get on retailer key-account, long-term planning calendars.

Prior to UPC scanning, consumer packaged goods companies only had to stay two to four months ahead in planning consumer promotions or trade deals. The exceptions were holiday promotions and seasonal products, such as cough and cold remedies and suntan lotion. While many companies often tried to plan out hypothetical consumer promotions for the fiscal year, in fact, the majority were revised or never ran as originally planned due to changing competitive pressures. As chains began to dominate and scanning became the norm, key account buyers demanded more lead time. This was also a function of line-extensions, and SKUs (stock-keeping units) running rampant in the 1960s and 1970s as food supermarkets scaled up from an average of 9,000 items to almost 25,000 items. Suddenly buyers were confronted with requests for more than 200 new-product presentations alone each month. All this overload resulted in the balance of power slowly shifting to the retail trade as often they had more up-to-date information than the seller. The net result was longer lead times to set up calendars as partners.

It is important to note that individual promotions often get revised and re-revised to adjust to ever-changing competitive deal pressures. Often entire programs are scrapped and revised, but it is important nonetheless to do the long-term planning to provide allocated budget dollars and get in line for sales department deal period slots, where often only a certain number of brands or deals can be sold at any one time.

The annual sales plan should include the following:
- Fiscal year budget in dollars
- Percent promotion dollars to sales dollars (range usually 5 percent to 15 percent)
- Number of deals (range usually four to eight per year, although in certain industries, such as soft-drink bottlers, deals can be weekly or biweekly)
- Percent dollars allocated to each deal and expected percent sales and dollar profit contribution from each deal
- Length of each deal period (this is usually the time it takes to cover all discounts, normally 30 to 120 days)
- Three- to five-year deal trend in dollars and percentage
- A clear deal strategy
- Individual brand specific deals and deal objectives
- Combined line deals with other company brands
- Specific itemization of whether all brand sizes are on deal or specific sizes only
- Coordination of consumer deals with integrated media support
- Absolute dollar cost per case or statistical unit of measurement

Exhibit 22.1 shows a sample annual sales promotion and trade deal calendar as merely a starting point and handy reference exhibit. Additional financial measurements could and should be added that will be actionable and useful to the users. Formats can vary by company and type of business. The exhibit is not intended to be a fixed template but rather a suggestion of one format that is useful. The reader is strongly encouraged to tailor the exhibit to his or her own company's specific use.

Some clues for analysis include (1) be careful not to spend 25 percent of the sales promotion budget on a program that might only deliver 15 percent of the annual year's sales (shipments) and 12 percent (for example) of the annual profit contribution; (2) consider keeping a contingency fund of 5 percent to 10 percent of the annual sales promotion budget for fire-fights, unexpected competitive deals that have to be countered, and putting in an extra or sweetener deal in the fourth quarter if it appears the annual sales and profit goals are not going to be met; and (3) measure any increases in brand share during the period through store audit services, such as Nielsen, IRI, or specifically constructed store panels.

THE ANNUAL SALES PROMOTION PLAN STRATEGY

The annual strategy needs a clear, actionable vision. Sales promotion should be a fit with the brand and reinforce the brand's image. A strategy is an overall stance and is not to be confused with individual promotion objectives.

Strategy. The strategy sets the marketing position the brand will take vis-à-vis its competitors, for example, brand X will strive to always have the lowest everyday shelf price and not be undersold by any national brand; or, brand X will strive to be priced above the national competitive brands so that everyday shelf price reinforces a quality, superior product image. An example follows.

Product Positioning:

This fine Swiss process hot chocolate combines the finest ingredients in the world to bring you the best-tasting hot chocolate.

Sales Promotion Strategy:

All consumer sales promotion visuals and elements will reinforce the fine Swiss process heritage. Key promotional programs for the year include...

— Trade contest sweepstakes trip to Switzerland
— Consumer self-liquidators of Swiss Army Knife with special logo
— Proof-of-purchase displays with Swiss Heraldic Crests and flags

EXHIBIT 22.1

Annual Sales Promotion and Trade Deal Calendar

	Q1			Q2			Q3			Q4		
Brand	Jan	Feb	Mar	Apr	May	Jun	July	Aug	Sept	Oct	Nov	Dec
Trade	2 free w/10 ◄───────►			10% off invoice ◄───────►			10% off invoice ◄───────►			10% off invoice ◄───────► 5% ad allowance Proof of performance		
Retailer	7,500 floor displays w/self-liquidator header card			25¢ FSI coupon 20 million households			5,000 39¢ salable sample trial size (pre-pak) 4 dozen pieces			35¢ Xmas Direct mail coop coupon - 15 million households		
Consumer	___											
Total Deal Cost	$___			$___			$___			$___		
% Annual deal (Budget)	15%			30%			15%			40%		
% Annual Sales	___ | ___			___ | ___			___ | ___			___ | ___		
% Annual Profit (Contribution)												

429

Objectives. Objectives provide finite actionable goals. They should not be written in broad generic terms, but rather in quantifiable specifics. Each sales promotion trade, retailer, and consumer component should be quantified if at all possible. Examples of each follow.

Trade Example:
— To increase average all commodity volume (ACV) distribution of the 8-ounce size from 67% to 75% during the deal drive period.
— To specifically increase "B and C" outlets from 65% to 70%.
— To obtain 60% ACV distribution of the new "lite" milk chocolate flavor in the decorator collectible European tin.

Retailer Example:
— To put up 7,500 floor displays for one week and two weekends and obtain 25% participation with "co-op best food day in-ad allowances" with 1,500 key accounts.
— To put up 12,000 Swiss flag shelf-talkers at existing shelf space locations.

Consumer Example:
— To obtain a 4.5% redemption of the $0.25 cents-off FSI (free-standing insert) store coupon.
— To put in place market research to determine if at least 15% of redeemers are new users and 20% are occasional past users.
— To obtain 10,000 self-liquidator mail-ins for the premium offer.

Following are some examples of often-used promotion objectives. While they are all not quantifiable as shown below, an attempt should be made, wherever possible, to put a pre- and post-goal on as many objectives as possible, particularly distribution goals.

- Increase key account on-shelf distribution from 70% to 85%.
- Expand facings on a specific size from 40% to 50%.
- Obtain secondary display out of category (for example, crackers in both cracker and cheese sections).
- Obtain end-aisle display during peak selling season.
- Expand distribution of new specific size or line extension.
- Obtain deep-discount feature price solo.
- Obtain deep-discount feature price as part of storewide retailer promotion or manufacturer's line multibrand promotion.
- Load consumers with multiple purchases to take them out of the market for two to three repurchase intervals to lessen the change of brand switching.
- Obtain complementary companion merchandising to stimulate sales of each (for example, vodka with tomato juice or whipped cream with espresso coffee).

This list is not intended to be all-inclusive but to provide some thought starters as the name of the game is obtaining off-shelf display, end-aisle display, feature pricing, and retailer feature advertising.

DETERMINING THE SALES PROMOTION BUDGET

Many of the so-called classical rules, norms, and ratios for budget setting that were gospel during the heyday of brand management in the 1950s and 1960s still apply occasionally, but the turmoil of the marketplace and the decline of media effectiveness have made trade dealing and consumer sales promotion a much more significant force than they used to be. Some of these classical rules or guidelines follow.

New Products.

- When introducing a new product, spend 75 percent to 100 percent of year one sales in media and promotion. This obviously results in a significant underwriting loss in year one, and often years two and three, until the brand pays out.
- While proportions vary significantly, a typical new products marketing plan is often skewed to the allocations shown in Table 22.1 in years one and two. Year two usually will have a dramatic cut in marketing funds in order to begin to return to a sustaining level. Marketing costs in year two rarely exceed 50 percent and by year three are even less.
- Trade deals alone should be at least 20 percent to 25 percent of year one sales in order to have attractive introductory deals.
- Consumer sales promotion — couponing, FSIs, and the like — should be at least 50 percent of the size of the media advertising budget.
- From 60 percent to 70 percent of the sales promotion budget should be spent in the first introductory two quarters; however, even with extreme front-loading of the introductory launch, be careful not to spend virtually all the funds in the first six months leaving very little to fend off competitive counterattack in the third and fourth quarters of the introduction.

TABLE 22.1
TYPICAL NEW PRODUCTS MARKETING PLAN

	Year 1	Year 2
Total trade deals	25% of sales	15%
Media	40% of sales	10%
Direct mail, FSI, couponing, etc.	25% of sales	7%
Displays, headers, shelf talkers, collateral, etc.	10% of sales	3%
	100%	**35%**

- Only sample when there is a superior product that achieves a minimum 55 percent to 45 percent win in a blind paired products comparison test. Sampling parity product rarely results in the subsequent repurchase necessary to pay out (note that a 60 percent to 40 percent win is even more desirable).

There used to be a media rule of thumb that stated the share of market objective is roughly one-half the share of advertising. For example, a 20 percent share of advertising would eventually yield a 10 percent share of market. But this no longer seems to hold as media glut and multichannels have proliferated. However, keep in mind that setting a market share objective higher than the share of media or promotion still is a red flag and is unlikely the brand can achieve its objectives.

Existing/Mature Brands.

- Here a strategic decision has to be made of "milk versus build." If a brand's profit is being milked (or maximized) there is usually a low-level maintenance media budget or no media budget at all, and the brand becomes virtually a 100 percent trade deal brand. The easiest method to set budgets is to gather all competitive deal sheets and make sure the brand is competitive with the custom of the category in which it competes.
- If a brand is a viable brand in the top three brands in its category, it will usually have a so-called A/S (advertising to sales) ratio (in reality, a percent of sales) in the 6 percent to 10 percent range. Whereas in the past, media outspent promotion, today trade deals, retailer displays and advertising allowances, and consumer couponing usually equals or exceeds the media budget. On many brands roughly two-thirds of all dollar sales is spent on sales promotion.
- To determine the cost of playing the game, outside audit services or trade intelligence should enable a rank order universe to be put together for the category with each major brand having an estimated percent and absolute dollar spending level. Comparing the numbers on a rank order basis should provide some insight into whether the brand's goals are realistic or not. Consider the following example in Table 22.2.

  The real issue is absolute dollars spent, since you can't take percentages to the bank. Also, recognize that unless you have a product advantage, or at least a target audience or positioning advantage, it is hard to win the game without a budget that at least equals the norm or median of the category. There are some notable exceptions, but they are few and far between and take long periods of time to build.

Table 22.2
Comparative Spending

	Promotion $	M/S*	Media $	A/S**
Brand A	$30,000,000	15%	$20,000,000	8%
Brand B	$25,000,000	12%	$17,500,000	10%
Your Brand	$22,000,000	15%	$15,000,000	10%
Brand C	$18,000,000	17%	$12,000,000	11%
Brand D	$15,000,000	18%	$10,000,000	12%

*Percent merchandising to sales.
**Percent advertising to sales.

Line/Size Extensions. Many brands attempt to specifically feature a given size or line extension to obtain trade promotion on the specific item in line with specific promotion objectives. A common objective is to step the consumer up to a larger size that (a) is more profitable and (b) takes the consumer out of the market for a longer period of time, thus lessening the ability to switch brands at the next repurchase interval. As a rule of thumb the ability to load-in specific sizes or line extensions is lessening. As proliferation of types, flavors, scents, and other variations has increased, the key accounts often prefer to feature the entire line. This often stems from consumer alienation because the consumers become upset if the size or type they prefer is not on feature price. The two current remaining exceptions are a small salable sample trial size (usually in a prepack or dump bin) or a deep-discount deal on the largest economy size.

Deals. A few words are necessary about the close relationship between trade (price) deals and sales promotion. In short, a price deal is simply a special price or discount on the open stock or list wholesale price. It is important to remember this is off the *wholesale* price because retail pricing can only be suggested and is in the domain of the retailer, not the manufacturer.

Deals can take many forms, and at one time there were different customs in many parts of the United States by industry. For example, one free with 11 in the drugstore business usually meant a dozen or 12 individual pieces, whereas one free with 11 in the grocery wholesale business usually meant one case with 11 or at least a gross, or 144 pieces.

However, as many food and household products companies packed out cases that could be six pieces of a large size or 24, 48, or 72 of a small size, one free with 11 in the grocery trade could result in myriad individual units. A short schedule of deal ranges follows:

Regular (existing product) deals:
- 1 free with 11, or 8 1/3% off
- 2 free with 10, or 16 2/3% off
- 5% to 16 2/3% off invoice

Introductory (new product deals):
- 2 free with 10 (low)
- 3 free with 9 (common)
- 10% to 25% off invoice

Many companies also construct performance deals that require proof of performance, and the remaining portion of the deal money is usually paid by credit memo upon proof of performance. Various forms of "proof" include feature advertising tear sheets, signed-floor display flooring sheets, or validation of deep-discount feature pricing. While credit memos for proof of performance were quite frequent in the 1950s through the 1970s, they are less universally used today because of the cost of policing and the trade's clamoring for simpler, easier deals.

Slotting Allowances. Slotting allowances emerged when a few grocery chains on the East Coast felt that helping to introduce a new product often cost them out-of-pocket money and, since numerous new products fail, they deserved some compensation. Slotting allowances soon mushroomed into a cause célèbre and stores began to demand extensive fees, dependent on what the market would bear. Apparently buried in history is if the term originally meant a computer slot for an SKU or not, but today the term *slotting allowances* is used to refer to both meanings. Many manufacturers have resisted paying slotting allowances because they feel the retailer should be a partner in introducing new products, which are the lifeblood of any industry. However, even companies that have refused to pay slotting allowances often will sell-in a new product with guaranteed sales or additional incentives to ensure the retailer does not get stuck if the product doesn't sell well.

Cooperative (Co-op) Advertising Allowances. A co-op allowance originally was a shared cost of the manufacturer and retailer to purchase retail advertising, direct mail flyers, or retailer inserts. It sometimes evolved into retailers offering space to manufacturers or expecting manufacturers to absorb more than 50 percent of the cost of a best-feature-day ad with additional case allowances over and above the trade deal to pay for media space.

Bank or "Street" Money. Bank or "street" money is usually a running pool of money that is a fixed absolute amount (but can also be a percent based on case volume). It provides the retailer an opportunity to tailor and localize promotions out of a "kitty" within flexible agreed-upon guidelines, rather than rely on simply executing a manufacturer-directed program. Often it is given quarterly but can also be banked for use during a given fiscal year.

Consumer Sales Promotion Tactics.

Sweepstakes or Contests. Ordinarily a sweepstakes or contest is a give-away with a grand prize and first, second, third (fourth or fifth) prizes. In order to be successful, the contest should attract new triers. It is hoped that at least 15 percent of the entries will come from new triers. Negatives, though, include "professional" contest enterers who are not loyal to any brand and clubs that enter contests and often reject the prize and split the cash proceeds or sell the prize back to a dealer. Most large companies award all prizes in order not to incur consumer backlash, but some companies still do not award all prizes if the winning entry has not been sent in. Obviously, the latter method allows running a contest with a higher multiple, because often as much as 75 percent to 85 percent of the winning numbers are never turned in. (Note: It is recommended that all prizes be awarded for best case public relations.)

Consumer Couponing. The sales promotion management should do the contract negotiating for all forms of consumer couponing — for example, FSI or direct mail. The sales promotion manager should also prepare redemption estimates and budgets and should always build in different face-value split runs in at least 1 percent to 5 percent of the U.S. to build up a database of "laddering" coupon values. It is also important to look at more than just the absolute redemption percents. A 2 percent redemption in a brand that has a 5 percent share of market is far better than a 5 percent redemption on a brand that has a 25 percent share of market. Sales promotion should also try to design coupons that fit the look and image of the brand. Too often this element is missing. A negative is making coupons into a permanent price-off for existing users who would have purchased anyway, rather than attracting new triers or defending the brand during a competitive attack.

Companion (Tie-in) Merchandising. Companion merchandising is one of the most important and logistically difficult domains of the sales promotion manager. The objective of companion merchandising, also sometimes called tie-ins, is to obtain additional off-shelf display, often in a new second location, for two complementary noncompeting items. Often the items may be made by two separate, noncompeting companies, though on occasion the two items exist within the same corporate framework. Some examples include: gin and tonic, cheese and crackers, ice-cream and syrup topping, bagels and cream cheese. In short, the obvious assumption is that the one is almost always or often used with the other. Some negatives of tie-ins include the occasional need for dual sales calls, nonequivalent inventory take away, tie-in deals from each brand that don't match, and two brands that are vaguely or only indirectly used together by a small percentage of users.

Self-Liquidators. A self-liquidator is usually a mail-in item wherein the customer either sends in an amount of proofs-of-purchase, boxtops, or labels, with or without money or a handling charge, to obtain a premium item. Technically, it can only be a true self-liquidator if the handling charge and/or fee covers the cost of purchasing the item and fulfilling it (postage, carton, insertion, handling). For example, $1.00 and two proofs-of-purchase for an Easter bunny cover the cost of purchasing the item and delivering it. The rule of thumb on self-liquidators is that they should enhance the image of the brand, present a value to the consumer that is better than the lowest discount store price, or be an item that is *not* readily obtainable elsewhere. Often the best self-liquidators are collectible or commemorative items with logos. A problem is that redemption is usually low (less than 1/2 of 1 percent return) and consumers can become alienated if they don't get the eagerly awaited item in the mail within four to six weeks. In addition, because the items are often customized and must be pre-ordered, the brand can either run out and be difficult to reorder or be over-ordered, resulting in thousands of dollars of virtually unsalable merchandise. Self-liquidators are usually not a primary promotion but are used as a glue-on to enhance coupon redemption or point-of-purchase on-pack sales.

Floor Displays. It is ordinarily the assignment of the sales promotion manager to work with sales, brand, and purchasing management to evolve functional and innovative permanent and temporary displays. These range from dump-bins and simple header cards to elaborate metal, plastic, and wood displays. In calculating display costs, the profit margin or direct brand contribution of the displayed production must be amortized over the lifetime of the display. For a cardboard bin, the life might be one weekend, or at best one week or two weekends if you are lucky. A dump-bin is usually an all-purpose tray with a stand and a feature or vertical header card with product randomly dumped in. Hence the term *dump-bin*. A prepack is specifically prepacked with product at the manufacturing point. Product is tightly packed to avoid breakage, and set-up at retail is often done by the salesperson who pulls it out of the back room where it has been shipped. Floor displays clearly accelerate case volume and are often necessary as a lever to obtain off-shelf or out-of-category display. There are several problems with floor displays. In large warehouse stores or key accounts, end-aisle displays would have resulted in selling in and moving out more product than a floor display could contain; therefore, critical mass lost sales can occur. Floor displays also are subject to breakage, and unless the cardboard bottom is plasticoated, wet mopping the floor can cause the display to buckle and collapse. Also, some store managers do not want to put up numerous floor displays because of "aesthetic clutter."

There is a growing trend to secure distribution of a new brand by giving a permanent display to the trade. These can range from metal or wood or plastic racks to operating chillers, refrigerators, or freezers. While these allow the brand to preempt floor space, the danger lies in competitive brands usually occupying 33 percent to 50 percent of the permanent display within a two-year period unless the brand has a store door delivery system in which the sales or route person can maintain and police the shelf sets.

Interactive Media/Promotion. Perhaps one of the fastest growing areas of interest is interactive media, which is defined as "promotion techniques combined with an active rather than passive consumer hook." Some examples include the following:

- *Coupon "robots."* Machines that dispense coupons in-store at the push of a button or activator mechanism. Pluses, obviously, are instant couponing and hopeful in-store comparison. Negatives include the ability of a consumer to obtain more than one coupon, albeit each requires a separate purchase.
- *Video/visual/audio monitors.* There are mini-commercials or infomercials usually run on television sets in the appropriate store section. (Infomercials are, in effect, ads that demonstrate product advantages with visualizations of actual use.) Some stores also sell radio-like announcements, while others might have specials of the day on illuminated programmable lightscreens. Shopping cart videos have also been introduced to replace the stationary ad signs that often embellish shopping carts. Integrating these techniques with UPC scanning is also available in some areas. The most commonly sought-after technique is targeting of current users of competitive brands. As customers check out, they can receive either a high-value coupon for a competitive brand or both a coupon and a brief commercial.

SETTING UP A TEST

There are many new companies jumping into the interactive media/promotion area. The jury is still out on many of them (as of this writing) and the largest problem has been the ability to quickly scale up an efficient national expansion of a successful local test. Capitalization also often presents a problem because companies often underestimate the funds necessary to scale up to national expansion, or even expansion into the top 25 markets. It should be remembered that it took more than 10 years for UPC scanning to get into the majority of the country. One of the most difficult aspects of interactive media promotion is the pricing. The supplying company must cover its costs and make a profit, but the end cost to the user may or may not bear any resemblance to existing costs or existing techniques. For lack of better benchmarks, the industry has (perhaps erroneously) moved to using the cost of an FSI coupon as a benchmark. Compounding the problem is the fact that very few sales promotion managers or account executives have experience in print or broadcast TV media planning, so financial comparisons with TV or print are often omitted. When they are done at all, the judgment factor is critical as the benchmarks again become arbitrary in the eye of the beholder. For example, is daytime network or spot TV or nighttime network or women's or men's magazines the best comparative? While all these decisions are related, they at least should be taken into consideration so that comparisons can be made. The best strategy is to determine (if at all possible) what the true cost is of obtaining a trier or keeping a current user from switching to a competitor. If managers began to work with accounting to determine new and innovative techniques to measure the actual or apparent cost of obtaining a trier, many of the current methods of analyzing comparative promotional media would be made more productive. Consider the following example.

Group A is 500 consumers who are exposed to high-frequency TV. Group B is 500 consumers who are exposed to the equivalent amount of money that would have been spent on high-frequency TV but instead see video shopping carts. Brand shares and actual purchases are measured before (pre-), during, and after (post) the test.

The marketing decision is based on which of the two expenditures of dollars (if any) results in the higher return on investment. It must always be remembered that a sales promotion or brand manager's starting point is "I have a limited amount of money. Are we better off putting more dollars in media, public relations, floor displays, sampling, interactive, giving deeper discounts, more FSIs, hiring more 'detail' salespeople, or what?" A brand overview should always accompany the necessary finite programs that eventually are put in place for the sales force to present and sell. Again, the question should always be "What is the best use of the budget to get the most sales and *profit?*"

Multibrand Line (Umbrella) Promotions. A classic dilemma is whether a brand should participate in a multibrand promotion or spend its money on a solo brand-specific promotion. The first rationale behind a multibrand promotion is there is more clout and critical mass in bundling together a group of brands under a common theme or idea than going to the buyer and presenting an extensive list of individual, brand-specific deals and promotions, each of which takes up the buyer's time and can create logistical headaches and confusion. The second rationale for a multibrand promotion is the so-called concept of "big brother helping little brother." By bundling together a group of large and small brands under a common theme or umbrella with an attractive trade deal, the buyer can — with one "yes" — order the entire program. Hence, the smaller or weaker brands are carried along by the larger, stronger brands. Multibrand promotions provide companies that have extensive brand lines additional clout in the marketplace since the name of the game in retailing is increasingly providing the trade customer with the largest array of product at the lowest deep-discount feature or special price. It is important to note that multibrand promotions do not always bundle together 100 percent of the brands in a company but often group together brands with similar seasonal patterns or with complementary tie-ins. When all (100 percent) of the brands in a company are presented together in a special promotion, it is ordinarily called a "corporate sale."

Corporate Sale/Promotion. A corporate sale is a high-velocity total program that is often worked out with senior field sales management and high-level key account buyers. While it can have a central theme, such as "Big Bonanza" or "Carnival Days" or "Truckload Sale" as an overlay, the primary attraction is deep-discount pricing that presents an extraordinary incentive for the consumer over and above the normal discounted price of a solo or multibrand promotion. In addition, there can be extra media support, truckload discounts, pallet sale discounts, and numerous extraordinary components that combine to provide the buyer with a special once-a-year package that is difficult to refuse.

A negative of both corporate and multibrand promotions is that many brand managers feel their brand has a special problem and will get lost in the shuffle. Yet, they are allocated, or assessed top-down from management, a dollar fee for participation. Often the brand manager will feel a brand-specific or solo promotion would be more efficient and would favor use of the brand's promotion/deal budget.

Solo Promotions. Solo, or brand-specific, promotions are one brand only and can even zero in on one specific flavor or size line extension. They are particularly effective if a new form or size is being introduced. The more innovative the form from the original or parent brand, the more likely the solo promotion will be successful. The difficulty with solo or brand-specific promotions is that unless the sales force is convinced there is really a point of difference, the brand could get lost in the shuffle or not even be presented to some accounts because there is only a limited amount of time a buyer will allot to each salesperson. While trade deals and practices are an ever changing kaleidoscope, often senior management will allocate or suggest to brand groups that if there is one promotion per quarter in a fiscal year, there should be, for example, one corporate sale, one solo, one multibrand, and a final brand solo. Whether the promotions are staggered (don't run two solos in a row) or whatever, must be part and parcel of an overall annual promotion strategy.

Case Example. The Swiss Milk Chocolate Company was planning to introduce an important line extension to its current line of ready-mix hot chocolate powder. While children preferred sweet mixes for both hot and cold milk, adults were calorie and fat conscious and preferred a slightly less sweet flavor. New "Lite" fulfilled these requirements and also had a more "European" bittersweet taste.

The marketing manager felt the product could obtain 85 percent ACV distribution and be a $25 million business, taking more than 40 percent of its volume from new triers. The sales department was less optimistic and felt 65 percent ACV distribution would be good and only 15 percent of the volume would be added business from new triers, with the rest being cannibalized from the existing franchise. Also, while brand management wanted more of the budget to be in consumer trial or pull vehicles, the sales department felt that better front-loaded trade deals, coupled with deep-discount in-ad allowances, would perform better and push the velocity of the brand.

In the introductory planning meeting, the sales promotion manager was asked to put together a plan to introduce the new line extension and carry it through its first fiscal year. After numerous meetings with outside suppliers, the sales promotion department came up with a comprehensive plan that filled numerous pages. An outline of the plan is summarized in Exhibit 22.2.

In evaluating this first-year promotional plan the committee of the brand manager, sales promotion manager, and field sales coordinator made sure they first reviewed what all their direct competitors were doing. All competitive deal sheets that could be obtained were tacked on the wall. In addition, a 10 percent reserve was set up in the budget so if a competitor countered with a one-time-only deep-discount deal, the brand group could counter it by sweetening the next promotion with additional allowances. In fact, as the year actually evolved, they found they had to modify two of the five promotions and deploy more money into the promotion just to be shelf-price competitive.

EXHIBIT 22.2

Overview:

Strategy — To indemnify the brand as the lowest-fat, healthiest adult hot chocolate drink with real European flavor.

Objectives — To ensure that all consumer promotional materials reinforce this strategy.

Trade — To obtain 75% ACV distribution in time for the hot chocolate season that starts October 1.

Retailer — To put up floor displays for the introductory promotion. To put up shelf-talkers for the introductory promotion.

Consumer — To provide couponing as an incentive to trial. To also offer self-liquidators that are perceived to have unique value.

Specific Plan:

Working together after numerous meetings, phone calls, debates, and compromises, the sales department coordinator identified five deal periods —four to run at 60-day intervals and a Christmas holiday promotion to run for 90 days.

I. Introductory Promotion

• Trade deal	15% off invoice with additional 10% ad allowance by credit memo
• Retailer promo	7,500 in-store floor displays prepacked 48 units to a bin; 12,000 shelf-talkers
• Consumer promo	$.50 introductory coupon via Donnelly co-op marketing with ROP (run-of-press) best-food-day coupon in selected top 100 B and C counties

II. Second Promotion

• Trade deal	Two free with 10 on small size only; one free with 11 on all other sizes; 5% ad allowance by credit memo
• Retailer promo	None
• Consumer promo	$.25 in-pack bounce-back coupon

III. Third Promotion

• Trade deal	10% off invoice on large size only
• Retailer/consumer promo	Salable sample prepack special; $.39 trial size with full retailer markup. Packed 72 to a pre-paid floor display with a $2.50 display allowance

IV. Fourth Promotion

• Trade deal	7 1/2% off invoice on all sizes
• Retailer promo	None
• Consumer promo	None

V. Fifth (Holiday) Promotion

• Trade deal	5% off invoice on all sizes; 10% ad allowance by credit memo
• Retailer promo	7,500 holiday header cards for end-aisle and card stacks features
• Consumer promo	Holiday FSI $.50 coupon with "Christmas in the Alps" sweepstakes

Robert E. Oliver is Project Manager for Frigidaire Company's Wet Products Group (laundry and dishwasher products). Oliver has more than 20 years of experience in consumer, medical, and industrial products marketing, including market research, brand management, sales management, international marketing, marketing strategy development, and new products. Since 1990 he has worked full time on developing a state-of-the-art product development system designed to improve the competitiveness of U.S. manufacturing industries by making new product introductions of higher quality and on faster implementation schedules. The system is currently being implemented within Frigidaire Company.

CHAPTER 23

SALES PROMOTION STRATEGY IN CONSUMER DURABLE PRODUCTS

In the United States, Canada, and the industrial nations of Europe and Oceana, the term *durable* consumer goods is most often used to refer to automobiles and large or "major" household appliances. Because of the initial purchase price, operating expenses, and extended payments necessary to own them, sales of consumer durable products, along with real estate construction and sales, form the backbone of virtually every measurement or index of what has come to be known as "consumer confidence."

In addition to being a major indicator of the consumer's willingness to spend money and incur debt, durables are important to the economy in other significant ways, too.

They remain at the very center of American manufacturing: employing large numbers of both skilled and semiskilled factory workers; providing important markets for steel mills, plastics, and electrical components manufacturers; and supporting additional thousands of jobs in the retailing and after-sale service sectors.

Since the early 1960s, the market for household appliances in the United States has become heavily dependent on replacement sales. Saturation statistics for durable products illustrate this convincingly: In 1989 more than 99 percent of U.S. households owned either a gas or electric range and a refrigerator, while 80 percent owned microwave ovens and 73 percent washing machines, dryers, or both. With a typical replacement cycle averaging 10–15 years, appliance manufacturers have only three or four opportunities to sell their products to consumers in an entire lifetime. Thus, it is not surprising that America's home appliance manufacturers place great value on satisfying, and (they hope) retaining, their customers. This essential tenet is reflected in the industry's advertising, personal selling, and sales promotion strategies. General Electric's current campaign "We bring good things to life," Frigidaire's new theme "Built for Generations," and even Maytag Corporation's headquarters address of "One Dependability Square" illustrate the pervasiveness of these ideals.

The U.S. major appliance business has become increasingly oligopolistic until, in 1993, only five large manufacturers were continuing to build appliances in the United States: Frigidaire, General Electric, Maytag, Raytheon, and Whirlpool. These same manufacturers similarly dominate the domestic Canadian home appliance market as well, either with export shipments from U.S. factories or wholly owned Canadian affiliates or subsidiaries. With replacement volume tied to population growth, housing starts, and consumer confidence cycles (consumers typically repair existing appliances during a recession, postponing replacement until better economic times arrive), the category has become intensively competitive.

All of this is reflected in appliance pricing, which for the period 1982–1989 increased just 5.9 percent (in "real" dollars adjusted for inflation) for home laundry equipment and only 3.0 percent for food freezers and refrigerators. For the same seven years, the U.S. Department of Labor's Consumer Price Index, usually considered the most comprehensive measurement of consumer spending, rose 24.0 percent.

As is characteristic of many sectors in the U.S. economy, the retail channels for major appliances have undergone sweeping changes in the last 20 years. The most important trend has been the decline of local, independent appliance retailers in favor of regional appliance and consumer electronics "superstores" such as Circuit City, Silo, and Best Buy Company. Like large-volume discounters in other mass market consumer product categories, the superstores have concentrated on wide product assortments, well-known (and advertised) brand names, and (usually) the sharpest pricing in their markets. In the largest markets where several superstore chains compete, such as Chicago, San Francisco, New York, and Houston, written guarantees of the lowest prices in the market on selected major appliances have become commonplace.

The success of the superstores has forced the large, traditional appliance retailers (Sears, Roebuck and Company and Montgomery Ward) to make significant changes in their operations. Montgomery Ward led the way with its "store within a store" concept, which it named "Electric Avenue." The concept involves a completely new look for the department, deeper merchandise assortments, and stepped-up advertising of brand names at extremely competitive prices. As a result, Montgomery Ward has become the largest retailer of both Maytag and General Electric appliances in the nation — two brands that have traditionally relied on their own (often exclusive) dealer networks.

After seeing its share of home appliance retail sales decline from a high of 40 percent in the early 1980s to an estimated 25 percent by 1987, Sears countered with a total overhaul of its traditional appliance department by test-marketing its first "Brand Central" in Indianapolis in 1988. Before Brand Central, Sears sold only Kenmore (a full-line, private-label appliance assortment not available in other stores) but now sells and services a full line of General Electric, Amana, Jenn-Air, and Whirlpool products as well. The effect has been to make Sears much more competitive, not only in product offerings and price but also in after-sale service (an advantage Sears has maintained against most of its superstore competition).

Along with the significant structural changes in both appliance manufacturing and retailing have come many changes in the ways these products are promoted. In all the consumer durables categories,

EXHIBIT 23.1

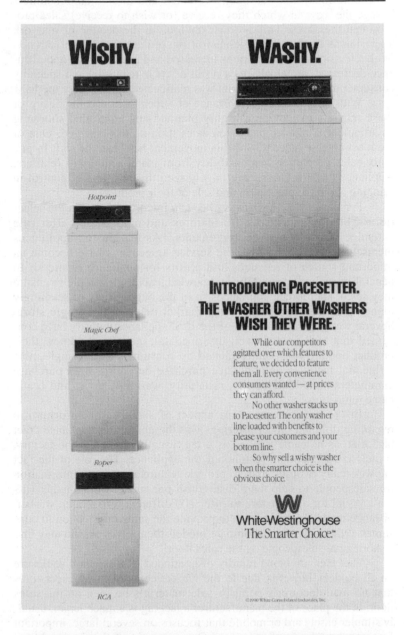

Example of trade advertisement for a new washing machine product line. Most sales promotional activities in the major appliance industry are directed at the retail trade.

the promotional mix has been evaluated and altered as consumers change the ways in which they receive (or wish to receive) sales promotional messages. This is most obvious in the decline of network television as the dominant element of the promotional budget. As network television advertising rates increased and audience size and affluence decreased, principally as a result of cable television and specialty consumer magazines, advertising was reallocated among these media.

With the increased importance of superstores and the desire of these retailers to provide a highly planned and controlled shopping environment, a new emphasis on sales training has emerged. One of the most notable outcomes of this movement has been the shift in primary sales promotion responsibility from manufacturers to retailers. Appliance manufacturers have largely seen this as a loss of control in bringing about the promotion and sale of their products.

Personal selling has always been an important factor in the selection of brand names, specific features and models, and after-sale extended warranty service agreements. (As margins on appliances themselves have diminished, the service agreements have become an important source of revenues and profits for appliance retailers.) In general many consumers rely on knowledgeable salespeople to ensure they select appropriate appliances from the huge variety of seemingly identical models available in the market or even at a single store. Several well-regarded surveys of the U.S. appliance industry have confirmed that well-trained, well-informed salespeople who know their product line are consistently ranked by consumers as the single most influential factor in an appliance purchase decision. Other purchase parameters include durability, reliability, warranty, price, and brand name reputation.

In the past an important aspect of salesperson information regarding different model offerings was the ubiquitous appliance "fact tag" that, as its name implies, is a tag, usually applied at the factory, summarizing important features of the appliance. The role of the fact tag was really twofold: first, to provide feature and benefit information for salespeople to help them distinguish one model from another (it's not unusual for a superstore to offer 100 different refrigerator, washer, or range models); and second, to provide the same information to consumers, who may wish to compare models themselves or who may find a shortage of salespeople on the sales floor.

Fact tags are being rapidly discontinued as a standard enclosure on all models, however, due to the requirements of many superstores that no manufacturer's point-of-sale materials be seen on the sales floor. In the place of the manufacturer's fact tag is a much larger, usually simpler easel card or mobile that focuses on several large, important features, brand name, and price. One outcome of this is that brand names tend to be somewhat de-emphasized while price (especially price point ranges) and feature comparisons are highlighted.

EXHIBIT 23.2

MULTI-CYCLE AUTOMATIC WASHER HEAVY DUTY

MODEL

AW700G

HEAVY-DUTY WASHING BENEFITS

- ☐ Large Capacity Wash Basket
- ☐ Double Scrub Washing Action
- ☐ Three Step Rinsing
- ☐ Bleach Dispenser
- ☐ Self Clean Lint Filter
- ☐ Automatic Safety Lid Lock
- ☐ Perm Press Cool Down

CONTROL PANEL FEATURES

- ☐ All Fabric Programming:
  - ☐ Automatic Agitate Spin/Speeds
  - ☐ Regular, Permanent Press and Knits & Delicates Cycles
- ☐ Four Wash and Rinse Water Temperature Selections
- ☐ Variable Water Saver Control to Conserve Water and Energy

HEAVY-DUTY CONSTRUCTION BENEFITS

- ☐ Heavy-Duty ½ hp Overload Protected Motor
- ☐ Strong, Quiet Transmission
- ☐ Stabilizing Suspension System
- ☐ Polypropylene Pump, Agitator and Tub
- ☐ Load Compensating Drive
- ☐ Ribbed PERMA TUB Wash Basket
- ☐ KNIGHT SHIELD™ Finish Top and Lid with Operating Instructions
- ☐ Durable Cabinet Finish
- ☐ Rear Self-Leveling Legs

Mix 'n Match with any Dryer

DIMENSIONS

- ☐ Overall Height 43 ⅜"
- ☐ with Lid Open 90°, 51"
- ☐ Height to Worktop 36"
- ☐ Depth 27"
- ☐ Width 27"

Before purchasing this appliance, read important energy cost and efficiency information available from your retailer.

FIRST YEAR FULL PARTS & LABOR WAR-
RANTY. FULL 25-YEAR PERMA TUB INNER
WASH BASKET WARRANTY. SECOND
THROUGH FIFTH YEAR EXTENDED TRANS-
MISSION WARRANTY. (SEE WARRANTY FOR
DETAILS.)

Parts & Service | **WCI** | **Nationwide**

WCI Consumer Parts & Service
White Consolidated Indus-
tries, Inc. maintains a vast
network of factory authorized servicers to provide
prompt, courteous, professional service
for your appliance anywhere you live or
move in the U.S.A.

(UL) Listed by Underwriters' Laboratories, Inc.

Kelvinator Appliance Company

An appliance fact tag that outlines features for both salespeople and consumers, a traditional means of product differentiation in the category.

EXHIBIT 23.3

A large fact tag used to increase point-of-sale merchandising of both features and warranty.

BRAND NAME IMAGERY: A STRATEGIC FOUNDATION

The role of brand names in consumer products marketing has been widely discussed and documented. In a number of high-volume, price-sensitive categories as diverse as disposable diapers, potato chips, toothpaste, and automobile rentals, successful market share positions have been built with generic or "no-name" products, usually at the expense of profitable, established, often historic brand names. Similarly, there is a class of simple, low-cost, "no-frills" product lines or single-product offerings within longer lines that reach low-end or very price-conscious consumers. Most evidence however, continues to support the traditional belief that extensive lines of well-featured and "stepped" products sold under well-known and respected brand names are what retailers and consumers still want most.

A classic example of the power of established brand names can be seen in the package goods offerings of Church & Dwight Company, Inc. Although in survey after survey upward of 90 percent of consumers don't recognize the name of Church & Dwight, an equal number express impressive confidence and trust in the quality and effectiveness of the company's most famous product, Arm & Hammer Baking Soda.

Only a few years ago it was likely that most retailers and consumers would have considered bicarbonate of soda — the chemical formulation on which baking soda is based — "uninteresting" and "mature" from a new product and marketing standpoint. Yet it is this simple, inexpensive, easy-to-produce chemical formulation that is at the center of a line of new products that now includes laundry detergent, toothpaste, and antiperspirant/deodorant offerings. So successful is this line of natural, healthy, good-for-the-environment products that other, much larger competitors are now rushing to develop and market baking soda derivative products themselves.

Church & Dwight has relied heavily on simple sales promotion techniques rather than media advertising for much of its growth, including extensive back-of-box copy explaining the many household uses of baking soda, free laundry room charts with much of the same information, and heavy price discounting with coupons and mail-in rebates to effect first-time trial use. A simple but illustrative measure of the success of these tactics can be observed by visiting a high school home economics class, where after years of advocating exotic (and expensive) chemical cleaning compounds, teachers are again enumerating the many uses and virtues of baking soda (usually with the familiar yellow and red box close at hand).

In the major appliance category, there has been a proliferation of brand names in the last decade, even though the number of manufacturers has continued to shrink. There are several interesting aspects to this phenomenon.

In 1980 there was no single brand name that offered a full line of major home appliances in the deluxe, high-end price point segments. Rather, certain brands dominated product categories in which they had established traditional quality and performance leadership. The case histories of three brand names — Maytag, Tappan, and Kitchenaid — are worthy of expanded discussion.

Maytag has always been known for its relatively short line of simple but high-quality and long-lasting washers. The company was well established and well regarded in the trade for its steadfast loyalty to a network of traditional, independent appliance dealers supplied by wholesalers in a classic two-step arrangement. While management was aware of the marketing advantages of the Maytag brand name in other appliance categories, it was careful to maintain its integrity (and margins) by adherence to strict quality standards in component sourcing, fabrication, and assembly.

Accordingly, Maytag's first offering beyond washers was clothes dryers (an obvious companion product) and then dishwashers. Expansion beyond these categories, however, required either sourcing of products from other manufacturers (which management considered risky as they were unable to completely control product quality and would be limited in product differentiation options) or building of additional factories (which in Maytag's risk-averse culture was seen as serious capital exposure).

In common with all appliance brands, however, Maytag needed to field a full line. It ultimately chose to do this by acquiring Magic Chef, Admiral, Norge, and Hoover, each of which brought new opportunities to the newly formed Maytag group of appliance enterprises. Magic Chef was well known as a low-end supplier of cooking products (free-standing and wall ovens and microwave ovens) and dishwashers.

Norge produced basic laundry pairs, which offered entry into medium- and low-priced markets not available to the Maytag brand. Admiral offered a line of refrigerators, which after a substantial retooling effort, provided models for Maytag, Magic Chef, and Admiral — all from the same factory. Finally, Hoover was purchased as a pure diversification play, providing the company with a leading floor-care market share in the United States and a strong household appliance presence in the United Kingdom.

To complete its metamorphosis, Maytag formed a major strategic alliance with Montgomery Ward (in the process, offering exclusive models to increase Ward's competitiveness and price point appeal). Today, Montgomery Ward is the largest retailer of Maytag washers and dryers in the nation.

Like Maytag, Tappan established its reputation in a single-product category. In the case of Tappan, however, it was in kitchen appliances, especially gas ranges, in which the company had grown from dominating its home territory in the Great Lakes states to a national presence and strong market share position. Soon after Tappan was acquired by Frigidaire Company, plans were announced to make the famous name a full-line appliance marketer.

This was a fairly obvious step in other kitchen product categories such as refrigerators, dishwashers, and disposers, but it was more difficult in laundry products where Tappan had no position or brand name recognition. The problem was solved in 1992 when an extensive line of Tappan washers and dryers was introduced into exclusive distribution by Montgomery Ward's Electric Avenue "store-within-a-store." Efforts by both Tappan and Ward are now under way to successfully seat and promote the new product line.

Kitchenaid's position as a supplier of high-quality kitchen appliances begins with its highly definitive name. (Frigidaire, a company with origins in the refrigerator, freezer, and air conditioner businesses, is another example of a descriptive brand name in the appliance industry.) For decades the company was best known for its leadership in dishwashers and heavy duty mixers. So attractive was the brand's consumer franchise that immediately after buying Kitchenaid's parent company — Hobart Corporation — Whirlpool decided to use the name to reach high-end consumers who would typically not buy its medium featured and priced Whirlpool brand.

This strategy has been implemented by offering unique features and styling that have created a Kitchenaid "look" not offered at lower

EXHIBIT 23.4

Product label used on export laundry appliances. In many markets, "Made in the U.S.A." remains an important selling point.

price points or by lesser brand names. Whirlpool is betting heavily there is a "Kitchenaid customer" who, having been satisfied by the brand in the past, will return for additional appliance purchases in the future.

BRAND POSITIONING: A CRITICAL ROLE FOR SALES PROMOTION

There is, of course, much more to taking a brand to market than simply giving it an image. The most effective brands in any field have strong, clear market positions in the minds of target consumer markets at all times, whether a purchase is planned or anticipated.

It is now widely understood that General Motors did enormous damage to the individual positionings of its brands when it tried to standardize "platforms" (basic automotive body stylings) across its five brands. At the height of this effort in the early 1980s, consumers were hard-pressed to see, describe, or understand the essential differences (other than sticker price) between Buicks, Pontiacs, and Oldsmobiles — GM's "brands in the middle." Even though it was quite clear that Chevrolet was GM's "starter" or low-end brand and Cadillac was its deluxe model, the confusion was further compounded with high-end Chevrolet Caprice models and low-end, stripped down, or compact-size Cadillacs. The situation reached its nadir in 1992 when stories appeared in the news media indicating that GM was unable to continue support for its Oldsmobile marque, and research was showing the brand no longer had a clearly understood following or target market with the public. GM stopped short of eliminating its Oldsmobile division and name, and it seems to be making headway in positioning Buick as a high-end "demand" brand just below Cadillac in its family of brands. Still remaining, though, is a need to find clearly defined and communicable market positions for Oldsmobile and Pontiac.

Frigidaire Company offers an interesting study with its five appliance brands sold in the domestic U.S. market: Frigidaire, Tappan, White-Westinghouse, Gibson, and Kelvinator. Each has a clearly delineated target market and sales promotion plan. The company expects that all of its appliances will provide certain consumer benefits including the following:

- Safety in operation and use
- Ease of use
- Excellent functional performance
- Optimum design and style
- Ease of maintenance
- Environmental responsibility
- High degree of reliability
- Excellent value for the money

The Frigidaire brand — the company's namesake and flagship product line — is clearly targeted to affluent, well-educated consumers for whom brand name recognition and status are important. Frigidaire brand products, while not trendy, are certainly fashionable and represent stylish good taste, which is immediately recognizable to this market segment. The brand appeals to those with a need to own appliances with the latest technology and innovative features and who are willing and able to pay for the best. Most Frigidaire consumers probably live in smart, upscale suburban communities.

As in automotive advertising and sales promotion activity, appliance manufacturers usually promote new features and benefits introduced at the beginning of each new model year. In the appliance industry this occurs at the National Association of Home Builders show held each February.

As Frigidaire Company's premier brand, important innovations or deluxe new features are offered first on Frigidaire brand appliances. In 1993 Frigidaire introduced its new Ultra Style design, and all media advertising (and much sales promotion) for the year focused on that line of Frigidaire appliances.

Full-line magazine ads (that is, ads featuring all appliance categories) were scheduled to run in the May–June and September–October periods, with supplemental refrigerator product campaigns from January through April and in July and August. These schedules were augmented with range and dishwasher campaigns running in April and September through December.

Working with the publisher of *Country Living, Better Homes and Gardens* and *Ladies' Home Journal*, Frigidaire developed a "Heart of the Home" sweepstakes promotion offering a free, full-color, 16-page Kitchen Design Guide featuring Frigidaire appliances. The magazines reached a combined total of more than 80 million home owners during the June–July period (when many kitchen remodelings are planned). Consumers who were motivated to visit their local Frigidaire dealers were eligible to register for the sweepstakes' grand prize — a fully equipped Frigidaire kitchen featuring new cabinets, appliances, and a $5,000 kitchen decorating allowance.

The dealer tie-in was, of course, the critical element in converting the promotion into additional sales of kitchen appliances, which both Frigidaire and its dealers sought.

In addition to the national advertising and sweepstakes promotion, four additional, product-specific sales promotions were also planned:

- **"Loads of laundry rebate"** — A special point-of-purchase (P.O.P.) display was prepared to offer consumers a $50 manufacturer's rebate on the purchase of qualifying Frigidaire washer and dryer pairs purchased at the same time from the same dealer.
- **Freezer tips booklet** — With the purchase of any Frigidaire food freezer, consumers received a free "Frozen Food

Preparation Guide" telling them how to get the most out of their new freezer. This information has become an important aspect of consumer satisfaction because many families no longer have a garden or prepare other foods to freeze, and the correct information about successfully freezing food may not be otherwise available.

- **Dishwasher installation allowance** — As with many ranges, dishwashers are often "built-in" appliances, and a $35 installation allowance from Frigidaire helped close prospective dishwasher sales by removing one more obstacle to purchase. The program applied to a wide range of dishwasher models and ran from April through June.
- **"Clean and quiet promise" program** — Another P.O.P. kit to sell dishwashers, this package guaranteed Frigidaire's new UltraPower wash system will clean better and run more quietly than the consumer's present machine or the purchase price would be refunded.

The Frigidaire product line is supported with attractively designed and produced, four-color, full-line and special refrigerator category brochures for consumers, and individual product line specifications sheets housed in a full-line binder for dealers.

Frigidaire's Tappan brand is positioned as the company's cooking products demand brand, variously described as a "cooking specialist brand" and "America's authority on cooking." Tappan's line of both gas and electric ranges and microwave ovens is the company's most complete with price offerings and feature content from basic to deluxe. Tappan appeals to many of the affluent, suburban consumers targeted by Frigidaire but with a discernible cooking-products orientation. Unlike Frigidaire, however, Tappan is sold through discount and wholesale ("warehouse") clubs where price competitiveness is a major promotional consideration. As part of a repositioning effort, Tappan's full line is offered nationally only in Montgomery Ward Electric Avenue stores whereas a network of dealers continues to merchandise the Tappan cooking products lines.

Tappan product literature features cooking products prominently, and dealers are offered a binder with some of the most complete cooking products specifications in the industry. To maintain full-line sales promotion in the Montgomery Ward account, Tappan has provided consumer brochures on its full line only in those stores. During the February through April 1993 selling period, off-invoice allowances on Tappan's gas and electric lines ranged between $6 and $25 per unit. Such allowances were designed to increase sales of slow-moving or especially profitable models and also encourage retailers to carry a larger product assortment.

Inventory financing — known as "floor planning" in the appliance industry — is always a concern to dealers, and Tappan used it as a major element of its microwave oven sales programs in the spring of 1993. Purchases of 10–24 units on a single invoice qualified for 30 days extra dating; sales of 25–49 units, an additional 60 days floor planning; and invoices totaling 50 or more microwaves were eligible for a full 90 days additional dating.

Finally, to generate dealer interest and excitement and provide an attractive "closer," consumers were offered a free cookware set on selected high-end Tappan ranges.

Next in the Frigidaire family of appliance brands is White-Westinghouse — the intriguing combination of names of Frigidaire's parent company in the United States (White Consolidated Industries) and one of America's best-known appliance brands, Westinghouse (who sold its appliance manufacturing and marketing operations to W.C.I. in 1975). White-Westinghouse is a value-oriented product line whose reputation has always been one of offering high-quality appliance features and performance at attractive pricing. At many price points, White-Westinghouse offers more features than its targeted competition (Hotpoint, Roper, Admiral, Magic Chef, and Kenmore). This position is proclaimed and supported by the brand's current tag line: "Helping You Live Your American Dream," an obvious reference to consumers' difficulty in maintaining living standards during recessionary times.

The brand is promoted to middle-income families who seek value for money in household purchases. Accordingly, the brand may be found in broad distribution across many classes of trade including warehouse clubs, superstores, and traditional two-step appliance retailers. If Wal Mart elects to offer a line of major appliances, White-Westinghouse would be an especially good strategic choice.

With no broadcast media advertising, White-Westinghouse relies heavily on sales promotion tactics to increase consumer awareness and sales. Salesperson "spiffs" (use of extra commissions to promote sales of selected models) and sales contests are routinely employed. In the spring 1993 selling period, White-Westinghouse offered its "Dream Deal" — $10 per unit spiff on 13 refrigerator, five freezer, two dishwasher, eight laundry, and nine range models mostly in the larger capacity or deluxe categories. The spiff program was supported by the brand's popular (and often repeated) "American Dream Bond Program" consumer tie-in promotion. With the purchase of eligible models, consumers were given a $50 U.S. Savings Bond. An extra incentive was given for a multiple-appliance purchase from a single dealer on the same invoice: If consumers purchased six appliances — for instance, a washer, dryer, freezer, refrigerator, dishwasher, and range — $1,000 (maturity value) in savings bonds would be rebated to the consumer.

Kelvinator, known to dealers and consumers as a "sensible, dependable, and affordable" brand, is Frigidaire's economy appliance line. Its short line is targeted to consumers who seek basic appliance features and performance in the "low-low" to "low-middle" price ranges. Despite the very American trait of "trading up" in purchases of durables as income permits, a large volume of appliances are sold at these budget price points. Frigidaire has recognized that younger consumers, perhaps those establishing a home for the first time, require simple, serviceable appliances. In the case of Kelvinator, however, simple models and low prices do not mean second-rate design. Cognizant that younger consumers have been exposed to high-technology features, performance, and styling in stereo and automotive products, Frigidaire's design center has given recent Kelvinator lines improved color and graphics treatment.

An important role assumed by Kelvinator is that of a branded "running mate" for both Frigidaire and White-Westinghouse. The brand is useful in filling in for either one as a complement to the higher-end offerings of the other two marques.

While still technically a "full-line" appliance company, Kelvinator does not sell countertop microwave ovens, gas ranges, or built-in appliances (all of which are provided in the Frigidaire and Tappan lines). This has all been done to further support a two-brand offering on many appliance dealers' floors.

Kelvinator is promoted with point-of-purchase displays, cooperative advertising, a series of product specifications for dealers, and sales contests. As with nearly all appliance brands offered by all U.S. manufacturers, there are important off-invoice price incentives to dealers who carry a full-line selection of Kelvinator stock-keeping units (SKUs).

Like its competitors, Frigidaire has watched the decline of independent appliance distributors that has occurred in the last 10 or so years. The company's Gibson brand is differentiated almost exclusively by its distribution strategy, for it is sold and merchandised exclusively by independent dealers. By maintaining a full but short line of machines for these dealers, Frigidaire has increased its market share in the remaining two-step distribution infrastructure. Said another way: Gibson represents a means of increasing business in a declining market.

The company believes that a segment of the consumer market remains loyal to independent dealers who continue to offer neighborhood stores and full installation and servicing facilities, personnel, and reputations. For these consumers, price is less important than quality, service, and warranty. Gibson serves these needs well with products and prices covering the "high-low to high-middle" range, and a "Golden Warranty" that offers best-in-class protection for consumers.

While Frigidaire, Tappan, White-Westinghouse, and Kelvinator are all focused on larger regional and national retailers, Gibson may be seen as a company within a company. Its sales promotion activities include larger-than-average fact tags with feature and performance information, an aggressive P.O.P. and full-line allowance program, and liberal cooperative advertising allowances.

WHAT ROLE FOR SALES PROMOTION?: THE BIGGER PICTURE

Having seen how sales promotion works to define a brand or product's image and how it can be used to effectively position a product offering in the home appliance market, how can the role of sales promotion in consumer durables be summarized?

From the standpoint of the manufacturer/marketer the first objective of any sales promotion effort is that measurable value be added at the dealer/retailer level. There are several aspects to this. First, dealers must be encouraged to carry a representative inventory of a manufacturer's product lines. The proper mix of stepped models must be selected, stocked, and merchandised if a brand is to maintain, or increase, its market share. Off-invoice allowances are the major sales promotion vehicle for achieving this objective; by providing an appropriate, attractive financial incentive, manufacturers can sell a feature and model mix that will maximize margins while meeting the dealers' requirements as well. The same approach can be used to encourage dealers to carry a larger assortment within a specific brand family by providing off-invoice allowances for dealers who display and/or merchandise more than a minimum number of models.

In home appliances, a market characterized in the U.S. by five manufacturers and some 20 brands, a key role for sales promotion is ensuring that display space and retail facings (SKUs) are achieved, maintained, and maximized wherever possible.

As mentioned previously, this has changed in recent years as superstores define what sales promotional materials will be allowed on their sales floors. The very thing that makes superstores attractive to consumers — a broad, deep merchandise assortment of well-known brands — creates a significant challenge for manufacturers — namely how to call attention to their SKUs in a plethora of possibilities. Today this is being achieved with product design (Frigidaire's new Ultra Style line is a good example of this tactic) and overhead, national advertising to bolster brand awareness in consumers before they visit the dealer's showroom.

In most other appliance dealerships, point-of-purchase displays remain a viable way to showcase a brand, product category, or specific model with minimum impact on floor space and at reasonable cost (expenses of larger P.O.P. units are usually shared between manufacturers and retailers). Frigidaire's new "Frigidaire Gallery" is one example of this approach. It creates interest and excitement on the retail floor due to colorful displays of product information (including racks for distributing brochures) and clearly promotes the brand's name and image to shoppers. Important or new features are promoted on the

EXHIBIT 23.5

Introducing The New Frigidaire Gallery.

An Exciting, New Way To Maximize Your Sales
With Minimum Floor Space.

FRIGIDAIRE
BUILT FOR GENERATIONS™

A Complete Line Of Quality Crafted Appliances

The Frigidaire Gallery. An example of an updated point-of-sale merchandising program used to build brand awareness and image.

columns that support the display. Little floor space is lost in using such a display, especially when used in end-cap positions.

Consumer sales promotions are often used to build traffic in appliance stores. Most Sunday newspapers in major metropolitan areas carry price-oriented major appliance advertising designed to "direct traffic" to dealers who carry well-known brands or especially "hot" models. Sweepstakes, rebates, installation allowances, and multiple-appliance purchase concessions also create new traffic and increase attentiveness and interest by in-store shoppers when properly merchandised. Although not as common today as in the past, promotions for trade-in allowances on old appliances have demonstrated considerable power in suggesting and encouraging replacement (and upgrading) of appliances.

Finally, all sales promotion activity must increase sell-through of product to the public. In a business where replacement makes up the majority of sales, real incentives are necessary to influence consumer purchases. Studies in recent years have concluded that price reductions below 20 percent off the suggested retail prices will not materially increase durable goods replacement buying. Major appliances, of course, are not impulse sale items; they have a long useful life and are still considered hard-working rather than glamorous products by the majority of U.S. consumers. Most replacement sales occur when existing appliances fail or become too costly to repair. Major appliance manufacturers have always been aware of the business potential of shorter, more frequent replacement cycles. If consumers could consider appliances as decorative or stylish (this is true to some degree with kitchen appliances such as dishwashers, ranges, and refrigerators), replacement cycles could be tied more closely to remodelings and thus better "managed" by manufacturers and dealers.

In the absence of greater demand for appliances, however, the price promotions most often "move the tonnage." Such promotions may take the form of manufacturers' or dealers' rebates, premiums, or purchase-with-purchase options (the classic example being a reduced price on automatic ice makers with purchase of a new refrigerator). Working closely with these consumer promotions are the always-present spiffs, which, of course, motivate salespeople to sell some models in preference to others. Spiffs can range from $1.00 to $10.00 per unit, and on a busy sales floor, daily commissions of $100 for top producers are not uncommon. Spiffs are especially valuable to manufacturers when new models are introduced. By putting an attention-getting spiff on the new offering, the manufacturer can be sure it will get the presentation time and selling effort needed for successful introduction.

The second objective of appliance industry sales promotional efforts is, of course, to persuade consumers to buy. In this hotly competitive field, promotions that raise brand awareness and improve brand imagery are especially valuable in meeting the manufacturers' objec-

EXHIBIT 23.6

THE CHANGING RULES OF APPLIANCE PLACEMENT

When it comes to placement of kitchen appliances, old rules are giving way to new trends. What's different about kitchens in the 90s is that designers are no longer lining up these products like soldiers along the wall. Appliances aren't found where they once were. There are other changes as well: heights of cabinets, countertops and islands are staggered; corners are rounded and base cabinets pulled forward for deeper countertops. The Maytag Kitchen Idea Center provides clarification on some of today's placement ideas.

Dishwashers

Designers are beginning to recognize that the dishwasher doesn't have to be located under a counter. One idea is to elevate this kitchen workhorse. Raising the dishwasher 12 to 18 inches off the floor minimizes stooping and bending and reduces the physical energy expended. It's a good idea, especially suited for those with back problems.

Raising the dishwasher 18 inches from the floor is a boon to bad backs and allows for wide drawer storage above and below the unit.

Since the dishwasher occupies the space of a standard 24-inch-wide cabinet, it is relatively simple to plan for an elevated dishwasher with cabinets above and below for storage. Remember, though, to have at least 18 inches of counter space between the sink and where the raised dishwasher begins for clean-up.

For larger families, a second dishwasher in the table area can enhance the efficiency of after-meal clean-up and entertaining.

Range/Cooktops

Since the 30-inch range or cooktop is one of the most used kitchen appliances, probably second only to the microwave and refrigerator, it should be placed in the primary work triangle--whether against a wall or in an island. The main rule to follow is that there should be 12 inches of space on either side of the range area for pan handles to hang over and for convenience and safety.

Wall Ovens and Microwaves

Jim Krengel, director of the Maytag Kitchen Idea Center, suggests placing wall ovens outside of the primary work area because they are the least used appliance in today's kitchen. He cites a recent study indicating that wall ovens are used only 15 percent of the time in meal preparation. Microwave ovens, however, are one of the most used kitchen appliances, and should be placed within or as close as possible to the main work area.

Aside from good looks, an angled wall oven turns the corner for easy access to nearby counters and cooktop.

A single wall oven should be installed at approximately countertop level or 36 inches off the floor. Another rule of thumb is that when the oven door is open, for

---

Information — even something as basic as where to place kitchen appliances for maximum convenience and efficiency — is an important component of sales promotion.

tive of keeping its brands in front of the public in a favorable way. This can be done quite effectively with attention-getting sweepstakes and smaller, local prize giveaways reinforced with broadcast and print advertising.

Spiffs, again, will keep salespeople interested in certain brands and models and will keep presentations (and sales) of those brands at higher levels than would otherwise be expected. Finally, although high-quality point-of-purchase brochures are the exception rather than the rule in appliance retailing today, their value shouldn't be overlooked.

Especially when several appliance purchases are pending, consumers often want to look over an entire line and compare features and prices away from sales floors and closing pressures. Such buyers can be effectively qualified with attractive, fact-filled product literature.

Selling is an obvious objective, but then there's the job of keeping the product sold and creating an environment for repeat purchases. Appliance manufacturers dream about "demand" brands, which command the full lifetime loyalty of consumers, but this is largely an illusion. More important to most appliance consumers than brand name are product features, perceived quality, economy of operation, freedom from service calls, and value for money.

The first step in attracting consumers to a major appliance product is attractive, functional, intelligent product design. It could be argued that much of our U.S. appliance industry was late in discovering the need for design, possibly due to its close affiliation and joint ownership with American automobile manufacturers.

This heritage lingers in 1993 when most household appliances are still sold on capacity and "features," and the leading brand of washing machines still has an aluminum control console with simulated walnut wood grain "styling." Despite this, there is a growing preference by consumers of the 1990s for appliance designs that are more like other products in their homes, especially televisions, stereo equipment, and furniture.

Besides design there are other requirements for big-ticket durable goods with which the consumer must live for 10 or so years. One of the most important of all is product warranties. In a category as close to commodity selling as appliances, after-sale "protection" has become a critical promotional consideration. In a market where porcelain-enamel washtubs are still the standard, Frigidaire Company caused some commotion when it began offering a 25-year full warranty on its polypropylene tubs.

Due to the tendency of porcelain tubs to craze and fracture, no other manufacturer has yet countered this selling advantage; therefore, warranty has become a major element in sales promotion.

More conventional consumer sales promotions in the appliance industry include manufacturers' rebates, installation allowances (to make replacement — especially of built-in appliances — less painful),

EXHIBIT 23.7

Frigidaire

TITAN TUB

FULL 25 YEAR WARRANTY*

A further commitment by the Frigidaire Company to build the most durable laundry appliances available. The Titan Tub is constructed of the latest, state-of-the-art material for washtubs, and is guaranteed not to break for 25 years from the date of purchase.

*See printed warranty for complete details.

Frigidaire Company established a new standard for warranty protection with a 25-year guarantee on its plastic washtubs in washing machines.

sweepstakes, premiums (especially those that are category-related), and multiple-product purchase incentives aimed chiefly at kitchen remodelings.

In conclusion, it is likely that major appliance manufacturers will continue to focus more sales promotional efforts and budgets on dealers than on consumers. This is a normal outcome in an industry characterized by brand proliferation, model proliferation, excess productive capacity, and price competition on products that many consumers see as essentially identical.

James C. Reilly, General Manager of Communications Services at IBM, joined the company in 1958. His experience within IBM is extensive, encompassing many communications disciplines including advertising, media relations, management communications, marketing communications, community relations, employee communications, customer publications, television, and business show events. He has worked in many organizational units within IBM including corporate, international, marketing, manufacturing, and development.

Reilly is on the board of directors of the Association of National Advertisers. He is a member of the association's management, taxation, and finance committees. He is also a member of the National Advertising Review Board.

He received his B.S. in Marketing and Journalism from New York University.

CHAPTER 24

SALES PROMOTION
IN BUSINESS-TO-BUSINESS MARKETING

INTRODUCTION

The tools and techniques of sales promotion are certainly among the most powerful resources available to the business-to-business marketer. By and large, the targets are well defined, and relatively easy to reach. This allows for a level of precision in assessing the costs and benefits of marketing activities — and generally enhances their effectiveness.

The question remains: How can you take advantage of this precision and power to solve difficult business-to-business marketing problems cost-effectively?

After a few brief sections on the nature of business-to-business marketing, a general methodology for finding answers to that question will be provided. There are two parts to this methodology.

The first is an analysis of the business-to-business marketer's business environment. This will help identify the unique opportunities and challenges facing a product sold within this environment and provide a framework for developing a successful strategy.

The second is an incremental analysis that will help to evaluate the potential return on promotional investment (ROPI). Calculating potential ROPI and then measuring realized ROPI gives one the ability to fine-tune spending and convert one's promotion budget from a corporate expense to a corporate investment with a demonstrated return.

Thus, the purpose of this chapter is to (1) familiarize the reader with business-to-business concepts, (2) provide a framework for developing a sales promotion strategy, and (3) help demonstrate the effectiveness of promotion programs.

THE BUSINESS-TO-BUSINESS ENVIRONMENT

There are many similarities between business-to-business and consumer marketing. First is the fact that in both cases the purchase is ultimately made by an individual, often with influence from other individuals. This means that sales promotions in both environments face the same psychological obstacles: media clutter, competition for a reader's time, and too little time to spare. It also means that the same basic communications techniques will work. People are attracted to a strong brand image, stand-out creative execution, and quickly grasped ideas.

Anyone working in packaged goods marketing already knows a great deal about business-to-business marketing. But there is one fundamental distinction between the two that cannot be overemphasized.

In business-to-business marketing, goods and services are being sold that enable business customers to sell goods and services to end-user consumers. In general, consumer products are sold on the basis of the intrinsic satisfaction they provide, while business products are bought for their potential to earn money.

The fundamental consumer marketing message is always some variation of "Buy this for satisfaction." The fundamental business-to-business message is "Here's the answer."

The business buyer is a professional evaluator of goods and services actively pursuing a solution to a specific problem. This means that the buyer is extremely interested in the product if it's relevant and completely uninterested if the product isn't. Other aspects of the business buyer's situation may include the need to conduct a formal review and make a recommendation to someone with the authority to spend the money, the need to justify any decision he or she makes, and a thorough and detailed specification and purchasing process.

The key to success in business-to-business sales promotion is finding the right people at the right companies for which a product will make a positive difference and getting them interested in that product's solution.

BUSINESS-TO-BUSINESS PRODUCTS AND CHANNELS

Consumables vs. Capital Equipment. There are, at the risk of being overly simplistic, two kinds of business products. There are consumables, including things like printer ribbons, industrial chemicals, and welding rods. Then there are capital investments, which include items such as computers, forklifts, and airplanes. Business services break into two similar categories, as well. Equipment or building maintenance and insurance meet ongoing needs, while a service such as consulting may be called upon to solve one particular (and particularly complex) problem.

Consumable goods or services are typically those bought repeatedly at relatively low cost, with little consideration given before each reorder. These goods often have relatively little impact on the profitability of the customer's business. Investments such as a mainframe computer, on the other hand, are decisions of the highest order. The choices, beginning with the decision to even look at all the options, involve financial, technical, and business operations experts over a long and painstaking period. The potential impact of a decision to change, taking advantage of an advance in technology to benefit the business, carries enormous risk. Not only will the decision makers be affected by a mistake, but so will the business, its employees, and its customers.

Direct vs. Distributed. The direct sales force is one of the differentiating factors between business and consumer marketing. Because business orders are often quite substantial, much is at stake. It often takes a full-time person to manage a sale. And even though it may seem like Company A is buying from Company B, it's important to remember that people buy from people.

Therefore, many traditional promotional activities, such as contests, coupons, rebates, and the like can be irrelevant in some business-to-business environments.

Other products are sold through the more familiar channels of distribution. For example, many products are effectively sold through catalogs. Here, the promotional activities dismissed in the direct sales environment can be quite effective.

BUSINESS-TO-BUSINESS SALES PROMOTION

Background. Business-to-business buying is often assumed to be a dry, scientific, fact-based discipline outside the influence of marketing activity. In truth, the marketplace is not dry at all, and business-to-business sales promotion is far more stimulating than many people think. Nevertheless, the buyer is a professional and not as impulse-driven as a consumer might be. This leads to some important points to keep in mind:

- Fact-based research, planning, and footwork are key to understanding the market, the prospect, and just how a product or service can be promoted.
- Discipline and objectivity are important. A single qualified lead from a call or reply card is far more valuable than massive responses from people who think the product does something it doesn't.
- Low cost is not the same as low price. It is a business-to-business marketer's job to show a prospect how his or her product or service can be the most cost-effective option — regardless of its price. The invoice cost of a raw material or part is but one item in a cost-of-goods-sold calculation. Product quality might, for example, drive a customer's cost of sales down because of an increase in repeat business, due to the new level of quality the product helped a customer attain.
- Getting the prospect's attention is a matter of delivering a message that makes sense to the prospective customer, in the language of the market.
- Getting to a prospect first is better understood as getting there at the right time — namely, when he or she is just beginning to focus on the problem and is forming a plan to solve it. The opportunity is to help solve the problem at hand by formulating the question in a way that one's product can most effectively answer.
- Making the sale is just the beginning of a relationship. Sales promotion, properly applied, can help ensure that a new customer becomes a repeat customer, not just for a particular product or service but for a company's brand in general.

Business-to-Business Sales Promotion Defined. Buying cycles will be discussed further in a later section, but for now, let it suffice to say that it is important to understand that in the time a business recognizes a need for a product, the time it gets bought, and the time it wears out, there are many steps. Each step begins or ends with a decision about whether a product deserves continued consideration.

Given the complexity of the buying cycle, business-to-business sales promotion needs to be more broadly defined than as a simple "buy now" incentive. Therefore, a more appropriate definition of business-to-business sales promotion might be as follows:

> Business-to-business sales promotion is any marketing or marketing communications activity that increases one's influence in any phase of the purchase path or that lowers one's cost of getting on and staying on a prospect's list.

THE BUYING CYCLE

In order to more thoroughly plan the strategic selection and deployment of any promotional activities, there are several purchasing cycles of which to be aware.

The Simple Case. In both the consumer and business-to-business environments, the basic buying cycle always reduces to four parts: need identification, purchase path, usage, and repurchase path. This basic cycle is also equally applicable to consumables and capital investments (see Exhibit 24.1).

Any of these steps can be simple or complex. In the consumer world they tend to be more informal, while in business-to-business, high-ticket capital investments, each step can be formalized and embellished beyond easy recognition.

Consider a simple cycle for bath soap, as shown in Exhibit 24.2.

1. **Need identified:** The prospect is about to run out of soap.
2. **Purchase path:** The prospect writes *soap* on a shopping list and looks for coupons. If a brand's free-standing insert (FSI) coupon broke at the right time, the prospect becomes a customer by buying that particular brand.
3. **Usage:** The prospect uses the promoted brand and likes it and is perhaps reinforced in his or her enjoyment by seeing advertisements in which other smart people use the soap.
4. **Repurchase path:** The prospect writes the brand name on the shopping list, goes to the store, and this time buys shampoo of the same brand name as well.

Note how the repurchase path worked to expand the brand's base at the customer's household.

It is the general goal of business-to-business marketing for both consumables and capital investments to influence the buying cycle

EXHIBIT 24.1

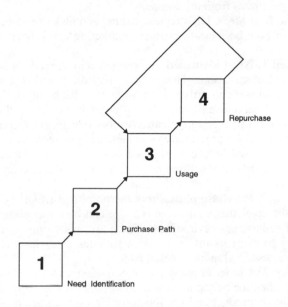

The four basic steps of any buying cycle.

EXHIBIT 24.2

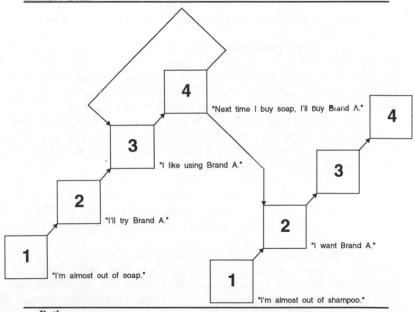

Bath soap case.

every step of the way, specifically for the purpose of expanding customers' purchases from the company.

The Four Steps. Let's review, define, and make some basic observations of how business-to-business marketing can influence the four steps:

Step 1: Need identified. A prospect may perceive a need based on internal observations. However, it may happen that a marketer's new technology can solve a problem of which the prospect was unaware. A marketer's direct sales representative can help the prospect see the need, using communications tools developed specifically for that purpose. The representative's influence is greater if there is a tradition of trust based on excellent products and service. Without a representative, a marketer must find other means of identifying and reaching this prospect.

Step 2: Purchase path. From the point that suppliers are evaluated to the point that a purchase is made can be rather complex in the business-to-business environment. There are many opportunities for a company to exert its influence through sales promotion techniques. These are described in more detail later.

Step 3: Usage. In many business-to-business situations, usage is the time when the next purchase is on the line. A company is expected to support its product and the relationships — both personal and professional — throughout the useful lifetime of the product. (This doesn't mean free support. It just means honoring commitments and making sure no one regrets buying the product.) Satisfactory performance here can give a company stronger influence than any of its competitors in Step 4.

Step 4: Repurchase path. Once any equipment has depreciated or has become obsolete, or once a consumable is consumed, the customer needs to make a replacement. If a business-to-business marketer has been a strong supporter of a customer's business, he'll effectively control the repurchase path and make the sale at minimal cost.

Business-to-Business Cycles. Within the corporate marketplace, actual buying cycles are significantly more complex and diverse. Purchase decision processes vary with often-changing priorities of price, quality, and delivery. Understanding whether a customer is a divisional purchasing manager at GM or the proprietor of the corner store sounds obvious; understanding just what appeals to the customer and why, and how one can best exert influence that favors one's product or service in the search for the best solution to the problem is rarely so clear.

Typically, a large or sophisticated business will go through a lengthy process in search of a solution. Many high-priced business products are one-time or rarely made purchases. The whole process becomes much more complicated because the actual buying process is more intricate and because the challenge is to turn that one-time purchase into a relationship that leads to add-on purchases of one's brand.

On the other hand, decision processes for repetitive purchases of consumables are typically fast, to the point of almost cursory investigation of quantity, price, and delivery questions. The opportunity, in this case, is to interrupt the automatic cycle and cause the purchaser to rethink the initial decision and incorporate one's own information in a new evaluation of needs.

Example: This is a typical buying cycle for a capital investment from a customer's vantage point:

1. Discover needs or problems.
2. Research options.
3. Present or try to solve these options internally.
   • Determine whether the scope of the problem requires an outside solution.
4. Evaluate external solutions.
   • Research available solutions.
   • Identify general suppliers of solutions.
   • Screen suppliers.
5. Short-list suppliers.
6. Request proposals from suppliers.
   • Provide specifications to suppliers for bid.
7. Receive presentations from suppliers.
8. Evaluate proposed solutions.
   • Decide among proposals.
9. Award the contract or make the purchase.
   • Implement the solution.
   • Review the effectiveness of the solution.
   • Close the case or refine the solution.
10. Evaluate and reassess the solution.
    • Evaluate the supplier for future needs.
11. Plan for future replacement.

Steps 1–3 comprise the need identification step in the four-step process. Steps 4–9 comprise the purchase path. Step 10 occurs over the usage phase. Step 11 is the initiation of the repurchase path.

To market effectively, one should mirror the customer's process:

1. Discover the customer's needs or problems.
2. Research the product or service options to solve.
3. Determine how the customer will try to solve.
   • Identify the prospect's search for options.
4. Research the problems from the customer's point of view.
   • Evaluate the competitor's solutions.
   • Identify general suppliers of solutions.
   • Research opportunities.

5. Gain attention of the customer with a solution.
6. Gain an invitation to bid.
   - Influence specifications to skew toward the solution.
7. Present the most effective and efficient solution.
8. Influence the customer's evaluation.
   - Gain the best reputation in the customer's mind.
9. Win the contract or purchase.
   - Implement the solution.
   - Review the effectiveness of the solution.
   - Maintain contact and follow up on refinements.
10. Continue to support for maximum satisfaction.
11. Watch for new opportunities to assist the customer in improving operations.

Note that even though a prospect's activity is internal at first, there are business-to-business promotion tools suitable for almost every part of the cycle (see Exhibit 24.3).

Ideally, all marketing communications activities should dovetail with the prospect's needs throughout this process. At each step, the job of the business-to-business marketer is to anticipate these needs and proactively address them.

A Close Look. By looking at each step in the hypothetical example given above, it is possible to derive suggestions with regard to how different promotional activities might be used to increase influence or lower the cost of getting and staying on a customer's list. It is not assumed, expected, or recommended that every suggestion is followed. Choosing the appropriate techniques for maximum impact and cost-effectiveness will be discussed in the sections on strategy and tactics. It should also be remembered that the brand image a prospect has of a company will influence that prospect every step of the way.

Step 1: Needs discovered. Within the prospect's company, there are almost always options and opinions about what these needs are and about which ones should be given the highest priority. A marketer can benefit from this ambiguity by helping a prospect notice and become concerned with the needs that the marketer's products fill. Tools available include advertising, newsletters, and direct mail addressing the customer's problems and giving a solution.

Step 2: Options researched. At this point, all options are still under consideration. Although the prospect still hasn't contacted a company, a company's influence through newsletters, direct mail, and collateral materials continues. If a company's promotion plan is integrated with advertising, some of the copy in rotation will address the reasons why its type of solution is the only reasonable way to solve the problem under discussion.

Step 3: Options presented. The internal presentation of optional solutions continues. The opportunity to expand one's influence in this

EXHIBIT 24.3

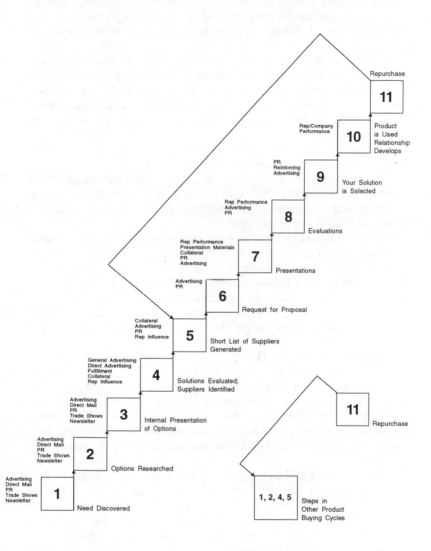

Even in a complex buying cycle, each step in the cycle can be influenced by business-to-business promotion programs.

step is to direct relevant promotional devices to the executive or jury involved with the decision. Because business-to-business mailing lists usually include job titles, there is a reasonable means by which to stratify materials and get the right level of information with the right slant on a particular solution to the right influences within the customer's organization.

The customer's decision to invest in a solution from outside the company is the first chance to be eliminated from the process — this is why marketing communications directed at specific problems and solutions are so important. The true initiators of many major business buys are the people on the lookout for solutions to specific problems; they are the kind of people who are hungry for information that can help them, who will read long copy when it pertains to the issues on their minds, and who send in coupons or call toll-free numbers.

Most important, if a business-to-business marketer has provided a satisfactory solution in the past, enjoys a good reputation with the company, and has an established relationship, decision makers will already be thinking of him or her.

Step 4: Solutions and vendors evaluated. As the field of solutions is evaluated, a company's image becomes more important because that image is an attribute of the solution. This is a good reason to support sales representatives with high-quality promotional materials such as collateral brochures and presentation aids. Here, attention-getting promotional activities that speak to the problems being solved are most important. Demonstrations and samples are sure to strike a nerve.

Step 5: Short-list. The quality and timeliness of a marketer's response to the prospect's inquiry is the most important source of influence in this step. One might think that appropriateness of the solution is paramount, but the disappointing fact is that unless there is an existing relationship or established brand image, all the prospect knows of a marketer and a marketer's product is how well that marketer's sales representative presented the solution through promotional materials.

Step 6: Proposal developed. At this stage, a representative diligently works on a proposal and negotiates a price. Different pricing programs and promotional packages should be available that can be offered to the customer to make the product more attractive. For example, magazines often offer merchandising credits to frequent advertisers, which can be used to generate a merchandising mailing or advertise at a trade show. The important point is that the promotional program should be a meaningful incentive to a customer.

Step 7: Proposal presented. Quality presentation materials are targeted, easy to understand, and personalized. A sales presentation must be consistent in tone and content with other promotion materials in terms of key benefits, significant points, and overall value. Quality presentation materials along with a quality sales presentation solidify a marketer's image.

Step 8: Evaluation. In these last few steps, a representative's personal influence has probably mattered more than the influence of any given promotion materials. This is why it is so important to work with the field people in developing collateral. They generally know what kinds of tools will help them the most. With balanced input from these individuals, the effectiveness of a sales force and the collateral promotion materials will reinforce each other.

Step 9: Solution selected. If a company gets the contract, it is because from the moment that prospect became aware of the need, the advertising, sales force, and sales promotion efforts have worked in concert to steer the prospect over to that company's solution. If the product is good and the marketing strategy was sound and well executed, it is inevitable that this company will be selected. Every time the customer thinks about the problem from any angle, that particular solution appears as the best choice.

Step 10: Ongoing evaluation. The work is never really done. Once a contract is won, it is time to analyze the process and refine the understanding of the purchase path and buying cycle. It might also be appropriate to start developing the next generation of promotion materials to reflect what has been learned from this successful experience. It is also time to cement a relationship with the customer through the sales representative by being responsive and responsible and by taking the time and effort to delight as many people in the customer's organization as possible.

Step 11: Repurchase. A company's success in winning the customer's business in the first place and its ongoing support and responsiveness build a base of trust that increases its influence in every step of the process next time around. In other words, everything that is ever done matters. If it has been done well, there may even come a time to start the next procurement initiative and help evaluate the customer's options.

THE PURCHASE PATH

It is important to keep in mind that the buying cycle is different from industry to industry, from product to product, and from year to year. The differences, particularly in the purchase path portions, can be profound.

The purchase path for large capital investments often involves far more meetings and presentations and individuals than has been indicated here, while many consumables are purchased automatically without thought. The point is that there is a cycle, and it is critical that the cycle be learned and understood for a product.

STRATEGIC ISSUES

In developing any strategy, it is wise to recall the familiar advice of Sun Tsu, the Chinese general who, more than 2,500 years ago, wrote in *The Art of War*:

> If you know the enemy and know yourself, you need not fear the result of a hundred battles. If you know yourself but not the enemy, for every victory gained, you will also suffer a defeat. If you know neither the enemy nor yourself, you will succumb in every battle.

To succeed consistently one must build a foundation of knowledge of oneself, one's competitors, the market, and the customers.

A good model for developing a sound sales promotion strategy begins with knowing five factors: product, assets and liabilities, resources, market, and challenges.

Product. Knowing one's product means understanding its position in the marketplace as well as its form, function, life cycle, purchase path, and profitability for the company. It is crucial to note that service and support are increasingly considered a fundamental part of many products.

By "position" in the marketplace, we mean that combination of awareness, reputation, relative price point, and other intangible, difficult-to-measure factors that form a prospect's preconceptions and differentiate a marketer from the competitors. Is the marketer's product the "gold standard" by which all others in the category are judged? Is it the "reliable standby" for customers who can't afford the very best? Is it the "risky bargain"? Do less sophisticated customers select it for its simplicity and comprehensive support, or is it favored by the most advanced customers because of its advanced features?

Perhaps most significantly, is the product always, sometimes, or never placed on the short list of the prospective customers? Why?

The point here is not to ask these general questions about a hypothetical product and market but to develop and answer specific, relevant questions about one's own product's position.

Assets and Liabilities. Assess the important assets and liabilities of the product that strengthen or weaken one's competitive posture. For example, a marketer may have either a particularly strong brand image that enhances interest in the products or a poor brand image that prejudices people against the products. With a weak brand image, interest in new products may not exist without significant positive publicity.

Another example of an asset may be the base of satisfied customers and its potential for additional sales. With a relationship already in place and knowledge of the customers' needs and ways of working, many sales are halfway to closing as soon as a need is recognized. Selling to a satisfied customer base saves the costs of prospecting and simplifies the purchase path. On the other hand, the customer base may be a liability if the customers are unhappy. In fact, the customer base can be thought of as a "word-of-mouth" communications engine. And it is well known that "word-of-mouth" is much better at spreading bad news than good.

Assets and liabilities must be assessed against the competition. For example, a marketer may have an excellent distributor network. However, if the market leader has a superior sales force with enviable customer relationships, the distributor network does not offer that marketer a competitive advantage.

Once the assets that offer competitive advantages have been identified, these assets can be used to their fullest to strengthen a company's position. Knowledge of liabilities can enable a marketer to convert them into assets or to avoid playing in a market if the liability does not allow a competitive edge. Marketers should also know their competitors' assets and liabilities and take advantage of them. For example, MCI challenged AT&T with its "Friends and Family" promotion. MCI could have been unwise to directly challenge the market leader in a very profitable business. However, AT&T could not retaliate with a similar program without losing significant profit. While MCI was gaining incremental profit, AT&T would lose profit by discounting. In this case, MCI was successful in taking market share from AT&T because it knew its competitor.

Resources. By resources we mean those marketing communications tools, information systems, personnel, budget, and other elements that can be deployed to achieve promotional goals. A well-constructed promotional plan will fail if resources are not available to support it.

Some resources such as budgets and information systems are obvious. Some resources are not so obvious but are still very important to a successful program.

For example, a sales organization is a powerful information resource. This is especially true with a direct sales force. A company's sales representatives know better than anyone else the concerns of customers and customer organizations. No one is in a better position to advise marketers on appropriate, realistic goals or the types of promotional activities that work best. Getting similar information from dealers and resellers can be more difficult, but it is still well worth the effort. Because dealers, resellers, and sales representatives are in contact with the customer base, they are in a uniquely efficient position for getting a promotional program (packaged by any of the techniques discussed in the later section on tactics) to the right person.

Another powerful resource is a database of customers. A database can be used to cross-merchandise or announce new products.

Market. "Knowing the market" means knowing the opportunities. This requires a comprehensive understanding of customers, both collectively and as individuals.

"Understanding customers collectively" means having an intimate knowledge of the dynamics of the market. This, in turn, breaks out into two general areas of inquiry: What is the market doing, and what is the product's position?

To know what the market is doing, it must first be defined. For example, a company may make programmable timers for industrial test equipment and consider its market to be every company that tests its own products. But these companies may be moving toward centralized computer control and no longer need discrete timing units. On the other hand, the timers may have other applications in new markets.

Is the market for a product growing or declining or is it stable? What is the long-term outlook? The answers to these all-important questions depend on the quality of the market definition and understanding of the product.

Then the product's penetration of the market must be addressed. The basic questions here are as follows: What is the market share, and is it growing, declining, or stable? Is the product on the verge of obsolescence or is it new? As we shall see in the section on challenges, comparing the movement of the market with the movement of market share is crucial to creating a cost-effective strategy.

"Understanding customers as individuals" basically addresses the following questions: Do prospects know the brand or company name and correctly associate it with the kinds of problems the products solve? Are the products automatically on the short list when prospects' needs arise? How does their buying cycle work? These issues are difficult to quantify or know for certain. They are nevertheless very important.

Challenges. The first step is to determine the potential value of a product's success on the market. A rough evaluation consists of superimposing the anticipated growth of market share over the expected growth of the market itself.

If the market is growing and the market share is growing with it, aggressive marketing activities may be justified to seize the opportunity. If interest in the product is declining within a stable market, an attempt to recapture market share may not be justified because of limited growth potential — promotional activities might instead maximize the profit of selling off remaining stock and gracefully exiting the market. If there is a growing share in a declining market, there is little or no incentive to invest in marketing activities.

When evaluated in the light of product profitability, this analysis can help a company decide how much time and money to invest. The same technique can be used for reaching decisions about appropriate marketing objectives, tools, and budgets.

The next step is a closer look at what a company knows about its product, assets and liabilities, and the market in order to precisely define the marketing challenges it faces.

Graphic analysis often helps. The key to successful employment of this tool is to be creative — in the most responsible sense of the word. What this means is seeking related variables and plotting them together to make relationships more explicit. A product's buying cycle can be mapped on a time line populated with customers and their production seasons to identify peaks in demand.

One of the most useful diagrams that a business-to-business promotion manager can make is a ladder of the product's buying cycle. Factors that influence each step should be included (see Exhibit 24.4).

The next step is to attach a product's assets and liabilities near the steps they influence most. A refinement would be to weight these influences with numerical values, but it isn't necessary (see Exhibit 24.5).

Between the analysis of the market and the ladder diagrams, the manager now has a concise, easy-to-understand statement of all the dimensions of the marketing challenge.

The next step is to review the resources that are available, to take these existing resources, and to apply them to the ladder diagram where they most naturally fit and can be most effectively deployed.

If existing resources fail to cover the product's most significant challenges, other tools, such as those discussed in the section on tactics, can be used to take appropriate action (see Exhibit 24.6).

Business-to-business promotion managers are urged to experiment and develop their own analysis techniques. The point of this whole section is as follows, if we may hear from Sun Tsu one last time:

> The general who wins a battle makes many calculations ... before the battle is fought. The general who loses a battle makes but few calculations beforehand. Thus do many calculations lead to victory, and few calculations to defeat; how much more no calculation at all!

As anyone who has ever studied physics knows, when you draw the right picture of a problem, the answer presents itself. Learn to draw.

TACTICS

In this section on tactics, we will look at some of the tools and techniques of sales promotion and discuss them in the context of business-to-business marketing and the methodology discussed above.

Sampling and Demonstration.

Type of product:	Any
Type of sales force:	Any
Delivery:	Mail, trade show, representative, POP
Where influential:	Early in the cycle
Effect:	Awareness, understanding, memorability

EXHIBIT 24.4

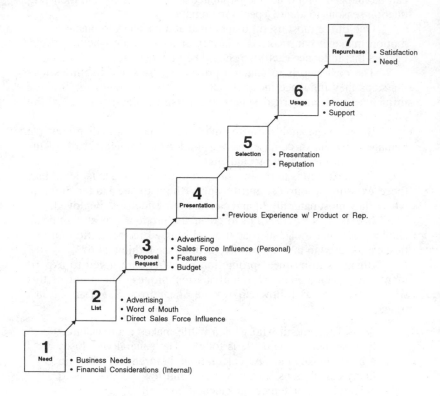

This diagram shows the purchase path and buying cycle as generated by a hypothetical producer of check printers, sold by a direct sales force.

EXHIBIT 24.5

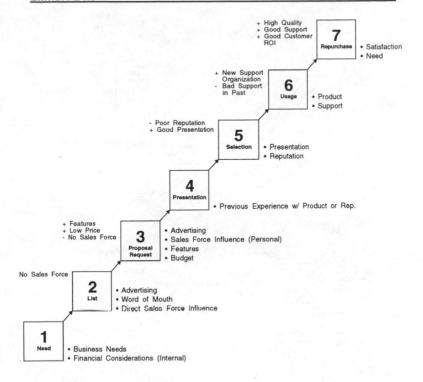

With assets (+) and liabilities (−) attached, it is clear that this company's selling task is daunted by a reputation for poor long-term performance.

EXHIBIT 24.6

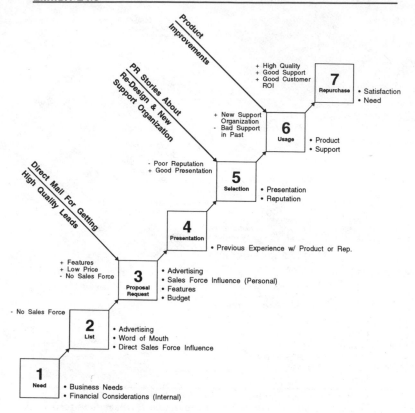

Without a strong sales force or dealer support, this company decided to use direct mail to lcap past steps 1–3 and put a simple demonstration in the hands of middle managers at customer companies. The budget was set using techniques of incremental analysis.

Sampling and demonstration can be highly effective in established markets and with new products. Their greatest impact will occur early in a prospect's buying cycle. A really strong product and demonstration may even initiate such a cycle.

If the product is self-demonstrating, meets an acknowledged need, and has obvious advantages, one can send a sample and let it do the talking. A business case must also be simple, such as obvious and immediate cost savings. Here, sampling works for business-to-business as it does for consumer marketing. The sample encourages the prospect to try the product, note its superiority, and — assuming you make it very easy to do so — order it for continued usage.

Compared to a sales representative's call, this is inexpensive. Packing a sample with a regular customer's order, for example, can cost next to nothing and gain trial in an environment where there is an existing relationship.

If a product is new and meets existing needs in an unexpected way or if it meets needs of which prospects are unaware, sampling can be effective if the product is easy to understand and is delivered with a powerful demonstration.

The key to successful sampling with a new product is identifying the right individual. Create a compelling demonstration, build an excellent list, and visit every prospect.

Alternatively, the whole package can be delivered. A marketer might, for example, send a sample and an automated demonstration with a professionally produced videotape in a creative, bulky package to a short but well-qualified list.

A memorable automated demonstration doesn't have to be elaborate. In fact, the simpler the better. A fireproof fabric might come with a sample of the new material, the current material, an ash tray, a box of matches, and a book of campfire songs. Compared to a consumer mailer, this would be pricey. But consider the potential return and note that this kind of sample/demonstration mailing will certainly cost less than making calls on every prospect. It may even have a better chance than a personal demonstration of being seen by the right person. Make an honest evaluation of return on promotional investment (ROPI); the results may be surprising.

Heavy machinery, new processes, and services such as consulting defy sampling. Nevertheless, creative demonstrations can go a long way toward making a sale. Likewise, samples of results could be sent to prospects.

To promote a laser drill that cuts difficult metals without raising a burr, for example, send a piece of metal with a clean laser-cut hole in one end and a sloppy hole cut the old way in the other end. To emphasize the bottom-line benefits, include the deburring tool and five one-dollar bills the prospect would have to spend to have the hole finished.

Before closing this section, note again that the purpose of sales promotion in business-to-business marketing generally isn't to make the immediate sale. It is to influence a step in the buying cycle and ultimately define the outcome. A successful sample or demonstration, particularly with expensive products, will result in an invitation to make a presentation. Therefore, as always, follow-up is the most important part of the promotion.

Couponing.

Type of product:	Consumables
Type of sales force:	Primarily dealer, mail order
Delivery:	Mail, trade show, representative, POP
Where influential:	Early in simple cycles
Effect:	Moves product, gains trial

As in the consumer world, discount coupons can be used with some products to boost sales in the short term, gain trials, and build or rebuild a customer base. Coupons are an excellent means of cross-merchandising across a product line, as well.

Of course, we're talking about low-priced products available through third-party distribution, such as office and cleaning supplies, in which a traditional retail model applies. And, as with consumer products, there are caveats. Don't let coupons erode the company's image. Don't train buyers to wait for coupons instead of paying the regular price.

Refunds and Rebates.

Type of product:	Consumables, light equipment
Type of sales force:	Dealer, mail order
Delivery:	Mail, trade show, representative, POP
Where influential:	Early and midway through in simple cycles
Effect:	Moves product, gains trial

Refunds and rebates are used primarily as temporary price incentives. Personal computers and peripherals are often sold in this way, as are other kinds of office equipment and hand tools. Business buyers can be motivated through such promotions to buy now rather than later, which allows a company to help turn the inventory at its distributors. This support can enhance a company's relationship with dealers, clear the channel for a new product, and boost sales for a given quarter.

With this kind of consumer-style promotion, telling customers about the offer can be just as important as the offer itself.

In addition to advertising, a promotion marketer should consider providing point-of-purchase displays and otherwise merchandising the campaign to more compellingly lead the customer to the decision. The main reasons for supporting dealers in refund or rebate promotions — or any promotion, for that matter — are twofold. First, a marketer retains control over the product's and the company's image.

Second, it will help the promotion work harder for the marketer and the distributor.

Direct rebates and refunds can appear to be of questionable integrity on big contracts for capital investments and large orders of consumables. And they can be quite expensive. Therefore, within the context of direct sales, rebates and refunds are often given as credit against accessories, support services, upgrades and the like.

Premiums and Premium Packs.

Type of product:	Consumables, capital investments
Type of sales force:	Dealer, direct sales
Delivery:	Personal
Where influential:	Early in simple cycles; as part of an ongoing relationship in capital equipment and simple cycles
Effect:	Can stimulate a sale, general goowill

Because buyers are professionals, premiums should be relevant and business oriented. This is a more flexible constraint than it may appear to be. A premium could be anything from a storage box for a new product to a no-cost/low-cost service agreement upgrade to go with a new printer.

If the premium is for the buyer's personal use at work, it should also be modest (obviously inexpensive, though never of low quality). Many companies have strict policies about gifts from suppliers, and an exceptionally nice premium may well become a liability.

With direct sales, this kind of promotion is limited in effectiveness. Products, such as production machinery, supply contracts, insurance, and consulting, are bought as needed and may not be needed very often. Prospects are not usually free to initiate negotiations just because a company is bundling accessories, services, and support equipment with its product.

Contests, Games, and Sweepstakes.

Type of product:	Any
Type of sales force:	Dealer, direct sales
Delivery:	Personal
Where influential:	With sales representatives and dealer employees
Effect:	Improved productivity and morale

In business-to-business promoting, contests, games, and sweepstakes are more often used to motivate the sales force. In fact, they are often quite effective, particularly when the prize is merchandised. For example, making an event out of the award presentation, providing a plaque as a permanent record of achievement, and getting the representative's picture in the local paper all add to the effectiveness of this promotion.

After all, the sales representative's life is a life of hard work and rejection. Contests, games, and sweepstakes provide a vehicle for the absolutely necessary recognition and encouragement required to maintain sales force morale — one of the keys to success. Performance-based contests can be used to achieve specific business goals, games can ensure that marketing materials are examined, and perhaps an occasional sweepstakes can serve as morale-building fun.

Should a promotion manager elect to attempt this sort of promotion with customers, he or she should be sure the prize and communications support the product's and the company's image. Just as important is sensitivity to the buyer's position. Accepting a valuable prize may not be allowed. Vacations are even more troublesome. Sending the buyer to Hawaii for two weeks, for example, is exciting but the buyer may not want to appear so expendable that he or she can disappear for half a month without negative effects.

Continuity Promotions.

Type of product:	Consumables, services
Type of sales force:	Dealer, direct sales
Delivery:	Automated in invoicing systems
Where influential:	During usage, repurchase path; early in simple cycles
Effect:	Product/brand loyalty — saves cost of getting a new customer; provides incentive for customer to switch to your product or company

Business-to-business marketing has given us what is perhaps the best known and most elegantly engineered continuity program running today: the frequent flier award. It has built brand loyalty in what has largely become a commodity market, and it has turned a liability into an asset by filling seats that would have probably flown empty anyway.

Business market retailers can run similar promotions to good effect. If an office supply store competes with another one nearby, corporate frequent-shopper accounts can build loyalty. If products are sold through a catalog, continuity programs are a good way to distinguish a product line.

One must be careful, however, not to over-reward customers who were loyal all along and are unlikely to switch to another vendor. All that happens then is cutting the profits.

Brand loyalty is difficult and sometimes expensive to cultivate, but it is extremely valuable. Continuity programs that pay off in discounts or appropriate premiums are among the simplest value-adds to implement — and among the easiest for a customer to appreciate.

POP and Merchandising.

Type of product:	Consumables, light equipment

Type of sales force:	Dealers
Delivery:	Personal visit, mail
Where influential:	On end-customers at the beginning of the cycle; on dealers as part of a relationship
Effect:	Stimulates interest in end-customers; demonstrates support for dealers

We've already touched upon this topic in discussions of refund and premium promotions. Traditional devices emphasizing a product and/or promotion should be developed for retail locations when a promotion is being run. The need for support materials goes beyond the retail environment, however.

In direct sales of major systems, services, capital equipment, and other products, the point of purchase is the conference room where the presentations and the negotiations occur. This leads to the next promotion topic.

Collateral and Presentation Materials.

Type of product:	Capital investments
Type of sales force:	Direct
Delivery:	Sales representative, mail
Where influential:	Throughout complex cycle
Effect:	Physical manifestation of brand image; assist customer in making internal presentations; provide reference for customer and representative

Collateral materials serve several purposes. They provide a reference for a prospect to peruse after the rep is gone. They provide a presentation tool for the prospect to use when taking the product up to his or her boss. They can be used to open a dialog with a prospect or as fulfillment to a direct response ad.

A sales representative will have uses for it as well. If a product line is extensive or complex, a good brochure will provide a quick refresher or primer for representatives who may have lost track of the benefits of a particular product. A representative may also use a new piece of collateral as a reason to visit a prospect.

The return on investment for collateral and presentation materials is difficult, if not impossible, to calculate. Yet their impact is palpable. A representative and a company can lose credibility, often with the result that the marketers have to work harder than the competition to be convincing. The easiest way to understand this is to compare collateral materials to clothes. A sales rep would never make a presentation in an ill-fitting, wrinkled suit — even though the facts are the same and there's nothing actually wrong with the outfit. Collateral materials, like clothing, make an impression that can have an unconscious but very strong impact.

Public Relations.

Type of product:	Any
Type of sales force:	Any
Delivery:	Media + newsletter
Where influential:	Throughout complex cycle
Effect:	Understanding and credibility

Public relations, or PR, in business-to-business marketing takes at least two shapes. When a product is released, there is often a press conference for the vertical publications and perhaps the general business press. If a press conference isn't appropriate, a press release is prepared and distributed to relevant publications. The purpose is to generate some coverage of the company's offerings.

More important to sales promotion is the magazine article that appears in the so-called trade press. One type of article features case histories of customers who are pleased with a given product, customers who have used a product in a new way or under extraordinarily difficult circumstances, or customers who have had some sort of problem that couldn't be solved any other way. In another type of article, one of the company's engineers works with a writer to tell the story of a recent breakthrough or insight. This would run in the technical publications that serve a particular industry. These articles can be prepared by in-house PR staff or a PR agency, which will also be responsible for making sure they are published.

The purpose of both types of articles is to gain awareness, or share of mind, in the important decision influencers. One of the most significant benefits is credibility. Even though the marketer basically wrote the article — and the prospects know this — seeing the story in print is often more compelling than seeing it in an ad or brochure.

To get the most out of PR stories, one should make sure to get massive quantities of reprints. Include them in fulfillment packages. Send them to customers whenever a new one is prepared.

Considering the prestige and credibility gained by running a story as an article and the possibilities for merchandising that article for a long time thereafter, PR is generally a good investment. Less quantifiable than other promotional investments, its impact, particularly when there's an ongoing stream of articles, can be great.

Direct Response Advertising.

Type of product:	Any
Type of sales force:	Direct, dealer, telemarketing
Delivery:	Media
Where influential:	Beginning of complex and simple cycles

Effect: Identify sales leads; gain greater
                                     understanding

Direct response advertising is one of the most powerful tools available to the business marketer. There are a number of reasons for this.

The main reason is that it's probably the most cost-effective way there is to make contact with relatively well-qualified prospects. Business publications targeted at highly specific industries, or even segments of industries, are avidly read by people who may become buyers of a product or service.

With the right creative, business-to-business direct response can be doubly cost-effective. First, it puts the message in front of a large mass of potential prospects — generally far more than one individual could possibly discover and cold call alone. Second, prospects will qualify themselves by responding to an offering only if it's relevant to their immediate needs; consequently, leads will be of higher quality and more likely to be worth the cost and effort of follow-up.

One estimate states that the average industrial salesperson in the United States spends something like 80 percent of his or her time servicing existing customers, 15 percent doing administrative work, and 5 percent or less —about 20 minutes a day — looking for new business. Because the five to 10 minutes it takes to confirm a lead over the phone comes out of that 20 minutes, it's important to design an ad to do as much of the qualifying up front as possible. This means that the best ad won't be the one that yields the greatest response. It will be the one that yields the best leads (the ones that lead to sales).

Most prospects at this point are usually just qualifying a potential source; therefore a call might be inappropriate or unwelcome under some circumstances. Therefore, direct mail's impact on the customer derives to some extent from the effectiveness of the fulfillment collateral materials.

Speaking of follow-up, it is important to respond in some way to everyone who responds to an ad and to do it fast. These are warm — sometimes hot — prospects, and this is a company's first opportunity to impress them with its service.

Also, keeping a record of the respondents is valuable. Direct response advertising is an excellent way to build a mailing list with accurate names, titles, and addresses.

Direct Response Mail.

Type of product:	Any
Type of sales force:	Direct, dealer, telemarketing
Delivery:	Media
Where influential:	Beginning of complex and simple cycles
Effect:	Identify sales leads; follow-up leads

The same highly targeted publications that make such a good platform for direct response advertising can also be helpful in executing a highly targeted mailing. Sometimes, they'll sell a good mailing list. Sometimes, they'll refuse but mail the company's pieces as part of an insertion agreement. And sometimes another source must be found for names.

The obvious place to start looking is in the company's own records. Service agreements, contracts, and advertising respondents are all prospects for a mailing. There are also brokers who specialize in business lists.

Once again, one should try to avoid the temptation to keep the creative costs way down. Do the math, then do the best creative that is affordable. Possible techniques were discussed under "Sampling and Demonstration." A prospect may be a busy executive whose mail is screened by a secretary. If a piece is sent in a large box, it may well get past that secretary. If the presentation is spectacular, the executive may act on the message or see that it gets into the right hands.

Also, the experience should be memorable, perhaps by including something such as a business or Rolodex card. The recipient may not have any present need of the services, but if the company makes a splash and provides an easy way to contact it, the chance for a sale is born, when and if the need should arise.

Newsletters.

Type of product:	Capital investments
Type of sales force:	Direct
Delivery:	Media
Where influential:	Usage/repurchase phases of complex cycles
Effect:	Maintain awareness; gain greater understanding; enhance professional relationships; enhance image

As you will recall, one of the general distinctions of business-to-business marketing is that prospects are intensely interested in useful solutions when there is a need and not at all interested when there isn't.

Therefore, even the best prospects will throw away promotions and skip ads most of the time. However, there are two strategies for dealing with this.

One strategy is to make ads and mailings as irresistible as possible and to run them as often as calculations indicate that the company can wisely afford to do it.

Another strategy is for a company to publish a newsletter for its own customers and prospects. The advantage of this approach is that it can build and maintain share of mind with the target. When the need for that company's solution arises, calling the company will then be the obvious course of action. The newsletter can also publish ads for various offerings in the product line, as well as complementary offerings from other companies. All in all, a good newsletter can give a company a high profile where it counts most — right in the prospect's office.

The disadvantage of publishing a newsletter is that it had better be a good one or it will be seen as just another form of direct mail advertising and will be thrown out. So let's look at what a good newsletter requires.

First and foremost, a newsletter demands quality editorial content. This doesn't necessarily mean the best writing that's ever been inked, but it does mean content that has some value to the reader. A company might run stories about the amazing things some of its customers are accomplishing with its products, solutions to problems that the products aren't generally known for solving, or little-known tips about the business. A newsletter can include book reviews or serial condensations or even run abstracts of articles printed in other publications (as long as permission is obtained to use anything that's been printed elsewhere). Another source of editorial content is the readers themselves. Invite submissions. Start a controversy and encourage them to write. Commission articles or editorials from luminaries in the field, such as editors, engineers, and business leaders. Newsletter editors can use their imagination.

Quality production is almost as important as content. A newsletter doesn't have to be a glossy four-color magazine, but it does have to be well designed, professional in appearance, and grammatically correct.

INCREMENTAL ANALYSIS

The most important single message in this chapter is a rather obvious but often overlooked fact: Promotional activities are investments, not expenses. The dollars that are spent in those areas should be expected to perform as well as the dollars that are invested in any other activity.

Return on promotional investment (ROPI) is not a simple calculation, but it is essential in order to make promotions work hardest while conserving resources.

First, one should determine how much it costs to sell the product without a promotion. How much do cold calls cost, how many turn into leads, how much does it cost to qualify the leads, how much does it cost to give a presentation, how many qualified leads are converted into sales, and how much does it cost to pay and support the sales force for pursuing and winning new business?

This information, along with profits, will allow the marketer to figure the return on sales support investment.

As this information is being collected, the marketing manager will also discover how much time the salespeople have for prospecting and pitching business. (Most people are usually surprised at how little this is.) This will give a good idea of the baseline new business development capacity.

Then one should collect the numbers generated by the promotions that were run in the past. This is difficult, but by knowing how one's own market responds to given stimuli, the models will yield more bankable approximations.

Next is to figure out, for every promotion, how much the leads cost, how many were obtained in a given amount of time, what it cost to qualify them, and how many of them converted into sales.

Comparing the incremental profits with the incremental expenses gives a clear picture of what the promotion dollars are earning.

Evaluating this return for a break-even point can be complicated by the role the product is intended to play in the market and in the company's strategy. If the product is a once-in-a-lifetime purchase and it's the *only* product, your ROPI has to be higher than it would be for a sale that's intended to result in repeat orders.

To put it another way, sometimes a company is spending against a single sale and sometimes its promotional spending buys the company a long-term revenue stream. A good ROPI calculation needs to take this into account.

Unless a company has already set up for this kind of tracking, the results cannot be completely accurate or precise. What's more, promotion techniques are rarely used alone, so a truly scientific quantification is most likely an unrealistic goal.

And when it comes to predicting ROPI, a company will have to do some serious interpolation and make some assumptions. After all, an investment is always a risk.

But with the high-quality marketing information at the company's disposal — through vertical publications, industrial mailing lists, and customer information — it knows exactly who the best prospects are and has the means to reach them directly.

CONCLUSION

In the beginning of this chapter, we promised to show how to use the precision and power of sales promotion tools and techniques to solve complex business-to-business marketing problems.

To accomplish this, we first defined the business prospect as a person who wants a solution to a problem. The prospect's problem is to find a better way for the company to make or save money.

The marketer's job in sales promotion is to help that person understand that his or her company has the best possible solution available and that it perfectly fits the need within the given constraints.

We then presented a framework for analyzing challenges graphically. As a tool for visualizing the entire buying cycle of a product along with its assets and liabilities, graphic analysis allows a company to pinpoint its key challenges.

After this, we examined important sales promotion techniques and tools discussed in this book (as well as a few others) from a business-to-business perspective. We saw the relative power and precision of each, and noted appropriate roles and capabilities.

Finally, in order to refine the cost-effectiveness of business-to-business marketing activities, we proposed a general method for calculating the return on promotional investments. With such a calculation, a company is equipped to set an optimal budget or design a sales promotion program gaining the maximum impact from whatever budget is given. Sales promotion is an investment, and like any investment, its purpose is to yield a profitable return.

The tools and techniques of business-to-business sales promotion are among the most powerful marketing tools available. Use them.

Edward O'Meara is an Account Supervisor at Ogilvy & Mather, Los Angeles. Prior to that position he was Vice President, Marketing Services, at Food World Promotions, a promotion marketing agency for leading supermarket and convenience store chains. There he managed both the account services and marketing teams, guiding the Reggie Award-winning Frequent Buyer promotion at ACME Supermarkets in Philadelphia and directing the development of Win$A$Fortune, an electronic, interactive game concept.

O'Meara is active in the Promotion Marketing Association of America, serving on the Retailer-Manufacturer Partnerships committee. He received his B.A. from the University of Georgia and earned his M.S. at Northwestern University.

CHAPTER 25

FOOD RETAILING PROMOTION STRATEGY

OVERVIEW

Advertising and promotion techniques have deep roots in the food retailing industry. Retailers, both large and small, have long sought to lure consumers into their markets and to motivate the purchase of primary goods. The growth of global-scale packaged goods competition, the rapid entry of alternative food retailing formats, and the increasing need for consumer motivation have brought sales promotion into the foreground of modern food retailing.

Trade promotion spending by packaged goods marketers has increased dramatically over the past decade. Exhibit 25.1 shows the spending changes over an eight-year period.

The rise in trade promotion funding has given the packaged - goods sales force and its customers (food retailers) increasing power in determining promotional activity. As Exhibit 25.1 indicates, funds have been moved from the traditional "brand" side of the business to the "sales" side. Trade promotion funds take many forms, including both currency (tangible dollars) and noncurrency forms. The most popular are in the form of price reductions. Retail power has evolved as more trade promotion money is offered to food retailers in exchange for merchandising and in-store promotion support.

Food retailers must decide how best to use temporary price reductions (TPRs) and other trade promotion allowances to (a) set competitive prices for products, (b) determine the most effective use of store resources (especially print, circular, and electronic advertising; shelf space; and display space), and (c) drive consumer traffic into the store. This chapter outlines the marketing environment and the basic promotion decisions faced by food retailers to meet these three business objectives.

INTRODUCTION

Retail Decision Making. Food retailers are organized like most companies. The management of the organization is responsible for item selection, store site selection, advertising, marketing, purchasing, and other critical functions. There is usually a senior vice president of marketing, of finance, and of operations. Within the marketing group, functional executives manage the various merchandising, buying, and advertising departments.

Advertising and promotion are a merchandising function similar to grocery, produce, and meat buyers. Each functional department (meat, grocery, produce) will include category managers and/or buyers and a promotion manager. These persons are responsible for individual

EXHIBIT 25.1
PROMOTIONAL CATEGORY SPENDING BY PACKAGED GOODS
COMPANIES

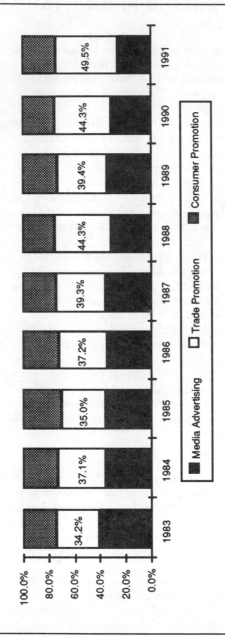

promotions on specific products or within categories. This is where many of the packaged goods trade promotions are analyzed. If these managers determine the right mix of incremental sales and profits on the item and within the category, they will recommend that the promotion be implemented. At the next level up, an executive will determine the overall store or chain marketing strategy. It is this strategic management level on which this chapter focuses.

Individual stores are staffed with managers and staff personnel whose responsibility it is to get product on the shelf and maintain the friendly atmosphere for customers to shop. Efficiency is a key criterion.

Generally speaking, food retailers resell packaged goods items. The marketing channel is represented by a simple diagram (see Exhibit 25.2). This diagram demonstrates the delivery of an item to the retailer at a given wholesale price (P_w), that is then offered to the consumer at a retail price (P_r).

Exhibit 25.3 demonstrates the modern retailing channel in which the manufacturer delivers the item to various retailers who then resell the item to the end consumers. Marketing investments are made both in the channel and outside the channel to improve the sell-through to end consumers.

Manufacturer Tactics: How to Gain More Retail Support Than Your Competitors. Manufacturers initiate a marketing "pull" strategy by communicating outside the sales channel directly with consumers through traditional advertising and promotion. The potential demand created by these promotions encourages retailers to support the product by ensuring adequate inventory levels, competitive price points, and merchandising support. To facilitate movement through the channel, the "push" element of the strategy, manufacturers may also offer a temporary price reduction (TPR) or other promotional incentive to integrate marketing efforts and maximize incremental sales to the retailer. Several tactics may be examined for better clarity.

Sales Channel "Push" Strategy:

- *Case purchase allowances:* A volume-based, monetary discount on purchases, typically requiring retail performance of advertising and merchandising support.
- *Slotting allowances:* A fee paid to offset the costs of obtaining new or additional shelf space within the store. These fees have been imposed as new product introductions and product line extensions continue their growth trends. The retail costs to be recovered by the fee include resetting the shelf, computer updating of the bar code and inventory tracking, and deleting existing items from that space.
- *Market development funds:* There are countless names for many incentive programs offered by manufacturers to increase retail commitments to their efforts. Sometimes they are also

EXHIBIT 25.2

EXHIBIT 25.3

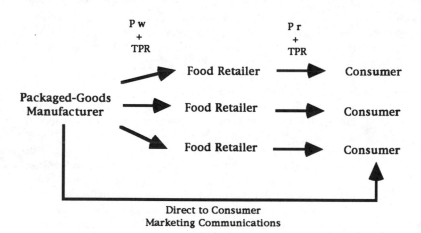

referred to as "street moneys." The noncommitted funds are available to regional or localized sales forces to accommodate special needs of the retailers in the market. Often, competitive pressures (such as local consumer brand preferences, or the use of the Brand Development Index [BDI] or the Consumer Development Index [CDI] in the market) are factors in the allocation and distribution of these moneys.

Consumer "Pull" Strategy:

- *Point-of-purchase displays:* Manufacturers may provide self-shipper units or collateral materials that create consumer attention and save retail labor costs. Retailers may also produce this material, either as part of their support or for a fee.
- *Special events and sweepstakes:* Consumer awareness and excitement may be developed through this tactic to promote incremental product purchases. These promotions also encourage retailers to support the product in terms of inventory maintenance and display to meet potential consumer demand.
- *Electronic couponing:* New hardware and software programs allow marketers to issue coupons to consumers based on the consumers' interests and purchasing decisions.
- *Database marketing and direct mail vehicles:* Using information from consumer letters, sweepstakes entries, and available databases, consumers likely to purchase the product are sent information and coupons to motivate product purchases.
- *In-store sampling and couponing:* Representatives located in the store hand out product samples and coupons and give product demonstrations.

Measurement of Successful Trade Promotion. The manufacturer both wants and needs retail "performance." This translates into discounts "passed on" to consumers in the form of lowered prices and visible promotional activity demonstrated in-store. Competitive pricing and supportive merchandising are the differentiating elements within successful retailer-manufacturer partnerships. The "brand" element is often a deteriorating consumer differentiating element.

Displays are large, standing areas within the store as end-of-aisle displays, "wing" or side displays, or stand-alone displays. Consumers have greater awareness of displayed or featured items and perceive that they are sale priced. This is the result manufacturers want. Merchandising variables are documented to increase sales that are more relative to other key variables, such as price, shelf signage, and feature advertising. Optimally, all elements are integrated, creating invisible interactions that geometrically increase sales volume.

The regulatory environment, primarily the Robinson-Patman Act and the Clayton Act, requires that manufacturers offer equal and proportionate prices and marketing allowances to all retail customers. It is the food retailer, then, that determines whether and how these funds are used to differentiate itself from the competition.

The Retail Dilemma: How to Take All Available Discounts and Promotional Offers? A TPR is offered to the retailer to offset advertising and promotion costs incurred by the retailer. Manufacturers want their promotional activity to receive the retail support they request. However, retailers carry 10,000 or more individual items, or stock-keeping units (SKUs). They can't afford to give all SKUs equal promotion and advertising support. Most stores have only 10 to 20 end-of-aisle displays on which to promote items.

Exhibit 25.4 illustrates the food retailer dilemma. In each category, there are dozens of manufacturers' brands, *all* offering trade promotion funds in the hopes of receiving retail advertising and promotion attention. Only four manufacturers are shown (this could represent one size and one flavor of one category, for example, 4.6 oz. of mint-flavored toothpaste).

Food retailers solve the problem by accepting all deals and compromising where necessary on performance. The number of outlets usually makes measuring performance difficult for manufacturer representatives. Retailers do what is possible to qualify for and receive all available funds. The balance of this chapter discusses how differentiation is made within their marketing framework.

EXHIBIT 25.4

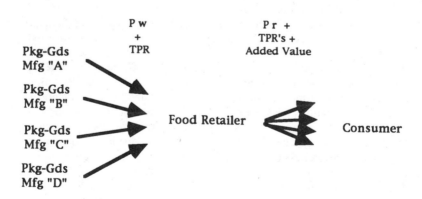

BASIC FOOD RETAILING STRATEGY

Food retailers have strategic objectives that drive their business. These strategic levers operate on a micro level.

Dimensions Affecting the Strategic Choice. The food retailer, like other corporate entities, must set its mission and outline its basic operating philosophies. The promotional elements then fall into place. Several different operating dimensions impact what type of promotion managers can use. Authors Scott Neslin and Robert Blattsberg have identified the primary dimensions affecting strategic choices in their book, *Sales Promotion: Concepts, Methods & Strategies* (1990, Prentice-Hall):

- Pricing
- Promotional level
- Customer service level
- Variety of product selection
- Number of specialty departments
- Convenience

These important elements determine the level and types of promotional activity that managers may embark upon. Retailers drive profits by the following methods:

- *Generating store traffic.* The more people in the store, the more total sales that are possible (assuming that average transaction stays constant). Higher revenues offset fixed operating costs, increasing profits.

- *Increasing the average transaction.* The total dollar volume sold in the shopping basket affects total revenue. The high fixed costs (and generally lower variable costs) of operations means that incremental consumer spending drives greater profits for a retailer.

- *Increasing gross profits.* Gross profits within certain departments (for example, deli or produce) have a dramatic effect on total profits within the store, dependent on each retailer's departmental strengths and weaknesses in the competitive set, and by local consumer demand elasticities for the department. Gross profits are more frequently measured at the category level. Category management activity focuses on total profit within a category (bar soap) and not directly on brand-specific sales (Ivory bar soap). This form of space, or shelf, management encourages managers to optimally sell product to consumers at the right price.

- *Quickly selling, or diverting, excess inventory.* Retailers may "forward-buy" inventory offered at promotional prices and then need to "turn" the inventory. Many products are date sensitive and need to be sold. Retail locations and warehouses are sensitive to space and inventory issues. Retailers use sophisticated financial models to determine how best to buy inventory and, in many cases, resell the inventory to other retailers who are unable to qualify for that particular discount. This may be due to either geographic or volume reasons. The largest national chains have moved toward centralized buying to maximize these buying efficiencies. This advantage may then be passed along to each of their "regional" divisions.

- *Enhancing store image.* Like consumers, retailers have different images, based on their consumer profile, locations, and product selection. These decisions may reflect the acceptance or rejection of curtailed promotional programs. Some retailers, for instance, will not allow manufacturer point-of-purchase (POP) material in their stores because of the resulting "circus-like" look of the combined materials of all manufacturers who wish to put up the POP.

- *Improving consumer price perceptions.* Retailers may choose to develop a certain price perception among consumers. This too affects the product choices, merchandising, and support decisions. The advertising may only affect those products that are on the consumer's regular shopping list (eggs, milk) and not other items that are less sensitive to consumers (pineapple juice, baking soda).

- *Fulfilling manufacturers' deal performance requirements.* Retailers who choose to accept all available deals may also minimize the support given to each. For example, competitive items may be both advertised and displayed, limiting the effect of the support.

- *Maximizing forward-buying of purchase deals offered by manufacturers.* Retailers may take advantage of manufacturers' deals by purchasing more supply than they know they would normally move during a promotion. They will carry this inventory beyond the promotion period, not buying the product in subsequent periods. The price spread (the difference between cost and retail price) is even greater during the post-promotion period if excess inventory purchased during the promotion remains for sale. Several retailers only purchase product on deal, switching among available brands in-store based on which product is on deal.

- *Defending against new market (retailer) entries.* When a new retailer, or alternative competing class of trade, enters the market, retail marketers notice and react. Complete changes in strategy have been noted recently as Wal Mart and Food Lion enter new marketing areas.

- *Matching retailer competitive pressures.* The market share leader may affect the reactions of retailers much the same way as new market entries.

Assessing the interactions of these strategic dimensions is often informal; senior management, to whatever degree, has developed an understanding of relevant dimensions and has made a decision to structure its marketplace positioning. It is important for marketers to understand these dimensions. They are indicators of promotional tactics that are in line with management's corporate strategy.

COMMUNICATIONS ISSUES

Developing retailer-to-consumer communications requires an understanding of several key issues. The number one issue is why consumers shop where they do. Is a food retailer a "brand" in and of itself, or is it simply a convenient location where consumers find the real "brands" they buy? The following discussion may help understand these issues.

Concentration of Volume at the Top. Food retailing volume is concentrated in fewer stores. There are approximately 170,000 stores generating $351 billion in sales, and 21 percent of the stores generate 73 percent of the total volume. The top 12,000 stores (8.5 percent of total) account for more than 50 percent of the volume. Fifty years ago the top three chains (12,000 stores) only accounted for less than 9 percent (8.5 percent) of the volume.

Volume is monitored in terms of all commodity volume (ACV). The most notable change in ACV share is for conventional grocery retailers. It has moved in the past 10 years from slightly more than 55 percent (55.2 percent) of all ACV to about 29 percent (28.6 percent). This decline is projected to continue. Store format changes not only affect the grocery competitive set but also the way in which suppliers and vendors interact with the trade channels.

The acquisition and consolidation of stores has had a great impact upon operations. As chains buy other store groups, they must deal with multiple operating systems and promotional strategies, especially computerized scanner systems. Often they are supporting as many as eight or 10 different front-end, point-of-sale (POS) systems. This makes it difficult to operate consistently from a marketing view. Most computer systems will have as many as 163 fields for each product or activity that must be able to cross these different POS platforms. This is a major problem for retail operations.

Newer operations, such as Wal Mart, have decided advantages. Their success lies in their power, both real and perceived. These operators have had the opportunity to start "fresh" and learn from others' mistakes. These are the result of consolidations, changing and merging of diverse formats, and operating systems. Wal Mart has uniform operations. In addition, their pricing strategies — primarily, every day low pricing (EDLP) — have closely followed consumers' attitudes in the declining economic climate. Finally, they have consciously utilized the latest in technology to create effective distribution centers.

Consumers' Shopping Characteristics. It is estimated that 50 percent of consumers don't even know the price that they paid for an item, even moments after picking it up off the shelf, even though consumers believe that they are price conscious. A study by Longman-Moran on consumer demand concluded that consumers have a pricing "zone of indifference" for many product purchases. Provided an item is priced within this zone, the consumer will purchase it without further price shopping. In fact, the average time spent before picking up the item was a scant 12 seconds. In this study, 61 percent of customers thought that the item they had just chosen was on special, but it wasn't.

Consumers' shopping habits have also changed. Less in total dollars is spent on food purchased for at-home use. In addition, the average shopping trip lasts only 22 minutes. A 1990 study by the Point-of-Purchase Advertising Institute (POPAI) reiterates this trend and takes the point further by segmenting the audience according to the purpose of the shopping trip to see how that affects the amount of the store shopped. This is shown in Table 25.1.

Consumers who are pressed for time are difficult to reach. Shopping trips are more focused, so marketers must fight to get shoppers moving through more of the store. Food retailers and brand marketers alike have learned to cater to shrinking market segments. New products, more shelf space, direct marketing, and special amenities have been adapted to the marketing communications mix to reach changing consumers. This is clearly important as consumers become more information driven and more likely to experiment with new products.

Media Changes. In 1980, network television reached 90 percent of consumers. In 1990 that figure fell to 65 percent, and the downward trend continues as cable and other alternative media vie for consumers. At retail, expenditures have changed also. Today approximately 30 percent of the marketing budget is spent on alternative (targeted) media, moving away from television and newspaper media. Some chains, such as Lucky's and Von's in California and Dominick's in Illinois, are

TABLE 25.1
SHOPPING ACTIVITY

Purpose	Time shopping (minutes)	% of store shopped
Stock-up	38	58%
Routine	23	44%
Fill-in	13	27%

Legend:
Stock-up shoppers purchasing 60%+ of total groceries.
Routine shoppers purchasing 20–60% of groceries.
Fill-in shoppers purchasing less than 20%.

exploring direct and saturation mailing programs that reach a greater share of the consumers.

Advertising Age reported that the southern California daily newspapers will lose more than $350,000 in ads this year alone and approximately $3 million in 1992 if the test proves successful. The goal, said one Lucky's executive, is to "create faster information flow."

Interestingly, Gene Hoffman (former president of Kroger Co. and former chairman of Super Valu Wholesale Food Co.) characterizes the opportunity for retailers to be the leaders toward integration of the marketing communications mix:

> Just close your eyes a moment and envision the Safeway Selling System, or Kroger Communication Central, or K-Mart In-Store Media Network, or, more cryptically, the Price Clubber, or "Sam Says," the Wal Mart Selling System.

The key implication is that media, as well as the marketer's attention, is continuing to move in-store.

STRATEGIC DECISION MAKING

Four Basic Food Retailing Strategies. Food retailers have industry terms for the four primary strategies. Strategies are visible in the product pricing structure of the retailers. Furthermore, each strategy may use various promotional tactics to promote products or motivate consumers to purchase items. An April 1992 study by *Progressive Grocer* asked both chain and independent executives to indicate their pricing strategy. Exhibit 25.5 demonstrates their responses.

Every Day Low Prices. The growing, if not dominant, trend in food retailing today is every day low pricing (EDLP). In perfect situations, this strategy reflects a cost leadership position. The retailer accepts lower gross margins, hoping to drive volume through the store. This general price theory follows a supply-demand equation that at different price intervals, different quantities will be sold. The mistake many retailers make is that price promotion is the most easily duplicated method of promotion, and it usually leads to a downward spiraling in prices within a given market. If retailer A lowers prices by 1 cent, then retailer B lowers them 2 cents, and so on. Eventually, many retailers within the market will realize no dramatic volume increases but very dramatic gross margin decreases. Prices will rise until a satisfactory equilibrium is reached.

However, price promotion works especially well for some retail organizations. These operators realize that to make a cost leadership strategy work, you must have the operational and buying efficiencies to survive at the lowest margins within a competitive set. Retailers with the lowest operating costs, including promotion and advertising costs, create lower price points, thereby influencing certain consumer

EXHIBIT 25.5
WHICH BEST DESCRIBES YOUR PRICING STRATEGY?

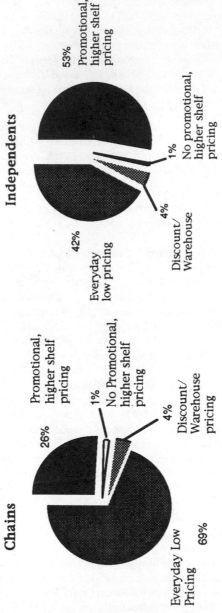

Source: Progressive Grocer 59th Annual Report of the Grocery Industry,
"Surviving the Squeeze," April 1992, p. 22.

segments. These retailers predominantly offer only price promotion in-store; product selection is limited to gain greater buying and stocking efficiencies, and there are longer "feature price" cycles. Profits in the store are volume based.

Advertising, if it is done, is image oriented; (often the CEO of the chain guaranteeing the lowest prices in the market.) Superior distribution centers, using the latest technology, keep operating expenses below the average. Older retailers who have not leveraged their capital in distribution have a difficult time competing head-to-head with EDLP operators. Successful examples combine centralized management and buying structures with national distribution and purchasing power.

This market leader philosophy requires a serious commitment to be profitable in the long term. While EDLP retailers appear to have a strategic advantage during poor economic conditions, this business is volume driven requiring larger shopping-basket totals. As consumers purchase fewer impulse items, the transaction size and store volume shrink, negatively affecting the total gross margin.

Club and Warehouse Formats. An astounding explosion of club stores and warehouse outlets has occurred in the early 1990s. Profits are volume based. Membership fees are charged to small businesses or other organizations to help cover overhead costs. Shoppers are encouraged to also do their home and business shopping at the locations. Business shoppers "feel" as though they are purchasing food for the home at specially reduced prices for businesses. This is a special advantage of the club stores.

Product is usually offered in unusual sizes and multipacks. In this respect, traditional retailers complain that unfair compromises are made by manufacturers that serve this market. These food and nonfood retailers are bare-bones operations. They enjoy very low distribution and operating costs. No traditional promotion or advertising is done, and a limited selection of items is carried. Item selection changes over time, based on available manufacturer deals. Items are selected for quick sales turns and impulse purchases.

High-Low Pricing. The high-low supermarket operator is very promotion oriented. This retailer offers consumers added value through deep discounts on selected items, usually high-interest, high-turn items. These "loss leaders" are sold at or slightly below cost to drive consumer interest. "Losses" are made up through higher-priced items within the consumer selection. Food retailers offer consumers the widest variety of items, including nonfood items. The goal is to create a one-stop shopping environment.

High-low retailers tend to be regional in nature, with a high concentration of locations. Many are independently owned and operated, are part of a national wholesale organization, or are a regional chain. The chain stores are larger, with suburban locations; whereas the independent may be located anywhere, in sizes varying from very small to very large. Advertising reflects values and services that the retailer offers.

In addition to higher levels of service, these retail operators also offer additional conveniences including bank locations, pharmacies, delicatessens, full meat and fish service, and video rental departments. The convenience factor, in both location and service, develops store loyalty among consumers. These additional sections have higher costs, as well as higher margins, requiring more stringent controls over the merchandising and gross profit mix of the entire store. There is also greater promotional freedom, using various department strengths to drive consumers into the store.

Limited Selection, Private-Label Retailing. Finally, there are limited selection, private-label retailers. Selling only key products allows retailers to increase their "support" of key brands, to drive greater volume purchases of those products, and to focus merchandising on private-label products. This format is popular in Europe where retail shelf space is scarce. Many retail private-label products sell better than the globally advertised brands. Both Sainsbury and Marks & Spencer have built strong consumer franchises with this strategy. In the United States and Canada, retailers, such as Wal Mart and the Loblows companies, have offered private-label products (Sam's Choice and President's Choice, respectively) in volatile categories such as soft drinks; and the private-label brands have beaten both Coke and Pepsi in consumer taste tests!

Food retailers are becoming more informed regarding product movement. With this knowledge comes the power to remove slow "turning" products off the shelf and increase the sales of preferred items. The category management revolution is even sparking some retailers to take more drastic measures. *Supermarket News* reported that Publix Supermarkets in Florida has elected to carry only one brand of paper products throughout the chain! Pundits report that this is just the beginning as food retailers struggle to find ways to improve both operating and promotional efficiencies in the competitive environment.

STRATEGIC TACTICS IN FOOD RETAILING

Third-party marketing services firms have long sold self-contained promotional tactics and concepts to retail executives. The changing financial conditions in food retailing, however, have led many food retailers to develop internal departments to both develop and administer profit-driven sales promotions. Whether done internally or bought from an outside supplier, promotional tactics have followed several conceptual categories that aim to produce increases in traffic, sales, image, or profits.

The development of some internal promotions, such as continuity programs, is an efficient practice for some retailers. In others — such as frequency marketing, games, and tape programs — there are definite advantages to engaging third parties to operate the programs. In all instances, proper legal counsel should first be sought. Federal and state governments have long monitored food retailing promotions for anticompetitive and predatory violations.

The *Progressive Grocer* study requested information on which promotional tactics food retailers used in support of their pricing and merchandising strategy. No cross-tabulation between the stated pricing strategy (see Exhibit 25.5) and the promotional tactics used was done in the study. Table 25.2 is consistent with expectations from the other information.

Promotional tactics have varying objectives and expected results. An annual study by the Association of Retail Marketing Services (ARMS) and Cornell University follows supermarket promotions as a guide to industry users. One measurement they use is retail managers' perceived effectiveness of promotional tactics. Table 25.3 lists the percentage of respondents reporting positive effectiveness.

Another measure of the study was to evaluate the cost of promotions as a percentage of sales during the promotional period. Table 25.4 gives the cost breakdown.

The study's authors note that there is a significant change in this spending over time. The average cost in the 1989 study was 1.73 percent, and in 1987 it was 1.54 percent. A brief discussion of each method may better define and illuminate the tactics and their impact on food retailing.

TABLE 25.2
WHICH PROMOTIONS DID YOU USE IN 1991?

% Using	Chain	Independent
Product sampling	94%	84%
Continuity programs	62	50
Theme sales	54	50
Bonus (double) coupons	44	41
Half-price sales	51	33
Register tape plans	54	30
Sweepstakes	22	16
Games	15	17
Frequent shopper programs	14	12
Electronic merchandising	12	2
None of these	0	4

TABLE 25.3
WHAT ARE THE MOST EFFECTIVE TYPES OF PROMOTIONS?

	Increase customer count	Increase transaction size	Maintain customer loyalty	Permanent new customers	Please most customers	Overall cost-effectiveness
Piece-A-Week Continuity	27.7	43.6	31.3	25.0	35.6	36.4
Tape-Plan Continuity	18.5	33.9	29.8	25.0	18.6	25.5
Frequent Shopper or Stamp Plan	10.8	12.9	20.9	25.0	16.9	12.7
Games	29.2	1.6	6.0	5.0	5.2	10.9
Sweepstakes	4.6	3.2	4.5	5.0	6.8	1.8
Other*	9.2	4.8	7.5	15.0	16.9	12.7

*Some of the "other" items listed were: Free Library Books, Community Services, Dollar Days, Apples for Students, and Double Coupons

TABLE 25.4
WHAT IS THE PROMOTION COST AS A PERCENTAGE OF SALES
DURING THE PROMOTIONAL PERIOD?

Low	0.03%
High	7.00%
Average	1.27%
Median	0.50%

Price Promotion. Price promotion takes many forms besides straight EDLP. Many retailers use price promotion as a way to drive consumer traffic. The advertising communications are used to alert consumers to the promotion. Events, seasons, departments, anniversaries, or any number of factors can be the "excuse" for the price specials.

Price promotion is usually considered in terms of "markdowns," or reduced prices from the normal retail price. Manufacturers allowances can be used to fund these markdowns, or they may be an existing part of the retail advertising budget. For example, a grocery chain may allocate the equivalent of 1 to 2 percent of its estimated sales for a featured item price promotion. This amount would be allocated among a fixed number of items on promotion for that period. Typically, these are the items featured in the advertising circular and in any electronic price-and-item commercials during the promotion period.

The most consumer-sensitive items (for example, eggs, milk, cereal, cola) would have the deepest markdowns and the largest amount of advertising and merchandising support. The next tier of items would have medium levels of markdowns and smaller amounts of advertising support. In this way, a price impression would be left for consumers on strategic items. A good mix of price-promoted items will encourage the shopper to travel through more of the store.

It is hoped that consumers will complete their normal shopping trip during that visit. Some items, such as cola, which are consistently priced below cost, lose consumer price perceptions and make it difficult to sell at a regular price. Extended markdowns, then, may have a negative impact on brand value perceptions.

Interestingly, research indicates that consumers are not as price sensitive as one would think. Consumers surveyed in the store at the time they select items typically do not know the price marked for the item. This is the strength of a high-low strategy using price promotion: Consumers perceive that all prices are low, and thus they do not comparison shop as closely as they think they do by looking at an ad circular.

Coupon and price promotions can give even the best food retailers nightmares. Heavy coupon users are very aware consumers. These shoppers are highly likely to cherry-pick many stores looking for the best price values at many chains. For high-low strategists, the risk is that consumers won't complete the shopping trip at their store. This creates lower actual sales against projected markdowns.

Stamp Plans. The "grandfather" of food retailing sales promotion is the stamp plan. Stamps have been around since 1890, when Edward Schuster of Gimbles began issuing Blue Stamps. The simple concept is that consumers receive stamps in exchange for a prescribed amount of purchase (usually one stamp for every one- or five-dollar purchase). As stamps are saved and put into a "saver book," they accumulate more value. Consumers can then redeem them for gifts, available through a catalog or at a gift center. This was a way for shoppers to "obtain" items from the "wish" book catalogs, at no direct cost to them, besides their shopping loyalty. One of the oldest and largest stamp companies, the Sperry & Hutchinson Company, is still in existence today.

Stamp programs have a simple goal — consumer loyalty. The more often you shop and the more you buy at the merchant, the more return value you receive through the stamps. The cost to operate the program is less than the actual value of the gift redeemed, and it represents a portion of the profits generated by the retailer through incremental sales of products to the consumer.

One of the factors that negatively affected the stamp industry was widespread imitation. Several large companies, including Top Value, Blue Chip, and Gold Bond Stamps, sold most food retailers a version of this stamp plan. Without the exclusive draw, consumers had difficulty choosing one program over the other. The core purpose of the promotion (exclusivity) became an insidious contradiction in terms.

A second factor was the "devaluation" of the gifts available. It took increasingly more stamps to receive gifts that were worth less. Both factors are lessons the airline industry has learned with their frequent flier programs.

Traditionally, stamp plans cost a retailer 2 percent of the gross sales. With low operating margins, this was a good strategy for food retailers. This was a fixed cost. In today's financial environment, in which retail price competition has reduced operating profits to less than 2 percent of sales, this type of program is no longer as cost-effective or realistic. Success is dependent upon gaining incremental market share and an incremental portion of the shoppers' total food dollars to offset any "cost" programs.

Frequency Programs. An offshoot of the stamp plans is the more recent frequency program. The stamp companies realized that the cost of their programs became too high to effectively operate. The concept was revitalized in the late 1970s and early 1980s. Rather than redeem stamps for items in a catalog, loyalty could result in lower prices in the supermarket. "Cash dividends" were offered by the Gold Bond Stamp Company as a way to differentiate their stamp product and lower the cost of the program. By offering discounts on existing product, often already marked down in price, food retailers were able to "control" their ad-featured markdowns. To qualify for dramatically low prices on featured items, customers had to shop frequently.

The most successful version of this concept was offered by Food World, Inc. Its "Frequent Buyer Savings Plan" won a PMAA Reggie Award for its work with Acme Supermarkets. In this program, consumers could save their Frequent Buyer "coupons" to be redeemed on selected high-turnaround grocery items for reduced prices (the average value was $.75), or they could be redeemed at over 4,700 associate merchants for values ranging from $1.00 to $25.00 per filled Frequent

Buyer "chek."

Acme gained more than two market share points in a highly competitive market, with no competitors able to match the value offered in the consumers' program. More than 90 percent of Acme's customers participated in the program, and more than 70 percent of all coupons issued were redeemed. The 26-week promotion was extended to two years of operation.

Several companies have attempted to conduct variations on this concept electronically. The programs work like this. Consumers are issued some identifying card (for example, a bar-coded magnetic strip card, or a card with a computer chip). These cards are read by special equipment at the point-of-sale system. Points are then issued and stored for each customer, based either on total purchases or on specific item purchases. These points can then be redeemed for gift merchandise or for reduced prices on future purchases. As consumer purchasing habits are tracked, special incentive offers for other brands can be issued. Monthly point statements are made available to consumers through either direct mail or some other in-store method.

Most visible has been Citicorp POS, a division of the banking conglomerate. Also involved have been Sperry & Hutchinson Company; Food World, Inc.; and a partnership between Procter & Gamble, A.C. Nielsen, Schlumberger, GTE, and others called The Vision Value Club. All of these programs have been tested in various markets around the United States and the Caribbean.

The key variables for electronic frequency program success are developing consumer interaction and managing the hard fixed cost of installation and technology. In stamp programs, food retailers simply handed out stamps. The new programs require consumers to present a personalized membership card, which the cashier then must activate with the on-line electronic frequency system. The companies "selling" these electronic programs must fund them from outside the food retailer (remember the cost problem with stamps?).

Most program funding has come from packaged goods companies that are willing to test the programs as direct-to-consumer advertising and promotion vehicles to drive incremental cases on specific brands and from start-up capital raised by the firms. The long-range future of these programs is promising as technology costs come down and consumers become more willing to participate and are more aware of their total shopping savings. The interactive nature of the technology offers direct marketing approaches that are much more efficient, and notably more effective, than are otherwise available.

Continuity Programs. Years ago, continuity programs were the way that many Americans "bought" their dinnerware, glassware, silverware, encyclopedias, luggage, towels, and pots and pans. With a minimal purchase, consumers could receive a free "piece-a-week" completer set. The idea was to channel consumers to spend a given amount each week in the store for a certain time period. Continuities are used heavily by food retailers at all retail levels, large and small, sophisticated and simplistic.

This is an inexpensive way to reward consumers with an added-value item. Most retailers purchase these items at a relatively low cost and receive return "guarantees" from the suppliers should all of the inventory not sell. The 1992 ARMS study noted that 97 percent of continuities have these return privileges (up from 91 percent in 1989), and that there is an average return of 15 percent of the product (up from around 10 percent in 1989). Some large chain groups will also "caravan" the product through one division and then another, to better monitor and lower their inventory levels. Most who go to this trouble also source and purchase the materials directly from the manufacturer to lower costs even further. This type of promotion serves for some companies as an additional profit item and not simply a promotion.

An example of one nonprofit continuity program is the Olympic Fund-Raising Committee Pin Set, licensed by the United States Olympic Committee through Sports Publishing Network. Each week several pins were available for $.99 with an item purchase. Each pin represented one of the Olympic events. The promotion raised funds for Olympic athletes and gave participating retailers the opportunity to seize consumer attention during the 1992 Olympics. Sponsoring packaged goods companies received in-store and media attention through the promotion (see Exhibit 25.6).

Tape Saver Plans. Tape programs are similar to frequency programs, but they are operated without a third-party apparatus (for example, stamps and stamp machines). The concept encourages customers to save the retailer's register tapes to qualify for special prizes or, more commonly, for donations to local schools. The most popular program is the Apples for Students program. School groups encourage parents to save the register tapes as a group. With different levels of register tape totals, the groups earn "money" for free Apple computers.

Other programs, such as the popular one from Motivational Technologies Company called "Upgrade," allow groups to save register tapes to purchase anything the group needs from band uniforms to school gymnasium equipment. Food retailers realize the power that local fund-raising programs like these offers. It truly generates traffic and sales when a minister or PTA president gets up to speak, reminding everyone to shop at a particular retailer because that retailer is helping the group to fund its programs. The public relations benefit and community goodwill that is developed are key benefits.

Like other programs before them, all of these programs have a high cost associated with them. Most programs hit the 0.5 to 1.0 percent of sales level. Likewise, the cost to monitor and administer the program is heavy. Many retailers, however, have generated such high volumes of incremental business and millions of dollars in free adver-

EXHIBIT 25.6

tising that they continue to offer these programs each fall as the back-to-school drive begins. They also find the cost of third-party adminis-tration is worth it.

Games, Contests, and Sweepstakes. Games of chance and other forms of contests fit well into retail promotions. Food retailers have long used *events*, such as holidays and grand openings, to drive con-sumers to the market. Anything to create excitement generates traffic to the store. But balloons and clowns aren't enough to compel time-pressed, working consumers to change their routine shopping habits. Food retailers have had to up the promotional ante.

One tactic already discussed was stamp plans. As that tactic struggled to differentiate retailers, the new goal was to offer consumers an alternative to trading stamps. This was also an opportunity for the retailer to break from the high 2 percent cost of sales associated with giving out stamps. From the early 1960s through the mid-1980s, games were either scratch-off instant-win games, probability games, watch and win games, bingo collector-board games, or lottery-type games.

Games of chance have one thing in common: There is no cost to the consumer to participate. Federal and state laws are very strict in their definition of "consideration." The laws vary widely by state, but they must be followed. For example, some states require that all avail-able prizes be given away. In Florida and New York, bonds must be filed in the state to protect consumers from fraudulent promotions. The Promotion Marketing Association of America has published a book of guidelines to help marketers understand these laws. No promotion, especially games, should ever be produced without proper legal counsel.

Finally, no game should be produced without the proper security measures and errors and omissions insurance. Many novice marketers have found trouble in do-it-yourself promotions when a printing error occurred. Specialty printers and promotion agencies have developed protective methods to ensure the legal and safe production of games.

Scratch-off games. Scratch-off games are big business. They are frequently used by many companies and by states for legal lotteries because of their inherent qualities. Consumers scratch off a latex coating on a game ticket and immediately know whether they win or lose. The games are easy to create provided one understands the strict state and federal laws pertaining to games of chance and lotteries. And, with better technology, the security aspects make scratch-off games a terrific method for a quick-fix game. Prize packages are tailored to the budget of the retailer, the competitive marketplace, and the consumer's appetite for winning. For example, HOOPLA was a scratch-off game tied to a basketball theme. Winners in the game could win free product items from sponsors, cash, or tickets to a featured college basketball game.

Scratch-off games can create instant store traffic. Typically, retailers experience a 5–10 percent gain in traffic and a small loss in the average transaction. This loss occurs because some new consumers visit the store just to play the game. Others may make more frequent visits, purchasing less during each visit, in the hopes of collecting more tickets, thereby increasing their odds of winning. Retailers hope that the traffic increase offsets the lost average "ring" of the register (see Exhibit 25.7).

Probability games. Probability games offer consumers equal chances to win the game. Every ticket has a winning combination. The luck of the participant, based on statistical probabilities, determines the winners. Consumer excitement is high because of the increased odds of winning. There are many dangers with this form of game promotion. Because every ticket is a potential winner, the liability exists that all participants could win.

Elaborate security measures have been developed to help marketers operate this game. However, many companies have had security codes "broken," and more consumers have won than were statistically determined to win. If prize levels are insignificant, this is a great opportunity to have fun. However, for serious levels of prizes, this method offers serious liability. Only professional game designers and security-print manufacturers should be used to create a winning version of a probability game.

EXHIBIT 25.7

Watch and win games. Watch and win games arrived some 28 years ago with "Let's Go to the Races, a promotion offered by TeleCom Productions. Consumers would obtain free game tickets and then watch a weekly, half-hour horse-race show to see if they had won. The game was fabulously successful with an up and coming television generation. *Bowling for Dollars, Wheel of Fortune, Jeopardy,* and *Murder, She Wrote* versions have followed (see Exhibit 25.8).

More recently CBS and Kmart partnered in a give-away game. The Kmart circular contained special numbers that would be shown on television. If the number on your circular matched the number displayed on television, you won. It was a great way to increase viewership of Kmart's commercials and readership of the circular. This promotion won the PMAA's Super Reggie Award for its innovation in the industry.

The big issues with watch and win games are cost and security. Security breaches can create serious liability issues for the promoter. One watch and win promotion was a very successful concept, featuring solutions to a television game show. Game tickets with possible puzzle solutions to a specific week of time were handed out by the food retailers to consumers. If the ticket solution matched the puzzle solution aired on the popular game show, you won a prize. Retailers had dramatic traffic and sales increases through this tie-in with the number-

EXHIBIT 25.8

one rated game show on television. Unfortunately, a mistake occurred. An episode was run through syndication in the marketing area where the consumer game was running. A puzzle solution featured on the syndicated episode closely matched the nonwinning solution on that week's game ticket. What was supposed to be a "common," or losing, game ticket became a winning ticket to millions of viewers. The prize value was $5,000! While the food retailer posted signs regarding the mishap, the state attorney general became involved in the episode. This is not the kind of liability that anyone wants from a game promotion!

Watch and win games produce traffic increases, as well as additional viewership for those who purchase commercial time during the airing of the weekly show. They also tend to post average transaction losses for similar reasons as cited with scratch-off games.

Bingo collector-board games. Bingo collector-board games have been around as long as the others. These games had catchy names such as Treasure Chest, Hunt-Bingo, Spell Cash, Gamarama, Diamond Jubilee Bingo, or retailer-insert-your-name-here bingo! These games are based on the bingo concept of filling in a grid until a row is completely filled horizontally, vertically, or diagonally.

Consumers receive a game board and game tickets, and they match the bingo number to the grids on the game boards. Besides, everyone knows how to play. The difference with this game is its collectable nature. It takes multiple visits to win. Food retailers were then encouraging more shopping visits, especially from new consumers. Food retailers understand that if they can acquire new consumers for multiple visits in a short period of time, they have a good chance of becoming part of that consumer's regular shopping routine.

This tactic drives repeat traffic and extends the life of a game. People don't know whether they win for four to five weeks. And everyone needs only one more piece to win. Again, traffic goes up, and average transaction goes down.

One of the turning points in "games" has been the advent of vendor involvement. The problem has been reframed: How do we sell more product as part of the traffic-building promotion? The day this question was asked, the first collect-the-brands game evolved. Instead of matching numbers, consumers collect and match pictures of brand name products. In the store, people were often heard to say, "All I need is Kraft Macaroni & Cheese to win $5,000."

Game boards with coupons attached were direct-mailed to the homes to inspire that first visit. To make it more fun, game tickets similarly changed to incorporate the new emphasis on selling product. In a game run by an IGA division, a NASCAR racing theme — a popular sport in the area — was featured. In-store merchandising followed the theme, and the game attracted lots of consumer attention. Consumers won NASCAR merchandise, free packaged goods products, cash, and tickets to a NASCAR event (see Exhibit 25.9).

Tickets became larger and included manufacturer coupons and free product prizes right next to the game markers. Guaranteed displays and ad-feature support were included. The game has become a merchandising event. Traffic increases. And the average transactions rise.

Lottery-type games. Lottery fever has swept the nation. Today, more than 35 states have legal lotteries, and it is estimated that more than 90 percent of the population has played a legal lottery somewhere. A few games have attempted to capture lottery fever, and add an in-store merchandising strategy to create an appealing game promotion.

Win-A-Fortune, for example, is a free electronic lottery game, playable in retail chains around the United States. Consumers are given a blank game card on which they can mark their favorite seven numbers. They then insert the ticket into the free-standing terminal. (Incidentally, one can also allow the machine to quick-pick numbers for you. This is just like the state lotteries.) Instantaneously, the card is read and verified. The number is burned into the card.

On the ticket bottom, a coupon or free product offer is imprinted, distributing manufacturers' offers selectively to consumers. Consumers then simply watch the live drawing on television during a predetermined time slot to see whether they've won the progressive jackpot. The odds of winning are one in 10 million. One retailer ran this promo-

EXHIBIT 25.9

tion and had a big winner of $525,000! It created quite a stir among other consumers (see Exhibit 25.10).

On average almost 80 percent of all customers participate in this kind of game. Over 70 percent of all prizes are claimed. The on-line nature of the promotion identifies where the consumers play and where the winners are after the live drawing. Retailers who have run this game indicate both sales and traffic increases in the double digits. And, the brands featured in the promotion move significant product volume. This incremental volume justifies their cost of participation in the promotion.

In-Store Advertising Programs. In-store advertising programs are the fastest-growing segment of the food retailing promotion business. Every available inch of retailing space is dedicated to these promotions. Manufacturers continue to discover new ways of advertising in the store. Shopping carts, clock and aisle markers, electronic kiosks, televisions, and hanging L.E.D. signs all have brand advertising on them. This developing area of promotion is primarily operated by third-party manufacturers of these products. ActMedia, for instance, sells the advertising space on many of these vehicles.

In-store promotions such as these are especially effective when coupled with the traditional promotional programs that retailers offer. The supply and demand of promotions are strictly controlled by retail-

Exhibit 25.10

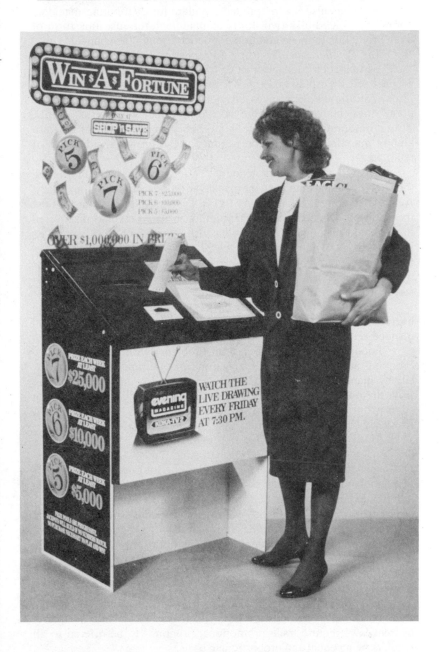

ers. Nowhere is this more evident than in the circular and display decisions. Retailers also use preprinted circulars for distributing manufacturers' coupons. Fully two-thirds of manufacturers use this form of trade promotion to move additional product through the channel.

The Retailer as Advertising Salesperson. Food retailers actively "sell" participation packages that contain all of the elements to increase product sales. Display space has a price. Advertising features have a price. Additional allowances are necessary to get the brand "price point" low enough to have the sustaining effect with the consumer. This promotional mix of elements is the primary cause of concern among manufacturers and the reason for the growing indication of retail power.

Changing consumers account for retailers actively marketing themselves rather than just the packaged goods products they carry. Active marketing is taking many forms. Dahl's, a Super Valu division, incorporated a frequent shopper program in its stores and discovered that it could raise the average dollar visit from $20 to $38 among its loyal shoppers, without affecting the $20 average of other shoppers. In fact, this program is attributed for raising dollar volume in test stores by more than 20 percent contrasted with 7 percent increases in control stores.

Progressive Grocer, among others, has followed the participation by retailers in these programs. Table 25.5 demonstrates current and planned activity for a number of the applications.

Food retailers perceive several problems with these programs. Programs are offered by third-party firms and are funded (if not founded) by manufacturers. Thus, the programs tend to have a bent away from the retail interest. Some of the key firms engaged in supporting such programs include Procter & Gamble, Kraft General Foods, Kimberly Clark, Ralston Purina, Sara Lee, and Philip Morris.

Many programs are also in "testing phases." Funding for the programs is coming out of special marketing funds, which are not normal manufacturer allowances. This raises the long-term issue of participation. Will the program be rolled out? Can it be rolled out? Many industry experts have claimed that manufacturers cannot afford these programs on a national scale, even if other media (such as FSI) are reduced or eliminated. To date, the majority of programs have been offered with no cost to retailers in test conditions. Can a retailer even afford these programs once they have to pony up to the table? Most special programs are not yet offered in all stores or to all retailers in the area.

The longer-term, legal issue resides in the Robinson-Patman Act's conditions. Programs are powerful if they are retailer exclusive. Current laws require trade promotional programs to be offered to all retailers on an equal and proportionate basis.

TABLE 25.5
ELECTRONIC MARKETING ACTIVITY

Application	Percent Active	Percent Planned
Electronic signage	14%	1%
In-store radio	13	—
Electronic coupons	12	31
Electronic rebates	6	5
Frequent shopper	3	8
Others	3	5

The Food Marketing Institute, the national organization of food retailers, has attempted to help guide retailers through this conundrum by publishing guides such as "Front-End Electronic Marketing" and "Targeting Food Customers." These volumes offer the basic concepts and lists of vendors that can help implement the programs. However, the third-party vendors underwrite the publications cost and thus editorialize these policy guidelines.

SUMMARY

Food retailing requires a strategic understanding of the marketing mix and a retailer's position within a competitive set. Different types of vendor promotions are offered to the retailer. Before promotion and merchandising decisions are made, retail executives must comprehend the impact on their total business. As consumers change their attitudes toward their time, the shopping experience, and brand name products, retailers will change their communications with the consumers and will find the most effective and profitable promotions to drive long-term business.

Jim Litwin joined Wunderman Cato Johnson/Chicago in 1988 as Director of Marketing and headed the team that worked with Taco Bell during the introduction of its Value Initiative. His current responsibilities as Vice President and Director of Marketing include strategic planning for the Kraft General Foods, Chevron and Pepsi accounts. Litwin developed several proprietary agency computer models, including PROMOBANK, the Tie-In Analysis, and the Frequent Buyer Economic Model.

Prior to Wunderman, Litwin worked at FCB/Impact on the Pepsi Cola account and at Frankel & Company on the McDonald's account, where he was responsible for the original Monopoly promotion and the NFL "Kickoff Payoff." Before entering the agency business, he worked in brand management at Heublein and Coors.

Litwin received his Master's of Management from Northwestern's Kellogg Graduate School of Management, with dual majors in Marketing and Finance. His Bachelor's degree was from Columbia College in Motion Picture and Television Production.

CHAPTER 26

QUICK SERVICE RESTAURANT PROMOTIONS

In 1985, Fred Turner, Chairman of McDonald's, banned the use of the phrase *fast food* and coined the term *quick service restaurant* (QSR). The use of the term spread quickly, and that is how the industry is known today. Every industry, of course, has its own terminology and acronyms, and the QSR category is no exception. Consumers are customers and POS (point-of-sale) is P-O-P (point-of-purchase) in QSR-ese. In fact, POS not only doesn't mean display material, in QSR-talk it means the cash register system. A seemingly minor difference unless POS is ordered and cash registers are received instead of counter cards! (It has happened.)

The QSR business was an almost $70 billion dollar industry in 1991. CREST (Consumer Reports on Eating Share Trends), the leading syndicated research company tracking the industry, defines QSR to include hamburger, chicken, pizza, ice cream, frozen yogurt, seafood, Mexican, Oriental, and barbecue quick service restaurants, doughnut shops, and convenience stores. National and regional chains comprise more than 60 percent of the total with hamburgers alone accounting for more than 30 percent. Most Americans frequent a QSR at least once a month.

THE QSR SALES EQUATION

The quick service restaurant is simply one form of retailing and shares the same basic business objectives with supermarkets, mass merchandisers, drugstores, and department stores — traffic, average check, and profit per square foot. Unlike these other retailing forms, QSRs generally do not sell manufacturers' brand names but have created their own "private label" brands such as the Big Mac and the Whopper. (Burger King has recently had some success with selling advertised packaged goods brands such as Snickers' ice cream bars, Famous Amos cookies, and Newman's Own salad dressings.) In a sense, QSRs have combined manufacturing and retailing under one roof. Because of this singular focus of effort, QSR promotion managers can exercise a degree of promotional control their packaged goods counterparts can only dream about.

As in any industry, the QSR promotion manager's overriding goal is to generate incremental dollar sales. But just saying "build sales" as an objective does not give much guidance on how to do this. The best place to start in the quest to "build sales" is the basic QSR sales equation. The two major elements in this equation are traffic and average check. The full sales equation works like this:

Traffic x Average Check per Eater = Dollar Sales

The traffic element has three major subcomponents:
- Reach (how many households visit in a given time period)
- Visit frequency (how often they visit in this time period)
- Party size (how many "eaters" there are in each group visiting)

Therefore, the full equation has five components, as follows:

(Reach x Frequency x Party Size) x Average Check
per Eater = Dollar Sales

As with any industry, the key to a strong QSR promotion program is a clearly defined set of promotion objectives. A careful analysis of a QSR's sales equation is critical to the formation of solid promotion strategies. These types of data can be obtained from the CREST report (see Exhibit 26.1). The most leverageable components of the sales equation should be given first priority when setting promotion objectives and building a promotion calendar (see "Promotional Calendar Planning" on page 534). Pursuing a reach strategy requires a completely different set of promotion tactics than does an average-check strategy.

THE THREE AUDIENCES — QSR STYLE

Most effective sales promotion efforts involve three audiences — usually the consumer, the trade, and the sales force. In the QSR business, there are also three audiences that need to be addressed. But, as discussed earlier, the consumer is the customer; the trade is the franchisee or restaurant manager; and the sales force is the "crew" working the counter or drive-through. Each is critical to the success of almost any promotion and should, at the very least, be considered.

THE QSR CUSTOMER — SEGMENTING APPROACHES

In the broadest sense, the QSR customer is anyone who needs a quick, inexpensive meal and who wants more than a candy bar or bag of chips but doesn't have the time, money, or inclination for a full-service, sit-down restaurant. How the food tastes is an important attribute, but speed of service is the overriding concern.

However, there are customers and there are customers. As in most businesses, the 80/20 rule applies. A disproportionately small number of heavy users typically represents the majority of sales. Not only are these folks visiting QSRs more often but also their average check is usually higher. Therefore, segmenting by usage and targeting promotions specifically to these heavy users can be profitable.

Who are these people? Generally, they live or work within a two- to three-mile radius or "trading area" of the restaurant. (The trading area theory does not apply in all cases. QSRs alongside major inter-

EXHIBIT 26.1

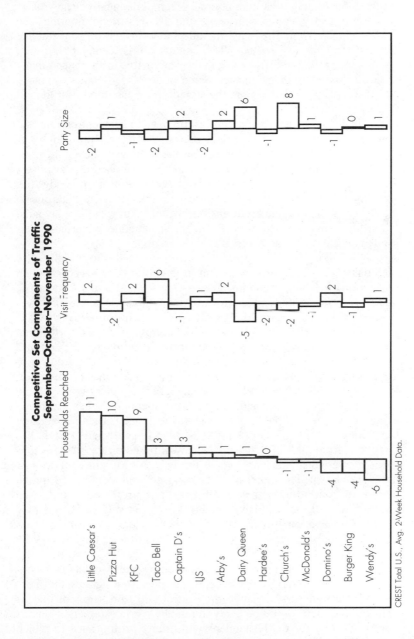

Competitive Set Components of Traffic
September–October–November 1990

CREST Total U.S., Avg. 2-Week Household Data.

527

state highways, in airports, and in shopping malls typically have a much larger trading area than normal.) Demographically, heavy users skew male and younger with teens and 18–34s predominating (see Exhibit 26.2). Their lifestyles include heavy usage of convenience products (microwave foods, ATMs, snack chips, candy bars), they spend a lot of time in their cars, and they are active in sports and many leisure activities (movies, music, theme parks, video games, going to clubs). In other words, they are the stereotypical fast food user that all QSRs are targeting!

Heaviness of usage is a very useful way to segment current and potential customers — it fits with the commonsense philosophy of "fishing where the fish are." But it is not the only way or even the most effective method. Niche opportunities can be overlooked if heavy users are the only promotional target. However, promotion of lighter, "healthier" menu items can attract the lighter QSR users that, due to their sheer numbers, can represent significant volume in key dayparts. Often higher margins on these items are sustainable because of their limited appeal (no competitors offer these items).

Another way to segment customers is demographically. McDonald's has been very proficient in targeting their advertising and promotions to young children, ages 2–7 ("Ronald age"), "'tweens," teens, seniors, Hispanics, and African-Americans. The key to effectively targeting demographic groups is "segmentation without alienation" — that is, to tightly focus the communication effort so that there is little spillover from one group to the other that may "turn off" that group. Running children's advertising only during children's programming is one way to do this. Placing a children's promotional P-O-P at the child's eye-level in the restaurant is another way.

Segmenting current and potential customers on the basis of brand loyalty is a new and potentially powerful technique. Using a research technique called the Conversion Model (developed by Dr. Jan Hofmeyer from the University of Capetown, based on the study of religious conversions and marketed in the U.S. by Market Facts), QSR users are classified as either users or nonusers and then ranked by the degree of commitment they exhibit to their preferred brands (see Exhibit 26.3). If the "available" group of users is very large, one may want to pursue a retention promotion strategy. Conversely, if the "convertible" group of nonusers is big, an acquisition campaign may be more in order.

Another use of customer segmentation by brand loyalty is in concept testing of promotions. Concepts can be tested against the more unavailable nonusers to gauge their attraction to a segment that, if induced to switch, would be likely to remain loyal customers. Contrast this to what undoubtedly happens with many promotions, in which convertible nonusers temporarily "jump ship" during the promotion and go right back to their regular brand when the promotion ceases.

EXHIBIT 26.2
PROFILE OF HEAVY USERS

		% U.S. A 18+	HFFU %	INDEX
Male		48%	48%	(100)
Female		52	52	(100)
Age	18–24	14	21	(145)
	25–34	24	34	(142)
	18–34	38	55	(143)
	35–44	20	23	(118)
	45–49	7	5	(77)
	50–64	19	12	(64)
	65+	16	4	(23)
Grad. College +		19	20	(110)
Att. College		19	23	(125)
Grad. HS		39	40	(103)
Non-grad. HS		24	16	(68)
Empl. Full-Time		55	67	(122)
Empl. Part Time		8	11	(128)
Not Empl.		36	22	(61)
Working Women		29	37	(127)
Full-Time Coll. Students		4	5	(152)
Part-Time Coll. Students		3	6	(192)
HHI	$60M+	17	19	(111)
	$50–$59,999	8	11	(133)
	$40–$49,999	12	14	(121)
	$30–$39,999	16	18	(116)
	$20–$29,999	17	17	(100)
	<$20M	30	20	(68)
Median HH Income		17	20	(116)
White		86	89	(104)
Black		11	8	(67)
Other		3	3	(126)
Spanish-Speaking		6	7	(108)

Universe (M):25,541   Source: Spring 1991 MRI

HFFU = Heavy fast-food user
HHI = Household income

EXHIBIT 26.3

THE CONVERSION MODEL

USERS' STRENGTH OF COMMITMENT				NON-USERS' BALANCE OF DISPOSITION			
The Four User Segments:				The Four Non-User Segments:			
SECURE USERS		VULNERABLE USERS		OPEN NON-USERS		UNAVAILABLE NON-USERS	
• ENTRENCHED	• AVERAGE	• SHALLOW	• CONVERTIBLE	• AVAILABLE	• AMBIVALENT	• WEAKLY UNAVAILABLE	• STRONGLY UNAVAILABLE
Staunchly loyal; unlikely to change in the foreseeable future	Comfortable with their choice; unlikely to change in the near future	Not ready to switch; but may be considering alternatives	On the threshold of change; psychologically divorced from the brand	Prefer the brand, but have not yet switched; the most likely prospects for new business	As attracted to the brand as they are to their current choice	Preference lies with their current brand, although not strongly	Strongly prefer their current brand

For _each_ brand not used, a person is in one of these four segments.

These so-called "promotionally responsive" customers do not usually represent high "lifetime value" to the promoting QSR.

The final way to segment customers is based on customer need states. This approach recognizes that people are totally different consumers depending on their physical or mental state and environment at each purchase occasion. Exhibit 26.4 depicts a hypothetical purchase decision model. Assuming a basic hunger level, there are a number of different need states a customer could be in at a particular time depending on circumstances as shown in the second column. Each need state has a corresponding "considered set" of acceptable choices as shown in the fourth column. These considered sets are based primarily on a combination of past product or service experience while in that need state, and the QSR's image as created by advertising and word of mouth.

The final decision regarding which QSR in the considered set to drive into often takes place while driving down "franchise row." Because there is usually more than one of the considered sets present in franchise row, this final decision is heavily influenced by which one has the easiest location to pull into and, to a lesser extent, external P-O-P offering promotional messages and radio advertising heard while in the car.

High-visibility external P-O-P such as banners and pole signs that feature a strong but simple promotional message can be very effective in swinging the final decision at the point of hunger. It's important to note that more than one-third of all QSR purchase occasions involve some sort of promotion. Promotions are often the tiebreaker in restaurant choice decisions, as well as in menu choice decisions once inside the restaurant or at the drive-through. Surveys have indicated that about one in 10 QSR restaurant choice decisions involve actual usage of a promotion, while more than 50 percent of menu choice decisions are influenced by promotion.

In summary, while everyone is a QSR customer at one time or another, there are many ways to "divide and conquer" these customers to maximize promotion expenditures.

OPERATIONAL ISSUES

A thorough knowledge of the operational aspects of a QSR is mandatory for any promotion manager. Ideally, the manager should spend significant time working in the restaurant in every position from clean-up crew to manager. Nothing will kill a promotion faster than overlooking an operational "mandatory." Typical problem areas to watch for include the following:

- Promotions that use up too much transaction time and slow down service
- Promotions that require the crew, manager, or customer to do too much
- Promotions that are too complicated for the crew or manager

EXHIBIT 26.4

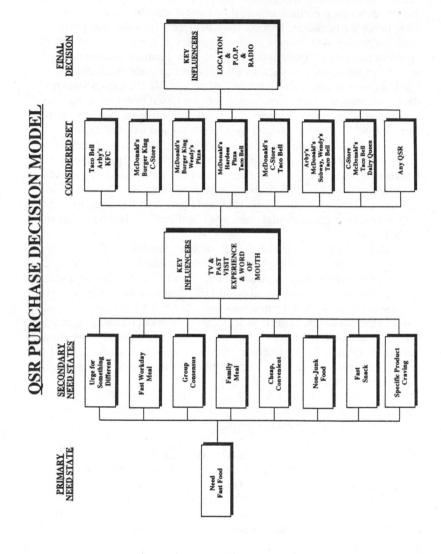

QSR PURCHASE DECISION MODEL

FINAL DECISION

KEY INFLUENCERS — LOCATION & P.O.P. & RADIO

CONSIDERED SET

- Taco Bell Arby's KFC
- McDonald's Burger King C-Store
- McDonald's Burger King Wendy's Pizza
- McDonald's Hardees Pizza Taco Bell
- McDonald's C-Store Taco Bell
- Arby's McDonald's Subway, Wendy's Taco Bell
- C-Store McDonald's Taco Bell Dairy Queen
- Any QSR

KEY INFLUENCERS — TV & PAST VISIT EXPERIENCE & WORD OF MOUTH

SECONDARY NEED STATES

- Urge for Something Different
- Fast Workday Meal
- Group Consensus
- Family Meal
- Cheap, Convenient
- Non-Junk Food
- Fast Snack
- Specific Product Craving

PRIMARY NEED STATE

Need Fast Food

to understand
- Coupons or game pieces that don't fit in the cash register drawer
- Premiums that take up too much space in the storeroom
- Promotions that work well in-store but not in the drive-through
- Packaging that won't fit through the drive-through window (yes, it's happened)
- P-O-P that blocks the view of the menu board

For anyone who hasn't worked in a QSR, it's a hot, noisy, pressure-filled environment for the crew members. If they're working a register during the lunch rush, the *last* thing on their mind is handing out premiums, coupons, or game pieces. The QSR manager's job is even more harried. A 40-hour workweek is something managers only dream about with all the forms they have to fill out as well as coping with crew absenteeism, shortages, and personal problems. Their lives are filled with major operational issues that seemingly threaten the ability of their restaurant to even open the next day. Complicated promotion manuals will certainly be the last thing to be read!

In summary, every promotion should pass through an operational screen that asks these questions:
- Will it significantly slow the speed of service?
- Will it work in the drive-through?
- Are the promotion communication materials simple and short enough so they will be used and understood by both managers and crew?
- Will the manager and crew be motivated to execute the promotion properly?

FRANCHISEE AND CO-OP ISSUES

Most QSR systems involve a mix of company-owned and franchised units. It is important to understand that franchisees are in no way obligated to run the franchisor's sales promotions. They usually can do whatever they want in this area, within reason. But having the majority of restaurants in a market running a promotion is critical to the creation of "promotion synergy." Therefore, a carefully planned "sell-in" campaign targeted to franchisees is a must for big promotions.

Franchisees in most markets make local advertising and promotion decisions in co-op meetings that typically occur once a month. These co-ops usually operate in a democratic manner in which votes are taken on each promotion program. Voting is typically done on a one-store-equals-one-vote basis. Therefore, multiunit franchisees or the company (if it owns enough units) can control some co-ops.

It's important to understand the political processes operating in a co-op, as well as the personalities of the key players. Generally speaking, franchisees respond best to hard test market evidence of the potential for success of a promotion. Videotaped testimonials from franchisees in the test market can be very compelling. Franchisees tend to be very "hands-on," operationally oriented people, so samples of the promotion elements for "show and tell" can be very convincing as well.

If no test market has been run, marketing research can sometimes work. Because many franchisees are not marketing-oriented by nature, complicated statistical results will usually fall on deaf ears. Videotaped focus groups, in which they can see people "just like their customers" responding to the promotions, can sometimes work miracles. A simple break-even analysis for each promotion can also help, if it is in a format the franchisees can understand and believe in. Allowing them to input key assumptions will give them ownership of the promotion and help "make the sale."

Once the promotion has been accepted by the franchisees and co-ops, the job is far from over. Proper ordering of sufficient quantities of the promotional elements (P-O-P game pieces, premiums, and the like) can make a huge difference in a promotion's sustaining itself throughout the entire promotion window. Unfortunately, franchisees tend to be rather frugal and conservative in their ordering, preferring to "save money" by under-ordering. They need to be educated to the fact that a small savings now can have a tremendous opportunity cost in lost potential profits. Often with games, they will under-order game pieces (or not encourage their employees to distribute the game pieces to all customers), on the theory that fewer game pieces distributed means fewer redemptions on food prizes. What they forget is that each food prize redemption usually involves significant add-on sales (and profits).

These facts need to be made clear to franchisees before they place their orders for promotional material. Again, some profit case histories of actual franchisees who ran out of game pieces two weeks into a promotion compared to those who ordered enough to last the full promotion period can be very convincing, especially if videotaped testimonials are used. Why bother going to the trouble and expense of putting up P-O-P, training the crew, and running TV spots if materials run out halfway through the program?

PROMOTIONAL CALENDAR PLANNING

There is no such thing as a bad strategy. Or a good one for that matter. Strategies have no inherent merit in and of themselves.... The achievement of tactical results is the ultimate and only goal of a strategy.
— *Marketing Warfare* by Al Ries and Jack Trout

Promotional planning should be an integral part of the overall marketing planning process for the QSR company. One would hope that the company has a clear, overall long-term business mission based on a sound analysis of its place within the industry, financial goals, operational constraints, and economic forecasting. From this longer-term perspective should flow a short-term (12-month) marketing mission, clearly defining the relative roles of advertising, promotion, public relations, and direct marketing within the context of new product introductions, planned operational charges, and pricing adjustments. Coordination of all the communication disciplines can result in a consistency of effort that can produce the synergy effect so critical to leveraging marketing budgets to the maximum. The sum of the marketing components should equal more than the whole.

Of course, the reality is that the planning process is fraught with obstacles and roadblocks that make coordination difficult. But, the synergy effect is a goal that should be strived for because it *can* work. Some companies actually do manage to achieve this synergy level more often than not.

The standard operating procedure is to build a 12-month "national" promotional calendar to help guide all the activities and thinking of the franchisees, marketing staff, and advertising, promotion, direct marketing, and public relations agencies (both local and national). Usually, the year is divided into 12 one-month-long periods, although there is no hard and fast rule on this. (Some companies use 13 four-week modules, and some work on a bimonthly or quarterly basis.)

Traditionally, calendar-building theory has held that advertising should take the lead role and all the other communication disciplines should coordinate with advertising's lead. Current thinking is to divide the year into broad "verticals," focusing on a particular product, subject, or aspect of the business and letting the most appropriate communication discipline for that subject take the lead.

Another approach is to utilize the QSR sales equation:

$$(Reach \times Frequency \times Party\ Size) \times Average\ Check$$
$$per\ Eater = Dollar\ Sales$$

The equation can be examined at different times of the year, and then broad promotion objectives can be assigned to each period, depending on what is most leverageable according to the CREST data. This can even be done by key user segment, dayparts, or even drive-through vs. in-store (for example, reach against teens, frequency among lighter users, average check at dinner, or party size in the drive-through).

Other approaches include the following:
- Anticipating competitive promotions and counterplanning against these
- Prioritizing objectives and placing those with the highest priorities into the ideal times of the year

All of these methods are valid and productive. The truth is that QSR calendar planning should be an iterative process with lots of give and take among the various methods and points of view. The calendar itself should remain flexible to accommodate major changes in the economy, the competition, and other factors. But it's critical to *have* a 12-month calendar with at least the next six to eight months fairly well locked in.

The key to an effective calendar is that it all hangs together and works toward the common goal of the company's overall business objective for the year. This does not mean that all the promotions should look and be the same, but simply that they are all moving the QSR system in the desired direction.

Using the Conversion Model from Exhibit 26.3 as a guide for this direction, the calendar could be designed to move everyone up the chain of commitment states. Current users should be moving toward becoming "entrenched," and nonusers should be moving toward "available." Using this approach, a year-long linked cycle of promotion objectives could be developed, starting the year with reach objectives (to gather in new and occasional users), then moving to frequency objectives (to get them coming in more often), progressing to average check objectives (to maximize dollar sales from the rapidly swelling group of users), and on to continuity promotions (to cement both the relationship and habit within this group). Then the cycle could begin again the next year to capture and then build and cement a relationship with a new group of users.

Another approach is to prioritize objectives for the year and fit the top priorities into the calendar when common sense and experience point to the ideal time periods. The following represent some current ideas on the best time periods for various objectives and strategies:

- *Average check — summer.* Traffic is usually at its peak in summer, and incremental traffic can be very expensive to obtain at this time. The most efficient use of the promotional dollar is to focus on increasing the average check of all the people crowding into the restaurant in the warm weather months. (Of course, if a QSR is experiencing traffic declines, this theory is invalid.)
- *Reach — January/February.* Bad weather invariably makes these months the slowest of the year. This is when it helps to use large coupon values and deep discounts on signature products (for example, $.99 Big Mac sandwiches) to really attract the customers.
- *Snack daypart — summer/back to school.* So many more people are on the road in the warm weather months that it pays to promote every daypart to take advantage. Snack promotions during late August/September can rebuild or reinforce the idea of after-school snacks at a QSR at the beginning of the school year, in the hope that they result in a year-long habit.
- *Promotion of "filling" products — winter.* Products that produce the greatest "belly-fill" effect are usually promoted in cold weather months.

- *Service promotions — winter/spring.* Lower traffic time periods allow a QSR a better chance of actually delivering on a service guarantee (for example, 60-second service). Also, the crew is more stable and experienced, having been on the job longer (since school began in the fall).
- *Increase female user base — January and presummer.* Promote low-calorie, low-fat menu items during the peak dieting months.

Other "rules" abound. Games are often run in the spring to build customer frequency that will carry through into the high-traffic summer months.

No matter how logically a national promotional calendar is put together, it's useless without the enthusiastic support of the franchisees and co-ops. As mentioned earlier, the planning process is an iterative one that works best when all parties have had a chance to express their points of view. Pro forma calendars are built and then improved. This democratic process gives a feeling of ownership to all parties involved. Of course, a senior officer of the QSR has to make the final decision on the calendar, and this decision should be based on a calendar that hangs together toward a common goal. (The worst possible scenario is a calendar that tries to please everyone equally. This calendar will invariably be a hodgepodge of conflicting objectives and strategies.) Some QSR companies have incorporated this democratic process into their corporate culture by inviting large numbers of franchisees and their local agencies to come to corporate headquarters several times a year to participate in planning meetings during which their voices can be heard by senior officers of the company.

Another technique to ensure support from the field is to build local "windows" into the national calendar in which local market co-ops are encouraged to run their own promotions. Usually a "vertical" theme is suggested, in which network media might be supporting a specific product or service and the local promotion would somehow coordinate with the theme in some fashion. The key is building numerous opportunities for local markets to "do their own thing" promotionally. Flexibility is the watchword when building national promotional calendars.

The last step in building a promotional calendar is the linking of promotion objectives to tactics and tactics to concepts. Exhibit 26.5 illustrates a number of tactical options for each promotion objective. After a tactic has been selected, the creative process begins and the promotion concepts are developed. (As mentioned at the beginning of this section, sometimes the development process begins with the concepts and works its way back to the objective. There is nothing sacred about where the process begins or whether it progresses downward or upward. The important thing is that one ends up with an objective and strategy for each promotion period and that they coordinate with the

EXHIBIT 26.5

Promotion Initiation Form Instructions

Use the chart below to aid in setting objectives and determining tactical preferences.

Objective	Frequency	Average Check	Reach/Traffic	Trial	Continuity

Tactical suggestions	• Bounceback in-store coupons
	• Everyday low price
	• Daily specials
	• Games
	• Daypart specials
		• Meal combos
		  - Order by number
		  - Meal pack
		• Super sizes
		• Container pack premiums
			• Games
			• FSI coupons
			• Electronic coupons
			• Tie-ins
			• LTO product
			• Free premium
				• Free with purchase
				• Sampling
					• Proof-of-purchase program
					• Collectible premiums
					• Punchcard
					• Rollover game card

Objective	Awareness/ Education	Excitement	Suggestive Sell/ Crew Motivation	Party Size	
Tactical suggestions	• P.O.P./ merchandising • Sweepstakes • Programmed learning • Tie-ins • Contests • Self-liquidating premiums	• Sweepstakes • Games • P.O.P./decor	• Sales contest • Mystery shopper • Crew apparel	• BOGO entree coupons • Children's Meals • Multi-packs	

P.O.P. Focus Areas

Use the lists below to prioritize key restaurant areas where a promotion offer can communicate to customers

Interior
• Front door
• Line/serpentine
• Counter
• Crew apparel
• Menu board
• Order pickup
• Dining room
• Table top
• Exit door
• Crew room

Exterior
• Street visible areas
• Pole sign
• Front of restaurant
• Parking lot
• Drive-through lane
• Side of restaurant
• Back of restaurant
• Menu board
• Menu board to pickup
• Pickup window
• Exit lane

other objectives throughout the year so the overriding business goal for that year is achieved.)

PROMOTIONAL TACTICS REVIEW

As mentioned in the previous section, the tactic is the engine that drives the QSR promotional calendar. Reviewed below are 15 tactical options that are important to the QSR category. Case histories are sprinkled throughout to illustrate the key elements of each type of tactic.

It should be noted that, as with media, customers who are into promotions are usually into most types of promotions. As heavy television viewers tend also to be heavy radio listeners and magazine readers, customers who are responsive to games are often responsive to the other 14 promotional tactics.

There is some evidence, however, that promotion responsiveness is not entirely uniform, which raises the intriguing possibility of combining complementary tactics to build overall "promotion reach" — for example, promoting a limited-time-only (LTO) product (to attract switches) while promoting a long-term continuity program (to retain regular users). More research needs to be done in this area before any hard and fast rules can be set.

1. Bonus Packs/Packaging. As with packaged goods, the bonus pack tactic involves offering extra product at no additional cost. Usually this takes the form of bonus drinks, fries, or other "side" dishes. Often the bonus size is available only as part of a meal combination to help build the average check. This provides a nice way to offer extra value to customers without the possible "cheapening" effect of a coupon or discount.

Bonus soft drink promotions are generally not as effective as bonus food portions. Much of this has to do with the impact of free refills offered at many QSRs. Bonus soft drinks may have their greatest impact during the lunch daypart when a bonus offer may encourage a soft drink purchase at the QSR rather than buying a beverage elsewhere.

Packaging changes that improve the delivery and convenience of the product or add an element of fun to the eating experience can also provide a significant sales lift. The "Tacos To Go" 6- and 10-pack box added a convenience factor to the lowly taco that made it the product of choice for group dining occasions. Spillproof cups can significantly boost drive-through incidence of beverage purchases. But the fun element of packaging can also sometimes work promotionally in the form of an adult "Happy Meal."

Case History — McDonald's Chicken McNuggets Shanghai. Chicken McNuggets had been introduced with great success in 1984. McNuggets are fun to eat and enjoyed by children and adults alike.

For a 1986 "vertical" centered on McNuggets, McDonald's decided to focus on the fun aspect of the product. A promotion called

Chicken "McNuggets Shanghai" that had been successfully run in Germany was adopted in the United States. Special oriental packaging was designed for the six- and nine-piece sizes. Four limited-time-only oriental sauces were developed especially for the promotion. And to cap off the fun, every McNuggets Shanghai came with a pair of chopsticks and a fortune cookie. (The TV spots emphasized the fun of dipping the McNuggets in the sauce with the chopsticks.) P-O-P featured store decor items that included a paper dragon and lanterns, and the crew was outfitted in kimonos with straw "coolie" hats (see Exhibit 26.6).

2. Charities or Causes. Charity- or cause-related promotions can be good for generating overall goodwill for a QSR chain but are unlikely to produce significant traffic gains. Customers are often skeptical about whether their contributions ever reach those in need, especially with a big national charity overlay.

Charity promotions *can* have an impact on sales if done on a regional or local-store-marketing (LSM) basis. Customers are more likely to take action if they know the money is going back into the community. LSM tie-ins to local schools and community organizations can be very effective in generating traffic, especially if a specific goal is communicated (for example, "buy a new computer for the 4th grade," or "build a new addition to the rehabilitation center").

3. Contests. Contests represent a very involving but underutilized tactic because of the operational expense of having to judge entries. However, these promotions can be very effective on an LSM basis. Because of the skill element, a purchase requirement can be required to play.

4. Continuity Programs. Continuity programs have traditionally been done on a single-store or regional basis with a punch card or on a larger scale with a collectible series of premiums. Continuity programs hold tremendous potential on a larger scale to not only build loyalty but also collect a database of customers that includes transaction data. This database can then be used to micromarket to individual customers who represent high "lifetime value." Again, the catch-22 is that heavy users don't like to carry cards or anything made of paper. Technology will undoubtedly provide some sort of electronic solution in the future.

Gift certificates can be a very effective form of continuity promotion. Traditionally sold in $5 booklets at Christmas time, they represent guaranteed traffic in January and February (again bridging from high to low traffic periods). Since they typically come in denominations of $1 or less and are typically given to kids, teachers, and mailmen, when redeemed, there are usually significant add-on sales involved.

There is also a fair amount of slippage (certificates sold and never redeemed) involved with gift certificates. This slippage money can be used to fund the printing of the gift certificates, promotions, and P-O-P or to support charitable organizations. However, an attorney

EXHIBIT 26.6

should always be consulted on the escheatment laws that control the status of unclaimed assets before making plans for the slippage money.

Gift certificate promotions don't have to be limited to Christmas. Other gift-giving periods can be used to sell them, such as Valentine's Day, Father's Day, Mother's Day, and Halloween.

A few words are in order on the operational aspects of gift certificates. Printing certificates is, in essence, like printing money. Typically, they are bought by the franchisee from the franchisor. When customers redeem them, the redeeming restaurant is compensated somehow. Because of the cash value of gift certificates, special security precautions need to be taken with the printing and handling of them. The certificates should be individually numbered and printed on special paper to make forgery difficult. In the restaurant, they should be treated like cash. It is highly recommended that gift certificates be printed as negotiable checks. This makes the reimbursement process for redeemed certificates simple. The manager simply deposits them daily at the bank along with the regular cash receipts.

Effectively managed, gift certificates can be a self-funding promotion that can build continuity, bridge traffic, and stimulate add-on sales.

5. *Coupons.* In general, coupons are the single most powerful tactic for building traffic. However, coupons are not necessarily the most *profitable* tactic.

The alternative to cents-off coupons are EDLP (every day low price) menus, as exemplified by Taco Bell's Value Menu. As covered later in the section on "Value Pricing," coupons have an advantage over EDLP in that not every transaction is offered at a discount. In fact, during the course of most coupon promotions, the majority of transactions do not involve a coupon. This has a lot to do with the fact that the majority of QSR customers are not regular coupon clippers and savers. Although most QSR users do use a coupon from time to time, most have a strong preference for promotions that require little planning, no gratification deferral, or no work on their part. The whole concept of coupon clipping fights the speed-of-service basis of the QSR's very existence.

Of course, there is a significant minority of customers who regularly stockpile and redeem coupons (probably less than 20 percent). These coupon "hobbyists" apparently derive some intrinsic gratification from the act of clipping, storing, and planning the usage of coupons. (Consumer thrift has also been popular for the 1990s.) Because these people typically have an inventory of QSR coupons at hand, they effectively avoid any delay in promotional gratification since there is always a coupon ready. These coupon hobbyists tend not to be the teens and young adults who are often the most frequent QSR visitors. Rather, they are the parents of large families, for whom coupon clipping can really pay off.

A few rules of thumb for effective and profitable coupons are as follows:

- Coupons on main meal products tend to perform much better than coupons for side items. (Main meal items generally distinguish one QSR from another.)
- BOGO (buy one, get one free) main meal coupons, such as BOGO large sandwich, tend to perform the best and build party size (since individuals probably can't eat two of the largest menu items by themselves).
- The more flexible the offer, the stronger the response. A BOGO of any large sandwich will generally do better than a BOGO Big Mac, for example.
- Common expiration dates pull better than staggered dates. Many QSRs run a free-standing insert (FSI) featuring a series of coupons, each good for two weeks. Typically, there are three sets of these coupons covering a six-week time period. The theory is that the "time-release" effect of staggered expiration dates will create a continuity effect over the six weeks. The reality is that having all coupons good for the full six weeks almost always generates a higher redemption rate. Because people have a larger window in which to use the coupons, their visit frequency goes up. Surprisingly, the pattern of redemptions is almost the same whether expiration dates are staggered or common. QSRs *don't* get a flood of redemptions in the first week with a common expiration date.
- The key to coupon profitability is to generate the most *extra visits* as a percentage of all visits. (An extra visit is defined as one that would not have been made without the coupon. As such, *all* profit generated is incremental.) The offer that generates the highest total response will not necessarily generate the highest percentage of extra visits. The extra visit percentage for various offers from a specific QSR can be determined by surveying a sample of coupon redeemers. Typically, coupon offers on unique "signature" products that are known for their ability to generate "cravings" produce the highest extra visit percentage.
- The optimal number of coupons on an FSI or mailer ranges from three to six. Six coupons reduces the cost of delivery per coupon and generates a higher total response, especially among heavy users. Six-coupon FSIs are best run in winter months when traffic is slow and comprised of mostly nonloyal heavy users. Three or four coupons tend to attract a higher percentage of new and light users. Although their total response rate is lower, three- or four-coupon offers may be more profitable because of a higher percentage of extra visits. An FSI with fewer than three coupons is usually not effective from a delivery cost per coupon standpoint. An FSI with more than six coupons tends to get cluttered, and total response,

while greater, tends to fall off on a per coupon basis rather quickly.

- Fifty cents seems to be the minimal acceptable value these days for a cents-off coupon. This hurdle can be overcome by not using cents-off as the offer but by promoting free product with a larger purchase that has an apparent value of $.50 or more.

There are many methods for delivering coupons. Coupons delivered in-store will not build reach but will increase visit frequency and/or average check among current customers. Coupons delivered out-of-store can build reach as well as increase visit frequency and/or average check. There are many options for out-of-store delivery and each has its pros and cons. Some of the major techniques include the following:

- *Solo FSI (free-standing inserts)* — Allows for maximum creative flexibility in terms of shapes, colors, and other design elements. There is no clutter but, of course, it has the most expensive upfront cost.
- *Co-op FSI* — Generally the lowest cost per coupon of all media-delivered vehicles, but in a very cluttered environment. However, one advantage co-op FSIs have over solo FSIs is that coupon users look for them in their Sunday papers. Co-op FSIs require long lead times.
- *Solo direct mail* — The most expensive medium but most targetable (and thus less wasteful). Through use of a survey-based list, such as Carol Wright's Share Force, one can actually target competitive users. However, direct mail is not sought out as an FSI is. Many direct mail pieces are thrownaway no matter how well targeted they are.
- *Co-op direct mail* — Much lower cost than solo direct, but little flexibility in distribution options, plus lots of clutter.
- *ROP (run-of-press) newspaper ad* — Can be implemented quickly at low cost. However, color reproduction is poor (if available).
- *Street distribution* — Can effectively target people in the trading area while they are deciding on where to eat. There is a relatively high cost per coupon. Street distribution works only in areas with lots of foot traffic (city centers, malls).
- *Tie-in partner distribution* — Can be very effective at a very low cost if the tie-in partners truly complement each other in terms of target audience. Distribution can be on-pack, in-ad, or in-store (depending on the partner's product or service). Usually, tie-ins are bartered deals in which each partner bounces traffic to the other. If each partner distributes the other's coupons as part of the regular service, the cost per coupon can approach zero.

The eternal debate over cents-off couponing's effect on "brand equity" has been waging for decades. There is some evidence to support all positions. The reality is that occasional couponing delivered with a creative presentation that is consistent with the QSR's current positioning probably has no impact on brand equity or loyalty if the QSR is also well supported through advertising and added-value promotions.

Of course, this debate raises the issue of just what is brand equity and how can it be measured? Many methods have been proposed:

- Size of customer base whose majority of purchases rests with a particular QSR company
- Attribute ratings over time (as determined by tracking studies)
- Size of the "entrenched" segment of users as measured by the Conversion Model

The important point is that this type of research is important to keep track of a QSR's overall business, as well as couponing's impact. It should be an ongoing component of a marketing plan.

6. Games. Games can be among the most powerful QSR promotional tactics, building traffic through reach, frequency, and continuity. Nevertheless, if improperly managed, games can be one of the highest risk promotion tactics, not only because of the high cost (game pieces, media, and prizes) but also because of the operational impact. Games typically have some of the highest break-even points of all promotions, often exceeding 5 percent (a 5 percent increase in overall sales is required to cover the *incremental* cost of the promotion). However, a well-designed, well-run game can produce incremental sales of 8 percent to 10 percent or higher.

The term *game* might be thought of as something of a misnomer because the winners are normally determined purely by random chance — skill is rarely involved. Yet the concept of "playing" makes a game emotionally different from a sweepstakes. (In a game, the "players" themselves discover by "playing" whether they are winners. In a sweepstakes, the winners are chosen by another person at random.) Also, the best games involve an element of fun that makes them much more attractive to the customer than the odds would imply.

The basic formula for promotion success (from the customer's perspective) holds especially true for games:

$$Fun + Value > Work$$

Translated, this simply means that the fun and the value of the promotion must exceed the perceived work effort that the consumer must expend to participate in the promotion — by a significant degree.

The work part of the equation refers to the simplicity of the game. The following are considered elements of work:

- Collecting game pieces over time
- Having to watch or listen for a broadcast to determine if one

is a winner
- Having to visit an in-store display to match a number
- Mailing in a winning game piece to collect the prize

The game with the least amount of work would involve scratch-off game cards that instantly tell customers if they've won anything and that could be redeemed immediately in the restaurant. (In the future, an even more effortless version might be an electronic instant-win game that eliminates the scratch-off reveal mechanism completely.) But a simple instant win game card has no element of continuity to it (unless the winner must return the next day or next week to redeem the card).

The value element of the success equation refers to the prize structure and the types of prizes. If the big prizes are truly spectacular in their appeal or if the odds are better than average, the value of playing the game increases. A good rule of thumb is to offer a minimum 1 in 12 odds of winning *something*. (During recessionary times, customers seem to pay a lot more attention to odds than usual. Recent games have been more in the 1 in 5 to 8 range.) If the goal is retention of current customers and it is known that the heavy user visits the QSR an average of once a week, it is relatively certain that the typical customer would win something if an eight-week game with odds of 1 in 8 was run.

The fun element of a game can be more important than value, if properly handled. Having the QSR game mirror a popular board game or casino game is one way to accomplish this (for example, McDonald's Monopoly or Scrabble games). Not only does this add the "borrowed interest" association of previous enjoyable experiences with the game, but it reduces the work side of the equation because customers already know how to play. It isn't necessary to pay licensing fees for the rights to use many popular games; games such as tic-tac-toe and checkers are in the public domain and are familiar to everyone. The key is to structure the game so it plays as much as possible like the actual game.

Fun can be added to the game through borrowed interest or through the selection of prizes. The critical goal in a QSR game creative promotion is to try to move a customer's assessment of the program from the rational side of the brain to the emotional side. If customers evaluate the game in a purely rational way, they will subconsciously focus on the odds and make a mental calculation of what it will cost them to win a prize (most people still believe there are better odds if something is purchased) compared to the value of the prize most likely to be won. If they're thinking like that, the game will almost certainly fail.

If, however, customers think about the fun of playing that game (with all the attendant childhood memories) or are enamored with a particular prize, amazing things can happen. Drs. Sobel and Ornstein at the University of California Medical Center have identified a command center within the brain that controls the decisions people make. Emotions are the primary force driving most decisions, not logic. The 85/15 formula, used by sales consultants to train salespeople, is based on the premise that people make decisions based 85 percent on their feelings and only 15 percent on the cold, hard facts. If the QSR game has struck an emotional chord, some customers will come in every day or even several times a day if they are really hooked. This emotional appeal is the whole premise behind why people play the lottery or gamble in casinos. Their rational side knows the odds are against them. Or, as someone once put it, "The net present value of a dollar spent on a lottery ticket is so close to zero as to be beyond the ability of normal calculators to detect it." But the emotional side overcomes all logic and causes people to play the lottery each week or travel to Las Vegas annually to lose money. People do crazy things when they're in love.

A few words are in order about prize structure. There are really two types: high-level, such as a $1 million, cars, and travel; and low-level, such as free food or discounts on food. High-level prizes provide the "sizzle" to attract attention and build awareness. They often provide the theme for the game and offer copy opportunities for outdoor P-O-P such as banners. ("Win $1 million" is a lot more attention-grabbing than "Win french fries.") Low-level prizes, if seeded at odds of 1 in 12 or below, provide the "permission to believe" that appeals to the customers' rational side and makes them think that "if everyone is winning something — I'm next." Even if an individual doesn't win a low-level prize on a particular visit, chances are that he or she will see evidence all around that people are winning (winning game pieces being redeemed in line, winners exclaiming "I won" while scratching their cards). It's the same phenomenon that occurs in the casinos. They publicize their big winners to draw in gamblers and, once inside, surround them with the artificially amplified sound of money dropping from slot machines. There is the sense that people are winning all around that makes people want to get in on the action. It's a powerful and compelling feeling that's linked to some elemental herd or mob psychology.

QSR games have traditionally provided a number of mid-level prizes, ranging from smaller versions of the top prizes to small cash prizes ($1,000 or less). The only reason the mid-level prizes exist is because of tradition. They serve no useful purpose and soak up a large portion of the available prize budget. A QSR game would be better served by eliminating the mid-level prizes and using this money to strengthen the offering of high-level prizes or the number of low-level prizes.

Coupons disguised as prizes have been used heavily in recent years to help improve the odds. This can be reasonably effective if used to make an "everybody wins" claim. However, clearly a prize of "50¢ off" does not have the same customer appeal as a totally free prize, even if the free item has a value of less than $.50. Consumers do not perceive coupons as prizes. If food discounts are to be used as prizes, the prize should not say "cents-off" on an item, but it should say, "You win (food item) for only (money amount)." For example, McDonald's has had some success recently with $.25 french fries as a low-level prize. People have recently become very sensitive to the odds and tend to perceive disguised coupons for what they are. A possible happy medium would be to offer a popular menu item for a very low price, but not have *everyone* win — possibly with the odds of 1 in 3 or even 1 in 2. There is a nice prize in addition to apparently great odds.

To keep the excitement level high and to maintain a sense of prize attainability, it's very effective to showcase the high-level winners in promotional advertising while the game is still running. Because games often run six to eight weeks (contrasted with the typical four-week window for nongame promotions), this often is quite possible. Lower level prize winners can be photographed and posted in the restaurant in which they won to accomplish this effect.

Finally, a word about the reveal mechanism. As mentioned earlier, instant win scratch-offs hold the highest attraction to the speed-oriented, heavy QSR user who usually has a strong need for immediate gratification. But the continuity element is missing, and unless the odds of winning are extremely good, most game pieces will become "instant losers," leaving a negative taste in the customer's mouth. One way to nullify the "instant lose" phenomenon and introduce an element of continuity is to make losing game pieces potential winners by letting the customer bring them in the next week (or the next day) to compare them to an in-store display that changes regularly. If they match that day, the losing piece becomes a winner. This game within a game combines the best of instant win games with a purchase continuity element (of course, it also introduces some negative operational considerations).

Another way to build continuity into instant win games is to incorporate a "rollover" element with an "everyone wins" feature. Simply put, the winning card cannot be redeemed until the next week. When the card is redeemed the following week, a new winning card is issued that is good for the week after that. Once customers are hooked in the initial weeks, they can be counted on for at least a weekly visit for the duration of the game. This is an excellent way to bridge traffic from a high traffic time of year into a slower period (for example, from December into January).

Case History — McDonald's Monopoly. Originally run for six weeks in the spring of 1987, Monopoly is about as close to a perfect QSR game as one can find.

First and foremost, McDonald's Monopoly incorporated most of the fun elements of the real Parker Brothers game (and Monopoly is synonymous with the word *game*). Customers could collect properties to win cash prizes, or they could win instantly. Even the prizes themselves were related to the game (such as Lionel train sets for collecting all the railroad properties).

The enthusiasm of the sell-in, combined with the sheer fun of the game, made for an almost 100 percent "take" by the McDonald's system. Part of this was probably due to the creative use of P-O-P to make the restaurant look like a giant Monopoly set. Giant blow-up posters of various parts of the game board were part of the P-O-P kit, including an oversized actual game board that framed the outside of the main door. All the P-O-P displays communicated the same message: "$40 million in prizes." (See Exhibit 26.7.)

Monopoly's sales results exceeded even the most optimistic expectations. The promotion was run again in 1988 with a few modifications and achieved excellent results.

7. *Local Store Marketing.* Pioneered by McDonald's, the local store marketing (LSM) technique recognizes the importance of the local trading area. A 1984 Gallup study showed that 66 percent of all customers traveled three miles or less to visit a QSR. And, as mentioned earlier, as few as several hundred of these local customers can represent the majority of a QSR's volume.

The first step is a trading area survey of current customers to reveal promotional opportunities and define customer segments. Even

EXHIBIT 26.7

more revealing can be a comparison of current customers to the demographics of everyone living and working in the trading area. Promotional opportunity "gaps" can be identified effectively in this manner. These "geodemographic" data are obtainable through a number of companies linking census data with various other databases to paint a portrait of the trading area.

Typical local store marketing targets include the following:

- Local high schools and colleges
- Seniors
- Ethnic concentrations
- Large office complexes and factories

Beyond these "opportunity groups," there are often localized occurrences or problems that are best addressed at the local trading area level:

- Grand openings
- New QSR competition in the trading area
- Softness in the local economy due to local plant closings
- Local school with a winning sports team

Specific promotions can be developed for each of these groups or situations. Local store marketing programs are often very similar even though the markets and their problems may differ. For someone responsible for a large chain of restaurants, it probably pays to invest in developing a number of canned local store marketing promotions that address a number of commonly occurring local store marketing opportunities. Franchisees or managers can then pull these promotions off the shelf as they have a need. If generic artwork has been developed for P-O-P displays, coupons, and so on, the individual store can then afford to handle the promotion in a professional-looking manner at a cost that it could have never afforded on its own.

8. Meal Combinations. Meal combinations are an effective way to build average check. These promotions are best run in high-traffic time periods to maximize dollar sales because additional traffic is expensive to achieve at those times.

Meal combos don't necessarily need to have a reduced price. Most customers don't bother adding up the individual items to see if there is an actual savings. Most consumers automatically assume that the meal combo is a deal in the same manner that a product promoted on an end-aisle display in the supermarket is assumed to be on special.

In addition to increasing average check, an "order by number" approach to meal combinations can actually improve the speed of service. Customers are increasingly overwhelmed with the number of choices offered on the average QSR menu board. For many customers, saying "Give me a number 3" is a lot less work than poring through several panels of choices. This approach can be particularly effective when many of a QSR's customers are unfamiliar with the products (as is often the case with ethnically oriented QSR concepts) and have to ask many questions.

9. *Point-of-Purchase.* Well-designed and properly placed, P-O-P can be *the* critical element in communicating a QSR promotional message. Consider these general truths:

- A significant number of restaurant choice decisions are made while driving down franchise row.
- The majority of specific product purchase decisions are made at the counter or while in the drive-through.
- Typically, 20 percent of a QSR's customers represent 80 percent of its sales.
- These customers visit frequently, sometimes several times a week.
- On a cost per impression basis, it may be cheaper to reach these heavy users through P-O-P than through traditional broadcast media.

Beyond the cost per impression advantages of P-O-P are the effectiveness factors. Potential customers are actually looking for P-O-P. Since they have usually already made the decision to eat out, many use exterior P-O-P to help them make the final decision regarding which QSR to visit (see Exhibit 26.4). Therefore, there is little waste with a P-O-P-delivered message.

Efficiency and effectiveness of P-O P can combine to produce some impressive results. One way to measure the impact of P-O-P is to choose a market in which the trading areas of all the restaurants of a particular chain are receiving the same weight of broadcast media exposure. Classify each restaurant based purely on the number of P-O-P elements present into minimum, average, and maximum; and then compare sales results during the promotion against the trend (vs. year-ago levels or pre- or post-levels). Factoring out other differences (new restaurants, no drive-through), usually reveals that P-O-P, by itself, can produce a 20 percent to more than 100 percent difference in incremental sales between minimum and maximum restaurants. Needless to say, this kind of study, while simple to perform, can be extremely effective in convincing franchisees to invest in P-O-P.

P-O-P can be developed to communicate a specific promotion or just to merchandise regular products more effectively. In either case, it's important to not overlook all the possible areas of the restaurant that can be used to potentially communicate a message. An effective way to do this is to think of the store as a map and envision all possible points of contact as the customer physically moves through it. Exhibit 26.8 illustrates an abbreviated communications opportunities "snake" for a hypothetical QSR. The drive-through/in-store split occurs early on in the process. The drive-through visit experience is quite different from the in-restaurant experience and must be treated with equal effort, considering that as much as 50 percent (or more) of a QSR's total business is generated there.

EXHIBIT 26.8

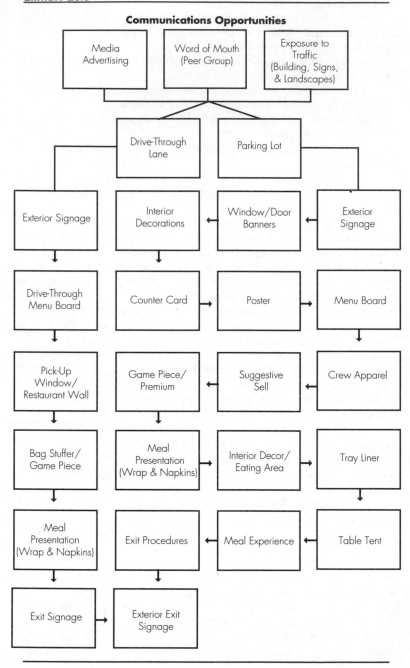

Communications Opportunities

In any case, the snake can be used at the outset of a promotion for planning which point-of-purchase elements to include in the "kit." There are literally several hundred surface areas that could be used for communication, but the typical kit can include only four to eight elements. Which area to focus on depends on the marketing objectives.

If reach is the objective, P-O-P efforts should be focused on the exterior with a simple and short message designed to catch the eye of the hungry QSR user who has a QSR chain in his or her considered set. Large banners hung on the front of the roof or the main pole sign are very effective here, if local zoning laws permit. If zoning regulations are an issue, large posters or decals in the windows can have almost the same impact. The key words are *large, colorful,* and *simple.*

The most effective messages for exterior P-O-P usually focus on a price point or a promotional product simultaneously being featured in broadcast media. The theory of image transfer holds that a shortened version of a heavily advertised message can stimulate viewers to replay the full spot in their mind upon viewing the banner. Regardless of whether this is true, coordinating a QSR's exterior P-O-P message with current advertising can be very effective if the message is motivating enough to finalize the purchase decision. For example, an advertising message that communicates the quality ingredients used in making the products may help the image of the QSR, but it is not the kind of message that will bring in traffic if it is communicated on a banner. Promoting the availability of a limited-time-only special product designed to induce craving is a much stronger alternative, especially if copy points in the banner are picked up from the advertising.

If the marketing objective is to stimulate trial of a new product, focusing on the areas of the store just before the point of ordering is an option in order to seed the idea in customers' minds — for example, the entrance area or the end of the waiting line area. In the drive-through, P-O-P placed along the lane before the menu board can serve the same purpose. Of course, P-O-P at the ordering point can also be effective but, by itself, may be too late for the customer who has not previously heard about the new product through advertising.

If the marketing objective is to build the average check, the point of ordering should be the main focus. P-O-P featuring meal combinations can achieve this goal, especially if the meal combinations make the ordering decision easier for the customer, as can be accomplished with an "order by number" meal combination.

If the goal is to build frequency from current customers, the dining area is a good bet. Tray liners and table texts can be effective in communicating a message that will positively reinforce the visit experience and increase the probability of a repeat visit on the next QSR-focused trip. Longer copy and more complicated messages can work here because customers have more time to read while eating their food. Take-out and drive-through customers can be similarly reached through exit P-O-P as well as bag stuffers and on-bag messages.

Add-ons such as desserts and side items can also benefit from exposure in the table area. While consuming the food, the customer — as a captive audience — is susceptible to appetizing suggestions resulting in additional purchases that round out the meal.

While the communications opportunities snake can be used to qualitatively help identify P-O-P focus areas, it can also be used to quantify each point of contact. In-market testing of different combinations of P-O-P elements in matched restaurants can determine the dollar sales value of each element. Of course, different promotional tactics will probably have different sets of P-O-P elements that support them best. For example, a counter card may have a very high value for a premium promotion but a low value for a new product introduction. Controlled testing over time should allow a QSR chain to develop a generalized set of guidelines for which point-of-purchase elements work best for each major promotion tactic. Of course, having a dollar value attached to each element can also be a very effective way of convincing franchisees to order the proper amount of P-O-P. Buying a $10 counter card becomes a lot easier to do if it's known that it can produce an incremental $100 in sales!

10. Premiums. Properly planned and executed, premium offers rank among the strongest sales generators in the QSR promotional arsenal. However, improperly done, they can lower average check, take up valuable storage space in the restaurant, and leave the QSR with large quantities of worthless inventory.

The success of a premium promotion is, of course, directly related to the appeal the item has to the target customer. The largest component of this appeal is usually the perceived value of the premium. The value of the premium can be increased by its uniqueness or the idea planted in customers that they can't get it anywhere else.

Adding a collectible element to the premiums can have a very strong continuity effect as customers strive to collect the set or, it is hoped, collect several sets. Due to the high purchase frequency of the QSR category, some fairly large collections can be built in a short period of time. The key to this is hooking the customer early in the promotion with a strong starter premium that cements a commitment to collect.

An often overlooked benefit of premiums is their ability to reinforce brand equity by extending a brand image. It's a good idea for the premium to at least have some connection to the QSR chain's advertising, decor, image, or product attributes. Barring this connection, the premium should be of high quality and built to last. Premiums can evoke positive memories of past visit experiences and can possess remembrance value that can carry on for years — but only if the premium doesn't break!

Premiums are easy to concept test (probably the easiest of all promotional tactics). Testing of actual prototypes that the consumer can touch provides the most accurate measure of a premium's appeal, but drawings and descriptions of the premium can also work. As with any promotion test, it's a good idea to include a premium for which there are sales results in the test to act as a reference point. It's also important to test the premium in the context of the promotional offer. The most attractive premium in the world will be a dismal failure if it's perceived as a poor value.

As with games, premiums are most effective when they work at the emotional level rather than the logical level. However, the rational side should not be ignored. If the premium has a practical use related to the food, it can develop continuity, especially if combined with an ongoing promotional offer, such as the perennial cup good for discounted beverage refills on future visits.

From the customer's perspective, premiums can be either free (usually requiring a purchase) or cost some additional amount. From the QSR's perspective, a free premium can be either a true added value, whose cost is paid out of the profit margin of the required food purchase, or a partial self-liquidator for which the food price includes some of the premium's cost. True self-liquidators have the customer paying all of the cost. There are advantages to each approach.

Free Premiums.

Customers will always say that they prefer free premiums over self-liquidators in research surveys. However, the very nature of free premiums limits the cost of the premium item. Although there are many examples of highly successful free premiums aimed at adults, children are more attracted to them in general due to their immediate play value. Adults have a more developed cost-benefit sense and tend to perceive some premiums as toys unless there is a significant borrowed interest element in the offer that increases their perceived value (see the Batman cups case history in the "Tie-In" section).

Children's Premiums.

Children are a segment that most QSRs cannot afford to overlook. One recent study revealed that children under 12 constituted approximately 40 percent of all parties during the dinner daypart.

It's important to think of the mother when designing premium promotions aimed at younger children because she is the gatekeeper to these purchase decisions. Mothers are interested in the quality construction of the premium, repeat play value, ease of assembly or operation, and clean up. Incorporating educational elements into the promotion will also win moms' approvals.

An additional motivation for determining the family's QSR purchase decision is a child who wants an advertised premium.

What makes a child desire a premium? Obviously, advertising targeted to children can plant the seed of desire. Displaying the actual premium in-store at eye level for the child can create the in-store insistence. If a display is built to showcase the premium, it's best to showcase future premiums (if any) to get the children excited about their collectibility.

What types of premiums appeal to children? First, it's important to segment children into younger (2–7) and older (8–13) groups at a minimum. The two groups are so different they seem to be almost from different species! The younger children aspire to be like the older group, who, of course, want nothing to do with the younger children.

The younger children tend to be fond of fantasy and fantasy characters. Borrowed interest through licensed characters can be effective, but QSR chains can establish their *own* characters as well. Mothers generally make the purchase decisions for this age group. Older children are starting to explore their independence. They're taken with fantasy, but cynical fantasy, not cute fantasy. Humor is very important. (Sometimes the independence, cynicism, and humor combine to yield "grossness.") Because peer approval and fitting in are so very important at this age, it's important to be in touch with what's "in" not only with this group, but with the group's aspirational target — teens. Ongoing research with a 'tween/teen advisory panel can help spot emerging trends. These children are often on their own after school with often hefty allowances provided by their dual-income parents. Never aim too young with this group — that's death.

Case History — McDonald's Happy Meals. McDonald's has set the pace for children's marketing in the QSR category since before the Happy Meal with its use of Ronald McDonald and its incorporation of playlands in many of its restaurants. While children by themselves represent a significant portion of the overall business, the true value of marketing to Ronald-age children (2–7) lies in the children's ability to influence the family QSR purchase decision.

The Happy Meal was a brilliant invention that further cemented this relationship with children. The best evidence of the success of the Happy Meal is the fact that almost every major QSR chain has some form of child's meal. It has essentially become the price of entry into the family segment.

Born as a packaged meal combination in McDonald's Kansas City co-op in 1977, the original Happy Meal was sold in boxes designed as circus trains, which were collected to form a set. The basic combination of sandwich, fries, soft drink, and a toy has remained unchanged since that time. The purchasing power of McDonald's full system has allowed McDonald's to offer increasingly high quality and original toys with each new Happy Meal, despite a recommended price decrease from $2.50 to $1.99.

11. Self-Liquidating Premiums. Self-liquidating premiums are attractive to the QSR because, as the name implies, there is little if any cost to the promoter. (In fact, some QSRs suggest a consumer price that allows the franchisee to a make a small profit on the item — usually just a few pennies. This makes the entire program more attractive and easier to sell-in, as well as compensates the franchisee for the extra effort.) Unlike self-liquidating premiums in the packaged goods arena, in which consumers typically mail in proofs-of-purchase to get their premium in the mail, QSR self-liquidators are usually fulfilled in-restaurant. This has the advantage of offering an immediate reward as opposed to the delayed gratification of receiving it through the mail.

Significant values can be offered to the customer on items that have a low per unit fixed cost. This is due to the typically large quantity discounts for which the bigger QSR chains can qualify. The addition of the borrowed interest of a licensed property can make the premium a "must have" for some customer segments. The *Indiana Jones* video-tape series offered by McDonald's in 1992 for $5.99 is an example of a high perceived value on a very desirable premium.

Although free premiums are rated as more desirable than self-liq-uidators in most customer research, collectible self-liquidators have some hidden advantages over the free premiums. Once the first in a series has been purchased, customers have a vested interest in returning to collect the set. Their involvement and interest are greater in the pro-motion because they spent their own money on it. An additional pur-chase both justifies and validates the wisdom of their original purchase decision.

Many QSR franchisees and managers don't like self-liquidating premiums because they don't want their customers spending any of their money on anything but food. A surprisingly large number of QSR customers have just a few dollars in their pocket at a given time. The concern is that a $5.99 videotape purchase, no matter how good a value, will not leave the customer with enough cash to buy a full meal. To avoid this "cash poor" situation, a good rule of thumb is to limit the customer cost of the premium to $.99 or less. Of course, rules were meant to be broken as illustrated by the apparent success of the *Indiana Jones* videotape offer.

Premiums that are meant to be used in conjunction with the con-sumption of the QSR's products can be exceptionally profitable. Beyond the free-refill coffee mug, these could include insulated bags for keeping food warm or trays for holding the food and drinks while in the car. (Ideally, these trays will only fit items from the promoting QSR!)

Case History — McDonald's Garfield Mugs. Collectible glass-ware promotions have historically been among the strongest top-line sales generators in the QSR category. McDonald's had great success in the late 1970s and early 1980s with several glassware promotions using licensed properties with a distinct child appeal; the two most notable were Peanuts and Muppets glasses. But in 1986, it had been five years since McDonald's last national glassware promotion, and its national marketing department felt the time was ripe for bringing back this venerable tactic. At issue was how to stand apart from the competition, which had continued to run glassware promotions throughout this period.

The solution was to tie in with the Garfield licensed character and offer a series of four collectible glass mugs, each featuring a different pair of typically droll Garfield cartoon frames. At the time, Garfield was the most popular cartoon character in the country, with appeal across all age groups, including adults. The strategy behind Garfield mugs was to have a property that appealed to both children and adults, and using the mug instead of the usual glass added to the adult appeal as well as set the promotion apart from the competition.

The promotion had been successfully tested in three cities in Pennsylvania earlier in 1986 at a $.69 price point, and this offer was extended to the national promotion. Each week in July, a different mug would be featured, each for $.69 with any purchase.

Results were phenomenal, with more than 32 million mugs sold in 7,500 restaurants during the month, making Garfield mugs the largest glassware promotion in the history of the industry.

12. Promotional Products (LTOs). Certain products are known to produce strong cravings among consumers, the most well advertised being the Big Mac (as in the "Big Mac Attack"). Sometimes these products generate strong sales during the introductory weeks but do not sustain these levels for very long. Customers seem to lose interest in these products after their initial craving has been satisfied.

These products are perfect candidates for limited-time-only (LTO) promotions. These promotional products are introduced with heavy advertising and then are withdrawn before sales start to slump (usually four to six weeks). If the LTO carries enough of the craving quotient, it can be very a powerful traffic builder.

The ideal LTO is operationally simple. Existing kitchen equipment is used to prepare the item, and little additional crew training is required. Often the LTO is based on an existing product with one or two ingredients changed. For example, a regular hamburger with a special sauce, bun, or condiment. Sometimes the product is tied thematically to a seasonal occurrence or holiday (for example, McDonald's Shamrock Shakes on St. Patrick's Day). This theme can often make the craving factor greater than the actual taste difference would normally warrant.

LTOs can be one way to test possible new products. Consumer tastes change over time, and products that haven't sustained sales in the past can in the future.

Case History — Taco Bell's Steak Burrito. Part of the success of Taco Bell's value strategy was a continuous stream of LTOs to keep the product news fresh and give some relief from a pure price message. Most of these LTOs were value priced at $.99 or less.

Several local Mexican QSRs had experienced considerable success with very large entree products. Going after this market, Taco Bell developed the Steak Burrito. This product was introduced nationally in 1992.

Initial results were spectacular. Transactions exceeded expectations and, more important, average check was up. Based on this response, the Steak Burrito was added to the regular menu where it remains today as a strong performer.

13. Sampling. Sampling is an underutilized technique that can be a real trial generator. Sampling is especially effective for new product introductions, particularly when the product concept is difficult to communicate with P-O-P or advertising and has a real taste advantage.

Typically, sampling is handled through coupons offering the product free or at a reduced price to reduce the risk of trial for the customer. But some products lend themselves to sample-size portions. Sampling of this type works best near the entrance so customers can try the product before they've placed their order.

14. Tie-Ins. Promotions are becoming very expensive for QSR companies to handle on a solo basis. Sharing costs and customers through a tie-in can make a lot of economic sense (and produce a lot of headaches if improperly planned).

There are two types of tie-ins: traditional and borrowed interest. The traditional tie-in matches two marketing entities whose equity lies in their products and current customer base. With the traditional approach, the first step in finding the ideal tie-in partner is to determine how many customers the partners have in common. This does not necessarily mean the partners have the same customers but that their target audience is the other's current customer. For example, a QSR chain that does well with seniors but poorly with families and wants to promote a new children's meal may wish to tie in with a toy company that has products children love but wishes to have greater appeal to grandparents.

A syndicated database such as MRI or Simmons can be used to measure cross-usage of products among tie-in partners. Such an analysis can also be used to help structure the deal between the two companies, because rarely does each partner benefit exactly equally in the tie-in. Whenever possible, it helps to quantify all aspects of the tie-in so that both partners know what they are getting into in advance.

The borrowed interest tie-in matches the QSR with a marketing entity whose equity lies in an event or licensed property (for example, movies, sports teams, celebrities, record companies, TV shows, or sports events such as the Olympics or the Super Bowl). These types of tie-ins are high-risk, high-return promotions. If the right property is chosen at the right time, the results can be phenomenal (see the Batman cups case history later in this section). However, it is difficult to generate borrowed interest tie-ins that have universal appeal. For every person motivated by a NASCAR race or a college football tournament, there are plenty of others who are profoundly disinterested in these events.

One way to reduce the risk of these types of tie-ins is to work with a proven property. Rather than tie in with the theatrical release of a film, tie in with the video release of a film that was a box office hit. Then it is known that there is an audience for this property, and research can show if this audience matches a QSR's target.

Case History — Taco Bell's Batman Cups. Taco Bell introduced its Value Menu in November 1988 with great success. However, one of the key components of the strategy was unlimited free drink refills. This was met with less than universal acceptance by the franchisees. There was also concern regarding whether the enormous sales gains experienced during the winter months could continue into the peak traffic warm weather months. Taco Bell was looking for a blockbuster promotion that could unite the system behind the free drink refills and drive sales to new heights. Coincidentally, a new dessert item, Cinnamon Twists, was scheduled for introduction in the late spring, to replace Cinnamon Crispas.

The movie *Batman* had received tremendous upfront publicity, thanks in large part to an exciting trailer that had run at the end of 1988. The frequent moviegoing set (essentially the same audience as the heavy QSR user) was eagerly anticipating the release of the movie scheduled for June 1989. The advance word was that *Batman* would be very dark and violent — not exactly family fare. Apparently because of this, none of the family-oriented QSRs made a serious attempt to tie in with *Batman*.

Taco Bell had cultivated an image as the alternative QSR through past advertising efforts (for example, the Jim McMahon "Born To Be Wild" campaign). Although families were an important part of Taco Bell's customer base, the idea of a "dark" Batman was not at odds with their image.

The decision was made to go with a series of four collector cups, each free with the purchase of a 32-ounce drink. The promotion creative focused on the word "free" (in addition to *Batman*, of course). This provided the perfect opportunity to unify the system behind free drink refills and to introduce the new dessert item with a free sample-size serving packaged in a Batman-logoed wrapper. Franchisees, of course, did not have to offer these additional items, but then they could not take advantage of the available P-O-P. The P-O-P kit included a number of unusual items that were designed to make the restaurant look like the Batcave (see Exhibit 26.9).

The results were spectacular. Even though the cups ran out in the third week of the promotion, more than 21 million were sold. Sales, which had been running at double-digit increases over the 1988 sales, almost doubled during this period. (Several sales records were set during the promotion.) Essentially 100 percent of the system started offering free refills. And sales of the new Cinnamon Twists exceeded all expectations. In fact, after the promotion ended, sales of the new item

EXHIBIT 26.9

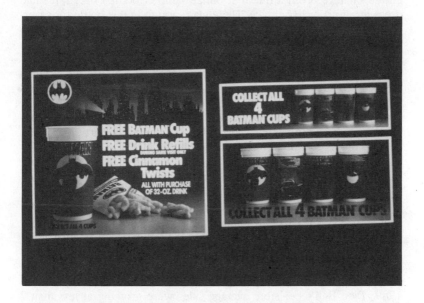

sustained themselves at a level significantly higher than they were before the promotion.

Batman kicked off the first summer of Taco Bell's value strategy with a bang and brought a lot of new people into the restaurants to experience the new Value Menu. This undoubtedly set the stage for the unparalleled success of this program in the next few years.

Case History — McDonald's and Kraft Salad Dressings. McDonald's rolled out its line of prepackaged salads with great success. These products allowed it to compete for a QSR customer who had been previously unavailable. These people had been eating at the salad bars of Burger King and Wendy's until that time.

Although salad sales were sustaining themselves well, some QSR salad lovers had lingering doubts about the salads' value relative to the competitions' salad bars. McDonald's wanted to erase those doubts as well as emphasize the quality of the ingredients used in preparing the salads.

The salad dressing category had always been very fragmented with no single brand dominating. Kraft had always been one of the top brands, but wanted to increase its penetration among heavy salad eaters. The possibility of tapping into known salad eaters among McDonald's 17 million daily customers held great appeal. (Kraft was also a major supplier of food products to McDonald's as well.)

The promotion worked as follows: Every customer purchasing an entree salad received a free four-ounce sampler bottle of a Kraft salad dressing of his or her choice. There was enough in this bottle for several servings of salad, so the customer typically took home a more than half-filled bottle. Attached to the bottle was a cents-off coupon good on regular size Kraft salad dressing.

15. *Value Pricing.* The concept of every day low price (EDLP) has been in vogue in recent years in many industries. If it is combined with a lessening in temporary price reductions such as couponing, promotional costs can be reduced and things made easier for the consumer. Participation is easy because all customers participate. (Of course, this is one of the hidden expenses in EDLP. There is no slippage. Even customers who never participate in promotions are affected by EDLP.) EDLP in the QSR category is usually called value pricing.

Case History — Taco Bell's Value Strategy. Value pricing took off on a national scale with Taco Bell's "Value Menu" in late 1988. Taco Bell reduced the price on its top item — the taco — from $.79 to $.49 in many markets. In other markets, it grouped a number of popular items into a $.59 Value Menu. Eventually, all markets moved to a three-tiered Value Menu structure with most items either at $.59, $.79, or $.99.

Sales results were phenomenal (see Exhibit 26.10). Prior to 1989, Taco Bell's per store average sales were growing at less than 2 percent — just matching the growth in the QSR category but significantly below the growth of Mexican foods in general in the country. The dotted line extrapolates that growth to 1992. The solid line represents actual sales. Since late 1988, that difference has been worth almost $2.5 billion in incremental sales to Taco Bell. More important, profit margins have also increased, despite the overall price reductions.

Taco Bell's Value Initiative was much more than an across-the-board price cut. Major operational changes were initiated to streamline product preparation and delivery so that speed of service and quality of product would not suffer with the increased traffic. Also, P-O-P was used on a much bigger scale to communicate and remind people of the news of the Value Menu.

Prior to 1988, Taco Bell restaurants were relatively void of P-O-P and had a distinctly sterile look. The P-O-P that was there was very subdued in design and copy. As part of the introduction of the Value Initiative, the restaurants were filled with P-O-P — both inside and out. Bright neon colors and bold designs were used to improve the attention-getting ability of the P-O-P and create a fun atmosphere.

Taco Bell had been testing "value" for several years prior to the national introduction. It had tested a Value Menu of items under $.99 in 1987 that simply highlighted the lower-priced side of the menu without offering any price reductions. QSR heavy users were very sensitive to price/value relationships and didn't buy it. Taco Bell tested the current Value Menu with little media or merchandising and had some ini-

EXHIBIT 26.10

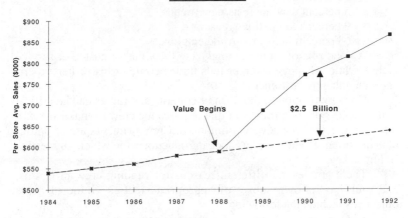

TACO BELL

tial success, but it was unable to sustain it. Only when it made the investment in both real price reductions *and* P-O-P *and* media did the customers start pouring in.

Traffic increases were amazing. There were 60 percent more customer transactions in 1990 than in 1988. Surprisingly, average check only dropped slightly. Customers were taking advantage of the lower prices by ordering more items. These facts, combined with operational streamlining, resulted in a 44 percent increase in operating profits in 1989 and a 33 percent increase in 1990.

Competitors were not slow to recognize the success of value pricing. Wendy's introduced a $.99 Value Menu. McDonald's reduced the recommended price of its hamburgers and cheeseburgers to $.59 and $.69 respectively and developed Extra Value Meal Deals — meal combinations offering significant savings.

An important element of value is to surprise customers with more than they expect. Taco Bell did this with its unlimited free refills. Most savvy customers said, "Why order large drinks anymore?" and took advantage of the system by going to Taco Bell more often. This "rip us off" approach brought in a lot more customers and profits than was lost on smaller drink average checks.

CREW MOTIVATION

Research shows that the six reasons why a customer stops patronizing a restaurant are as follows:

- 1 percent die
- 3 percent move
- 5 percent new interests/new friends
- 9 percent competitive reasons
- 68 percent indifferent/rude employees

A good rule of thumb in analyzing the value of customer service is that, while a happy customer tells three people of his or her experience, an unhappy customer tells 10.

Crew motivation in the form of contests and rallies can be critical to the success of any promotion that requires the crew to make an extra effort (which is almost every promotion). Crew members are of particular importance with new product introductions for which suggestive selling is key.

There are several different reasons for running crew programs, and each has its own subset of appropriate tactics. Some of these objectives include the following:

- *Operational Training.* Promotions designed to train the crew in a new operational procedure or one training program related to a promotion. One approach might be a contest to see who can perform the new procedure the quickest or the most accurately.

- *Motivational.* To motivate the crew to perform its job better with the end goals of reducing employee turnover and improving service. An example might be a video sneak preview of upcoming promotions so that the crew feels more involved and "plugged in" to the bigger picture.

- *Suggestive Selling.* The critical ingredient in higher new product trial rates or increased average check. A simple question — "Would you like to try...?" — asked of all customers (or selected customers ordering specific items) at the point of ordering can yield dramatic sales increases. Usually, a suggestive selling promotion takes the form of a contest. Suggestive selling can be measured either directly through a "mystery customer," who issues awards to those "caught" doing the suggestive selling; or indirectly through a sales contest in which actual sales are measured. Sales should always be measured in some uniform manner that compensates for traffic differences between shifts — for example, "new product units sold per thousand transactions" or "highest average check."

In structuring these contests, the scope of the competition is important to achieving overall restaurant objectives. Contests can be as simple as the manager announcing, "$10 to the person with the highest sales during the lunch rush" to the counter crew. This is an excellent short-term program for employees working the cash registers and will almost certainly get them to improve the areas they can control, such as suggestive selling to build average check. But this does nothing to motivate the rest of the crew that supports the counter.

One way to do this is to organize teams of employees to compete against each other. For example, the lunch shift vs. the dinner shift might be one way to go. (Again, it's important to measure performance in a way that reduces or eliminates differences in traffic between day-parts and other factors not controlled by the crew.) To encourage over-all restaurant performance with the team approach, it's always a good idea to include performance measures that cover every major crew activity (not just sales or transactions). For example, an independent judge could rate the cleanliness of the lobby and restrooms, the accuracy of orders, portion size, properly cooked product, holding times, speed of service, and other important variables not immediately affecting sales.

Other options include store vs. store and region vs. region. However, the larger the size of the team, the less meaningful the competition becomes to individual crew members, because they feel that they can make less of an impact individually.

The type of prize awarded to winners can have a big impact on the success of the program. One thing that should be part of any program is recognition of superior performance. In many instances, recognition can be enough of a motivator by itself, especially if there is some relatively permanent record of achievement (a pin or badge that can be worn or a plaque on the wall). Cash as a prize is a strong motivator that has universal appeal but little remembrance value. Noncash prizes such as extra break time and days off also have universal appeal but little remembrance value. Remembrance value can be found with merchandise awards that employees constantly see or use and that remind them of their achievement. Clothing and electronics are good examples of merchandise with good remembrance value.

Effectively communicating the program to the crew is almost as important as the program itself. Communication can be as simple as a five-minute meeting with each shift or as complex as a regional crew "rally" staged at a local auditorium. The ideal communication technique takes crew members away from the work environment so they're totally focused on the subject at hand. But on-site programs can also be effective. A well-produced video that can be watched during a break can work. A poster describing the program can be hung in the break room and serve as both a reminder and a reference point for the contest. The critical point is that crew members understand how the program works as well as have a good feeling that the whole experience will be fun and that they have a reasonable chance of winning something.

PROMOTION ANALYSIS

Post-Promotion Analysis. Regular, in-depth analysis of promotions is critical to understanding what works and what does not for a particular QSR company. Eventually, a "war chest" of proven promotions will be built up for use as needed.

Good data are at the core of effective promotion analysis. The widely used CREST report, a syndicated service of the NPD group, is based on a diary panel of 13,000 households. These households complete a two-week diary of all their restaurant eating activities for all members of the household, including information on items ordered, check size, and use of promotions. This information is reported quarterly to subscribers of CREST.

The value of this kind of information lies in the fact that the results can be compared to previous waves in order to project trends. It can also be cross-tabulated against demographic data on the households to yield a clear picture of who is participating in the promotions, where any gains have been made, and from whom share is being taken. This can be done for a given chain along with its competitors. CREST data can allow one to see patterns in a competitor's promotions and hypothesize what its overall marketing plans may be (assuming the competitor has any).

If volume declines are being experienced. CREST data can pinpoint whether the problem is due to reach, frequency, party size, or average check, as well as show how this problem changes during different times of the year. The data can also pinpoint problem dayparts or products. To a limited extent, the data can pinpoint problems (or opportunities) in different regions of the country.

Another very effective way to pinpoint problems is through a monthly tracking study in a QSR's major markets. Many of the major chains conduct telephone surveys of QSR users on a regular basis to track trends for their chain and their competitors on key attributes such as cleanliness, quality of product, price/value, or speed of service. Additionally, advertising and promotion awareness can be tracked. As with CREST, these trends can be very revealing over time. The advantage over CREST is that the data from these surveys are usually available within days (vs. weeks) and can be run as frequently as necessary (vs. quarterly for CREST). Problems and opportunities can be identified and reacted to while they are still hot. This allows for "midcourse" corrections, often while the promotion is still running. Another advantage of a regular telephone survey is that the data are proprietary and not available to competitors.

Pre-Promotion Research. As mentioned earlier, testing of promotions while in the concept phase can provide critical early feedback on improving promotions that possess at least a modicum of customer interest. This concept testing can be as simple as focus groups for qualitative feedback or as complicated as multimarket, in-depth, one-on-

one interviews with statistically significant results. These testing techniques can be combined with segmentation research techniques such as the Conversion Model to measure customer interest in both loyal users and nonusers. Financial questions can be asked to gauge customer depth of interest in spending disposable income on incremental visits. Data can then be plugged into a promotion payout analysis to actually estimate the net profit potential of a promotion. This kind of analysis can be very critical to the sell-in of the promotion to the franchisees.

Break-Even Analysis. A break-even analysis is a very useful financial analysis that should be run on every major promotion concept before it ever sees the light of day. The break-even analysis simply estimates the incremental sales increase necessary to cover the cost of running the promotion. (Incremental promotion cost should include only those items that are due to the promotion. Normal P-O-P should not be considered incremental because P-O-P would be used whether or not the promotion ran. Incremental costs usually include extra P-O-P, game piece costs, prize costs, and premium costs.) Mathematically, the equation looks like this:

Incremental Sales Increase x Profit Margin =
Incremental Promotion Cost

For example, if a promotion was estimated to cost $100,000 and the overall profit margin was 40 percent (average across all menu items), it would require $250,000 of incremental sales to just cover promotion costs ($100,000 ÷ 40 %). If this was a four-week promotion and overall system sales were normally $5,000,000 during this period, $250,000 in incremental sales would mean a 5 percent increase over the normal baseline ($250,000 ÷ $5,000,000). See Exhibit 26.11.

The break-even percentage can act as a "reasonableness check" for the promotion by comparing it to previous promotions of its type. For example, if the 5 percent promotion described above involved a self-liquidating premium and past self-liquidating premium promotions had never done better than a 3 percent increase in sales, then the promotion concept should undergo major retooling to reduce the costs. If, however, the promotion was a game and past games had averaged a 7 percent incremental sales increase with a high of 12 percent and a low of 3 percent, then the promotion at least would seem reasonable.

A low break-even point is not necessarily a good thing. Weak promotions can have very low break-even points, yet barely move the sales needle. The break-even point must be examined relative to the type of promotion being run and the historical incremental sales rate associated with these types of promotions.

The break-even analysis does not necessarily have to look at overall restaurant sales. If the promotion is aimed only at a specific menu item during a specific daypart, then the break-even analysis could be performed using only that item as the baseline. For example,

EXHIBIT 26.11

QSR BREAKEVEN ANALYSIS

ASSUMPTIONS

Promotion Type:	Game
Promotion Period (weeks):	4
Expected baseline sales	$5,000,000
Promotion incremental cost	$100,000
Profit margin:	40%

BREAKEVEN POINT CALCULATION

Incremental Sales Needed To Breakeven	Total Sales Needed To Breakeven	Incremental Sales Increase To Breakeven	Historical Probability Of Game Achieving This
$250,000	$5,250,000	5%	

BREAK EVEN TABLE

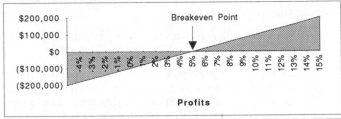

Percent Sales Increase	Total Sales During Period	Profit or Loss	R.O.I.	Historical Probability
-5%	$4,750,000	($200,000)	-200%	
-4%	$4,800,000	($180,000)	-180%	
-3%	$4,850,000	($160,000)	-160%	
-2%	$4,900,000	($140,000)	-140%	
-1%	$4,950,000	($120,000)	-120%	
0%	$5,000,000	($100,000)	-100%	
1%	$5,050,000	($80,000)	-80%	
2%	$5,100,000	($60,000)	-60%	
3%	$5,150,000	($40,000)	-40%	
4%	$5,200,000	($20,000)	-20%	
5%	$5,250,000	$0	0%	
6%	$5,300,000	$20,000	20%	
7%	$5,350,000	$40,000	40%	
8%	$5,400,000	$60,000	60%	
9%	$5,450,000	$80,000	80%	
10%	$5,500,000	$100,000	100%	
11%	$5,550,000	$120,000	120%	
12%	$5,600,000	$140,000	140%	
13%	$5,650,000	$160,000	160%	
14%	$5,700,000	$180,000	180%	
15%	$5,750,000	$200,000	200%	

if a promotion is designed purely as a breakfast promotion, it doesn't make a lot of sense to include lunch and dinner sales in the base. Of course, narrowing the focus only works if there are other, similar breakfast promotions with which to compare it.

Payout Analysis. A break-even analysis is a good first-pass method to check on the reasonableness of a promotion. Once it's been determined that a promotion is at least in the ballpark of profitability, the next step is to estimate what the actual net profit will be.

The QSR net profit equation looks like this:

$$\text{Net Profit} = (\text{Profit Margin x Extra Visit Sales}) + (\text{Trade Up/Down Profits}) - (\text{Promotion Costs})$$

where Extra Visit Sales = Sales resulting from a customer visit that would not have been made without the promotion. Because these are totally incremental visits, all profits from these visits can be added to the net profit of the promotion.

Trade Up/Down Profit = Profits resulting from a regular, planned visit that involved a customer trading up (or down) from his or her normal purchase to something different to take advantage of the promotion. Represents the profit difference between the normal item and the promotional item.

Promotion Costs = The incremental cost of running the promotion (extra P-O-P, prizes, game pieces, premiums). As defined earlier, if free food is used as a prize, then the food, paper, and labor costs associated with that item should be considered part of the promotion cost (not the retail price of the item).

The best way to estimate net profit payout is to set up a spreadsheet showing each menu item involved in the promotion and the current number of customers who buy that item during the time of the promotion. Estimates can then be made of participation rates and extra/regular visit ratios among each group of users to derive a total net profit.

Exhibit 26.12 shows a simplified payout analysis for a hypotheti-

EXHIBIT 26.12

Payout Analysis

HYPOTHETICAL EXAMPLE FOR A PROMOTION
All large hamburgers are 99¢ for one month only. Each large hamburger
purchaser also gets a free premium.

		REGULAR USERS OF:			
		STANDARD	LARGE	EXTRA LARGE	PROMO PROFIT
1	Regular Price	$0.79	$1.49	$1.99	
2	Cost of Goods	$0.34	$0.49	$0.74	
3	Profit (1 - 2)	$0.45	$1.00	$1.25	
4	Promo Price	$0.79	$0.99	$1.99	
5	Profit at Promo Price (4 - 2)	$0.45	$0.50	$1.25	
6	Customers/Month	12,000	5,000	2,000	
7	Participation Rate	30%	100%	20%	
8	Number Participating (6 x 7)	3,600	5,000	400	
9	Extra Visit Percent	40%	10%	30%	
10	# Extra Visits (8 x 10)	1440	500	120	
11	Profit Per Extra Visit*	$1.50	$1.50	$1.50	
12	Extra Visit Profit (10 x 11)	$2,160	$750	$180	$3,090
13	Regular Visit Percent	60%	100%	70%	
14	# Regular Visits (8 x 13)	2,160	5,000	280	
15	Unit Trade Up/Trade Down**	$0.05	($0.50)	($0.75)	
16	Tot Trade Up/Down (14 x 15)	$108	($2,500)	($210)	($2,602)
17	Promotion Profit (12 + 16)	$2,268	($1,750)	($30)	$488
18	Incremental Promo Cost***				($300)
	NET PROMO PROFIT				$188

---

* Assumes $3.00 average check at 50% profit rate.
** Equals profit on promo item minus profit on item normally ordered (line 4).
*** Incremental P.O.P., premiums, etc.

cal QSR selling three types of hamburgers — standard size, large, and extra large. The promotion is for one month, and the large size will sell for $.99 instead of its regular $1.49.

A payout analysis is driven by a series of assumptions. The first set of assumptions is contained in the participation rate line (line 7). This shows the percentage of each item's customers who will take advantage of the promotion during the month. For example, 30 percent of all customers normally buying the standard hamburger will trade up to the large to take advantage of the promotion. Of course, 100 percent of regular large customers will be buying at the promotional price.

Lines 9 and 13, "Extra Visit Percent" and "Regular Visit Percent," are key to the profitability. Of the 3,600 transactions in which people who would normally have ordered standards now order larges, it was estimated that 40 percent of the visits (or 1,440) will be extra visits (would not have been made without the promotion) and 60 percent will be on regular, planned visits. (Note that it is assumed that current users of the large hamburger will increase their overall visits 10 percent to take advantage of the promotion.) All of the $1.50 profit on the extra visits is attributed to the promotion. Only the trade-up, trade-down profit on the regular visit is attributable to the promotion, because the customer would have made the visit whether or not the promotion was there.

Obviously, the participation rates and extra/regular visit ratios are the key assumptions that can make or break a promotion. There are two ways to estimate these figures:

1. Pre-promotion research among each item's user group to measure "intent to participate" in the promotion, how often the group would take advantage of the promotion, and other variables
2. Surveys conducted during similar promotions run in the past to learn these ratios

This same sort of analysis can be applied to any type of promotion. With games, keep in mind that there is usually a game piece *distribution* phase, when customers might make extra visits to pick up pieces. There is also a *redemption* phase, when customers who have won food prizes come in to redeem them (and typically, buy additional items).

Payout analysis can become very complicated and include lots of subjectivity in estimating the various ratios. However, if the assumptions are reasonable, they can be good indicators of what can be expected from a promotion and, as such, what can be used effectively to sell-in the promotion to franchisees.

PROMOTION MANAGEMENT ORGANIZATIONAL STRUCTURE

Most QSR chains have a marketing department that is structured functionally like most packaged goods companies, albeit with different job titles. Instead of brand managers, there are usually project managers who are responsible for specific promotion modules (as well as responsible for ongoing marketing efforts against key dayparts, target segments, and product groupings). Sometimes the entire marketing department is split between strategy and execution. (Typically, promotion falls into the executional side.)

Partners with the project managers are usually a promotion agency or agencies to develop the creative on P-O-P and promotions, as well as perform strategic analysis and promotion fulfillment. (Depending on the size of the QSR chain, the ad agency may handle those functions.) However, the larger QSRs tend to delegate these responsibilities to the promotion agency. Due to the specialized nature of QSR promotion, tight timetables, and the ever changing competitive climate, these agencies are often on retainer with the QSR so the agency can dedicate permanent account staff to the client.

One major difference between the packaged goods and QSR marketing structures is in QSR's emphasis on regional promotions. Usually, QSRs have advertising managers in each major market who are responsible for developing marketing plans with the local co-ops. This responsibility extends to hiring and managing local agencies, selling in national promotions, and coordinating local promotions with national headquarters.

At the store level, the customer relations rep (CRR) takes local marketing one step closer to the individual customer. CRRs are individuals who, besides their regular restaurant duties, coordinate local store marketing programs for a single restaurant or group of restaurants. Often CRRs have exhibited some talent or interest in marketing and are interested in a career with the QSR. Typically, they are recently graduated college students who majored in marketing, advertising, or mass communications. Not every QSR can financially justify even a part-time CRR. Sometimes several restaurants will band together to appoint a CRR. The problem with this is that this person will not be as intimately familiar with an individual restaurant's trading area as the CRR who focuses on one restaurant.

One way around this is for several noncompeting retailers (for example, a quick oil change shop, a drugstore, and a department store) to band together with the QSR to hire a CRR to cover all local store marketing activities for the retailers within a specifically defined trading area. This can be very difficult to coordinate, but very efficient, because the CRR becomes the expert in that trading area. For example, if the CRR is arranging a special price for local high school students, it's just as easy to set this up for three stores as for one.

Finally, constant communications among all parties involved in the execution of a promotion is critical. Franchisees and store managers typically receive a lot of mail from headquarters, not all of which is top priority. Very often this mail is ignored for some time. One way to get them to read truly urgent material is to incorporate all the critical communications into one monthly mailing. As long as this communication vehicle isn't abused, franchisees and store managers will learn to look for this mailing and read it when it arrives.

Another technique to keep field and headquarters marketing managers coordinated is through weekly conference calls. Although this can get to be expensive, local reactions to new promotions and products and competitive happenings can be communicated to everyone on a very timely basis. Mid-course corrections can be communicated and executed in this manner.

THE FUTURE

To better prognosticate the future of QSR sales promotion, it's good to start with a re-examination of its roots in the 1940s and 1950s.

The original QSRs achieved their initial success by offering a quality product in a convenient location at an inexpensive price. Automation and production line techniques were applied to the restaurant business in a way that fit perfectly with the developing, modern-American, on-the-go lifestyle. Rather than being repulsed by the lack of human interaction, Americans were fascinated with the QSR's robotlike efficiency.

While the breadth of the typical QSR's product offerings has expanded significantly since then (perhaps too much), the same basic need for speed exists. One only need look at other products and services often used by QSR heavy users to see what the future holds. These people demand speed and convenience more than ever, but now they want personalization as well. They are much less willing to accept "one size fits all" than their 1950s counterparts were.

Technology will undoubtedly guide the future of the QSR industry once again in many ways:

- ATM-style ordering
- Scaled-down operations in nontraditional locations, such as shopping malls and schools
- Totally automated vending operations

ATM-style ordering will provide the opportunity for the next breakthrough in QSR promotions — true micromarketing (marketing targeted to the individual), based on a transactional database. If customers identify themselves as individuals to the ATM, the following promotions are then possible:

- Menus customized to each person's tastes
- Electronic suggestive selling based on past purchase history
- Electronic discounts or added-value offers based on a customer's projected "lifetime value"
- Electronic frequent user programs to develop customer continuity and loyalty

There are many mechanisms by which the customers can identify themselves, varying from the straightforward to the practically science fictional:

- A PIN number punched in by the customer.
- A mag-striped or bar-coded card run through a reader by the customer (this could be a card created just for the QSR chain or an existing credit card). A central QSR computer could maintain the customer's purchase history, linked by modem to each outlet.
- A "smart card" containing a small computer chip that contains the customer's entire purchase history. Although expensive on a per card basis, this approach eliminates the need for the computer linkage between outlets.
- A radio frequency smart card in which the chip interacts with an electronic "reader" without having to be retrieved from the customer's wallet. This system is being tested on tollway systems where cardholders merely drive through a special lane that automatically deducts the toll from the smart card's chip without having to slow down significantly.
- A TV camera in the drive-through lane that optically reads a car's license plate.
- Fingerprint or voiceprint ID systems.

Another major trend of the future is the growth of home/office delivery service that will continue to be demanded by the time-pressed and aging American consumer. In addition to providing another means of identifying the customer as an individual, this will provide fertile ground for tie-in promotions for competing QSR operators serving a similar customer base (demographically speaking). The logical extension of the continued growth in drive-through and off-premise consumption is the "restaurant without walls" — a QSR operation 100 percent dedicated to delivery service.

In addition to the potential of true micromarketing, technology will almost certainly offer the means to overcome P-O-P clutter both inside and outside the restaurant. Rather than keeping up the same P-O-P 24 hours a day, technology will allow the message to change to fit the daypart or weekpart. This could range from a TV monitor in the menu board programmed to play silent commercials appropriate for each daypart to a scrollable translite that rolls back and forth to portray a different featured product (much like a bus route sign is changed).

Technology will undoubtedly make the total QSR experience faster and more pleasant in the future. But it will not replace the need for a creative approach to promotion development that never loses sight of the fundamentals of fun, value, and work. All other things being equal, creative will always be the tiebreaker in the future as it has in the past.

PART IV
ISSUES

Keith M. Jones has spent his entire career in consumer packaged goods marketing management. As Director of Worldwide Promotion for Colgate-Palmolive Company, he oversees both consumer and trade promotion, database marketing, and syndicated business analysis, while advising Colgate's international subsidiaries on promotion strategies.

In the mid-1980s, Jones developed the Brand Hostage Index to assess trade promotion, and he became a Vice President in the Summa Consulting Unit of Nielsen Marketing Research. He conceived, fielded, and published The First Annual Survey of Manufacturer Trade Promotion Practices. *The survey, now in its fourth year, has become one of the industry's foremost trade promotion publications.*

Prior to Nielsen, Jones was Vice President of Marketing for the Mott's USA Division of Cadbury Schweppes, Vice President of Sales for Schweppes USA, and New Products Marketing Manager at Anheuser-Busch, Inc. Jones began his marketing career in the Pepsi-Cola Division of Pepsico, Inc.

Jones has published articles on promotion effectiveness in many trade publications and is a frequent speaker on the topic. He is a Director of the Promotion Marketing Association of America and is a Steering Committee member of the Marketing Science Institute's Consumer Product Group.

Jones received an MBA from Harvard in 1972.

Chapter 27

PROMOTION AND BRAND EQUITY

Do promotions have a long-term effect? If so, do promotions erode or enhance the value of a brand franchise over time? Professional opinion, promulgated mostly by advertising agency executives in the absence of facts, has suggested that promotions somehow devalue brands, while advertising builds brand equity. Is this really true, or is it simply marketing folklore?

This chapter addresses these deceptively simple questions by first developing working definitions of *promotion* and *brand equity* and proposing a way to measure their interaction. Following this, the most recent behavioral research findings are reviewed, which quantify the impact, if any, of reduced price promotions on brand loyalty over time. Next, a practitioner's perspective is offered for both reduced price and consumer value-added promotional approaches. The chapter closes by summarizing this learning in a few actions that promotion professionals can take to protect and enrich the value of brands.

PROMOTION MORE BROADLY DEFINED

Today, separating advertising from promotion is not the black-and-white issue it was in the 1950s when television first emerged as a powerful mass medium. Is a direct mail piece, extolling the benefits of a product or service, while offering a trial incentive, an advertisement or a promotion? Consider a television spot with an 800 number that invites entry to a vacation sweepstakes. Is it advertising or is it promotion? And how do we categorize a product sample that has been delivered to the home? Unless the medium has truly become the message (in which case the whole idea of brand equity is irrelevant), a product sample may well be the most elegant advertising form of all. Yet most texts, including this one, classify sampling as a promotion tool.

The fact is, what we call "advertising" and "promotion" are both simply forms of consumer communication. A simultaneous fragmentation of mass consumer markets and proliferation of new marketing communication delivery systems has created a new portfolio of marketing tools that defies traditional labels. We have Prodigy (the shopping network for personal computer users), in-store television that broadcasts a succession of brand deals, in-store electronic coupon dispensers at the cash register, and Whittle Communications printed material in medical and dental offices. Meanwhile, the ubiquitous T-shirt has emerged as the outdoor advertising medium of the 1990s.

Our task of understanding the long-term effects of promotion is further complicated by the emergence of powerful retailers elbowing their way between manufacturer brands and consumers. I am not just talking about the Wal Marts and Krogers of the packaged goods world. Giant travel agencies peddle even the strongest airline and hotel brand names. Fast food franchises tout branded products, such as Oscar Mayer cold cuts at Subway and Coca-Cola at Burger King. Or is it Pepsi this year? Toys R Us. Home Depot. Blockbuster Video. Everywhere we look, strong players in the distribution system are imposing their will on brand marketers. General Cinema. Hertz Car Rental. These distribution powerhouses have built their own brand names by using supplier brands to enhance their own equity. As a result, what a marketer considers a promotion (for example, package art and a price cut in a trade circular) is viewed as advertising by the retailer. That's no small advertising medium either. The average food retailer, for example, has more than 15 branded frankfurter ads a year. If you are a hot dog manufacturer, it doesn't matter whether the circular is "advertising" or "promotion." It's a form of marketing communication with the consumer that is absolutely necessary.

In short, the world of 1950s' marketing has been turned on its head. The one-size-fits-all, mass-market consumer has exploded into a multitude of segments (Prizm offers 64 psycho-geo-demographic consumer cells) while the fragmented retail trade has concentrated. There used to be one consumer and a universe of retailers. Now we have a multitude of consumers and a few powerful trade factors. As the art of marketing approaches the 21st century, let's move beyond the simple labels of advertising and promotion. They are both tools for communicating with consumers. It is more helpful to think of the practitioners' portfolio as containing short-term communication tools (promotion) and long-term communication tools (advertising).

Short-term communications ask for action, using price, quality, value added, or a combination of the three to close a sale; long-term communications impart information, usually about the user, the usage occasion, or the product or service itself. For the sake of simplicity, the terms *advertising* and *promotion* will continue to be used throughout this chapter; however, the reader should think of them in this broader sense.

A WORKING DEFINITION OF BRAND EQUITY

Now let's also move beyond the simple assertion that short-term marketing communication is per se a devaluator of brand equity. Let's look for factual proof. What is the impact of a prolonged succession of short-term marketing communications on the value of a brand name? While the answer is still not perfectly clear, a number of marketers and researchers have attacked the issue objectively. But, before examining their findings, we first have to get a handle on what we are trying to measure. Brand equity. What exactly is "brand equity"?

There is no universal definition for the value, or equity, of a brand name. The financial community looks at the profitability of a business, return on shareholder investment, or the potential acquisition value of the property. Consumer researchers suggest that equity lies in the minds of consumers and is reflected in the pricing premium that consumers are willing to pay for a given product or service. Marketers think of equity in terms of extendability of a brand name into new entries. Many retailers believe that they influence the value of a brand by the amount of support given (or withheld). Richard Owens, Senior Vice President of Kroger, Inc., has said that his company can make any brand it chooses into the market leader, and he went on to dramatize canned tuna brands as mere pawns for the greater equity called Kroger. Recognizing a diversity of opinion on the issue, the Marketing Science Institute has conducted conferences for managers, researchers, the investment community, and retailers to work out a consensus about brand equity — with inconclusive results.

After 20 years as a brand marketer, I've reached the conclusion that brand equity resides in the product or service itself. As augmented by packaging and the cumulative impact of marketing communications (both long and short term) this product equity is rewarded by consumers in the form of brand loyalty. And, importantly, this consumer loyalty can be measured!

William Moran, President of Longman-Moran Analytic, offers a relatively simple way to measure loyalty: substitutability. Moran argues that "reducing substitutability gives a brand more equity and makes it more profitable."[1] He goes on to describe a pair of survey questions that any marketer can ask consumers in tracking substitutability over time:

1. Which brand did you buy last time?
2. What would you have done if that brand had not been available? (a) Wait, (b) Go to another store, or (c) Buy another brand — and if another brand, which one?

Based on the responses to these questions, Moran is able to profile the substitutability of a brand and the power of a brand to send loyal users to another store. By repeating these questions over time, marketers can understand the direction in which brand equity is moving and develop their own conclusions about the role of specific marketing communications as causal factors behind these movements.

RECENT BEHAVIORAL RESEARCH ON PROMOTION AND BRAND LOYALTY

Fortunately, 17 years ago, Tod Johnson, President of The NPD Group, Inc., began keeping diary panel records of individual household purchase behavior for major packaged goods brands. First published in 1984 in "The Myth of Declining Brand Loyalty" in the *Journal of Advertising Research*, Johnson's biannual updates of reported household behavior have repeatedly found that "while promotion expenditures are growing tremendously, they are not adversely affecting brand loyalty/brand franchises that are effectively supported by manufacturers."[2]

Now, this is a sweeping conclusion that demands a closer look at the methodology involved! The NPD Group's packaged goods diary panel (acquired by Nielsen Marketing Research in 1987) tracks purchases and prices in thousands of households. Johnson's analysis draws on this database by examining behavior for loyal buyers of 50 brands in 20 product categories during six-month periods every other year, beginning in 1975. He defines loyalty in a number of different ways. One way is as a brand's "share of requirements." Loyal users are consumers who make at least three purchases of a given brand in the six-month period and for whom that brand constitutes more than a 50 percent share of total category requirements. In other words, all competitive brands substitute for less than half of the loyal users' purchases.

Of the original 50 brands in 1975, 45 are still major leading brands today, with relatively little deterioration in brand loyalty as measured by "share of requirements." Together, these 45 brands index at 92 percent of their 1975 loyalty level, while more than two out of five index at 100 percent or better (see Table 27.1).

TABLE 27.1

SHARE OF REQUIREMENTS SATISFIED[3]

Year	'75	'77	'79	'81	'83	'85	'87	'89	'91
Index	100	100	99	94	94	91	92	92	92

100 = 1975 level (each brand weighted equally).

Johnson goes on to point out that in most cases where brand loyalty (as measured by share of requirements) has declined, it has resulted from manufacturer segmentation strategies or from reducing advertising share of voice below share of market — not from increased price promotion activity. Manufacturers often induce substitution among loyal users of their brands by line extensions into new segments. For example Tab diet soft drink was virtually destroyed when Diet Coke was introduced. And today mighty Budweiser is losing volume in the beer industry as Bud Light and Bud Dry challenge the Bud user to substitute.

Johnson's analysis then compares the 17-year share of requirements index of brands having the greatest recognized increase in promotions with the brands having the smallest recognized increase. As shown in Table 27.2, except for the years 1983 and 1985, the two groups have virtually the same trend over time.

In 1978, Donnelley Marketing Company's first annual survey of promotion practices among manufacturers of nondurable goods revealed that trade promotion (retailer deals and incentives) represented 25 percent of total marketing expenditures. The 13th annual survey,

TABLE 27.2
SHARE OF REQUIREMENTS SATISFIED

	'75	'77	'79	'81	'83	'85	'87	'89	'91
23 brands with highest levels of consumer recognized promotion	100	101	98	95	91	88	92	90	91
22 brands with lowest levels of consumer recognized promotion	100	99	101	94	98	94	92	94	93

completed in 1991, found that trade spending had escalated to 44.3 percent of the collective industry marketing budget (the remainder in consumer promotion and advertising). That's almost a doubling of resources behind price promotions without adjusting for inflation! Yet, during this period, the NPD diary panel data cannot identify a significant impact on consumer loyalty for 45 major brands in 20 product categories among 6,500 to 10,000 households.

The NPD findings are supported by another study, completed in 1991 at the London Business School. Led by Professor A.S.C. Ehrenberg of the Centre for Marketing Communications, this report, titled "The After-Effects of Large Consumer Promotions," examined more than 100 leading brands in some 210 grocery product categories in Japan, Germany, the United Kingdom, and the United States. Using scanner data and household purchase panel data covering more than three years of behavior in 1,000 to 8,000 households, the London Business School team focused on 170 short-term promotion sales peaks that lifted sales per week by at least 25 percent over the normal rate. These peaks lasted anywhere from a week to up to two months. By isolating the largest and most distinct price reductions, the purchasing after-effects could then be tracked to determine the impact on brand loyalty, the repeat buying rate, and new user generation. Like the NPD work, this study involved established high-turn packaged goods brands and did not involve new products, services, or durable goods. However, both British Airways and the Prudential Insurance Corporation were among the study sponsors.

Remarkably, the study findings parallel Johnson's observations from the NPD data. The London Business School team concluded that large price discount "promotions for established brands have no noticeable effect either on subsequent sales or brand loyalty. The promotions had large immediate sales effects (often at a high cost) but do not appear to be brand building."[4] The authors go on to observe that price promotions were ineffective in attracting totally new users to the brands and that the incremental volume came from prior users of the brands.

WHY THE FACTS DON'T SUPPORT MARKETING FOLKLORE

Together, Johnson's and Ehrenberg's separate works directly challenge the anecdotal marketing assumption that somehow increased price promotion activity erodes brand equity. How can this be? Perhaps it is because we are dealing with a false base period. Consumers have always switched from brand to brand to a certain extent, and the assumption that consumers of the 1940s, 1950s, 1960s, or whenever relied on a single brand for all their purchases is probably a false assumption. As the families depicted in *Leave It to Beaver* and *Father Knows Best* were fictitious, so too may be the belief that these families were more brand loyal than today. After all, no one has ever presented hard evidence from the "golden age" of brand equity, whenever that was, to show that consumers were ever exclusively loyal to a single brand.

All right. So price promotions may have little long-term relationship with brand loyalty (as defined by user substitution behavior), so long as the brand's fair share of long-term marketing communication is maintained. Surely there must have been some consumer impact from more than 300 billion dollars in consumer packaged goods trade deals in the past 20 years! Well, there has, and professors James Lattin and Randolph Bucklin at Stanford University may have put a finger on it. Using IRI scanner data to examine the purchase behavior for ground coffee in 67 households over two years, they found that consumers learn from retail price discounting and modify their purchasing patterns accordingly. Consumers develop price discount expectations about future purchases based on their previous experiences. Lattin and Bucklin call this expectation the "reference priced discount," and their brand choice model shows that consumers simply adjust their purchase activity in order to capture deals on their preferred brand or brands. Over time, the authors suggest that "overly intensive discounting may end up (1) redistributing demand, (2) lowering baseline sales, and (3) increasing the proportion of sales made at discounted margins."[5] In other words, consumers stock up on their favorite brands when they are attractively dealt, and they delay purchasing when not. With the emergence of everyday low price outlets, such as Wal Mart, they may even transfer purchasing decisions on a category from one class of trade to another. In the same way that food stores shifted business away from drugstores for many personal care items in the 1960s and 1970s, mass merchandisers are now taking the same categories away from food stores. So, consumer brand loyalty may be relatively unchanged over the past 20 years, but when, where, and at what price brands are purchased may have substantially changed!

THE PROMOTION ADVANTAGE OF MARKET LEADERS

While price discount promotions don't appear to either build or erode brand equity, they do play an important role in helping brand leaders sustain their leadership over long periods of time. Major brands with market share leadership have an advantage. They occupy the high ground in a zero sum environment. And, like a well dug-in defense in infantry warfare, they have a statistical edge. From experience, I have observed that market leaders enjoy three specific promotion advantages, cumulatively providing a reason why brand leaders in stable, established businesses are rarely dethroned:

1. Lower cost per unit for fixed promotion expenses, such as slotting allowances, feature ads, end-aisle displays, and FSI couponing;
2. Greater ability to expand total category sales during a promotion;
3. Greater variable-deal cost efficiency as retailers are more likely to pass the full deal of leading brands on to the consumer, while pocketing a larger share of discounts from weaker brands.

Let's explore each of these assertions in more detail, beginning with the greater efficiency of fixed cost events. Every brand, whether packaged goods, durable goods, services, or transportation, incurs lump sum, fixed promotional costs. For a packaged goods brand sold in food stores, one of these expenses is the cost to participate in a trade newspaper feature ad (such as the Pathmark chain in New York at a going rate of $25,000) or the increasingly more prominent direct mail circular. Generally, this participation fee is the same amount whether the brand has a 40 percent, 20 percent, or 10 percent share of market. As a result, the cost to the 10 percent share brand may be four times the cost per unit for the 40 percent share brand.

The same principle applies to couponing. The cost of a full-page newspaper free-standing insert (FSI) is about $7.50 per thousand. A national run of 50 million circulation costs a brand about $375,000. Because high share brands will incur higher coupon redemptions (as a percentage of circulation), this fixed cost is spread over more retail unit purchases. In most packaged goods categories, a brand must offer three to four national coupon programs each year to compete. That is well over a million dollars in FSI distribution cost! Because about 70 percent of all coupon redemptions, according to both of the leading coupon clearinghouses, are from current brand users, secondary brands experience lower redemption rates than leading brands. If a weak brand is redeemed at half the rate of a leading brand, then the leader will have a half-million-dollar marketing efficiency on coupon distribution examples. This is just simple mathematics. What is not so obvious is that leading brands enjoy a double advantage. Their share of fixed promotion events can be less than their share of market! This double whammy for leadership brands was quantified by Nielsen (Schmitz) in a 1987 study for *The Nielsen Researcher* quarterly.[6] During a four-year period (1982–1986), purchase behavior of 13,238 grocery shoppers in 24 U.S. markets was correlated with retailer feature ad activity in the same markets. In 36 product categories, 144 brands were examined. As illustrated in Table 27.3, brand leaders, averaging 25.2 percent market share, required a significantly lower share of feature ad support (16.7 percent). Conversely, the three-share brand required feature ad activity nearly 25 percent higher than its share of market! Clearly, the leading brand enjoys an advantage of marketing scale.

Now let's look at the second promotional advantage for brand leaders — the ability to expand the category during promotional events. Every marketing professional working on a leadership brand can document this phenomenon. When American Airlines offers low discount fares, total airline passenger count increases. When McDonald's runs a $.99 hamburger promotion, total fast food hamburger sales increase. And Heinz Ketchup or Campbell Soup brands increase food store category sales during their promotions. Brand leaders have greater category expansion power because they cannibalize the other brands less. This effect was captured by Robert Blattberg and Kenneth Wisniewski at the University of Chicago in a working paper titled "How Retail Price Promotions Work: Empirical Results."[7] Using scanner data from Jewel Food Stores in the Chicago market, Blattberg and Wisniewski analyzed the effect of retailer price promotions for the flour, margarine, bath tissue, and tuna fish categories. They found that, excepting flour (where commoditization may neutralize the effect of branding), the leading brands exhibited a lower category cannibalization than did secondary brands. Intuitively, if not with scanner data, retailers know that market leaders can expand category sales during promotions and reward leading brands with enhanced merchandising support (see Table 27.4).

A third advantage for the leadership brand is the greater likelihood that the trade will pass a cents-off deal, penny for penny, on to the consumer, while pocketing a few pennies of the weaker brand allowance. Therefore, secondary brands may have to offer deeper deals just to get the same trade support as the market leader. From personal experience in the carbonated beverage business, I learned early on that

TABLE 27.3
RELATIONSHIP OF RETAILER AD SUPPORT TO
SHARE OF CONSUMER PURCHASES

	Leading Brand	Second Brand	Third Brand	Store Brand
Share of Purchases	25.2%	13.6%	8.0%	8.8%
Share of Features	16.7%	13.2%	9.7%	6.4%
Number of Brands	36	36	35	37

Source: *The Nielsen Researcher*, Summer 1987, p. 10.

TABLE 27.4
CANNIBALIZATION COMPONENT OF DEAL SPIKE

(Deal Discount = 20%)

	Brand Market Share Due to Cannibalization	% of Spike
Flour		
Pillsbury	19.7%	27.1%
Gold Medal	11.9	10.1
Ceresota	10.5	3/1
Jewel Maid	9.2	9.5
Margarine		
Imperial	14.3	10.3
Land O Lakes	11.3	24.9
Parkay	7.2	22.0
Chiffon	5.9	63.4
Blue Bonnet	3.0	62.8
Blue Brook (Disc)	39.7	.8
Sunnyland (Disc)	7.1	56.3
Bath Tissue		
Charmin	15.0	19.6
Scott Tissue	14.6	22.7
Northern	7.2	31.9
White Cloud	6.7	96.8
Soft 'N Pretty	3.9	47.7
Coronet (Disc)	—	100.0
Jewel	1.8	44.9
Tuna Fish		
Chicken of the Sea	16.9	8.8
Bumble Bee	8.4	18.9
Starkist	6.8	14.0
Blue Brook	—	18.1

the third-rated cola brand, Royal Crown, needed to offer a greater deal allowance per case in order to get the same reduced retail price as Coca-Cola or Pepsi. Over the long term this distribution reality ensured that Royal Crown could never muster the funds to mount an equity-building marketing assault on the co-leaders.

Cumulatively, these promotion advantages are one of the reasons why leading brands in established, stable product categories are rarely toppled from their thrones. The Campbell Soups, Heinz Ketchups, Tide Detergents, and Coca-Colas of the packaged goods world benefit from the fact that it costs more to capture market share than to defend it in a stable industry. Therefore, it is clear that price promotion can be an effective tool for high market share brands to protect their share over time. So, while short-term price promotion may not function to either erode or build equity, it can be a technique for preserving equity over a long period.

WHEN LEADING BRANDS STUMBLE

Despite the promotion advantage, brand leaders do fall from grace. Consider the case of Ivory Liquid dishwashing detergent over the past 16 years. Procter & Gamble's Ivory Liquid was the market share leader in 1976 with 24 percent of the market. Despite advertising and promotion support levels equal to the primary competition (Palmolive and Dawn), Ivory has plummeted to fourth place in the dish liquid derby by mid-1992 with less than half its 1980 market share (see Table 27.5).

TABLE 27.5
LIQUID DISHWASHING DETERGENT SHARE TRENDS

Brand	1976	1980	1985	1989	1992
Ivory	24.0%	22.5%	15.1%	12.2%	9.1%
Dawn	6.5%	19.0%	19.4%	21.4%	26.0%
Palmolive	18.0%	16.5%	5.4%	6.8%	16.4%
Sunlight	n/a	n/a	10.0%	8.8%	10.8%

Sources: 1976/80 P&G sales brochure; 1985 SAMI; 1989/92 Nielsen Scantrack.

Did the Ivory Liquid equity decline? Of course! Did promotion have anything to do with the decline? Absolutely not! So what happened to one of America's leading brands under the management of perhaps the world's most astute marketing company? In a word, the consumer changed. Ivory was originally positioned to women as the product that was mild on the hands because it was 99 and 44/100% pure. Palmolive liquid was positioned as mild on the hands but effective in cleaning dishes. And the Dawn brand was introduced by Procter & Gamble in 1975 as the brand that cuts grease. Because new, younger users of dishwashing liquids wanted a brand that was tough on grease and spent less time in the kitchen than their mothers, they didn't value mildness as much, and so they used Dawn. As the Ivory user base aged and American demographics changed, the Ivory brand lost its appeal.

Remember, as I suggested at the beginning of this chapter, the equity of a brand is bestowed by the consumer because the product, its packaging, and its marketing communication meets his or her needs. When a brand loses equity, it is because these elements no longer appeal to the consumer, not because the brand or service has been promoted to death.

Let me summarize what we have learned so far about the relationship of short-term (price) promotion to brand equity for leading, or high-share brands:

1. As long as a brand maintains its fair share of advertising voice, short-term price promotions neither erode nor enhance brand loyalty. The assertion that promotion per se somehow destroys brand equity is simply unsubstantiated by fact.

2. Market leaders enjoy a promotion advantage over secondary brands. This advantage can protect the existing equity of a leading brand over long periods of time in businesses with little technological change or new product activity.

PROMOTION AND WEAK BRANDS

Up to this point we have examined large, leading share brands because the only available studies have focused on brands for which brand equity or loyalty can be presumed to actually exist. What about secondary brands? Does price promotion have a different effect on these weaker brands over the long term? As Blattberg's work with the Newel chain suggests, and our friend Richard Owens of Kroger insists, weak brands are more easily influenced by the negotiating power of strong retailers. I call this process "trade hostaging."[8] Hostaging occurs when a low-equity brand shifts a disproportionate share of marketing resources into trade promotion over time in a misguided attempt to build sales volume and market share. I first experienced the hostaging effect in the early 1980s, when as the marketing vice president for the apple products subsidiary of a large corporation, I tried to grow our apple juice business in low-development markets, relying almost exclusively on trade promotion. We dealt deeper and deeper in an attempt to build share, but it never happened. Why not? It was because the trade simply pocketed much of our allowances and made sure we didn't cannibalize their large, private-label apple juice business, while consumers only bought our brand on deal. Yet, if we cut back on trade deals, our business virtually dried up. And with all our resources tied up in deals and coupons, we never had a chance to build a consumer franchise. In short, the brand was a trade hostage!

Taking these insights into the consulting business, I developed an approach that measured the degree to which a brand was hostaged and tracked the hostaging process over time. The idea was to identify brands under heavy trade pressure while there was still time (and resources) to prevent death in captivity, and to put new strategies in place to free brands that were already captured. The first step was to develop the "Brand Hostage Index," a proprietary figure composed of four elements:

1. Percentage of volume shipped to the trade under a deal

2. Deal depth as a percentage of gross sales
3. Trade spending as a percentage of total marketing spending
4. Percentage of market held by private label/generic brands

Together, these factors represent the level of trade influence on a brand as represented by the calculation of an annual "hostage index." The countervailing force of brand equity is measured in terms of market share. By graphing the brand's hostage index vs. market share over several years, we can identify a curious phenomenon: Weak brands may increase their trade spending each year, yet simultaneously lose market share. These hostage brands use heavier and heavier doses of trade deals to accelerate their own decline!

The following actual case history illustrates my point (see Exhibit 27.1). A weak national powdered laundry detergent brand in a fragmented market (10 national brands) shows the typical hostage profile.

This weak brand is skewing increasingly more of its resources to the trade, as exhibited by the rising hostage index, while the ever weakening consumer franchise results in declining share of market. The next step for this detergent brand is trade delisting. Remember Fluffo Shortening, Bon Ami Cleanser, Nehi Orange Soda, Gleem and Pepsodent toothpastes, and Morton TV Dinners? These brands have disappeared either from the shelves or from consumers' minds or both.

After applying the hostaging analysis to 26 brands in different categories, it was clear that many (but not all) secondary brands do suffer from the long-term effects of excessive dependency on trade promotion. The bottom line for a weak brand is clear: Either build a point of difference into the marketing mix or retreat to an everyday low price/value point; but don't try to promote your way out of the hostage box.

CONSUMER PROMOTION AND BRAND EQUITY

We have been focusing on short-term, price-driven promotions for two reasons. First, if any form of promotion has a propensity to affect brand equity, it would surely be visible in the substitution effects of deals. Second, virtually all the consumer packaged goods hard data, be they scanner retail movement, household panel, or manufacturer shipments, lend themselves more readily to the analysis of short-term programs. There is another category of promotion, consumer promotion, that communicates a message while seeking action and may have a longer-term (if any) effect upon consumer behavior.

Sweepstakes; contests; sampling programs; event marketing; premiums; continuity programs; in-, on-, or near-pack offers; direct mail offers; coupons; rebates; and cause-related tie-ins — these consumer promotions all can produce incremental sales volume, but do they influence brand equity? The answer is much less clear than for price promotions because the long-term effect cannot be separated from the effects of other elements of the marketing mix, such as packaging graphics, advertising copy and weight, and product improvements. Rather than

EXHIBIT 27.1 DETERGENT BRAND HOSTAGE TREND

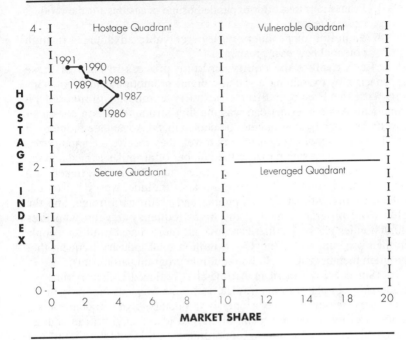

HOSTAGE INDEX CALCULATION

	1986	1987	1988	1989	1990	1991
Percentage on deal	88.5	90.2	95.2	92.5	100	100
Percentage of deal depth	22.7	25.9	30.1	33.5	35.2	35.5
Trade % of mix	69.3	75.0	81.4	85.6	89.9	90.5
Private label share	5.7	5.8	5.4	5.6	5.5	5.2
Hostage index	2.6	2.8	3.1	3.3	3.4	3.4
Market share	3.2	3.5	2.2	1.9	1.7	1.1

resort to marketing folklore, let's look for instances in which products or services have relied on consumer promotions as a primary marketing tool over a long period (at least 10 years) and have enjoyed marketplace success. Using this criterion, there are at least four types of consumer promotions that can build brand loyalty or equity:

1. Continuity programs involving long-term purchasing behavior for which the reward is more of the product or service itself;
2. Promotions that transfer an advertising equity into a tangible

consumer activity;

3. Promotions that offer expanded usage occasions for the product or service; or

4. Sampling of products with perceivable advantages to high potential new user prospects.

Let's explore the equity building process in each of these approaches by examining a specific brand promotion campaign, starting with the Frequent Flier continuity campaign pioneered by American Airlines. American was the first airline to offer a consumer loyalty program by introducing the personalized Advantage Program in 1981. Every month after customers travel, they receive a computerized account statement summarizing the number of air miles earned and the requirements for converting these miles into free airline tickets (on American, of course). The program also includes special discount offers; tie-ins with car, hotel, phone, and credit card usage; and the elite Gold program aimed at the high-frequency traveler who flies 40,000 miles per year. American now has more than 11 million people in their program out of the 13–18 million total industry frequent flier program membership, excluding multiple program participants.

Since 1981, American Airlines has replaced United Airlines in leadership in total passenger miles, and their frequent flier program is one of the reasons why. Not only is the database of frequent fliers a potent tool for targeting special offers, but also American can address specific route traffic-building opportunities while coddling their best customers with specialized personal treatment. Why is this promotion considered an equity building tool? For three reasons. First, program members will avoid other airlines in order to rack up more miles on American. Second, the reward for flying American is free American tickets — the reward for loyalty is more of the product itself! This is important because the quality of the American product consistently is the highest among U.S. airlines according to industry consumer research. People view free travel on American as an aspirational goal. A similar continuity program run by Holiday Inn was less successful. Why? Because a free weekend night at a Holiday Inn was not so desirable. The third equity ingredient is the longevity of the program. Participants know that the program will still be in place a year from now, so they are confident that flying American today will pay off for them, even if it takes a year or two to accumulate sufficient miles to earn free tickets.

The final proof that the Advantage Program works to build loyalty for American is that the airline cannot afford to discontinue the program, even if it wanted to. Loyalists would be irate, and switchers would flee to competitive frequent flier programs. The promotion has now become part of the product itself; the promotion is now part of the brand equity!

Another way in which consumer promotion can enhance brand

value is by transferring an advertising equity into action. Perhaps the most vivid example of this approach is the promotional use of the cowboy accessories by Philip Morris Company's Marlboro Cigarettes when broadcast advertising was eliminated by the government in 1960. Recognizing that the "Marlboro Man" was as much a part of the equity as the product itself, a decades' long promotion campaign helped personalize the cowboy and his cigarette to brand users. Utilizing the actual clothing and cowboy gear worn by the "Marlboro Man" as self-liquidating premiums, Philip Morris Company opened the Marlboro Company Store through point-of-sale materials, print offers, and in-pack leaflets. Loyal users could own actual sheepskin jackets, cowboy boots, shirts, leather chaps, and western headgear just like the "Marlboro Man." Every few years, new items were added to the line (rain slickers, belts, work gloves) culminating in the 1992 offering of a hand-tooled, monogrammed-rodeo champ-style brass belt buckle. The possibility that a loyal user could be fully garbed from head to toe in Marlboro clothing is an inspiration for promotion professionals everywhere!

Together with a consistent print and outdoor advertising thrust, these promotions helped build and sustain Marlboro as America's leading brand cigarette with more than 20 percent share of market for the past 25 years. The use of an advertising equity in consumer promotion is not limited to Marlboro. In fact, many strong brands use promotion to make an advertising personality more tangible and intrusive. Consider the Budweiser Clydesdale horses (available as premiums in several forms as event marketing mainstays), the Pillsbury Doughboy (plus doll liquidator), Kool-Aid's smiley face pitcher (point-of-sale materials, T-shirts, self-liquidating premium with proofs-of-purchase), Snuggle Fabric Softener's "Snuggle Bear" (self-liquidating premium with proofs-of-purchase), and Campbell Soup's "M'm! M'm! Good!" theme with the Campbell Kids. Or how about Green Giant Vegetables plush "Little Sprout" doll? What about the California Raisin Council's raisin characters as liquidated premiums, Quaker Oats' Captain Crunch Cereal Where's the Captain quiz contest?, or Camel Cigarettes' "Old Joe" character T-shirt with multiple purchases? Or Wendy's hamburger pitchman "Dave?" By actually using "Dave" to present and tout special promotional meal offerings, Wendy's ensures that price alone is never the message to its users. All of these promotions work to build brand loyalty for two reasons: The promotion has become part of the product itself (not just borrowed interest), and the user builds a physical rapport with the brand through the promotional offering. Strapping on a gleaming Marlboro belt buckle is a tremendous rapport builder!

The next way that consumer promotion works to build brand equity is by creating and communicating extended usage occasions for products or services. This approach focuses on the current user and simply provides more ways for product use. Many food products use recipe collections for this purpose. For example, Jell-O gelatin for more than 20 years has offered recipe extensions into salads, fruit-based desserts, beverages, and frozen desserts. Most of the Jell-O recipes involve multiple purchases or proofs-of-purchase to receive a recipe book or recipe-related accessories. Pillsbury dessert mix brand accomplishes the same thing with its annual Bake-Off Contest in which loyal users compete for recognition for the most imaginative and tasty new recipe. The Bake-Off is more than 15 years old, and it may be one of the reasons why the Pillsbury brand has overtaken Duncan Hines to vie with Betty Crocker for category leadership in the dry cake mix business. Grey Poupon Mustard (gourmet recipe book), Kraft cheeses (home entertainment guide and snack recipe book), Chex cereals (holiday snack mix recipe and premiums), Ocean Spray Cranberry Juice ("Sea Breeze" mixed drink promotion), and Lipton soups (snack dip and casserole recipe promotions), among many others, have used promotional techniques to involve consumers in new and different uses of their products. A classic user of promotion to expand loyal user consumption is Jack Daniels Distilleries. The premium priced "sippin' whiskey" has been extended into rich cake and pastry recipes through promotional offerings and the direct mail communication of Jack Daniels' exclusive "Kentucky Colonel" membership club.

While packaged goods food and beverage products have made the greatest use of this equity building approach, the approach works in other businesses as well. Baskin-Robbins Ice Cream's franchised outlets use direct mail to send free cone certificates on children's birthdays in an attempt to make the birthday a new usage occasion in their stores. Financial institutions use new services such as safe deposit boxes, savings-bank life insurance, and annuities as promotional offers, working to extend their relationship with existing users. One of the strongest equity brands in America, Kodak has used the new-usage approach successfully, developing the disposable camera, creating new usage occasions for its film, and promoting the camera heavily during the vacation season to spur film sales.

The fourth promotional approach for building brand value is to deliver product samples to high potential new users. No product can sustain its equity without adding new users to the franchise. However, most promotional tools, such as coupons, refunds, deals, and rebates, work best against current users. Nielsen, for example, estimates that more than 70 percent of coupon redemptions are from current users. Throw in the 20 percent usually ascribed to misredemption, and new usage is even further reduced. Other studies by Information Resources Incorporated (IRI) and Carolina Manufacturer Services (CMS) support this contention. The bottom line is that in most cases new users are not drawn to products by temporary price reductions, but by the inherent utility of the product itself. This point was also made earlier in this chapter in the London Business School deep price discount study led by Ehrenberg. Therefore, one of the best ways to win new users is by placing a cost-free product sample in their hands.

Brands with strong brand equity are best suited to make sampling work for them. My favorite example is Apple Computer's 1987 sampling program for its Macintosh line. Called "Test Drive a Mac!", the offer invited consumers to use the Mac PC in their home free for 30 days. Since then the Macintosh business has tripled. Of course, the test drive is not a new idea for high-ticket items. Rolls Royce and Mercedes automobile dealers don't sell cars. They encourage a test drive! The car then sells itself. Prestigious perfumes and colognes are sampled by elegant models in high-fashion outlets. Perrier dispensed free samples of sparkling water on New York's stylish Fifth Avenue and Chicago's chic Michigan Avenue in the late 1970s when its mass-market new-user drive commenced. Today, Mars candies are still sampled at family-oriented sporting events around the globe, and Mars remains the world share leader in its category. Low-ticket supermarket brand leaders from shampoo to laundry detergent are sampled weekly through direct mail or at point-of-sale by the manufacturer because new users continually enter the marketplace.

It's hard to think of a leading brand that has not sampled high potential prospects in order to keep building the franchise. Still, one caveat applies to this equity building tool: the more visible the product benefit, the more effective sampling will be. Remember the old rule that "the fastest way to kill a lousy product is to advertise it." Well, sampling an inferior product will speed its demise even more quickly.

Of course, the examples I have offered to illustrate the equity building role of several consumer promotion strategies are exceptions rather than the rule. The fact is that most of the hundreds of thousands of brand consumer promotions bombarding the consumer annually are one-shot efforts designed to build short-term sales volume. And we have not even discussed couponing, a $3.5 billion a year business! What is the impact on a brand of dozens of coupons, rebates, sweepstakes, contests, events, premiums, and their hybrid derivations over time? Probably very little. Like less sophisticated price promotions, most of these consumer promotions deliver increased sales volume, maybe even excite a few sales managers, retailers, or consumers, then are forgotten by all parties.

In Summary

The relationship between promotions and brand equity is an elusive affair that is just beginning to be scrutinized. Yet, so many variables can affect a brand franchise that I suspect the specific role of promotions may never be satisfactorily isolated for scientific study. New developments in database-targeted "relationship marketing," electronic point-of-sale tools, third-party loyalty programs such as air miles, and emerging every day low price (EDLP) strategies will find their respective niches in the marketing mix to further complicate our analysis.

So, what is the promotion practitioner to do? While we wait together for scholars, researchers, suppliers, and marketers to get a tighter fix on the equity building role of promotions, let me in summary offer a few suggestions:

1. Develop a systematic approach to measuring the value of your brands over time, and stick with it. Every year take a reading from consumers of your brands on one or more of the following equity measures:

   a. Product substitutability — as measured by percent share of requirements among brand users.

   b. Brand loyalists — as measured by the percent of brand users who use your product exclusively.

   c. Trademark value — as measured by product attribute and purchase intent ratings on both a find and identified basis. The response differential measures the power of the brand name.

   d. Economic value — as measured by the price premium per unit that users pay vs. the lowest available competitive price.

2. If your product or service does not already possess a strong equity, don't expect to build one through promotion. No matter how equity is defined, I am unable to cite examples of weak brands that developed long-term strength on the basis of promotions alone. In fact, the evidence suggests that leadership brands benefit from significant promotion advantages vs. the also-rans.

3. If your brand enjoys a strong franchise, promotions can be powerful tools to defend and maintain the equity. Keep the product and its packaging contemporary and relevant, keep advertising share of voice near share of market, and promote as often and creatively as your budget permits. This is not to say that promotional waste should be tolerated. Offering the trade deeper or more frequent deals than can be passed through to consumers is wasteful. National FSIs for brands with distribution gaps is wasteful. Higher than necessary coupon values and longer than necessary coupon expiration dates are wasteful. Promoting to nonusers, such as disposable diapers to households without children, is wasteful. A strong brand has more to fear from promotional waste than from equity deterioration.

4. If your brand enjoys a strong franchise, some consumer promotions can enhance brand equity. As discussed earlier, four types of consumer promotion merit consideration for building brand value:

   a. Long-term continuity programs where the payoff is more of the product or service itself.

   b. Promotions leveraging specific advertising equities.

   c. Promotions creating new usage occasions.

   d. New user sampling when perceivable advantage exists.

Admittedly, the evidence is both ad hoc and circumstantial, but most strong brands build one or more of these approaches into their annual marketing plan. When repeated over a number of years, these consumer promotions can enrich the value of a brand.

Finally, after considering the preceding suggestions, stop worrying whether promotion is harming your product.

Archaeologists have found evidence in the ruins of ancient Rome and Egypt that merchants used promotions to build their businesses. I suspect that centuries from now, men and women in business will still be concocting promotions to help peddle their wares. After all, promotion is still a field where creativity, imagination, excitement, and just plain fun have a place in the marketing mix. And *that* is a form of professional equity that we all can share.

REFERENCES
1. William Moran and Kenneth Longman, "Signals of Marketing Profitability," *Marketing Insights*, Summer 1990, pp. 25–32.
2. Tod Johnson, "The Inherent Value of Brands: Results from over 15 Years of Brand Loyalty Data," *The NPD Group*, 1991, p. 9.
3. Tod Johnson, "17 Years of Brand Loyalty Trends: What Do They Tell Us?," *The NPD Group*, 1992, p. 10.
4. A.S.C. Ehrenberg, Kathy Hammond, and G. J. Goodhardt, "The After-Effects of Large Consumer Promotions," London Business School Centre for Marketing and Communication, December 1991, p. 2.
5. James M. Lattin, and Randolph E. Bucklin, "The Dynamics of Consumer Response to Price Discounts," Marketing Science Institute Working Paper #88-111, Cambridge, Massachusetts, 1988.
6. Robert A. Schmitz, Jr., "The Long-Term Relationship Between Trade Promotion and Brand Sales Share," *The Nielsen Researcher*, Summer 1987, vol. 1, no. 3, p. 10.
7. Robert C. Blattberg and Kenneth K. Wisniewski, "How Retail Price Promotions Work: Empirical Results," University of Chicago Working Paper #42, December 1987, pp. 23–24.
8. Robert C. Blattberg, and Scott A. Neslin, *Sales Promotion: Concepts, Methods, and Strategies.* New Jersey: Prentice-Hall Inc., 1990, pp. 478–481. See also David N. Martin, *Romancing the Brand*, New York: American Management Association, 1989, pp. 20–26.

Peter Lucas has been a writer and editor on several publications over the past ten years and has written extensively about the banking industry. He is currently the editor of CardFax, a daily news service sent via facsimile machine. In addition he is associate editor of Credit Card Management, *a monthly magazine for the credit and debit card industry. Prior to this, Lucas was an associate editor for the banking newsletter,* Bank Network News, *assistant editor for* Computer Reseller News *of CMP Publications, Inc., and before that, sports editor for* News/Voice Papers, Inc., *coordinating sports coverage for a chain of eight weekly newspapers.*

Lucas graduated from Monmouth College in Illinois with a Bachelors degree in English and History.

CHAPTER 28

FINANCIAL SERVICES AND COBRANDING

When it comes to financial services, GE Capital Services Inc. is king. From its modest origins financing General Electric Co. appliances during the depression, the company has compiled an enviable record, producing double digit gains in a variety of businesses, including credit cards.

With its finger in multiple pies, including auto financing, mortgage lending, corporate financing, and securities brokeraging, GE Capital has scored so many financial services successes it appears to have the Midas touch. The company, which is just one of twelve GE offspring, posted record earnings of $1.5 billion in 1992, or one-third of GE's total earnings. Assets have more than doubled the past five years to $155 billion. Credit cards, which account for 10 percent of those assets, generate a large part of GE's income. In 1992, GE was the third-largest owner of credit card receivables.

GE's high ranking in the credit card business reflects just how lucrative credit cards are and marks a big change in the traditional financial services market. More nonbank companies than ever are gaining a foothold in financial services through credit cards. The diversity of the three leading card issuers supports that trend. Sears Roebuck & Co. ranks first, Citibank ranks second, and General Electric is number three. Only Citibank is a true financial institution.

Other corporate giants have muscled in on the card business, too. Many represent services marketers expanding their base into financial services such as AT&T Co., GTE Corp. and Western Union Corp. General Motors Corporation has started its GM Card success story as a durables manufacturing giant. These are but a few who have seen how nicely plastic sells things like automobiles and long distance service, in addition to fostering greater customer loyalty among their user bases.

The highway being provided for the entry of nonbank companies into credit cards are the Visa and MasterCard systems. Visa U.S.A. and MasterCard International are marketing and administrative associations that were established in the 1960s by banks seeking to create national credit card brands. The two associations have established Visa and MasterCard as household names. In addition, the merchant network offered by the Visa and Mastercard names is tremendous. In 1992, for instance, Visa and Mastercard could be used at 10.4 million merchant locations. This kind of mass acceptance by merchants is crucial to the success of a credit card brand. The familiarity of the Visa and MasterCard brands and their corresponding merchant networks make it possible for almost any corporation to establish a Visa and/or a

MasterCard program with the approval of the Visa and MasterCard boards.

Companies like AT&T and GM are taking advantage of this immense brand equity and these merchant ties by stamping their names on Visa and MasterCard cards to get more mileage out of their own marketing budgets and to boost sales.

The strategy is called *cobranding* and it has raised the stakes in the financial services market and general-purpose credit card business to unprecedented levels.

Cobranding Ventures

Cobranding has spread like a brush fire among Visa and MasterCard issuers. What makes cobranding attractive to consumer goods companies is that it is workable for almost any kind of product or service — the possibilities are endless. Cobranded cards can offer discounts on everything from long distance services to airline tickets and purchases from select national retailers. The extra value is what consumers want from credit cards in the 1990s.

The list of cobranded cards is impressive. A sampling of a few includes:

- **The AT&T Universal Card:** Charter members pay no annual fee for life provided they use the card once a year. In addition, charter members receive 10 percent discounts on calls made outside the residence and billed to the card. AT&T still offers no-fee cards and calling card discounts on a limited basis. The card also carries a variable interest rate of the prime rate plus 8.9 percent.
- **The Ameritech Complete Card:** Patterned after the AT&T's Universal card, the Complete card has no annual fee and features year-end 10 percent cash-backs on local and long distance calls billed to the card. Interest rates are tiered, based on the size of the balance revolved.
- **The GM Card:** Charges no annual fee and a variable interest rate of the prime plus 10.4 percent. Cardholders earn 5 percent rebates redeemable toward the purchase of GM vehicles. Rebates are doubled to 10 percent when the card is used at any of GM's merchant partners, which include Mobil Oil Co. Rebates are capped at $500 annually and $3,500 over seven years.
- **The GE Rewards Card:** Offers 2 percent cash rebates on every $500 spent and quarterly discount coupons redeemable at 27 national merchants and on GE appliances. The card has no annual fee and a tiered interest rate, which is assigned based on the cardholder's credit history.
- **The MCI Card:** MCI's answer to the AT&T card. MCI, however, gave its card a unique identity. The card is not a calling

card, rather cardholders earn coupons for 15 minutes of free residential long-distance service per month, based on spending, with a maximum of three free hours of long-distance service annually. Cardholders pay no annual fee as long as they are MCI customers. Cardholders who switch their long-distance service pay $20. The card also carries a variable interest rate of prime plus 9.4 percent.

- **The Ford Card:** Offers 5 percent rebates on purchases redeemable toward the purchase of a Ford, Lincoln, or Mercury vehicle. Ford's point of differentiation is that cardholders can earn higher annual rebates, $700, allowing them to reach their maximum rebate level of $3,500 in five years, two years faster than they can on the GM card.
- **The Western Union Card:** Western Union Corp., which has skirted the financial services business for decades with its money transfer and bill payment services, is using cobranding as an entree to secured cards, which are issued to people who can't use plastic without collateral and so represent the last source of largely untapped cardholders. The card pays interest on prime minus 1.5 percent on funds cardholders place in escrow to secure credit lines of equal value, well above the rate paid on most savings accounts.
- **The H&R Block Card:** Tax preparation giant H&R Block began testing in 1993 secured and unsecured versions of a cobranded card that offers rebates on its services. The card carries a $9 annual fee and an interest rate of prime plus 9.9 percent. Secured cardholders earn 3.5 percent on minimum deposits of $500 to secure a credit line of equal value. In 1992, Block prepared 12 percent of the 108 million tax returns filed in the United States.

Looking back, AT&T was one of the first corporate powerhouses to recognize the value of the Visa and MasterCard brands for selling products other than consumer revolving credit. AT&T's intention was to use the Visa and MasterCard system to gain an edge against its competitors by combining a calling card with a general-purpose credit card offering discounts on long distance calls billed to the card. AT&T launched its Universal card in 1990.

A shrewd marketer and a veteran of some nasty promotional scuffles with MCI Corp., AT&T broke new ground by not charging an annual fee for the card. AT&T's offer of "No annual fee for life" for cardholders booked in the first year was practically unprecedented at the time in the Visa and MasterCard business. It is an idea that has caught on and redefined consumers' expectations of value in a credit card.

While Discover Card, which Sears launched in 1985, was the first general-purpose card issuer to offer a no-fee card technically, Discover did not take advantage of the merchant network in the Visa and MasterCard system and had only a handful of participating retailers when it launched. Building a merchant base from scratch is a hard slog. While initially consumers flocked to Discover's offer, they found they couldn't use the card in as many places. Sears threw in the towel and sold Discover Card Services to the public through the stock market. Selling Discover didn't mean that Sears was out of the general-purpose card business. Sears considered a Visa or MasterCard franchise so valuable, it sued Visa for the right to issue Visa cards. The case was still pending in 1993 and is expected to eventually go before the U.S. Supreme Court.

American Express has had considerable success outside the Visa/MasterCard systems, even though it has a lesser merchant base — nearly three times smaller than Visa and MasterCard. It has been successful because its merchants are the type with which its cardholders do frequent business. As a travel and entertainment card, AmEx targets business executives, the affluent, corporations, and small businesses. Its merchant network is comprised mainly of airlines, hotels, restaurants, and resorts. In recent years, AmEx has tried to broaden its merchant base to appeal to a more general audience, but still lags far behind Visa and MasterCard in this respect.

One thing is certain. The power of cobranding is immense and can thereby be lucrative for both the bank issuer and the corporate sponsor of the card. The GM Card, for example, had booked 5.25 million accounts within 30 days of its launch, and cardholders were cashing in rebates earned from balance transfers to purchase cars much faster than GM expected. Within a year, GM had sold almost 50,000 vehicles to cardholders cashing in rebates. The card issuer, Household Bank, got a lucrative new source of accounts and volume. The card also accumulated $4 billion in receivables, propelling issuer Household into the ranks of the 10 largest Visa/MasterCard issuers, based on receivables.

Because of this kind of documented cobranding success, others will undoubtedly enter the cobranding arena as well. Prospective players include oil companies, retailers, more automobile manufacturers, and other regional Bell operating companies.

But before a corporation and card issuer jump into the cobranding fray they must first ask themselves some key questions. What position in the market do they want to protect? What is the creditworthiness and profile of the cardholder likely to be attracted by the offer? What is the contribution of the marketing partner? And how much is the issuer willing to spend on the venture? How does one make the card competitive? How is value defined in the consumers' minds?

THE VALUE MESSAGE

Posing the questions is easy. Finding the answers, however, is far more difficult, because not every cobranded card is a success right out of the chute. Issuers and their corporate partners must find a value that will have long-term appeal to consumers and price the card appropriately.

Since the advent of the AT&T card and GM card, issuers have experimented with various no annual fee offers, lower interest rates, and cash rebates — or a combination of the three. These, however, have had a minor effect. Price alone is no longer sufficient to close a sale — consumers want "value." Any issuer who doesn't understand that value is more than price will face a tough challenge.

AmEx tried to give value its own posh twist by offering cardholder rewards, such as weekend getaways, tickets to special performances by select entertainers, and even the opportunity to shoot hoops with a National Basketball Association player. This kind of added value goes beyond the more typical price-value orientation that many cards use to attract consumers.

GE's Rewards card is an example of how a cobranded card can fall flat if it is not careful to offer the right value and communicate that value to consumers. Although initially, Rewards proved to be an unqualified direct mail and telemarketing success, with hit rates of 6 percent and 15–20 percent respectively, this growth was not at the level of other successful cards such as the GM Card or AT&T Universal Card.

Stunting the growth of the Rewards card, card experts say, was GE's decision to charge an annual fee and its failure to communicate a straightforward marketing message about the card's value. Card experts argue that GE's marketing message was too complex for consumers to grasp. Furthermore, the card's merchant partners ranged all over the map, making it tougher to zero in on a target audience for the card. Merchants included discounter Kmart and eyeglass maker Lens Crafters, as well as automobile manufacturer Volvo North America Corp. To some experts, it appeared as though GE was unsure and trying a little of everything to see which merchant type offered the most value to potential cardholders.

Shortly after the GE card's launch, the annual fee was dumped and rebated to those cardholders who had paid it, and a new interest rate tier was added to the card to increase its appeal. GE's quick action gave the card a second chance in the cobranding market but the lesson remains — a card must demonstrate value to be successful.

GE's experience does not mean that annual fees are dead. On the contrary, several issuers still charge fees for value-added cards. They just must be prepared to give up something of real value — and to explain that value in simple terms to consumers. Citibank, for one, charges a fee for its cobranded Ford card, in return for which it offers 5 percent rebates redeemable toward the purchase of Ford vehicles. Citibank also cushions the impact of the fee, and in turn sacrifices some pretax profit, by waiving the fee in the first year and crediting a rebate to the cardholder's account when the fee is paid in subsequent years.

Pinpointing just what type of value can sustain an annual fee and still draw enough accounts is daunting. Card executives agree that there is no universal offer that will excite all cardholders. And the influx of creative rebate programs has dulled the luster of many offers.

For instance, Discover's cash rebate on purchases of up to 1 percent was one of the first entries in the value-added market, but now looks like a laggard in a field crowded with more potent givebacks. Discover executives admit the card is no longer alone in offering rebates. However, they contend the card still offers value to people who put a premium on cash. Trouble is, some say the industry has raised the bar on cash rebates. Cash back still excites people, but credit card experts say that it has to be more than 1 percent. Credit card consultant Donald M. Berman, president of Plainview, N.Y.-based Cardholder Management Services, believes 2 percent is about the maximum an issuer can afford to give back on a cash rebate. But if you are going to give up that much, it may be more economical to share the rebate with a partner.

WHO PAYS?

The economics of cobranding are too great for card executives to ignore. If issuers structure their cobranding deals correctly, the cobranding partner will pick up the bulk of, if not all, the marketing costs. This lowers the issuer's account acquisition costs, allowing the issuer to comfortably underwrite its portion of the rebate.

Household Credit Services has cracked the nut when it comes to implementing this strategy with its Ameritech partnership. Ameritech pays all marketing costs for its cobranded card issued by Household, while Household coordinates marketing for the card, owns all receivables, and provides customer service.

Many suspect that Household has struck a similar deal with GM. Card experts surmise that GM is footing the bill for most of its card's marketing costs, as well as picking up some of the tab for the rebate. If an issuer can eliminate marketing costs, it provides more flexibility in other areas of the cobranding deal.

Giving marketing partners responsibility for picking up the tab for marketing or account acquisition expenses is not outrageous since most manufacturers, service companies, and retailers include discounts and rebates as part of the marketing budget. "It's an accounting procedure for GM, because it has built the cost of the rebate into its business as a marketing expense," says Bill Hodges, senior vice president of marketing for Discover Card Services. "GM is funneling more of that money through the card program. As long as it sells cars and get incremental sales, GM can afford its part of the giveback."

CAPPING REWARDS

As competition increases in the cobranded market, the temptation to give up too much will be almost irresistible. Giving up too much pretax profit to cardholders is a sin no issuer of a corporate partner should commit. Incentives must be capped to prevent cardholders from draining too much profit from the program. Issuers of airline affinity cards, which offer cardholders one frequent flier mile on a specific airline for every dollar spent, learned this painful lesson. Issuers reportedly surrendered 2 percentage points of sales volume revenue (interchange) to help fund the cardholder giveback, a steep sacrifice for a quick share gain.

When the bill for givebacks came due, issuers and their airline partners realized that profits were flowing out of the door as cardholders racked up more miles than projected. Compounding the problem was that a high percentage of airline affinity cardholders paid their balances in full each month, thereby dramatically reducing the card issuer's interest income. As a result, these issuers were later forced to cap cardholder rebates and push annual fees into the stratosphere — as much as $60 for standard cards — to hold the line of profits. FCC National Bank, which issues the United Airlines Mileage Plus card, capped rebates at 10,000 miles a month and 50,000 a year. The rewards expire three years after the date of transaction.

Since then, no cobranded card program has made the same mistake. GM caps rebate dollars at $500 annually and $3,500 over seven years for standard cardholders, and at $1,000 annually and $7,000 over seven years for gold cardholders.

Although Ford has a higher annual cap of $700, it gives up no more in rebates overall, $3,500, than GM. Ford's point of differentiation is that cardholders can earn their maximum rebate two years sooner than they can on a GM card.

COBRANDING ECONOMICS

If issuers have to give up some margin, the question is how much? That is a question that must be answered by individual issuers, since each financial institution has a different threshold on profits. Most card executives agree, however, that 25 basis points to one percentage point of interchange is about the maximum an issuer can give-up on a no-fee, low-rate, value-added card.

Interchange is a fee paid to the card issuer by the merchant bank. Interchange is funded by merchant discount fees, which are what merchants are charged by banks that handle their Visa and MasterCard transactions. Merchant banks take their cut of profit from the discount fee.

Paying out up to 1 percent of interchange to fund a cardholder giveback is a hefty sum, considering that cobranded and value-added cards tend to attract primarily convenience users, which means little interest income. Sustained profits will come to those who match what they give up to what they can generate in incremental charges.

That means attracting cardholders who will be profitable over the long haul. Without a large cache of revolving cardholders, issuers are likely to wind up funding the giveback largely from interchange revenue, which is hardly enough to sustain long-term profits. It takes almost $5,000 in annual spending for an issuer to break even on a nonrevolving account, according to *Credit Card News*, a publication that tracks the credit card business. Interest income provides 80 percent of an issuer's revenue stream.

Convenience users are a ticking bomb in cobranded and value-added portfolios, and issuers know it. While these accounts can provide swift share gains, they can drain long-term profits by cashing in incentives without generating any finance revenue. Unfortunately, value-added cards attract convenience use. Screening out likely convenience users using statistical scoring models enables issuers to identify accounts that are likely to defect to more compelling offers. Armed with this information a card issuer can focus on better servicing accounts that are likely to jump in order to keep them in the fold and hopefully maximize revenues on those accounts. This may mean dropping or lowering the annual fee and offering discounts, which not all cardholders receive.

Another way to hedge against convenience users is to charge an annual fee. This is tricky, however, because annual fees can lead to positioning problems, a la GE's Rewards card. Issuers can usually only get away with an annual fee if the value of their card justifies a fee. While no-fee cards are currently in vogue, most consumers are smart enough to appropriately weigh the annual fee against the value offered.

FORGING A MARRIAGE THAT WORKS

Striking successful cobranding deals requires that each party in the partnership be sensitive to the other's objectives and desires. Almost always in cobranding, each partner has a different objective for the card. However, there must be a willingness to subordinate egos and work together to forge a deal that meets both sets of objectives and makes both partners equally as successful in the venture.

Indeed, a clash of agendas can cause a deal for a trend-setting card to slip right through an issuer's fingers. That's what happened to Bank One, Columbus, which originally had the contract to issue the GM card. Ronald N. Zebeck, GM's managing director of credit card operations, recalls that GM pulled its GM card from Bank One because Bank One wanted to maximize its return on assets by (1) limiting the size of the cardholder portfolio to about one million accounts, (2) charging an annual fee, and (3) maintaining a higher interest rate. That plan didn't satisfy GM, which wanted a card that would offer the kinds of incentives that would sell cars.

Banks, however, are not in the business of developing cards that do not provide a solid return on investment. A bank is concerned with meeting certain returns and this is based on funding costs. With low-cost funds, an incentive-based card can be profitable, but as the cost of funds rises the profit margins are reduced. This caution characteristic of most banks is the reason that some say that banks are not necessarily always the best issuing partner for corporate entities looking for an entree into the cobranding derby — they are focused on protecting their card profits at the expense of aggressively expanding their card portfolio. Holding the line on profits and protecting share can work against a card's competitiveness in growing its cardholder base.

For GM the object was obviously to sell cars. For the issuing bank, Household, the goal was to gain a lucrative source of transaction volume and interest income on receivables. In the end, Household was willing to acknowledge that the primary purpose of the GM card was to sell cars, not Household's credit. The value that GM brought to the card, however, served Householder well in reaching its goals, too. It is thought that issuers like Household, which are not banks because they do not accept deposits or sell retail bank products, are more willing to be flexible with a cobranding partner, as they bring very little brand equity to the partnership themselves. Cobranding allows these issuers the ability to move cards into millions of wallets largely on the name of their cobranding partners.

Banks such as Bank One, Columbus, the 12th largest Visa and MasterCard issuer in 1992, are not focused only on cards and so cannot always afford to tie up huge sums of capital in one area of the bank. Bank One Senior Vice President Mark Tonnesson argues that long-term profits are more important to banks than short-term share gains. "Our interest is not in volume, but in profits for ourselves and our clients. If people say we (banks) lack creativity because we aren't willing to give up profits to a cobranding partner, then we are guilty as charged."

Cobranding partners view incentives differently. For Ameritech, the cost of discounting telephone rates for Complete card users is worthwhile when the market share gain is factored into the balance sheet. Ameritech mailed more than $1.5 million in annual rebates in the first 30 months after the card's launch.

NOT EVERYONE NEEDS A PARTNER

For those issuers who are loath to take on a cobranding partner on anything less than their own terms, the alternative is to find a way to add value without the baggage of a partner. The benefit for a card issuer without a partner is that it really doesn't matter what department gives up more because all the benefits from the card are kept under one roof.

An example is Wells Fargo bank, which has linked its value-added card not to somebody else's product, but its own. Wells' California Advantage card has drawn accolades from card executives as an example of the creativity banks need to keep from being squeezed out of the value-added card market. Wells' California Advantage card gives cardholders rebates on purchases toward the principle of a Wells Fargo mortgage. Its success proves that a bank or financial institution doesn't necessarily need a partner to add value.

Some question Wells' decision to attach an annual fee to its cards, but the card's value is so attractive it may indeed justify a fee. Because the card can reduce the cost of buying a home in a market where real estate costs have gone through the roof, it offers a real value on its own. While the success of Wells' California Advantage could boost card profits, it might also help the bank to win back a large share of the mortgage business, 50 percent of which is owned by nonbanks. There is speculation that the program could also attract higher-quality customers who do not want to risk denial on a mortgage application because of delinquencies on past credit card accounts.

The program can also provide a blueprint of how banks can recapture some of the share lost to nonbanks in the credit card market. Nonbanks controlled 25 percent of the card market in 1993, up from 19.4 percent in 1990. Most of the gains in that span were due to proliferation of nonbank-issued cobranded cards.

PROTECTING THE COBRANDING INVESTMENT

Quality accounts are crucial to the success of a card program. Delinquencies or loans charged off the books because they have been deemed uncollectible can sink a card program. Therefore, there is a high premium on scoring models, the mathematics behind identifying portfolio hoppers and high-profit customers.

Booking cardholders with pristine credit ratings is certainly the goal of all credit card issuers, but the pickings are slim — about 10 million, card experts estimate. The small pool means there will be a lot of churn among that group. Thus, issuers have to dip lower into the risk pool. To protect against losses with riskier cardholders, many issuers are offering performance-based pricing that rewards the best customers with lower interest rates. Rewards are also limited to non-delinquent cardholders. Performance-based pricing covers the risk of chronic delinquents because the most costly part of a program — the incentive — is not at risk. By avoiding delinquency problems, there is a good profit spread as people spend more regularly to attain the best rate.

Still, performance-based pricing can set off some land mines. Issuers who tie interest rates to prime may find that they can no longer pass along a rate hike to cardholders without suffering reprisals in the form of attrition. It may mean having to eat profits or charging an annual fee. The card industry did just that in the 1980s when the cost of funds rocketed and issuers were afraid to crack the 20 percent barrier on interest rates.

A more plausible solution, however, is to renegotiate the sharing agreement with the cobranding partner if the partner has the margins to offset the cost of funds. Partners in bad deals often renegotiate contracts or kill the program before losses spiral out of control. Those who are most successful with the cobranding strategy are financially shrewd. They didn't get into these deals to lose money.

The key to renegotiating contracts is proving to manufacturers, service companies, and retailers that plastic is a successful marketing tool for merchandise, such as automobiles. More and more cards are becoming successful at doing just that. For instance, the airline cards, which though they may not have always worked for the banks, have sold plenty of seats for the airlines.

Today, with intense price competition, issuers need to be savvy when cutting a cobranded deal. Inevitably, issuers will have to give up some portion of profitability. In the case of cobranding, no deal is forever. What was negotiated with a marketing partner once can be renegotiated if the profit squeeze gets too tight.

With card pricing expected to remain in a state of flux for at least a couple more years, issuers running in the cobranding derby will need to emphasize long-term planning and flexibility to adjust to swift market changes. Those who survive will be the ones who get the highest response rates for their marketing dollars.

Just how far issuers will go to achieve that goal is unknown. What is certain is that issuers aspiring to reach the heights yet to be attained in the card business will use cobranding as their springboard.

Robert G. Brown is founder and CEO of the SPAR Group, an international organization of promotion, in-store merchandising, and information and research service companies with over 2,000 representatives in the United States, Canada, Australia, New Zealand, Asia, and the United Kingdom. Dubbed the "guru of price promotion" by Fortune Magazine and the "master of trade promotion analysis" by Advertising Age, he has worked with over 80 percent of the major consumer packaged goods companies in the world on such issues as improving incremental profits and sales from promotions, the impact of EDLP, building long-term brand franchises, forward buying, and diverting. SPAR operates in-store programs in major retailers such as Kmart, Wal Mart, and Toys 'R' Us. Based on Brown's pioneering work on baseline technology in the 1970s, SPAR's approach has been used by many marketers to evaluate and improve promotions worldwide.

Brown is a featured speaker at many international conferences, speaking for organizations such as the Association of National Advertisers, the American Marketing Association, the Advertising Research Foundation, the Grocery Manufacturers of America, the Promotion Marketing Association of America, EOSMAR, and PROMO. He has written articles and commentaries for numerous trade publications.

CHAPTER 29

DIVERTING AND FORWARD-BUYING

Throughout the history of business, the area of marketing and sales has always been witness to significant waste. It is probably the one area in which, despite the known waste, the practice of spending large amounts of money continues because the spending that does succeed makes such a tremendous impact.

JC Penney's famous quote about knowing that 50 percent of his advertising money is wasted, but not knowing which 50 percent is wasted, is more true today than ever before. More than 50 percent of the spending on trade promotion is currently inefficient due to forward-buying and diverting. Yet most manufacturers offer, at best, lip service to the problem and, almost without exception, write it off as a cost of business.

Diverting is very simply the practice in which retailers buy product and resell it to other retailers. The increased inefficiency of local marketing money, the incorrect payment of commissions, and an inability to track product in the event of a recall are some of the more serious ethical and business issues caused by diverting. In addition, the inability to control the factors contributing to diverting has already led to significant increases in forward-buying and paying discounts on turn business.

With billions of promotional dollars being wasted on forward-buying and diverting, and the problems presented due to these, it is important to understand these practices in more depth and to figure out how and why such waste and inefficiencies are not only tolerated but also actively encouraged by many major manufacturers.

OVERVIEW OF THE PROBLEM

Diverting, while an old practice, has recently become a major problem for manufacturers. With estimated industry growth rates of more than 50 percent per year for the last few years, with the subdivision of manufacturers into regional offices and an emphasis on local and regional marketing, with more sophisticated "wires" or electronic communications about product rates among diverters, and with a strong commitment by retailers to profit from diverting (including the hiring of full-time diverters), the problem has become a potential time bomb for manufacturers.

The position taken by Winn-Dixie in the fall of 1988 to monitor regional discounts — buying at the best possible price — is an inevitable result of the manufacturers' "decoupling" of promotional money from national programs and monitored performance. Many major manufacturers have moved away from national promotions toward local programs or toward a "trust the retailer" program. This trend will intensify the pressure on manufacturers to continue local promotions. If manufacturers try to resume national promotions, they will find themselves at a relative disadvantage to other manufacturers, since a national program is directly contrary to the strategic objectives of local marketing and prevents manufacturers from capitalizing on the benefits of local marketing.

Diverting, or even the perception of diverting, is highly disruptive to a coordinated and ethical local promotional or marketing program. The feeling of being "cheated," even if untrue, creates major issues with brokers, customers, and sales staff. Most manufacturers, from the perspective of their employees and brokers, do not have a policy on diverting and have not taken action to prevent diverting. A failure to act rewards diverting, and in a very real sense, the actual policy becomes one of rewarding those who participate in diverting.

In many respects, an inability to identify the actual amount of diverting has created a feeling among those involved that they are "suckers" and are not treated fairly because of their "honesty." This issue, when not satisfactorily addressed, consumes abnormal amounts of time and energy, all of which is highly unproductive. In many situations, such as in New England, the real amount of diverting may be less than the suspected amount, and the ability to clearly quantify the amount of product diverted could be a very positive initial step in addressing some of the major issues. The perception of the problem must be prevented from exceeding reality.

Because of the complexity, and to some extent due to the sudden appearance of the problem in its current magnitude, many manufacturers are just now developing clear policies and programs to address the issues. Many manufacturers, however, along with their employees, representatives, and brokers, encourage or tolerate diverting for what they perceive as their own advantage.

DIVERTING AND FORWARD-BUYING

Diverting. Diverting refers to a practice whereby sales intended for certain customers under a promotion or pricing schedule are "diverted" or resold by one retail customer to other customers for whom the pricing or promotional allowances are not available.

Diverting is a highly profitable and easy-to-run business. The retailer establishes a "diverting desk," often hiring full-time people solely to buy and sell the diverted product. All promotions that are offered with "hot prices" are sent to the retailer's diverting desk. These products are then put on the "wire," which is often a fax sent to other retailers who buy the diverted product. If the diverter's promotional price is less than another retailer's current manufacturer price, these retailers send in their orders, which are combined with the diverting retailer's legitimate order, and the total is given to the manufacturer as an order.

The diverter generally keeps $.50 per case, plus any discount (usually 1 percent or 2 percent) for payment to the manufacturer within a specific period of time. While $.50 per case doesn't sound like a lot of profit, at 1 percent margin (typical retailer net profit), this is equivalent to selling $50.00 of product to the consumer. Considering that a truckload of product is often diverted, and the diverter is merely handling paper, it is easier than the work involved to sell the product at retail. The economic viability of diverting is clear.

Forward-Buying. Forward-buying occurs when a price discount is offered for a short period of time. Not wanting to pay full price when the promotion ends, the retailer purchases extra product for later sale when the promotion ends.

Forward-buying is one of the most expensive and inefficient practices in moving products from the manufacturer to the consumer. A rational approach to keep costs down and quality high is to maintain the lowest level of inventory possible. Yet many estimates show that inventory levels for many major brands are double what is needed to adequately service the consumer. Many retailers have built or leased warehouse space to hold inventory due to forward-buying.

In addition to direct costs (for example, warehousing, insurance, interest, spoilage), there are indirect costs caused by manufacturing excess product for short periods of time, which are for forward-buying, and then having manufacturing plants with no demand while the forward-bought product is sold to the consumer.

Today, the amount of product obtained through forward-buying is based on a set formula that usually considers factors such as discount, margin, turns, interest, insurance, and cost of storage. The retailer purchases sufficient product on discount so that the discount covers the cost of holding the product. If the cost of storage is 1 percent per week, and the discount is 10 percent, a rational retailer will forward-buy 10 weeks' worth of product.

Since retailers typically forward-buy sufficient product of heavily promoted brands to last until the next promotion, this deal-to-deal buying means that a retailer never pays list price, and the new list price effectively is the promoted price. This new price is called the "dead net price."

Every Day Low Pricing (EDLP). EDLP is an attempt by some retailers and manufacturers to get away from the artificially high list prices and shelf prices that surround "hot features." In 1991/1992 Procter & Gamble announced they would move all their brands to EDLP. Since excess forward-buying and diverting almost always accompany this high-list, deep-deal policy, EDLP eliminates the cost of this approach.

TYPES OF DIVERTING

International Product Sold Domestically. Many companies offer special pricing on packaging for overseas sales. The price is often lower because of the following reasons:

1. There are no U.S. taxes.
2. The manufacturer is offering lower prices since it doesn't have the high sales or marketing expenses incurred in the U.S.
3. Overseas sales are based on incremental revenue and costs and, therefore, have no fixed component in pricing.
4. The product is excess merchandise.
5. The product is below U.S. standards.

When product is sold for foreign consumption, there are usually legally enforceable contracts, and the diversion of products back to the United States is illegal. But the product is sometimes shipped outside the country and reshipped back to the U.S. Sometimes it is never shipped outside the country, but the title is passed. Since it is an area of questionable legality, tracing the product and who is responsible is often difficult. Some companies (for example, Hershey Foods) have successfully sued and won legal suits against diverting of overseas product. While overseas diverting can be a problem for some companies, as a percentage of overall diverting, this is a relatively small percentage.

Forward-Buying for Resale. Some diverting is really a combination of forward-buying and diverting. It occurs when a manufacturer offers a sufficiently large discount on low-bulk, deep-deal, high-value products (usually health and beauty aids products) to cover the cost of significant forward-buying. After the promotion ends, the product is resold by diverters to other retailers in the market at a price below the manufacturers' normal retail selling price. In essence, the diverter or reseller now is competing against the manufacturer, selling the manufacturer's own product at a lower price than the manufacturer.

This type of diverting is becoming less significant because manufacturers who pay the most promotional allowances now sell 100 percent of the product on promotion, thus eliminating the price variance among retailers that prompts diverting.

Selling to Noncompetitor Retailers. The largest and fastest growing type of diverting is the instance of product that is purchased on promotion in one market and then resold in another market where the promotional allowance isn't offered or the promotion is less.

Transshipping Within Chains. National chains such as Kroger have developed a very sophisticated computerized system for purchasing product in one region of the country and shipping it to all their stores nationally. This is profitable considering the cost of shipping against the extra discount generated by buying product to divert within the chain.

Selling Across Trade Channels. Manufacturers that sell "similarly" packaged products to wholesale or price clubs for lower prices than they charge other retailers create the opportunity for this product to be diverted into more traditional channels in which significant marketing and selling expenses result in higher list prices. Another variation of this is the practice of repackers who buy lower weight or multipacks on discount and then resell the single packs now separated to those retailers who buy the full product or purchase single packages.

One example is of candy companies that sell a lower weight product for sale in vending machines at a lower price, sell bonus packages (extra candy bars for free), or sell lower-weight bars in multipackages. Repackers purchase these products, break them into traditional quantities, and resell them profitably for a lower price than the full-weight product.

Another example involves appliances that are sold overseas without warranty and at a lower price. These are then diverted and sold through traditional channels of distribution.

DIVERTING ISSUES

There are a number of issues with respect to diverting that are often not realized or are overlooked by manufacturers.

- *Product recall.* Under the Manufacturers' Fair Practices Act, manufacturers have an obligation to code and track product in the event of a product recall that could pose a health or safety problem. What could be a minor recall in one market could turn into a national nightmare if tainted product shipped to a market has been diverted and no records exist of where it was shipped.
- *Legal issues.* A manufacturer who has knowledge that product is being diverted into markets where other retailers are not getting equal access to available promotional money is in violation of the spirit, if not the letter, of the antitrust law.
- *Incorrect sales commission.* Commissions are paid on sales to a market. When product is diverted out of a market, the salesperson where the product is diverted loses the commission. Since the salesperson or broker not receiving the commission is still expected to service the retailer, this obviously creates many significant organizational and morale problems.
- *Increased local marketing funds (LMFs).* Most retailers add LMF money to the off-invoice amount to get a dead net case price. Since diverting occurs from markets with low dead nets to markets with higher dead nets, this increases the amount of LMF spent. A further impetus to increase LMF money is from the retailer who is buying the diverted product and who often asks for LMF from the manufacturer to run a specific program at retail. Manufacturers almost always give this money because they expect this type of retail program to generate

extra sales. While it does increase retail sales, manufacturers gain no additional sales. In fact, the manufacturer has paid off-invoice and two different LMFs to sell the same case of product.

- *Inability to analyze sales.* When significant quantities of product are diverted, it completely distorts any ability to judge the sales personnel and the various marketing and promotional programs. Sales personnel who fail to meet sales objectives, yet accomplish their objective by spending promotional dollars and selling to diverters, are in the end judged successful. Those sales personnel who service the retailers who buy from diverters and keep promotional spending down are often judged as poor performers. The result is that not only are poor personnel rewarded over good personnel, but also a standard is soon set that the company rewards those who sell to diverters and punish those who do not.

- *Ethical misbehavior.* When brokers and sales personnel are put in a position in which they have to sell to diverters to gain additional commissions or to make quota, it creates ethical issues for the manufacturer. The best-run organizations set high ethical standards to which they expect their employees to adhere. When senior managers close their eyes to violations of company policy (not to sell to diverters), then they implicitly set criteria in which violations of company policies are condoned. It then becomes more difficult to tell employees which company policies they need to observe and which ones they don't.

- *Unequal treatment of retailers.* Because very few diverters are unknown to manufacturers, the manufacturers are participating in programs that allow unequal treatment of competing retailers. When retailers find out that competing retailers are obtaining merchandise at lower prices than they are, their discovery creates a difficult selling environment, and the manufacturer often has to spend promotional money to match the diverting price. Since most manufacturers make a significant effort to treat all their customers (retailers) fairly and on an equal basis, this conflict is counterproductive.

- *High retail prices.* While individual retailers gain an advantage by buying and/or selling diverted product, the diversion of product adds costs to bringing a product to market. Additional promotional spending and the cost of additional shipping and warehousing of products, plus the diverter's profits, are all eventually reflected in the retail price.

How Diverting and Forward-Buying Distort
Promotion Analysis

It is important to understand how much of a product sold by a manufacturer during a promotion to a retailer is for forward-buying and diverting.

Table 29.1 shows incremental volume from seven promotions broken into normal baseline sales, sales from forward-buying, sales due to incremental consumption, and diverted product sales. While promotions 6 and 7 look best, most of the additional sales are coming from diverted product. A failure to measure this could easily lead a manufacturer to conclude that promotions 6 and 7 are the best. To continually run these promotions which are more expensive will result in ever-increasing quantities of diverting and significant waste of promotion dollars.

Measurement of Forward-Buying. Forward-buying is actually fairly easy to measure. Many software packages are available that calculate a baseline (what would be sold without a promotion). Exhibits 29.1 and 29.2 show a typical promotion and the incremental sales and trade inventory loading during the promotional period. As seen, trade inventories are run down prior to the promotion in anticipation of it, while incremental buying is reduced after the promotion due to forward-buying.

TABLE 29.1
ANALYSIS OF PROMOTION VOLUME

Promotion	Base Consumer Franchise	Forward-Buying	Incremental Volume	Diverting
1	2516	5102	830	0
2	3110	3437	3312	0
3	3716	3826	3526	3241
4	1679	2478	4463	1801
5	1416	3719	3832	1963
6	1360	2616	3438	8142
7	4006	3682	3888	14216

EXHIBIT 29.1

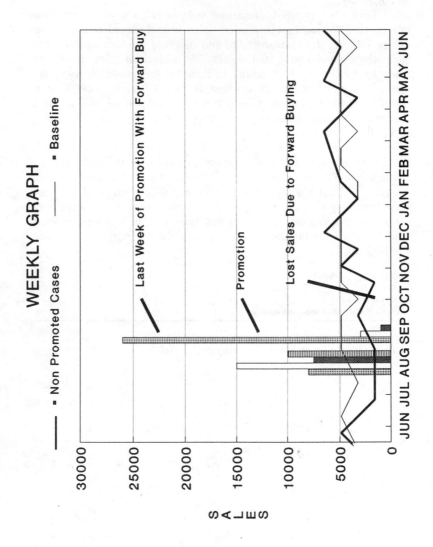

EXHIBIT 29.2

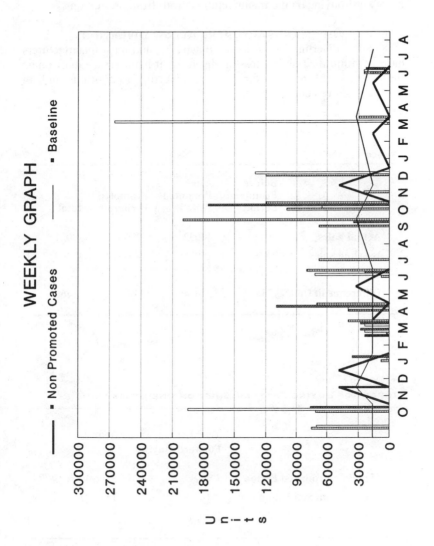

WEEKLY GRAPH

■ Non Promoted Cases ⎯⎯ ■ Baseline

Units

Another example of the importance of forward-buying is shown in Tables 29.2 and 29.3. Table 29.2 shows the weekly sales to a retail account. This retailer has a good record of supporting promotions but has shifted to deal-to-deal buying. Table 29.3 shows the impact of this in forward-buying on the manufacturers profit from promotions.

WHY MANUFACTURERS ALLOW DIVERTING
Since diverting has so many drawbacks, and most manufacturers have it within their ability to stop diverting, it is necessary to examine the reasons why manufacturers allow diverting to continue and, in some cases, even encourage it.

TABLE 29.2

	Before Promoted Period	After Promoted Period	Promoted Period	Total
Actual Sales	2643	40022	17266	59931
Baseline Sales	3428	15928	29109	48465
Difference in Units	-785	24094	-11843	11466

TABLE 29.3
IMPACT OF BUYING PATTERN SHIFT ON ONE STORE

	Year 1 Forward-Buying	Year 2
Avg. Post-Promoted Period	3 weeks	8 weeks
Avg. Incremental Volume	280	151
Avg. Incremental Profit	$121.30	$32.70

- *Retailer resistance.* Many retail buyers are judged on the amount of promotion allowances they get from manufacturers. In addition, many systems and procedures have been developed that revolve around forward-buying. Any attempt to eliminate forward-buying will be met with strong resistance by a very entrenched bureaucracy whose very job might be at stake. In late 1991 and early 1992, Procter & Gamble switched all brands to an EDLP approach, and this has been met with considerable resistance from retailers.
- *Short-term earning loss.* Any reduction in trade inventories will have a negative impact on manufacturers. Manufacturers earn sales and profits by selling to retailers. Each case in retail inventory reduction is one less case sold by a manufacturer. With pressure for short-term earnings, most manufacturers are not willing to accept this type of short-term earnings reduction.
- *Pressure to make quota.* The major reason manufacturers tolerate diverting is that they often need to sell the extra volume to diverters to make their quota or plan.
- *No "smoking guns" to indict.* When manufacturers want to stop diverting and punish offenders, clear evidence is often lacking. Since an accusation is a serious charge, clear evidence must exist. Diverting, by its nature, is done secretly, and rarely does anyone admit to selling to a diverter nor do retailers admit to diverting.
- *Individuals don't care.* Except for those salespeople who have product being diverted into their markets, there is little economic incentive to go to considerable effort and create the confrontation necessary to stop diverting. This is particularly the case if the belief is that management won't do anything to punish large customers.
- *Afraid to challenge major customers.* Manufacturers often know which of their major customers are involved in diverting. But one of the prime objectives of a manufacturer's sales department is to build good relationships with major customers. Threatening to stop selling to them unless they stop diverting is not generally thought to be in the manufacturer's interest.
- *Senior management doesn't want the facts.* This is not an issue that senior managers like to address. As long as business is successful, the attitude of most senior managers is one of benign neglect. Manufacturers offer general policy statements against diverting but only very rarely enforce this policy. Generally, senior management feels that little diverting is occurring even when those close to the retailer know it is happening continually.
- *It's an inexpensive way to promote.* Smaller manufacturers

can offer promotional monies to known diverters who will divert the product into retail chains in large markets. This allows a smaller manufacturer to get selected lower prices without offering the promotion in the large market, a cost that is prohibitive.

Expected Benefits or Savings from Stopping Diverting. There are several benefits to the manufacturer who puts an end to diverting. Stopping the diverting accomplishes the following:

1. It increases the ability to trace product in the event of a product recall.
2. It reduces the time wasted by management, sales, and brokers who are focusing on the diverting problem.
3. It lowers the percentage of cases forward-bought or diverted on discount.
4. It reduces manufacturing and distribution expenses.
5. It results in a savings or reallocation of LMF by eliminating double promotion spending on diverted cases.

Assessing a Company's Diverting Problem. In order to assess the magnitude of the diverting problem, Spar/Burgoyne, Inc. has developed 10 simple questions to ask. By scoring the answers in the manner prescribed, and adding up the 10 for a total score, a company's "diverting health" can be immediately diagnosed.

1. Diverting has increased for my company.
Yes (3) No (1) Don't Know (3)

YES: An increase in diverting for your company indicates a dangerous trend has started, and operational policies are occurring that allow these increases. Unless these policies are reversed, the increased diverting is likely to continue.
NO: The fact that diverting is not increasing shows that your company has instituted sound policies. Diverting is growing at an incredible rate (100 percent in the last 18 months), and your ability to move contrary to these trends is a very positive sign.
DON'T KNOW: Lack of knowledge of whether diverting is increasing shows a lack of focus on the issue, and an inability to measure a critical problem. Because it isn't being monitored, it is probably increasing at least at an industry rate (100 percent in the last 18 months).

2. Diverting accounts for 5 percent of my company's annual sales.
Yes (2) No (1) Don't Know (3)

YES: If more than 5 percent of your sales is diverted, you are probably worse off than other manufacturers. It is estimated that 2 percent to 10 percent of dry grocery is diverted.

NO: If less than 5 percent of your sales is diverted, you are probably not significantly worse than other manufacturers.

DON'T KNOW: Not knowing how much of your product is diverted is a danger signal. A potential time bomb is not being correctly monitored; therefore, there won't be any warning until after it explodes.

3. Diverting accounts for more than 25 percent of total trade forward-buying.
   Yes (4)   No (1)   Don't Know (4)

YES: Diverting has reached a very significant level for your company and is having a significant impact on the profitability and success of your trade promotions, as well as any regional marketing and pricing programs. The fact that your current policies have already resulted in such a significant level of diverting indicates the problem is going to get considerably worse in a very short period of time unless immediate action is taken.

NO: Since diverting represents a small percentage of your total forward-buying, it indicates that your policies and programs in total have not resulted in diverting having a significantly negative impact on your trade promotions or local marketing and pricing programs.

DON'T KNOW: The fact that you are unaware indicates a serious lack of good information. Most companies that have not been able to quantify this number find the problem is significantly worse than they anticipated when the data do become available. Immediate steps should be taken with your MIS or marketing research department to quantify the percentage of forward-buying that is going into diverting.

4. Diverting increases in the last quarter of the year.
   Yes (3)   No (1)   Don't Know (5)

YES: The fact that diverting increases significantly in the last quarter of your year is an indication that your company not only sanctions the policy, but also, in either subtle or direct ways, actually encourages diverting to occur. The result of this will be a company culture and a way of doing business that will be very hard to reverse.

NO: The fact that diverting does not increase in the last quarter of the year probably means that individuals within your company do not use diverting to help them reach their departmental goals in sales, marketing, or profits. This indicates that your company has already taken significant steps to address the diverting issue, which is a very healthy sign.

DON'T KNOW: The fact that your company doesn't know whether diverting increases at the end of your fiscal year is a sign that there is a complete lack of information and control. This is worse than the situation in which a company knows it has a problem, but has not done anything about it. The fact that your company doesn't even know if it has a problem indicates that it probably does, and will not be taking any action to correct it.

5. The identity of who diverts more than half the product is known.
   Yes (0)   No (2)   Don't Know (3)

YES: If you know who diverts more than half your product, you are now in a position to take corrective action. Knowing the problem and the cause of it goes halfway toward solving it.

NO: If you don't know who is diverting your product, it is going to be almost impossible to implement any programs to try to control it.

DON'T KNOW: If you don't know the companies who do more than 50 percent of your diverting, it means there is a tremendous lack of interest or focus on the subject. The idea that managers within the company haven't identifed diverters means diverting is a low priority issue. Because of its low priority, the chances are that the diverting problem is likely to get out of control before anyone starts to address it at all.

6. Programs already in place have significantly reduced diverting.
   Yes (0)   No (2)   Don't Know (4)

YES: Your company has already addressed the diverting issue and has successfully reduced the amount of diverting that is occurring. This is a very healthy sign and clearly indicates that the problem can be and has been addressed by your company.

NO: The fact that your company has not yet put programs into place to reduce diverting is a dangerous sign. Many packaged goods companies have successfully addressed the issue and have reduced the amount of diverting that is occurring. Since diverting across all manufacturers is increasing considerably, chances are the amount of diverting that is occurring for your company is also increasing.

DON'T KNOW: The fact that your company has not disseminated information on whether the programs they have attempted have been successful in reducing diverting is a very unhealthy sign. This is an indication that either no attempt has been made by your company, or that such a low priority is placed on this subject that basic information about the success of the program has not been passed on to key managers.

7. My company believes it can't do anything about diverting.
   Yes (5) No (1) Don't Know (2)

   YES: The fact that your company believes that nothing can be done about diverting means that any attempts to address the issue will probably be halfhearted and doomed to failure. Unless management's attitude is corrected, the diverting issue can only get worse.
   NO: This is a healthy sign that indicates your management has looked at the issue and believes the problem can be successfully addressed. This in itself does not guarantee that you will successfully address the issue, but it does indicate a good, healthy, positive attitude by management.
   DON'T KNOW: The fact that your company doesn't know if it can do anything about diverting is not a healthy sign. However, since it hasn't concluded that it is merely "a cost of doing business," there is still a chance it will recognize the seriousness of the issue and determine to do something about it.

8. My company believes total diverting of all products will increase over the next two years.
   Yes (1) No (5) Don't Know (3)

   YES: The fact that your company believes that diverting will increase over the next two years is a very positive sign because it means there is recognition of what is happening in the industry. This recognition of reality will make your company sensitive to the issue and the magnitude of the potential problem.
   NO: The fact that your company does not believe diverting will increase significantly is an indication that it is not likely to take the problem seriously and address it in the near future. The attitude or belief that diverting is not a problem is very much an ostrich-with-its-head-in-the-sand approach.
   DON'T KNOW: The fact that your company doesn't know if diverting will increase significantly in the next two years indicates a lack of perception of what is going on in the marketplace; therefore, it's an indication that serious action is not likely to be taken.

9. Senior management always backs up all policies to reduce diverting.
   Yes (3) No (1) Don't Know (2)

   YES: The fact that management always supports all policies to reduce diverting is an indication that a clear and focused program is not in place. Many policies that are suggested and implemented are not likely to work and are often counterproductive. A good senior management program discriminates between the good and bad policies and only supports those that have proved effective at other companies in the past.

NO: The fact that senior management doesn't back up all policies is an indication that it is making an attempt to discriminate between effective and ineffective programs. The biggest risk is that senior management either doesn't back up any of the policies or is inconsistent in its enforcement, communicating a message to line management that the policies are for show only.

DON'T KNOW: If you don't know whether your senior management backs up policies to reduce diverting, then there has not been a clear communication of senior management's intent and actions throughout the company. Without this visible commitment of senior management, line managers cannot be expected to take on that type of policy setting or decision making on their own.

10. The company is moving toward more local use of trade promotion money.
    Yes (3)   No (0)   Don't Know (2)

YES: The local use of trade promotion money is one of the largest contributors toward diverting. It is almost impossible for headquarters to control how the money is spent or have it spent in such a way that it does not increase diverting.

NO: Since local use of trade promotion money is one of the largest causes of diverting, one of the major causes of future diverting will not be present at your company.

DON'T KNOW: If you don't know what your company's future policies on the local use of trade promotion monies are likely to be, your company will not be able to determine what impact this is likely to have on diverting. Not knowing the future magnitude of diverting that is likely to occur in your company will mean that any policies to address diverting are likely to be put off for some time.

Add up your score to get an instant diagnosis of your company's diverting health.

0–10   Diverting policies are very strong, and while you should not be complacent about the issue, diverting has been successfully addressed.

11–14   Your company has the right approach. While some problems exist, they should remain at tolerable levels. Remain vigilant so the problem does not suddenly escalate into a serious issue.

15–18   Your company has a major problem. If immediate corrective action is not taken, future efforts are likely to be more disruptive and costly. Begin addressing the tactical issues and develop a company philosophy on what should be done to solve the diverting problem.

Over 18   Diverting is probably completely out of control, with management believing that "it's the cost of doing business." Not only has significant control of the distribution been given away by line management, but also competitors are probably starting to gain a long-term competitive advantage. Only a strong effort by selected managers can solve the problem. Immediate action is required. The best strategy is to recognize that this will be an area of competitive weakness for years to come unless you move quickly.

A SOLUTION

The solution to the diverting problem consists of four parts:

1. A clear policy and set of objectives needs to be set and stated by management. Senior leadership and direction are essential. Therefore, the first recommendation is to devise a policy statement, along with suggested penalties for those failing to comply. This recommendation will ensure that senior management's ongoing commitment to this program is perceived by the organization.

2. A program to measure how much product is being diverted, who is diverting the product, and who is buying the diverted product is essential. Without these measurements, it will be impossible to tell how much improvement is being made, or even if any is being made.

3. The front line in stopping the growth of diverting is the sales organization. The salespeople need tools and training sufficient to do the job. The only viable solution to stop diverting before it occurs is to compare orders against expected volumes. In addition to common sense, sales organizations uniformly believe this is the best approach. An example is shown below in Table 29.4.

TABLE 29.4

Account	% ACV	% YTD Purchases	Flag	% YTD Consumer Sales
ShopRite	18	19		18
Pathmark	17	16		17
Waldbaums	10	15	*	9
A&P	8	5		8
Grand Union	7	8		7
Foodtown	8	14	**	7

* Outside anticipated range — should be investigated.
** Far outside anticipated range — immediate action required.

4. Set local spending policies that don't create an environment in which controlling diverting becomes even more difficult. A corporate policy across all brands is not practical, but each brand needs a promotional policy that doesn't encourage diverting and that is consistent with strategic objectives and tactical competitive situations. That a manufacturer's own promotional policies can contribute to diverting can be seen by levels of forward-buying, which is driven by some of the same factors that cause diverting.

Richard H. Lenny has had an impressive career working in marketing and sales at Kraft since 1977. Starting in brand management, he was quickly promoted through the ranks to hold the title of Vice President in several divisions, including marketing and sales promotion, and sales planning. He is now the Executive Vice President of Sales for Kraft, USA. He is a member of the American Marketing Association and was voted by Advertising Age *as one of the Top 100 "Best and Brightest" in 1986.*

Lenny received his MBA with Distinction in Marketing and Finance on a full tuition scholarship from the Kellogg School of Management at Northwestern University, where he is now on the Board of Directors. His Bachelor's degree is in Marketing from Georgia State University where he graduated magna cum laude.

CHAPTER 30

WORKING WITH RETAILERS

"NOTHING HAPPENS UNTIL A SALE IS MADE"

The business system in which consumer packaged goods operate is depicted straightforwardly in Exhibit 30.1.

EXHIBIT 30.1

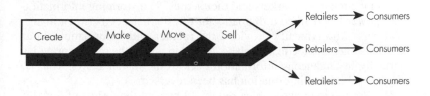

The business system or "value chain" starts with research and development's product development (create). Manufacturing then takes over the broad-scale production of the product (make), and distribution ensures its movement into the pipeline (move).

However, it is the selling organization that is closest to the customer and, therefore, completes the process. It is imperative that the selling organization fully understand the needs of the customer ("buyer") in order to satisfy the needs of its organization — that is, maximize shareholder value. Marketing is a functional discipline operating across the business system to ensure that consumer needs are being identified and met.

The focus here is on this buyer-seller relationship. The relationship between a manufacturer's selling arm and its retail customer is a classic one, yet one that is evolving at almost a revolutionary pace. This chapter is limited to retailers. Wholesalers that supply retailers are a critical link in the supplier to retailer relationship. Many of the principles mentioned here can and must be applied to wholesalers as well, in order to win in the marketplace.

The traditional one-to-one selling process is being replaced by a matrix approach — from both sides. And the key to winning and creating a long-term competitive advantage is maximizing the benefits desired for both sides in the most cost-effective manner.

THE CHANGING RETAIL ENVIRONMENT

One of the most critical aspects in terms of working with retailers is the recognition of the rapidly changing retail environment. While the primary focus here is on the consumer packaged goods industry through supermarket stores, many of these changing conditions have applications across a multitude of industries. There are four primary changes that have dramatically affected the buyer-seller arrangement between manufacturers and retailers.

1. Shifting Balance of Power. Over the past several years with the advent of in-store scanning capabilities, retailers have been flooded with a wealth of data. In many instances, these "data" have been turned into powerful information to better understand consumer buying trends within the retailers' markets and their stores. Transforming information into power has marked a dramatic shift in the balance between manufacturers, who typically provided the retailer with information about the consumer and the marketplace, to one in which the retailer provides virtually instantaneous information back to the manufacturer. That is, the flow of critical information has been reversed.

Not too long ago a sales rep might present the results of a major promotion run by a supermarket chain several weeks after the promotion had taken place, and the retailer was most appreciative to have this "up-to-the-minute" information. This information was cursory at best, such as cases sold and gross profits earned. However, the new reality is that the day after a promotion runs, the retailer can summon the same sales rep into his office and state "your promotion was a success" or more often than not "your promotion did not move the incremental volume that you stated in selling us the promotion!"

More important, what constitutes a "successful promotion" is changing as well. Gone are the days of simply stating success in terms of cases moved. Retailers now want incremental movement per stock-keeping unit, at different price points, and with various levels of merchandising support, for example, feature ads, displays, or co-op TV. In short, what had been analogous to one-dimensional checkers is rapidly moving toward three-dimensional chess.

This shifting balance of power will only accelerate as store level and zip code buyer behavior becomes readily available and easily accessible to retailers, almost regardless of their level of sophistication.

As retailers have recognized the difficulty of harnessing this new technology, they have responded by hiring MBAs — typically those who might have pursued a career on the manufacturer's side. In essence, retailers are now able to go toe to toe with a manufacturer's sales rep.

2. Retailer Concentration. Similarly, over the past several years, there has been an increasing concentration of buying power in both the retail and the wholesale environments.

In the early 1980s, the top 20 retailers accounted for 25 percent of the total business, and there were 390 wholesalers. By the early 1990s, the top 20 retailers generated 51 percent of the business, and there were only 240 wholesalers.

Moreover, geographic concentration intensified as well. In the early 1980s, five of the top 20 markets were controlled by four supermarket chains. In fewer than 10 years later, 18 of the top 20 markets were controlled by four chains. One of the key driving forces behind this concentration has been the creation of nationwide retail customers (American Stores) and the expansion of national chains such as Kroger. Wholesalers such as Fleming, SuperValu, and others are expanding their presence to better capture and lever economies of scale.

Additionally, many of these retailers have gone through leveraged buyouts (LBOs) over the past several years and with high debt service have positioned themselves to gain as many monetary incentives from their suppliers as possible. For perspective, in the early 1980s, 14 of the top 15 chains were publicly held; by the 1990s, 11 of the top 15 chains are foreign-owned, LBO, or private.

In essence, for the LBO firms, these "cash-poor retailers" are becoming "power-rich market leaders." The advent of alternative formats, such as clubs and mass merchandisers, is creating even more leverage and power at the retail level.

3. Slow Growth Categories. With the formation of households growing at a scant 1 percent per year, virtually most of the categories that comprise the large consumer packaged goods businesses are experiencing slow to no growth. In fact, real food dollars have declined slightly since late 1990. With the investment community still expecting double-digit profit gains, manufacturers are forced into aggressively promoting their products through price to the retail trade in order to stimulate revenue growth.

Additionally, the proliferation of new products (most notably in variety and size alternatives) to achieve necessary share gains further creates a "buyer's market" for the retailer. With "new news" hard to come by in the categories, retailers can in certain instances pick and choose those new items they wish to carry and, thus, can in many instances demand stronger concessions from some manufacturers for shelving and new product distribution.

Slower category growth and more demanding retailers have helped create more price sensitive consumers. Consumers shop for specials or rely on the retailer for every day low prices (EDLP) — a retail strategy employed to position oneself as the place to shop day in and day out.

4. Multiple "Stake Holders." Another significant change is that the one-on-one buying relationship (sales rep vs. buyer) is evolving into a team approach. The one-on-one selling process that typically was the norm is now being supplanted by a problem-solving approach.

For example, in addition to satisfying the needs of the buyer, a manufacturer must also satisfy the needs of customer service, logistics, and accounting.

Another way to think about this is that the retailer (customer) has its own value chain. As such, the retailer is developing strategies to maximize each link in the chain and, therefore, needs a supplier who can help solve multiple problems. This requires a broad range of skills and resources.

Therefore, the most successful approach is to create a team of individuals from the manufacturer who represent different yet complementary disciplines to penetrate these various levels of a customer. While the sales rep to buyer relationship is still the cornerstone for making the sale, long-term success will be dictated by a manufacturer's team working in concert with a similar team from the customer.

The implications to the manufacturer from this changing retail environment are clear:

- *Have a deeper understanding of customer needs.* It is imperative that the selling organization fully understand what the customers' needs are and that these needs now transcend just the "buyer to seller," going into areas such as customer service, logistics, and store operations. Only by understanding a customer's entire business system (or value chain) can a selling organization successfully add value to the customer.

- *What customer problem can the manufacturer solve?* Critical to a successful sale in a changing environment is to identify the problem inherent in the customer's business system and how the manufacturer's sales rep and "team" can provide the correct solution. For example, if the supermarket chain is promoting itself as the price leader in a market, how can the sales rep present a promotion that enables the retailer to compete on price but that still creates value for the brand and value for the retailer? If a retailer's strategy is to offer superior in-store services, perhaps the supplier will recommend a joint promotion that offers its national brand of microwave popcorn with a free video from the customer's video rental department.

- *Create the proper selling organization.* A manufacturer must ensure that its selling organization is properly aligned with the "multiple stake holders" of the customer. More often than not, one structure will not meet the needs of all customers. Within any one geographic area, competing retailers can use distinctly different strategies that coincide with their respective market position. Therefore, a supplier has to be flexible in how it services that retailer.

  This does not mean "n + 1" organization structures. What it does mean is that there should be an organizational foundation grounded in sound strategic principles able to make different applications based on an individual customer's needs.

The goal is to fit your selling organization to each customer — not his to yours. If you don't, you can believe someone else will. The marketplace of the 21st century will reward speed, innovation, and flexibility.

THE CREATION OF VALUE

Despite the changing retail environment, the one aspect that has not changed on both sides of the buyer-seller equation is the desire to create maximum value. What makes it both interesting and challenging is that the seller, in this instance the manufacturer, is trying to create brand loyalty, whereas the buyer, the retail customer, is attempting to maximize store loyalty.

This is referred to as the classic horizontal versus vertical orientation. In a consumer goods company, the marketing and selling organizations are attempting to sell a "few" products horizontally across the entire country, that is, a few brands to a lot of people. Conversely, the retailer or supermarket customer (given its relatively narrow trading area) is attempting to sell a "lot" of products to a few people, thus penetrate vertically within a marketplace.

Creating further tension in this classic buyer-seller negotiation is that the retailer oftentimes is trying to extract the most money for the least value given, whereas the vendor (manufacturer) is trying to gain the most value for the least money expended. As such, in order for both sides to be successful, a partnership or "alliance" must truly be created.

For example, in the soft drink business a retailer can create customer traffic by offering several brands of soft drinks at an attractive price. The retailer in many instances is indifferent in terms of the soft drink promoted. To be sure, there are market leading brands. But, consumers will choose from a set of acceptable alternatives when heavily discounted.

Remember, the retailer wants to maximize store traffic to shop a broad range of categories; in this instance, the "draw" is soft drinks. More often than not, each week it's a different category. But only those high household penetration, frequently purchased categories are used as "traffic builders."

However, the manufacturer in its attempt to build share wants that retailer to promote its product to the exclusion of competing brands. In order to be successful, the manufacturer must demonstrate that promoting its brand at an attractive price point can do two things: (1) generate more total category profit for the retailer and (2) contribute to that retailer's desire to create store loyalty. Again the retailer's goal is to differentiate its store from that of its competitors, not necessarily to differentiate brand "A" from brand "B."

Now the trick for the manufacturer is to create unique but equally compelling "selling stories" for its different retailers. The manufacturer will suboptimize its effectiveness and not build market share if it attempts to use the same approach with all retailers. The goal is the same, namely to outperform the competition. However, the approaches used can be and should be vastly different.

A FORMULA FOR SUCCESS

There are several elements that can create a formula for successfully working with retailers.

Conduct Fact-Based Situation Analysis. The most important aspect is to start with a well-grounded analysis of what's happening within the marketplace and why. Only by carefully analyzing the situation can you determine who's winning and why and what your goals and action plans (to achieve these goals) should be.

Some key elements of a good situation analysis are as follows:

- Customer(s) performance within the marketplace, its share of the category, the market, and so on. If specific scanner data aren't available, there are "proxies" for determining relative market positions and growth rates. At a minimum, you know what you sell to each customer and you know your growth with each customer.
- Strengths/weaknesses/opportunities/threats (SWOTs). This simple matrix (Exhibit 30.2) helps assess advantages/disadvantages for the three fundamental players (three *C*'s) within the market.

   It's critical to conduct a SWOT analysis for yourself (company) and competitors in relation to how you do business with your customers (see Exhibit 30.3). The key is to lever your strengths to exploit market opportunities while correcting your weaknesses to overcome competitive threats. For example, if you are the leading brand in a marketplace but you have a weak position with the leading retailer, your marketplace strengths (brand loyalty, consumer drawing power, profit potential) can improve by establishing a growth program with that leading retailer.
- Learn the retailer's strategy. That is, how does the retailer compete in the market? One of the best ways to do this is to track its tactics. Does it advertise on price or offer unique services? One approach is to observe how the retailer promotes other noncompeting categories. Track its co-op advertising and interview some of its shoppers to determine how its customers position the retailer — then act accordingly. Again the key is to build your customer's business, which will build yours.
- Learn about the sources of competitive advantage that your customer(s) has, for example, size, format, price, or services, against its competition within the market. Table 30.1 is a simple analytical template for assessing a marketplace.

EXHIBIT 30.2

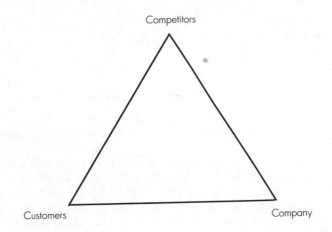

EXHIBIT 30.3
SWOT ANALYSIS

Yours			Competition		

Strengths	Weaknesses
Opportunities	**Threats**

Strengths	Weaknesses
Opportunities	**Threats**

TABLE 30.1

Source of Competitive Advantage in a Market	Retailers				
	A	B	C	D	E
Store size					
Location					
Low price/no frills					
Shopper loyalty					
Services					

Establish Specific, Timely, Quantifiable Targets. As the saying goes: "If you don't know where you are going, any road will take you there."

The above situation analysis answers what's happening and why. It is now time to set out to positively change your results. If you're growing, you want to grow faster or perhaps expand your profit margin. If your volumes are soft, yet the margins are good, you may want to invest a couple of margin points to build your market position, that is, to gain share.

Typical targets that you might set are volume, share, profit, return on investment (ROI), and sales expense as a percent of revenue. Whatever goals you choose, they need to be material. Don't set a goal that will not confer competitive advantage if you achieve it.

When possible, set goals for each retailer (or customer segment). While this is harder to do, it helps focus your strategies and action plans customer by customer, which is the only way to win. As stated before, your marketplace is an aggregation of individual retailers just as a consumer franchise is an aggregation of loyal users, brand switchers, first-time triers, and others.

Create Retailer-Specific Promotions. Because the situation analysis included a blueprint of each retailer's strategy, you are now in a position to create those promotions (or business-building activities) that will have maximum impact. That is, develop promotions that will create maximum value for you and your customer — again, aligning yourself and your business with that of your customers.

Many times, a selling organization will be in a position in which it has to execute promotions developed at headquarters, far removed from the local market and often very homogeneous in nature — macro promotions for micro applications. How then do you tailor these national events (an FSI, rebate offer, or special pack promotion) to achieve maximum retailer penetration and drive customer satisfaction?

The way to win is to "think nationally and act locally." Typically, the national promotions have been designed to address very broad strategic issues based on the aggregation of consumer buying behavior. Most often these national promotions are designed to achieve broad trial and/or repeat objectives. But in order to maximize their effectiveness, the in-market influences, that is, your retailers, must act synergistically. A national event with maximum local retailer support will be far more effective than a "stand-alone" national offer.

To add value to the national (or regional, market-level promotions) you must tailor the event to the account's way of doing business.

Create a Mutually Beneficial Information Network. Regardless of the level of sophistication, the future relationships of manufacturer and retailer will be information driven and co-dependent. Again, to win, you must solve a problem that your retailer has, and the more action-oriented your information network, the greater the likelihood of building a long-term relationship with your customers.

Maintain Adequate Lead Time. The retail trade typically works many weeks out in terms of scheduling promotions for its stores. As such, a manufacturer needs to present its promotions well in advance to secure adequate support.

Most retailers have their own annual planning cycle and promotion calendar. The smart manufacturer knows that and targets specific activity at the time its customer is promoting its stores. The simplest examples are key holidays. Most retailers run big events around July 4th, Thanksgiving, and Christmas. Depending on the market and your category, there are numerous holidays or "local events" to secure customer support for your national promotions.

Remember, the customer is interested in differentiating its stores from its competitors' stores. The better you can contribute to that differentiation, the greater likelihood of success.

SUMMARY

The marketplace has changed and will continue to evolve. Retailers have become more powerful and sophisticated. Long gone are the days of simple "relationship" selling.

Sellers must now be more fact-based and hard-nosed analytically. The keys to winning are having the right information applied creatively to the differing needs of each customer.

Each retailer has a different strategy for competing in the marketplace and, thus, has a different position in the marketplace. As such, a thorough situation analysis must be conducted before initiating any major actions.

Once the situation is well understood, quantifiable goals need to be set. These goals must be material — if you achieve them, you gain competitive advantage.

Next, recognizing that differences do exist among retailers, customer-specific promotions must be developed and executed. The goal is to help each retailer differentiate itself from its competitors. As the manufacturer is building brand loyalty through product quality, packaging, or advertising, the retailer must build store loyalty. The more you can tailor your promotions to your customer's store strategy, the more that customer will support your products.

Working with retailers requires a unique balance. As a manufacturer, you must do what's in the best interest of your business. Yet to be successful, you must obtain maximum retailer support for the right price.

In the long term, creating and fostering sound strategic alliances with your retailers will help you achieve the above goals.

Sandi A. Lawson is Executive Vice President in the firm she cofounded in 1986, Perry Lawson & Associates, which focuses on consumer products marketing and promotion projects for clients such as Sony, Pepsico International, and Walt Disney Company. Prior to starting her own company, Lawson worked for 17 years as Consumer Promotion Manager for the Clorox Company, having responsibility for a wide range of consumer products.

Lawson is a member of the Promotion Marketing Association of America and has served on its Board of Directors.

Marshall A. Perry, President and cofounder of Perry Lawson & Associates, has 20 years of experience in marketing consumer packaged goods for companies such as Procter & Gamble and the Clorox Company. From 1981 to 1987 he was the Senior Marketing Executive for the Kingsford Division of Clorox, responsible for the national and international marketing of the Kingsford and Match Light brands of charcoal. Perry provides expertise not only in marketing established consumer products but also in new product introductions.

CHAPTER 31

NEW PRODUCT INTRODUCTIONS

INTRODUCTION

The purpose of this chapter is to describe the role of sales promotion in the context of new product introductions. The effectiveness of sales promotion depends — perhaps equally — on technical (promotion) skills, creativity, and the degree to which the promotion person has been incorporated into the multifunctional introductory team. The planning and team requirements outlined in this chapter apply to all types of market placements for new products (limited test markets, simulated test markets, regional rollouts, national expansions). Planning time can typically be shortened for testing — but thinking cannot! This is because tests, done properly, should project real-world marketplace results; done improperly, they mislead, perhaps unknowingly and disastrously.

OVERVIEW

Sales promotion, working in conjunction with other marketing elements, is the primary tool for achieving distribution and consumer trial. For new products, however, it is important to understand that promotion cannot be an effective contributor if it is viewed as a separate entity from the overall marketing function. The statistics are not encouraging: more than nine out of 10 new products introduced in the past five years are not on retail shelves today. Most don't get past the buyer; most of the rest fail at the trial stage. However, new products with significant product differentiation, adequate funding, and effective planning are nearly always successful.

Effective planning is the key. If promotion works hand in hand with other primary marketing elements, it can be one of the most important tools to improve chances for marketplace success on new products. It is very important for the person responsible for promotion to understand the structure of the broader marketing plan picture. In a marketing plan, like in a jigsaw puzzle, it is essential to know your particular piece — say, the promotion piece — but also how the entire picture is going to look once assembled into a finished plan. This chapter, then, will discuss both the thinking and the puzzle/organizational aspects of promotion as they relate to new product introductions.

THE FOUR KEYS TO PLANNING

There are four keys to developing an effective marketing plan. They are the team, the timetable, the integration of the four marketing tools, and the recognition of trial and repeat effects. The following is a discussion of each of the four keys.

The Team. In the beginning, there must be a marketing team responsible for successfully introducing the new product. Teams should be made up of strong individuals with experience in accomplishing difficult objectives, and they should have experience using the multidisciplinary talents of a group. These individuals should fully appreciate the synergistic benefits of a team approach.

The team should also include people with experience in new product introductions over a wide range of situations (for example, size, spending, competitive set, product uniqueness). Since each new introduction should be considered unique, be particularly wary of "formula solutions" from any member. Recognize that something new is being brought into existence, something that needs to be strong enough to wrest market share away from (perhaps) entrenched competition. It will take a new approach — a novel, interesting plan — to stir up the necessary trade and consumer attention, at least enough to switch.

The sales promotion professional must be a strong component of this marketing team. Team interaction is a two-way street in the sense that the promotion person needs to also actively contribute to the team's objective while the balance of the team must be able to contribute necessary input for the promotion person's complete understanding. For example, if advertising is being considered for the introduction, the promotion person should be advised of the copy strategy, media strategy, and target audiences, as well as advertising timetables. Using this information properly, the promotion person will contribute strategies and plans that complement the advertising efforts. This is key because, too often, strategy and plan development are prepared independently by separate functions. The result, at worst, is discordance; at best, a forced fit. Think of fitting parts of a car together as an analogy. Things go much better at assembly if the door maker has worked closely with the body maker, the wheel people with the axle people, and so on.

Also, by being part of the marketing team, the sales promotion person will have direct access to marketing facts such as the overall marketing objective, marketing strategies, and budget guidelines for expenditures. With this knowledge, sales promotion objectives, strategies, budgets, and timetables can be delivered that lead to an introductory consumer and trade promotion calendar.

The team's core group has primary responsibility for completing and implementing the promotion calendar. This group relies heavily on several support groups to ensure that the promotion ideas are creative and executable on budget and in a timely fashion. The support groups are selected as needed after considering what is required in order to achieve the marketing objectives and to execute the strategies. The core group brings a sense of realism to the planning to ensure that ideas are not "pie in the sky." The promotion person is responsible for ensuring that the creative, breakthrough promotional concepts developed by the team are implemented as efficient and effective promotions. Key members of the core and support groups are as follows:

Core Group

1. **Product management group:** Has overall marketing responsibilities for the new product.
2. **Promotion group:** Plans, develops, and implements the promotion.
3. **Sales and merchandising group:** Sells the new product to and through identified distribution channels.

Support Groups

1. **Outside promotional vendors:** Typically assist with creative and promotion execution issues.
2. **Advertising agency:** May assist in creative development and can assure that the promotional creative work is consistent with the product's overall creative direction and tone.
3. **Media group:** May assist with placing promotional media.
4. **Creative and design groups:** May assist in creative development, for example, on point-of-sale materials.
5. **Other possible groups:** R&D; public, and corporate relations.

The Timetable. Assuming the new product is being introduced nationally, you should allow about one year prior to the introductory date to prepare the promotion plan. Less time is likely required for simple introductions (if there ever really is a simple introduction!), such as for line extensions or product improvements. However, short-cutting the one-year timeline on complex introductions could spell disaster and lead to an inability for the new product to achieve its objectives. Lesser problems include delayed executions, exposed redemption liabilities, inadequate creative, poor consumer acceptance, embarrassment to the product franchise and company, and financial losses.

As shown in Table 31.1, you can see that it can take the full year to plan, produce, and implement a new product introduction. The sample schedule starts with Week 1, about one year prior to the start of planned promotions.

Integration of the Four Marketing Tools. The primary tools for any new product introduction are trade promotion, advertising, public relations, and consumer promotion. Most any new product will use all four tools to one degree or another. The most significant difference among products is the inclusion or absence of advertising (excluded or reduced, usually due to its extraordinarily high costs). Spending levels for each of these areas vary with the product category and distribution channels, as well as the objective. In some cases the category is more trade supported so that the trade spending portion of the budget is larger than the other marketing elements. With other products, the consumer

TABLE 31.1
THEORETICAL INTRODUCTORY PLANNING CALENDAR

Step	Time	Task(s)
(1)	Weeks 1–6	Develop test and national promotion plans
(2)	Weeks 7–19	Produce sales promotional materials and ship to field distribution points
(3)	Weeks 20–28	Sell-in of new product
(4)	Weeks 29–33	Achieve on-shelf distribution level of at least 80% of target
(5)	Weeks 34–41	Start of advertising
(6)	Weeks 42–52	Implement consumer promotion calendar

franchise is the most important element and, as a result, the majority of the budget is allocated to awareness-building goals that can be achieved through advertising, public relations, and consumer promotion. A typical new product spending mix, split for the four marketing tools in the introductory year, might look like the sample in Table 31. 2.

TABLE 31.2

	Percentage of Total Spending
1. Trade promotion	40%
2. Advertising	25
3. Consumer promotion	25
4. Public relations	10
	100%

Recognition of Trial and Repeat Effects. Sales promotion is the most valuable means of surmounting a new product's greatest hurdle: the achievement of satisfactory initial consumer trial. Additionally, sales promotion allowance programs and other trade incentives assist the sales department in accomplishing retail distribution objectives — a necessary first step without which absolutely nothing can follow. Although distribution is the first step, it is of little value unless we can find ways to follow by initiating and then stimulating consumer take-away from the shelf. The trade may give a new product a set amount of time — for example, six months — to reach its particular movement or turnover requirements for the item — perhaps stated as one case moved per store per week, or 10 percent sell-through each week. Again, the task for promotion working in tandem with advertising is to stimulate consumers' interest in buying their first package of the new product.

The fulcrum of success turns fundamentally on trial, not distribution. Distribution is often achieved with "push" tactics and heavy spending and may or may not be based on intrinsic project merits (because these are not yet known by the consumer at this stage). The trial phase is 100 percent "pull" by comparison. This doesn't mean that you cannot throw a lot of money at gaining trial (you haven't even imagined a budget until you've priced out physical sampling to 45 million households). It's just that consumer response (as against trade response), once the awareness is present, will be more driven by need than by weight.

Once distribution is achieved, a three-part "dependency string" is created with each succeeding element being completely dependent upon accomplishment of the prior one. The dependent relationship is due to the fact that in each successive step, the level achieved can never be any higher than the prior step's highest level. Thus, 60 percent awareness puts a ceiling on the trial level (that is, 60 percent) which also defines the maximum for the repeat phase. So, repeat purchases are driven by trial, which is driven by awareness. It makes sense, too. No one can ever try a product if he or she is not aware of it, and no one can buy it again (that is, repeat) if he or she hasn't bought it the first time.

The awareness level for a new product should be at least 65 percent among the product's target audience for a successful introduction. This first element, awareness, is brought about through a combination of store placement, merchandising, advertising, and promotion.

Trial, however, is the brainchild, domain, and responsibility of promotion. The trial rate for a new product will depend on a number of things, not the least of which is a company's financial requirements. Typically, there is some limit to the budget that can be spent on a new product introduction; therefore, the goal is to generate as much trial as is affordable.

It is hoped that all conditions following purchase are favorable for the consumer (the product performs, exceeds expectations, demonstrates some sort of advantage over existing products, or proves to be a good value). These conditions set up the possibility of the vital repeat purchase curve on which the product's fundamental and long-term business is built. This curve will vary by product category. To be successful, products with shorter purchase cycles typically require higher repeat purchase rates than products with longer repeat rates.

Over the longer haul, the profile of a brand's business can be described as primarily repeat (largely a function of the purchase cycle) with a smattering of trial volume. So, repeat business equates fairly well with product shipment levels and, when considering the entire product category, the product's market share.

SIGNIFICANT ACTIVITIES BEFORE INTRODUCTION

This section can serve as a checklist of must do's for the team.

Step I: Market Research. Regardless of the type of product or category, confirming the underlying consumer need and trade acceptance for the product are the two most important preconditions for a successful product launch. Knowing factual data early allows for better — more factual — decisions in product development, package design, product positioning, and sales promotion. Research is the customary realm of marketers (product managers or brand managers), and involvement of the team at this stage might be considered unusual. The following information also explains the reasons for sales promotion involvement in market research.

Consumer Research. Identify overall consumer appeal and purchase intent levels by conducting research among likely consumer targets for the product. Beyond bare-bones purchase intent and overall interest data, this is a great opportunity to gain promotion input, such as learning the relative appeals of various trial devices.

- **Qualitative** — A probable first step in identifying consumer reaction to the product concept. This is not projectable information to the population or the target audience as a whole. But it is of value in learning consumer feelings toward the product (likes, dislikes, primary reasons for interest, a "stepping-stone" means to designing the next level of quantitative research). A typical type of qualitative research — focus groups — is an opportunity to connect the team directly to the consumer early in the project. The team literally sits on one side of a one-way glass while a group of 8–10 consumers is on the other side. Such involvement often triggers promotion ideas and concepts for later evaluation.

- **Quantitative** — Confirms consumer target audience, purchase intents, and key product benefits. This research will project to at least the geographic area where it was conducted, or it can "mirror" the U.S. if conducted among large enough groups of respondents in at least eight U.S. markets. Beyond product, per se, quantitative research is a perfect opportunity to gauge consumers' reactions to trial activities when coupled with the product they had previously rated.

Trade Research. Interview all channels of distribution possible (usually wholesalers and retailers). Frankly, the trade is often overlooked as a source of information. Yet, if members of the trade don't purchase the product, the introduction will fail. The irony is that they understand the consumer and can give valuable opinions about how they themselves will treat the product long before the first sales call — excellent input for the salespeople. These are qualitative studies in that the number of respondent interviews is small. However, respondents should be selected from a cross-selection of accounts (consider size, geography, type of business). Trade research may still project broadly (in a nonstatistical sense) because even a few interviews may be held, but with trade decision makers who dominate their markets. For example, in the San Francisco Bay Area, interviews with just two grocery buyers — one from Safeway, one from Lucky's — represent input from factors who control 50 percent of the grocery volume in the market. This is the type of interview for the promotion person to learn current trade perspective on trial events, such as demos or FSIs, because the information will be valuable in itself and as an indicator of trade support to follow. Also, the trade will likely share current "requirements" for slotting, stocking, and movement allowances. In true Trojan Horse fashion, this is a great opportunity to learn of any willingness to swap consumer promotion spending for trade allowances.

The following are the usual respondents in trade research:

- The internal sales force, brokers, or sales representatives will help you establish the appropriate distribution channels and the selling price of the product. They will also provide an indication of trade acceptance, concerns, and opportunities.
- Wholesalers, distributors, and retailers will provide reactions to the product, its packaging, their expectations for it, in-store placement possibilities, price points, and possible assistance in developing sales promotion incentives for both the trade (themselves) and the consumer.

Step II: Category Review. Your understanding of the new product's category will strengthen the team's marketing plans. This information can often be obtained (one time and often at no charge) from market measurement companies such as A.C. Nielsen. Obtain key data such as:

- Size and trends of the category, current and longer term;
- Major products within the category;
- Unit and dollar volume;
- Competitive promotion spending;
- Promotion responsiveness;
- Size and trends relative to other close-in categories; and
- Regional differences (related to all of the above information).

Step III: Product Development and Manufacturing. There is value in sharing relevant team data on a continuous basis with the R&D and manufacturing functions. These groups' better comprehension of consumer expectations and other learning from the team can help ensure that the final product is more on target.

- Modify product performance or capabilities based on research results.
- Qualify all raw material sources.
- Finalize package structure.
- Finalize the manufacturing plan.

Step IV: Package Design. The package is often the only communicator of product positioning and benefits to the consumer.

All team members should participate in the key design steps (initial meeting, one or two midpoint reviews, final proposal). The package "crystallizes" the product concept; it provides the key communication that leads to consumer trial, and the promotion person needs to understand this dynamic. Also, more materially, promotion materials should reflect key package design elements, such as colors and graphics. A better understanding of the designer's objectives and thinking are gained here.

KEY ANSWERS NEEDED BEFORE INTRODUCTION

A bare-minimum checklist would include the following elements:

A. Overall business strategies, volume forecast, and ROI (return on investment)
1. What business strategies will allow the new product to establish an ongoing solid business?
2. What volume will be needed for Years 1–5 in order to achieve the overall business objectives?
3. What pricing is needed to achieve the new product's financial goals?

B. Marketing objectives, strategies, and budgets
1. What objectives and strategies will allow the product to establish a strong acceptance level with the trade?
2. What objectives and strategies will allow the product to gain maximum consumer trial and repeat purchase levels?
3. What spending levels allow the product to achieve its marketing and financial goals?

C. Selection of distribution channels
1. Will this product be introduced nationally or regionally?
2. What distribution channels are most likely to achieve the product's volume objectives?

D. Selection of sales force
1. What type of sales force is most appropriate for the targeted distribution channels?
2. Should a direct sales force be used, or should the new product be sold by an outside company such as brokers or manufacturer's reps?

E. Selection of marketing tools
1. Advertising
a. What is the most effective method of advertising the new product: print, television, radio, or a combination?
b. What levels of consumer awareness are needed to achieve the new product's Year 1 volume objectives?
2. Public relations
a. Can and should public relations be used to supplement the new product's advertising and promotion campaign?

    b. Should public relations be used as the only tool to build the new product's awareness?

  3. Promotion

    a. What types of trade allowances and incentives are needed to encourage excitement and trade support?

    b. What level of spending is needed to achieve the new product's Year 1 volume goals?

    c. What are the best consumer promotion incentives that will allow the new product to generate consumer trial and repeat purchase?

F. Testing

  1. How much testing is needed to sufficiently reduce risk and improve odds of marketplace success?

  2. What type of testing best accomplishes this with the least impact on cost and time?

G. Choice of new product sales promotion tools

  1. Trade allowances and incentives are typically established by:

    a. Reviewing the category to determine competitive spending levels

    b. Interviewing key trade factors for each distribution channel in order to obtain current practices among the product's category

    c. Relying on overall company experience and current customer relationships

  2. Consumer incentives

    a. Explore all sales promotion tools that will efficiently generate trial among consumers, for example, sampling and high-value or free-product couponing.

      i. Consider direct mail or cross-ruff delivery for high redemptions and quicker trial or use.

      ii. Consider FSIs not only because of high redemptions but also because of their broad reach capability.

    b. Explore all sales promotion tools that will encourage repeat purchase of the new product, for example, high-value couponing (instant coupons, cross-ruff coupons, and FSIs) or high-value refunds.

Promotion Calendars. Calendars vary by type of product and category. What's important, however, is to start all promotion activity after the product has strong distribution and consumer awareness. A typical calendar will range from two to four consumer promotions per year. During the new product's introductory year, the promotions are scheduled to establish initial trial at the start of the introduction and thereafter to assure that the consumer repeat levels will provide a strong ongoing business. Other factors that influence the overall promotion calendar are as follows:

    • *Seasonality.* Consumers can be more easily encouraged to try new products if promotions are scheduled during peak category consumption periods. This is not a factor for products that are consumed relatively evenly on a year-round basis.

- *Competitive trends.* These trends should be acknowledged when planning a new product introductory plan. Typically, competitive spending and timing will assist the promotion person in determining the most efficient and effective promotion calendar for the new product. The competitive analysis can help determine that the promotion budgets or the number of promotions needs to be increased or decreased. The key is to have a meaningful share of voice (SOV) amid the competitive advertising and promotion over time. While the budget will often not allow for spending levels equal to the established brands, new products should strive to come as close to competitive promotion spending levels as possible.
- *Availability of promotional budget.* Promotional budgets vary by product category. Categories with higher budgets will typically have more frequent promotions, for example, one per quarter. For products with lower budgets, it is more effective to have fewer but stronger promotions.

Promotional Pitfalls. The following are examples of pitfalls common to new product introductions:

1. Implementing consumer promotions before the product has achieved its minimum distribution level (80 percent all commodity volume [ACV]);
2. Implementing consumer promotions before the product has achieved a sufficient (65 percent) consumer awareness level;
3. Blindly duplicating a competitive promotion that is not faithful to the new product's objectives and strategies;
4. Creating promotional budgets that are excessive and inconsistent with overall profit goals. There is a tendency to overspend on new product promotion because of the paranoia about creating trial. Spend dollars efficiently, not extravagantly.
5. Consumer promotions timed too closely together. Timing is a function of a product's purchase cycle, and no two products' cycles, even competitive products, are necessarily the same. Spending too much on promotion too early will often result in wasted promotion duplication with little incremental trial gains. For this reason, it is better to spread the limited budget over the first two to three quarters rather than load it all into the first quarter of an introduction.
6. Consumer promotions reaching the wrong target audience.

New Product Evaluation. Product evaluation is measured by reading actual monthly volume figures against established goals — case shipments, sales dollars, or perhaps share levels. In larger companies, the marketing team will use an outside service to monitor the product and its competitors. Typically, these reports are purchased on a monthly or bimonthly basis. Smaller companies will read their monthly shipments and will compare these on a monthly basis with their goal. When available, product performance is compared to the past year's data, as well as to the current year's objectives. Exhibit 31.1 provides an example.

Wayne W. LoCurto was elected president and CEO of ACT-MEDIA in 1989. ACTMEDIA is the leading supplier of in-store advertising and promotion services in the U.S., Canada, and the U.K. Prior to joining ACTMEDIA, LoCurto was vice president of marketing consulting with Glendinning Associates and, before that, president of Whittle Communications, where he launched the company's international division. He began his career with 11 years in marketing and management positions at Richardson-Vicks.

LoCurto is a graduate of Dartmouth College and The Amos Tuck School of Business Administration.

CHAPTER 32

IN-STORE MARKETING

In-store marketing has grown faster than any other marketing communications discipline over the last 10 years. The rising influence of in-store marketing has particular significance for sales promotion professionals who are being given more and more of the marketing budget and from whom ever bigger and better results are expected.

The arena in which these results are expected — the store — is a challenging one in which the only constant is continuous change brought about by demands from consumers, manufacturers, and retailers.

Fragmenting consumer audiences, changing relationships between manufacturers and retailers, declining brand loyalty, and the rising costs and declining impact of mass media are the dynamics that have fueled in-store marketing's growth. And, while this chapter will concern itself primarily with supermarket retailing, these forces are affecting virtually all retail channels. Sales promotion professionals who work mostly through chain drug, mass merchandise, wholesale clubs, and many other formats will find the techniques discussed here relevant and helpful to their own work.

SHIFTING CONSUMER AUDIENCES

Twenty years ago the marketing community was skeptical, to say the least, about what was then a startling new concept: in-store marketing. Marketers then were raised on the power of the mass media to build dominant consumer brand franchises among the mass audience. But the advocates of in-store marketing saw big changes coming. With the absolute clarity of hindsight, these changes seem obvious and their impact significant: Today there are between 10 and 15 companies that offer national in-store programs, and over 50 companies and many retailers that offer some form of in-store marketing programs; within the next five years, in-store marketing should be a $1 billion industry.

Perhaps the biggest change was taking place in what marketers call "the consumer audience" — what everyone else knows as "the American public." The standard family of the '50s, '60s, and early '70s, with mother, father, two or three young children, and only the father working outside the house, is now just one of many diverse lifestyles. In fact, this "traditional" family now represents only 12 percent of all U.S. households; single-parent families now comprise 20 percent, and single people account for another 25 percent.

New family structures resulted in new family roles. Mom is not necessarily the key grocery shopper any longer. Research from the Point-of-Purchase Advertising Institute (POPAI) indicates that 40 percent of men and 92 percent of teenagers participate in family food shopping, and that consumers over age 55 are the most frequent visitors to supermarkets. So, marketers and retailers have had to adjust to a diverse store population. And, they've come to realize that the only place to reach the mass audience is in the store.

FRAGMENTING MASS MEDIA

As the mass audience disintegrated into increasingly diverse and hard-to-reach "niche" audiences, mass media has changed and, in some cases, disappeared altogether. Gone are the days when network television regularly captured 90 percent of all TV viewers. There are now hundreds of TV channels to choose from, with separate networks devoted to everything from cartoons and science fiction to sports and weather. Television developments of the last decade or so, including cable and the VCR, are still evolving and changing the way information is received. The convergence of video and telephone technology promises to bring enhancements in interactive and pay-per-view television, the impact of which promises to be dramatic, but hard to define right now.

For instance, network TV has changed dramatically:
* Network share of TV usage was 73 percent in 1983; in 1991 it was down to 51 percent.
* The cost to reach 60 percent of total households was $67,906 in 1965; in 1990 it was $678,917. And, in 1965, 18 percent of all viewers could recall the last commercial they saw; in 1990 that number was down to 4 percent. Put in everyday language, it now costs 10 times more to reach an audience and only 4 percent of that audience can recall the average commercial.

Changes have been dramatic in print media as well. Just as mass-circulation magazines like *Look* and the *Saturday Evening Post* gave way to scores of specialized magazines in the 1960s and '70s, the technology now exists to personalize virtually every copy of a given publication.

Change has come also to promotional media and methods. Couponing has been on the rise since the 1970s and is the major force for the increases in manufacturers' consumer promotion budgets. About 90 percent of all coupons are distributed through free-standing inserts (FSIs). But, as more and more coupons are distributed, and something like 320 billion were delivered in 1992, redemption rates are declining, averaging just 2 percent (4 percent for grocery products), and retailers do not automatically lend strong merchandising support to coupon programs like they used to. Several electronic coupon delivery programs, such as the Instant Coupon Machine, are radically changing the couponing industry.

DECLINING BRAND LOYALTY

Another significant force behind the rise of in-store marketing is the decline of brand loyalty among consumers. Again, the traditional family unit has changed, and this has had impact on the shopping roles of various family members. These different shopping roles have led to different shopping habits. With 70 percent of women working outside the home, and the rise in dual-income families, time is at a premium. This becomes clear when considering these facts:

- Consumers face too many product choices. The typical supermarket offers between 20,000 and 25,000 different products. Plus, each year more than 10,000 new products come on market.
- Brand loyalty is decreasing. In 1975, according to Burke, 75 percent of consumers were loyal to the majority of products they used. By 1987, that was down to 54 percent; and in 1991, only 29 percent of shoppers consistently used a single brand, according to Simmons.
- The consumer solution to huge selection and declining brand loyalty? They now make brand decisions in the store. Point-of-Purchase Advertising Institute research shows that more than two-thirds of all purchase decisions are made in-store. That means that despite the best efforts of manufacturers and marketers, most consumers arrive at the supermarket with minds that are clean slates; they decide which brand to buy as they are walking down the aisles.

TIME TO INFLUENCE IS IN-STORE

With all the changes among consumers, retailers, and manufacturers, there is one essential fact that remains unchanged: The one place where a manufacturer can count on finding the consumer is in the store. The vice president of marketing for Campbell Soup Company puts it this way: "We believe there's no better time to reach consumers than when they're in the store with a fistful of dollars."

To get the most out of the in-store environment, sales promotion professionals need to have a working knowledge of micromarketing or target marketing techniques, as well as understand the optimal uses for the wide variety of in-store products and services.

The advent of scanners at checkout counters is certainly the most widely acknowledged technological change in the retail industry over the last decade. Computer technology now gives retailers the ability to quickly evaluate shelf space allocations, return per square foot, direct product profit, and return on invested inventory. This means that retailers are rethinking the store virtually every day. It also means that the retail buyer has emerged as a category manager. They often have MBAs, sell in-store programs, and focus on category share and profit growth. It is important that sales promotion professionals develop programs that address these new retailer needs.

In-store promotion can be defined as programs that offer the consumer an immediate inducement or direct incentive to purchase any given product. Promotions are especially effective when the marketing objective is to gain trial, such as during new product launches. For already established products, promotions are used best as a short-term tactic.

Each in-store promotion technique has different strengths: The brand objective should dictate which combination of techniques should be used. Couponing generates brand switching, particularly for unplanned or impulse purchases; couponing and sampling work to encourage trial purchase. And they bring the power of one-on-one selling to the retail floor.

In-store promotions also work well at gaining trade support. This is particularly true of in-store demonstration, sampling, or customized events, as well as in-store couponing which, because of faster and higher redemption rates, generate added retailer support and merchandising programs.

Coupons distributed in-store, either singly or as part of a co-op, account for an increasing percentage of total coupon distribution. Co-op programs generate, on average, redemption rates about 1.5 times those of FSIs. Programs such as ACTMEDIA's Instant Coupon Machine, where the coupon is offered at the shelf with the couponed product, have seen redemption rates average 17 percent, with some programs going as high as 70 percent. Given the proven impact of in-store coupons, it is essential that in-store coupon program providers communicate with the retailer so inventory is available and they can put other merchandising support in place.

<h2 style="text-align:center">MICROMARKETING</h2>

While shifting consumer demographics and changing media patterns have contributed to the emergence of the store as perhaps the most powerful promotion arena, which store or stores are right for any given promotion? In which of the 30,000+ supermarkets, 53,000+ chain drug stores, or the tens of thousands of other stores would a marketer most efficiently reach his or her best consumers? Each year manufacturers and retailers spend collectively $6 each week on every man, woman, and child in the country. That's a huge expenditure, and any successful effort to make it more efficient can have an important bottom-line benefit.

Sales promotion planners for years have relied on a variety of demographic analysis tools — from zip code segmentation to analysis of consumer values — to define target audiences and tailor promotional offers. But all of these tools rely primarily on U.S. Census data, which is only updated every 10 years; population dynamics are changing so quickly that 10 years is much too long to rely on such data. Within less than the next 10 years minorities will account for about 30 percent of the population. Black and Hispanic populations are now growing at rates of 50 percent more than the general population, and the Asian population in the U.S. has increased 60 percent since 1980. Each of these minorities has many subsegments with vastly differing tastes and cultures. Factor in different preferences and attitudes found in the country's various regions, and it is easy to understand why it is important that sales promotion planners have accurate information about an individual store's shopping population.

Technology has now made that information available, at least within the supermarket universe, on a store-by-store basis. This means that the potential now exists for store-specific marketing. Some call it "community marketing" or "micromarketing," but whatever it's called, it means knowing enough about a given store's shopping population and its product preferences to decide, on a store-by-store basis, if a specific store is right for any given promotion. This is a huge step forward in an era of growing marketing efficiencies.

One senior retailer in Southern California explains micromarketing this way: "Information flow between a supermarket and its suppliers ... will result in more accurate and timely merchandise transfers from supplier to retailer. Our ultimate goal is to send our point-of-sale data to our suppliers, to enable us, in partnership, to make micromarketing decisions at a level heretofore not possible.

"The bottom line is that the mass market is terminal. We must tailor product mix, services, and presentation to the particular needs of the residents of a given neighborhood trading area," he concludes.

As an example of the micromarketing information available, a small, cutting-edge firm, called Market Metrics, produces detailed profiles of 30,000 individual supermarkets in the United States. Profiles include such information as neighborhood traffic patterns, per capita food expenditures, and neighborhood population densities as well as store size, sales volume, and exact measurements of the amount of space devoted to individual brands (by SKU) or categories. Store shopping populations used to be determined by drawing a series of concentric circles with the store at the center. Now, each store profile provides a more accurate assessment of shopping population by taking into account local conditions such as highway traffic patterns and natural boundaries, like rivers or railroad tracks.

The strength of this type of information is best shown by an example. Using Market Metrics information, two stores from the Jewel chain, the leading supermarket retailer in Chicago, can be compared. These stores are not far apart physically, but their shopping populations are very different.

Store A draws from a shopping population of 5,889 people who skew heavily toward shoppers 45–70 years old. They are predominantly white, college-educated, and with professional or manager-level jobs and incomes of $75,000 a year. The families on average have one wage earner.

Store B has a significantly larger population, 13,034 people, with a high percentage of them less than 34 years old. The population has a broad ethnic mix, some black and Hispanic populations, and an average income that ranges from $15,000 to $50,000. They have some high school and some college education, and job categories are mostly blue-collar or service-oriented. Store B's families have, on average, two or more wage earners.

An interesting point about both stores is that they have a significant number of families with five or six persons. Without going into great length about these stores' product mixes, the essential point this makes is that sales promotion professionals need to build their promotions on a store-by-store basis. It's not good enough anymore to target a region, a city, or even a specific chain within an area. One must choose each store on its own merits.

REAL TIME MARKETING

As a corollary to the detailed information now available on a store-by-store basis, that same level of detail is now available on a promotion-by-promotion basis. A program called "Real Time Marketing" combines the market research potential of a sophisticated, scanner-generated analysis with the marketing strength of the country's leading in-store field force to give sales promotion planners accurate, store-by-store information about how well a given promotion is working.

Instead of relying on data that is usually weeks, if not months, old, manufacturers and retailers can now get immediate information from checkout scanning systems about sales, pricing, and merchandising on a store-specific, next-day basis. Then, armed with the information, the manufacturer can deploy the largest in-store army in the country, ACTMEDIA's 13,000-member field force, to modify a promotion or find out what the competition might be doing to counter it. Now manufacturers or retailers can "tweak" promotions while they are up and running, based on solid sales data, instead of realizing weeks later that the promotion didn't work, with all the weeks and dollars that went into planning it wasted.

START WITH THE STORE

Today there is a new starting point for sales promotion professionals. The new starting point is mandated by the advent of store-specific information, the increasing need for efficiency in the marketing function, and the existence of national networks of effective, proven in-store marketing programs and services. That new starting point is the store. Promotion planning needs to start with the place where 100 percent of the target audience is reached; where that audience is hearing or seeing a message at the exact moment when they are making a purchase decision. Plans that start with the store and work outward, instead of the traditional plans that drive people into the store and then leave them at the front door, will be the success stories of the new marketing generation.

IN-STORE PROMOTION SERVICES

What follows is a brief description of various in-store promotion services, from couponing programs to in-store signage.

National Networks. National networks are defined as having a broad mix of promotional products and services in a minimum of 5,000 food stores, which allows marketers to run programs with a significant national impact. ACTMEDIA's In-Store Marketing Network is one of the most comprehensive national networks in the in-store industry. It provides a full range of products, including signage, print, video, electronic and audio displays, promotional sampling and couponing, and events and live demonstrations. It also provides such services as arranging and planning in-store strategies and post-event analysis and consultation.

Couponing Programs. In-store couponing generates brand switching, particularly on impulse items. It also offers savings to consumers who don't clip coupons, forget to bring them to the store, or don't receive them through traditional methods, such as direct mail and FSIs. Plus, because it has higher and faster redemption rates, in-store couponing gets stronger merchandising support from retailers. Two specific programs include the Instant Coupon Machine and the Checkout Coupon.

ACTMEDIA's Instant Coupon Machine is an on-shelf, electronic coupon-dispensing device available in food stores and chain drug stores nationwide. The machines are placed directly in front of each couponed brand and offer state-of-the-art coupon security. Catalina's Checkout Coupon program is linked to the UPC scanner, issuing coupons and other purchase incentives to shoppers at the checkout in supermarkets based on actual purchase behavior. For example, a coupon may print automatically when a competitive product is scanned. Cost is determined by product category and number/type of coupons distributed.

Frequent Shopper Clubs. Modeled after the airline's successful frequent fliers' clubs, frequent shopper clubs have been tried unsuccessfully in supermarkets since the mid 1980s. Such established companies as Citicorp, Sperry & Hutchinson (of S&H green stamp fame), and GTE have pulled out of the business after spending millions of dollars. These clubs aim to build brand and store loyalty through a combination of database marketing and consumer incentive programs. Right now, most frequent shopper clubs are run by retailers.

Vision Value Network is a combined electronic marketing, financial services, and frequent shopper program. Through enrollment forms, shoppers give retailers demographic data that can then be matched with purchase patterns to form the basis for a wide variety of promotional programs. The system has the capability for dispensing coupons at the checkout lane and for developing well-targeted promotions. According to Advanced Promotion Technologies (APT), research shows club members consistently spend more than nonclub members.

Sampling/Demonstration Programs. Essentially, there are two types of in-store sampling: distribution of prepacked, trial-sized samples, and distribution of "live" samples. Prepacked samples are meant to be taken from the store for consumption later. Live samples are meant to be consumed immediately. In-store sampling is much more efficient than direct mail or other out-of-home options. Live sampling programs give manufacturers the power of one-to-one personal selling, and the demonstrator is an important part of the sale. Coupons are often distributed to encourage immediate purchase. Given the importance of the demonstrator or sample distributor, it is essential to use a well-trained field force. Live sampling and demonstrations are particularly effective in new product launches or relaunches. Specific programs include:

- Impact — A program from ACTMEDIA that provides customized store events, such as sampling, couponing, premium distribution, and product demonstrations. A turnkey program, Impact includes program planning, retailer sign-up, demonstrator training and supervision, quality execution, and program results. Impact has its own permanent, part-time demonstrators who maintain a consistent appearance through identical aprons and materials. Impact events are generally located in the front of the store, but can be set up in other locations at the manufacturer's request. Costs are based on a per-store basis and can vary depending on level of service required. Standard reporting includes coupons and samples delivered plus pre- and post-inventory counts and products sold. Most clients receive redemption rates five times an FSI.
- ActNow Retailers' Choice — A unique, cooperative in-store couponing and sampling program. Professionally trained, uniformed ActNow representatives distribute cooperative coupon booklets, solo coupons, samples, and premiums to shoppers during each of five annual events. The cost-per-thousand ranges from $18.50 to $60, depending on the scope of the program. Samscan Audits and Nielsen Marketing Research audits have shown an average sales increase of 22 percent. National or regional programs are both available.
- Marketplace Solutions' In-Store Support Services and National Retail Demonstration Network — This service provides specialized, high-quality in-store demonstrations for sampling, food preparation, couponing, premium distribution,

and product demonstrations. Customized merchandising efforts can also be executed. The program includes training and supervision, quality execution, and program results within 10 business days. ISS standard costs are on a per-store-day basis, varying depending on markets. Reporting includes top-line figures, pre- and post-inventory counts, and product sold.

Radio/Audio Programs. P-O-P Radio is a broad-spectrum satellite and tape-delivered electronic system that delivers a DJ-hosted, chain-customized FM radio program during store hours. Available in both food and drug stores, Simmons Market Research Bureau (SMRB) estimates that P-O-P Radio reaches 49 percent of all U.S. adults, with a frequency of 5.4 times over a four-week period. P-O-P Radio programming capabilities are flexible enough so that direct promotional and/or pricing tie-ins are possible. Research conducted quarterly by Nielsen Marketing Research demonstrates an average 9 percent increase in unit movement of advertised product in food stores and an average 11 percent increase in drug stores.

Musak's Superlink Network is an integrated program of 20-second audio ads, shelf-talkers, and at least one additional mandatory merchandising event (display, print support, and/or price reduction). Music, ads, and E-mail are satellite-delivered to stores, emphasizing B, C, and D counties.

Grocery Carts. Grocery carts are a natural in-store vehicle on which to place advertising or promotions. Several alternative services are available:

- ACTMEDIA Carts have signs attached on the front-inside and front-outside of grocery shopping carts. The program is available in 8,000 stores nationwide, including 24 of the top 25 chains. Advertising is sold in four-week cycles on a category-exclusive basis and monitored quarterly by Nielsen Marketing Research and monthly by ACTMEDIA's Quality Control Audit Group. Audience is measured by both SMRB and MRI. SMRB has determined that this cart program reaches an average 64 percent of all U.S. adults, with a frequency of six times over each cycle. More than 600 independent tests have demonstrated an average sales increase of 11 percent.

- Videocart, Inc. offers videocarts where a videoscreen is mounted on cart handles, providing such information as price promotions and product locations. The technology provides push-button, paperless coupons that are transmitted to the checkout. Additional features include store maps, *USA Today* news, and entertainment and sports at the checkout. Monitored electronically from a central location (in Chicago), this service is available in 2,200 stores nationwide. Research conducted by Information Resources Inc. showed market share gains of from 12 percent to 33 percent.

- Ad-Strap delivers advertising messages on children's safety straps in shopping carts. The program is in all 50 states, Puerto Rico, Canada, England, and Australia, and covers 50,000 grocery and mass merchandise outlets. Advertisers run their messages and logos on belts, which they usually purchase from Ad-Strap and provide to the retailer in exchange for in-store consideration, such as end aisles or promotions.
- Inbasket is a program whereby signs are attached to all four sides of hand-carried baskets. Also, there are signs on the basket holders located around the store in high-traffic areas. There are almost 2,500 participating supermarkets. Advertising is sold in 26-week cycles and is available on a category-exclusive basis. Inmarket, the parent company, monitors compliance and performance. The company uses Promotion Decisions, Inc., to conduct matched-pair store testing for national advertisers.
- MediaOne's Cartclip is an advertising unit attached to the shopping cart handle, featuring a clip that holds shopping lists or coupons. The program is sold in four-week cycles on a category-exclusive basis. It is monitored periodically by Information Resources, Inc., and Nielsen Marketing Research, as well as the company's own organization. Research by various organizations have shown sales increases of 6 percent to 18 percent, with an average of 12 percent.
- Shoppers Calculator, through ADDvantage Media Group, is a unit mounted on cart handles that includes a calculator, along with an advertising space. The program is installed in grocery stores and in selected Wal Mart and Kmart stores. In product-movement tests, Shoppers Calculator increased advertised product sales 13.1 percent on average.

In-store Signage. ACTMEDIA's Aislevision offers signs and directories that are suspended above store aisles. Usually one to two signs are available per aisle, with only two advertisers per aisle. It is sold quarterly and in four-week cycles with category exclusivity available. Nielsen Marketing Research audits the network on a quarterly basis, and ACTMEDIA's Quality Control Group provides additional monitoring. Audience is measured by SMRB and MRI. Aislevision reaches 48 percent of all U.S. adults, at a frequency of 5.5 times over a four-week cycle. More than 100 tests conducted by Audits and Surveys show an average sales increase of 8 percent.

The Health Monitor Center is a free-standing unit that provides computerized health information. Advertising messages, educational material, and product purchasing incentives are integrated into each center. Retailers rent the units as a consumer service. The centers are monitored by Health Monitor Marketing's national field force. Marketing Analysts, Inc. conducts pre- and post-tests, including control stores, for all participants, and research results are free to participating advertisers.

MediaOne Lights are two-sided, backlit advertising signs, located at each checkout lane, incorporating a header card to direct consumers to the aisle where the product is stocked. TakeOne is a lucite holder affixed to a MediaOne light pole within reach of the consumer. This feature allows manufacturers to promote mail-in rebates, premium offers, health tips, and recipes.

Robert Horton is president of Horton Berman, Inc., a marketing public relations company with offices in New York and Los Angeles. Prior to founding the agency in 1988, Horton was senior vice president, management supervisor with Symon & Hilliard, a New York advertising agency. Before that, he worked at Burson-Marsteller, one of the world's largest public relations companies. Horton began his career as a newspaper and wire service reporter.

Horton is a graduate of Tufts University.

CHAPTER 33

INCORPORATING MARKETING PUBLIC RELATIONS INTO PROMOTION PLANS

It is a pretty good bet that when evaluating a consumer promotion idea, very few brand or promotion managers ever ask themselves: Is there any news here? Instead they ask: Are we making a compelling offer to consumers or the trade? Does it add value to my brand? Will it sufficiently differentiate my brand from the competition?

Those are all good questions, but by overlooking news, brand managers are overlooking what is one of the most compelling parts of people's lives. Americans have a huge appetite for news. Television networks interrupt programming for news flashes. Every year hundreds if not thousands of magazines are started with the idea of offering something new to readers. There are all-news radio stations, 24-hour news TV networks, computer on-line news services, and newsletters on everything from pet care to professional wrestling.

Yet with the ability of news to "break through the clutter," public relations is too often an afterthought in consumer promotion planning. Most brand or promotion managers consider the very term *marketing public relations* an oxymoron. Public relations is publicity, pure and simple. Can it really have any marketing muscle or build sales?

The answer is yes. Public relations can be a dynamic marketing tool, but it requires careful planning to achieve meaningful results. Usually, public relations is called in at the last minute. "We're running a promotion in two weeks in which we're giving away baseball cards with every package of our Honey-Dipped Hot Dogs. Can you get us some publicity?" While the agency or in-house PR department will try to help, they should really just say no, because chances are it's already too late to be of any great help. The promotion will most likely be structured improperly from a PR perspective.

That answer would frustrate everyone, most of all the public relations people. Consumer promotions are, with few exceptions, months in planning. Public relations should be part of the promotion team assembled at the outset. When this happens, the promotion's architecture is such that media attention is not only possible but also likely.

PR's Point of Difference
Knowing what makes news is what differentiates public relations experts from their colleagues in other marketing communications disciplines. Understanding media and the news is the starting point for PR. Just as good brand and promotions managers should understand their brand's equity with consumers and the trade, public relations managers need to understand the brand's news equity. What information is

believable coming from the brand?

Consider the Honey-Dipped Hot Dog brand mentioned earlier, Chicken Little Hot Dogs, and the baseball card promotion from a news equity perspective. Certainly hot dogs and baseball can evoke a strong emotional response: eating hot dogs while sitting in the stands watching a ballgame is almost an American rite of passage. So, in the broad sense, baseball and hot dogs form a logical connection. But that connection alone does not provide news equity.

If the baseball cards offered are the same ones available with bubble gum or in stand-alone packs, then there is nothing intrinsically new about the offer. To develop news equity, one would need to alter the baseball card to include new information in order to generate media interest; to give the promotion true marketing muscle, the information provided must generate news that is sufficiently motivating to the target audience.

For Chicken Little Hot Dogs, the primary target audience is mothers of young children, with the young children themselves as the secondary audience. If the baseball card offers interesting new information about the players, most coverage would end up on the sports page, the section of the paper with little interest to young mothers. But if the baseball card were to include, say, the players' favorite after-game meal, or the recipes his mom used to make for him, that information would be of interest to food or lifestyle editors who preside over sections of the paper best read by mothers of young children.

THE VALUE OF NEWS

Consumer and trade promotions have grown dramatically over the past decade. Clearly, promotion is working for marketers, or it would have gone the way of restroom billboards. And in most cases it has worked with little or no support from public relations. The value of news, and therefore PR, to a promotion is not just to make the promotion more compelling, but to communicate the offer through editorial channels, whether print or broadcast. Not only is that a different way to communicate with consumers, it's the most believable way and lends great credibility to the offer.

PLANNING THE PROMOTION

Any promotion planning team should include people who are expert in consumer and trade promotion, marketing public relations, and consumer advertising. They should all be present for the same briefing. And they need to talk to each other. The more they understand about the brand's objectives, its position with the trade, and the competition, the better served the promotion will be. Today people call this approach part of integrated marketing. Before it had that label, smart marketers were doing it instinctively. By having all viewpoints and expertise contributed at the beginning, a stronger product promotion will result in the end.

In the preparations for a briefing, a brand's news equity must be considered. The answers to the questions below can serve as a good start toward making a promotion newsworthy.

1. In what areas can the brand be considered an expert? As an example, a condiment such as mustard or ketchup could be seen as experts in picnic trends, the move toward easier, more convenient meals, or children's nutrition.

2. Has market research unearthed any information that would be of interest to the media? Before automatically answering yes, one must follow with a realistic assessment of whether anyone would read a story about the information.

3. The types of magazines, newspaper sections, or TV shows that appeal to the brand's target audience should be identified. What kinds of stories do they carry? What can the brand contribute to those kinds of stories?

4. The news exploration shouldn't be limited to only the brand. There could be news equity in other elements of a promotion. For example, are celebrities involved with the brand? Are there charities who could benefit from the promotion?

5. What makes news? What gets reporters or editors to cover something? A promotion must provide them with topical, relevant information that is not seen as overwhelmingly self-serving.

6. Do the results of a promotion lend themselves to news coverage? If there is a contest involved, especially if it involves some skill, the results can generate good coverage and extend the impact of the promotion.

Robert L. Sherman is a partner in the New York office of Paul, Hastings, Janofsky & Walker. He specializes in intellectual property law, with an emphasis on litigation involving trademarks, copyrights, unfair competition, and false advertising, as well as all aspects of direct marketing, advertising, and promotion law. He provides legal services in advertising compliance, FTC regulations, sweepstakes, mailing list transactions, database marketing, and consumer privacy.

Sherman's experience spans more than 20 years representing a wide range of clients across many industries. His cases typically are brought in federal court and have resulted in a number of noteworthy decisions.

Sherman is also General Counsel to the Direct Marketing Association. He is regularly called upon by industry and government to help fashion laws and Federal Trade Commission rules that have an impact on direct marketers. He has participated, by invitation of the Special Advisor to the President for Consumer Affairs, in a series of White House meetings on the issue of consumer privacy as it is affected by advanced technology and database marketing. Sherman is a frequent industry speaker and teaches Direct Marketing Law and Ethics in Northwestern University's Medill School of Journalism.

He is a graduate of the University of Rhode Island and The American University Law School, where he was a member of the Law Review.

CHAPTER 34

DATABASES AND PRIVACY

For direct marketers, the collection, storage, and use of marketing information in the form of databases usually results in a process that involves the compilation and transfer of lists of names and addresses — commonly referred to as mailing lists.

These lists may be developed from a variety of sources, discussed more fully below. Thus, although this discussion revolves around mailing lists (really marketing lists inasmuch as telephone lists and lists for use in other media are included), it should be kept in mind that, as such, they constitute a species of the generic category of "information" that may be derived from such systems. It is this use, for direct marketing purposes, in which advertisers, promoters, and direct marketers are interested. Following will be a description of how mailing lists are used for direct marketing purposes and the lack of harm involved in this activity. Further, there will be an explanation of certain specific court rulings that underscore the First Amendment concerns involved in attempting to inhibit this process.

Finally, there is included an outline of the social and economic benefits that flow from direct marketing, underscoring how various segments of society (commercial, political, and charitable) rely on these techniques to communicate information about products, services, and ideas.

It should be understood that industry applauds all reasonable and responsible efforts to safeguard individuals' privacy. Marketers do not have any interest in, nor would they condone, any activity that truly invades personal privacy. However, in the laudable pursuit of privacy protection, legislators and regulators sometimes fail to consider the potential for inadvertent suppression of public benefit.

All told, for reasons that shall be shown, inflexible regulation of mailing lists (which for economic reasons can amount to a ban) is counterproductive to the interests of consumers. The absence of any significant degree of harm, detriment, or endangerment to individuals arising from the fact that their name and address remains on a mailing list raises serious questions regarding a restrictive mandate to owners or users of mailing lists that would impose unnecessary costs or restrictions upon their activities. It must inevitably be consumers and the economy in general that shoulder such burdens. These conclusions are consistent with those of the federal Privacy Protection Study Commission (PPSC), which were reached after many months of public hearings and intensive study. In essence, the PPSC recommended against government regulation and in favor of industry self-regulatory efforts.

The Commission believes that the record keeper with which the individual has a relationship should accept responsibility for notifying him and seeing that his objections, if any, are respected. However, because it is acutely aware of the difficulty and the undesirability of forcing record keepers to assume that responsibility, and because so many appear to be willing to assume it voluntarily, the Commission believes that voluntary implementation is likely to be a successful as well as adequate solution to the problem. (Report of the Privacy Protection Study Commission at p. 151.)

Direct marketers always have been sensitive to the issue of consumer "privacy." As one example of industry activity in that area, the Direct Marketing Association (DMA) has had in place since 1971 its Mail Preference Service (MPS), which provides the means by which individuals may have their names removed from mailing lists. This service is promoted widely, for example, in nationally circulated magazines and in action line columns.

MPS provides a central location where the names of individuals who have expressed a desire to have their names removed from unsolicited national mailings are stored. Typically, mailers who are about to send their messages to persons they believe will be receptive to them obtain the MPS computer tapes, compare the names on their list to those on the MPS tapes, and delete those names that match. In that way, MPS provides an individual with the opportunity to get off mailing lists. The Direct Marketing Association encourages and closely monitors MPS usage. More recently the Direct Marketing Association's Telephone Preference Service was developed to provide a corresponding mechanism for those who want their names removed from telephone marketing lists.

THE NATURE OF DIRECT MARKETING AND DIRECT MAIL

It is important to bear in mind the many economic and social benefits of direct marketing. An ever increasing number of businesses — large and small — are turning to this form of marketing to sell products and services. It is an effective and efficient way to communicate information about available goods to targeted audiences.

As a measure of its economic importance — and consumer acceptance — mail order consumer sales volume has expanded to billions of dollars annually.

The benefits to consumers are many. This increased activity has intensified competition, leading to broader consumer choices and sharper competitive pricing. Direct mail — including cataloging and an infinite variety of promotions — provides consumers with more specific information on product characteristics, prices, colors, and sizes than any other major advertising medium.

For many consumers — particularly those who reside away from major metropolitan areas — shopping by mail provides special opportunities to seek a wider selection of products that would otherwise be unavailable.

Finally, and most important, direct marketing and promotions provide maximum convenience because of the virtues of shopping at home. Needless to say, this benefit is of particular significance to the elderly as well as to the increasing number of families with both heads of the household working.

In addition to its benefits to consumers and commerce, direct marketing has proven to be an indispensable fund-raising and communications medium for charitable causes and the political process. Direct marketing is simply promoting and selling things directly to consumers through the mail or private delivery services.

Mail is only one of many media used to carry a sales promoter's or direct marketer's message to its intended audience. In addition, direct response techniques are also used in radio, television, newspapers, magazines, cable TV, telephone sales, etc.

Just as sales promoters or advertisers select various kinds of media vehicles to effectively and efficiently reach an audience of general demographic characteristics, which make it a good prospect for their product (such as one magazine rather than another), so, too, they will look for a mailing list of individuals having traits in common that suggest they will have above average interest in the product. Sales promoters or advertisers have no more curiosity about who any of the addressees might be or about the details of their personal lives than they have about the individual subscribers to a magazine in which they advertise and thus use to reach, let us say, business executives, homemakers, young brides, or any other select category of potential customers.

The sales promoter or advertiser has no concern or use for such individualized information, and suppliers of mailing lists provide nothing more than a list of names and addresses. The only consequence to individuals on a mailing list is to receive mail, which they can read or throw away as they choose.

THE NATURE OF A RIGHT TO PRIVACY

The issue with which sales promoters and marketers are concerned relates to whether the use of mailing lists violates individual rights of privacy and, if so, to what extent; and, as has been suggested, whether a person maintaining a mailing list must have prior consent or should be legally required to remove an individual's name and address from the list upon that individual's request. Again, the term *mailing list* is used throughout as a shorthand for the marketing information maintained in databases from which the actual list is generated.

Although it would seem an inescapable prerequisite to any legislation that there be a clear concept of what is meant by "right of privacy," such a concept is lacking. Actually, the supposed constitutional right of privacy, which the Supreme Court has expounded and exemplified in certain cases, is not one found or defined as such in the Constitution itself. Rather, as cogently analyzed in *Griswold v. Connecticut*, 381 U.S. 479, 484 (1965), it is a "penumbra" or "zone" attaching to other guarantees in the Bill of Rights.

> Various guarantees create zones of privacy. The right of association contained in the penumbra of the First Amendment is one, as we have seen. The Third Amendment in its prohibition against the quartering of soldiers "in any house" in time of peace without the consent of the owner is another facet of that privacy. The Fourth Amendment explicitly affirms the "right of the people to be secure in their persons, houses, papers, and effects, against unreasonable searches and seizures." The Fifth Amendment in its Self-Incrimination Clause enables the citizen to create a zone of privacy which the government may not force him to surrender to his detriment. The Ninth Amendment provides: "The enumeration in the Constitution, of certain rights, shall not be construed to deny or disparage others retained by the people."
>
> The Fourth and Fifth Amendments were described in *Boyd v. United States*, 116 U.S. 616, 630, 6S. Ct 524, 532, as protection against all governmental invasions "of the sanctity of a man's home and the privacies of life."

It is, however, quite apparent that, for example, the Privacy Act of 1974 was not intended to protect any right of privacy simply as an abstract or philosophical concept. The enactment clearly and narrowly focuses the legislative concern upon prevention or minimization of specifically designated kinds, or at least magnitudes, of "harm," or endangerment, to individuals "by the misuse of certain information systems" which make "use of computers and sophisticated information technology." The nature and scope of the harms or dangers contemplated by the enactors are such as involve "the opportunities for an individual to secure employment, insurance and credit, and his right to due process, and other legal protections" (sec. 2(a)(2) and (3)). The enactment's objective is to guard against such records and information systems "result(ing) in *substantial harm,* embarrassment, inconvenience, or unfairness to any individual on whom information is maintained" 5 U.S.C. &552a(e)(10) (emphasis added).

That, then, is the scale against which any legislature should measure the impact upon individuals of finding unsolicited mail in their mailboxes or of having their names and addresses included in a mailing list from which they might believe (perhaps through misunderstanding) they would prefer to have it deleted. But sales promoters and marketers should do everything within their power to avoid giving legislatures reason to enact restrictive laws that inhibit their ability to do business. They should be sensitive to consumer privacy and should provide every consumer with the opportunity to opt out of the system. Sales promoters and marketers should never place consumers in the position where they might be harmed.

The above definition is also the level of detriment or endangerment that is necessary to qualify as the "right of privacy (that) is ... protected by the Constitution," and with which the Privacy Act is concerned (sec.2(a)(4)), as the Supreme Court has made clear in *Roe v. Wade*, 410 U.S. 113, 145 (1973):

> The Constitution does not explicitly mention any right of privacy. In a line of decisions, however, going back perhaps as far as *Union Pacific R. Co. v. Bottsford*, 141 U.S. 250, 251, 11 S.Ct. 1000, 1001, the Court has recognized that a right of personal privacy, or a guarantee of certain areas or zones of privacy, does exist under the Constitution. (Citations and brief discussion thereof.)

> These decisions make it clear that *only personal rights that can be deemed "fundamental" or "implicit" in the concept of ordered liberty ... are included in this guarantee of personal privacy.* (Emphasis added.)

Moreover, the U.S. Supreme Court has made it equally clear that the concept of "liberty" has not singled out other rights as candidates for special protection. *Paul v. Davis*, 424 U.S. 693 (1976) (reputation or defamation violations have not been converted to constitutional rights of due process even where violated by the government).

Only certain activities within the imprecise definition of a "right of privacy" have received judicial protection. Such matters as those relating to marriage, procreation, contraception, family relationships, child rearing, and education are the ones on which it has been held that there are limitations on the government's ability to substantively regulate conduct (*Id.* at 713). In the absence of an infringement of rights in those areas, one does not make out an intrusion into the sphere that is considered to be "private."

Nonetheless, perception sometimes becomes reality. If sales promoters and marketers overstate the nature and depth of the information they maintain on consumers, the perceived invasion of privacy might suffice to elicit legislative action. Thus, sales promoters and marketers must refrain from employing copy that leads consumers to believe the marketers know more about that consumer than they truly do.

More recently, added to those activities are those that threaten the sanctity and privacy of the home, even when cloaked in an otherwise protectible form. Thus, a local ordinance that prohibited "focused picketing taking place solely in front of a particular residence" was upheld in the interest of residential privacy.

One important aspect of residential privacy is protection of the unwilling listener. Although in many locations, we expect individuals simply to avoid speech they do not want to hear, the home is different. "That we are often 'captives' outside the sanctuary of the home and subject to objectionable speech ... does not mean we must be captives everywhere." Instead, a special benefit of the privacy all citizens enjoy within their own walls, which the State may legislate to protect, is an ability to avoid intrusions. Thus, we have repeatedly held that individuals are not required to welcome unwanted speech into their homes and that the government may protect this freedom. *Frisby v. Schultz*, 487 U.S. 474, 484-85 (1988).

Judicial analysis has resulted in the characterization of a right to privacy as involving at least two different kinds of interests. One is the individual interest in avoiding disclosure of personal matters (confidentiality), and another is the interest in independence in making certain kinds of important decisions (autonomy). *Whalen v. Roe*, 429 U.S. 598, 599 (1977) (a patient disclosure requirement for users of particular drugs was held not to be an invasion of privacy notwithstanding the potential for an immediate and threatened impact on the reputation or independence of the patients involved).

It must be noted that the U.S. Supreme Court limited its characterization while expressly and fully recognizing the threat to privacy implicit in the accumulation of vast amounts of personal information in computerized data banks or other massive government files (*Id.* at 605). It specifically refrained, however, from addressing the issue of unwarranted disclosure of private data by a system that did not contain adequate security provisions.

Thus, it is clear that the mere collection and storage of data, which is in itself legitimate, is not rendered unconstitutional simply because new technology makes such operations more efficient. Although it is recognized that the central storage and easy accessibility of computerized data may increase the potential for abuse of that information, in the absence of a demonstrated violation of rights involving the family-linked personal areas described above, there does not appear to be an invasion of a personal right to privacy.

To be constitutionally protected by a right of nondisclosure, therefore, personal information must concern an area of life itself protected either by the autonomy branch of the right of privacy or by other fundamental rights. At least that appears to be the thrust of the decisional law to date, although some question exists regarding whether the right of confidentiality protects a broader array of information than that implicated by the autonomy branch of the right of privacy. *Borucki v. Ryan*, 817 F.2d 836, 841 (1st Cir. 1987).

Again, although the concept of a constitutional right of privacy still remains largely undefined, it might simplistically be viewed as protecting (a) an interest in independent decision making, or autonomy, and (b) an interest in avoiding disclosure, or confidentiality. *Plante v. Gonzalez*, 575 F.2d 1119, 1128 (5th Cir. 1978) (concerning financial disclosure requirements placed on state officials, but holding that financial privacy does not fall within the autonomy right on its own); *Igneri v. Moore*, 898 F.2d 870 (2d Cir. 1990) (upholding a statute requiring extensive financial disclosure by political party chairmen on the ground that they had foregone their right to privacy to a limited degree by deliberately entering the political arena). *See also, Plowman v. U.S. Dep't of Army*, 698 F. Supp. 627 (E.D.Va. 1988) (information concerning individuals' medical condition not constitutionally protected as private). At least one of the federal circuit courts has interpreted the Supreme Court as holding that the Constitution does not encompass a general right to nondisclosure of private information. *J.P. v. DeSanti*, 653 F.2d 1080, 1090 (7th Cir. 1981).

What is becoming clear, however, is that in determining whether a privacy violation has occurred, although the autonomy strand requires a "strict scrutiny" analysis, the confidentiality strand involves a balancing standard between the interests any legislation would serve with those it would hinder (*Id.* at 1134). *See also, Barry v. City of New York*, 712 F.2d 1554 (2d Cir. 1983).

Indeed, when asked to address the respective rights involved in disclosing specific financial information of state officials, and the argument that financial disclosures should be made in terms of ranges (for example, that an asset is worth between $10,000 and $15,000), rather than specifying the precise value of an asset (for example, that an asset is worth $13,217), the *Plante v. Gonzalez* court determined that while sufficiently narrow ranges would convey much useful information, increasing the specificity would increase the value of the information. The Court then held that while the incremental benefit may be slight, the incremental harm is even slighter (*Id.* at 1136). Nonetheless, certain types of information, due to their personal and private nature, or the circumstances under which they initially were disclosed, should not be used for marketing purposes. Consumer expectation requires that they be kept confidential.

Medical Data. It must be recognized that an unwarranted disclosure of one's medical records or condition generally constitutes an invasion of privacy. *See, e.g., Schaill By Kross v. Tippecanoe County Sch. Corp.*, 864 F.2d 1309, 1322 n.19 (7th Cir. 1988) (recognizing a substantial privacy interest in the confidentiality of medical information); *In Re Search Warrant (Sealed)*, 810 F.2d 67, 71 (3rd Cir.) (recognizing that patients have a constitutionally protected privacy interest in their medical records), *cert. denied sub nom., Rochman v. United States*, 483 U.S. 1007 (1987); *Trade Waste Management Ass'n., Inc. v. Hughey*, 780 F.2d 221, 233-34 (3rd Cir. 1985) ("One personal matter that has been recognized as protected from random governmental disclosure is personal medical history."); *United States v. Westinghouse Elec. Corp.*, 638 F.2d 570, 577-78 (3rd Cir. 1980) ("There can be no question that an employee's medical records, which may contain intimate facts of a personal nature, are well within the ambit of materials entitled to privacy protection.").

The above notwithstanding, a person's privacy interest in medical information and records is not absolute. There may be occasions when such an interest must be weighed against other societal interests in disclosure. *United States v. Westinghouse*, 638 F.2d 570, 577 (3rd Cir. 1980). *See also, Fraternal Order of Police Lodge No. 5 v. City of Philadelphia*, 812 F.2d 105, 110 (3rd Cir. 1987) (adopting a balancing approach in evaluating claims of the right to confidentiality as derived from the privacy right); *Taylor v. Best*, 746 F.2d 220, 225 (4th Cir. 1984), *cert. denied*, 474 U.S. 982 (1985). It is difficult, however, to imagine a marketer's interest that would rise to a sufficient level to overcome an individual's objection to disclosure of his or her private medical information.

In *Westinghouse*, the Third Circuit held that the National Institute for Occupational Safety and Health (NIOSH) could compel the production of employee medical records from a private corporation. The court noted that governmental intrusion into medical records is permitted only after a finding that the societal interest in disclosure outweighs the individual's privacy interest on the specific facts of the case (*Id.* at 578). The court stated that the factors to be considered include (1) the type of record requested; (2) the information it does or might contain; (3) the potential for harm in any subsequent nonconsensual disclosure; (4) the injury from disclosure to the relationship in which the record was generated; (5) the adequacy of safeguards to prevent unauthorized disclosures; (6) the degree of need for access; and (7) whether there is an express statutory mandate, articulated public policy, or other recognizable public interest militating toward access (*Id.*). The Third Circuit affirmed the trial court's finding that NIOSH's security precautions sufficiently assured nondisclosure by the agency, thereby authorizing the production of the documents.

It is not obvious what societal or public interest direct marketers could advance to justify the collection, use, and transmittal of private medical information.[1] Such data appear to be of a nature that should not be used for marketing purposes.

Financial Data. With respect to data that may be considered personal by all reasonable standards, reasonable consumer expectation provides the foundation from which a determination may be made of whether the information is private. In that regard, *financial data*, a potentially broadly defined term, must be viewed from multiple perspectives.

The source of the financial information, the circumstances under which it was provided, the method or means of collection, the purpose for which it is stored and used, and ultimately whether it is transferred are factors that all contribute to determining whether a consumer reasonably would understand such information to be personal or private in nature. As a general proposition, financial information such as bank or checking account balances, income, debt, size of credit lines, and the like constitutes information that most consumers would reasonably expect to be kept private between them and any fiduciary to whom they reveal such information.

Although the use of such information in broad-range categories for purposes of classifying individuals as qualifying for different marketing lists may not pose any serious threats to the personal or financial safety of the individual, the likelihood is that an individual would consider unauthorized release of such information to be a violation of his or her personal privacy. An even stronger case could be made out when the government is the intruder into the privacy of such data.

Accordingly, federal statutes that have been enacted addressing the privacy of financial matters are, by and large, geared toward preventing government intrusion. For example, Congress enacted the Right to Financial Privacy Act in 1978 in response to a pattern of government abuse in the area of individual privacy (12 U.S.C. &3401 *et seq.*). The act is intended to protect customers of financial institutions from unwarranted intrusion into their records, while at the same time permitting legitimate law enforcement activity. Seeking to strike a balance between the customers' right of privacy and the need of law enforcement agencies to obtain financial records pursuant to legitimate investigations, the act mandates compliance with strict procedures when federal agencies request access to customer bank account records. The basic thrust of the act is to entitle customers of financial institutions to receive notice of any government request for customer financial records and to an opportunity to challenge the request. Financial records or information that does not identify a particular customer may be disclosed without compliance with the procedures described by the act. The law also excludes state agencies and local governments, as well as private employers, from its coverage.

As an amendment to the Privacy Act of 1974, the Computer Matching and Privacy Protection Act of 1988 regulates computer matching of federal data for verifying eligibility for federal benefits programs or for recouping delinquent debts. 5 U.S.C. &552(a). In order to protect an individual whose records are used in matching programs, the act requires the government to give that individual a chance to respond before it takes adverse action. It further requires formal agreements prior to agency disclosures for matching; verification of any data generated by a match before the data may be used as a basis for an adverse decision against an individual; and the establishment of "Data Integrity Boards" to review and justify recurring matching programs. Notice may also be required to be sent to individuals whose records are matched.

Additional laws not specifically directed toward the government also have been enacted to protect consumer privacy. For example, The Fair Credit Reporting Act of 1970, enacted to protect the privacy of individual citizens and of records maintained by credit reporting agencies, bars those agencies from sharing credit information with anyone but authorized customers. 15 U.S.C. &1681. The act was designed to prevent consumers from being unjustly damaged because of inaccurate or arbitrary information in a credit report. It provides each individual with the legal right to know the nature, substance, and sources maintained by a consumer reporting agency, and requires that an individual be notified of any adverse action taken on the basis of a report from a consumer reporting agency, such as denial of credit, insurance, or employment. The Fair Credit Reporting Act does not apply to reports used for business, commercial, or professional purposes, and thus credit reporting agencies do not have to satisfy the consumer protection provisions of the act when they share information with firms reasonably believed to have a "legitimate business need."

Congress, in enacting the Electronic Communications Privacy Act of 1986, intended to strike a balance, through stringent regulation of the uses of electronic surveillance, between protecting individual privacy and permitting limited government surveillance in accordance with carefully designed and strictly controlled procedures. 18 U.S.C. &2510 *et seq.* Enacted as part of Title III of the Omnibus Crime Control and Safe Streets Act of 1986, the offense includes three essential elements: there must be a willful interception, the oral communication must be uttered by a person exhibiting an expectation that the communication would be private, and the communication must have been under circumstances justifying an expectation of privacy.

Finally, the Privacy Act of 1974 governs the responsibilities of federal agencies in the disclosure of, access to, and content of their records concerning individuals. The purpose of the act is to give consumers greater control over the gathering, dissemination, and accuracy of agency information about them. 5 U.S.C. &552(a). In the absence of written consent of the individual, any disclosure of information covered by the Privacy Act is prohibited, unless authorized by one or more of 12 specific exceptions. The "routine use" exception enables an agency to disclose an individual's record without written consent for uses that are compatible with the purpose for which the information was collected. The act, therefore, bars federal agencies from allowing information they collect for one purpose to be used for a different purpose.

As can be seen, even in those statutes that do not directly address the privacy of financial data, many of the precepts voluntarily followed by responsible members of the direct marketing field have found their way into legislation. Honoring consumer requests, use of data only for the purpose for which they were collected, consumer opportunity to object, and the like, are the foundation of many federal statutes. Under the circumstances, it appears that sales promoters and marketers should continue their support for keeping financial information that was disclosed under confidential circumstances private and confidential.

THE TRANSFER OF LISTS DOES NOT INVOLVE THE USE OF INFORMATION OF A PERSONAL OR PRIVATE NATURE

Unfortunately, those who claim that the rental or exchange of lists is an "invasion of privacy" that somehow threatens the unauthorized disclosure of highly personal information perhaps misunderstand what mailing lists are and how they are used.

What is a list, where does it come from, and how is it used? A list is a simple series of words, names, or numbers. It can be a grocery list, a Christmas list, or a list of things to do. Or it can be a list of names from almost any source such as the telephone directory, newspapers, customer files of a retailer, subscribers to magazines or cable TV, or donor files of a charity. When people have enough in common to be on the same list, it is assumed that they also comprise an identifiable potential market for some product or service.

Virtually everyone shares some characteristic or interest with a number of other people. Thus, each person "qualifies" to be placed on a list. In essence, the only way not to belong on some kind of list is to become a hermit — totally withdrawn from society, belonging to no organization or social group, subscribing to no magazine, owning no real property, and buying nothing by mail. Even then, one could find oneself on a list that has been compiled from public records.

There is no material difference among lists derived from retailers, charities, or subscribers to magazines or cable TV systems, except perhaps the physical or technical means by which they are developed. A retailer may maintain a list of its customers; a charity, of its contributors. Each may, of course, attempt to categorize or segment individuals, for example, by product or service on the one hand, or by frequency of purchase or donation and type on the other.

It is common practice for a list owner (for example, a retailer with customers, a charity with donors, a magazine with subscribers, or a telephone company with a directory) to permit the one-time use of its list by another, frequently by an advertiser. By way of example, the advertiser may choose to make a mailing to the names on a particular owner's list in an effort to provide the addressee with information about his or her goods or services. The following is illustrative of how this works.

A mailing list transaction prohibits the list user, by legally enforceable contractual obligation, from copying or making a record of the names and addresses on the list. The purpose and function of a mailing list is solely to furnish names and addresses to be used in the process of mailing promotional material of the user to the listed addresses. It is not to convey any information for any cognitive purposes and never purposely discloses anything beyond the name and address of each person on the list and, by implication, that he or she falls within the generic category of persons that the list catalogs. Transposition of names and addresses from a list to the mailing pieces is done mechanically, electronically, and automatically. List users gain no information or knowledge regarding the contents of the list by having the list, which in its physical form consists of magnetic tapes or sheets of labels, transmitted to them or received by them.

Thus, in many mailing list transactions (indeed, perhaps in the majority of them), the magnetic tape or mailing label list itself is delivered temporarily to an independent lettershop engaged by the advertiser, or to the advertiser itself, for the single mailing involved. However, each list made available to the advertiser typically contains tens of thousands of names and addresses; the essential point is that it is made available not to enlarge the advertiser's reservoir of information or to gain details about any individual on the list, but solely to be mechanically transposed onto a set of envelopes or other mailing wrappers that he or she will never see or consult. To repeat, a list user is under a legally enforceable contractual obligation not to copy or in any other way make a record of or retain the names and addresses on the list.

The plain, simple, and obvious fact is that the list user has no interest in finding out from the list that Mr. John Jones lives at 123 Maple Street, Elm City, New York; the user does not in reality employ the list to ascertain that gem of information, or any other. He or she simply utilizes the list to get a particular mailing into the mailboxes of a stated number of potential customers who remain, in true effect, anonymous so far as the list user is concerned. The list communicates neither individual knowledge nor intelligence.

In those respects, a mailing list is a unique vehicle. It provides means for both mass communication and for individual attention; but the individual attention is provided to the listed persons in the form of receiving something they are likely to be interested in, not by disclosing anything about them as individuals.

The essence of a mailing list is its ability to provide the means to transmit a message to individuals who share certain common and relevant interests; it is merely the physical manifestation of an attempt to correlate potential receptivity and activity. Sales promoters and direct marketers are continually making that attempt. To succeed they must deliver their messages to the right prospects. A mailing list is the impersonal aid used to reach that goal.

THE PRIVACY PROTECTION STUDY COMMISSION

A federal law in 1977 provided for the establishment of a Privacy Protection Study Commission (PPSC) composed of seven members — three appointed by the President of the United States, two appointed by the President of the Senate, and two appointed by the Speaker of the House of Representatives. The commission was chaired by David Linowes.

One of the PPSC's initial and principal directives was to report to the President and the Congress on whether a person engaged in interstate commerce who maintains a mailing list should be required by federal law to remove an individual's name and address from such a list upon request of that individual. After much deliberation, based on many months of hearings and thousands of pages of testimony, the PPSC concluded that the answer to this question should be "no."

The PPSC's principal reason for reaching the conclusion it did was that "the balance that must be struck between the interest of the individuals and the interest of mailers is an especially delicate one" ("Report of the Privacy Protection Study Commission" at page 147). The PPSC recognized and respected the importance of direct mail to nonprofit organizations, to the champions of unpopular causes, and to the many organizations that create diversity in American society, including business. It never seriously doubted the substantial economic significance of direct mail marketing.

In supporting its finding that no legislation or regulation was needed in the mailing list arena, the PPSC showed great respect for the testimony provided by the U.S. Postal Service through its then Director of the Office of Product Management, who told the PPSC:

> We can find no evidence that the present use of mailing lists in the direct-marketing process constitutes a significant or peculiar invasion of privacy. The economic pressures of the marketplace provide mailers with a strong incentive to direct their advertisements away from those individuals who might find them annoying. By its very nature, direct mail must be aimed at individuals who have some desire to receive it. Moreover, the recipient of unwanted mail matter has the option of throwing it away. Indeed, an individual probably finds it easier to avoid reading his mail than to escape from any other form of advertising. (Testimony of United States Postal Service, Mailing Lists Hearings, December 11, 1975, pp. 253-54, incorporated into the "Report of the Privacy Protection Study Commission" at p. 149.)

Good business practices demand that mailers be responsive to their customers' wishes. No one wants a dissatisfied customer, and no one wants to mail to an individual who is not likely to be responsive. Mailing lists provide the means by which to reach the right audience — people who are interested in getting the message.

The PPSC thus concluded that voluntary self-regulation by the industry, in the form of providing adequate means for people to have their names removed or withheld from lists, was the appropriate action, not governmental regulation. Established and effective vehicles to this end are the Direct Marketing Association's Mail Preference Service (and now also Telephone Preference Service), as well as individual mailers' name removal options, which provide customers an opportunity not to have their names placed on mailing lists.

Nonetheless, it is recognized that legal precedent exists for laws that would prevent unsolicited communication to those who have expressed a desire not to be contacted. Such requests should be honored.

> The Court has traditionally respected the right of a householder to bar, by order or notice, solicitors, hawkers, and peddlers from his property. ... In this case the mailer's right to communicate is circumscribed only by an affirmative act of the addressee giving notice that he wishes no further mailings from the mailer.

Rowan v. United States Post Office Department, 397 U.S. 728 (1970) (concerning an individual's ability to stop delivery to his private residence of advertisements that offer for sale sexually provocative material, but without interfering with the mailer's general right to disseminate its materials to willing recipients).

In yet another commercial setting, a federal appeals court upheld the validity of a state statute that prohibited the solicitation by a real estate broker of permission to sell residential real estate once the owner had given notice that he did not wish to sell the property.

> ... The right to privacy sets America apart from totalitarian states in which the interests of the state prevail over individual rights; moreover, the unique importance of the right to privacy *in the home* has, from time immemorial, been amply demonstrated in our constitutional jurisprudence. ... When the fundamental right to privacy clashes with the right of free expression, the interest in privacy does not play second fiddle when the speech is merely intended to propose a commercial transaction.

Curtis v. Thomson, 840 F.2d 1300 (7th Cir. 1988) (emphasis in original). The court explained why the Illinois statute restricting solicitation was valid under the First Amendment by stating:

Our holding today is narrow: once a homeowner gives notice to a person that he or she does not desire to have the home listed for sale and that he or she does not desire to be contacted by real estate brokers who have previously been made aware of the decision, the right of the homeowner to decide what he or she will or will not hear, under the right to privacy, plainly outweighs the right of a real estate broker to continue to contact that person in his or her home. Once actual notice is received by a real estate agent, that agent is barred from contacting the homeowner for the purpose of persuading him or her to list the residence for sale. Our holding prevents neither a buyer nor a seller of real estate from contacting any person who has not notified the particular broker that he wishes to be left undisturbed. *Id.* at 1304 (footnote omitted).

The analogy between the court's reasoning and direct marketers' traditional notice to consumers with an option to opt out of the mailing list/direct marketing process is remarkable. In the same manner that direct marketers recognize the need and the benefit of providing their customers with notice of their list rental practices and providing the opportunity for those customers to opt out of the process, a federal court determined as a matter of law that once a potential customer has been solicited and has expressed his or her desire not to be recontacted for that commercial purpose, the solicitor of the business must honor that desire and refrain from recontact. Thus, it is clear that the system and process urged and followed for some time by responsible direct marketers has, by analogy, received judicial approval.

Certain federal statutes more directly pertinent to direct marketers already have taken advantage of the legal precedent that requires one to honor such consumer requests. As a miscellaneous provision of the Cable Communications Policy Act of 1984, a subscriber "privacy" provision was enacted. Under the terms of that statute, a cable operator would be permitted to disclose personally identifiable information only if the cable operator had previously provided the subscriber the opportunity to prohibit or limit such disclosure. However, the disclosure could not reveal, directly or indirectly, the viewing habits of the subscriber or the nature of any transaction made by the subscriber over a cable system. Specifically excluded from the term personally identifiable information are any aggregate data that do not identify particular persons. Thus, a cable operator could disclose the fact that individuals subscribe to services but may not disclose the particular selections of the subscribers.

Accordingly, the Cable Communications Policy Act recognizes the legitimacy of disclosure in a manner consistent with that used by direct marketers. Only where information is personal and identifiable to an individual subscriber would its disclosure be prohibited. In substance, the act adopted and codified the voluntary name removal option employed by responsible direct marketers and the Mail Preference Service (and Telephone Preference Service) procedure whereby individuals may have their names removed from national mailing lists.

On November 5, 1988, the Video Privacy Protection Act was signed into law. Under the provision of that statute, a videotape service provider (one who sells or rents prerecorded video cassette tapes) is prohibited, except under specified circumstances, from disclosing personally identifiable information concerning any consumer. Among those exempt circumstances under which disclosure of such information is permitted is disclosure for the exclusive use of marketing goods and services directly to the consumer. Thus, videotape service providers may disclose the names and addresses of consumers if they have provided the consumer with the opportunity to prohibit such disclosure and the disclosure does not identify the title, description, or subject matter of any specific videotapes, although the subject matter of such materials may be disclosed.

Once again, Congress essentially adopted and employed the voluntary procedures used by direct marketers, including the essential features of DMA's Mail Preference Service (and Telephone Preference Service). These examples may be viewed as a codification of customary direct marketing industry practice and the adoption of legal precepts from circumstances as diverse as sexually provocative material on the one hand and real estate on the other. Nonetheless, they are sound in their logic.

More recently, Congress enacted the Telephone Consumer Protection Act of 1991 (effective December 20, 1992) that, in recognition of consumers' right to privacy, requires individual companies to maintain in-house suppression files in order to honor the wishes of those consumers who have requested that their names be removed from telephone marketing lists. The act also restricts the use of automated telephone dialing systems and artificial or prerecorded voice messages for unsolicited advertisements.

By Using Aggregate Data, Mailing Lists Can Only Be Positive. To think of private mailing lists as data banks with limitless capacities for computerized compilation and retrieval of the most intimate personal information is alien to reality. Mailing lists attempt to select out of the total marketplace those individuals who are most likely to be interested in, and persuaded by, an appeal to purchase a given type of product or service or yield to an appeal for support — monetarily or ideologically — of a particular institution, cause, political candidate, or the like. Where credit sales or extension are involved, they may also be intended to include trade prospects who are more likely to be good credit risks.

None of this possesses any true capacity to endanger or harm in any substantial way the individuals who are on the lists. Quite the contrary. No mailing list is conceivable that would be constructed on the basis of unfavorable information regarding the names on it. Lists that constitute reports regarding the credit status of individuals are, of course, not mailing lists, and, in any event, they already are governed by the Fair Credit Reporting Act. However, it should be pointed out that there, too, there is no invasion of privacy if the reporting company satisfies all the requirements of the law. *Tureen v. Equifax, Inc.*, 571 F.2d 411 (8th Cir. 1978). Similarly, lists compiled for purposes other than for direct marketing are not mailing lists as that term has been defined.

Moreover, whatever demographic information may be represented by a given mailing list is necessarily in terms of averages, or means, or broad characterizations, which cannot be specifically relied upon or applied with respect to any particular person on the list, other than the basic, and objectively generic, designation of the list itself (for example, newly married couples, purchasers from a particular company of a particular product or service). From there on, the rest is assumption, made at the peril only of the surmiser.

By Using Aggregate Data, Mailing Lists Cannot Be Used to Derive Individual Profiles or Dossiers. Mailing lists simply cannot realistically be used to develop multifaceted private data about an individual, even were a mailer to have some strange irrational desire to do so. Suppose, as an example, that someone should wish to investigate John Jones of 123 Main Street, Elm City, New York, seeking to construct a profile of some aspect of his lifestyle. There is no central bank of data to which the investigator could turn, punch in the name and address, and pull a printout of all information available concerning Jones that relates to any particular phase of his lifestyle. It would be necessary to rent every kind of mailing list that deals with one or another of the relevant segments of lifestyle (such as automotive and accessory purchases, air conditioners, stereos and other electronic items, home owners, home furnishing equipment of all various kinds, vacation and entertainment services, sporting, hunting, and fishing equipment, club memberships, book and magazine purchasers, clothing, wines, foods, or business executives.

One mailing list in each category would not be enough, for Jones' name and address might be missing from 20 lists but be present on the twenty-first. The investigator would then have to run the tapes or search the gummed labels or otherwise examine separate mailing lists to ascertain whether Jones' name and address were on it, and then make his or her own compilation and draw his own "profile" deductions from, at best, highly broad and nonspecific *assumptions* of the characteristics that might be *inferred* from the presence of a name and address on each kind of list, which might or might not be safely attributed to Jones.

The fundamental fact is that mailing lists are singularly poor sources for detailed information that specifically concerns any given person, particularly facts of a private nature. Mailing lists are made up in one of two manners: either they are compiled, by firms that make the effort to do so, from publicly available sources (such as directories of various kinds, open government records, voter registration records, club or association membership lists, lists of licensees of various kinds), or they are generated by a company from its own customer records.

Even when the second type, the customer list, may reflect some relatively private information (such as may have been required in order to establish a line of credit), the mailing list does not itself embody any such data; it communicates to others than the list owner (to whom the personal details have been voluntarily and knowingly supplied by the individual) nothing more than the names and addresses of the owner's customers — possibly further broken down by categories of products or services purchased. Inferences regarding economic status or personal buying habits that may be assumed from the fact that one has bought, for instance, a luxury automobile, a piece of jewelry, or clothing, are not greater, and no more private, than such as would follow upon members of the public seeing the purchaser driving or wearing such items.

THE LAW AND JUDICIAL PRECEDENT DISASSOCIATE MAILING LISTS AND INVASION OF PRIVACY

Since privacy, like any mental state, is essentially subjective, it is not easy to fix the scope of any right encompassing its precepts. The ordinary dictionary definition lists privacy as "the quality or state of being apart from observation: seclusion." One Supreme Court Justice has referred to it as the "right to be left alone." As previously discussed, its status as a constitutional right is ill-defined.

Amorphous as it may be, however, legal scholars and the judiciary have put their gloss on the more general (not constitutional) "right of privacy":

> The right of privacy is the right of a person to be left alone, to be free from unwarranted publicity, and to live without unwarranted interference by the public in matters with which the public is not necessarily concerned. *Housh v. Peth*, 165 Ohio St. 35, 133 N.E.2d 340 (1956).

Concerning the tort of invasion of privacy, the same court has stated:

> An actionable invasion of the right of privacy is the unwarranted appropriation or exploitation of one's personality, the publicizing of one's private affairs with which the public has no legitimate concern, or the wrongful intrusion

into one's private activities in such a manner as to outrage or cause mental suffering, shame or humiliation to a person of ordinary sensibilities. *Id.*

According to Dean Prosser, in his *Handbook of the Law of Torts*, invasion of privacy is not a single tort but consists of four distinct torts. They may be analyzed as follows:

1. Intrusion upon the plaintiff's seclusion or solitude or into his or her private affairs;
2. Public disclosure of embarrassing private facts about the plaintiff;
3. Publicity that places the plaintiff in a false light in the public eye; and
4. Appropriation, for the defendant's advantage, of the plaintiff's name or likeness.

Additionally, Prosser states (at page 813 of his handbook) that "thus far no expansion has occurred; and there is as yet no decided case allowing recovery which does not fall fairly within one of the four categories with which the courts have thus far been concerned."

In 1967, in a federal court in New York,[2] a plaintiff commenced an action against the Commissioner of Motor Vehicles on the ground that the statute permitting the Commissioner to contract with the highest responsible bidder to furnish copies of records of all vehicle registrations violated his "right of privacy" as well as the right of all those similarly situated, inasmuch as it subjected him to "considerable annoyance, inconvenience and damage ... by reason of the large volume of advertising and crank mail and other solicitation to which he was subjected."

In finding the plaintiff's contentions "plainly unsubstantial," the court dismissed the complaint and denied the plaintiff's request to have the constitutionality of the statute decided by a special, three-judge court. The court simply refused to accept the superficial argument proffered by the plaintiff and flatly stated:

> The mail box, however noxious its advertising contents seems to judges as well as other people, is hardly the kind of enclave that requires constitutional defense to protect "the privacies of life." 269 F. Supp. at 883.

Continuing, the court made the simple, yet obvious, and legally conclusive statements:

> The short, though regular, journey from mail box to trash can ... is an acceptable burden, at least so far as the Constitution is concerned.

> In his contrary thesis, plaintiff proposes to stretch the constitutional dimensions of "privacy" far beyond any rea-

sonably foreseeable limits the courts ought to enforce. *Id.* at 883-84.

Of special interest was the court's further observation:

> Indeed, questions more troublesome than plaintiff's might arise if the State adopted a policy of "privacy" or "secrecy" with respect to such information. *Id.*

The lower court's decision was affirmed on appeal; the Supreme Court refused to accept review.

Similarly, in the Ohio state court decision of *Shibley v. Time Inc.*, a plaintiff's contention that he and other magazine subscribers had suffered an invasion of privacy by the rental of their names, and that the defendants had been unjustly enriched thereby, was dismissed.

In that case, the plaintiff conceded, as he had to, that his claim did not fit into the orthodox framework of the traditional invasion of right of privacy case. Relying on the definitions and the legal precedents discussed above, the court dismissed both of the plaintiff's claims — the invasion of privacy cause on the ground that no legal claim was stated and the unjust enrichment clause on the ground that no invasion of privacy having taken place, the sales by the defendant were not wrongful (no unjust enrichment).

On appeal, it was clarified that "appropriation of one's personality" refers to those situations in which the plaintiff's name or likeness is displayed to the public to indicate that the plaintiff endorses the defendant's product or business — not to those in which "personality profiles" are only used to determine what type of advertisement is to be sent.

What becomes apparent is that any linking of mailing lists and the "right of privacy" is inappropriate. Logically, operationally, and legally, the two simply do not interact; emotionally, they must remain separate.

It follows that justification for restrictive legislation in the database or list area must be based on new evidence of the existence of substantial harm. The question that must be satisfactorily answered is, "does the use of mailing lists result in demonstrated substantial harm?"

As has already been demonstrated, no harm, and much benefit, accompanies the use of mailing lists. There are no "victims." Mailing lists do not victimize. They are a tool to market products, sell ideas, and raise funds; and although not everyone will like the product nor accept the idea nor contribute money, few, if any, would feel victimized solely as a result of being asked.

The focus of any legislation must be on true privacy questions and not based on nuisance and nuisance only. It is not necessary to elaborate here on the long list of items that people term a nuisance. Suffice it to say that the list is substantial and varies according to the irritation quotient of the person involved. Although there are some nuisances shared almost in unanimity by all, no such unanimity exists concerning the receipt of advertising mail or the rental of mailing lists without individual permission of the names on the list.

To the contrary, the large number of mail order companies with growing lists of satisfied customers would indicate that the nuisance level of direct mail ranks far down the list of minor irritations to a small group of individuals. For every person who may be driven to distraction by the presence in his or her mailbox of direct mail, there are many others who find such missives unobtrusive, interesting, and useful or, at worst, conveniently disposable. In any event, those few who seriously do not wish to receive direct mail are protected by existing industry practices — the DMA's Mail Preference Service and Telephone Preference Service, and individual mailers' name withholding and removal options.

THE FIRST AMENDMENT PROHIBITS GROSS RESTRICTION OF THE RIGHT TO COMMUNICATE AND OF THE RIGHT TO RECEIVE COMMUNICATIONS

It is a well-established tenet of constitutional law that the First Amendment not only protects the speaker's right to be heard but also guarantees the listener's right to receive information of interest to him or her. The United States Supreme Court has upheld such protection in a commercial setting in which the speaker is an advertiser and the potential audience consists of prospective consumers.

> Commercial expression not only serves the economic interest of the speaker, but also assists consumers and furthers the societal interest in the fullest possible dissemination of information. *Central Hudson Gas & Electric Co. v. Public Service Commission*, 447 U.S. 557, 100 S. Ct. 2343, 2349 (1980). Also, *Virginia State Board of Pharmacy v. Virginia Citizens Consumer Council, Inc.*, 425 U.S. 748, 765 (1975). *See also, Bolger v. Youngs Drug Products Corp.*, 463 U.S. 60 (1983) (commercial speech is protected even where offensive to some).

In doing so, the court laid down certain precepts delimiting governmental power to abridge commercial speech, at the same time precluding states from restricting commercial speech easily and excessively.

> The State must assert a substantial interest to be achieved by restrictions on commercial speech. Moreover, the regulatory technique must be in proportion to that interest. The limitation on expression must be designed carefully to achieve the State's goal. Compliance with this requirement may be measured by two criteria. First, the restriction

must directly advance the State interest involved; the regulation may not be sustained if it provides only ineffective or remote support for the government's purpose. Second, if the governmental interest could be served as well by a more limited restriction on commercial speech, the excessive restrictions cannot survive. *Id.* at 2350.

Subsequently, in the matter of *State University of New York v. Fox*, the Supreme Court retreated slightly from its "least restrictive manner" requirement and held that a "narrowly tailored" requirement must be satisfied instead. The court made it clear that its test did not insist on the absence of any conceivable alternative that was less restrictive, but only that any regulation not burden speech more than is necessary to further the government's legitimate interest.

What the Supreme Court now requires is a fit between the legislature's ends and the manner chosen to accomplish those ends. That fit may not necessarily be perfect, but it must be reasonable. It may not be the single best disposition, but it must be one whose scope is in proportion to the interests served, one that employs not necessarily the least restrictive means but a means narrowly tailored to achieve the desired objective.

However, there could be no more utter or discriminatory means to abridge commercial speech than a requirement that, for example, all subscribers to a magazine or purchasers from a catalog must give their prior consent before their names could be included in a mailing list of such subscribers. Such a concept, which provides no definition or specificity or identification of the substantial state interest being asserted (beyond invocation of the buzzword privacy), and which promotes blanket restrictions, cannot survive.

Given that, as a general First Amendment proposition, a heavy burden of proof must be satisfied before protection can be diminished, it can only follow that something more than an amorphous reference to "invasion of privacy" must be present before an agency of the state may abridge marketers' and consumers' freedom of speech. *Procunier v. Martinez*, 416 U.S. 396 (1974); *Shelton v. Tucker*, 364 U.S. 479 (1960); *Kusper v. Pontikes*, 414 U.S. 51 (1973); *Beneficial Corp. v. FTC*, 542 F.2d 611 (3rd Cir. 1976); *Terry v. California State Board of Pharmacy*, 395 F. Supp. 94, 105 (N.D. Cal. 1975) (three-judge panel), *aff'd*, 426 U.S. 913 (1976).

Returning to the imperatives set forth by the Supreme Court in *Central Hudson* and *S.U.N.Y. v. Fox*, a legislature, in order to dam the free flow of commercial information (1) must assert a substantial interest to be achieved by restriction on commercial speech and (2) must employ a regulatory technique that must not be disproportionate to that interest.

With respect to the ever-present threat of restrictive legislation, it is unclear what state interest would be advanced if a statute were enacted prohibiting the transfer of magazine subscribers' names, for example, on a mailing list. Such a matter does not provide a state interest basis for abridging commercial speech. If others exist that do, they must be singled out, and proposed restrictions refined and limited to only so much as would "directly advance the state interest involved" (*Central Hudson* and *S.U.N.Y. v. Fox, supra*).

Presumably, there has not been an analysis of what kind of restrictions proposed legislation would place on mailing list transactions. It is clear, however, that any across-the-board prohibition would be excessive and, therefore, would fail to satisfy the constitutional requirements that a narrowly tailored restriction be used, and that it not be disproportionate to a specifically identified, substantial interest of the state.

Imposing a requirement that a prospective recipient of a piece of mail give prior permission before it may be delivered has been held by the United States Supreme Court to be unconstitutional as an impermissible limitation on the addressee's First Amendment rights. *Lamont v. Postmaster General of the United States*, 381 U.S. 301 (1965).

The Court, there considering a statute that required an affirmative act (returning a reply card) before mail that had been determined to be "communist political propaganda" could be delivered, concluded that no statute could impose such a limitation on "the unfettered exercise of the addressee's First Amendment rights."

> The addressee in order to receive his mail must request in writing that it be delivered. This amounts in our judgment to an unconstitutional abridgment of the addressee's First Amendment rights. The addressee carries an affirmative obligation which we do not think the government may impose on him. *Id.*, concurring opinion at 309.

So, too, would any prior consent or preapproval requirement placed on a prospective recipient of direct mail advertising abridge the First Amendment. And any argument that such an imposition involves only "inconvenience" and not an abridgment has been rejected by the same court where it stated that "inhibition as well as prohibition against the exercise of precious First Amendment rights is a power denied to the government" (concurring opinion at 309).

> The dissemination of ideas can accomplish nothing if otherwise willing addressees are not free to receive and consider them. It would be a barren marketplace of ideas that had only sellers and no buyers. *Id.* at 308.

In the case of direct mail advertising, such an inhibition would be almost total. It would make the compiling and renting of lists economically unsupportable.

Again, under *Central Hudson* and *S.U.N.Y. v. Fox* standards of advancing a substantial state interest in a narrowly tailored manner, a statute may not perpetrate a blanket intrusion on addressees' rights to receive information (including commercial information).

The statute under consideration, on the other hand, impedes delivery even to a willing addressee. In the area of First Amendment freedoms, government has the duty to confine itself to the least intrusive regulations which are adequate for the purpose. *Lamont v. Postmaster General* at 310.

Any effort to justify a ban on a particular method of speech under the guise of exercising a state's police power similarly will not hold up. *Ad World, Inc. v. Township of Doylestown*, 672 F.2d 1136 (3rd Cir. 1982) (an ordinance that prohibited the delivery of unrequested door-to-door advertising material was stricken as violative of the First Amendment notwithstanding the distributor's willingness to stop delivery when a resident so requested, although affirmative consent for delivery was not obtained, under the theory that the unsightliness of accumulated deliveries during a resident's absence might tip off burglars that a home was unoccupied). It was determined that the freedom to disseminate information to all citizens wherever they desire to receive it was so vital to the preservation of a free society that, aside from reasonable police and health regulations of time and manner of distribution, such freedom must be fully preserved.

As earlier discussed, there are many who want and enjoy receiving mail and many who do not appreciate the full implications of opting to have their names removed from lists. Accordingly, any statute that in an across-the-board manner interferes with the First Amendment right to be a recipient of information by means of that medium cannot withstand constitutional scrutiny. It is, after all, the medium about which it has been said:

> The United States may give up the post office when it sees fit, but while it carries it on, the use of the mails is almost as much a part of free speech as the right to use our tongues.[3]

As the direct marketing industry has become more sophisticated, so has the Supreme Court's analysis of First Amendment issues in that area. In the context of lawyer advertising, the Court has analyzed the differences and corresponding rights between general mailings and targeted mailings.

In *Shapero v. Kentucky Bar Association*, 108 S.Ct. 1916 (1988), the Court was asked to determine whether targeted direct mail solicitations that were not false or misleading could be, consistent with the First Amendment, categorically prohibited by the state. The statute distinguished between sending nondeceptive letters to potential clients known to face particular legal problems (prohibited by the statute) from sending them to persons not known to need legal services but who might in general find such services useful (permitted).

In holding the ban to be violative of the First Amendment, the court observed that although, for First Amendment purposes, it had distinguished written advertisements from in-person solicitations in the past — *Ohralik v. Ohio State Bar Association*, 436 U.S. 447 (1978) — and other courts have distinguished literature from telephone calls — *National Funeral Services, Inc. v. Rockefeller*, 870 F.2d 136 (4th Cir. 1989) — the Supreme Court has never distinguished among the various modes of written advertising to the general public. The court had previously equated advertising in telephone directories with newspaper advertising — *Bates v. State Bar of Arizona*, 433 U.S. 350 (1977) — and mailed announcement cards with newspaper and telephone directory advertisements — *In re R.M.J.*, 455 U.S. 191 (1982).

Critically, the Supreme Court stated:

> But the First Amendment does not permit a ban on certain speech merely because it is more efficient; the State may not constitutionally ban a particular letter on the theory that to mail it only to those whom it would most interest is somehow inherently objectionable. *Shapero v. Kentucky Bar Association* at 1921-22.

Although the Court distinguished written solicitations from face-to-face solicitations, it noted that the printed word, including targeted direct mail solicitations, poses much less risk of overreaching or undue influence than does its in-person counterpart.

It then observed that:

> The recipient of a letter and the reader of an advertisement... can effectively avoid further bombardment of [his] sensibilities simply by averting [his] eyes. A letter, like a printed advertisement ... can readily be put in a drawer to be considered later, ignored or discarded.... [It is] conducive to reflection and the exercise of choice on the part of the consumer.... Nor does a targeted letter invade the recipient's privacy any more than does a substantively identical letter mailed at large. *Id.* at 1923.

Although no opinion was rendered on whether the discovery of facts about the recipient creates any privacy violation, the court expressly stated there was no such violation by the mailer's merely confronting the recipient with the discovery.

Although the court recognized that a personalized letter, under certain circumstances, could lead the recipient to overestimate the sender's familiarity with the recipient's situation, it held that "merely because targeted, direct-mail solicitation presents [one] with opportunities for isolated abuses or mistakes does not justify a total ban on that mode of commercial speech" (*Id.*). In addressing the *Central Hudson* requirements, the court reaffirmed the decision's vitality and stated:

> And so long as the First Amendment protects the right to solicit ... business, the State may claim no substantial interest in restricting truthful and non-deceptive ... solicitations to those least likely to be read by the recipient. *Id.* at 1924.

The United States Supreme Court also struck down an ordinance that attempted to restrict a particular form of communication (there, the posting of "For Sale" signs).[4] The court reasoned that such a ban could not be defended as a mere regulation of the time, place, or manner of speech inasmuch as each medium has its unique qualities, and an entire medium's complete removal results in constitutional deprivation.

> Serious questions exist as to whether the ordinance "leave(s) open ample alternative channels for communication," *Virginia Pharmacy Bd., supra*, 425 U.S. at 771. Although in theory sellers remain free to employ a number of different alternatives, in practice realty is not marketed through leaflets, sound trucks, demonstrations, or the like. The options to which sellers are realistically relegated — primarily newspaper advertising and listing with real estate agents — involve more cost and less autonomy than "For Sale" signs (citations omitted); are less likely to reach persons not deliberately seeking sales information (citations omitted); and may be less effective media for communicating the message that is conveyed by a "For Sale" sign in front of the house to be sold (citations omitted). The alternatives, then, are far from satisfactory. *Linmark Associates* at 93.

A statute that prohibits the free transfer of names and addresses alone or with the information that implicitly, albeit anonymously, accompanies a list, cannot survive the constitutional tests of *Central Hudson/S.U.N.Y. v. Fox* (advancement of substantial state interest in a narrowly tailored manner), *Lamont* (prohibition against requiring addressees' permission or request before delivery of targeted mail), *Shapero* (protection of targeted messages), or *Linmark Associates* (prohibition against restricting one medium of communication).

CONCLUSION

It is hoped this has shed useful light on some of the unsupportable cliches that are commonly repeated by critics of database marketing, sales promotion, and direct mail. Although users of databases and direct marketing have substantial rights to continue their form of communication and selling, they should be mindful of the threat of restrictive legislation should they fail to be sensitive to consumer privacy expectations. Those who use databases should provide their actual and potential customers with the opportunity to have their names removed from the future mailings by employment of the Direct Marketing Association's Mail Preference Service and Telephone Preference Service, and by providing their own removal option. Only by providing the means of opting out of the system will the system be preserved.

FOOTNOTES

1. This, of course, does not include the use of such information for insurance purposes (not marketing purposes) in which insurance is sold by direct marketing methods.
2. *Lamont v. Commissioner of Motor Vehicles*, 269 F.Supp. 880 (S.D.N.Y. 1967), aff'd, 386 F.2d 449 (2d Cir. 1967), *cert. den.*, 391 U.S. 915 (1968).
3. *United ex rel. Milwaukee Social Democratic Pub. Co. v. Burleson*, 255 U.S. 407, 437 (1921) (Justice Holmes, dissenting opinion).
4. *Linmark Associates Inc. v. Town of Willingboro*, 431 U.S. 85 (1977).

Kathryn K. Mlsna is a Senior Corporate Attorney for the McDonald's Corporation, having day-to-day responsibility for the legal review of the national advertising and promotional programs produced and conducted by the 9,000 McDonald's restaurants in the United States.

She is immediate past Chairman of the Board and President of the Promotion Marketing Association of America (PMAA), having served as a Vice President (1989–1992), Chairman of the Legal Committee (1989–1992), and Chairman of the 7th Annual Promotion Marketing Law Conference. She is currently the Chair of PMAA's Integrated Marketing Committee. She is also a frequent speaker at industry meetings on advertising and promotion law.

Mlsna is a member of the American Bar Association and the Illinois Bar Association. She holds a Bachelor of Arts degree in sociology and a law degree from Northwestern University's School of Law.

Gregory Griffin is a partner in the law firm of Levett, Rockwood & Sanders in Westport, Connecticut. He practices corporate law, with a focus on marketing, advertising and promotions, antitrust and trade regulation, and intellectual property. He is a past Director of C-I-L Corporation of America, a Canadian-based chemical company, and Business Express, Inc., a regional airline serving the northeastern United States and Canada.

He is a member of the Business and Antitrust Sections of the American Bar Association and of the Connecticut Bar Association. He is on the Legal Committee of the PMAA and has spoken on advertising and promotion topics before a variety of industry groups.

Griffin graduated from The Taft School, Williams College, and Harvard Law School. He served four years as an intelligence officer in the U.S. Navy.

Edward B. Chansky is an associate in the law firm of Levett, Rockwood & Sanders, concentrating in the areas of copyright, trademark, advertising, sweepstakes, promotions, entertainment, antitrust, and trade regulation.

He is a member of the Patent, Trademark and Copyright Section of the American Bar Association and the Executive Committee of the Intellectual Property Section of the Connecticut Bar Association. He is an Associate Fellow of Berkeley College at Yale University.

Chansky is a graduate of Yale University and Harvard Law School.

CHAPTER 35

PLANNING A LEGAL PROMOTION: SALES PROMOTION LAWS AND REGULATIONS

INTRODUCTION

No thorough discussion of promotion marketing would be complete without consideration of the laws and regulations that govern promotions and the other legal issues that promotion professionals face. A working knowledge of applicable federal, state, and local laws is an essential element of any successful promotion. Because these laws affect every aspect of a promotion, from initial concept to final execution, they cover a wide spectrum of issues. They do, however, have one thing in common. Each law is a governmental response to a perceived abuse in the marketplace. For example, state prize prenotification laws were enacted to cure the problems that resulted from programs that notified people they had won a valuable prize but failed to inform them of substantial, time-consuming, and sometimes expensive prize claim procedures or the full and sometimes unappealing details of the prizes themselves.

Similarly, the promotion professional must have some awareness of the nonregulatory legal risks and issues that arise in the creation and execution of promotions. What are the risks and issues in a coupon offer? Who should take what responsibilities in putting together a premium offer?

This chapter has three goals. First, it will highlight the major current legal issues of which any marketing professional should be aware when developing a promotion to be conducted in the United States. It is not intended to be an exhaustive study of all legal issues but is intended to be a tool to help avoid the major mistakes that can seriously impair or prematurely terminate an otherwise creative and effective program.

Second, this chapter is intended to encourage its readers to work with a promotion marketing lawyer. Because it highlights only the major current legal issues, this chapter should not be used as the sole legal resource when developing a promotion. There are many laws governing promotions which simply cannot be covered in this space. Furthermore, there are general laws governing truth in advertising which are relevant in most promotions, and legal questions involving transshipping and diverting that are often associated with promotions, but for reasons of space those topics cannot be addressed here.

Therefore, readers should use this chapter to identify legal issues and take full advantage of a lawyer's expertise. A lawyer will be able to determine which laws apply to each element of the promotion, and how the promotion can be structured to comply with and even take advantage of those laws.[1]

The third goal of this chapter is to make the job of marketing professionals easier and more rewarding. We will present this summary of key laws and interpretations in a "reader-friendly" manner, with the intention that readers use this chapter often during all stages of planning a promotion.

The legal references in this chapter were current as of the date we went to press. Be aware that changes in the law or its interpretation may occur. Consult a promotion lawyer for the most up-to-date information.

What the Pros Know. Laws and enforcement policies change. What was legally acceptable one month could be completely unlawful the next. This chapter and a marketing lawyer should be consulted in the planning of each promotion, even if the promotion is a rerun of a prior one.

Experienced professionals also know that the presence of a promotion in the marketplace is no guarantee of its legality. Just as all promotions cannot be characterized as successful merely because they have been executed in the marketplace, not all programs in the marketplace should be assumed to comply with all applicable laws. As noted above, laws or enforcement policies might have changed after the prior program ran. That prior promotion might not have undergone careful legal scrutiny. And just as enforcement authorities do not pull over every speeding driver, they do not take action against every promotion that might violate the law — but they are free to take action against a company if a promotion does violate the law.

Depending on its nature, a violation of laws governing the promotion industry can result in civil as well as criminal penalties. Violation of laws governing games of chance, for example, can be pursued as violations of gambling laws. While it is not common for enforcement authorities to pursue criminal penalties in the promotion law area, such penalties are available, are more likely to be used in extreme cases, and provide enforcement authorities with powerful leverage if a violation occurs.

Generally, professionals know that compliance with the letter of the law is not enough. Designing a program to comply with the letter of the law, but not the spirit of the law, is inviting legal as well as business trouble.

Compliance solely with the letter of the law can avoid technical legal problems, but it is not a guarantee that expensive, time-consuming, and reputation-damaging legal challenges will not be brought against the marketer. Further, compliance with simply the letter of the law, and not the spirit of the law, can be shortsighted because promotions are generally governed by consumer protection laws, which are very broad and which are liberally construed against the marketer to prevent deception and unfairness.

The letter of the law is a specific requirement stated in that law. For example, sweepstakes disclosure laws require a description of the prizes to be offered. The spirit of the law is the purpose of that law. In the promotion marketing area, the spirit of the law is consumer protection. In this example, drafting official rules that include a craftily worded prize description of a mid-level-quality prize, which includes the few required specifics surrounded by many superlatives such as *best*, *fabulous*, *unequalled*, might comply with the letter of the law but might not comply with the spirit. Disappointed prizewinners, inquiring attorneys, and unhappy sponsors are the likely result.

PROCEDURES

In order to know which specific laws and regulations apply to a promotion or which legal issues are raised by a promotion, the marketing professional should regularly follow a few basic procedures. These procedures will be discussed first. Later we'll look at the key laws and regulations and other key legal issues connected to the various forms of promotion.

Planning. Brand managers, account executives, creative directors, and other marketing professionals should get into the habit of thinking about legal review early. Legal issues can arise long before it is time to "run it past the lawyers" for a last-minute approval. Many problems can be avoided by seeking legal advice when *planning* the concept, execution, and fulfillment of the promotion. It is really true that an ounce of prevention can be worth a pound of cure.

When consulting an attorney, put all the cards on the table. Describe the promotion completely. Explain exactly what the terms of the offer should be, who plans to run the program, where it is planned to run the promotion (geographically, as well as in which media), the product(s) promoted, the prize(s) offered, the intended audience (especially if it includes children), and what the marketing objective is.

With this information, a promotion lawyer usually can determine whether a program is lawful. Sometimes the answer won't be clear. Many of the laws in this area are subject to varying interpretations. Promotions often fall into "gray" areas. Moreover, enforcement of the law is not always consistent with the letter of the law. Taking these factors into consideration, a lawyer who is given all the facts is in a position to suggest adjustments or alternatives consistent with the marketing objective to try to avoid problem areas.

In addition, the lawyer can begin to identify issues to be dealt with down the road. These include legal copy in ads, registration requirements, and the like. Getting these items into the pipeline early can help relieve pressures when the promotion is ready to enter the marketplace.

Review. Develop a standard system for reviewing promotions.

Begin by requiring outside suppliers and agencies to review their own materials before they send them to the promotion team. Then conduct an in-house review. Take steps to minimize any litigation risks that are identified along the way. Try to make the promotion as clear and simple as possible. This helps avoid consumer confusion and complaints.

The review process should also include a strict approval system. Such a system forces review by and accountability of the whole promotion team from beginning to end. An authorized representative of the sponsor should be designated to approve every stage of the promotion. Other personnel, including any outside promotion house or agency, should fully inform the authorized person of all relevant issues. This requires more than having a lawyer take a quick look at a camera-ready mechanical an hour before it has to go to press. It means making sure that the sponsor's authorized representative is aware of any legal risks and has time to evaluate them.

The Lawyer's Role. Like the marketing professional, the lawyer should be proactive. The lawyer should seek out the brand manager, the account executive, or other "client" to talk about and understand the promotion. Effective lawyers will (almost) never say "never"; they should look for ways to make a promotion work and try to suggest changes that resolve legal problems without interfering with the marketing objective. The lawyers should understand the time pressures of promotion work and be flexible whenever possible. However, they should resist giving bad advice if they haven't been given adequate information or time to think properly about an issue. Finally, the lawyers should follow up with the promotion team. If they don't hear about a project for a while, they should find out why. This helps catch projects that have gone in new directions or that have fallen off the track of legal review before they become problems.

Dealing with Problems. Despite the best planning and review, some problems inevitably will arise. When they do, fix them. Do what's right — for the consumer, the brand, the client, and the company. And do it fast. Legal problems usually get worse if they are allowed to linger.

GENERAL LEGAL PRINCIPLES

As a general rule, a promotion is an offer by its sponsor. The sponsor tells consumers that they are entitled to something (a discount, a free item, cents off a purchase price, or a chance to win a prize) if they perform some act (purchase something or submit a proof-of-purchase or coupon). If consumers accept the offer by performing the act, a binding contract is created, and the sponsor is required to give what it offered. The important thing to note here is that this kind of contract is as binding as the multipage, fine-print, signed-at-the-bottom document that has the word Contract at the top. Furthermore, the general rule is that all material conditions and details of the offer, wherever they appear (for example, advertising copy, coupon copy, package copy) can become part of the contract. Therefore, a sponsor should be certain that it communicates the exact offer and leaves no room for doubt.

COUPONS

A coupon is a form of offer. However, because third parties redeem coupons as agents of the issuer, all terms and conditions should be stated on the coupon itself and not in other places. (An exception might be the terms and conditions offered by the issuer to the redemption agent — for example, the grocer or other retailer. Some companies put those terms and conditions in separate agreements and only summarize key points on the coupon.)

When preparing a coupon offer, the promotion professional should ask the following questions:

1. **What benefit does the coupon offer?** The product or service should be described and illustrated accurately. What product? What discount? What size? What service?

2. **What must the customer do to redeem the coupon?** The requirements should be clearly stated. What is the required purchase? What proofs must be submitted?

3. **What is the redemption deadline?** The date by which the coupon must be redeemed should be clearly stated. To decrease the potential for fraud, coupons without expiration dates should generally not be used.

4. **Where can the coupon be redeemed?** A list of the participating locations (if possible) or a statement that the coupon is redeemable at participating locations should be included.

5. **Does the coupon have a stated cash value?** The states of Indiana, Utah, and Washington require coupons to state a cash value: 1/20 or 1/100 of a cent is a common cash value declaration.

6. **Is the coupon redeemable in conjunction with other coupons or offers?** All conditions should be clearly stated. Some coupon issuers state that the coupon cannot be redeemed with another coupon in order to prevent the customer from aggregating coupons and receiving a totally free, rather than discounted, product.

7. **Can a customer use a coupon for more than one product?** The number of products or services to which the customer is entitled for a single coupon should be specified. For example, consider a coupon redeemable for a free 10-oz. can of soup with the purchase of a 20-oz. can of soup. If the issuer wants to limit the redemption of each coupon to one free 10-oz. can of soup, the issuer should state this detail clearly on the coupon in order to prevent a customer from purchasing 25 20-oz. cans of soup and expecting to redeem 25 free cans.

8. **Will the merchant be reimbursed by the issuer?** Reimbursement is common and expected. The grocer, for instance, redeems coupons issued by a food company and then requests reimbursement from the company. The Grocery Manufacturers' of America Association has compiled an extensive list of recommended coupon disclosures in this regard. (Sometimes these are in separate policy statements, which are incorporated just by reference in the coupon.) These provisions are intended to clarify the terms of the reimbursement and to decrease the possibility of fraud. Some manufacturers use short deadlines to help combat fraud; they reimburse only if coupons are remitted promptly (for example, 60 days) after the coupon expiration date.

9. **Does the coupon use the words *free* or *cents off* or words with similar meaning?** Recognizing that these words are highly motivating, the Federal Trade Commission (FTC) issued a guideline in 1971 that governs the use of these words and should be referred to prior to making such an offer. The guideline:
   - Specifies the recommended frequency and duration of such offers. (Briefly, "free" or "discount" offers that run too long or too often are viewed as misleading.)
   - Describes the recommended placement of qualifiers. (Briefly, qualifiers should appear in appropriate type size immediately after the words being qualified, rather than in a footnote at the bottom or on the reverse side of the coupon.)

   Several states, including Connecticut, Florida, Illinois, Massachusetts, Michigan, Minnesota, Ohio, Oregon, and Wisconsin, as well as New York City, have adopted similar laws.

10. **What other limitations are appropriate?** For example, if the coupon issuer wishes to restrict the transfer, sale, and reproduction of its coupons, it should include a statement to that effect on the coupon. (Most manufacturers do impose such restrictions on their cents-off and free coupons to reduce the risk of fraudulent redemption. To discourage counterfeiting, some manufacturers also use special papers and inks that resist photocopying.)

11. **Will the coupon be enclosed in and featured on a package?** The package that contains the coupon should state the redemption deadline and other important details so that customers know what the coupon offer is before they purchase the package. Coupon expiration dates should take into account normal shelf life.

12. **What are the other considerations in preparing a coupon promotion?**

a) **UPC code.** Most scanners use them; they're essential for redemption tracking.

b) **Store or manufacturer coupon.** The kind of coupon should be specified, so it's clear who is making the offer.

c) **Consumer pays sales tax.** If the consumers must pay any applicable sales tax, say so. This is especially important with "free" offers.

d) **Void where prohibited or taxed.** This statement makes it easier to withdraw the offer if a law or regulation changes or is discovered after the fact.

Exhibit 35.1 is an example of a well-drafted coupon.

OTHER COUPONING ISSUES

Many of the points discussed above are raised because of some unique laws and issues that affect couponing.

Cross-Couponing Laws. Several states have enacted cross-couponing laws that govern coupons redeemed by an entity other than the coupon issuer. For example, Company A distributes a coupon that is redeemable by Company B. Briefly, California, Washington, Wisconsin, and Kansas regulate cross-couponing. Several of those states require the issuer and redeemer to enter into an agreement stating that the issuer will redeem the coupon if the intended redeemer fails to do so and require the coupon to state the name and address of both the issuer and redeemer.

Trading Stamp Laws. A number of states have adopted what are known as trading stamp laws. Generally, these laws regulate, license, and/or tax the provision and/or use of certain coupons issued in connection with the sale of a product or service. Eleven of these states have adopted a basically standardized trading stamp law, which provides a specific exclusion for coupons and similar items that are used by a manufacturer or packer of a product when advertising or selling it: California, Connecticut, Florida, Maine, Maryland, Massachusetts, New Hampshire, New Jersey, New Mexico, New York, and Vermont. Fourteen other states and Puerto Rico specifically regulate trading stamp/couponing activity:

Alabama	Utah
Indiana	Virginia
Kansas	Washington
North Dakota	West Virginia
Ohio	Wisconsin
Oklahoma	Wyoming
Rhode Island	Puerto Rico
South Dakota	

Corporate Procedures. Compliance with all applicable laws is

EXHIBIT 35.1

Used by permission of Campbell Soup Company.

sometimes not enough. A number of companies have developed internal guidelines governing the drafting of coupons. These guidelines might dictate elements such as format, type size, wording, and terms for redeeming merchants. The marketing professional should inquire about the existence of any guidelines before becoming too attached to a particular coupon style.

Coupon Fraud. Coupons are money. The design, production, distribution, and redemption of coupons should be treated with the same level of care as the printing and handling of money. Unfortunately, a significant illicit business has developed that fraudulently exploits the willingness of companies to give money (that is, coupons) to people who buy their products or services. Volumes can be written about the detection, handling, and prevention of coupon fraud. This point is discussed in Chapter 6, "Couponing." Let's discuss several of the highlights here.

Retail and Clearinghouse Fraud.

Issuers of coupons should know the retailers who handle their coupons. Is the retailer submitting coupons in a quantity consistent with its historic or expected sales volume and actual product inventory? If not, the coupons submitted may not actually have been redeemed by consumers. For example, the retailer whose redemptions of a particular cereal coupon indicate that the sales volume of that cereal far exceed what would be expected for that product or retailer would merit a closer look by the coupon issuer who receives from that retailer a questionable quantity of redeemed coupons for reimbursement.

Several years ago, the U.S. Postal Service conducted an investigation of a number of retailers by analyzing redemptions of a coupon for a fictitious detergent. Many coupons were submitted by retailers to the "detergent" manufacturer, even though the product never existed.

One typical chain of retailer coupon fraud works like this. A retailer (or someone holding himself out as a retailer) obtains a quantity of coupons for which he wants to obtain reimbursement from the issuer. He has obtained these coupons, however, not from customers but from printer waste or coupon clipping "clubs," for example. The coupons are cut and handled to give them the "handled" look and feel. They are then sent to the clearinghouse for accounting and processing, after which time they are forwarded to the issuer for "reimbursement" to the submitter (who had not made the required retail sale to the consumer). Another typical chain of fraud involves the clearinghouse, which has obtained a quantity of coupons that have never been in customers' hands.

Consumer Fraud.

The "nonexistent detergent" investigation was interesting not only for what it revealed about certain retailers but for what it revealed about certain customers — those people who submitted the coupons to retailers for redemption or to bulk-buying middlemen for cash without having purchased the specified (though nonexistent) product. This same process occurs at a less dramatic level when consumers attempt to redeem coupons for products and sizes other than those specified on the coupon.

Coupon issuers have an interest in ensuring that customers redeem coupons for the intended product or service. Customers fail to redeem properly for one of two reasons: honest mistake or intentional fraud. Clear wording can help to avoid the former. The recommended procedures and coupon language developed by the Grocery Manufacturers's of America Association were designed to combat the latter. Further, the Coupon Information Corporation's Coupon Information Center is a useful resource to any marketers wishing to manage the risk of fraud.

PREMIUMS

Many federal, state, and local laws, regulations, and industry standards govern the manufacture, shipment, and distribution of merchandise premiums in the United States. We cannot examine each one in detail, but we will discuss the hottest issues. These can be divided into two types: marketer and supplier protection and consumer protection.

Marketer and Supplier Protection.

Producer Agreement. Any marketer and any premium supplier involved in the development of a premium promotion should insist that all parties enter into a producer agreement. This agreement will provide essential protections that the marketer and the supplier will want when working with one another. From the marketer's perspective, the producer agreement is attractive because it requires the supplier to produce the premium ordered, by a specified date and in the exact quantity required. In addition, the supplier must stand behind its product in the event of a problem. The agreement is attractive to the supplier because it gives it clear specifications with respect to the product ordered and it describes the terms of payment.

A producer agreement should be executed before a purchase order is issued and, if premiums are being specially manufactured, before any product is produced. A well-drafted producer agreement should include the following terms and any others that are appropriate to fully describe the parties' expectations:

1. The marketer agrees to provide the necessary artwork, copy, and sample approvals in the specified form (written is recommended) and by the specified dates.
2. The supplier agrees that the premiums will be produced according to approved samples.
3. The parties specify who will own all trademark, copyright, and patent rights in any original works.
4. The parties specify the quantity of premiums to be delivered.

5. The parties agree on important dates (inspection, production, shipping, and delivery).

6. The supplier agrees to be responsible for compliance with all applicable federal, state, and local laws; industry standards; and other requirements governing the manufacture, shipping, and delivery of the premium. The supplier is typically required, among other things, to submit the premium to safety testing pursuant to regulations issued by the Consumer Product Safety Commission or the Food and Drug Administration, as well as a number of states.

7. The supplier agrees that if it materially fails to live up to the terms of the agreement (for instance, if it does not deliver the product on time, or if it delivers a product on time but it is the wrong product), it will be responsible for the costs of the product, packaging, advertising, and point-of-sale materials that cannot be used; and for the costs of replacing that promotion.

8. The supplier agrees to be responsible for any losses or damage caused by its premium. The marketer, on the other hand, agrees to be responsible for any losses or damage arising out of any acts or omissions on its part.

9. The supplier and marketer agree to obtain insurance to back up their obligations under the agreement.

10. The supplier and marketer agree to maintain the confidentiality of information that either party obtained while working with the other.

11. The marketer agrees to pay the supplier a specific amount for the premiums on a specific date.

12. The parties agree on the terms of any buy-back. For example, must the product be unopened and in original condition?

13. The supplier and marketer should determine whether the same or similar product can be made available to any other entity for a period before, during, and after the promotion.

14. The supplier agrees to actively assist in the resolution of customer, governmental, or other inquiries or complaints.

15. The parties agree whether the supplier may subcontract any of its responsibilities.

16. The parties specify whether the supplier may refer to the purchaser as a client in promotional materials.

17. The purchaser and supplier might want to decide whether the supplier will be given the exclusive right or a right of first refusal to produce the same or a similar premium for a subsequent promotion.

18. The parties specify when the agreement can be terminated. Bankruptcy, failure to perform any obligation, the making of a false or misleading representation or warranty, and "acts of God" beyond the control of either party are typically cited as

reasons to terminate an agreement.

Premiums Bearing Trademarks. If the marketer wants to place its trademark or logo on a premium, the producer agreement should include additional language that:

1. Authorizes the supplier to place the trademark or logo on the premium on behalf of the marketer.
2. Protects the supplier from any claims of trademark infringement.
3. Requires proof that no excess product was produced (which could find its way to the marketplace and dilute the effectiveness of the promotion).
4. Makes it clear that no right or license to use the trademark is being conveyed to the supplier.

Consumer Protection. It should go without saying that a premium must be safe. A creative, motivating, and successful-beyond-your-wildest-dreams premium will become the nightmare explained to the CEO if the premium causes an injury or death.

Many premiums are small, low-cost, high-volume, mass-produced premiums of foreign origin. Sometimes, they are designed just for the promotion in question. The risk of product defects and of safety problems can be higher with such premiums than is the case when off-the-shelf, proven consumer products are used for premiums.

Whatever premium is under consideration, it must meet whatever legal, industry, and internal company safety standards might apply to it. The company must determine — and the supplier must identify — what those standards are.

It is important to know that all elements of the premium must be safe. This means that the item, packaging, and accompanying literature must be safe. For example, some companies insist that their paper packaging be made of special flame-resistant material.

Premiums should be safety-tested during the design and manufacturing process to ensure that they are safe. Marketers should require their suppliers to test their products and warrant that their products are safe. Many suppliers choose to have their premiums tested by independent labs in addition to or in lieu of in-house testing.

Two special categories of premiums merit separate mention:
- Children's premiums
- Quick service restaurant premiums

Children's Premiums. In addition to general considerations regarding the safety of all premium items, there are special rules for premiums intended for children. Premiums intended for children must comply with special safety regulations because children require special protection.

The Consumer Product Safety Commission (CPSC) is one of the principal federal agencies charged with ensuring that consumer products are safe. The CPSC has issued regulations that help marketers and suppliers determine whether their premiums and other products are safe. These regulations define numerous products or items deemed potentially hazardous or unsafe. Examples include items that present mechanical hazards (sharp points, small parts, sharp edges); or electric or thermal hazards; items that contain lead or other toxic substances; items that risk injury through skin or eye irritation or hearing loss; certain projectiles, such as lawn darts; items that are flammable, explosive, or radioactive; and items that may suffocate infants or small children (such as poorly designed cribs and pillows).

The CPSC has special regulations governing toys, which are often applicable to premiums, and these should be checked and complied with.

Toy premiums either must be safe for children of all ages or should be labeled as being appropriate for particular age groups. For example, the regulations require that a toy with small parts must be age-labeled as intended for children ages 3 and older. (The rationale is that children under age 3 are most likely to put small objects in their mouth, nose, and ears and are likely to be injured.) A premium that has sharp points must be labeled as intended for children ages 8 and older. Caution must be exercised here. Labeling a premium as appropriate for a certain age group might not be sufficient if the marketer or supplier has reason to believe that the premium will be made available to or have play value for a younger (more vulnerable) age group.

Advertising of these premiums should include a reference to the appropriate age groups.

Quick Service Restaurant Premiums. In 1983, the CPSC issued a statement of enforcement policy stating that it considered premiums distributed by quick service restaurants to be in a special class. The CPSC stated that because restaurants did not offer a wide array of toy selections as would a retail toy store, and because the parent of a young child at the restaurant would be under a great deal of pressure to give the child a premium even though it might not be safe for that age group, these restaurants would be permitted to distribute only those premiums that are safe for children of all ages or distribute age-graded premiums but also make available an alternative premium that is intended for children of all ages. The alternative premium must be of comparable cost and play value to the age-graded item.

Consumer products is one area of the law, in particular, in which the marketer must not assume the promotion is acceptable to run this year just because it ran last year. The CPSC, in response to newly developed research, is continually updating its standards and enforcement practices. All marketing professionals will want to keep current.

Other Premium Issues.

Country of Origin Labeling. The Federal Trade Commission requires that premiums be labeled with the country of origin. "Made in

Japan" is an example of such labeling.

Art Materials. Certain types of art materials intended for use in the household or for use by children must be reviewed by a toxicologist and then labeled either to (a) state that the product conforms to applicable standards, or (b) include detailed chronic hazard warning information.

Industry Standards. Over the years, a number of industry groups have adopted standards that supplement government regulation. This activity is a notable initiative to self-regulate the activities of the consumer product industry. The following is not an all-inclusive list of groups, but, for example, these bodies have issued guidelines that might affect a promotion:

- American National Standards Institute
- National Bureau of Standards
- American Society of Testing Materials
- Toy Manufacturers Association
- American Association of Textile Chemists & Colorists

In addition to the industry groups that have issued guidelines governing premiums, a number of organizations, including the following, have developed recommendations that affect other segments of the premium industry:

- Children's Advertising Review Unit of the National Advertising Division of the Better Business Bureau
- Direct Marketing Association
- Grocery Manufacturers' of America

In- or On-Pack Premiums. Enclosing or attaching a premium in or on a food, drug, or cosmetic package can be a problem if the premium or its placement affects the product or its package. For example, a product could be deemed misbranded (a) if the placement of the premium obscures information that is required to appear on the label, or (b) if the product's net weight declaration includes the weight of the premium. Similarly, a product could be deemed adulterated if the premium causes the product to become impure. Federal and state food, drug, and cosmetic laws regulate this area.

The lesson here is that premium promotions should not be conducted by amateurs. Know the law, know the suppliers, and know the product.

CONTESTS AND SWEEPSTAKES

Contests and sweepstakes are discussed elsewhere in this work, in Chapter 8, "Sweepstakes, Games, and Contests." Here, we focus more heavily on the legal issues presented by these forms of promotion, which are heavily regulated. Federal, state, and local laws apply. The Federal Trade Commission, Federal Communications Commission, the U.S. Postal Service, state attorneys general, and local district attorneys all may be looking over the company's shoulder.

Fortunately, most of the regulation in this area fits into one of three basic categories: anti-lottery laws, consumer disclosure requirements, and formalities (registration, posting bonds, providing winners lists, retaining records, and the like).

We will discuss the three basic categories of regulation separately. We will then address some special concerns that apply to specific industries and types of promotions. Finally, we review some of the important points to remember about drafting rules for contests and sweepstakes.

Anti-Lottery Laws. Generally speaking, gambling is illegal. This includes lotteries (unless run by a state government). An illegal lottery exists when a person gives "consideration" in the hope of obtaining a "prize" which will be awarded by "chance." Anti-lottery laws must be considered when developing sweepstakes or contests. That is because when all three elements are present in such a promotion — consideration, prize, and chance — there is an illegal lottery. When any one is eliminated, the program generally is legal (though some exceptions may apply).

Consideration. The most common way to avoid a lottery is to eliminate "consideration." "Consideration" means something of value. Usually it means money (such as the purchase price of a product or service or the cost of a 900-number phone call to enter). It also may include a substantial expenditure of time or effort. A promotion generally is not an illegal lottery when the consumer is not *required* to pay money or make a substantial expenditure of time or effort in order to get a chance to win a prize. This is why most contest and sweepstakes copy begins with the words, *no purchase necessary*.

"No purchase necessary" tells consumers that they have a purchase-free alternative way to get a chance to win a prize. The rules of the promotion will explain the alternative method. The alternative method must allow a reasonably comparable chance to win as the primary method of participation. It commonly will involve requesting an entry or game piece by mail.

Although postage stamps cost money, the cost of ordinary postage generally is recognized as an exception to the definition of consideration because it is not a payment to or benefit for the sponsor. This is true under federal and state law. Nebraska, Vermont, and Washington deem *return* postage to be consideration, but currently only Washington appears to enforce its law. Thus, in Washington, a mail-in option cannot require the entrant to include a stamp on a self-addressed return envelope, and some conservative marketers take the same position with respect to Vermont and Nebraska.

Some states also are more strict than others regarding the amount of time and effort they deem to constitute consideration. In general, the marketer can require the consumer to do ordinary things such as watch a television show, fill out an entry form, mail an envelope, make a toll-free phone call, or visit a local store to enter a contest or sweepstakes (though store visit requirements occasionally have been questioned, particularly in Ohio and Michigan). A few states (such as Washington) define precisely which kinds of efforts may be required without amounting to "shoe leather" consideration. Similarly, some states, such as Minnesota, Wisconsin, and Alabama, require sponsors of in-pack or on-pack games to make game cards available locally, so that participants do not have to expend much effort getting them.

A growing number of states now also prohibit requiring a winner to give consideration to *receive* a prize after he or she has already won. These post-consideration laws sometimes can pose problems, especially when a prize consists of a discount coupon for an item, rather than the item itself (occasionally pursued as unlawful in California) or where a person must make a subsequent visit to a location to claim a prize (a problem in Vermont).

So watch out. Plan ahead. Explain all the details of the promotion to a lawyer. A seemingly small detail sometimes can make the difference between a successful promotion and an illegal lottery.

Chance. After consideration, chance is the element most often eliminated to avoid the lottery laws. (The prize element usually cannot be eliminated, since it typically is the key to the promotion.)

Chance is eliminated in a promotion in which everybody "wins" or receives the *same* "prize." Note, however, that chance is not eliminated merely if "everybody wins." There is still an element of chance if it is uncertain which of several prizes a participant might win.

Contests of skill do not involve chance. As a result, most states (though not all) allow consideration to be required to take part in a contest of skill. However, consideration may not be required, even in a skill contest, in Arizona, Florida, Maryland, or Vermont.

To qualify as a contest of skill, winners must be selected *purely* on the basis of skill. Chance cannot play a part in the process. Examples of genuine contests of skill include essay contests, photography contests, puzzle contests, and trivia contests. But be careful. Entries must be judged strictly in accordance with the announced rules, based on objective criteria. Solutions to puzzles and answers to questions must not be so easy that no real "skill" is required. And ties cannot be broken by a random drawing. In short, to avoid the lottery laws as a skill contest, a promotion must completely remove the element of chance.

Disclosure Requirements. In addition to telling the consumer how to take part in a chance promotion without a purchase, what else must be disclosed? And where? We address these two questions separately.

Content of Disclosures. A contest or sweepstakes is an offer to the consumer. Like any offer, it should communicate the essential terms, and it should not be deceptive or misleading. In general, this means disclosing at least the following things: the methods of participating; the deadlines for entries and prize claims; the eligibility requirements; the number and value of prizes; the odds of winning; how to get a copy of the full rules of the promotion, if they are not already included in the offer; and any other information the consumer may need to take part in the promotion.

Some state and federal rules specifically require additional disclosures. Such disclosures may include the geographic area covered by the offer, whether entries must be complete to be eligible, whether winners may have to sign affidavits or releases, whether prizes may be substituted or redeemed for cash, whether participants will be required to listen to or attend a sales promotion (if otherwise legal in a given state), and that taxes on prizes are the winner's responsibility.

Thus, it is important to know where the company's promotion will run. Applicable state laws often vary. The disclosures made generally will be dictated by the law of the strictest state where the promotion appears. This avoids having to keep track of different versions of disclosures for different states. A company may voluntarily make additional disclosures to communicate special provisions in the promotion rules. (See the discussion of rules below.)

Location of Disclosures. Disclosures should appear where consumers are likely to see them. This protects the consumer. It also protects the company. Whenever possible, therefore, the full terms of the offer should appear in close connection with the consumer's opportunity to participate in the contest or sweepstakes — for example, on the back of the game card in a scratch-and-win game, on an in-store poster in a match-and-win game, and on the outside of specially marked packages in an in-pack game.

Advertisements can be trickier. The consumers may not yet be in a position to participate in the promotion when they see the advertisement. (Perhaps a store visit is required.) So what kind of disclosure is appropriate? State laws vary widely on this question.

A few states, notably New York and Florida, require a sponsor to publish the full rules and regulations of a promotion "in all advertising copy." This requirement applies whenever the total prize pool is worth $5,000 or more. These states further require that the full rules be posted conspicuously in every retail location where the promotion is offered. These are the strictest disclosure requirements in the nation. Although, at the time of printing, these requirements are neither rigorously enforced nor complied with, it is obvious when a sponsor fails to comply with them. As a result, many sponsors publish full contest and sweepstakes rules in all their national print advertisements. In fact, some sponsors publish the full rules in any situation in which they give a consumer an opportunity to participate directly in the promotion (for example, instant-win games) because the rules are the full contract with the consumer. Those sponsors regard it as important for the consumer to have the full rules in hand at the time of participation.

If the company's promotion is not running in New York or Florida, check the particular states where it appears in order to make sure all the necessary disclosures are included. As a general rule, the more that is disclosed, the better, because there will be less opportunity for confusion or mistake.

Finally, broadcast ads generally are treated differently from print advertising. Legal authorities recognize that air time is limited. They usually allow minimal disclosures on-air, provided that the sponsor informs the consumer where to find the full details on the contest or sweepstakes. The major television networks have published guidelines that specify standard minimum disclosures. Individual promotions, however, may require additional disclosures to explain any unusual features to the consumer.

Procedural Requirements. In addition to anti-lottery laws and disclosure requirements, some state and federal agencies require sponsors to observe certain procedures. In New York and Florida, for example, a chance promotion with total prizes worth more than $5,000 must be registered with the state. Further, the sponsor must post a bond or establish an escrow equal to the value of the prizes, and winners' lists must be provided to the state to release the bonds. In Rhode Island, a chance promotion sponsored by a retail establishment must be registered if the prize pool is worth more than $500.

In the gasoline and food retailing industries, federal regulations require that game pieces be mixed and distributed on a completely random basis; that a game may not end prior to distribution of all game pieces, regardless of the scheduled termination date; that there be a certain period of time between promotions at the same establishment; and that the sponsor retain records relating to the game for a specified period of time.

The above procedures are not a complete list. They illustrate only a few common types of requirements a sponsor may need to know about. The actual formalities required in a particular promotion will vary depending on where the promotion runs, the type of promotion, and the industry and products involved.

Regulated Industries and Chance Promotions — Special Issues. Alcohol and tobacco are heavily regulated. Thus, it is not surprising that contests and sweepstakes in these industries also are regulated. For example, federal law prohibits in-pack chance promotions for cigarettes. And some states (currently Massachusetts, Michigan, and for retail games, Virginia) do not permit the use of chance promotions in connection with cigarettes.

Other regulated industries are not as obvious. Dairy is a good example. Several states restrict chance promotions in connection with dairy products. Some restrictions apply only to milk. Others apply to a wider array of dairy products. Gasoline stations and grocery stores are other examples. Several states prohibit chance promotions altogether in connection with retail gasoline sales. Others, like Washington, severely restrict the ability of retail grocers to conduct chance promotions. Analyzing these laws can become complicated where a convenience food store and a gasoline station are attached to each other. It becomes even more complicated if the convenience store has a license to sell beer or wine, which may trigger additional alcohol control regulations.

The key here is to make sure that the company (and its lawyer) know exactly where the promotion is planned to run. What works for soft drinks may fizzle for milk. And what drives sales at a department store may be forbidden at the corner gas station.

Special Types of Chance Promotions. The format of a promotion may trigger special legal concerns. Some states, for example, prohibit anyone other than a licensed charity from conducting "bingo" games or promotions that resemble "bingo," regardless of whether consumers can play for free!

In-pack chance promotions also trigger special rules. For example, Wisconsin and Minnesota require the sponsor to make free game pieces available for in-store distribution upon request from retailers. In Alabama, a soft drink bottler was required by a state court to make free bottle caps available in-store in its bottle cap promotion, regardless of whether the retailers had or had not requested them.

Pay-per-call or "900-number (and 976-number)" promotions are also becoming heavily regulated. The legal landscape regarding these promotions is changing rapidly. The change is occurring in part through new laws and regulations (both federal and state) and in part through interpretation of laws already on the books. So far, most states appear content to treat 900-number chance promotions like other promotions — that is, 900-number promotions are legal so long as they offer a free alternative means of participation, and the proper disclosures and formalities are observed. The FTC and other states, however, require special and extensive disclosures and formalities for 900-number promotions. And a handful have suggested (though not yet definitively) that 900 number chance promotions may constitute illegal lotteries, even when an alternative means of entry is provided. Until the law in this new area stabilizes, the smart marketer should approach 900-number contests or sweepstakes with caution.

Contest and Sweepstakes Rules. Contest and sweepstakes rules are contracts. The sponsor offers a prize on certain terms and conditions. If the consumer complies and the terms and conditions are met, the sponsor is bound to award the prize.

The sponsor therefore wants the rules to be clear and complete. Although every promotion requires certain tailor-made rules, a good set of rules generally will cover at least the following points:

1. **No purchase necessary.** Explain the ways and places a consumer can participate, including deadlines, limits on number of entries, and other rules.

2. **How to play.** Tell the consumer how to participate.

3. **How to claim a prize.** Instruct the consumer exactly how to submit a claim, including deadlines.

4. **Validations.** Inform the consumer that the judging organization's decisions are final; that materials are void if they contain errors or are forged, incomplete, duplicated, or tampered with; that the consumer may have to sign an affidavit and release; that entries will not be returned; and that the sponsor is not responsible for late, lost, or stolen mail.

5. **Eligibility.** Define who is eligible and who is not. Age, residence, and affiliation with the sponsor commonly determine eligibility.

6. **Prizes.** Describe the prizes precisely to avoid disputes. Disclose the retail value and the odds of winning each prize. Inform the consumer of any restrictions or limitations, such as travel date restrictions for trips, when prizes will be delivered, and whether they may be substituted or transferred.

7. **Winners' list.** Tell the consumer how to get a copy.

A good example of a thorough set of rules is shown below:

McDonald's® Match Three Game Official Rules

1. NO PURCHASE NECESSARY. MUST BE 16 OR OLDER TO PLAY. Beginning April 10, 1992, get one McDonald's Match Three game card, per visit, while supplies last, at any participating McDonald's in the states of Minnesota, Wisconsin, Iowa, South Dakota, North Dakota, Northwest Michigan, West Central and Northern Illinois, Northeast Nebraska and Eastern Montana. Michigan residents only will receive one game card while supplies last, by mailing a self-addressed, stamped envelope accompanied by a single signed handwritten request to McDonald's Match Three Game, Game Card Request, P. O. Box 700, Beverly Hills, CA 90213-0700. All written requests must be received by May 7, 1992. All visits to the same McDonald's within a two-hour period constitute a single visit. One prize per card redeemable per person on future visit.

2. HOW TO PLAY: Carefully open perforated doors on the front of the game card. Match three identical symbols exactly in a row across on the same card and win the prize indicated (subject to verification). Prizes available are listed in the Odds Chart.

TO VERIFY AND REDEEM OFFICIAL GAME CARDS FOR PRIZES OF $50 CASH OR MORE. Sign full legal signature in ink across the face of the official game card. Then, request from the manager of any participating McDonald's a pre-addressed redemption envelope. Legibly print or type all of the information requested on the envelope. Then insert official game card and send it to the Redemption Center via REGISTERED OR CERTIFIED MAIL, for official verification and award of your prize. **McDONALD'S RESTAURANT PERSONNEL CANNOT VERIFY OR REDEEM GAME CARDS FOR PRIZES VALUED AT $50 OR MORE.** MANAGER'S SIGNATURE ON THE REDEMPTION ENVELOPE DOES NOT MEAN THAT THE GAME CARD HAS BEEN VERIFIED AS A WINNER.

TO VERIFY AND REDEEM OFFICIAL GAME CARDS FOR PRIZES OF $2 CASH, $5 CASH, OR FOOD PRIZES. Sign full legal signature in ink across the face of the official game card. Note: It is not necessary to sign official game cards for food prizes. Any participating McDonald's will redeem $2 Cash, $5 Cash, and food prizes upon presentation and verification, but only on a *future visit*, and only during the hours that the food product is served. Not valid in combination with any other offer. Only one prize redeemable per eligible person per visit. Official game cards must be presented for redemption before placing order. No substitution for food prizes will be allowed, but McDonald's reserves the right to substitute a food product of equal or greater retail value for food prizes.

DO NOT SHOW OR GIVE ANY POTENTIAL WINNING GAME CARD FOR PRIZES OTHER THAN $2 CASH, $5 CASH, OR FOOD PRIZES TO ANY McDONALD'S EMPLOYEE.

3. REDEMPTION OF PRIZES: A participant may win more than one prize, but you are not a winner of any prize until your official game card has been verified at a participating McDonald's or the Redemption Center, whichever is applicable, and until you have complied with all the terms of these Official Rules.

4. CONDITIONS OF PARTICIPATION: The submission of official game materials is solely the responsibility of the participant. Participant assumes all risk of loss, damage, destruction, delay, and misdirection of game materials and is advised to obtain postal insurance, where appropriate. **Protect potential winning Official Game Cards.** Game materials submitted become the property of McDonald's and will not be returned. Prizes and Official Game Cards may not be assigned or transferred prior to award. By participating, participant agrees to abide by and be bound by these Official Rules and decision of judges which are final and binding in all respects. Participant waives the right to assert as a cost of winning any prize, any and all costs of verification and redemption or travel to redeem said prize and any liability which might arise from redeeming or seeking to redeem said prize. Prizewinners may be required to sign an affidavit of eligibility and release and any applicable forms required by tax authorities and will be responsible for all applicable taxes on prizes. No cash substitution will be made for any food prize. Prizes will be awarded only if participants comply with these Official Rules. *By participating and redeeming a prize, winner releases McDonald's Corporation, its franchisees, affiliates, and subsidiaries and respective directors, officers, employees, and their agents, including advertising and promotion agencies, from any and all liability with respect to any prize.* By accepting a prize, prizewinner agrees to the use of his/her name, address (city and state) and/or photograph, videotape, or any likeness for advertising or publicity purposes and to the use of statements made by or attributed to prizewinner relating to McDonald's and any and all rights to said use without further compensation. McDonald's reserves the right to suspend or terminate the game for one or more days should production, seeding, printing, or other errors cause more than the stated number of prizes in each category to be available and/or claimed. In such event, not yet awarded prizes will be awarded in a random drawing from all prize claimants in the category. It is your responsibility to ensure that you have complied with all of the conditions contained in the Official Rules. Promotion void in whole or part where prohibited by law.

5. ELIGIBILITY: Participation is open only to persons 16 years or older who are legal residents of the United States of America. Persons in any of the following categories are NOT eligible to participate or win prizes: (a) persons who from and after November 1, 1991, were or are employees or agents of McDonald's Corporation, their subsidiaries, or their franchisees; employees or agents of service agencies or independent contractors of any of the above organizations; (b) individuals engaged in the development, production, or distribution of materials for this game; (c) persons who are immediate family of, i.e., mother, father, sister, brother, daughter, son, or spouse, regardless of where they live, or who reside in the same household, whether related or not, as any person in any of the preceding categories.

6. VERIFICATION: All game materials are subject to verification at a participating McDonald's or the Redemption Center, whichever is applicable. Official game materials are null and void and will be rejected if not obtained through authorized, legitimate channels, or if they are from other games, and may be rejected if any part is counterfeited, illegible, mutilated, or tampered with in any way (except for the legal signature of the potential winner) or if they contain printing, typographical, mechanical, or other errors. All decisions of the Redemption Center are final, binding, and conclusive in all matters. IMPORTANT: ANY ATTEMPT TO FORGE GAME MATERIALS OR TO DEFRAUD IN ANY WAY IN CONNECTION WITH THIS GAME WILL BE PROSECUTED TO THE FULLEST EXTENT OF THE LAW.

7. GAME SCHEDULE AND AWARD OF PRIZES: The game will begin on April 10, 1992, and is scheduled to end on May 7, 1992. Regardless of the scheduled end date, the game will officially end when all game cards have been distributed. Some participating McDonald's may complete distribution of their supply of game cards before others, but the game will continue until all other participating McDonald's have distributed their supply of game cards. Therefore, as the game progresses, game cards may be available at some McDonald's but not at others. Although these McDonald's are no longer distributing game cards, they will continue to distribute redemption materials and redeem food prizes in accordance with these Official Rules. All game cards must be received for verification by a participating McDonald's or the Redemption Center, whichever is applicable, on or before May 22, 1992, or no more than 15 days after all game cards have been distributed, whichever is later. All official game cards received after this date are null and void and will be ineligible for prizes. Major prizes won by minors or other persons who have an appointed legal representative may be awarded in the name of that individual's parent or legal guardian in trust for the minor. Prizewinners will be notified by mail within 15 days of official verification, or as soon thereafter as is reasonably possible. Unawarded or unclaimed prizes shall not be awarded.

8. LIST OF PRIZEWINNERS: For a list of major prizewinners, mail a self-addressed stamped envelope, accompanied by a signed handwritten request to:

McDonald's Match Three Game
Winners List P.O. Box 700
Beverly Hills, CA 90213-0700

All requests must be received between May 22, 1992, and June 30, 1992.

© 1992 McDonald's Corporation
ALL RIGHTS RESERVED
NO PURCHASE NECESSARY
PRINTED IN THE UNITED STATES OF AMERICA

PRODUCT LICENSING AND TIE-INS

Product licensing and tie-ins typically involve the use by one company of another company's trademarks and service marks. In the product licensing situation, the owner of a trademark will authorize another company to use one or more of its marks on the product of that company. In the tie-in situation, two companies use each other's trademarks in a joint marketing effort.

It is a basic tenet of trademark law that the trademark owner must control the use by others of its marks or risk losing them to the public domain. The trademark owner will want to negotiate a number of terms in the trademark license agreement, including the following:

- Identity of the trademarks being licensed
- Description of the products on which the trademarks may be placed
- Geographic area where the products can be distributed
- Period of time in which distribution can occur
- The method of distribution (if retail, which retailers), and any methods of distribution that may not be used (for example, some trademark owners will not let their marks be used on premium or tie-in items)
- Disposition of products after the specified distribution period (transferred to trademark owner, destroyed, or sold during an authorized sell-off period)
- Documentation required by trademark owner to substantiate the number of products which will bear the trademark
- The amount of the royalty and the basis upon which it will be calculated (based on number of products manufactured, sold to a distributor, or sold to consumers)
- The quality standards the trademark owner will require and the approval rights the trademark owner will retain over product samples, packaging, and production
- Whether the licensee will indemnify, insure, and hold the trademark owner harmless from any loss arising out of a product liability or other claim
- The form of trademark notices the owner will require to be placed on products and labeling

The licensee that is authorized to use the marks will, of course, be interested in the above terms and will have a list of its own:

- Whether the licensee will be the exclusive licensee during the specified period
- Whether the trademark owner will indemnify and hold the licensee harmless from any losses arising out of a claim of trademark infringement
- Whether the trademark owner or the licensee will be responsible for handling and resolving consumer inquiries or complaints

CONTINUITY PROMOTIONS

Continuity promotions take many forms — for example "frequent flier" programs, "frequent purchaser" credit card programs, and "collect and win" games. Since these promotions ask the consumer to make repeated transactions to receive a benefit, it is particularly important that the terms of the offer be developed carefully and communicated clearly. Also, since many of these promotions involve tie-ins among multiple sponsors (for example, earning airline "miles" for staying at particular hotels), it is important that the contracts among the sponsors clearly specify the rights and obligations of each party. If the promotion involves chance, the company may need to update certain disclosures — especially the odds of winning — during the promotion.

RETAIL ADVERTISING AND FEATURING

Retail advertising and featuring is an area that has enjoyed a surge of attention on the part of marketers who wish to target the ultimate consumer, to take advantage of increasingly sophisticated databases with consumer information, or to respond to the increasing power of retailers (who have the most direct access to the consumer and to such data). Retail advertising and featuring is no different from other types of advertising with respect to requirements that such advertising and featuring not be false or misleading, or infringe upon the trademarks, trade names, copyrights, publicity and privacy rights, and other rights of third parties. In addition, to the extent it is paid for or provided by the manufacturer or distributor, retail advertising and featuring must comply with the requirements of other types of trade promotions governed by the Robinson-Patman Act; and the agreement between the manufacturer and in-store media must be clear regarding which party will be responsible for compliance, which will be discussed later. Also, the state and federal laws governing heavily regulated products such as alcohol and tobacco frequently have specific provisions on the nature of in-store advertising that may be undertaken. For example, otherwise permissible in-store liquor ads may not be allowed in some states if they are on shopping carts that can migrate outside the store. Similarly, treatment of in-store video ads for tobacco products may or may not violate advertising restraints, depending on whether they are fed from outside or inside the premises.

Finally, some of the more advanced forms of retail advertising and featuring raise special issues that would need to be addressed in any arrangement between a retailer and a manufacturer or distributor. For example, with respect to in-store media — such as video shopping carts, in-store radio, in-store demonstrators, automatic coupon dispensers, and in-store product sampling — the parties providing for such activities should agree in writing on issues such as who owns any in-store equipment and any software that operates it; who maintains it; who has liability for its failure or for injuries caused by it; who pays for the activity; who is responsible for printing, shipping, and securing coupons or product samples, and returning them (or destroying excess coupons) after the promotion is finished; and, if there are persons supplied to demonstrate or distribute products, coupons, or advertisements in the store, who is responsible for hiring, monitoring, paying, controlling, and otherwise managing such persons.

SAMPLING

We have referred in the previous section to sampling as one method of retail advertising and featuring. Indeed, as indicated in Chapter 5,

"Sampling," sampling has grown steadily as a promotion technique. What are the legal issues that arise in connection with sampling?

The most prominent legal considerations are contractual. To be certain that a sampling program runs properly, the parties involved should rely on the process of negotiating and executing contracts to identify the key tasks to be performed, allocate responsibility for their performance, and spell out who's accountable if they are not properly performed.

The points to cover are identified in some detail in Chapter 5, and include the specific responsibilities of samplers or demonstrators and their supervisors; procedures to be followed in the setting up, conduct, breakdown, and cleanup of sampling operations; exclusivity of the sampling service; training of samplers in the product and its preparation, presentation, and key attributes; responsibility for equipment and supplies; availability of adequate stock to support increased purchases stimulated by the sampling; responsibility for the security of coupons, if any are included in the program; prechecking retail outlets to be sure they are ready for the program; data gathering and reporting during and after the program; handling of consumer complaints, questions, and claims; provision of appropriate insurance by the sampling service and retail outlet; proper documentation of performance and expenses by the sampling service; securing the right to conduct a sampling program on premises or locations not owned by the manufacturer; fees to be paid, when, and how; and the timing of all critical elements of the program.

Depending on the product, sampling by mail or in person can raise additional legal issues. Some federal and state laws prohibit the unsolicited leaving behind, or delivery by mail, of certain products such as intoxicating liquors, drugs, or other products that could harm children, certain fragrances, and contraceptives. Even where laws do not explicitly prohibit unsolicited sampling, the nature of a product or its packaging may make it inappropriately risky to sample by mail, or by hand delivery if the sample is not delivered in person but is left behind. Examples are aerosol, flammable, breakable, or perishable items, or products such as tobacco products that may not lawfully be delivered to persons under a certain age.

DIRECT RESPONSE MARKETING

Special rules apply to direct response marketing, above and beyond the general laws governing advertising. The most important of them are summarized below.

FTC Mail Order Rule. Mail-order sellers must ship merchandise within the time stated in the solicitation. If no time is stated, they must ship within 30 days of receipt of a properly completed order. They must notify the consumer of any delay and provide the option to cancel and a cost-free means to do so (for example, business reply mail or

800-number). Special rules apply when the delay will exceed 30 days. Created in 1975, the rule applies to merchandise ordered through the mails and by telephone. The rule has been applied to an on-pack premium offer that wasn't shipped on time, leading to a substantial fine against the marketer. Exemptions apply to magazine subscriptions (after the first shipment), sales of seeds and growing plants, photo-film, COD sales, and transactions covered by the Federal Trade Commission "Negative Option Rule" (discussed below).

FTC Negative Option Rule. Commonly used by book and record clubs, a "negative option plan" involves an announcement to a subscriber that she will receive a particular item (and be billed for it) unless she returns timely notice to the seller *not* to ship. A negative option plan cannot be used unless the consumer affirmatively agrees in advance to participate. The initial solicitation must clearly and conspicuously disclose all the material terms. Subscribers must be given at least 10 days to respond to announcements. Penalties for violating the rule can range as high as $10,000 per violation.

Unordered Merchandise. Except for free samples *clearly and conspicuously marked as such*, federal law prohibits a seller from shipping unordered merchandise. The recipient is entitled to treat unordered merchandise as a gift and to keep it without obligation to the sender.

FCC Telemarketing Restrictions. The Telephone Consumer Protection Act of 1991 and Federal Communications Commission (FCC) Regulations prohibit using automatic dialers or artificial or prerecorded voices to call any emergency telephone line, health care facility, or any phone for which the party called is charged (for example, cellular phones). They also prohibit sending unsolicited advertisements by facsimile machine, as well as using automatic dialing systems to tie up two or more lines of a multiline phone system simultaneously.

Residential telephones cannot be called by businesses before 8:00 a.m. or after 9:00 p.m., unless the caller: (1) has the express permission or invitation of the person being called; (2) has an established business relationship with that person; or (3) is a tax-exempt organization. In addition, any business making nonexempt calls must maintain a list of persons who do not wish to receive telephone solicitations from that business. The FCC Regulations specify procedures for creating and maintaining these "do not call" lists.

EVENT MARKETING

Sponsorship of events — such as sports, theater, or concerts — can be extremely effective. And it can be extremely complicated. One key to effective sponsorship is the contract. It identifies the parties (there often are more than two) and their respective rights and responsibilities.

The Parties. A potential sponsor needs to know who controls the various aspects of an event. In a concert tour, for example, the artist and his or her management may control what happens on stage, but national and/or local promoters often control the choice of venue, placement of advertising, sales of merchandise, and concessions. For major sports events, the broadcaster, producer, or syndicator may control the commercial time. This may be more important to the sponsor than the event itself. Frequently, a sponsorship opportunity is presented to the marketer by a packager who offers to take responsibility for assembling the necessary parties and serve as a kind of general contractor for the promotion. Whatever the situation, understanding who the parties are and clarifying what each will be required to deliver is essential.

Rights and Responsibilities. Once the parties are identified, it is important to define their respective rights and responsibilities. These will vary from event to event. Certain provisions, however, will be important in most situations. These include the following:

- *Liability insurance.* The presenter needs adequate coverage. The sponsor wants to be indemnified and held harmless. If consumers are invited to attend/participate, and risky or dangerous activities are involved, they should sign releases.
- *Cancellation protection.* Provide for a refund or other remedy if the event fails to take place.
- *Advertising time/space.* Specify how much will be delivered, by whom, and at what cost.
- *Concessions.* Make clear who controls sales of food, T-shirts, and other merchandise. Quality control, choice of brands, profit sharing, and exclusivity must be addressed.
- *Trademarks.* The sponsor should retain control and approval over how its trademarks are used.
- *Logistics.* Be sure the event presenter can deliver everything he promises.
- *Exclusivity.* If sponsorship exclusivity is important (either complete or by product category) think about whether it can be enforced against "ambushers." Sometimes it can't. For example, if a contract is with a sports producer, the television network covering the event may be selling time around the event to the company's competition.

The above list only touches a few highlights. If you are considering special event marketing, take the time to draft a thorough contract. It can save a lot of headaches later.

SPECIAL PROMOTIONS

What do live animals, gasoline, and alcohol have in common? These, along with several other types of premiums and promotions, are the subject of regulations that vary by state.

Live Animals. Many states prohibit the use of live animals as premiums. In California, for instance, it is unlawful to offer live chicks, rabbits, ducklings, or other fowl as inducements to enter a contest or a business establishment. Illinois prohibits the use of chicks and ducklings as novelty items. Chicks and other fowl cannot be dyed.

Gasoline. Some states (for example, New Jersey and Rhode Island) prohibit giving free or discounted motor fuel as a premium for the purchase of any product. They further prohibit giving *any* premiums in connection with the sale of motor fuel. State law restrictions in Maryland, Massachusetts, Nevada, New Hampshire, New Jersey, and Virginia prohibit chance promotions by motor fuel sellers; and numerous states indirectly regulate promotions through laws prohibiting below-cost sales of gasoline.

Alcohol and Tobacco. Because of the nature of these products, promotional activity in this area is heavily regulated by federal and state law, making it difficult to conduct a national promotion. Generally, these products cannot be given as premiums, and they cannot be promoted to children. Television advertising is either prohibited (cigarettes and liquor) or closely regulated (beer and wine). Chance promotions and below-cost sales often are prohibited. Manufacturers and importers of alcoholic beverages are severely limited in the types of promotional services and allowances they may provide to retailers.

Banking. Banks are subject to various regulations, depending on the type of bank (such as commercial or savings and loan) and whether the bank is federal or state-chartered. California, for example, restricts the value of premiums state banks may give away. It also prohibits charging customers for any part of the cost of the premium. Idaho limits not only the value but also the number of premiums that may be given per account within a 12-month period. Federal regulations impose strict limits on give-aways by federal savings associations, but only where state law imposes similar restrictions on state banks.

Real Estate Sales and Time-Share. Widespread abuse has led to widespread regulation in this area. Many state laws require specific disclosures, including the actual market value of any premiums offered; the method of selecting "winners"; the odds of receiving any particular prize or gift; the actual number of premiums available; and all rules, terms, requirements, and conditions that must be fulfilled to receive the premium, including whether the consumer must attend a sales presentation. Some states go so far as to prescribe the type size of such disclosures and require them to be made on the first page of any solicitation.

Dairy. Almost 20 states restrict promotion of dairy products. Most are aimed at prohibiting below-cost sales. They typically restrict free offers, rebates, cents-off coupons, or discounts that reduce the price the consumer pays for dairy products. Some prohibit promotions of any kind for such products. Some states apply their laws to all dairy products; others only to fluid milk.

Furs and Fibers. Federal laws impose strict disclosure and labeling requirements for fur and textile products. A fur product is "misbranded" (an unfair trade practice) unless it bears a label showing, among other things, the names of the animals that produced the fur; the manufacturer; the seller, transporter, or distributor; the country of origin (if not the U.S.); and whether the product contains bleached, dyed, or artificially colored fur. Clothing and other household textile products must be labeled with similar types of information, including a listing of the percentage of each constituent fiber in the product.

Stock. An offer to give a share of stock as a premium with the purchase of a product can be deemed to be subject to rigorous and costly registration and disclosure requirements under federal and state securities laws. Although some requirements might be avoided by offering to give away securities issued by third parties and purchased by the sponsor in the open market (as distinguished from stock in the sponsor's own company), this is a highly sensitive area and rarely worth the risk or expense.

Plush Toys. A number of states have enacted laws that require safety testing, product labeling, recordkeeping, and periodic filings with the state in connection with the distribution of plush toys in those states.

TRADE PROMOTIONS

Trade Allowances. To help promote resale of its products, a manufacturer sometimes pays a retailer to provide promotional services or facilities (such as advertising or in-store displays). Or the manufacturer might provide promotional materials directly to the retailer at no charge. Under the Robinson-Patman Act, such payments and materials are legal, provided the manufacturer informs all competing customers of the availability of its promotional services and allowances and makes them available to all competing retailers and dealers on proportionally equal terms. Otherwise, the manufacturer risks violating the antitrust laws. This rule is an extension of the antitrust prohibition against charging competing resellers different prices for the same product.

Co-op Advertising. Co-op programs are subject to the same requirements under the Robinson-Patman Act as other trade allowances — that is, they must be made available to competing customers on proportionally equal terms. A recurring question is whether the manufacturer can discourage discounting of its products by requiring retailers to publish the manufacturer's suggested retail price in co-op ads. The courts have said no. It is a per se violation of the antitrust laws to require a retailer to resell at a price agreed upon with the manufacturer. However, a few courts have held that, where the manufacturer pays for the ad (in whole or in part), it can require a discounting retailer to exclude all prices from the ad. Since this area of the law is still developing, it would be wise to seek legal advice prior to imposing restrictions on retailers' price advertisements.

Sweepstakes/Prizes. With minor exceptions, all the usual rules governing sweepstakes and prizes apply in the trade context. In addition, the sponsor must avoid inducing its customers' employees to push the manufacturer's products without the knowledge and consent of their employers. The sponsor should take steps to assure that the employer is aware of any offer directed toward the salespeople, should state expressly that prizes are awarded subject to the winner's company policy regarding acceptance of prizes, and should abide by such policies.

Slotting Allowances. Manufacturers sometimes pay retailers to gain access to the retailers' shelves for new products or to gain preferential shelf space for existing products. Such payments are called "slotting allowances." Both types of slotting allowances are common, but both have been attacked as antitrust violations by manufacturers who claim to be denied access to retail outlets when they cannot afford the payments and by retailers who allege they are disadvantaged if they do not receive the same amounts paid to their competitors. In addition, some state legislatures have recently considered passing laws prohibiting the payment of slotting allowances altogether. The question of whether slotting allowances do or don't comply with applicable laws is highly dependent on the facts of the particular situation. Therefore, the smart marketer will seek legal advice before agreeing to pay slotting allowances.

Tied-House Laws. With very limited exceptions, manufacturers and importers of alcoholic beverages engaged in interstate commerce are prohibited from providing promotional services or allowances of any kind to resellers. These "tied-house" restrictions are intended to prevent the manufacturers and importers from controlling bars, restaurants, and package stores. While viewed by many as unnecessary, these laws remain in effect and are enforced by the federal government. Many states have similar laws.

CHARITABLE PROMOTIONS

Supporting a charitable cause is a powerful marketing tool. It also is regulated. Charities generally must register in states where they seek to raise money; so must paid solicitors, in more than 40 states. In approximately a dozen states, "commercial coventurers" also must comply with certain regulations. A "commercial coventurer" is a person or company who offers goods or services based on a representation that the purchase thereof will benefit a charity or a charitable purpose. The regulatory requirements may include having a written contract between the manufacturer and the charity, including certain required terms in the contract, filing a copy of the contract (or at least the key financial terms) with the state, making certain disclosures to consumers in all advertising, and registering and obtaining a bond.

The Philanthropic Advisory Service of the Council of the Better Business Bureau has published standards for charity–business promotions. These standards deal with many of the same issues addressed by state laws. From the consumer's perspective, the most important standards deal with disclosure. For example, where the benefit to the charity depends on the volume of sales made, the amount of the benefit should be clearly disclosed, either as a dollar amount or a percentage of what the consumer pays in each transaction. If there is a cap, that should also be disclosed. If a "flat" amount will be donated regardless of sales, that fact should be disclosed, and the ads should not imply that the consumer's purchase of the goods and/or services will affect the amount the charity receives.

900-NUMBER PROMOTIONS

Pay-per-call or "900-number (and the local 976-number)" promotions are controversial. Viewed by marketers as a major breakthrough in interactive marketing possibilities, they are under attack by many consumer protection groups and legislative bodies. The FCC and FTC have issued special rules governing these promotions. Most of the legislative action concerns disclosures.

Advertisements must tell the consumer how much the call will cost. This may be a fixed amount or an amount per minute. Either way, it must be clear. Some state laws require this disclosure to be stated *each* time the phone number is given and in the same size type. On television, it may have to be spoken as well as shown on the screen. Other required disclosures may include that the caller must be 18 or older.

Each call to the 900-number must begin with a "preamble." Generally about 10 seconds long, the "preamble" must inform consumers of the name of the service they have reached, the cost of the call, and that they have the option to hang up before the program begins in order to avoid being charged for the call.

The use of 900-numbers for chance promotions is the most regulated part of the "900" area and has already been discussed.

RIGHTS OF PUBLICITY/UNFAIR
COMPETITION/TRADEMARKS/COPYRIGHTS

Promotion sponsors often hope to attract attention through the use of well-known images, names, or personalities. This is a great way to boost the effectiveness of a promotion, but it is risky business if the sponsor doesn't have the necessary permission.

One potential problem may arise when a manufacturer's promotion offers the product of *another* manufacturer as a premium, without entering into an agreement with the second manufacturer. For example, a camera company might offer the film of a well-known manufacturer with the purchase of every camera. The offer itself is legally permissible. A problem may arise, however, if the camera company features the film manufacturer's name and/or logo so prominently in the promotion that it suggests an endorsement or cosponsorship that does not exist. If consumers are likely to assume such a connection, the film manufacturer may have a claim for trademark infringement. To avoid the problem, the camera company should consider either de-emphasizing (and thereby diluting) the impact of the film manufacturer's name or logo or getting a license agreement with the film manufacturer. Including a disclaimer in the ad is helpful but will not by itself carry much weight if the ad is otherwise likely to cause confusion.

A similar problem arises with celebrities. *Any* unauthorized use of a live or deceased celebrity's name or likeness is likely to infringe on the celebrity's rights. Indeed, in some recent cases, the use of sound-alikes and look-alikes to imitate certain celebrities (for example, Bette Midler and Woody Allen) and even non-look-alike parodies (Vanna White) has been found to infringe on their rights of publicity. In short, it is very risky to use names or likenesses without permission.

A less obvious area of concern involves giving tickets to events as prizes or premiums. This time-honored practice has recently come under attack from event sponsors. They feel it is a form of "ambush" marketing in which the giver of the tickets tries to pass himself off as a sponsor of the event without paying to be a sponsor. Some event sponsors, notably the NCAA, have started to print restrictions directly on their tickets stating that they may not be used as prizes without the NCAA's express permission. While the enforceability of such a restriction is questionable (at least where the give-away promotion does not otherwise create a likelihood of confusion regarding sponsorship), more and more event sponsors are moving in this direction.

In sum, the owners of well-known names, images, and events are becoming keenly aware of their rights, and they are policing them more vigilantly than ever. The marketer will need to analyze the risks carefully before using or suggesting another person's product, image, or mark in connection with a promotion.

Finally, the review of any promotion should include proper attention to basic trademark and copyright issues. Trademark considerations have been referred to in this section and elsewhere in this chapter, for example, in the discussion of licensing and tie-ins.

In addition, however, the creators of a promotion must be sure that the name of their promotion and any other catchy taglines or phrases are not the trademarks of some other party. Trademark searches should be conducted, either by in-house or outside counsel. The use of other persons' trademarks should be made with caution and, depending on the circumstances, only with their owners' permission.

Similarly, the creators of a promotion must be mindful of copyright law, which protects original works of all kinds that are fixed in tangible form. This is rarely an issue, since promotions are usually created afresh for a particular purpose. Nonetheless, if the creators of a promotion wish to use artwork, copy, illustrations, photographs, music, film clips or stills, or any other creation of another person, the law of copyright may prohibit that use without the permission of the creator or owner. This is an area in which involving a promotion lawyer early in the planning can avoid significant problems later on.

CONCLUSION

In this chapter we have addressed in general terms a wide variety of legal issues that arise in the sales promotion field. Rules and regulations in this field derive from legislative efforts to protect consumers. Almost every aspect of sales promotion raises at least some legal considerations, although some areas are more heavily regulated than others, such as sweepstakes and games of chance.

Therefore, it is important for the sales promotion professional to be mindful of the legal implications of a proposed promotion. Since the laws in this area are complicated and numerous, and since new laws and regulations are frequently implemented and legal enforcement policies occasionally change, it is wise to involve a promotion marketing lawyer at the outset. All of the details of the proposed promotion should be shared with the lawyer, so that he or she can offer the most helpful input possible. When in doubt, it is safest, most defensible, and fairest to do what is best for the consumer.

FOOTNOTES

1. A useful and more complete source of information on promotion laws and regulations is *Promotion Marketing Law* (1993 Revision) by Frank T. Dierson, Esq., General Counsel to the Promotion Marketing Association of America (PMAA). The book is updated periodically and is available to PMAA members.

Alan Rosenthal is an Evanston, Illinois-based editor and author of books and articles on marketing, technology, and other aspects of business. His work has appeared in publications such as Forbes, Advertising Age, Business Marketing, Consumers Digest, Chicago Tribune, *and* Crain's Chicago Business. *In the past, he has served as editor of magazines such as* Crain's Illinois Business *and* Success *and* Online Access, *a magazine devoted to on-line computer services.*

The author wishes to acknowledge the following sources who provided background information for this chapter: Robert Horton, president, Horton Berman Communications, New York, New York; Fred Schneider, executive director, Smart Store, Andersen Consulting, Chicago, Illinois; Sandy Goldman, president, ShopperVision Inc., Norcross, Georgia; Kenneth Dulaney, vice president, Gartner Group, Stamford, Connecticut; Noel Ilberg, president, MicroMarketing, Port Washington, New York.

CHAPTER 36

ELECTRONIC TECHNOLOGY'S IMPACT ON SALES PROMOTION

Anyone who's considered buying a new personal computer or copy machine recently knows about the fast pace of technological changes. It seems as though advancements in electronics are hitting the market so quickly that your PC or laptop is obsolescent before you get it out of the box. Tonight's TV news or tomorrow's *Wall Street Journal* will announce a new model that's smaller, faster, and more capable than yours. Wait 90 days and there may be an entirely new breakthrough in the field.

These mind-boggling advances are affecting the field of sales promotion, as well. Maturing computer technology has created miniaturized chips that store reams of information, as well as massive databases and artificial intelligence that enable marketers to assess data and promote in new ways. Developments such as electronic couponing, scanners, video screens on shopping carts, interactive cable TV, CD-ROMs, CD-I, PDAs — the whole alphabet soup of Buck Rogers paraphernalia — are opening up new possibilities for promotion marketing. And who knows what will be coming along once we get up to speed on the so-called information superhighway?

So, any discussion of the effects of technology on sales promotion must carry the caveat that a new gizmo or concept may be developed tomorrow. This chapter presents an overview of the state of electronic technology today; some views on what's coming down the road; as well as an analysis of how the new technology is affecting promotion marketing.

In addition to changing the marketplace, technology is blurring the traditional borders between promotion marketing, advertising, and sales. In retail outlets, electronic monitors or signs "remind" shoppers of commercials they've seen on TV and mix in promotional offers. Closed-circuit TV and radio networks in shopping malls and retail stores broadcast advertisements and promotional offers. If you shop via on-line computer services from your home or workplace, incentive messages may come up on your computer screen as you browse through the "electronic mall." If you buy products or services via interactive TV at home or through an interactive computer in a kiosk at a mall, the system may trigger sales promotions automatically.

To provide perspective, let's look first at today's technology. This will paint a pretty good picture of how developments in electronics are affecting promotion marketing, how the field is changing already, and what additional developments we might expect in the future.

One good place to examine the state of the art is inside what

Andersen Consulting calls its Smart Store, housed in a converted warehouse near downtown Chicago. Here, the management consulting firm has constructed a mock supermarket to show food-industry clients how using new technologies can help them run their businesses more effectively. Smart Store is an idea center, where consultants can demonstrate equipment and management processes that are currently in various stages of research and development.

ELECTRONIC ADVANCES CHANGE THE MARKETPLACE

The Smart Store's supermarket section contains displays that envision how grocery outlets might be changed to make use of new technologies. Picture this scene:

Huge supermarkets with long, space-consuming aisles containing thousands of boxes and jars are gone. Instead of maneuvering up and down aisles with a shopping cart, you are issued a handheld scanner wand (about the size of an oversized fountain pen). With this you stroll, unencumbered, to a series of small display racks with placards depicting product packages, complete with label information, such as ingredients and preparation instructions. No actual products are on the shelves. An electronic price label and bar code are adjacent to each placard. If you want an item, you simply run the scanner wand across the bar code, and the selection is transmitted by radio frequencies to an order-collection center in the store. There, groceries are assembled and bagged, cost tallied, and purchases charged to a credit or debit card. Special promotions and electronic coupons can be displayed on these racks, as well, and the offers may be adjusted on a real-time basis to reflect changes in a promotional campaign. Discounts are credited automatically as you make your selections.

Other electronic systems are based on so-called smart-card technology. Frequent-shopper cards with magnetic stripes, similar to credit cards, are issued to regular customers. Often, customers are asked to fill out questionnaires detailing demographic information in order to receive the cards. Promotional prices on various items are offered to cardholders; the savings are registered automatically at the checkout after the card is "swiped" past the scanner. These systems not only encourage store loyalty; they gather valuable information on each customer's shopping habits. This data, in turn, may be used to fashion other promotion marketing campaigns targeted to groups or even individual households.

Or, in another scenario showcased at the Smart Store, you might stroll the aisles of a more traditional-looking supermarket, pushing a basket equipped with a small video screen. You would swipe your frequent-shopper card through a scanner at the side of the unit, allowing the store's computer to tap into your personal demographics and record of past purchases. Then, as you approached various categories in each aisle, promotional offers would be transmitted to your cart's screen, enticing you to buy certain products right at the time you're considering your purchases. These incentives would be targeted directly to you, since the computer would compare promotional offers to your purchasing profile. For example, say the database shows you buy infant-related products. The video screen might display a message offering a promotional price on disposable diapers. A touch of the screen would record your selections, "capture" the electronic promotional "coupon," and transmit charges to the checkout counter.

Some Smart Store mock-ups showcase technology that's already well accepted in the marketplace. For example, electronic units at checkout counters automatically spew out coupons as the bar codes on your purchases are passed over the register's scanner. Depending on how commands are programmed into the system, they may be coupons for another of the same product or a line extension, a competitor's product, or a related product. Thus, if you buy a six-pack of Coke, you might receive a coupon for a case of Coke or Cherry Coke, cans of Pepsi, or a bag of pretzels or potato chips. In other words, the promotions may be used to sell more of the same or a related product; to entice the customer to switch brands; or to encourage purchases of complementary products. And, since the coupons are good only at the issuing store, they stimulate customer loyalty and return visits.

The Smart Store also envisions grocery shopping from home, via interactive TV or computer. In the Smart Store's section that replicates a typical American kitchen there are TV monitors and computer screens that demonstrate existing and developing electronic media designed to simulate the supermarket shopping experience. As you electronically "enter" an area on your screen — the bakery goods section, for example — the system displays special promotions on selected items that day or hour. (Notably, these promotional offers can be changed instantly from a control center.) If you wish to purchase the promoted item, you indicate your selection through a keyboard, mouse, or remote-control device. Your purchase and the promotional price are recorded, and the amount is charged to or debited from your account. Merchandise may either be picked up or delivered to your home.

The technology demonstrated at the Smart Store is gaining growing acceptance in the grocery and convenience-store industry, and it's already moving beyond the supermarket setting into other areas of retailing. Electronic couponing and scanner technology are being utilized by drugstore chains, warehouse clubs, and discount stores. The more than 4 million subscribers to on-line computer services (such as CompuServe and Prodigy) have 24-hour access to "electronic malls," enabling them to buy items ranging from jewelry to office equipment at the touch of a keyboard or click of a mouse. And several companies that offer interactive cable TV services are conducting field tests that include home shopping for groceries, drugstore items, hardware products, compact discs, and cassettes. Typically, promotional messages are added at the bottom of the screen.

Proponents of promotion marketing based on these electronic media point to the huge market reached by these means. One major advertising agency has identified 30 million "electronically advanced consumers" in America today, and the number is growing rapidly. These consumers, it's noted, typically are upscale people who are willing to try new products and methods of shopping. The fact that most of the coming generation of Americans are already computer-literate and comfortable with the techniques makes marketers even more optimistic about the prospects for acceptance of the new technologies.

And the potential audience for interactive TV is even larger. An estimated 98 percent of U.S. households now have at least one TV set — more homes than have running water — and more than 60 percent of those households are hooked to cable. So the possibilities for promotion marketing campaigns carried by these media are exciting.

Sales promotion is taking advantage of other advances in electronic technology, as well. Marketers are utilizing point-of-sale radio and TV monitors in venues such as supermarkets, discount stores, shopping malls, health clubs, and even airport terminals to promote certain products. Instant coupon machines and shelf-talkers next to products tout promotions in grocery stores and other retail outlets. New computer technology has enabled companies to target individuals by name, sending personalized promotions through direct mail or in magazines delivered to the prospect's mailbox.

Making use of the information superhighway, other marketers transmit promotional messages and offers via on-line computer services such as Prodigy, CompuServe, and America Online. Often, users are encouraged to download a demonstration document onto their own personal computer, then try out the product on their own. Promotional computer disks, CD-ROMs, and videotapes mailed to potential customers allow the target audience to see a product in action. The prospect can manipulate the interactive message on his computer, determine how the product or service can be useful to him, then, in some cases, automatically contact the seller (by mail or modem) and receive a premium for purchase. Marketers are already using interactive disks to promote everything from computer software, to automobiles, to financial-planning services.

Interactive kiosks — freestanding units with computers, screens, and printers — also provide an effective means of delivering promotional messages and incentives to prospective customers. Users communicate with the computer through a keyboard or touch screen, receiving product information, learning about promotional offers, printing out incentive coupons, and even ordering products and charging them to their credit cards. To date, these units have achieved relatively limited acceptance in shopping malls, discount centers, and music stores, but industry analysts predict that more than half a million interactive computer kiosks will be used to promote goods and services by 1997. Already, Kmart Corp. is utilizing a couponing kiosk in many of its stores, and the Tower Records chain is testing the units in its music stores.

TECHNOLOGY'S IMPACT ON SALES PROMOTION

What effects have the new technologies had on the field of sales promotion? How can promotion marketers take advantage of the advances in electronics to promote more effectively? Industry experts point out that today's technological developments provide a variety of benefits for adept marketers. Some of these are:

- *More knowledge-based promotional campaigns.* Advances in computer technology have led to integrated databases and artificial intelligence. These developments have enabled marketers to store massive amounts of data on individual sales prospects — their purchasing histories, buying preferences, even their lifestyles — and then to massage this information and relate various aspects, providing increased knowledge and perspective on the big picture. With expert systems (a type of artificial intelligence that enables computers to make deductions and suggest solutions), managers can correlate the information with marketing goals and plan a range of promotional campaigns.

- *More precise market segmentation.* Bar-code scanners and the so-called smart cards provide a huge quantity of quality information about customers. Marketers no longer must depend merely on demographic data about the potential customers in a given geographic area. Now, this information can be correlated with actual buying habits and preferences of specific households — even individuals within a household — providing a valuable database of details. Marketers can learn what products customers buy; how often; what their brand preferences are; how loyal they are to certain brands; and what types and values of incentives are likely to coax them to switch brands or move up to higher-profit purchases.

- *More effective micromarketing.* This information, in turn, enables a company to target promotional campaigns more narrowly. Managers can tailor a program more effectively, delivering promotions of one type and value to one potential buyer, while promoting another product or service to the household or business next door. In addition, promotions can be offered only to individuals who are the best prospects, precisely at the time that the prospect may be ready to make a purchasing decision. For instance, if a supermarket learns that Customer A regularly buys dog food every fourth week, it can target an incentive to him just as he's about to buy this product, influencing the purchase. This precision tailoring minimizes waste in marketing campaigns, making promotional efforts more cost-effective.

- *More valuable incentive marketing.* The corollary to this benefit of technology is that each promotional device can offer more value to the customer. Coupons delivered through newspapers or magazines, on the other hand, have to be of relatively low value (20 cents off or less, for example), since millions may be issued. The paltry value of these offers is one of the reasons that only about 2 percent of these coupons are redeemed. However, when technology enables a company to target only the best prospects, each promotional offer may carry a much higher value, making it much more likely that the coupon will be redeemed or the promotion accepted. In other words, micromarketing of promotions greatly increases the probability that the incentive will have the desired effect.

- *Rapid response.* Because electronic technology provides daily, even hourly, feedback on how a campaign is doing, marketers can track results on virtually a real-time basis. This is a sea of change for promoters; in the past, results could not be assessed until weeks after a promotional campaign was over. With scanners and expert systems, managers can now analyze data quickly, allowing them to change or adjust promotions while the campaign is still in progress. If, for example, a supermarket manager sees that a coupon offer is not achieving the desired results, she can electronically increase the value or extend the offer immediately. Incentives delivered by electronic means — via interactive TV or on-line computer systems, for example — can be changed, extended, moved, increased in value, or withdrawn at the flick of a switch. Likewise, promotions offered through point-of-sale broadcast media can be adjusted instantaneously. Electronic coupons, offers on computer disks, and incentives delivered through interactive kiosks can be changed as quickly as a computer can be reprogrammed — in a matter of minutes. This gives the promotion marketing manager a new level of flexibility, allowing him to adapt quickly to changing circumstances. Quick reaction can salvage a campaign that isn't meeting goals or increase the effectiveness of an already successful promotional program. In addition, a manager can quickly adapt to developments in a business environment — countering the promotional offer of a store down the street as soon as it's detected, for instance.

- *Flexibility.* Technology gives the marketing manager the ability to customize incentives for individual customers, based on their previous usage and store and brand loyalty patterns. She might, for example, offer one type of incentive to induce someone to switch brands; another promotion to encourage someone to trade up within a brand; and still another to entice someone to buy a related product or service. Multiple-purchase incentives could be targeted to heavy users, while medium or light users could be given a trial/conversion incentive, followed by a continuity program.

WHAT'S AHEAD

As indicated previously, the heady pace of technological developments is rapidly changing the ways retailers, manufacturers, and service providers promote and market. As you read this, hardware and software developers are testing new electronic, interactive, and multimedia systems that will provide imaginative new means of delivering and tailoring promotions to potential customers. And, in the research labs, engineers are devising systems that promise a new era in marketing and promotion. Here are a few of the possibilities currently being explored:

- Utilizing smart-card technology, extensive databases, and artificial intelligence software, one developer has devised a supermarket promotion system linked to individual customers. When the consumer swipes his frequent-shopper card through a device at the store entrance, it spits out a custom-designed shopping list based on previous buying habits and projections of the customer's desires and needs. If, for example, the store's artificial intelligence technology decides that the consumer is due to buy a box of cereal that day, it will put cereal on that shopping list — and perhaps add an offer of $1 off on a brand the customer doesn't usually buy. Incentives are offered just before the moment of purchase (the most influential timing), and they can be high-value offers. Discounts are credited automatically at the checkout, after the buyer has swiped the card across the scanner.
- Using a handheld scanner, a customer will soon be able to "collect" paperless coupons electronically. He or she merely will run the device across a bar code shown in a newspaper or magazine advertisement, then redeem the coupons by again passing the device through a unit in the store.
- A variation of this system envisions a handheld device that will be able to capture coupon values right off the TV screen at home. In this scenario, TV commercials will include electronically encoded symbols representing promotional offers; consumers will point a device at the screen, press a button, and — zap — the incentive is stored in the device, to be redeemed at the retail outlet. This system might be used for everything from high-value coupons on groceries or cosmet-

ics, to sweepstakes offers, to promotional offers on cars or durable goods.

- In mall kiosks, interactive computers may be used to promote a variety of consumer products. To sell cosmetics, for instance, they might be programmed to take a picture of you, then to reconfigure the photo to show you with blonde hair instead of black, for example. Then it would spew out a coupon to buy hair coloring and, perhaps, other incentives for related cosmetic products.

- Interactive TV will soon be merged with artificial reality software to achieve a new level of home shopping. A customer will tune into an electronic supermarket, drugstore, or hardware outlet and see shelves full of products on a TV screen. Using a remote-control device, the customer will be able to "approach" a shelf; select a product; electronically pick it up and manipulate the package to read the labeling on all sides; and then buy the product with another click on the device. Promotional offers will be presented automatically as a customer "enters" the store or "approaches" a certain aisle or product category; electronic coupons can be captured on-screen with the remote control. Through artificial intelligence, when the customer selects an item, she can be offered other promotions on related products. Another click on the remote control, and she will be "teleported" to the shelf showing those items. In the future, the system may have the capability of calling up multimedia displays on the screen, with full-motion and sound videos showing uses of the product or offering advice to encourage purchases. Items purchased would be delivered to customers. Test markets of several interactive systems similar to this will be conducted soon, beginning with grocery and drugstore simulations; other outlets, such as toy stores, record shops, hardware stores, and discount centers, may be added shortly.

A WORD OF WARNING

Electronic technology is exciting, sexy, and exhilarating. It can provide efficient, comprehensive means of achieving your sales promotion goals. But, remember, *your sales promotion goals* are the operative words here. Be sure to keep your eyes on your goals and ask yourself: Does it meet our needs? It's easy to be dazzled by the gadgetry, enticed by the gimmicks, and seduced by all the gee-whiz feats that advanced technology is capable of producing. In the romance of it all, you may lose track of what you're trying to accomplish: providing incentives to affect prospective customers' behavior and induce prospects to make purchases.

The hardware and software associated with this technology are relatively expensive and, as we've noted, quickly outmoded by new developments. So, before you sign up for the electronic revolution, you should examine how the new technology would fit in with your company's existing systems and needs, what the payback might be, and how long the likely results might be effective. Also, it's important to assess whether the electronic technology helps to accomplish your marketing goals better and/or less expensively than other means.

Laurie Petersen is Editor-in-Chief of The Cowles Report on Database Marketing, *a newsletter published by Cowles Business Media, Stamford, Connecticut. She is also a contributing editor to* Direct Magazine. *She was previously a columnist and editor at* Adweek's Marketing Week. *She was founding editor of Adweek's* Promote *and has lectured on promotion and marketing at universities, companies, and conferences around the country.*

Petersen spent five years in electronic on-line publishing and the development and promotion of interactive media for The New York Times *and CBS. Her career began in the newspaper business as a reporter and editor with the* Daily Record *in Parsippany, New Jersey.*

She received a B.A. in communications from Glassboro State College, Glassboro, New Jersey.

CHAPTER 37

THE FINAL CHAPTER — FUTURE TRENDS

So where's it all headed? It's risky to commit to paper one's prediction of the future, which is why this chapter is left to a journalist. But what better spot to sit back and assess how the convergence of consumer behavior, marketplace developments, and emerging technologies will affect marketing, and more specifically promotion marketing, in the years to come?

Through repeated and accelerated use, the 1980s carefully taught the consumer how to identify and interpret promotions. Consumers became accustomed to looking for the best price in a favored set of brands. Stockpilers and switchers took the place of brand loyalists. But as the recession took hold, consumers also became more demanding about what they received for their dollar. The consumer of the 1990s seeks quality, convenience, service, and reliability. This real shift in attitude means inferior products cannot get by on low price alone. A catchy advertising slogan is meaningless to an educated public if it is contradicted by experience. The lowest price is not the calling card if it requires too much sacrifice in quality. A time-pressed population needs to know that a marketer stands behind its products or services and is accessible on the consumer's schedule. That attitude affects buying behavior for the most ordinary of package goods as well as clothing, appliances, automobiles, and financial services.

Today's consumer is smart. Successful promotions of the future require marketers to consider these consumer values as well as the added value of the promotional offer. The car manufacturer who throws in free pick-up and drop-off service or a free rental car during repair periods offers a benefit more relevant to the 1990s' consumer than a mere price rebate. Volkswagen failed to reverse sales declines when it offered to pay for car and insurance payments if a buyer lost his or her job. But the promotion did show some ingenuity by addressing the consumer's greatest fear about making big-ticket purchases: the specter of losing a job.

For some audiences price will never be an issue but access is. The retailer who lets preferred customers preview new merchandise, cherry-pick sales, or get special shopping assistance may win out over the discounter. The trick is to know your customer and understand his or her hot buttons. American Express catered to its Platinum Card members' neéd for exclusivity by first polling the card members to determine their interests and then offering them unique relevant privileges "By Invitation Only" to those who hold the top-line card.

Altruism is of interest to this more enlightened consumer but not

at the expense of self-interest. Hanna Andersson, the West Coast cata-
loger, taps into this double standard beautifully. The company offers a
Hannadowns program that helps to build the brand's reputation for creating clothing of such a quality that it is virtually certain to outlast the
needs of one child. Buyers can recycle their Hannas and receive a 20
percent discount off the original purchase price. These recycled clothes
are then distributed to needy families and charitable organizations.
This type of promotion is a sure signal of future trends.

Consumers will continue to demand simplicity. There needs to
be a clear offer they can take advantage of without putting in inordinate
amounts of time, effort, or money. Continuity programs that require
consumers to collect and save cash register tapes and record and clip
proofs of purchase and bar codes for a meager reward will be less likely to fly with the contemporary consumer. There's neither the time nor
the inclination.

Changing demographic patterns will also influence how promotions are conducted. The trend continues toward more families of the
nontraditional ilk. More single-parent families. More step-families.
More single-person households. More empty nesters with money to
burn. For the first time in the latest census, the growth of single-person
households outpaced that of married households. More men are
becoming single parents. Dominant age groups are changing. One in
eight Americans is now above the age of 55. Ethnic groups that were
once the "minority" will become the majority in the population by the
turn of the century. These lifestyle trends demand new approaches to
promotion beyond the cookie-cutter FSI coupon or sweepstakes event.
How each of these segments is reached varies dramatically; what motivates them varies as well.

Event marketing and sports marketing will continue to offer
ways for marketers to relate to specific consumer segments during their
leisure time. So will the continued segmentation of media offerings,
the proliferation of cable television options, and new forums such as
on-line special-interest groups who use computer networks. In fact,
many consumers of the next generation will have cut their teeth on
some form of interactive media. For years already, Ford and Buick
have used personal computer disks to provide prospects with specific
details about their product lines. The interactive nature of these ads lets
the user play all sorts of "what-if" games to better understand a specific
car's offerings. As these technologies advance, consumers will be able
to interact directly with the marketer through a modem.

Media companies will continue to act as promotion innovation
catalysts in the quest to both promote themselves and gain back advertising dollars that otherwise would divert to retailers or purely promotional media. Magazines and newspaper companies are looking for
ways to offer targeted portions of their subscriber bases for marketers
who want to promote only to those segments. Turner Broadcasting

System's Turner Private Network operates an Airport Channel at airport waiting lounges. Physicians' and dentists' offices, hospitals, and health clubs have all been subjected to so-called "place-based media" experiments. In the skies, several organizations will use the airplane seatback to deliver interactive marketing messages. Already, Sky Mall lets airplane passengers use airplane telephones to place orders from an airborne catalog. The orders are delivered within 24 hours. Who is more captive than the airplane traveler?

And you know the world has changed forever when the CBS television network figures out that the way to give itself impact is by using its national mass media clout to get supermarket display space for itself and a full assortment of Nabisco cookies and crackers.

Expect renewed attention to consumer communication as the decade winds up. Nothing short of a revolution in manufacturer and retailer relations will make that happen as marketers' dollars are actually placed against something that enhances image and sales.

A watershed event of 1992 was the decision by Procter & Gamble to put down its foot and declare war against trade promotion spending. The shift of marketing dollars over the 1980s from consumer-focused messages and promotions into retailers' pockets was the underlying factor driving everything that happened in marketing — that and the obsession with short-term results. For years, marketers railed against the destructiveness of street money, but those who had tried to pull back found the repercussions too severe.

It took a manufacturer with the clout of Procter & Gamble and brand assets such as Tide and Ivory to seize the initiative and say, "Enough is enough." In retrospect, the only surprise is that it took so long. Retailers did not sit back idly kowtowing to the packaged goods behemoth of Cincinnati. Some removed Procter & Gamble products from their shelves. The company suffered a short-term setback and discontinued brands and sizes that were not making money. The move's sheer logic argues in its favor. And it has provided an opportunity for other packaged goods manufacturers to wrest themselves from the bondage of trade promotion spending. (Of course, the other opportunity is to take the short view and leap into the void that Procter & Gamble created. Some did.)

If the trade's lock on marketing dollars can be broken, that money can be diverted into marketing efforts to help create brand preferences and drive consumers into stores. Marketers can then refocus on selling their products. No more obsession with slotting allowances, presentation allowances, and delisting allowances. No more worrying about diversion.

The message a consumer gets at the store will still be critical. Indeed, the dollars once spent for the privilege of a little shelf space may still be used at the retail level. But the efforts will be more promotional in nature, involving sampling, in-store events, displays, and partnered promotions with retailers.

What is done will be evaluated for its payback. The tools will finally be available for the marketer to assess if the money spent on the front end yielded a profit or a loss on the back end. Indeed, the idea that promotion is efficient because it is so easily measured is a prevailing myth that has been effectively exposed. Only as marketers and their sales forces have ready-to-use tools offering easily interpretable results will real evaluation occur.

How will this ability to measure efficiency translate? Already promotion efforts are being focused on where they have the greatest impact. Look for more of the homely mainstays, but some big spenders will cling to the high-publicity glitz events. The humble Kraft Holiday Homecoming, combining FSI coupon spreads with a holiday entertainment and recipe magazine, offered space to each participating retail chain to provide the promotion of its choice. The splashier Diet Pepsi "Uh-Huh" Month, meanwhile, tried to take over the store linking live karaoke singing contests to the cola's Ray Charles advertising campaign. (But don't think the soda would sell without a price discount.)

Just where the consumer shops, however, may force a dramatic revision of where the promotional message is offered. The actual point-of-purchase may not be a retail setting. Computerized and telephone shopping services, food subscription clubs, and catalog shopping all promise to increase in importance as consumers find less and less time to shop for the mundane. Consequently, shopping for groceries using a computer makes the computer the point-of-purchase. Picking up staples at a warehouse store is a different psychological experience from visiting a supermarket. Promotions of the future, therefore, must work in concert with retailer needs and be flexible enough to accommodate an ever growing variety of shopping experiences. How will these changes translate into tactical promotion practice? Despite the protestations of clutter, clutter, clutter, coupons will follow us into the next century. But how they are distributed will evolve. Marketers will be forced to look for new points of contact with consumers, and the net result should be a decline in volume.

Nielsen Clearing House Promotional Services predicted a 13 percent increase in coupon distribution by the end of 1992, meaning more than 330 billion coupons went out into the system in the United States alone. These are merely the trackable traditional coupon offers. They don't include the daily onslaught of discounts pouring into American homes for film processing specials, restaurant discounts, car wash reductions, and even two-for-one cemetery plots.

The successful marketer will be one who can identify at what point a coupon is most likely to be acted upon. For different industries, this will mean completely different things. But expect distribution to migrate to points-of-purchase or direct delivery based on previous purchase or lifestyle behavior. In fact, completely new product lines are already being developed based on knowing where to look for the customer base that needs the product. Promotion will surely play more of a role in identifying these customer bases. Then once identified, future promotions can be delivered in ways that are obvious only to the market that is interested. That message may be tailored to a market of one.

What does that mean? Relevance, for starters. One packaged goods company markets a rust-removing cleanser that is said to be a godsend to people who live in areas where the water quality creates toilet or bathtub stains. Through previous promotions, it has gathered a database of people who need and use its product. That database is now a homing device for hot spots across the nation that have this type of problem. If one person has it, surely his neighbors do too, because they use the same water supply. Thus, the marketer can deliver promotions in the mail to neighbors of the consumers in its database. Or specialized media buys can zoom in on specific markets based on the knowledge gained through the database. Cost efficiency isn't the only reason to take this approach. It's smarter marketing. Cultivate a relationship with these customers and you can exploit it to develop future products. Even a mass marketer like Pepsi Cola is trying out some continuity. Its "Gotta Have It" cardholders would be an ideal base on which to test the appeal of future products, sponsorship opportunities, or even advertising messages.

Promotions will continue to gain importance as a way to position brands. Keystone Beer, the "value" brand marketed by Coors Brewing Company, identified anglers as a key target audience. To position itself as the fisherman's beer of choice, it launched a self-liquidating 900-number hotline that offered information about fishing holes around the country. It was a regularly updated service for fishermen to find out where the fish were biting at that moment. Take that notion a step further and it's easy to envision Coors running special events and providing custom promotions for the folks who call.

The idea of market-specific promotions and more individualized promotions means the world 10 years from now may be much more promotional in nature but appear much less so because of targeted messages.

Nongrocery retailers, whose margins are higher, are already using what they know about their customers to deliver the right promotions at the right times and to boost the bottom line. NBO Stores, a discount chain of menswear stores on the East Coast, set up a Dress for Success Club consisting of 10,000 customers who spend at least $500 in the store and make at least two visits a year. Analysis of customer spending patterns revealed these 2 percent made a full 11 percent of annual purchases. The club was set up to offer benefits that go beyond a mere price discount. Club members get free lifetime alterations, in case they gain or lose too many pounds. They can come in for seasonal "tune-ups" enabling them to get seams mended, missing buttons replaced, and the like. These benefits are service- and convenience-oriented. The idea is to make other customers aspire to become a V.I.P. customer.

The automotive industry is moving to the database with tremendous speed. Pick up a magazine announcing new car lines and you're bound to find some response device somewhere within. It may be a discreet toll-free number embedded in the fine print. But it's there. This enables the company to learn something about people who are interested, however remotely, in their cars and trucks. It also helps measure the efficiency of specific media purchases.

General Motors Corporation has gone so far as to introduce a product that is a promotion itself. The GM Card offers a 5 percent rebate on every purchase. That rebate goes into an accumulating fund that can be applied to the purchase of a General Motors vehicle. GM is trying to establish its vehicles as the upfront goal for every consumer who signs up for its branded MasterCard. The automaker will also be able to target specific car promotions to specific credit card customers, varying the percentage accumulated for promotional periods or making special prices available to GM cardholders.

MCI Communications created Friends & Family, which was really a promotion designed to get people to switch their long distance carrier or influence their friends to do so. But Friends & Family is also more. It's a built-in retention program. Once in the circle of friends, the consumer risks more than annoying a phone company by dropping out. The program is already credited with lifting MCI's consumer long-distance telephone share by more than 2 percent. And now MCI has a platform on which it can promote to different segments of its Friends & Family database. The possibilities are limitless.

If it's becoming harder to distinguish what is and what isn't a promotion, that's the whole point. Events such as the launch of a GM Card or a Friends & Family promotion are indicators of the trend toward the holistic marketing promotion. The smartest marketers will be the ones who figure out long- and short-term ways to gain customer loyalty. It won't be done using tricks. It will be done offering legitimately good deals that are easy to understand and easy to participate in. That's a future trend anyone would predict with confidence.

APPENDICES

APPENDIX 1

PROMOTION MARKETING SERVICES

Here are explanations of the categories from *PROMO's* annual spending breakdown for 1992, as shown in chapter One, "Introduction and Overview."

Premium Incentives: $17.7 billion. This figure covers consumer premiums and incentives, including travel.

P-O-P Advertising: $15.7 billion. The Point-of-Purchase Advertising Institute reports revenues of $3.65 billion for design and production of food and paper product displays; $3.05 billion for transportation products; $2.58 billion for personal products; $2.14 billion for health and beauty aids; $847 million for hardware; $418 million for household products; $164 million for farm and garden displays; and $993,000 for miscellaneous products.

Couponing: $7.03 billion. Manufacturers paid $4.21 billion to consumers for face-value redemptions; $1.77 billion to newspaper insert, direct mail co-op, and other companies for various types of delivery systems; $606.7 million in handling fees to retailers; and $83.4 million to redemption agencies for coupon processing.

Specialty Advertising: $5.2 billion. This figure, reported by the Specialty Advertising Association International (SAAI), covers specialty items that are given away to consumers as "goodwill" items bearing the donor's name or logo.

Promotion Licensing: $4.4 billion. The $4.4 billion figure is a *PROMO* estimate based on discussions with industry analysts as well as several licensing agency executives who represent some of the most popular properties. Most said that promotion accounted for between 5 and 10 percent of their business last year. We split the difference and took 7 percent of the $63.5 billion generated last year from the retail sales of license merchandise to come up with our figure.

Special Events: $3.2 billion. According to the International Events Group, publishers of *Special Events Report*, corporate sponsors spent $1.88 billion on sports events; $382 million for music events; $294 million for festivals; $206 million for cause-related events; and $176 million on the arts.

Specialty Printing: $2.4 billion. This category includes the printing of in-pack/on-pack promotion offers, game cards, coupons and labels. The figure we arrived at includes the U.S. Department of Commerce figures for the commercial printing industry along with confidential information shared with *PROMO* by various specialty printers.

Promotion Fulfillment: $2.2 billion. Of the total, $450 million includes handling, administration, packaging, and warehousing of prizes and premiums, and rebate face value redemptions. The $1.5 billion figure is an estimate based on internal reports that several companies were willing to share with *PROMO*. The figure does not include automobile rebates.

Promotion Agencies: $950 million. This figure covers promotion agency gross revenues and is a *PROMO* estimate based on industry data and reported revenues. The figure does not include the share of promotion revenue generated by advertising agencies.

Promotion Measurement: $728 million. Marketing research is reported to have accounted for $3.4 billion last year, but the portion that is devoted to promotion is relatively small. Information Resources, Inc. (IRI) and Nielsen Marketing Research account for the bulk of spending in this category through their scanner-based research products and services.

Product Sampling: $176 million. This figure covers both outdoor and mail/in-store delivered product samples. Outdoor pertains to samples that are distributed at fairs, festivals, and other special events, as well as on street corners and at other high-traffic outdoor locations. This method accounted for $100 million in revenues in 1992, a figure we arrived at by multiplying an estimated 500 million samples that were distributed outdoors in 1992 by a conservative $.20 per sample distribution charge. Sampling by mail covers the distribution of product samples primarily through co-op programs that also deliver coupons. We counted only the revenue generated by the samples, not the coupons that may have been included in the same kits, and came up with a figure of $53 million in revenues for 1991. In several cases we "dissected" the actual sample kits that different companies distributed and determined how much revenue was generated from each program by counting up the samples, looking at the companies' rate cards, and then doing some simple arithmetic. Also included in the figure is in-store sampling, such as the kind offered by ActMedia through its Impact program and also by Stratmar Systems. Here is where there may be some overlap with Merchandising Services, because demonstrators are often hired to hand out product samples in-store. But since we've kept our estimates on the conservative side, the possibility of inflating the figure is minimized.

In-Store Advertising: $117 million. This category includes the revenues generated by delivering in-store advertising messages, both electronic and display. Once again, ActMedia dominates the category, accounting for nearly half the revenue generated, primarily through its

AisleVision, CartVision, and ShelfTalk programs. Also gaining ground are In-Store Advertising and MediaOne, both of which continue to add stores to their networks while forming strategic alliances with consumer magazine groups and other partners to increase participation in their programs.

Merchandising Services: $238 million. There are at least 139 companies that offer merchandising services, which include demonstrations, product resets, display assembly, and customized coupon and sample distribution. A survey conducted by the National Association of Demonstration Companies (NADC) indicated that most of these companies generated revenues of between $250,000 and $3 million in 1991.

Telepromotions: $435 million. The telepromotion industry has continued to grow, largely due to manufacturers' continued acceptance of the telephone as a legitimate marketing tool. Industry efforts to clean up the image of 900-numbers, coupled with some notable promotion success stories, helped increase revenues in 1991 for carriers and service bureaus alike. These figures were reported by Strategic TeleMedia, a New York–based company that tracks telecommunications industry expenditures.

APPENDIX 2

PROFESSIONAL AND TRADE ASSOCIATIONS

Promotion marketing is a wonderfully diverse process, given the sheer variety of methods, media, and activities available to the practitioner today. Many such activities are represented by trade and professional associations, which often serve as information sources and referral services for potential users. The following list of organizations, along with their own mission statements, was compiled by the editors of *PROMO* magazine.

Advertising Research Foundation (ARF)
641 Lexington Avenue
New York, NY 10022
Telephone: (212) 751-5656
Fax: (212) 319-5265
Contact: Michael Naples, President

The ARF is the only industry-wide, not-for-profit association dedicated to increasing the effectiveness of advertising through objective and impartial research. Founded over 50 years ago by the American Marketing Association (AMA) and the American Association of Advertising Agencies (Four-A's), ARF includes among its members advertisers, advertising agencies, research firms, media companies, and educational institutions.

American Association of Advertising Agencies (Four-A's)
666 Third Avenue
New York, NY 10017
Telephone: (212) 682-2500
Fax: (212) 953-5665
Contact: John O'Toole, President

The mission of the Four-A's is to improve and strengthen the advertising agency business in the U.S. by counseling members on operations and management, by providing the collective experience of the many to each, by fostering professional development, by encouraging the highest creative and business standards, and by attracting excellent people to the business.

American Marketing Association (AMA)
250 S. Wacker Drive
Chicago, IL 60606
Telephone: (312) 648-0536
Fax: (312) 993-7542
Contact: Michael Wukitsch, Interim President

The AMA is an international professional society of individual members with an interest in the practice, study, and teaching of marketing. The role of the organization is to urge and assist the personal and professional development of its members and to advance the science and ethical practice of the marketing discipline.

Association of Coupon Processors (ACP)
500 North Michigan Ave., Suite 1400
Chicago, IL 60614
Telephone: (312) 661-1700
Fax: (312) 661-0769
Contact: Joan Carter, Executive Director

The ACP is a coupon redemption industry trade association whose primary purposes are to improve coupon industry business conditions, to assure the continuance of coupons as a viable sales and marketing tool, and to provide for the resolution of common industry concerns in the development, distribution, and redemption of coupons.

Association of Incentive Marketing (AIM)
1600 Route 22
Union, NJ 07083
Telephone: (908) 687-3090
Fax: (908) 687-0977
Contact: Andrew Bopp

AIM is the professional association of those who provide incentive merchandise and services. It is dedicated to promoting the education, quality, and highest ethical standards of the incentive marketing field.

Association of In-Store Marketing (AISM)
66 North Van Brunt
Englewood, NJ 07631
Telephone: (201) 894-8899
Fax: (201) 894-0529
Contact: Virginia Cargill, Marc Kalan, Committee Co-Chairs

AISM, under the auspices of The Point-of-Purchase Advertising Institute (see below), was created to build a stronger voice for the in-store media/marketing industry by promoting the awareness and use of in-store media/marketing programs; working toward the development of standards for in-store research methodologies; and developing a speakers bureau to conduct industry presentations at marketing forums and conferences.

Association of National Advertisers (ANA)
155 E. 44th Street
New York, NY 10017
Telephone: (212) 697-5950
Fax: (212) 661-8057
Contact: DeWitt Helm, President (through Nov. 1993)

ANA is the only organization exclusively dedicated to serving the interests of corporations that advertise regionally and nationally. The association's advertiser membership is, in composite, a cross section of American industry. With more than 2,000 subsidiaries, divisions, and operating units, ANA members market a variety of goods and services and collectively account for over 80 percent of all annual regional and national advertising expenditures in the United States.

Association of Retail Marketing Services (ARM)
3 Caro Court
Red Bank, NJ 07001
Telephone: (908) 842-5070
Fax: (908) 219-1938
Contact: Gerri Hopkins, Executive Director

ARMS represents suppliers of incentive services to retailers and direct marketers in all industries. It is dedicated to educational, research, and information programs that promote sound incentive use and enhance the professionalism of its members.

Council of Sales Promotion Agencies (CSPA)
750 Summer Street
Stamford, CT 06901
Telephone: (203) 325-3911
Fax: (203) 969-1499
Contact: Marilyn Esposito, Executive Director

CSPA's mission is to be the preeminent, worldwide industry

association for qualified, full-service sales promotion agencies and to inform and educate the client community of the strategic role/function of the promotion agency, as distinct from the advertising agency and direct marketing agency, in the overall mix of marketing service providers. Also, the organization expects to raise the level of recognition and professional respect for promotion agencies while promoting the value of its services to a broad range of clients.

Direct Marketing Association (DMA)
11 West 42nd Street
New York, NY 10036-8096
Telephone: (212) 768-7277
Fax: (212) 768-4546
Contact: Jonah Gitlitz, President

The Direct Marketing Association is a service organization dedicated to encouraging and advancing the effective, responsible, and ethical use of direct marketing through conferences and meetings, information, education, and by representing the interests of direct marketers to government, the general public, and media.

Food Marketing Institute (FMI)
800 Connecticut Avenue, NW
Washington, DC 20006-2701
Telephone: (202) 452-8444
Fax: (202) 429-4519
Contact: Tim Hammonds, President/CEO

The FMI is a non-profit association conducting programs in research, education, industry relations, and public affairs on behalf of its 1,500 members — food retailers and wholesalers and their customers in the United States and around the world. The organization is designed to help the grocery retailer and wholesaler discharge their responsibilities to the customer in moving food from the producer to the consumer in the most efficient possible manner.

Grocery Manufacturers of America (GMA)
1010 Wisconsin Avenue, N.W., Suite 900
Washington, DC 20007
Telephone: (202) 337-9400
Fax: (202) 337-4508
Contact: Jeff Nedelman, Vice President of Communications

GMA is a trade association of the manufacturers and processors of food and non-food products primarily sold in retail grocery stores throughout the United States. GMA's mission is to forcefully advance the public policy and trade relations interests of grocery manufacturers through aggressive, strategic government relations, communications, legal, regulatory, scientific, and education advocacy — and by forging cooperative industry alliances to improve the productivity and distributional efficiencies of the industry. GMA is committed to advancing these objectives through the participation of member company executives in a dynamic policy setting process, with strong direction from senior executives serving on the Industry Productivity and Government Affairs Councils and the CEO-led Board of Directors.

Licensing Industry Merchandisers' Association (LIMA)
350 Fifth Avenue, Suite 6210
New York, NY 10118-0110
Telephone: (212) 244-1944
Fax: (212) 563-6552
Contact: Murray Altchuler, Executive Director

LIMA represents more than 475 companies and individuals engaged in the marketing of licensed properties. The group's mission is to establish a standard reflecting a professional and ethical management approach to the marketing of licensed properties; to become the leading source of information in the industry; to communicate this information to members and others in the industry through publishing, public speaking, seminars, and an open line; and to represent the industry in trade and consumer media and in relationships with the government, retailers, manufacturers, other trade associations, and the public.

National Association of Demonstration Companies (NADC)
P.O. Box 1189
Bloomfield, NJ 07003-1189
Telephone: (800) 338-NADC
Fax: (201) 338-1410
Contact: Robert Jay Lieberman, President

NADC is a group of approximately 200 individual organizations located throughout the country. They are united as a common body for the purpose of strengthening the direct marketing industry through combined efforts and actions. It is the goal of the membership to improve and stimulate the acceptance, performance, reputation, and use of in-store demonstrations, as well as a range of other marketing assistance services.

National Association for Information Services (NAIS)
1250 Connecticut Avenue, NW, Suite 600
Washington, DC 20036-2603
Telephone: (202) 833-2545
Fax: (202) 833-1234
Contact: Bill Burrington, Executive Director

NAIS is a non-profit national trade association representing the interests of the ever evolving and changing interactive telemedia industry. The NAIS advocates the business and public policy interests of a diverse range of companies involved in the interactive telephone, television, and multimedia industries. Members include cable television companies, long distance carriers, regional Bell operating companies, major publishing companies, service bureaus, and a wide variety of information providers.

The Point-of-Purchase Advertising Institute (POPAI)
66 North Van Brunt
Englewood, NJ 07631
Telephone: (201) 894-8899
Fax: (201) 894-0529
Contact: Richard K. Blatt, Executive Director

POPAI is the only international non-profit trade association exclusively dedicated to serving the interests of advertisers, retailers, and producers/suppliers of P-O-P products and services. The 57-year-old association provides its members with a variety of benefits designed to promote, protect, and advance the broader issues of point-of-purchase advertising.

Promotion Marketing Association of American (PMAA)
257 Park Avenue South
New York, NY 10010
Telephone: (212) 420-1100
Fax: (212) 982-PMAA
Contact: Christopher Sutherland, Executive Director

PMAA is the leading non-profit association representing the multi-billion-dollar promotion marketing profession. PMAA's purpose is to encourage the highest standards of excellence in promotion marketing through education and information. PMAA's membership consists of more than 650 companies nationwide and around the world reflecting all segments of the promotion industry. As the industry "voice," PMAA represents member interests and promotes better understanding of the importance of promotion within the marketing mix. The PMAA has four councils that are charged with addressing the specific needs of their constituencies. They are: The Entertainment Council for Entertainment Marketing; In-Store Marketing Council; Product Sampling Council; and Small Business Council.

Specialty Advertising Association International (SAAI)
3125 Skyway Circle North
Irving, TX 75038-3526
Telephone: (214) 252-0404
Fax: (214) 258-0949
Contact: H. Ted Olson, President

SAAI's mission is to lead a vital and growing promotional products industry and to help its members prosper in an evolving business environment.

APPENDIX 3

AWARD PROGRAMS

There are two major associations in the United States whose sole orientation is promotion marketing. One is the Promotion Marketing Association of America (PMAA). The other is the Council of Sales Promotion Agencies.

The goal and purpose of PMAA is to foster an understanding of the benefits of promotion marketing to the consumer, trade, supplier, and promotion marketers. The approximately 650-member trade association is 82 years old. Half of its 24-person Board of Directors represents service and supply companies; the other half, corporate, brand, product, and promotion managers. Member services include legal updates on recent legislation, Washington lobbying, and annual conferences.

PMAA sponsors the Reggie awards, which go to clients and agencies for successful promotion campaigns. The awards are given at PMAA's "Update" conference in March. There is also a Leadership Conference in June and a Law Conference in November. PMAA has local chapters in New York, Chicago, and Southern California.

The Council of Sales Promotion Agencies (CSPA) is a much smaller organization, comprising the principals, partners, and presidents of promotion agencies. A promotion industry's version of the American Association of Advertising Agencies, its membership is by invitation only.

CSPA is truly international in nature, with spring and fall meetings taking place in the U.S. and overseas. There are fewer than 75 member agencies, but they are as geographically diverse as the U.S., Canada, U.K., France, Italy, Spain, Greece, Germany, Japan, Australia, New Zealand, Brazil, and Mexico.

CSPA sponsors an annual "Awards of Excellence" program judged by the promotion, advertising, and marketing trade press and announced at the organization's spring meeting. The award is given to an agency for excellent results from a promotional campaign run the previous year.

General marketing associations with promotion divisions are the American Marketing Association and the Association of National Advertisers. The American Marketing Association sponsors the SPIREs (suspended in 1993), an acronym for Sales Promotion Industry Recognition of Excellence. The American Association of Advertising Agencies, also known as the Four A's, has a promotion marketing committee but neither an awards program nor a full-fledged promotion conference.

There are two non-association awards programs, both of them

sponsored by *PROMO* magazine and both given out at the magazine's fall conference. The PINNACLE Awards, judged by corporate brand, product, and promotion managers, go to marketing services companies for promotion innovation, marketing relevance, and industry leadership. The PRO Awards, established in 1990, go to art directors, copy writers, and producers at agencies for creative excellence in promotion advertising.

Trade groups organized around various types of promotion delivery vehicles are the Direct Marketing Association, the Point-of-Purchase Advertising Institute, the Association of Retail Merchandisers, and the International Mass Retail Association (IMRA), and several others.

Appendix 4

THE POPAI GUIDE

Foreword

The power of education has remained the leading "safeguard" for competing in the tumultuous marketplace of today. As one noted scholar once said, "Knowledge is the ultimate ally and when used properly can conquer most limitations." Without the power of information, one cannot hope to fulfill his or her potential.

It is in this vein that POPAI is proud to publish the first complete P.O.P. Desktop Reference, an easy-to-use compilation of jargon, buzz-words, key phrases, and technical terms for P.O.P., sales promotion, advertising, and marketing.

Someone also once said, "A little knowledge is dangerous," which is why this glossary is so complete. Over 1,200 terms are defined and cross-referenced, providing one of the most comprehensive and current listings available on the market today. POPAI is confident that you will find this reference an indispensable "partner" in your day-to-day agenda.

This publication is part of POPAI's overall dedication to providing educational tools and programs for the new and established professional, as well as for the academic community. Our efforts will continue to expand as we focus on the true power of information and the advancement of professionalism in the P.O.P.-related industries.

John M. Kawula
President, POPAI

A.B.S. — A tripolymer material made of three substances: acrylic, butadien and styrene. Used in the manufacture of P-O-P signs.

ASCII (American Standard Code for Information Interchange) — The assignment of numbers (for computer use) to printable characters (letters, digits, punctuation symbols) and other special characters.

A-Board — A curb sign used by the oil industry, in which the two sides lean together at the top and are connected by a cross brace, forming an A.

Access Time (electronic) — The time it takes to find, retrieve, and display a piece of recorded information. Access time is usually measured at its worst, the longest time to get from one piece of information to another. This is generally a matter of minutes on videotape, two or fewer seconds on video disc players, and milli- or micro-seconds in a computer.

Acetate — a tough, clear plastic film that accepts ink well. Widely used in P-O-P work.

Acerkman-Johnson — a type of masonry fastener used in the installation of outdoor P-O-P signs.

Acrylic — 1: An optically clear cast resinous plastic that can be screen-printed and heat-formed. 2: A class or group of plastics that exhibit fairly high impact strength, rigidity, and compatibility with other plastics. Often used as base compounds in formulating ink and adhesive systems.

Acrylic Emulsion — A water based latex made of acrylic polymer that is used for coatings and/or impregnations.

Acrylite — See Acrylic Emulsion.

Ad Reprint Holder — A framing device containing reprints of advertisements, usually displayed on counters.

Adherend — A body that is held to another body by an adhesive.

Adhesion (adherence) — The phenomenon in which surfaces are held together by interfacial forces.

Adhesion — Specific adhesion between surfaces that are held together by valence forces of the same type as those that give rise to cohesion.

Adhesive — A substance capable of holding materials together by surface attachment. Adhesive is a general term that includes cement, glue, mucilage, paste, etc. These terms are all essentially interchangeable. Various descriptive adjectives are often applied to the term adhesive to indicate certain characteristics, as for example: physical form, e.g., liquid adhesive, tape adhesive; chemical form, e.g., silicate adhesive, epoxy adhesive; materials bonded, c.g., paper adhesive, metal-plastic adhesive, can-label adhesive; conditions of use, e.g., cold-setting adhesive, hot-setting adhesive.

Adhesive, Cold-Setting — An adhesive that sets at temperatures below 20 degrees centigrade.

Adhesive, Hot-Setting — An adhesive that requires a temperature at or above 100 degrees centigrade to set.

Adhesive, Intermediate-Temperature-Setting — An adhesive that sets in the temperature range of 31 degrees–99 degrees centigrade.

Adhesive, Pressure-Sensitive — An adhesive made to adhere to a surface at room temperature by briefly applying pressure alone.

Adhesive, Room-Temperature-Setting — An adhesive that sets in the temperature range of 20 degrees–20 degrees centigrade in accordance with the limits for Standard Room Temperature specified in the Standard Methods of Conditioning Plastics and Electrical Insulating Materials for Testing (ADTMDD618).

Adhesive, Solvent-Release — An adhesive that releases solvent vapor during cure.

Adhesive, Warm-Setting — A term sometimes used synonymously with intermediate-temperature-setting adhesive.

Advertised Brand — A brand advertised nationally to the consumer and the trade; distributed by competing wholesalers and stocked by competing retailers.

Affixed Merchandise — Products glued or otherwise fastened to the display to keep the display intact.

Aided Recall — A research technique used in measuring the level of advertisement perception, in which the interviewer gives respondents a clue to refocus attention on the original exposure situation.

Air Rights Display — A display hanging from overhead above traffic or merchandise.

Airbrush — In artwork, a small pressure gun shaped like a pencil that sprays watercolor pigment by means of compressed air. Used to correct and obtain tone or graduated tone effects.

Aisle Jumper — An overhead wire that reaches from aisle to aisle, jumping the space between flags and pennants announcing advertising messages that are draped over the wire. Differs from an arch in that it is just the frame.

Alphanumeric — Refers to a character set consisting of both letters and numbers in a display.

Alpo — Trade name for a hard, inexpensive, long-lasting, baked enamel finish that gives the appearance of thousands of little "hammer marks" spread across the surface. "Hammerloid" and "Vidreo" are other trade names for this type of finish.

Altruistic Display — A display featuring additional products of other advertisers besides those of the advertiser who pays for the display. Also, a store-wide program featuring seasonal products that includes the advertiser's product but does not specifically name it.

Alumina Hydrate — An extender pigment used in certain inks, particularly lithographic inks. It is used to make an ink "go farther." Not frequently used today as most printing calls for deep-full colors and alumina hydrate tends to water down or weaken a color.

Anchor Bolts — The large threaded steel rods used to secure a sign base to a concrete foundation. This term applies to outdoor installations only.

Animation — The use of motion in displays.

Animation (electronic) — 1: The ability to make electronic graphics appear to move. 2: (Animation function) A function on an electronic display that makes graphics move.

Anodizing — The process of preserving metal by adding a protective oxide film by an electrolytic process.

Apron — The open area of a filling station or other retail outlet where displays and/or signs are in evidence and/or merchandise is sold.

Arch — A display designed to go from one gondola to another, over and above the aisle.

Art — All illustration copy used in preparing a job for printing. Also referred to as art work.

Artwork, Comprehensive — Design produced primarily for customer approval of layout, etc.; not necessarily camera ready. Color work may be indicated by overlays to show color areas over the black and white base design.

Artwork, Separated — Artwork produced to indicate separations of color areas; i.e., a separate layout for each color.

Assembly — 1: The process of erecting display component parts into a single, integrated display unit. 2: A group of materials or parts that have been placed together for bonding or that have been bonded together.

Assembly Time — The time interval (either necessary or permissible) between spreading the adhesive to the surfaces and the application of pressure, heat, or both, to assemble. The open assembly time is the optimum time interval after applying the adhesive when surfaces should be joined.

Assortment Display — A display designed to offer the customer a choice of size, color, type of item, etc. Also, a display offered with the purchase of a product assortment.

Attach-To-Merchandise Display — A display that may be larger or smaller than the merchandise that it advertises, usually giving some informational copy, and attached directly to the product or to a group of products.

Audience — The total number of people who have the opportunity to read a point-of-purchase advertising message. This term is also applied to all other advertising media.

Audio Still Frame (electronic) — The commentary, music, or sound effects accompanying a single still image (artwork or slide). The soundtrack may be recorded using some version of compressed audio for greater economy.

Audio Video Display — Custom display that utilizes computer electronics to convey audio and video messages to the consumer. These are well used for products that require a high degree of information or cross-referencing by the consumer.

"Audioprint" — Trade name for the process that combines sight and sound for unusual impressions.

Audiovisual — A display using sound as well as sight to convey its advertising message. Also the hardware used for that purpose.

Author's Alterations — In art or composition, changes and additions to the copy after it has already been prepared for proving and printing.

Authoring (electronic) — The preparation of a computer program, often using a structured "authoring language" or "authoring system" that allows people without formal training in computer programming to prepare applications for computer-based systems.

Auto Centering — The ability to automatically center text on the electronic display screen without manually counting spaces.

Autoclave — A type of oven used to provide heat during, or upon conclusion of, a manufacturing process.

Autoclave Molding — A modification of pressure bag molding in which the entire assembly is placed in a steam autoclave at 50–100 psi after lay-up. See **Bag Molding**.

Autolock Style — A carton or tray that, when erected, forms a bottom automatically without requiring manual locking, gluing, or taping.

Automatic Mold — A mold for injection or compression molding that repeatedly goes through the entire cycle, including injection, without human assistance.

B

B Flute Corrugated Paperboard — One of the wave shapes in the inner portion of combined corrugated board. It is 3/32 of an inch in height and the most widely used corrugated in display production. Provides a good printing surface and die-cutting performance.

Back-Bar Display — A display designed to be used behind the bar, or on the mirror behind the bar or fountain.

Back Card — A card unit attached to the back of a dump bin, floor bin, or counter merchandiser and presents the advertising message at eye level.

Back Draft — An area of interference in an otherwise smooth-drafted encasement; an obstruction in the taper that would interfere with the withdrawal of the model from the mold.

Back-Light Display — See **Transparency**.

Back Pressure — The resistance to the forward flow of molten material in an extruder.

Back-Up Merchandise — Merchandise not on display but kept available for restocking displays.

Backing Plate — A plate used in molding that backs up the cavity blocks, guide pins, bushings, etc. Sometimes called the support plate.

Backing-Up — Printing on the other side of a printed sheet.

Bag Molding — A molding technique in which consolidation of the material in the mold is created by the application of fluid pressure through a flexible membrane.

Baked Enamel Signs — Signs usually printed by the screen process on metal, employing synthetic resins, and baked at high temperatures to speed up the drying process and prolong the life of the sign.

Ballast — Stabilizing mechanism used in outdoor illuminated signs.

Balloon Testing — Testing a desired height and location of an outdoor sign using a helium balloon.

Banner — A piece of plastic, cloth, or paper, usually in the form of a rectangle or triangle, suspended by its top in windows, from walls or ceilings, or outdoors on ropes or wires between poles. Outdoor banners are usually printed on heavy canvas and have metal grommets for stays.

"Banner Tender" — Trade name for a vertical and horizontal cloth banner attached to poles.

Base Color — A first color used as a background on which other colors are printed.

Basic Material Supplier — A manufacturer who supplies component parts or materials to the P-O-P producer/supplier.

Basis Weight — (of corrugated paperboard) — Weight of the linerboard or the corrugating medium expressed in terms of pounds per 1,000 square feet (MSF).

Battery Back-Up — A feature on an electronic display that allows the memory to be retained even if power is interrupted.

Baud (electronic) — A measure of transmitting computer characters. 300 baud is 30 characters per second, 1200 baud is 120 characters per second, etc.

Beach Puncture Tester — A laboratory testing device, widely used and universally accepted, in the paper and paperboard industry. It establishes the strength of the material and its resistance to puncturing.

Benday — An engraving process that permits the production of halftone or color effects without halftone work. This is done by placing a plastic sheet previously printed with black or white dots over the original art. Bendays are measured by percentages — such as 10% or 20%.

Bending — Used in the phrase "proper bending qualities" to mean that the corrugated paperboard must be capable of bending along creases or score lines in forming the box so that the container-board is not ruptured to a point where it seriously weakens the box.

Bimetal Plates — Lithographic plates in which the printing image base is formed of one metal and the nonprinting area of a second metal. Generally, the printing area is formed of copper, while the nonprinting area may be nickel, chromium, or stainless steel. Some plates employ a third metal as a base or backing and can be regarded as trimetallic, multi-metallic, or polymetallic. Both surface and deep-etch platemaking techniques are used in the making of such plates. With a plating of chromium or copper sheet, the resist stencil of deep etch method permits etching chromium from image to reach copper or stainless steel base. Surface platemaking methods temporarily protect the image while the copper is etched away to expose stainless steel for nonprinting areas of plate.

Bin — A holder for bulk merchandise. Can be made of wire, wood, corrugated, sheet metal, etc.

Binary (electronic) — The base-two number system. It uses only the digits 0 and 1 and is the basis of computer coding and calculation.

Bi-Pole — A structure or sign mounted on two poles.

Bit (electronic) — 1: An abbreviation of the words "binary digit," the smallest unit of information. 2: A single character in a binary number. 3: A unit of information capacity in a storage device.

Black & White — A photograph without color. Originals or reproductions in a single color.

Black & White Artwork — A sharp, black, pen-and-ink or brush line drawing on a smooth or textured white board that is camera ready.

Black Printer — In color reproduction, the black plate is made to increase contrast of neutral tones and detail.

Blank Dummy — A mock-up, full-sized, serviceable model of a display with no printing or art, sometimes used as a sample.

Blanket — In offset printing, a rubber surfaced fabric that is clamped around a cylinder, to which the image is transferred from the plate, and from which it is transferred to the paper.

Blanket Cylinder — The cylinder where the blanket is mounted. This cylinder receives the inked design from the plate cylinder and "offsets" or transfers it onto the surface to be printed.

Blanking (electronic) — During the time it takes for a video disc to search from one sequence to another, the video image is turned off. This results in a blank screen or screen blanking. The search interval between sequences is referred to as "blanking."

Blanking Area — The area between the outside edge of a poster and the inside edge of the molding which is covered with white paper and serves as a mat for the poster design.

Bleed — 1: The part of the original artwork that is carried beyond the illustration or background so that when the finished unit is cut or die-cut, no portion shows. 2: That area of one color that overprints another for the purpose of ensuring registration between the two colors. 3: Term applied to a lithographic ink pigment that dissolves in the etch and causes tinting.

Bleed Loss — The part of the bleed that is cut off.

Blind — A dot on a photographic negative or positive that lacks density and has become so transparent that any light going through it falsifies the values desired. To be photographically effective, all dots must be opaque and all transparent areas must be absolutely clear.

Blind Embossing — A design that is stamped without metallic leaf or ink, giving a bas-relief effect.

Blister — An undesirable elevation of the surface of an adherent, somewhat resembling the shape of a blister on human skin; its boundaries may be indefinably outlined and it may have burst and become flattened.

Blister-Pack — A card containing an item covered with transparent casing or cap attachment. Usually a non-food item or premium with a packaged food. Facilitates stacking and displaying and deters pilferage of small items.

Block Colors — Those colors printed solid, i.e., with near identical opacity and density over the entire surface and without gradations, tints, or shading, in poster style.

Blocking — Undesired adhesion between touching layers of a material; occurs under moderate pressure during storage use.

Blow Molding — A method of producing hollow objects by injecting a parison of hot melt into a hollow, two-part mold, then inflating the parison against the cool mold surfaces where it "freezes" into shape.

Blow Pin — The pin (or needle) through which air is injected into the parison during the blow molding process.

Blowing Agent — A chemical that is added to plastics to cause expansion.

Blow-Up — A large-sized picture of the product or the advertising message.

Blowup Ratio — In blow molding, the ratio of the mold to the cavity diameter.

Blueline — A blueprint type paper which, when laid over an offset plate, shows size, position, die outlines, etc.

Blueprint — A photographic print, usually by contact with negative on paper, glass, or metal. Serves as a guide for artist in making "keyed" art for multicolor; also used as a method of securing a copy of unit negatives for checking layout and imposition. Ozalid prints used for prints from photographic positives.

Board — Abbreviation for various paperboard. See **Boxboard**, **Chipboard**, **Containerboard**, **Fibreboard**, **Linerboard**, and **Paperboard**.

Bond — *v*: To attach materials together by an adhesive. *n*: The attachment at an interface between an adhesive and an adherend. See also **Joint**.

Border Line — A line or design surrounding the whole or portion of a design to set it apart from the rest of the design or to emphasize the whole.

Bottle Glorifier — A display designed to fit on a bottle, or to serve as a background for the bottle, usually having a cutout area or recess to hold the bottle in place.

Bottle Pourer — A plastic or metal configuration that fits over the opening of a liquor bottle and is used to facilitate pouring or to pour a specific quantity while carrying the advertising message.

Bottle Topper — A small cardboard display designed to circle the neck of a bottle and carry an advertising message. More modest than a bottle glorifier.

Box — A rigid container having closed faces and completely enclosing the contents. See also **Fibreboard Box** and **Container**.

Boxboard — A general term designating the types of paperboard used for making folding cartons and set-up paper boxes.

Brand Awareness — The process, style, graphics, or size of a promotional piece or program by which the advertised product name becomes familiar to the consumer.

Brand Consciousness — The degree of awareness consumers have of a particular brand.

Brand I.D. — Brand identification. Sometimes the trademark and signs used for the purpose of calling attention to the name.

Brand Image — The qualities attributed to a particular brand by consumers. Can be real or imaginary.

Brand Loyalty — Consumer faithfulness toward a brand, measured by length of time or regularity of use.

Brand Name — A name selected by the advertiser to identify a product to the consumer, and to set it apart from all other products. Several product variations may exist within a designated brand, i.e. flavors.

Brand Selection — The customer seeks a particular item but has no brand preference, or has two or more brands in mind. When selection of the brand is made in the store, it is called "in-store brand selection."

Brand-Switching — The action whereby a customer buys a brand different from his or her customary brand. A "brand-switch" may be planned prior to store entry or it may be made at the point of purchase, usually from some form of in-store stimulation.

Break for Color — In artwork and composition, to separate the parts to be printed in different colors.

Breaker Plate — A perforated plate located at the rear of the die in an extruder. It also supports the screens that prevent foreign particles from entering the die. Also used without screens in injection-molding nozzles to improve distribution of color particles in the melt.

Breathing — The opening and closing of a mold to allow gases to escape early in the molding cycle: also called degassing.

Broadside — Any large advertising circular or poster.

Brochure — A pamphlet bound in booklet form.

Broke — The paper waste from the print production process.

Broker — A trader who purchases materials or commodities and resells them at a profit without making any alteration in the materials or commodities. Sometimes misapplied to point-of-purchase advertising agencies that design and sell but do not manufacture point-of-purchase materials.

Bubble-Maker — A machine for producing bubbles and ejecting them into the air. The bubbles are sometimes scented.

Bubble-Pack — See **Blister Pack**.

Bubble-Up — A hollow glass rod or tube with a ball on one end that contains a gas and a liquid. Warmth activates the gas causing a steady movement of bubbles within the tube. "Bubble-ups" are used on Christmas trees to give sparkle to the light and in beer mugs or glasses in displays to give the beer a look of freshness.

Build-Up — Multiple layers of corrugated pads glued together to give a desired thickness; normally used for interior packing.

Bulk Factor — The ratio of the volume of a molding compound or powdered plastic to the volume of the solid piece produced; the ratio of the density of the solid plastic object to the apparent density of the loose molding powder.

Bulk Shipments — Refers to components/parts shipped unassembled.

Bump-Ons — Small vinyl, plastic, or metal feet often used on the bottom of wooden countertop displays or wall hangers.

Burn-In — The technique of double exposing film. This is often done to make a logo or text appear on a photo or background.

Bursting Strength — Term used to describe or identify the strength of corrugated paperboard. The strength will vary depending on the liner-boards used which, when combined, make the corrugated construction. This is done by a piece of laboratory equipment known as a Mullen Tester. It is universally used to authenticate the strengths of shipping containers.

Bushing — The outer ring of any type of a circular tubing or pipe die that forms the outer surface of the extruded tube or pipe.

Butadien — A plastic polymer material that, when mixed with acrylic and styrene polymers, produces A.B.S. material which is widely used in P-O-P manufacturing.

Butyrate — Common name for a tough cellulose acetate thermoplastic used for signs, etc.

Buyer — A person responsible for purchasing point-of-sale materials.

Buying Habits — The usual manners and actions of a consumer in purchasing products and/or services.

Byte (electronic) — A group of eight bits treated as a unit to represent a character in a coding system.

C.A.D. — Abbreviation for Computer Aided Design, a process whereby circuits, schematics, and other designs are generated by a computer.

CD (electronic) — Stands for compact disc. A relatively new audio-video-computer format that digitally encodes sound on a 12 cm laser disc. The sound is decoded by an optical laser for exceptionally high quality audio playback. This format was originally envisioned as a home electronics update or replacement for vinyl LP sound recordings.

CD-I (electronic) — Stands for compact disc interactive. A new technology released in 1987 that combines the data storage capabilities of CD-ROM with the storage standards for audio and video. It will provide 660 megabytes of memory. It can carry still graphics and motion video as well as audio. This could mean a possible 7,000 natural still pictures, up to 32,768 colors for user-manipulated graphics, and up to 256 colors for full programmed animation. It can deliver 2, 4, 8, or 16 channels of audio information, as much as 16 hours of monaural or eight hours of stereo sound. CD-I machines will be able to play standard CD programs.

CD-ROM (electronic) — Stands for compact disc read-only memory. This format uses the CD format as a computer storage medium and can handle 550 megabytes of data on a disc about the size of a traditional 5-1/4 inch floppy. This format, introduced in 1987, can deliver the complete *Encyclopedia Britannica* on one disc with room to spare. CD-ROM will be used as an adjunct to mini and personal computer memory systems.

CL — Abbreviation for carload. In rail transportation, a shipment filling one freight car.

C.P.M. — Abbreviation for Cost Per Thousand. A method of determining the cost of 1,000 exposures of an advertising message to potential customers for a product. Most advertising media recognize this means of cost measurement.

CPR (Cost Per Return) — A method of measuring the effectiveness of a marketing program. The CPR is calculated by taking the cost of a promotion and dividing it by the number of responses to it.

CPU (electronic) — See **Central Processing Unit.**

CSA — (Canadian Standards Association) — Electrical P-O-P in Canada requires CSA approval.

C Flute Corrugated — One of the wave shapes in the inner portion of combined corrugated board. 9/64ths of an inch in height. Most widely used flute for applications that require increased structural strength, such as shipping containers, support pieces, pads, etc.

C-Print — A color print made from a film negative.

"Cab-O-Sil" — Trade name of shredded, finely divided silica used as fillers. Used with resins, it makes them thixotropic.

Calendar Rolls — In the production of paperboard, the setting of these rolls determines the thickness, density, and finish of the paper being produced.

Calendar Stock — Same as calendar rolls.

Caliper — The thickness of a sheet measured under specific conditions, expressed in thousandths of an inch. Thousandths of an inch are often called "points."

Camera Ready — Copy and/or art that is ready for photography.

Can — See **Sign Cabinet.**

Cantilever — A steel supportive structure or racket projecting from a main support column. Used in installation of some outdoor signs.

Car Topper — A display that can be attached to the top of a car or truck, either permanent or expendable, for showroom or street use.

Cardboard — A term erroneously used as a synonym for corrugated fibreboard. Not an applicable term for container materials.

Carpet Selector — A display that coordinates carpets or carpet samples by color, size, quality, etc., for selection by the customer.

Cart — See **Mobile Floor Stand.**

Cart Wrap — A printed advertising message on paper, light cardboard, etc., designed to wrap around shopping carts.

Carton — A package generally made from a bending grade of boxboard and used for merchandising consumer quantities of product. A "carton" may be a corrugated or solid fiber shipping container that does not necessarily have to comply with Universal Freight Classification (UFC) Rule 41 or National Motor Freight Classification (NMFC) Item 222-Series.

Case Card — Product riser or header that is attached to, or inserted into, a case containing the actual product.

Case Dividers — Strips of any material to fit in display cases or food freezers that carry an advertising message and help the retailer to organize the case; sometimes referred to as a case organizer.

Case Strips — Plastic or cardboard strips designed to snap into the channel molding of food cases or shelving.

Case Wrap-Arounds — A decoration or sales promotion sheet designed to wrap around a case of merchandise. It's usually made of singleface corrugated with printing on the flat or fluted side. Used as a display or as the base for a display.

Cash Register Display — A display designed to be mounted on a cash register at a checkout spot in self-service stores. Usually designed to hold high-impulse items such as candy, cigarettes, razor blades, etc. Also a sign, usually illuminated, mounted on the cash register on the bar or back bar.

Casting — The process whereby a liquid polymer is poured into an open mold where it hardens without application of external pressure; also the finished product of a casting operation. The term is not to be used as a synonym for molding.

Catalog Items — Year-round, institutional, or permanent point-of-purchase units.

Cavity — The depression in a mold; the space inside a mold wherein the resin in poured; the female portion of the mold; that portion of the mold that surrounds the molded particle or that forms the outer surface of the molded article (often referred to as the die).

Cellulose Acetate Butyrate — See **Butyrate**.

Cellulosic Fibres — Made by chopping, beating, and shredding wood and paper stocks. When at the fibrous stage it is used in the production of paper.

Cement — *n*: See **Adhesive** *v*: See **Bond**.

Central Processing Unit (C.P.U.) — The "command center" through which all information must pass in an electronic display, usually a microprocessor "chip" and its associated hardware.

Certificate, Box Maker's — A statement printed on a corrugated fibreboard box identifying and locating the box maker and guaranteeing that all applicable construction requirements of the carriers have been observed.

Chaining (electronic) — The ability to link, or "chain" separate messages together so they will run in sequence in an electronic display.

Chair Easel — A vertical riser held in place by a chair-like projection in front and dependent on the weight of the merchandise for full stability. Sometimes called an easel stocker, easel back, or chair back display.

Chalking — A lithographic term referring to the improper dying of ink; in chalking, the pigment dusts off due to lack of a binding vehicle caused by rapid absorption of vehicle into paper.

Change Holder — A rubber or plastic mat with a "nubbly" surface to keep coins from rolling off the counter when the clerk puts them down for the customer. Usually carries an advertising message.

Change Maker — Any small counter display or device that holds products near a checkout or register to generate an impulse purchase from small change after another purchase has been made.

Change Pad — See **Change Holder**.

Change Tray — Receptacle on cashier stand for customer change. Usually featuring an advertising message.

Changeable Letter Sign — A sign that, in addition to identification, provides for changing the advertising message by the use of removable letters.

Channel Strip — Extruded metal molding covering the front edge of a retail display shelf for price, unit cost, or other data.

Channelized Letters — Independent letters mounted on a beam-like structure that house electrical connections or any background that is so designed to permit easy/sure anchoring of letters and numbers. Can be for indoor or outdoor P-O-P.

Chapter (electronic) — A consecutive sequence of frames.

Chapter Stop (electronic) — A code embedded in the vertical interval of the video disc that enables certain video disc players to locate the beginnings of chapters.

Character (electronic) — Letters, numerals, punctuation marks, symbols, etc., on a computer.

Chase — The main body of the mold that contains the molding cavity or cavities, or cores, the mold pins, the guide pins or the bushings, etc.; an enclosure of any shape used to shrink-fit parts of a mold cavity into place, to prevent spreading or distortion in hobbing, or to enclose an assembly of two or more parts of a split-cavity block.

Check Disc (electronic) — A disc that is used to evaluate video material prior to the replication of release copies.

Checkout Counter Pieces — A point-of-purchase device at the checkout counter that performs a consumer service (dispenses matches, gives time, etc.) and contains an advertising message to stimulate impulse buying.

Checkout Stand — A stand for checking purchases and bagging them in a self-service store. The cash register is a feature of the "checkout stand."

Chip — An electronic circuit in a compact, uniform package (also silicon chip, integrated circuit).

Chipboard — A paperboard often made from reclaimed paper stock. Used for many purposes including partitions and the filler (center ply or plies) of solid fibreboard. The substrate to which a litho is mounted to create a cardboard display.

Choke — A plug or similar device located in a channel in a blow-molding manifold designed to direct and restrict flow to a desired path or to equalize pressures.

"Chromacom" — A trade name for a highly sophisticated computer color separation laser scanner capable of electronic retouching and stripping.

"Chromalin" — A trade name for a photographic proof of a color separation showing color quality.

Chrome — A color transparency with a positive photographic image on film.

Cladding — An affixed facade to an existing sign pole or base that can be added after the sign is built. It may not have been planned for or known at the time the sign was installed.

Clamp Nail — Special fastener used to join sides of wooden frames.

Clamping Pressure — In injection-molding and in transfer molding, the pressure that is applied to the mold to keep it closed; it acts in opposition to the fluid pressure of the compressed molding material.

Classification, Freight — Publications maintained by the railroads and the motor common carriers that include the rules and regulations governing the acceptance of freight in transportation. These rules designate the forms of packaging that are acceptable and specify the minimum requirements for shipping containers. These requirements must be met to avoid penalty increases in freight charges.

Clean — In reference to a display program that involves minimum effort on the part of the retailer. It eliminates complicated paperwork, special pricing, or special handling.

Cleavage — A method of rupturing adhesive bonds between rigid materials that can be described as a prying action.

Coating — The process of applying protective films on signs, especially to fireproof them. Coating may also add to the luminosity of signs. The process by which any material can be given color or a gloss, satin, matte, or protective finish.

Cohesion — The phenomenon by which the particles of a single substance are held together by primary or secondary valence forces.

Cold Molding — The shaping of an unheated compound in a mold under pressure, followed by heating the article to cure it.

Cold Pressure — A bonding operation in which an assembly is subjected to pressure without the application of heat.

Cold Slug Well — In injection molding this is an undercut section of the mold that holds the plastic material being molded in an accessible fashion so the machine operator or a robot device can easily grasp and remove the just-molded part. See **Sprue Lock**.

Cold Type — A trade term denoting the use of composition methods not involving hot metal type. Most common forms are typewriter composition, paper letters, photo composition on photo paper, and mechanical lettering instruments. Photographic composition on film is a form of cold type composition.

Collar — Any flange that encircles or surrounds another piece or section, standing up to protect or hold the other piece or section. Also, a flat printed piece carrying an advertising message and designed to encircle the neck of a bottle in a display by following the contour of the bottle.

Collotype — A direct, screenless printing process that reproduces continuous tones with maximum fidelity. See also **Photogelatine**.

Color Correction — Any method, such as masking, dot-etching, re-etching, and scanning, used to improve color rendition. Can be done on screened or continuous tone separation negatives, or by corrective work on the halftone printing plates.

Color Plate — A printed plate that carries all the elements of an advertisement to be printed in a specific color.

Color Process Work — Also called Process Color. A reproduction of color made by means of photographic separations. Also the method or the copy requiring such operation.

Color Proofs Progressive — A set of color proofs consisting of color proofs of each plate, singly, and in combination with other proofs as the job will be printed. For example, yellow by itself; magenta; yellow and magenta; cyan; yellow; magenta and cyan; black by itself, and all four colors combined.

Color Separation — A photographic negative exposed through one of the tricolor filters and recording only one of the primary colors; in platemaking, manual separation of colors by handwork performed directly on the printing surface. The pre-separation of colors by the artist using separate overlap for each color executed in black or gray tones ready for the camera.

Color Separation Negative — A photographic negative exposed through a color filter and recording only one of the primary colors in full color work or one of the two colors in two-color work; in platemaking, manual separation of colors by handwork performed directly on the printing surface. The negative is a gray tonal record of the intensity and the color it is reproducing, being light where the color is strong in the copy and dark where the color is weak in the copy.

"Color-Stik" — Trade name for pressure-sensitive stickers for color-keying packages.

Color Swatch — A small, usually square solid print used with the sketch, negative, positive, or printing plate to identify a color. A guide in color separation and correction operations.

Color Transparency — A full-color photographic positive on a transparent support. Ektachrome and Flexacrome are examples.

Colorama — A giant-sized color transparency, usually photographic.

Column — A vertical row of LED in an LED matrix.

Combination Features — Two or more products offered together at a single unit price.

Combination Plate — One engraving which combines line and half-tone reproduction.

Combined Board — The term used to indicate a completely fabricated sheet assembled from several components, such as 'corrugated' fibreboard or 'solid' fibreboard.

Combo Display — Parts so designed and included that it can be used as a counter display if there isn't enough floor space for floor placement.

Combo Pack — Combination package of two or more items; can be joined by a band or on a card; common in the food and health-and-beauty aids industries.

Comprehensive Mock-Up (or "Comp") — Finished or semi-finished piece of art; a drawing or model. A physical sample with semi-finished artwork or photography applied to the unit for preproduction evaluation or studio photography.

Compression Mold — A mold that is open when the material is introduced and that shapes the material by heat and by the pressure of closing.

Compression Testing — See **Deflection**.

Computer Generated (electronic) — Usually text and graphics created, stored, and produced entirely by a computer — either by the elaborate equipment in a professional editing suite, or by the external computer used in a Level 3 interactive video configuration.

Computer Graphics — The interactive production and layout of graphic material, text, and images by means of computer keyboard, light pen, digitizer, mouse, and other hardware/software integration.

Conditioning Time — The time interval between the removal of the joint from the conditions of heat and pressure, or both.

Conduit — A tube or protected trough for electrical wires. Used in outdoor illuminated sign installations.

Contact Molding — A process for molding reinforced plastics in which reinforcement and resin are placed on a mold and cured either at room temperature, using a catalyst-promoter system, or by heat in an oven. No additional pressure is used.

Contact Screen — A halftone screen which is placed in direct contact with a photographic positive or negative. It is used to produce halftone positives of halftone negatives for making screen printing plates.

Containerboard — The paperboard components (linerboard, corrugating material, filler chip) from which corrugated and solid fibreboard are manufactured.

Continuity Distribution — Denotes a specific time frame in which all display and collateral material must arrive at the retail store level at numerous geographic locations.

Continuity Program — A promotion that builds regular shopping visits by consumers. Usually consists of an offer each week for a new piece to a set, such as a dinner plate. These are sold at low prices.

Continuous Tone — A photographic image that contains gradient tones from black to white.

Contrast — Tonal comparison of high lights and shadows in an original or reproduction. The tonal difference in detail, i.e., contrast copy, refers to accentuated detail in both light and dark areas.

Co-op Contract — Cooperative display contract between the advertiser and retailer that is frowned upon by the Robinson-Patman Act unless it is offered on equal terms to all retailers.

Copy — The printed advertising message. The manuscript or text furnished to printers. Although the term "copy" is widely applied to photographs and different types of artwork submitted for reproduction, a better term for these items is "original" because it is from them that the reproduction originates. In photographic plate making there are two kinds of copy, line and tone, photographed without, and with, the halftone screen, respectively. Line copy is that in which the design or image of the original is composed of lines or dots of solid color. Tone copy is that in which tones, shades, or solid colors appear.

Copy Area — That part of a sign or display carrying the message. Also called "live" copy area.

Copy Platform — The formulation of the basic ideas for an advertising campaign and the designation of the importance of the various selling points.

Copy Preparation — In photomechanical processes, the directions indicating desired size and other details for illustrations and the arrangement into proper position of the various parts of the page to be photographed for reproduction. Also the work of preparing copy in paste-up form of text and art as a unit, termed a mechanical paste-up. In typesetting, the careful revision of copy to ensure a minimum of changes or corrections after type is set.

Copy Slant — The style in which a selling point is presented. Copy is usually said to be "slanted" toward a particular audience.

Copy Testing — Research performed to evaluate the appeal and/or clarity of proposed selling messages.

Core — A channel in a mold for circulation of heat-transfer media; part of a complex mold that forms undercut parts.

Core Vents — Slotted vents used to get steam into expandable polystyrene.

Corepin — A pin for forming a hole or opening in a molded piece.

"Corobuff" — Bemiss-Jason Corp.'s trade name for a single-face corrugated that is made of flute plus a layer of paper. This is often used as a decorative wrap for case stacking.

Corona Treatment — An electrical process for making certain plastics printable.

Corrugated Board — The structure formed by gluing a fluted (corrugated) inner member to a flat facing (singleface) or between flat facings (singlewall). Other combinations of inner members and facings are used to form doublewall and triplewall board. These can be of varying strengths and densities.

Corrugated Board, Doublewall — The structure formed by three flat facings and two intermediate corrugated members.

Corrugated Board, Singleface — The structure formed by one corrugated member glued to one flat facing.

Corrugated Board, Singlewall — Also known as doubleface. The structure formed by one corrugated inner member glued between two flat facings.

Corrugated Board, Triplewall — The structure formed by four flat facings and three intermediate corrugated members.

Corrugated Plastic Sheets — A twin wall of extruded plastic sheets spaced apart by a ribbed or fluted center section. Used as a screen printing and display substrate.

Corrugating Material or Corrugating Medium — Paperboard used in forming the fluted portion of the corrugated board.

Corrugation — See **Flute**.

Corrugator — A machine that usually takes containerboard from three roles and combines it into a corrugated board consisting of two exterior facings and an intermediate fluted member. The corrugator forms the intermediate material into a series of arched trusses and attaches the facings to them with adhesive applied at the tips of the flutes. The resulting board is called singlewall corrugated fibreboard. By taking containerboard from five rolls, it also produces a corrugated board, commonly known as doublewall, consisting of three facings and two corrugated mediums. By adding another corrugated medium and facing, triplewall corrugated fibreboard is produced. The machine also cuts the fibreboard to size and may score it in one direction.

Counter Card — At the point of purchase, a card with brand name and product information designed for use on the checkout or service counter. It may be placed with the merchandise to serve as a reminder.

Counter Mat — A flat mat of any material bearing an advertising message on the counter.

Counter Occupancy — The amount of area or space a display occupies in square inches or square feet. This is an important factor in gaining retail acceptance and placement of a counter display.

Counter Stand — A small display piece designed to fit on an average store counter.

Coupon Pad — A deck or pack of coupons serrated or so taped for easy tear-off. Usually features a mail-in premium or a price rebate.

Coverage — The area over which a given quantity of coating material can be applied at a specified thickness.

Crazing — Fine cracks that may extend in a network on, under the surface, or through a layer of adhesive.

Crease Score — A line indentation made to facilitate a partial fold in paper or board, such as displays, cartons and other items that are shipped flat and then assembled. Also see **Scoring**.

Crease Sheet — C/Sheet — Corrugated or chipboard that has an impression for bending.

Crop Marks — To eliminate portions of the copy, usually on a photograph, indicated on the original by "crop marks." Sometimes referred to as "tic" marks. Usually placed in the margin to denote the area of an image to be reproduced. To cut off an edge or trim.

Cross Merchandising — See **Related Display**.

Crosshead — A device that is attached to the discharge end of the extruder cylinder, designed to facilitate extruding material at an angle (normally, at a 90-degree angle to the longitudinal axis of the screw).

Crossmarks — Register marks to make possible the accurate positioning of images in composing, double-printing, and multicolor printing, and in superimposing overlays onto a base, or to each other. Commercially available in a variety of forms for pasting on copy.

Crow's Feet — A pair of metal brackets that fit into pole slots at right angles to each other and form feet for a pole display. May also be constructed from corrugated board.

Cubic Size/Cube — The measurement of volume of a display piece for shipping, storage, and/or set-up dimension of a display unit. Usually an outside dimension.

Cull — The material remaining in a transfer chamber after the mold has been filled.

Curtain Coater — A coating machine that spreads an even thickness of low viscosity liquid (clear or adhesive) across a flat sheet or surface.

Customer Profile — An estimate of the number of people and their demographic or geographic composition who will probably buy a given brand. This may also include their purchasing patterns.

Cut-Case — A shipping carton designed to be cut into shelf trays, each tray carrying product and a product message. The outer shipping container can be shipped with a tear tape or perforations to aid in the display's set up.

Cut-Off — 1: In web printing, the cut or print length corresponding to the circumference of the plate cylinder. 2: The line where the two halves of a compression mold come together; also called flash groove or pinch-off.

Cut-Score — A method of die-cutting a fold where the material is cut halfway through. Commonly used in corrugated paperboard and polypropylene plastic displays to increase the flexibility of the fold.

Cyan — One of the subtractive primaries and the hue that is used for one of the four-color process inks. It reflects blue and green light and absorbs red light.

DCE (electronic) — See **RS 232** and **RS 422**.

DMA (Designated Marketing Area) — A market defined in geographic terms and based on media coverage.

DOS (Disk Operating System) (electronic) — The set of systems programs that operate a disk drive.

DS Mirrors — Indicates the strength and thickness of the glass. DS

1/8", for instance, is commonly used to refer to P-O-P work. The DS indicates the glass is "double strength" and 1/8" duplicates the thickness. See also **SS Mirrors**.

DTE (electronic) — A formal standard for serial communications between computers. See **RS 232 and RS 422**.

Dangler — A display panel that is suspended from the ceiling or one that snap-fits into a price channel strip. Either style moves with air currents and store traffic.

Database (electronic) — A collection of information in a form that can be manipulated by a computer and retrieved by a user through a terminal.

"Day-Glo" — Trade name for daylight fluorescent paint or ink used in advertising.

Deal — An offer by an advertiser giving a free display, free merchandise, cash, or other considerations to the retailer for using the display, buying a specified quantity of merchandise, or performing other functions.

Deal Pack — Special-pack merchandise that usually carries the marketers' promotional pricing graphics.

Deal Sheet — A printed sheet (black and white through four-color process) that carries an image of the display and all pertinent information relating to size, floor occupancy, product load, dealer costs, dealer margins, etc., for the purpose of establishing production quantities or quantities of produced units to be shipped.

Dealer Acceptance — Refers to how well a display piece is received by the retailer or the merchandising staff.

Dealer Copy — The space for the retailer to put his name, price, or other message on the advertiser's sign or display; also the copy he puts in.

Dealer Incentive — A display having as an integral part some useful or desirable take-home unit for the dealer, for example, tables, carts, grills, etc. Can also be used as a "prop."

Dealer Loader — See **Dealer Incentive**.

Dealer Survey — A survey performed exclusively among proprietors or managers of retail stores.

Dealer's Privilege — A P-O-P sign that carries an advertisement on one side and a message from the dealer to the customers, e.g., "Thank You, Call Again," "Please Pay When Served," etc., on the reverse side. The P-O-P sign may have more than two sides.

Debossed Sign — A sign in which all or part of the copy area is recessed or "pushed in" from the flat surface, yet is an integral part of that surface.

Decal — Short for decalcomania. A printed plastic or specially treated paper sign usually affixed to windows, doors, products, or any smooth surface. May be of the water-immersible or pressure-sensitive type.

Decalcomania — See **Decal**.

Deflashing — The operation in which the excess material of pinch-off and flash is removed from blown containers.

Deflection — Refers to the deformation or reduction in dimensions in the testing direction between established pre-load and ultimate failure load in compression testing.

Delamination — The separation of layers in a laminate because of failure of the adhesive, either in the adhesive itself or at the interface between the adhesive and the adherend, or because of cohesive failure of the adherend.

Delivery System (electronic) — In interactive video, the set of video and computer equipment actually used to deliver the interactive video program.

Demand Color(s) — Refers to additional colors used during four-color process printing that are solid colors not produced by using "dots."

Demo Kit — Self-adhesive stickers or cards that can be attached to a product to point out features, usually attached to the sales floor "demonstration" model.

Demographic Characteristics — The vital statistics of a population group or a derived sample, such as age, sex, education, etc.

Demonstration Stand — A display stand that offers facilities for showing the practical use of the product, e.g., vacuum cleaner and attachments are demonstrated in cleaning dirt off a rug, electric juicer squeezing oranges, etc.

Demonstrator Display — A display that shows the function of a unit.

Densitometer — An electric instrument designed to accurately measure optical density, or tone values, and used in place of the human eye for such purposes. Two general types: visual and photoelectric. Transmission densitometers measure the full density range of negatives, and reflection densitometers measure the reflection range of opaque copy. If a photocell "search unit' is provided, the instrument can be used as an illumination meter on the ground glass of camera.

Density — A measurement that is used to determine the hardness of the foam plastics. It is expressed in pounds per cubic foot (PFC).

Department Maker — A display and/or collateral material used to dominate or provide a large or strong theme in a specific department in a retail store.

Departments — Large merchandising stands featuring the variables of one product or a brand line.

Die — 1: An assembly of parts which, when attached to an extruder, is used to form an extrudate into a desired shape. 2: Any of various tools or devices, originally cubical in form, for molding, stamping, cutting, or shaping.

Die-Cut — A cut made with special steel rule dies. The act of making a part or container by cutting and scoring to shape by such tools. Also used to denote a board that has been die-cut.

Die-Cut Sign — A sign where the shape is altered or cut by other than straight lines in order to give configuration to the sign for purposes of design.

Die-Cutting — The process of cutting out special shapes by means of a die made for the purpose.

Die-Stamp — A steel plate that is used to apply gold or silver leaf.

Die-Strike — A "first-off" proof from the die that is used to determine cutting accuracy.

Digitized Images (electronic) — A photographic or three-dimensional image electronically transferred to a computer memory and displayed on a screen.

Diisocyanates — A group of plastic compounds valuable for use in display work due to their ability to cause a chemical reaction when mixed with a polyglycol or polyester material. The resulting product is urethane. See **Urethane**.

Dioramas — Elaborate color displays of a scenic nature that are almost always three-dimensional and illuminated. Motion is often included.

Direct Profit Profitability (DPP) — The term used to describe a particular SKU's direct contribution to a store's profitability and sales volume.

Direct Shipment — Shipment of point-of-purchase materials directly to the dealer, either automatically, as part of the complete merchandise order, or at the special request of the dealer. This type of shipment is employed extensively by smaller advertisers with limited sales forces.

Discrete (electronic) — A single-element LED. Turns on just one lighted area.

Disk Drive (electronic) — A device that reads digital instructions or information and stores, or recalls it, from a thin, round plastic record called a floppy disk.

Dispenser — A sign or display containing a literature pocket or a tear-off pad, or a merchandise display containing a stock of merchandise for active selling.

Display — A device or an accumulation of devices which, in addition to identifying and/or advertising a company and/or product, may also merchandise, either by actually offering product for sale or by indicating its location. A display characteristically bears an intimate relationship with the product whereas a "sign" is more closely related to the name of the manufacturer, the retailer, or the product.

Display Card — A piece of display advertising, printed or mounted on cardboard, for attachment to a display of merchandise. See **Shelf-Talker**.

Display Carton — A carton, printed inside and outside, that is designed to fold out into a display without removing the product. Also referred to as a shipper display or an inside/outside shipper display.

Display Device — The medium through which information is displayed in an electronic display; examples would be LED, LCD, vacuum fluorescent, incandescent bulbs, and flippers.

Distribution — The total number of outlets through which an advertiser's product is sold.

Distribution Checklist — Printed form on which the complete distribution plan of shipment of point-of-purchase materials to distributors and retailers is detailed. It is frequently consulted to ensure coordination between arrival of merchandise in retail outlets and the placement of point-of-purchase units.

Distributor — The agency responsible for the marketing of an advertiser's product.

Doctor Blade — A scraper mechanism that regulates the amount of adhesive on the spreader roll or on the surface being coated.

Doctor Roll — A roller mechanism that revolves at a different surface speed, or in an opposite direction, resulting in a wiping action for regulating the amount of adhesive supplied to the spreader roll.

Domed (electronic) — A discrete or monolithic LED that has a dome-shaped lens.

Dot — The individual elements of a halftone.

Dot-Etching — Tonal correction of halftones, positives, or negatives in photolighography by judicious and controlled reduction of dot size through the action of chemical reducers. Tray etching for all-over reduction of dots; local etching done by an artist with a small soft brush.

Dot Matrix — 1: Term used to describe an array of LED. 2: Any configuration of LED, LCD, flippers, incandescent bulbs, or vacuum fluorescent segments arranged to display alphanumeric and graphic characters.

Doubleface — 1: Corrugated board with two smooth sides. 2: Any sign or display finished on two sides.

Doubleface Display — A display with a sales message on both the front and back.

Double Mounting — Term used interchangeably with duo mounting.

Double-Ram Press — A press for injection or transfer molding in which two distinct systems of the same kind (hydraulic or mechanical) or of a different kind, create, respectively, the injection or transfer force and the clamping force.

Double-Shot Molding — A means of producing two-color parts in thermoplastic materials by successive molding operations.

Double Stroke (electronic) — A routine that displays characters or graphics at twice their normal width.

Dowel — A pin, fitted into one part of the mold, that enters a hole in the other part so that when the mold is closed the two parts become accurately aligned.

Download — To transmit information from a central storage area to a terminal.

Draft — The taper or slope of the vertical surfaces of a mold designed to facilitate removal of molded parts.

Draft Angle — The angle made by the tangent to the surface at that point and the direction of ejection.

Draw — Stretching of a plastic face over a die to obtain the desired configuration for an embossed or debossed sign.

Draw-Down — In ink making, a term used to describe ink chemist's method of roughly determining color shade. A small glob of ink is placed on a piece of paper and drawn down with the edge of a putty knife spatula to get a thin film of ink.

Drop-Out — Portions of originals that do not reproduce, especially colored lines or background areas.

Drop Shipment — Timed shipping of small batches of a large order, or simultaneous shipping to multiple destinations.

Drop Shipper — The advertiser who ships directly to the customer upon receiving orders from a salesperson or organization that performs the selling.

Drop Testing — A series of tests done to a container or shipping box to see if damage occurs to its contents.

Drum — See **Sign Cabinet**.

"Duco" — Brand name of a line of nitrocellulose lacquers, enamels, paints, varnishes, cements, etc.

Dummy — A mock-up of the finished sign or display. Can be rough or well-finished.

Dummy Merchandise — Empty packages, or bottles filled with colored water, etc., used instead of the live merchandise for purposes of display.

Dump-Bin — A bin-shaped holder designed to stand on the floor containing merchandise in random order, so called because the merchandise can be "dumped" in from the case.

Duo Mounting — The process of laminating a printed sheet to both sides of cardboard to exact register.

Duo Tone — Term for a two-color halftone reproduction from a monochrome original and requiring two halftone negatives for opposite ends of gray scale at proper screen angles. One plate usually is printed in dark ink, the other in a lighter one.

Duplex Display — See **Shipper Display**.

Dwell — A pause in the application of pressure to a mold, made just before the mold is completely closed, to allow the escape of gas from the molding material.

Dye Transfer — In photography, a process of producing color prints by thinning photographic emulsions and using them to transfer dye solutions to film or paper coated gelatin.

E Flute Corrugated Paperboard — One of the wave shapes in the inner portion of combined corrugated board. 3/64ths of an inch in height. Provides an excellent printing surface and shows little washboarding (bumps) as compared to the larger flutes. This is the smallest corrugated flute, yet it offers increased strength over tag and chipboard stock.

EPS — See **Expanded Polystyrene**.

Earth Colors — The toned-down variations of the more intensive primaries, prepared from various ores and oxides found in the earth, such as iron or manganese oxides with aluminum silicates.

Easel — Free-standing floor unit of wood, plastic, or metal to support signs, large cards, and frames, or a support attached to a display card to enable it to stand.

Easel Stacker — See **Chair Easel**.

Easeling — Process of attaching point-of-purchase signs and displays to easels.

Ejection — The process of removing a molding from the mold impression, by mechanical means, by hand, or by the use of compressed air.

Ejection plate — A metal plate used to operate ejector pins; designed to apply a uniform pressure to them in the process of ejection.

Ejection Ram — A small hydraulic ram fitted to a press for the purpose of operating ejector pins.

Ejector — An attachment to a hydraulic press used to operate ejector pins. It may be mechanically, pneumatically, or electrically operated.

Ejector Pin — A pin or thin plate that is driven into a mold cavity from the rear as the mold opens, forcing out the finished piece; also called a knockout pin.

Ejector Rod — A bar that actuates the ejector assembly when the mold is opened.

Elastomers — An ingredient put into adhesives to develop an elastic or soft, rubber-like bond, as opposed to a hard or brittle bond.

Electric Spectacular — An outdoor sign in which lighting forms the design.

Electronic Display — A generic term for electronic programmable displays using LED, vacuum fluorescent, LCD, or a flipper matrix.

Electrostatic Film — A plastic sheet that has been electrostatically charged so that it "clings" to any highly polished surface without adhesive, offering easy removal and re-use capability.

Electrostatic Painting — A process for spray painting metal that involves invoking opposite electrical charges between the paint and the metal display component, resulting in a lower usage of paint (less overspray).

Electrotype — A duplicate of the original engraving plate.

Embossed Design — A molded plastic or metal design (or part of a design) cut out and mounted on a flat surface. Embossed elements are distinct from an embossed sign by not being an integral part of the background material.

Embossed Sign — A sign on which all or part of the copy area is raised so that it stands out from the flat surface, yet is an integral part of that surface.

Embossing — Process of raising prints, designs, patterns, etc., so that they are raised above the flat surface of signs or displays.

Emulsions — Liquids used in connection with photographic work. See **Dye Transfer**.

End-Aisle Display — A display built for placement at the end of a store aisle that accommodates a large group of product units. Also known as "end-cap displays."

End-Cap Displays — See **End-Aisle Displays**.

End Displays — Mass displays stacked against the end of a gondola or tier of groceries.

End User — The consumer of a product or service.

Entrance Angle — The maximum angle at which the molten material enters the land area of the die, measured from the center line of the mandrel.

Epoxy — Generic name for a group of thermosetting resins having strong adhesive qualities and chemical resistance.

Expanded Metal — Sheet steel that is slotted and stretched to form a geometric pattern.

Expanded Polystyrene — Light-weight foam beads bonded together through the use of heat and pressure inside a mold to form display components. Varying densities are used as required to increase or decrease the strength and detail.

Exposed Merchandise — Merchandise kept in sight of consumers on shelves and counters that is readily accessible to clerks and customers.

Exposure — The individual consumer's sensual contact with a P-O-P unit or other advertising media.

Extended Color — The extra area of color necessary for trimming or die-cutting when the printed image goes to the very edge, to avoid a white area due to inaccurate cutting of paper.

Extender — A substance, generally having some adhesive action, added to an adhesive to reduce the amount of the primary binder required per unit area.

Exterior Illumination — Sign illuminated by externally mounted lamps shining onto the faces.

Extrudate — Word sometimes used to identify an extruded piece or extruded section.

Extruded Aluminum — A finished piece of aluminum that has been produced by conforming it to shape by passing it through the die.

Extruder — The machine that is designed to position the die or dies through which plastic or metal is pushed or forced to manufacture the desired extruded shape. The lengths of such extrusions can very greatly.

Extrusion — Formed part created by forcing raw material through a die creating desired shape.

"Eye-Beam Display" — Trade name for an unmounted display, based on a unique construction principle in which the display can be rolled and shipped in mailing tubes, yet will be rigid when set up.

Eyeletting — The process of punching small holes, which may or may not be reinforced, for purposes of lacing or tying parts of a display together or attaching hooks, cords, etc.

FCC Approval — Indicates an electronic display has passed a test administered by the Federal Communications Commission (FCC) and certifies that the device has, at most, an acceptable level of radio frequency (RF) interference; FCC certification is mandatory by law in almost all computer-based products.

Fabric Banner — An advertising banner of woven or knitted cloth, usually suspended from a horizontal pole and often fringed on bottom and sides.

Face — Refers to either style of type or the raised portion of type that produces printing. Also refers to the front or "face" of a display.

Face Cover — Protective cover for the decorative or functional part of a sign.

Facings — The number of packages of an item on the front line of the store shelf or in a merchandising display.

Fade Proof Inks — In printing, certain inks that have a quality of resistance to fading when exposed to extreme sunlight. The "fade-ability" of inks will vary with geographic location and time of exposure to sun. No ink is totally fade resistant.

Failure Load — The maximum amount of weight pressure a construction or shape can withstand without breaking or being damaged.

Fascia Sign — A flush-mounted wall sign.

"Fastex" — Trade name for a one-piece extruded rubber fastener designed with button anchor for use in carding and packing merchandise.

Features — A term for products being given sales promotion.

Feet — Various styles of display stands made of wire or corrugated board. See also **Crow's Feet**.

"Fiberglass" — A trademark for finespun filaments of glass woven into sheets often used in sign fabrication.

Fibre or Fibreboard Box — A container made of either corrugated or solid fibreboard. For classification purposes, when the term 'box' is used, the structure must comply with all requirements of UFC Rule 41 of NMFC Item 222-Series.

Fibreboard — A general term applied to fabricated paperboard used in container manufacture. May be of either corrugated or solid construction. See also **Combined Board**.

Filler — A relatively nonadhesive substance added to an adhesive to improve its working properties, permanence, strength, or other qualities.

Fillet — A rounded bead or a concave junction of sealing compound over, or at the edges of, structural members.

Finish, Dry — A finish obtained on paperboard that has not been dampened before going through the calendar rolls. The surface is not as smooth as water-finished paperboard. See **Finish, Water**.

Finish, Water — A relatively hard and glossy finish produced on paperboard by spraying water on one or both sides as the material passes through the calendar rolls. See **Finish, Dry**.

Finished Art — Art that is complete in all respects; a true prototype of the anticipated reproduction; camera ready.

First Surface — Outside surface of a sign face.

Fixative — A chemical substance applied to signs to give permanency and to prevent fading.

Flag Testing — Testing a desired height and location for an outdoor plastic illuminated sign by suspending a flag in the location.

Flange — Projecting rim around sign or part of a display to hold it in place.

Flange Sign — A sign made so that it can be mounted vertically to the surface of a wall, building, or post from which it projects. It has "sell" copy on both sides.

Flaps — The closing members of a fibreboard box. The flap length is parallel to the slot and essentially equivalent to its dimension. The flap width is parallel to the flap score and essentially equivalent to its dimension.

Flash — The extra piece of plastic attached to a molding; it must be removed before the part can be considered finished.

Flash Gate — A long, shallow, rectangular gate.

Flash Groove — A groove ground in a mold to allow for the escape of excess material.

Flash Line — A raised line appearing on the surface of a molding and formed at the junction of mold parts.

Flash Mold — A mold designed to permit the escape of excess molding material. Such a mold relies upon back pressure to seal the mold and put the piece under pressure. See **Molds**.

Flash Ridge — That part of a flash mold along which the excess material escapes until the mold is closed.

Flasher — A light that flashes on and off at timed intervals to attract attention.

Flat (electronic) — 1: A discrete or monolithic LED lens that is flat as opposed to domed; generally flat lenses give wider angle readability. (In lithography.) 2: The assembly of photographic negatives or positives on goldenrod paper, glass, or vinyl acetate for exposure in a vacuum frame while in contact with sensitized metal press plate. Equivalent to a typographic form and containing text as well as art.

Flat Etching — See **Silhouetting**.

Flexo Printing — See **Flexography**.

Flexography — A variation of rotary letterpress using flexible rubber plates and rapid-drying fluid inks. Also known as "flexo printing."

Flexural — **See Test, Edgewise Compression**.

Flipper (electronic) — A display device that consists of a disk, door, sphere, or cube that is electromagnetically opened and closed to show either a colored or black surface; used primarily in outdoor electronic displays.

Floating Chase — A mold member, free to move vertically, that fits over a lower plug or cavity, and into which an upper plug telescopes.

Floating Platen — A plate located between the main head and the press table in a multi-opening press, and capable of being moved independently.

Flocking — An electrostatic spraying process producing a velvety finish on any surface.

Floor Bin — See **Bin**.

Floor Mat — A mat of any type carrying a product message on the floor. Also a step-on mat used to trigger sound, motion, etc., in a display.

Floor Occupancy — The area or space a display occupies on the floor in square feet. This is an important factor in gaining retail acceptance and placement of a display unit.

Floor Pyramid — A display of merchandising rising from the floor in which products are stacked in the form of a pyramid.

Floorstand — A P-O-P display that is placed on the floor.

Floppy Disk (diskette) (electronic) — A small, 5-1/4" or 3-1/2" direct-access magnetic storage device resembling a phonograph record. Used to record or read information. General storage capacity 256,000–1,024,000.

Fluorescent Ink — An ink with high light-reflecting properties, hence it is attention-getting. It is most effective when surrounded by black or very dark color.

Flush — The vertical alignment of printing. Copy is usually spoken of as "flush left" or "flush right," meaning vertical alignment on the designated sides. Copy aligned vertically on both sides is called "adjusted."

Flute or Corrugation — One of the wave shapes in the inner portion of combined corrugated fibreboard. The flutes most commonly used are:

	Flutes Per Linear Foot	Approximate Height*
A-flute	36 +/- 3	3/26"
B-flute	50 +/- 3	3/32"
C-flute	42 +/- 3	9/64"
E-flute	94 +/- 4	3/64"

*Not including thickness of facings

Flute (or Corrugation) Direction — The normal direction of the flutes is parallel to the depth of the box. In "end-opening" boxes and in wrap-around blanks, the flute direction may be parallel to the length or width. With the latter construction, the designation is "horizontal corrugation box" or "horizontal corrugation blank."

Foam Board — A family of rigid, foam-centered sheets and boards, made of a variety of laminate materials.

Foil Paper — A very thin metal sheet laminated to a paper backing or support sheet, usually with permanent adhesive for use as a single-element substrate.

"Fome-Cor" — Trade name for a board with an expanded foam plastic core covered on both sides with Kraft paper.

Font — Characters, numbers, and punctuation in a given type face/size.

Force — The male half of a mold, which enters the cavity, exerting pressure on the plastic and causing it to flow; either part of a compression mold.

Four-Color Process — See **Process Color**.

Four Conductor Wire (electronic) — Standard telephone cable as can be found in ordinary household applications; also used for connecting a network of electronic displays.

Fragrance Strip — A fragrance delivery device for use at the point-of-purchase comprised of microencapsulated fragrance sandwiched between plys of paper.

Frame (electronic) — A single, complete picture in a video or film recording. A video frame comprises two interlaced fields. Film runs at the rate of 24 frames a second; video at 30 frames a second in NTSC standard systems, 25 frames a second in PAL and SECAM (European standard) systems.

Frame Grabber (electronic) — The logic element of a broadcast teletext decoder that "captures" a designated, numbered frame as it is transmitted.

Frequency — In point-of-purchase exposure, the number of time an individual sign or display is exposed to individuals within a specified time period.

Frequency (electronic) — Time varying changes of signal measured in Hertz (Hz), which is cycles per second.

Front-End Merchandisers — Displays that are accessible only from the front. The sides and back are "closed."

Fugitive Colors — Inks made from pigments or dyes that are not very light resistant and that lose color rapidly when exposed to light, heat, and other environmental influences.

Galley Proof — A proof of text copy before being made into pages.

Gate — 1: In wooden display racks, the fronts of shelves or bins. Often screen-printed or embossed with copy. 2: In injection molding and in transfer molding, the narrow orifice through which material is injected into a mold cavity from the feed; the molded material removed from the orifice in the process of extracting the mold.

Gazebo — A display fixture (generally free-standing and open on all sides like a gazebo structure) with several types of products. A large island display.

Gear Streaks — In printing, parallel streaks appearing across the printed sheets at the same interval as gear teeth on the cylinder.

Giant Replica — An oversized reproduction of the product or trademark.

Glow Panel — Luminescent lighted panel bearing an advertising message.

Glue — Originally, a hard gelatin obtained from hides, tendons, cartilage, bones, etc., of animals. Also, an adhesive prepared from this substance by heating with water. Through general use the term is now synonymous with the term "adhesive."

Goldenrod Flat — The method of assembling and positioning lithographic negatives (or positives) for exposure in contact with a light-sensitized press plate. The goldenrod paper used is translucent enough to see penciled layout on underside, or master layout on separate white paper beneath. Film negatives can be attached to goldenrod paper in the proper position with red scotch tape. The goldenrod paper beneath image areas is cut away before flat is reversed to place emulsion-side of negatives to emulsion on metal plate. Flat is also used for making blueprint of form for checking imposition. Sometimes referred to as a form. A lithographic flat corresponds to a typographic form.

Gondola — Island shelving, open on two sides, common to self-service stores.

Gondola End — A display designed to be used at the end of a gondola (set of shelves) in a self-service store. "Gondola ends" are usually large displays.

Gondola Topper — A two-sided display to rest on the top of the gondola in such a way that it can be seen from numerous aisles, or coming and going in both aisles.

Grain — In papermaking, the direction that most fibers lie; this corresponds with the direction the paper is made on a paper machine.

Graphics Monitor (electronic) — A video monitor or terminal capable of displaying graphics.

Gravity Feed — A merchandiser designed to use the force of gravity to bring more merchandise into view. This can feed a single unit or a quantity in succession.

Gravure — Printing by means of an engraved cylinder produced through a photoengraving process. This printing process permits a number of impressions to be made in a single operation at high speed, usually associated with large quantity runs.

Gray Scale — A strip of standard gray tones, ranging from white to black, placed at the side of original copy during photography to measure tonal range obtained, and in the case of color separation, negatives used to determine color balance or uniformity of the separation negatives. A commercial product available either on paper or on transparent acetate for use with transparencies.

Gripper Bite — The amount of paper that extends beneath the press gripper. Sometimes called gripper margin.

Gripper Edge — The unprintable blank edge of a sheet that gives allowance for mechanical fingers to pick up the sheet and carry it through the printing or die-cutting press, this edge is usually 1/2" wide.

Gripper Margin — See **Gripper Edge**.

Grommet — A metal eyelet used for fastening.

Grommetting — The process of placing metal eyelets in displays.

Ground Mounted — A sign mounted in the soil rather than on a structure (i.e., sign, sign pole, building, etc.).

Guide Marks — A method of using crossline marks on the offset press plate to indicate trim centering of sheet, centering of plate, etc., as well as press register in multicolor work. Not to be confused with register marks used for stripping elements to register.

Guide Pin — A pin that guides mold halves into alignment on closing.

HO (High Output) — Refers to fluorescent lighting.

Halftone — Any photomechanical printing surface and impression therefrom in which detail and tone values are represented by a series of evenly spaced dots of varying sizes and shapes. The dot areas vary in direct proportion to the intensity of the tones they represent.

Halftone Printing — A printing technique to reproduce artwork with tonal variation. The original artwork is photographed through a screen that separates the design into small varied sized dots, producing continuous tone variation.

Halftone Screen — See **Halftone Printing**.

Handshake — 1: (hardware) A method of controlling communication between two or more devices; in serial communications, several wires may be used to let a device know if the line is clear for data transmission; these wires are known as handshake lines. 2: (software) The act of agreeing on which device sends and which device receives is called handshaking.

Hanging Sign — A sign that hangs from a mounting bracket that usually projects from a wall, building, or post. It usually features copy on both sides.

Hard Disk (electronic) — Disk storage device using rigid disks rather than flexible. Can generally store more information and access it faster.

Hardboard — A fabricated board material often used in displays.

Hardener — A substance or mixture of substances added to an adhesive to promote or control the curing reaction by taking part in it. The term is also used to designate a substance added to control the degree of hardness of the cured film.

Head — The end section of a blow-molding machine in which the melted plastic is transformed into a hollow parison.

Header — A message board projecting above the display and giving the headline or the advertising message. Usually larger or more intricate than a riser.

Heat Blending — A process whereby plastic is locally heated in order to bend the material to a desired angle without cracking the material. This is widely used on small countertop plastic signs.

Heat Motor — A small rotating element that is operated by the heat of an inside light. May be used to give the illusion of such effects as falling water, blowing drapery, etc., in a display.

Heat Seal — To bond or weld a material to itself or to another material by the use of heat. This may be done with or without the use of adhesive, depending on the nature of the materials.

Heat Sink — A fin to conduct heat away from a surface or electronic device.

Hickeys — An imperfection in lithographic presswork that can be caused by dirt on the press, hardened specks of ink, or any dry hard particle working into the ink or onto the plate or offset blanket.

High Contrast — Refers to the relationship of highlights to shadows on a negative, whether continuous tone or halftone. In such a negative the highlights are very black and the shadows very open according to the tonal scale.

Highlight — In photomechanics, the lightest or whitest area of an original or reproduction, represented by the densest portion of a continuous-tone negative, and by the smallest dot formation in a halftone negative and printing plate.

Highlight Halftone — A halftone reproduction in which the highlights are devoid of dots for accentuation of contrast.

High-Pressure Molding — A molding process in which the pressure used is greater than 1000 psi.

Hinged Side — The side of a doublefaced sign that would hinge open for servicing.

Hob — A master model used to sink the shape of a mold into a soft steel block.

Hob Punch — The hardened-steel master tool used in hobbing; the male part of a mold.

Hollow Lumber — Square cardboard tubes for display construction.

Honeycomb — Tissue-paper sheet with alternate gluing that stores flat, but opens into a honeycomb effect and makes three-dimensional bells, balls etc.

"Hook-Ups" — Trade name for plastic buttons with a metal hook and sticky back used to hang small signs or displays.

Horizontal Arrangement — The stocking of a line or variety of products full length on a single gondola or wall shelf.

Host Computer (electronic) — A computer and associated database that, although run as a separate entity, can be accessed through a network.

Hue — The attribute or dimension by which one color is distinguishable from another, by a particular color name but with no qualification as to tone or intensity.

I

IC (Integrated Circuit) — See **Chip**.

"INT" (Image and Transfer) — A trade name for a process of producing type transfers or rub-offs.

"I" Beam — A metal sign shaped like an "I" in its vertical section.

Ident — Identification as on a sign; the brand name.

Identification Sign — A sign furnished by the advertiser and in addition to the advertising message, bearing the firm name of the retailer, bank, etc. Also, a sign giving the firm name only in a place of business.

Illuminated Signs & Displays — Any signs or displays with light in any form.

Imposition — Arranging and fastening negatives or positives to a supporting flat for use in offset lithography platemaking. Multiple imposition is the exposure of the same flat in two or more positions on the press plate.

Imprint — To reproduce letters, symbols, marks, etc., by pressing.

Impulse Buying — Making an unplanned purchase.

Impulse Items — Those products that have a high appeal to the consumer and cause him/her to make an unplanned purchase. Items are described as "high" or "low" impulse.

Impulse Sales — Sales for retailers resulting from consumers making unplanned purchases of "impulse items."

Inflatable — A plastic creation that assumes three dimensions when filled with air or gas. May be used as a premium or an integral part of the display.

Infra Red (electronic) — An invisible frequency of light just below the color of red, used to communicate without wires between the keyboard and an electronic display.

Injection Blow Molding — A blow molding process in which the parison to be blown is formed by injection molding.

Injection Molding — The method of forming a plastic to the desired shape by forcing the heat-softened plastic into a relatively cool cavity under pressure.

Injection Ram — The ram that applies pressure to the plunger in the process of injection molding or transfer molding.

Ink-Receptive — Having the property of being wet by greasy ink in preference to water.

Inner Packing — Materials or parts used in supporting, positioning, or cushioning an item in an outer shipping container.

Inner Supports — In cardboard dump bins or floorstands the egg-crate construction used to strengthen those parts of a display that are designed to hold merchandise or are subject to stress.

In-Pack Coupon — Store redeemable coupon enclosed in a product package, for use later by the product's buyer; may be redeemed on a subsequent purchase of the same product, or on a different product (cross-couponing). Generally promoted on the exterior of the package.

In-Pack Premium — A premium packed inside a product package as an incentive for consumer purchase.

Input (electronic) — Generic term for circuit or information coming into an electronic device; in an electronic display this would be a keystroke from the keypad or serial communications.

Insert — 1: An advertisement packaged with retail merchandise. 2: An integral part of a plastic molding consisting of metal or other material that can be molded into position or pressed into the molding after the molding is completed.

Insert Cards — Display cards that can be inserted into a permanently mounted frame.

Installation Service — Service offered by a company that contracts to place displays in retail outlets for the advertiser at a per unit cost.

Instant Coupon — Cents off, or other discount or promotional coupon, affixed to, or inserted in, a package.

Instruction Sheet — Printed instructions giving directions for setting up a display.

Intaglio Printing — Printing from a depressed surface. Lines to be printed are cut below the surface of the engraved plate. When flooded with ink and wiped clean, only the inked design remains. Gravure and photogravure are forms of intaglio printing.

Integration — Term used to describe the use of point-of-purchase advertising in conjunction with other media — television, radio, newspapers, magazines, etc.

Intensity (electronic) — Brightness of the LED.

Interactive (electronic) — Relative term indicating a user's ability to input commands and receive a response from a system. often erroneously used as a synonym for "two-way."

Interactive Display — A display requiring the consumer to actively participate in the selling process by supplying information about needs and preferences through the use of a computer keyboard or touch-sensitive screen. The computer, in turn, processes the consumer's needs and the product attributes, and makes a buying recommendation.

Interactive Video (electronic) — The convergence of video and computer technology; a video program and a computer program running in tandem under control of the person in front of the screen. In interactive video, the user's actions, choices, and decisions genuinely affect the way in which the program unfolds. The opposite of interactive video is linear video, e.g., a television program or a video tape.

Island Display — A display designed to stand alone with merchandise available from all sides.

Island Floorstand — A floorstand designed so that it is accessible from all sides.

Item 222-Series — Provisions in the National Motor Freight Classification of the motor common carriers containing requirements for corrugated and solid fibreboard boxes.

Itinerant Display — An expensive display or exhibit that is scheduled and moved from one outlet to another.

J-Hook — A hook that projects from a shelf to carry a display of merchandise.

Jet Molding — An injection-molding process in which most of the heat is applied to the material as it passes through a nozzle or jet, rather than in a heating cylinder as in conventional presses.

"Jewelite" — Trade name for decorative plastic trim used to attach faces to metal drum in sign manufacturing.

Joint — 1: The location where two adherends are held together. 2: That part of the box where the ends of the scored and slotted blanks are joined together by taping, stitching, or gluing. When accomplished in the box manufacturer's plant, it is known as a manufacturer's joint; created when the box flaps are sealed in a box user's plant (usually on automatic equipment), it is called a user's joint.

Joint, Lap — A joint made by placing one adherend partly over another and bonding together the overlapped portions.

Joint Scarf — A joint made by cutting away similar angular segments of two adherends and bonding the adherends with the cut areas fitted together.

Joint, Starved — A joint that has an insufficient amount of adhesive to produce a satisfactory bond.

Jumble Basket — Similar to a dump bin in that articles for sale are tossed in haphazardly. A jumble basket usually contains many different kinds of products; a dump bin only one.

Jumble Displays — The loose arrangement of items in a display container.

KD — Abbreviation for "knocked down" display. A KD display is assembled at the spot where the display is to stand.

KD Display — A display that is shipped partially assembled for reasons of economy in shipping, storage, or actual production. The degree of KD varies.

KD Tooling — Tooling that is constructed for fabricating parts of a display, then torn down and reconstructed to fabricate completely different parts. This type of tooling is usually inexpensive compared to more permanent varieties.

Key Line & Paste-Up — A set of drawings, one for each color included in the finished print, which are keyed to each other for successive printing runs. This usually consists of a board on which various elements are pasted down with overlaying plastic sheets on which other elements intended for different colors are pasted.

Keyhole Slot — Recessed slot machined in wooden, wall-mounted displays to facilitate hanging.

Keypad (electronic) — Input device for an electronic display used to program and operate the electronic display (also keyboard).

Kick Band — Strip at the bottom of a floorstand, usually dark in color, that withstands accidental scuffs, kicks, mopping stains, etc., when in use in the retail outlet.

"Kleen-Stik" — A trade name for tape with transferring adhesive used to install signs, posters, or lightweight displays. Also, a trade name for self-sticking papers.

Knife Lock – A small slot that is die-cut into a paperboard display to accept a tab. The tab and slot lock securely.

Knocked Down — See **KD**.

Knockout — Any part or mechanism of a mold used to eject the molded article.

Knockout Pin — See **Ejector Pin**.

Kraft — A word meaning strength applied to pulp, paper, or paperboard produced from wood fibres by the sulfate process.

"Krylon" — Trade name for a line of aerosol type acrylic spray coatings.

LCD (Liquid Crystal Display) — A display device using crystals that can selectively become opaque or clear when exposed to a controlled voltage; commonly seen in calculators and digital watches.

LCL — Abbreviation for Less Than Carload. In railroad transportation, a shipment of materials filling less than one carload of space.

LED (Light Emitting Diode) — A display device using a material junction that glows a characteristic color (red, green, yellow) when exposed to a current.

LTL — Abbreviation for Less Than Truckload. In truck transportation, a shipment of materials filling less than one truckload of space.

Laminate — A product made by bonding together two or more layers of materials.

Laminating — A process that consists of spreading a clear, bright, thin coat of plastic over a printed surface, giving a high degree of brilliance and protecting the surface against wear. Also see **Litho Laminating**.

Laminator — A machine that adheres two or more plies of paper or fibreboard. For corrugate fibreboard, this usually encompasses laminated facings or corrugating medium to provide enhanced functional properties and/or more attractive graphics.

Lamp Pulls — See **Light Cord Hangers**.

Land — The surface of an extrusion die parallel to the direction of melt flow; the portion of a mold that separates the flash from the molded article; in a semipositive or flash mold, the horizontal bearing surface.

Land Area — The whole of the area of contact, perpendicular to the direction of application of pressure of the seating faces of a mold; those faces that come into contact when the mold is closed.

Landed Force — A force with a shoulder that seats on land in a landed positive mold.

Laser Disc (electronic) — The name popularly used to describe the reflective optical video disc. A high-density video system storing tens of thousands of images on a 12-inch disc encoded with 10 billion tiny pits beneath a plastic layer. These pits are read by a low-power laser beam on a video disc player and decoded to a readable video screen.

"Latex" — A trade name for a material made by a suspension in water of fine particles of rubber and/or synthetic rubber.

"Latex 61-1000" — Trade name of a special form of latex.

Lay-Up — The face of a mold that establishes the character, appearance, and configuration of a finished reinforced plastic sheet. See **Vacuum Bag Molding**.

Lazy Susan Display — A display turned by hand or push-button motor on a turntable base. Also see **Spinner Display**.

Lead Time — The time between the arrival of signs and displays at their ultimate locations, and the date the promotion is due to break.

Ledge Display — A display designed to go behind the counter, on the top of a bar or shelving (in which case it is flat on the back), or on top of a gondola (in which case it can be round, or two-sided).

Lenticular — A grooved plastic sheet with certain light properties that give a different visual angle at different light angles, creating a three-dimensional effect when either printed or preprinted.

Letterpress — Oldest method of mechanical printing in which printing ink is transferred from raised metal or rubber to paper, board, etc. Also see **Rubber Plate Printing**.

Level 0 (electronic) — The bottom of the scale designed by the Nebraska Videodisc Design/Production Group to describe interactivity in videodisc players. Level 0 represents domestic-standard players that have no potential for interactivity.

Level 1 (electronic) — Represents the basic features expected on consumer equipment: frame, addressability, remote control, the "search" facility, still-freeze frame, forward and reverse motion, chapter stop, picture stop and quick scan, slow motion, and step frame replay.

Level 2 (electronic) — A level 2 industrial player uses level 1 capabilities plus its own on-board microprocessor; can offer multiple choice, branching facility and scorekeeping, and improved access.

Level 3 (electronic) — Effectively the top of the Nebraska Videodisc Design/Production Group scale. Level 3 represents a level 1 or level 2 video player, industrial or domestic, linked to an external computer (mainframe, mini, or micro). Level 3 offers by far the greatest versatility of any interactive configuration.

Levels of Interactivity (electronic) — The potential for interaction determined by the capabilities of the video disc hardware.

"Lexan" — Trade name for polycarbonate manufactured by General Electric Corporation and used in production of outdoor illuminated signs. Also used indoors when strength and durability are needed for a display.

Light Box — A box-shaped display unit in which a transparency forms one face of the box and is backlighted.

Light Cord Hangers — Cardboard advertising messages suspended at the end of a lamp chain or cord.

Light Thief — A display that has no illumination of its own but gives a lighted effect due to the use of transparencies seen against a store light source or due to use of reflective surfaces that trap and focus light.

Line Copy — Any copy suitable for reproduction without using a screen; copy composed of lines or dots as distinguished from copy composed of continuous tones, but are still regarded as line copy if they can be faithfully reproduced without a screen.

Line Cut — A line engraving that is reproduced without tonal variation. Tonal variation is possible with halftone engraving.

Line Screen — See **Screen**.

Liner — A creased fibreboard sheet inserted in a container that covers all side walls.

Linerboard — Paperboard used for the flat facings in corrugated fibreboard; also as the outer plies of solid fibreboard.

Linerboard, Wet Strength — A facing that has been chemically treated in the containerboard mill to impart higher resistance to rupture when saturated with water.

Linkage — Connections from the motor to the moving parts of a motion display. This can become complicated depending on the type of motion required.

Literature Holder — A display that holds customers' products or service brochures at the point-of-sale.

Literature Pocket — A literature holder that is attached, or built into, a display.

Literature Rack — A floor or counter holder for stimulating use of sales brochures, or for selling periodicals or books.

Litho Laminating — The process of combining a litho printed sheet of SBS board with singleface corrugated to produce a structural sheet of corrugated board. The printed sheet is then ready to go directly into die-cutting.

Lithography — A printing process in which the art is photographed on a sensitized metal plate, and treated so that the plate will accept ink only in those areas from which an imprint is desired. This method is based on the repulsion between grease and water; the design is put on the surface with a greasy material; and then water and printing ink are successively applied. The greasy parts that repel water absorb the ink, but the wet parts do not. This type of printing is used in offset lithography, offset printing, photo-offset, photo-lithography, and planography.

Live Area — The area on a sign or a display header that's fully visible when set up.

Live Merchandise — The actual product on display. When the display is in a position vulnerable to pilferage, small items such as pens, etc., are sometimes cemented, or otherwise affixed, to the display.

Living Hinge — Common expression for the repeated flexing ability of a polypropylene sheet.

Load — The product or mix of products being displayed. Also denotes the weight of the product in a display.

Locating Ring — A ring that serves to align the nozzle of an injection cylinder with the entrance of the sprue bushing and the mold to the machine platen.

Locking Pressure — In injection and transfer molding, the pressure that is applied to the mold to keep it closed (in opposition to the fluid pressure of the compressed molding material).

Locks — On cardboard or corrugated displays, tabs that secure display sections or pieces in the intended position.

Logo — The advertiser's stylized trade name or trademark to be used repeatedly in advertising.

Logotype — Printing plate used to reproduce advertiser's logo; also refers to two letters joined in one block of type.

Loose — Articles "dumped" in a box, package, or other container.

Loose Punch — The male portion of a mold, so constructed that it remains attached to the molding when the press is opened and is removed from the mold with the molding (for the purpose of extraction).

Low-Pressure Molding — Molding at a relatively uniform pressure, i.e., of about 200 psi or less, with or without application of heat from an external source.

Lumen — Measure of unit of light.

Luminescence — A phenomena of light emission by a chemical composition that is film-forming and that absorbs light, releasing it when extraneous light sources have been removed. A "glow-in-the-dark" capability.

Magenta — One of the subtractive primaries, the hue of which is used for one of the four-color process inks. It reflects blue and red light and absorbs green light.

"Magic Base" — Trade name for a floor display with a device that elevates the back product area. May also be called a pop-up tray.

Make Ready — Preparing for the production of materials by setting up production facilities, making special adjustments, etc.

Makeup — The arrangement of printed messages on signs and displays.

Makeready — 1: On an offset press, the adjusting of feeder, grippers, side guide, pressure between plate and offset blanket cylinder, putting plate on press, and ink in fountain to be ready to run the press. 2: On a photo composing machine, the preparatory work of positioning negative in holder, plate on back, and getting ready to start exposures in step-and-repeat operation of platemaking; the "set-up" work.

Mandatory — Usually copy required by law. May also be copy required by the advertiser in every advertising message.

Mandrel — An insert in the flow channel of a die that converts the flow from a solid cross section to some type of hollow or annular cross section. The outer surface of the mandrel guides the flow of the inner surface of the plastic melt before leaving the discharge end of the die.

Manifold — The distribution or piping system that takes the single-channel flow output of the extruder or injection cylinder and divides it to feed several blow-molding heads or injection nozzles. (The term is used mainly with reference to blow-molding and sometimes to injection-molding equipment.)

"Market-Diser" — Trade name for a battery-operated, transistorized tape message-repeater device that creates sound for displays.

Masking — 1: Covering, usually with a tape, a printing plate or die to prevent ink or paint from being applied (appearing) in areas not to be covered. 2: In photography, to block out areas on a negative that are not wanted on the print to be made.

"Masonite" — Trade name for panels made from exploded wood chips pressed into dense boards.

Mass Display — A display featuring a sizable grouping of the product plus a message. Also see **Pallet Display**.

Mast Arm — Perpendicular extension off of pole to hang sign.

Master Pack — 1: A shipping container complying with UFC Rule 41 or NMFC Item 222-Series used to overpack or unitize a number of individual containers. 2: An outer fibreboard box in accordance with UFC Rule 41, Section 3, Note 8, or NMFC Item 222, to enclose and unitize two or more boxes of uniform dimensions and complying with other requirements.

Mastering (electronic) — A stage in the production and real time process in which the premaster videotape is used to modulate a laser beam onto a photosensitive glass master disc (from which all subsequent discs will ultimately be pressed).

Matched Metal Molding — A process for manufacturing reinforced plastic in which matching male and female metal molds are used (similar to compression molding) to form the part, as opposed to low-pressure laminating or spray-up.

Matrix Panel (electronic) — An array of LED used primarily to display text, graphics, and animated sequences of graphics. (Also known as a graphics panel.)

Mats — Carpets or mats bearing an advertising message that are placed on the floor immediately in front of a product or leading to and from a store entryway. See also **Floor Mat**.

Mechanical — See **Key Line & Paste-Up**.

Mechanical Book — a motion display consisting of a giant book that automatically turns its pages. The pages are mounted on a horizontal cardboard cylinder that revolves slowly and continuously from back to front, ferris wheel style. Power is provided by a midget alternating current motor.

Mechanical Paste-Up — A method of assembling all copy elements into a unit for photographic plate making (copy ready for the camera). May include all copy except text, or be complete with text as well as line and tone copy proportional and positioned.

Media Support — Schedules in television, radio, magazines, newspapers, etc., that back up display promotion.

Medium — See **Corrugating Material** or **Corrugating Medium**.

Medium, Wet Strength — A medium that has been chemically treated in the containerboard mill to impart higher resistance to rupture when saturated with water.

Memo-Changer — Compact counter piece with room at the top for the customer's change and memo paper, usually locked next to the cash register in liquor stores. The back of the unit serves as a handy storage compartment for the retailer.

Memory (electronic) — 1: A circuit that allows permanent or temporary storage of text, graphics, and numbers in an electronic display. (Also RAM, ROM) 2: A specific message within the electronic display.

Memory Loader (electronic) — A device that loads complete, precomposed messages into an electronic display.

Menu Board — A point-of-purchase display that enables the retailer to list offerings and prices.

Menu-Driven (electronic) — A program built around a series of menus, or tables of contents, that guides users through the options available.

Merchandiser — A display containing merchandise for immediate sale.

Merchandising — Promoting a company's in-store effort to the salesforce, wholesalers, and dealers. The promotion to consumers of the product by use of point-of-purchase materials, in-store retail promotions, and stock maintenance.

Merchandising Awards — Awards given by POPAI during an annual competition to companies whose displays have best met merchandising challenges.

Merchandising Kit — A display kit promoting a general event or a selected group of related products, consisting of different types of display units to be used throughout the retail outlet.

Message Repeater — Endless film or sound tape where message is repeated in some form of box display for indoor or outdoor use. Film is usually backlighted.

Metallize — To give a plastic or other substrate a metallic appearance by depositing a microscopic layer of metal.

Metamerism — A condition in which colors match under one light source but do not match under another light source, due to different pigment having been used to produce the sample colors.

Mezzotint — The dots that form a contact screen for making simulated halftone effects and that are irregular in shape and size and non-uniform in position. The end result can resemble a manually produced crayon effect on rough surfaced stock.

Microcapsule (microencapsulation) — A microscopic plastic resin sphere containing a liquid such as a fragrance oil.

Microcomputer (electronic) — Computers with central processing units that are microprocessor chips. Microcomputers consist of personal computers, small business computers, and desktop computers ranging in prices from $200 to $20,000.

Microencapsulated — See **Microcapsule**.

Microprocessor (electronic) — A central processing unit (CPU) implemented on a chip.

Middletone — In halftone, any neutral tone intermediate between the highlights and shadows of an original and reproduction therefrom.

Miniature — A small scale model of a large and/or expensive display. Also a small sketch very much under scale and usually rough.

Mobile — A display consisting of several counter-balanced pieces suspended in such a way that each piece moves independently in a light current of air.

Mobile Floorstand — Floorstand that has wheels so that it can be moved from one area to another. Also known as a cart.

Mock-Up — Facsimile sample of P-O-P signs and displays indicative of proposed production unit.

Modem — (Electronic) — Modulator/Demodulator. A device that converts a digital signal to an analog signal suitable for telephone transmission and vice versa.

Modified EPS Bead — Erector set system, permitting the building of a variety of displays from a few basic units.

Moire — Undesirable patterns occurring when reproductions are made from halftone proofs or steel engravings, caused by conflict between the ruling of the halftone screen and the dots or lines of the original; a similar pattern occurring in multicolor halftone reproductions and usually due either to incorrect screen angles or misregister of the color impressions during printing. Moire can also be caused by the regular pattern of fabric threads intersecting the halftone screen pattern.

Mold — The cavity or matrix into, or on which, the plastic composition is placed and from which it takes form; the assembly of all the parts that function collectively in the molding process to shape parts or articles by heat and pressure.

Mold Insert — A removable part of a mold cavity or force that forms undercut or raised portions of a molded article.

Mold Pins — Devices used to separate the two mold sections after the molding cycle has been completed. These pins push the two parts away from each other so the part just produced can be manually or automatically removed from the mold.

Mold-Release Agent — A material used to prevent sticking of molded articles in the cavity. See **Release Agents**.

Mold Seam — The line on a molded or laminated piece, differing in color or appearance from the general surface, caused by the parting line of the mold.

Mold Shrinkage — The immediate shrinkage that a molded part undergoes when it is removed from a mold and cooled to room temperature.

Molded Urethane — A molding process utilizing a foaming urethane material that expands to fill every detail of a capped-off soft silicone mold. A high degree of detail and some undercuts are possible. Material has the look of wood and is easily painted or stained.

Molding — The shaping of a plastic composition within, or on, a mold, normally accomplished under heat and pressure; sometimes used to denote the finished part.

Molding Compound — can be 1: *thermoplastic*, which means the material can be formed by heating and can be reheated and reformed upon application of heat at any time, or 2: *thermoset*, which is a class of materials that assumes a desired shape by applying (usually) high heat. However, in this case, reheating will not melt or soften the material.

Molding Cycle — The period of time necessary for the complete sequence of operations on a molding press to produce one set of moldings; the sequence of operations necessary to produce one set of moldings.

Molding Pressure, Compression — The unit pressure applied to the molding material in the mold. The area is calculated from the projected area taken at right angles to the direction of applied force and includes all areas under pressure during complete closing of the mold. The unit pressure is calculated by dividing the total force applied by this projected area.

Molding Pressure, Injection — The pressure applied to the cross-sectional area of the material cylinder.

Molding Pressure, Transfer — The pressure applied to the cross-sectional area of the material pot or cylinder.

Molds — Patterns or forms from which metal or plastic signs and display elements are produced.

Monochrome — A negative or printing plate that is used in a press to print one color on the material being run, usually paper or plastic.

Monolithic (electronic) — see **Discrete**.

Motion Displays — Any signs or displays with moving elements to attract attention.

Mounting and Finishing — Bonding the printed sheet on reinforcement, die-cutting, scoring, etc. Joining parts in sub-assembly or assembly.

Movable Merchandisers — A merchandiser, usually made of metal, with two or more wheels to allow the retailer to move the entire display without disturbing the merchandise. These displays are often constructed on the handtruck principle.

Movable Platen — The large back platen of an injection-molding machine to which the back half of the mold is secured during operation.

Moving Letter Sign — A horizontal panel having many lights. The successive lighting of these lights in pattern makes the letters seem to move.

Mucilage — An adhesive prepared from gum and water. Also in a more general sense, a liquid adhesive that has a low order of bonding strength.

Mullen Tester — See **Bursting Strength**.

Multicolor Printing — Any finished display element that has more than one color on any single piece, or component, in a display or sign.

Multideck — A display fixture with vertical shelf arrangement.

Multiple-Cavity Mold — A mold with two or more mold impressions; a mold that produces more than one molding per molding cycle.

"Mylar" — A trade name for colorless or colored metallic finish often applied to signs and displays; film base.

"Mystik Tape" — Trade name for a self-sticking tape.

NEC — Stands for National Electric Code.

NMFC (National Motor Freight Classifications) — This is the universally accepted book of rules governing proper packaging and protection for all items when shipped by truck. The section pertinent to each situation must be located after the description of the item(s) to be shipped are known.

National Brand — A brand familiar to consumers throughout the country because of its universal distribution.

Near-Pack — A display that contains a premium giveaway and carries the promotional message placed in close proximity to the product being promoted. Can also describe a display knocked down flat and packed in a container with product still in shipping cases for set-up and loading at the retail level.

Neck Extender — A pole extension with end fitting of a sleeve on one end and an adapter connection on the other. One or more may be used between the top and bottom pole sections of a pole display.

Needle Blow — A specific blow-molding technique in which the blowing air is injected into the hollow needle that pierces the parison.

Neon — Gas-filled glass tubing producing various colors and configurations.

Network (electronic) — A group of electrical displays that are connected together by wire and/or modems, and can be programmed individually or as a group from any point within the network.

Nitrocellulose — Common gun cotton, used as a wadding material in display work much as it was used long ago in tightly packing (stuffing) an explosive charge. Used to force a more perfect shape or form.

Node (electronic) — Refers to a branching or exchange point in networks.

Non-Commit — A situation where the advertiser is not sure how many P-O-P units are required and places the risk on the producer/supplier who produces and stocks the item, selling it to the advertiser as ordered, a few pieces at a time, at a higher cost to the advertiser.

Non Glare (electronic) — Refers to the acrylic face plate of an electronic display; the surface of the acrylic is frosted in order to disperse ambient light, or glare.

Novel Paper Stock — Base stock mounted on cardboard made from distinctive paper, e.g., mother-of-pearl, velour, star-studded, Christmas paper, brick design, etc.

Nozzle — The hollow, cored, metal nose screwed into the extrusion end of the heating cylinder of an injection machine or a transfer chamber (where this is a separate structure). A nozzle is designed to form, under pressure, a seal between the heating cylinder, or the transfer chamber, and the mold.

Off-Pack — A display containing product and premiums, or just premiums, that are not physically connected to each other.

Offset — Wet ink that is undesirably transferred from one sheet to another in a load of freshly printed sheets.

Offset Blanket — A rubber blanket used in offset printing. see **Offset Printing**.

Offset Press Plate — The engraving plate on an offset printing press. See **Offset Printing**.

Offset Printing — A process in which impressions are transferred from the engraving plate to a rubber blanket and then printed on paper.

Olfactory — Relating to the sense of smell.

On-Pack — See **Out-Pack**.

Opaque Ink — 1: An ink that conceals all color beneath it. 2: Local application of opaque ink to photographic negatives or positives; blocking-out.

Optical Density — Determining the tone values of colors by relying on the human eye. See **Densitometer** for the instrument used today.

Optical Disc (electronic) — A video disc that uses a light beam to read information from the surface of the disc.

Out-of-Stock — Having no supply of a product on the shelf available for purchase. May also apply to having no back stock.

Out-Pack — A premium fastened to the outside of the merchandise package to give appeal and attention value to the product.

Out-Pack Shipper Display — A prepack group of premiums in a shipper display device, alongside stacks of the products, wherein the consumer is on the "honor system," taking both premium and product to the checkout counter. Also describes a display that is knocked down flat in its own shipping container and shipped with cartons of product strapped to, or wrapped with, the display shipping container.

Output (electronic) — Generic term for circuit, or information, going out of an electronic device such as a computer.

Outsert — separate printed matter attached to a package.

Overlay — 1: In artwork, a transparent, translucent vinyl or mylar that is placed over the copy where color break, instructions, or corrections are marked. Also transparent or translucent prints that, when placed one on the other, form a composite picture. 2: A transparent sheet that carries the object lines of a cutting die in order to check printing and graphic layout/position/registration during preparation and production before die-cutting occurs. Can also identify variations of additional details affixed over a graphic rendering. 3: A sheet of paper fastened on the printing surface of a press to make a heavier impression.

Overlay (electronic) — The ability to superimpose or key computer-generated text and graphics over a video picture, moving or still.

Over-Pack — One or more items packed together in one outer carton. Frequently, product plus display.

Overrun — Displays or elements that exceed the number ordered. This is necessary whenever more than one operation is required to produce the final product. The producer must gamble on how many pieces will be required to offset accidental damage in each intervening process so that he or she may come out with at least the number ordered.

Over-The-Wire Banner — A long rectangular piece of paper with the product message printed twice (head to head) on one side of the paper. When thrown over a wire, the messages are back to back and can be seen from either side. These banners are also used over T-bars. Frequently, a series of smaller banners are used over one wire.

Oxide Film — Applied to metal surfaces to provide a preservative coating. See **Anodizing**.

Ozalid Prints — A process that provides blueprint-type sheets from photographic positives. See **Blueprint**.

PLC (electronic) — A generic term for a programmable logic controller that reads inputs and sets outputs accordingly.

P-O-P — Common abbreviation for point-of-purchase advertising.

P-O-P Merchandising Agency — A creator, programmer, and supplier of point-of-purchase advertising materials who operates without manufacturing facilities, but with creative facilities geared to client needs.

P-O-P Producer/Supplier — A supplier of point-of-purchase advertising materials who may own production facilities, as well as creative facilities, for supplying P-O-P materials.

POPAI (Point-of-Purchase Advertising Institute, Inc.) — POPAI is the trade association representing the producers and users of advertising signs and displays. Pronounced "popeye."

P.O.S. (Point-of-Sale Advertising) — Used interchangeably with P-O-P.

P.S.F. — Pounds per square foot.

P.S.I. — Pounds per square inch.

Pack 1, 2, 3, 4, etc. — Denotes a display pack knocked down flat, singly, or in multiples in a shipping container.

Package Band — A premium offer announcement or special advertising message wrapped around a package.

Pad — A corrugated or solid fibreboard sheet or other authorized material used for extra protection or for separating layers of articles when packed for shipment.

Painted Wall — An outdoor advertisement painted on a wall visible to a shopping area with a high frequency of shoppers.

Painter's Guide — A line drawing in which the colors to be used are indicated on the various elements of the design.

Pallet Display — A mass display of product built on a pallet and contained in corrugated or other structural components. The entire pallet load of products is designed to be moved into place on the retail floor ready for display by just removing the protective shrouding.

Panel — A poster that can be used indoors or outdoors. Also, an area of a corrugated display that may accept graphics. Such panels are usually numbered.

Pantone System — a patented printing ink color matching system involving a range of stock colors that, when mixed in prescribed combinations and amounts, create a wide range of tints, tones, shadings, and intermediate hues.

Paper-Coated Gelatin — Paper specially treated to receive dye transfers. See **Dye Transfers**.

Paper Sculpture — Cut-out and folded paper figures that give the illusion of three dimensions.

Paperboard — The broad classification of materials made of cellulosic fibres on board machines, encompassing fibreboard, linerboard, corrugated medium, and piles of solid fibreboard. Most commonly made from wood pulp or paper stock.

Parallel (electronic) — A form of communications that sends all bits of information at once.

Parison — In blow molding, the hollow plastic tube from which an article is blow molded.

Parting Line — The mark on a molding or casting where the halves of the mold meet in closing.

Partitions — A set of corrugated or solid fibreboard pieces slotted so they interlock when assembled to form a number of cells into which articles may be placed for shipment.

Paste — A soft plastic adhesive such as that obtained by heating starch and water together.

Paste-Up — See **Key Line & Paste-Up**.

Paster — Machine that applies an adhesive to two or more plies of paperboard and combines them into a single sheet of solid fibreboard.

Peel — To separate a bond of two flexible materials or of a flexible and a rigid material by pulling the flexible material from the joined surfaces.

Pegboard — A name copyrighted by the Masonite Corp. for hardboard panels featuring holes drilled or pushed. Designed to receive wire hooks and other devices. See **Perforated Board**.

"Peg-Tube" — Trade name for paper tube that accommodates hooks and fixtures.

Pencil Rough — Pencil drawing of the proposed sign or display usually in the preliminary stages and in a loose style. Roughs can also be produced by other implements such as chalk.

Penetration — The degree of effectiveness of advertising in terms of its impact on the public.

Pennant — Same as a banner, but pointed at the bottom.

Perforated Board — The generic term for hardboard panels when not produced by the Masonite Corp. The holes and spacing are standard but special spacing and signings are available. Can be designed to hold displays or product.

Perforated Board Hooks — Hooks that fit into holes in perforated boards to support products, displays, etc. Usually made of formed wire.

Perforated Metal — Sheet steel or other metal die-cut in an all-over geometric pattern.

Permanent Display — A display designed for use for an indefinite length of time (often defined as one year). Example: large outdoor signs.

Personalized Display — A display that carries a retailer's name, etc., to personalize it.

Photo Stamps — High-gloss photographs in postage stamp form reproduced from photographs, negatives, or artwork. They are made available in sheets with gummed backs and are perforated.

Photocell — For use in P-O-P, see **Densitometer**.

Photoengraving — See **Gravure**.

Photogelatin — A direct, screenless printing process that reproduces continuous tones with maximum fidelity. It allows facsimile reproduction of any original copy; in fact, any type of artwork, monotone or multicolor. This method is used for printing point-of-purchase transparencies and vinyl. The printing plate in this process consists of a thin film of chemically treated gelatin, which has been spread over a special metal plate.

Photogravure — See **Gravure**.

Photolithography — See **Halftone** and **Copy Preparation**.

Photopolymer — A photo sensitive material used in the manufacture of raised letterpress printing plates. Primarily used in the flexo and pre-print printing processes.

Picking — Removal of part of the surface of paper, during printing. Picking occurs when the pulling force of the ink is greater than the surface strength of the paper, whether coated or uncoated.

Pick-Up Roll — A spreading device in which the roll for picking up adhesive revolves in a reservoir of adhesive.

Picture Stop (electronic) — An instruction encoded in the vertical interval on the video disc to stop the video disc player on a predetermined frame.

Pigtail Sign Holder — Wire-formed double-circle sign holder that allows for insertion of a header sign between the wire circles.

Pigments — Manufactured chemical colors, inorganic or organic; the former generally opaque and produced from basic materials including metals; the latter includes coal tar dye lakes formed by precipitation on alumina hydrate and widely used for lithographic transparent inks.

Pilfer-Proof — Usually said of a display used on the counter that shows the product to the consumer, but allows access only to a clerk behind the counter. "Pilfer-proof" displays on the floor sometimes have ingenious locking devices. Product itself is locked into card or container. Most are actually "pilfer-resistant," not "pilfer-proof."

Pin Holes — A substitute for core vents (air passages) in molds designed for production of expandable polystyrene.

Pinch-Off — In blow molding, a raised edge around the cavity in the mold that seals off the part and separates the excess material as the mold closes around the parison in the blow-molding operation.

Pixley (electronic) — 1: One LED dot within an LED matrix. 2: One dot of any display device within that device's matrix.

Placement — Use and acceptance of the display offered by the advertiser.

Planogram — A schematic drawing or other depiction describing the relative shelf placement and number of facings alloted for each SKU. Usually limited to a particular product category.

Plaque — A message or figure mounted on backing of a regular shape and having a more or less formal effect.

Plastic Transparency Display — A display unit that shows the body of a product upon which transparent slides are dropped in various combinations to show different colors available to consumers. The most commonly used products in this display category are automobiles.

Plasticate — Changing plastic pellets into a viscous melt by applying heat and pressure. See **Screw Plasticating Injection Molding**.

Plastisol — A suspension of a finely divided vinyl chloride polymer or copolymer in a liquid plasticizer that has little or no tendency to dissolve the resin at normal temperatures but becomes a solvent for the resin when heated. At the proper temperature the resin is completely dissolved in the plasticizer, forming a homogeneous plastic mass which, upon cooling, becomes a more or less flexible solid.

Plate — A metal or plastic sheet engraved with the reverse image of material to be printed.

Plate Cylinder — See **Cut-Off**.

Plate Making — See **Separations**.

Platens — The mounting plates of a press, to which the entire mold assembly is bolted.

Plating — Bright nickel, nickel-chrome, brass, or zinc finishes for displays. Usually relates to displays made from wire.

"Plexiglas" — Trade name for acrylic plastic sheets.

Plunger — A ram or piston used for the displacement of fluid or semi-fluid materials in transfer-, injection-, or extrusion-molding methods; also called piston, pommel, force, force plug, and pot plunger.

Ply — Any of several layers of solid fibreboard.

Pneumatic — A system that develops pressure by compressing air or gases to drive some machines, or to open, close, or activate a production cycle.

Point — Term used to describe the thickness or caliper of paperboard, a point being one thousandth of an inch.

Point-Of-Purchase Advertising — Telling the product or brand name story to customers at the retail outlet.

Point-Of-Purchase Advertising Institute — See **POPAI**.

Point-Of-Purchase Advertising Materials — Those devices or structures located in or at the retail outlet that identify, advertise, and/or merchandise the outlet, service, or product as an aid to retail selling.

Point-Of-Sale Advertising — A term used interchangeably with point-of-purchase advertising.

Pole — Round cardboard tube to hold display above a stack of merchandise, usually in several sections. Also a metal pole on which display or sign is erected.

Pole Display — A display mounted on a footed pole designed to be used with massed merchandise, and to be seen above it. The pole is mostly hidden in use.

Pole Sign — Single or doublefaced sign, attached to poles at gasoline stations, and other outlets.

Pole Topper — The part of a pole display that carries the advertising message.

"Polecat" — Trade name for one-piece telescoping pole support for displays and lights.

Polycarbonate — A thermoplastic material with high impact strength, low water absorption, and good electrical and optical properties.

Polyester — A thermosetting plastic composition with the capability of being drawn into extremely fine strands or thread that can be woven or knitted into many types of textiles including screen printing fabric. A common trade name in the general textile field is Dacron.

Polyglycol — A plastic polymer that reacts with diisocyanate to produce urethane material. See **Urethanes**.

Polymer — Any of numerous natural and synthetic compounds of unusually high molecular weight consisting of repeated linked units, each a relatively light and simple molecule.

Polypropylene — One of the more widely used compounds of the "plastics family." In sheet form it can be bent or flexed many times without breaking. Sometimes referred to as the living hinge.

Polystyrene — A clear, colorless plastic material used for molding sign faces, trays, parts of displays, etc.

Polyurethanes — See **Urethanes**.

Polyvinyl Acetate — A vinyl polymer used for coatings and adhesives.

POPAI — The Point-Of-Purchase Advertising Institute, Inc.; the trade association representing the P-O-P industry.

Pop-Up — A display where the display or portion of it is set up automatically as it is opened.

Pop-Up Bin — A corrugated display bin constructed so that it can be set up with one motion.

Porcelain Signs — Signs of porcelain on metal, usually printed by the silkscreen process, each color being applied and fused separately onto the metal. Extremely durable and long-lived, they are used extensively by companies whose advertising approach remains constant for extended periods of time.

Porosity — The quality or state of being permeable, i.e., of sufficiently loose texture to permit passage of liquid or gases through pores. One measurement is the rate of air movement through a test specimen. The relationship between porosity of corrugated fibreboard and the action of vacuum cups on automatic equipment that opens, loads, and seals boxes is often misunderstood.

Portable Display — A floor display with folding legs that is easily transportable.

Portable Reefer — A refrigerator case on wheels that can be moved to various locations.

Positive Mold — A mold designed to apply pressure to a piece being molded with no escape of material. See **Mold**.

Post-Testing — Store audits or other research techniques employed after a display has been installed to determine the rise in sales and/or brand awareness brought about by the use of the display.

Poster — A printed plastic, paper, or cloth banner or sign for window or interior use.

Poster Frames — Frames for posters and blow-ups of advertisements. Layers of ads may be mounted on one frame whereby the top ad can be torn off to reveal a new one.

Pot — A chamber to hold and heat molding material for a transfer mold.

Pot Plunger — A plunger used to force softened molding material into the closed cavity of a transfer mold.

Pourer — See **Bottle Pourer**.

Powder Coating — A durable spray paint finish that is applied dry and baked onto a metal component of a display. Can be made from epoxy, urethane, or polyester resins, or hybrids of these. Applied as a dry powder, the metal can first be heated to create a thicker finish.

Powder Molding — Techniques for producing objects by melting polystyrene, usually against the inside of a mold, either stationary (slush molding) or rotating (rotational molding).

Preform — A pre-shaped fibrous reinforcement formed by distribution of chopped fibres by air, water flotation, or vacuum over the surface of a perforated screen to the approximate contour and thickness desired in the finished part; also, a pre-shaped fibrous reinforcement of mat or cloth formed to a desired shape on a mandrel or mock-up prior to being placed on a mold press; also, a compact "pill" formed by compressing pre-mixed material to facilitate handling and control of uniformity of charges for mold loading.

Pre-Mastering (electronic) — The stage in the production of a video disc involving the coding, editing, assembly, evaluation, revision, checking, and preparation of intermediate materials onto a master tape for transfer onto the master disc from which all subsequent discs will be pressed. Sometimes called final assembly.

Premium — An item of some value used to attract attention to the displayed product in a secondary manner. An item of interest that can be received through the mail at a discounted price, free with purchase of primary (displayed) product, or as a cash-back offer. Also, a premium container (such as a decorative glass jar or tin box) that is reusable by the consumer.

Pre-Pack — A display designed to be packed with merchandise by the advertiser and shipped as a unit. A more refined version of a shipper display. This type of display is often favored by retail management because little time is required to assemble the display in the market, and little or no handling of product is required.

Pre-Press Proofs — Proofs made by photomechanical means in less time and at lower costs than press proofs.

Preprinted Linerboard — This is a printing operation performed on linerboard while it is still in roll form. Line art printing through four-color process printing in which several demand colors are available. Screen values to 120 lines are achievable. Liner is then corrugated and processed over die-cutting and conventional presses without the need to print.

Pre-Production (electronic) — That part of the production schedule leading up to the actual still or in-motion shooting of material on video or film, including script writing, storyboarding, flow-charting, and software design.

Press Proofs — Actual press sheets to show image, tone values, and colors as well as imposition of form or press plate in advance of the production run.

Press Run — The total number of copies printed.

Pressure Bag Molding — A thermoforming process in which pressure is used to press the sheet to be formed against the mold, as opposed to vacuum forming in which the sheet is drawn down onto the mold by exhausting the air between the sheet and the mold.

Pressure Pads — Reinforcements of hardened steel distributed around the dead areas in the faces of a mold, to help the land absorb the final pressure of closing without collapsing.

Pressure-Sensitive — A common adhesive material usually available in strips or solid coverage used to adhere signs, etc., to posting position desired.

Pre-Testing — A few display samples are tried in store locations to determine their effectiveness before the entire order is placed. Can be misleading if sites are not carefully selected; a test market.

Price Channel — The metal strip on the front edge of retail store fixtures or shelving that is designed to hold price and weight/size information about the product located at that spot on the shelf. Usually these plastic or paper pieces will snap-fit into the channel, and they can slide easily to adjust to product spacing.

Price Sign — A sign carrying a price.

Primary Colors — In printing ink, this refers to yellow, magenta (process red), and cyan (process blue). Of light, the primary spectral colors are red, green, and blue.

Primer — A coating applied to a surface, prior to the application of an adhesive, to improve the performance of the bond.

Printing Plates for Corrugated Board — Flexible, molded rubber, synthetic rubber, photosensitive solid polymer, and cured photosensitive liquid polymer blankets bearing images and used to transfer inks to paperboard substrates.

Privilege Copy/Panel Area — Part of display for private or exclusive use of retailer.

Process Color — Four ink colors — yellow, magenta, cyan, and black — which, when printed in sequence, one over the other, give the effect of natural color. Also known as "four-color process."

Producer — See **P-O-P Producer/Supplier**.

Product Identifier — A miniature printed plastic sign (self-sticking) or label affixed to the product itself. Informs and sells product on display. Usually carries the brand name.

Product-In-Use Display — A demonstration-type of display showing how the product is to be used by the customer.

Product Load — See **Load**.

Product Spotter — Small shelf sign or device designed to call attention to a particular product or brand that might otherwise be missed.

Product Switching — The customer enters the store planning to buy a particular item but instead purchases a different one.

Production (electronic) — In video terms, this refers to the stage in the job when still of motion video or film footage is actually shot.

Profile — 1: Ornate shape machine on edge of wooden display components. 2: The cross-sectional shape of the extrudate; usually reserved for complex shapes. Also, the extrudate with a complex cross section.

Profile Extrusion — An extrusion process that produces an essentially finished extrudate, as against one that produces a coating on wire or an intermediary material or parison.

Program — A planned, coordinated series of displays.

Progressive Proofs (Progs) — Proofs made from separate plates in color process work, showing the sequence of printing and the result after each additional color has been applied.

Promotional Display — In the broad sense, all displays are "promotional," but "promotional" is also used to indicate a display that is designed to be used only for the duration of a particular promotion, as opposed to those pieces that are designed for use for an indefinite period. (See **Permanent Display** and **Semi-Permanent Display**.)

Promotional Message/Copy — The copy on a display that makes the feature/benefit or value statement to the consumer. Usually appears as bold copy to facilitate reading and grab attention.

Proof — A trial impression taken at each stage of the printing process.

Prototype — Original model.

Proximity Sensor (electronic) — A device (sonar or infra red) that senses a user approaching and activates the related equipment.

Public Service Display — Display containing a clock, thermometer, baseball scores, etc., of interest to customers but not necessarily related to the product.

Pump Topper — Display used on top of gasoline pumps.

Puncture Test — The strength of the material expressed in ounces per inch of tear as measured by the Beach puncture tester.

Pylon — A tall identifying sign. Also can refer to the post or pole supporting an outdoor sign.

"Q-Tabs" — Trade name for stand-up, pressure-sensitive die-cuts for flash messages, shelf-talkers, and attention-getters.

R

RAM (electronic) — Stands for Random Access Memory. 1: The part of a computer's memory that can both read (use and display) and write (load) information, and that can be updated or amended by the programmer or user. 2: Storage device for chip hardware.

Ram — In molding, a ram is a piston or plunger that forces molten polymer through the head and die of an accumulator-type injection- or blow-molding machine.

Ram Force (molding) — The total load (normally expressed in tons) applied by a ram, and numerically equal to the product of the line pressure and the cross-sectional area of the ram.

RDA — See **Retail Display Agreement**.

RGB (electronic) — Stands for red-green-blue. A high-quality screen used with many computers, and increasingly with video systems as well.

RJ 11 (electronic) — Modular-type connector commonly used with telephones; also used for connecting electronic display networks.

ROM (electronic) — Stands for Read Only Memory. The smaller part of a computer's memory, in which essential operating information is recorded in a form that can be recalled and used (read), but cannot be amended or erased (write).

RS 232 (RS 232C) — A formal standard for serial communication between computers (DTE) and other devices (DCE); the complete, formal standard is rarely implemented; generically, a three- or four-wire serial link between devices; one wire to receive, one to send, and one for reference.

RS 422 — A standard for serial communication between computers (DTE) and other devices (DCE); generically a four-wire link using two wires to send, two wires to receive.

Rack — A floorstand featuring shelves, pockets, or hooked arms, usually of wire, designed for special display of a group of related items — sometimes a subdepartment — for customer self-selection and/or self-service. Racks may or may not also carry an advertiser message.

Rack-Jobber — A contractor who places the racks in the retail outlet and maintains them with merchandise, usually non-food.

Redemption Coupon — A coupon that, when mailed to the advertiser or presented to the dealer, entitles the consumer to acquire the advertised product at a discount or without charge.

Re-Etching — See **Color Correction**.

Reflection Copy — In photography, illustrated copy that is viewed and must be photographed by light reflected from its surface.

Register — 1: Exact correspondence in the position of pages or other printed matter on both sides of a sheet or in its relation to other matter already ruled or printed on the same side of the sheet. 2: In photo-reproduction and color printing, the correct relative position of two or more colors so that no color is out of its proper position.

Related Display — The combination of several related products in a single display. A counter display, floor bin, or other unit with several products having a seasonal, functional, or other commonality. Sometimes referred to as "cross-merchandising" when the products being promoted are from two or more advertiser firms.

Release Agent — Materials that are sprayed on mold surfaces to prevent sticking of molded shapes when the mold is separated. Facilitates removal of molded part.

Reminder Sale — A sale consummated when in-store stimulation causes the customer to remember a product for which a conscious intent to buy has been established.

Reset — Removing or adjusting an existing product configuration to accommodate a new product line, a replacement product line, new packaging, new shelving/displays, or an improved configuration as determined by the retailer.

Resolution (electronic) — Refers to the density of a dot matrix in electronic displays. The more "dots" in a dot matrix, the higher the resolution.

Retail Display Agreement (RDA) — Common in the paperback book and magazine field in which the retailer agrees to display the publications in return for remuneration from the wholesaler or publisher.

Retainer Plate — The plate on which demountable pieces, such as mold cavities, ejector pins, guide pins, and brushings, are mounted during molding; usually drilled for steam or water.

Return — Any portion of a display that bends 90–180 degrees to form a closed or clean edge for the purpose of better eye-appeal or to trap or hold another part in place.

Revolving Display — A turning display that can be motor-activated.

"Rhoplex AC-33" — Trade name for acrylic latexes. AC-33 contains 46 percent acrylic solids in an aqueous emulsion; it is a non-ionic emulsion.

"Rhoplex AC-55" — Same as AC-33 but with approximately 50 percent solids. AC-55 is an anionic emulsion.

Riser — That part of a display that projects above the merchandising presentation — or a sign or display that rises from the top shelf of an aisle or is placed atop a pole and is visible from other parts of the store.

Riveted Display — A metal display, the parts of which have been finished and decorated in the flat and assembled by means of rivets.

Robinson-Patman Act — A law enacted by Congress and that is interpreted by the Federal Trade Commission, which is the official authority on such matters. This act requires that each similar retail establishment receive equal treatment from suppliers, manufacturers, wholesalers, distributors, etc.

Robotape — An audio sales message repeater that automatically operates a product or display for a self-animated sales demonstration.

Rotating Display — A hand-turned display or one that is motorized and activated by a switch.

Rotational Molding (or Casting) — A method used to make hollow articles from plastisols or powders. The material is charged into a hollow mold capable of being rotated in one or two planes. The hot mold fuses the polymer after the rotation has caused it to cover all surfaces. The mold is then chilled and the product stripped out.

Rotogravure — A printing process in which the graphics to be printed are etched on a copper cylinder.

Rough — See **Pencil Rough**.

Rubber-Plate Printing — The process of reproducing from rubber plates, usually on combined corrugated board, eliminating the need of printing on lithograph sheets and then mounting to corrugated. Primarily used to reproduce bold line artwork. Some coarse screen work is also possible.

Rule 41 — A rule in the Uniform Freight Classification of the rail carriers containing rail shipping requirements for corrugated and solid fibreboard boxes.

Run-Long — See **Overrun**.

Runner — The secondary feed channel that runs from the inner end of the sprue in an injection or transfer mold to the cavity gate; the piece formed in a secondary feed channel or runner.

Run-Short — See **Underrun**.

SBS Board — Solid bleached sulphate board stock which, when litho printed, may be laminated to singleface corrugated. May also be referred to as folding carton stock.

SKU — See **Stock Keeping Unit**.

SS Mirrors — Indicates the strength and thickness of the glass. For instance, in the P-O-P field, SS 1/16" tells that the glass is 1/16" thick and that it is single strength. See also **DS Mirrors**.

S.U. Display — Abbreviation for Set-Up Display. One that is shipped set up and requires no assembly at the retail level.

Satellite Network (electronic) — A broadcast programmer or information system operator employing transponders on synchronous orbit satellites to transmit television or data communications to large numbers of users.

Sawtooth Hanger — Common device attached to the back of wall-mounted signage, wood frames, plaques, etc., so unit can be easily adjusted to hang level.

Scanner — An electronic device used in the making of color and tone corrected separations.

Schematic — Pertaining to, or in the form of, a scheme or diagram. A structural diagram such as a drawing of an electrical or mechanical system.

Sconce — A wall bracket to hold signs, displays, lights, mirrors, etc. Usually in pairs.

Scoring — A partial cut through corrugated or cardboard or a crease impression to allow for bending of material along that line.

"Scotchlite" — Trade name for outdoor sign letters used for their great light-reflecting properties.

Scrap — Any product of a molding operation that is not part of the primary product, including flash, culls, runners, sprues, and rejected parts. Can often be reused or sold for reuse.

Scratch 'N Sniff — Generic description for a coating of encapsulated fragrances that releases a fragrance when scratched.

Screen — In photoengraving, a transparent plate ruled with two sets of parallel lines running at right angles to each other, used in the halftone process. The more lines per square inch, the finer the reproduction.

Screen Printing — See **Screen Process**.

Screen Process — A method of printing one color at a time through a stencil securely affixed to a porous surface on a screen of nylon. The color used in this process is a paste, which, when pushed through the pores of the silk, leaves an even coating on stock placed under the screen. All parts of the design not to be printed have been rejected by an impermeable substance. Previously referred to as silk screen process when the screen was made of silk. The use of "silk" in this process is out-of-date.

Screw Plasticating Injection Molding — A molding technique in which the plastic is converted from pellets to a viscous melt by means of an extruder screw that is an integral part of the molding machine. Machines are either single-stage, in which plastication and injection are done by the same cylinder, or double-stage, in which the material is plasticated in one cylinder and fed to a second for injection into a mold.

Seam — The junction created by any free edge of a container flap or wall where it abuts, or rests on, another portion of the container and to which it may be fastened by tape, stitches, or adhesives in the process of closing the container.

Search (electronic) — The facility in interactive video systems to request a specific frame, identified by its unique sequential reference number, and then to instruct the player to move directly to that frame, forwards or backwards, from any other point on the same side of the disc or tape.

Second Surface — The back side of an outdoor sign face to which most copy is applied.

Self-Liquidating Point-Of-Purchase Unit — A P-O-P unit that the retailer pays for in whole or in part.

Self-Liquidator — A display offering a premium at a price that makes the offer entirely customer-supported.

Self-Selector — A display containing merchandise organized in such a way that the customer may readily select color, size, style, etc.

Self-Sticker — Pressure-sensitive sign or spotter.

Semi-Commercial — A display or merchandising aid that gives the retailer or salesperson benefits over and above the advertiser's goal.

Semi-Permanent Display — A display sturdy enough to be used for a seasonal promotion, such as Christmas or spring, but not intended for indefinite use. It would customarily outlast several short-term promotions and would serve as the encompassing carrier of a seasonal theme.

Semipositive Mold — A combination of the positive and flash-type molds; a mold that allows an amount of excess material to escape when it is closed. It is used where close tolerances are required. See **Molds**.

Semi-Spectacular — A painted outdoor bulletin with special effects, cut-outs, lighting, or animation.

Separate-Pot Mold — Refers to a type of mold that is used in a method of transfer molding in which the transfer pot or chamber is separate from the mold.

Separation — In color photography, the isolation or division of colors of an original into their primary hues, each record or negative used for the production of a color plate. The act of manually separating or introducing colors in printing plates. In lithography, direct separations are made with the use of the halftone screen; indirect separations involve continuous tone separation negatives and screened positives made from these.

Serigraphy — A term used by fine artists to denote the result of the screen printing of original art. Used also to denote the fine arts reproduction phase of the screen printing industry.

Service Cover — Panel providing ready access to an area of a sign for maintenance purposes.

Set — To convert an adhesive into a fixed or hardened state by chemical or physical action, such as polymerization, oxidation, vulcanization, gelation, dehydration, or evaporation of volatile constituents.

Setback — The requirement established by local code restrictions governing the distance a sign is set in from a specific point (i.e., property line, power line, sidewalk, etc.).

Shade — The value of a color. Can vary from deep/intense to light/pastel. See **Tints**.

Shadow Box — Illuminated transparency holder with forward-projecting frame, frequently with provision for a changeable message. Frequently has concealed interior illumination.

Sheet-Fed Press — Any printing press that uses paper cut into separate sheets before printing.

Sheet Wise — The use of a form or offset plate that prints just one side of the sheet when both sides are to be printed; a method of press production.

Shelf-Extender — A display in the form of a small tray, designed to be fastened or clamped to a shelf and to project from it, thus extending the space of the shelf. It is usually used for related item sales or introduction of new products.

Shelf-Miser — A small display designed to fit on the shelf and to hold more units in the same space than would ordinarily be on the shelf. These frequently have a spring or gravity-feed arrangement to keep the front of the facing full.

Shelf Organizer — A device used to present products in an appealing, organized way. Lanes or channels provide specific areas for on-shelf display.

Shelf-Strip — A device of tag stock, plastic, wire, or other material, pressure-fit into the price railing under a product, as an attention-getting device.

Shelf-Talker — A printed card designed to lay on the shelf under the product and project out and down to carry an advertising message that will call attention to the product. The flap end is frequently die-cut. It is sometimes held in place with pressure-sensitive adhesive.

Shell — A sheet of corrugated or solid fibreboard scored and folded to form a joined or unjoined tube open at both ends. Used as inner packing.

Shipper Display — Usually larger and more elaborate than a carton display. Parts are all included in one shipper, along with prepackaged merchandise. Sometimes referred to as a duplex. May be countertop or floor standing.

Shipping Container — In a self-service store, a movable basket for holding shopper selections and wheeling them to the checkout stand. They often have advertising messages attached.

Shot — The yield from one complete molding cycle, including scrap.

Shot Capacity — The maximum weight of material that an injection machine can inject with one forward motion of the ram.

Shrink — The difference in the size of a pattern and the finished plastic part.

Side Guide — A device employed in printing to pull the sheet to a certain spot on the printing plate. All printing and die-cutting is performed using the side guide and the gripper edge as the point of reference.

Sign — Any device that identifies a company or a product and/or carries an advertising or directional message. Signs may be separate entities, or an integral part of a display. "Signs," as commonly used, mean separate entities.

Sign Cabinet — That part of a sign that houses the lamps, ballasts, etc., and supports the faces.

Silhouette Halftone — A halftone with all screen background removed.

Silhouetting — Opaquing out the background around a subject on a halftone or a continuous-tone negative. On a positive this can be achieved by staggering the subject and by flat-etching the background until it is entirely transparent.

Silica — A crystalline compound that occurs abundantly as quartz or sand (primarily) but is found in other materials as well.

Silicate — A compound that contains silicon, oxygen, and a metallic organic radical.

Silk Screen Process — Same as screen process; use of "silk" is outdated. See **Screen Process**.

Silver-Colored Foil — A foil used extensively in combination with cardboard to produce interesting optical and attention-getting effects. Silver-colored foil can be rendered in any color with dye or can be purchased in a desired color and mounted to cardboard for printing and die-cutting.

Singleface — Corrugated board with one smooth face, usually printed on the corrugated side. Any sign or display finished on one side only. Also the stock to which SBS is laminated.

Sink Mark — A dimple-like depression with well-rounded edges, in the surface of a part where it has retracted from the mold.

Sizing — The process of applying a material on a surface in order to fill pores and thus reduce the absorption of the subsequently applied adhesive or coating, or to otherwise modify the surface properties of the substrate to improve the adhesion. Also, the material used for this purpose. The latter is sometimes called size.

Skid — A platform support for a pile of cut sheets that facilitates shipping and handling by forklift trucks.

Slip Sheet — 1: A flat sheet of material with tabs on one or more sides, used as a base upon which goods and materials may be assembled, stored, and transported. 2: Paper sheet used between sections of a display or in between the display and the carton, in packing for shipment. 3: Sheets used between freshly oriented sheets to prevent rubbing.

Slit — A cut made in a sheet without removal of material.

Slit-Score — A cut made in a sheet that extends through only a portion of the thickness, which enables the sheet to fold back on itself.

Slot — A cut made in a fibreboard sheet, usually to form flaps and thus permit folding. Widths of one-fourth and three-eighths inch are common.

Slush Casting (or **Molding**) — A method for casting thermoplastics in which the resin in liquid form is poured into a hot mold where a viscous skin forms. The excess slush is drained off, the mold is cooled, and the molding stripped out. See **Casting**.

Snapper — An extra incentive used to stimulate consumer purchase of a special product.

Sniffer — A display that uses odor to attract attention to enhance the product.

Soft Pack — A partially assembled prepack-style display that may be opened to accept product on a production/packing line. Commonly used where a production environment does not lend itself to assembling display components. Also called a "Pack-Rite."

Software (electronic) — A collection of instructions to a computer spelling out the exact order of actions to perform. Such software can be used with every size and capability graduation of the computer field, from the smallest microprocessor (individual unit) to a CPU (Central Processing Unit) into which any number of terminals might be eligible to access.

Soil Bearing — A numerical factor normally expressed in pounds per square foot that relates to the ability of unconfined soil to support a weight such as a footing or foundation for an outdoor sign, pole, or pylon.

Solid Fibreboard — A solid board made by laminating two or more plies of containerboard.

Solid Matter — Lines of type set without spacing between lines.

Solvent Cement — A "tacky" solvent that facilitates the bonding of plastic materials.

Solvent Molding — A process for forming thermoplastic articles by dipping a male mold in a solution or dispersion of the resin and drawing off the solvent to leave a layer of plastic film adhering to the mold.

Sore-Thumb Display — A display designed to attract immediate attention by virtue of its size or unique style.

Space Management — The technology used to determine the optimum placement of, and shelf space allotted to, brands and SKUs within a product category. Used to generate a planogram.

Special Display — Space allocated for the promotion of a product other than its regular shelf space.

Spectacular — A large permanent outdoor sign equipped with special lighting and motion effects. Also, a large display either designed to stand free or to be used in a free-standing stack of merchandise, often incorporating elements of light and/or motion that is used indoors.

Spider — The membranes supporting a mandrel within the head/die assembly.

Spinner Display — A display with its components and product arranged around a central pole. The components holding the product rotate, allowing the consumer to shop the entire display while standing in one spot.

Spinner Sign — A sign, with a wall-mounted bracket, that revolves in the wind.

Split-Cavity Blocks — Blocks that, when assembled, contain a cavity for molding articles having undercuts.

Split Mold — A mold in which the cavity is formed of two or more components held together by an outer case. The components are known as splits. See **Molds**.

Spot Display — Merchandise prominently displayed and accentuated by an extraordinary attention-getting device.

Spot-Welded Display — A metal display, the parts of which have been fabricated and assembled by means of spot welding and then finished and decorated.

Spread — The quantity of adhesive per unit joint area applied to an adherend. It is often expressed in pounds of adhesive per thousand square feet of joint area. Single spread refers to application of adhesive to both adherends of a joint.

Spreader — A device to hold a display, customarily shipped flat, in an open position.

Spreader Roll — The roll that is in contact with the adhesive and that can be adjusted to set the amount of adhesive being applied. Can be used with certain coatings as well.

Spring Pole — Pole display supported by spring tension, floor to ceiling.

Spring Wire — Wire that produces motion without electricity. It quivers from vibrations and air currents. Can be used for floor, wall, counter, and shelf display locations.

Sprue — The main feed channel that runs from the outer face of an injection or transfer mold to the mold gate in a single-cavity mold or to the runners in a multiple-cavity mold; the piece formed in the feed channel.

Sprue Bushing — In an injection mold, a hardened steel insert that contains the tapered sprue hold and has a suitable seat for making close contact with the nozzle of the injection cylinder.

Sprue Lock — In injection molding, a portion of the plastic composition that is held in the cold slug well by an undercut; used to pull the sprue out of the bushing as the mold opens.

Squeegee — A tool used to force ink through the openings of a screen printing when in contact with a substrate, consisting of a rubber or plastic strip or blade held in the edge of a wooden or metallic handle. A variety of blade shapes and hardnesses are available.

Stabile — Display suspended from the ceiling, having several elements similar to the mobile, sometimes reaching from ceiling to floor, but unlike the mobile, having immobile parts.

Stabilizer — An ingredient used in the formulation of some adhesives, especially elastomers, to assist in maintaining the physical and chemical properties of the compounded materials at their initial values throughout the processing and service life of the material.

Stacker Display — A display with an arrangement for projecting or suspending the advertising message from stacked merchandise.

Standard Art — See **Syndicated Art**.

Stapling — See **Stitching**.

Static-Free — In plastics, a formulation with additives that eliminates annoying and dangerous static electrical discharges.

Steel Rule Die — Metal blades, with different cutting values, inserted in hardwood backings (flat or curved) to produce impressions or die-cut pieces. Used when special shapes or angles are required on a component. Used to cut many different materials.

Stencil — The component of a printing screen that controls the design to be printed.

Stepover — In multiple imposition on a lithographic press plate, the procedure of repeating the exposure of a flat by stepping it along the gripper edge; side-by-side exposure.

Stereotype — A duplicate printing plate cast from a paper matrix.

Stiffener — A hem strip that folds back to strengthen an edge of the display.

Still Frame (electronic) — A graphic of any kind that is presented as a single, static image rather than as moving footage. The economical storage of still frames is one of the strengths of the video disc.

Stirrer-Holders — Receptacles for holding stirrers, napkins, and other bar accessories, for use on the bar or fountain. They carry an advertising message, frequently on a riser.

Stirrers — Long sticks of various shapes for stirring drinks. They carry an advertising message and are usually made of plastic.

Stitching — Application of metal fasteners to form the joint of fibre boxes or to close boxes. Stitches are machine-formed using wire drawn from a spool.

Stock Item — A brand or product commonly sold in great quantity by a retail outlet and perpetually kept in stock.

Stock Keeping Unit (SKU) — The term applied to each unique variation of a particular brand, including, but not limited to, size, count, style, flavor, ingredients, etc., for which a different UPC (bar code) is required.

Storage Life — The period of time that a packaged adhesive can be stored under specified temperature conditions and remain suitable for use. Sometimes called shelf life.

Store-Wide — See **Merchandising Kit**.

Story — See **Theme**.

Streamer — A printed plastic, paper, or cloth banner for window or interior use.

Stringing — The stretching of signs on one wire to produce an orderly row, usually spelling out an advertising message.

Stripper Plate — A plate that strips the molded article from mold pin, force, or cores.

Stripping — 1: The act of positioning or inserting copy elements in negative or positive film to a unit negative; the positioning of photographic negatives or positives on a lithographic flat for form imposition. 2: The condition under which steel rollers fail to take up the ink on lithographic presses, and instead are wet by the fountain solution.

Stroke — The length of ram travel on a press.

Styrene — A plastic material used in vacuum forming and injection molding processes. It is used for its high strength properties and its ability to be colored.

Substrate — A material (usually a paper stock, wood, or wood derivative) to which is applied a label or a finished material. A substrate may support or "carry the load" but it is not seen. It is the "base" material.

Supplier — See **Basic Material Supplier**; also **P-O-P Producer/ Supplier**.

Surprint — In photomechanics, a print from a second negative superimposed upon a previously printed image of the first negative, and differing from a double print in that one image is superimposed on the other rather than being photo printed into or around the first image. Surprinting is commonly used to superimpose the print from a line negative on a previously made print from a halftone or other line negative. Line work surprinted will reproduce as solid black and with no screen.

Syndicated Art — Low-cost point-of-purchase material supplied to various advertisers for different brands of a commodity in separate market areas.

T-Bar — A T-shaped bar to hang two signs, or to hold a large paper poster that can be draped over it and thus seen from both sides.

TL — Abbreviation for Truck Load. In truck transportation, a shipment of materials filling one or more trucks completely.

"T" Molding — Metal or vinyl molding often used to hide raw edge of wood display shelves secured in a slot cut into the shelf edge in lieu of mechanical fasteners or adhesive material.

T-Nut — Recessed fastening device often used in KD wood display units.

Tab — A small flap fastened to the edge of displays, sometimes conveying an extra advertising message or reminder. Also, a locking device that attaches the same or different materials to a receiving slot.

Table Tent — See **Tent Card**.

Tack — Stickiness of an adhesive.

Tack, Dry — The property of certain adhesives, particularly nonvulcanizing rubber adhesives, to adhere on contact to themselves at a stage in the evaporation of volatile constituents, even though they seem dry to the touch. Sometimes called aggressive tack or contact bonding.

Tacker — Small metal sign.

Tacker Sign — A sign made so that it can be tacked or nailed to a building, a fence, etc. It has copy on one side only.

Tag Stock — A thin flexible cardboard.

Take-One Pad — A pad for customer tear-off used as part of a sign or display.

Talker — See **Shelf-Talker**.

Tape — A narrow strip of cloth, paper, or plastic film (sometimes having a filler or reinforcement) that is coated on one side with an adhesive. It is used to form the joint on a fibre box or to close or reinforce such a box. Closure and reinforcement can also be created with pressure-sensitive tape.

Taping — The running of a cloth or plastic binding.

Tap-Marker — A display to be attached to a bar or fountain tap handle for a particular brand of beer or soft drink.

Tapper — A motorized device for tapping a window or other sound producer to attract attention.

Tear-Off — See **Take-One Pad**.

Tent Card — Single fold card, set like a tent, for use on counters, bars, or tables, carrying an advertising message. Frequently has messages on front and back of tent.

Test — When not otherwise modified, refers to the bursting strength of linerboard and combined board except for those grades of corrugate in which a puncture test is substituted for bursting strength.

Test, Bursting Strength (Mullen) — Measurement of the resistance of a material to bursting expressed in pounds per square inch. The test is made on a motor-driven Mullen tester.

Test, Compression — Involves the application of force applied by two flat surfaces of a machine to opposite faces of a box, such as top and bottom, the two ends, or the two sides. Usually, the test is performed on individual empty boxes, and measurement is taken of the load applied in pounds and the deflection or deformation in one-tenths of an inch. The test is related to the forces that filled boxes encounter while being transported and while stacked in warehouses.

Test, Corrugated Linerboard (CLT) — This test measures the on-edge stiffness of the material in terms of the amount of force required to crush a narrow specimen of linerboard held upright in a special clamp.

Test, Corrugating Medium (CMT) — This test measures the amount of force required to crush a specimen of fluted corrugating medium that has been formed into a strip of singleface by application of pressure-sensitive tapes.

Test, Drop — This determines the resistance of a filled container to shocks caused by dropping it certain ways onto a solid surface (i.e., on corners, edges, faces, etc.). It measures how well a container and its inner packing (if any) will protect the contents against the handling encountered in shipping.

Test, Edgewise Compression (Short Column) — This is a measure of the edgewise compressive strength of a short column of corrugated fibreboard. This property, in combination with the caliper or flexural stiffness of the combined board, relates to the top-to-bottom compressive strength of corrugated shipping containers.

Test, Flat Crush — The force required to crush the corrugations in a specimen of combined board. Force is applied to the flat surfaces of the specimen and the load per square inch required to cause the corrugations to collapse is determined.

Test, Flotation — A measure of the resistance to water of corrugated which has been surface-coated with a wax blend. A specimen of predetermined size is formed into a tray and floated on water. A fixed quantity of water is also poured into the tray. The percentage of water absorption is determined by weight after a designated exposure.

Test, Incline Impact (Conbur) — Determines the resistance of a packaged item to damage from impact. In the test, the container, complete with contents, is positioned on the front end of a dolly which is released from a predetermined point on an inclined set of tracks to strike against a solid wall at the bottom. The impact force can be measured with a suitable shock recorder.

Test Market — See **Pre-Testing**.

Test, Puncture (Beach) — The resistance of fibreboard to puncture and, when a modified procedure is used, a measure of the stiffness of the specimen. In the test, a pyramidal metal point is driven through a specimen of fibreboard by the swinging action of a pendulum from which the point projects.

Test, Revolving Drum — Determines the resistance of a packaged item to shocks encountered by rotating it inside a drum that is usually seven feet in diameter and which has six flat faces. Baffles, or fins, are mounted in a standard design on the faces and force the box to fall on different sides, edges and corners as the drum is rotated. The test is often continued to the point where the contents spill from the container.

Test, Ring Stiffness — This establishes the on-edge stiffness of material and is applicable to linerboard and corrugating medium. It establishes the amount of force required of containerboard inserted into a holder with a circular groove.

Test Store — A retail unit where product sales tests are made to determine buying and merchandising practices.

Test, Tear (Elmendorf) — The amount of energy required to continue a tear of specified length of tape, or other material, once the tear has been started by an intentional pre-cut.

Test, Vibration — This test subjects the container with contents to shaking or vibration and produces, on an accelerated basis, forces similar to those encountered in transportation.

Test, Water Absorption — A procedure published in those tariffs to the railroads that provide specifications for fresh fruit and vegetable shipping containers. This procedure is also incorporated in Federal Specification PPP-B-1163. The test measures, as a percentage increase in weight, the amount of water absorbed by 4" x 4" specimens of fibreboard during a one-hour period of immersion. The test applies only to boxes made of fibreboard treated with wax or chemicals (see **Wax Impregnated**) to impart water and moisture resistance. The detailed procedure and permissible levels of water absorption are designated in the tariffs.

Test, Water Wicking — A measure of the resistance to water of corrugated fibreboard that has had the corrugating medium (and, optionally, the facings as well) infused with a wax or wax blend. A specimen of predetermined size is processed by cutting through the corrugations at their approximate center for a specified distance along one of the edges. After the resultant sections are folded back to form a T-shaped column, the specimen is allowed to stand in one-inch of water for 24 hours with the corrugations in a vertical direction. Wicking, as evidenced by discoloration above the surface of the water, is recorded for each facing and the corrugating medium.

Theme — The central character or feature of a display program that is present in all elements of a P-O-P promotion and that serves to tie them all together for better consumer identification. Can also relate to a single display such as a "Father's Day Special."

Thermography — A printing process in which the ink, while still set, is dusted with a resinous powder that adheres to the ink, after which heat treatment causes the powder particles to fuse together giving a raised effect.

Thermoplastics — Plastic materials and adhesives that are formed by high temperature and that, once set, will not soften or melt when successive heat is applied.

Thixotropic — A state in which a resin is gel-like at rest, but fluid-like when agitated. By making a resin thixotropic, you can paint on a vertical surface without rundown.

Three-D — see **Lenticular**.

Three-Step Finish — In wood displays this is often referred to as "furniture quality" finish. This most commonly refers to stain, seal, and lacquer.

Thumbnail — A miniature or rough sketch.

Ticky-Tack — Very rough permanent model put together to judge size and overall looks.

Tie-In — Cooperative advertising effort between multiple products featured together on one display unit, usually at a money-saving combination price, e.g., toothbrush/toothpaste; razor/shaving cream/aftershave lotion. Products are sometimes manufactured by different companies.

Tint — A color made lighter by adding white to the color; a degree of color lighter than normal.

Tints — Various tones (strengths) of a solid color. For rough work, sometimes handled on the copy by pasting down a piece of stock shading sheet and handled as line copy; or patented drawing board is used by artist and tint areas are developed with chemicals. Photographic (halftone) tints are stock developed film (negative and positive) in various strengths of tone (25%, 50%, etc.) and usually 133-line screen prepared by the camera department and inserted by stripper as indicated on copy.

Tip-On — A special card that may be "fused on" to a given display to call attention to a special sale or other feature.

Toluene — A colorless, very mobile solvent. It is characterized by being strongly refractive, having an odor like benzene, and a burning taste. See **Diisocynates** and **Urethanes**.

Tone (audio-electronic) — A selectable sound found on some electronic displays; used for attracting attention during a message.

Tone (color) — A degree of color made darker than the original hue by adding its complimentary or black. See **Shade**.

Tooling — The process of readying productive facilities for mass production of point-of-purchase materials. Also spoken of as "tooling up."

Tooling Charges — Charges for machine tools necessary for production that are usually the same, regardless of run quantity.

Topper — That part of a pole display that tops the pole. See also **Pole Topper**.

Torpedo — A streamlined metal block placed in the path of flow of plastic in the heating cylinder of extruders or injection-molding machines, and used to spread the plastic into thin layers and force it into contact with the heating areas.

Touch Plate — In screen printing, the use of an additional or fifth screen to reproduce a "non-reproducible color" in process printing, such as a fluorescent or a white.

Touch Sensitive Screen (electronic) (Touch Screen) — Technology in which the user activates a computer system or interactive laser disc by touching the display screen's appropriate menu choices. Infra red, LED, and membrane versions are available.

Trade Name — A name that identifies a company and its products to the public.

Trademark — The registered name of a company or product in its stylized form.

Traffic Count — The number of potential customers passing a display during a specific time period.

Transfer Chamber — See **Transfer Molding**.

Transfer Molding — A method of molding in which the plastic is first softened by heat and pressure in a transfer chamber, and then forced by high pressure through suitable sprues, runners, and gates into the closed mold that establishes the desired shape and, upon cooling down, the part can be removed from the mold without change in the shape or size of the molded part.

Transformer — A device used to step-up or step-down voltage using electromagnetic induction.

Trans-Lite — See **Transparency**.

Translucent — A term indicating the property of a substrate or other material to permit passage of some light rays in a diffused manner so as not to clearly establish the design or object from which the rays are reflected.

Transparency — 1: A monochrome or full-color photographic positive or picture on a transparent support, in which the image is intended for viewing and reproduction by transmitted light. 2: In photography, also refers to the light-transmitting power of the silver deposit in a negative and is the inverse of opacity. 3: Inexpensive, semi-permanent window posters printed on high grade onion-skin paper for application to glass surfaces. 4: The property of an ink that permits light to pass through it. Lack of hiding power.

Transparent Ink — A printing ink that does not conceal the color beneath. Process inks are transparent so that they will blend to form other colors.

Trapping of Inks — The property of a printing ink that makes it possible to superimpose one color on another, both in wet and dry printing; may be used to obtain a third color, which is a combination of the two applied, or to hide the first by overprinting the second with an opaque color.

Traveling Display — Displays designed to be shipped from place to place so they can be reused in various retail outlets.

Traveling Tape Sign — A sign, usually illuminated, in which an advertising message, brand identification and pictorial elements appear on a tape that moves across the open face of the sign, with the motion generally supplied by an electric motor.

Tray — that part of a display that holds the merchandise or a change tray; may be integral or separate.

Tri-Color (electronic) — An LED that is capable of displaying three colors: red, green, and yellow.

Triple Message Sign — A sign with rotating triangular louvers that turn in unison and compose a different message as each of the three faces are exposed.

Tripolymer — See **A.B.S.** Can refer to any three substances that are combined to furnish desired manufacturing and finished properties.

Truck Topper — See **Car Topper**.

Tube — A sheet of combined board, scored and folded to produce a multi-sided form. This may be either an element of a box style or a unit of interior packing to add protection and compression strength. When used for the first purpose, it is joined by gluing, stitching, or taping. As an interior piece, it may or may not be joined.

"Tuffak" — Trade name for polycarbonate manufactured by Rohm & Haas. Often used as the facings for outdoor plastic illuminated signs.

Turntable — A rotating table to display all sides of a single piece of merchandise, or a selection of various pieces. May be turned mechanically or by hand.

Twinwall — See **Corrugated Board, Doublewall**.

Two-For-One Sale — The offering of two units of a product for the price of one.

UFC Rule 41 — Refers to a section of the National Motor Freight Classification stating the structural strength requirements for shipping boxes made from corrugated paperboard or solid fibreboard.

UL — Commonly used abbreviation for Underwriters Laboratory. See **Underwriters Laboratory**.

UPC — Abbreviation for Universal Product Coding of products. UPC facilitates quick pricing at checkout and assists in inventory and reorder procedures.

Ultrasonic Sealing — A means of sealing two pieces of styrene together with sound waves.

Ultraviolet Curing — Polymerization created by ultraviolet rays.

Ultraviolet Drying System — Any system that utilizes ultraviolet rays to effect the drying or curing process of inks, coatings, or adhesives. More correct term is ultraviolet curing system.

Undercolor Removal — In process multi-color printing, color separation films are reduced in color in areas where all three colors overprint and the black film is increased an equivalent amount in these areas. This improves trapping and reduces ink costs.

Undercut — A condition often designed into flexible molds (made from rubber, vinyl, etc.) for use with numerous plastics. In the case of aluminum molds for expandable polystyrene production, this is not possible since the molds are rigid.

Underrun — The number of displays or printed material short of the number specified in the order. See also **Overrun**.

Underwriters Laboratory (UL) — The UL mark means that the electrical device has passed the appropriate tests administered by the Underwriters Laboratory and is safe.

Unselfish Display — A unit that accommodates related item merchandise not sold by the advertiser, or a storewide program that does the same. See also **Altruistic Display**.

Upstroke Press — A hydraulic press in which the main ram is situated below the moving table, and pressure is applied by an upward movement of the ram.

Urethanes — Substances produced by a reaction between diisocyanates (especially toluene diisocyanate) and polyglycols or polyesters. Flexible or rigid, these materials are used in flexible upholstery in furniture, as well as in rigid insulation, coatings, and adhesives. Widely used as a substitute for natural wood. A material used to mold permanent displays, signs, and components.

User Programmable Graphics (electronic) — An electronic display user's ability to create and store his/her own graphics and illustrations on the matrix.

"Uvex" — A trade name for cellulose acetate butyrate sheets used for signs, panels, and letters.

Vacuum Bag Molding — A process for molding reinforced plastics in which a sheet of flexible transparent material is placed over the lay-up on the mold and sealed. A vacuum is applied between the sheet and the lay-up. The entrapped air is mechanically worked out of the lay-up and removed by the vacuum, and the part is cured. See **Bag Molding**.

Vacuum Fluorescent (electronic) — This device uses a gas-filled tube to create alphanumeric characters. Color is a function of the gas used in the tube, commonly orange and blue. One of the systems or methods used to "light up" the picture or viewing area on an electronic display.

Vacuum Forming — An inexpensive process for shaping flat plastic sheets into contours for 3-D effects by heating the sheet until flexible over a mold with the desired shape or contour, then withdrawing the air from between the heated plastic sheet and the mold or die.

Vacuum Metallizing — A technique for depositing a very thin film of metal on a substrate, thus producing a metallic foil appearance on its surface.

Valance — A long narrow sign or display designed to be used above eye level.

Valence Forces (chemistry) — As used in adhesives, cohesion strength is developed through an atom's or a group of atoms' ability to combine, thereby increasing the bonding strength.

Varnish — A thin, protective coating applied to a printed sheet for protection or appearance.

"Velox" — A trade name for a small photographic process print with small black dots in a white field to represent highlight areas, and small white dots in a black field to represent shadow areas; a screened photoprint. A photographic paper print made from a screen negative.

Vent — A shallow channel or minute hole cut in the cavity of a mold to allow air to escape as the material enters.

"Verplex" — Trade name for a process simulating the effect of an oil painting through special embossing.

"Versa-Panel" — Trade name for a type of sign having a four-panel screen for bulletin display.

Vertical Arrangement — The stocking of a line or variety of products on shelves above and below each other.

Video Disc (electronic) — A generic term describing a medium of video information storage that uses thin circular plates, primarily composed of translucent plastic, on which video, audio, and various control signals are encoded, usually along a spiral track. Optical disc systems use a laser beam to read the surface of the disc.

Video Merchandisers — Custom merchandising units that utilize computer electronics to convey graphics and visual messages to the consumer. These are well used for products that require a high degree of information or cross referencing by the consumer.

Vignette — An illustration in which the background fades gradually away until it blends into the unprinted paper.

Vinyl — Plastic formed by the polymerization of compounds. This material is durable and virtually nonbreakable.

"Vue-More" — Trade name for a mechanical turntable.

Vulcanization — A method or process of treating rubber with sulphur and subjecting it to intense heat. This makes the rubber more durable and more adaptable for various purposes. In P-O-P work this relates primarily to rubber-based adhesives.

W

Wagon Merchandiser — Movable wagon designed to hold merchandise and carry an advertising message.

Wall Banner — A large advertisement on a wall or suspended from a wire and stretched across a store.

Wall Flush — Refers to a sign mounted flush against a wall.

Wall Mount — Refers to any singlefaced sign mounted to a wall.

Wall Panel — A display or merchandiser made for mounting to a wall.

Warp — A significant variation from the original, true, or plane surface.

Water-Resistant — To give a board some resistance to damage or deterioration by water, it is "sized," meaning it is treated with water repellent materials.

Wax Blend Surface Coated — Combined board made from unimpregnated components and coated on one or both sides, as desired, with a hot melt wax blend.

Wax Cascaded — Combined board impregnated by vertically cascading molten paraffin wax or wax blend over corrugated without blanks. This processing is frequently employed as a substitute for wax dipping.

Wax Dipped — Combined board impregnated by dipping it into a hot paraffin wax or wax blend such that the resultant wax content of board is not less than 40% of the weight of the board prior to dipping.

Wax Impregnated — Combined board having one or more components infused with a paraffin-type wax or wax blend to a minimum of 5 lbs. per 1,000 sq. ft. per impregnated component (4 lbs. per 1,000 sq. ft. for conventional weight corrugating materials lighter than 33 lbs. per 1,000 sq. ft.).

Wax Impregnated Plus Wax Blend Surface Coated — Combined board having one or more components infused with a paraffin-type wax or wax blend to a minimum of 5 lbs. per 1,000 sq. ft. per impregnated component (4 lbs. per 1,000 sq. ft. for conventional weight corrugating materials lighter than 33 lbs. per 1,000 sq. ft.) and, in addition, coated on one or both sides, as desired, with a hot melt wax blend.

Waxing — The application of wax as a finishing process to signs and displays.

Web-Fed Press — A printing press in which a roll of paper is printed and then cut into separate pieces. This equipment can only be used on long runs (high-quantity unit orders).

Web Printing — See **Web-Fed Press**.

Weight of Facings — This is the summation of weight per thousand square feet of all facings in the board structure excluding the weight of coatings and impregnates as well as the corrugating adhesive.

Welding — To unite by heating to a plastic or fluid state the surfaces of the parts to be joined, and then allowing them to flow.

Window Display — A retail outlet display placed in the windows facing outside to attract the attention of pedestrians passing the establishment.

Window Streamer — A long narrow advertisement attached to a store window.

Window Strip — An advertising message carried horizontally at the bottom of a window.

Wire Feet — See **Crow's Feet**.

Wire Wobbler — A spring steel wire extended to hold a display card that oscillates with light air currents caused by store traffic.

Wobbler — A lightweight display that hangs from a wire over a frozen food case or in other positions and bobs and turns with the air currents emitted by the case.

Wood Failure — The rupturing of wood fibres in strength tests on bonded specimens, usually expressed as the percentage of the total area involved that shows such failure.

Wood Grain — Application of a woodlike finish to metal, paper, and other materials other than wood.

Wooden Indian — A standing wooden image of an American Indian formerly used for advertising out in front of a tobacco shop. Said to be the original point-of-purchase display used in America. A stylized version of this symbol is used for POPAI's OMA (Outstanding Merchandising Achievement) Award statuette, presented to winners of POPAI's annual merchandising awards contest.

Working Life — The period of time during which an adhesive, after mixing with a catalyst, solvent, or other compounding ingredient, remains suitable for use.

Wraparound — A roll of continuous printing, usually on singleface corrugated or heavy soft sheets designed to decorate the space between a counter or tabletop and the floor. Also, a display card of special design that "hugs" or wraps around a project.

Wraparound Blank — A cored and slotted sheet of corrugated without printing that is formed into a box around its contents. The user seals the box with both the flap (seam) and body joint closures.

Wrapped In Fibreboard — Envelopment of the packaged item(s) in corrugated or solid, not necessarily complying with the provisions of UFC Rule 41 or NMFC Item 222-Series.

Wrinkle Finish — Application of a baked enamel decorative finish that is characterized by a pattern of "wrinkles."

Yellow — One of the subtractive primaries, the hue of which is used for one of the four-color process inks. It reflects red and green light and absorbs blue light.

GLOSSARY:
WORDS IN PROMOTION

PROMOTION MARKETING ASSOCIATION OF AMERICA, INC.
(PMAA)

ACKNOWLEDGMENTS
The most significant change in product and service marketing over the past decade has been the growth in sales promotion spending as a proportion of overall marketing expenditures. In 1977 promotion marketing expenditures represented 58 percent of total spending. In 1990, promotion represented over 65 percent.

This unprecedented growth has created industries within our industry. We are truly integrated marketers. A few short years ago *database marketing* had little meaning to package goods marketers; *joint ventures* were only popular in the oil and technology industries, *customer retention and relationship marketing* was still being defined.

The general public, educators, legislators, and industry are now hearing a whole new language — the language of the Promotion Marketing Industry.

Because the media, the PMAA, and industry continue to be inundated with questions about our industry and its growth, the PMAA decided it was time to publish "The New and Revised PMAA Glossary." This glossary provides much needed legitimacy to and understanding of our business.

In helping to write this glossary of terms, I was fortunate to work with many wonderful professionals in our industry. Thank you to all committee members, and a special thank you goes to Emilie Lion, whose soft pushes kept this project on target and made it happen.

Gary Weisbaum, Marketeam, Inc.
Chairman-Glossary Committee

Account Opener: A direct premium offered to the buyer to secure his business (e.g., a premium offered by a bank to a depositor to open a new account).

Ad Slick: Reproducible artwork, which is used as a master in the offset printing process.

Advanced Premium: One given to a new customer in expectation that he/she will earn it by later purchases; a technique originated by home-service route firms.

Advertising Allowance: A payment or service by a manufacturer of goods to a merchant for advertising a product of the manufacturer.

Advertising Specialties: A form of direct advertising. Products that bear the name, address, and/or slogan of a business firm are given away free by the advertiser to present or prospective customers. Sometimes called remembrance advertising.

Affiliated Chain: A regional group of retail stores associated with other noncompeting stores for the advantage of large-scale purchasing or for exclusive territorial rights to the marketing of certain brands.

Affiliated Retailer: A retailer who is affiliated with a voluntary chain. Also refers to a retailer who participates with others in a cooperative wholesale purchasing operation.

Affiliated Wholesaler: A wholesaler who sponsors a voluntary chain of affiliated retailers. Also, a wholesaler who is a member of a voluntary chain of wholesalers.

Agency of Record: An agency that purchases media time or space for another agency or a group of agencies who happen to serve the same client. Abbreviated A.O.R.

All Commodity Volume Basis: See distribution. Abbreviated ACV.

Allocation (in promotion): A pre-assigned quantity of merchandise to be made available or sold to an individually designated area or customer. Also allotment.

Allotment: Predetermined distribution of product for which the demand often exceeds the supply; for example, a special pack. Also, the total amount available of a particular special pack in a particular area or to a particular customer (e.g., a price pack allotment).

Allowance: A temporary price reduction or discount offered to the retailer by the manufacturer. Sometimes given in the form of free goods, like one case free with twelve.

Automatic Distribution: Distribution of goods by a wholesaler or by the headquarters of a chain to individual retail stores without a specific order; usually done on a guaranteed-sale basis.

Bait Advertising: Advertising that offers an unusually low price for an item to draw a customer into a store where the low-priced item is usually not available. Then the customer is convinced to buy a more expensive similar product. Also known as "bait and switch" advertising. Not an ethical practice regardless of what it is called.

Ballot Test: A sample mailing of special mail-in offer leaflets to randomly selected U.S. households to learn about consumer responsiveness to the offer and its probable cost if used broadly.

Banded Pack: Two or more packages are banded together and sold at a reduced price. The packages can be the same or related products.

Barter: The furnishing of products by an advertiser as full or partial payment for broadcasting time or free mentions on television or radio. Time so purchased is called barter time, and its purchase is usually arranged by a broker.

Best-Food-Day (BFD): The day on which a newspaper runs editorial material on food, making that day's edition the most advantageous for retail grocers' advertising and hence, for the advertising of food manufacturers; usually Wednesday evening or Thursday editions, depending on the market.

Billback Allowance: A merchandising allowance in which the discount is not given to the retailer until he provides proof he has complied with the merchandising requirements of the seller. Also billback.

Bill of Lading: A bill of lading is a written account of goods shipped, signed by an agent of the transportation company, acknowledging receipt of the goods and promising to deliver them in good condition at the place directed.

Bleed: Excess areas of printing plates extending beyond edges of final trimmed sheet, thus eliminating a white margin along the edge.

Blind Offer: An offer placed inconspicuously in the body copy of a print advertisement; often used to measure reader attention to the advertisement. Also buried offer, hidden offer.

Blister Pack: A package consisting of a card faced with a plastic casing enclosing the product. Also bubble card, skin pack.

Bonus Goods: Salable merchandise given by a manufacturer to a retailer as a reward for a large purchase (see free goods; allowance).

Bonus Pack: A specially packaged product designed to provide purchasers with an extra amount of product at the usual price.

Borrowed Interest Promotion: A promotion that uses the recognition and/or impact of a well-known event or personality to capture the attention and interest of the target audience.

Bottle Hanger: A promotional or advertising collar designed to hang around the neck of a bottle.

Bounce-Back: A second promotion offer made to consumers in order to encourage additional purchase(s); e.g., a coupon for a second purchase placed within a product package, or a second offer of a different premium enclosed when the first premium is mailed.

Box-Top Offer: An offer of a premium based on the return of the box top from a package or other appropriate proof-of-purchase.

Brand Development Index: A measure of the concentration of a brand's consumption; typically, the units or dollars of a product consumed per thousand population in a year's time.

Brand Image: The pattern of feelings, associations, and ideas held by the public at large regarding a specific brand. Also brand personality.

Break-Even Calculation: A technique to determine the absolute or percent sales increase needed to pay for the cost of a promotion:

1. Total cost known
   Divided by margin per case
   Equals total volume needed
2. Unit costs known
   Divided by margin per case
   Less base volume
   Equals incremental volume needed

Broadside: A giant folder, often sent as a self-mailer, used especially (but not exclusively) in direct mail advertising to the trade.

Broker: An agent in the purchase or sale of goods; as the agent of a seller, especially of packaged goods, serves to supplement or supplant the seller's sales force in return for a commission.

Business Gift: A gift to a customer, stockholder, employee, or other business friend as an expression of appreciation. There is an upper dollar limit for purposes of a business tax deduction.

Business Reply Mail: Advertising mail that includes an envelope or card that enables the recipient to reply without paying postage.

Buy-Back Allowance: An allowance that is based on the amount of product purchased on a preceding deal.

Cannibalize: To draw sales away from another product of the same manufacturer in a manner diminishing the maker's profit; said of new competitive products, flanker items, or line extensions.

Canvass: A round of visits to retail and wholesale customers in a territory for some specific purpose.

Carrier Route Presort: Sorting mail into nine-digit zip code sequence so that it is ready to be distributed to individual U.S. Postal Service carriers. Saves additional postage over five-digit code sequencing.

Carryover: Orders written and recorded as orders but not yet recorded as shipments.

Case Allowance: An allowance by a manufacturer to a retailer. The allowance is proportional to the number of cases purchased, either continuously or in increments.

Case-Count Method: A form of acceptance of a wholesale delivery by a retailer on the evidence of the number of cases listed in an invoice rather than after a physical count of cases delivered.

Case Rate: A figure used commonly to indicate the marketing expenditure behind a brand by showing support per case sold. A brand's "case rate" is determined by dividing its total annual marketing budget (advertising, promotion, etc.) by its total case volume. For example, a brand with a $500,000 budget and a volume of 100,000 cases would have a "case rate" of $5.00.

Cash Refund Offer: An offer by a manufacturer for a refund of money to a customer who mails in a label or a designated proof-of-purchase.

Central Location Study: Research conducted among a selected group of consumers to determine relative consumer preference and/or acceptability of a premium or product concept. If consumers are recruited to a specific place, it is called a *Consumer Panel Study*. If the researchers go to a shopping center, it's called a *Shopping Mall Intercept*.

Central Location Testing: A market research testing technique that uses a permanent facility in a high-traffic location to recruit qualified respondents. This technique gives monadic and relative rankings of promotions. Diagnostic data can also be obtained using this technique. The technique also permits rankings of consumer satisfaction and can be done using the package. Costs are similar to Ballot Testing and the text can be accomplished in less time.

Clearinghouse: An organization that counts and rebates coupons sent from retailers, and, in turn, sends them to the manufacturer's redemption center for payment, or rebates coupon value and handling charges to retailer from manufacturers impress funds.

Collection Promotions: These promotions require multiple purchases to participate. Many also have some minor reward for a single purchase.

Combination Sale: A tie-in of a premium with the purchase of an item at a combination price, sometimes self-liquidating; often an on-pack.

Consignment Selling: A system of retail selling under which a supplier is paid only as his goods are sold, the retailer having the right to return undamaged goods unsold after a certain date.

Contest: A promotion device in which a prize is awarded to an entrant judged to have qualified by virtue of superior skill; entrants may be required to furnish a consideration (usually proof of product purchase), without violating lottery laws in many states. (Any element of chance involved with the prize award would make the promotion an illegal lottery.)

Continuity Program: A continuing promotion offer with inducements to make additional purchases of the product (e.g., get one teaspoon for a label and $1, and the next spoon for a label and $1, etc.).

Control Area: A geographic area in which a brand's shipment level and/or sales, under imposed conditions of normal advertising and promotion weight, may be viewed in contrast to a test area where extra advertising or promotion weight, or a change in advertising or promotion weight, is expected to increase the brand's business. In other words, an area used to help measure the effectiveness of a test.

Controlled Brand: A brand of merchandise distributed exclusively by one wholesaler, retailer, or group of stores in an area (see franchised label; private label).

Controlled Store Test: A means of testing the potential success of brand promotion offers by providing the offer in a small number of retail outlets. In the controlled store test, agency or research personnel establish and maintain test conditions and keep track of product movement. Sometimes they note customer preferences and interview customers to help evaluate consumer reaction to the promotion being tested.

Co-operative Advertising: Advertising run by a local advertiser in cooperation with a national advertiser. The latter usually supplies the copy, plates, or reproduction materials; the two share both the cost and the mention of their names.

Cooperative Association: A group of independent retailers who combine under a common name for purposes of purchasing merchandising (see voluntary chain).

Cooperative Coupons: A group of coupons that are delivered together in the same vehicle for increased efficiency or impact.

Cooperative Merchandising Agreement: A contract between a manufacturer and a retailer or wholesaler in which the manufacturer agrees to pay for specified merchandising services, such as featuring display, price reduction, etc. Abbreviated C.M.A.

Co-ops: Print ads or direct mail efforts shared by more than one different brand or advertiser.

Cost-In-The-Mail (CIM): Refers to the cost of getting an item to the customer, including the costs of the item, handling, postage, and mailing carton charges.

Cost Per Package Moved: The Cost Per Redemption divided by the required number of proof/packages per redemption.

Cost Per Return: A measure of the effectiveness of a communications medium in promoting a sales offer, contest, coupon promotion, etc., that invites a direct response from the public; computed by dividing the advertising/promotion cost involved by the number of returns.

Cost Per Redemption: A number indicating how much each coupon or offer redeemed costs a promotion's sponsor. It includes all costs and all legitimate redemptions.

Cost Per Thousand: The cost of advertising needed to reach one thousand persons, homes, or other audience units. With periodicals, the advertising rate or actual advertisement cost is divided by the circulation, interpreted as the estimated number of readers or ad-noters. With television and radio, the rate charged for commercial placement is divided by the average number of persons or homes tuned in. Abbreviated C.P.M.

Count and Recount Allowance: An allowance to a retailer or wholesaler paid for each unit of a manufacturer's specified merchandise sold to customers in a stated period of time. Involves inventory at beginning of period (count) plus purchases and final inventory (recount) to determine retailers' sales to customers during deal period.

Coupon: A certificate with a stated value (in money or merchandise) that the customer presents to a retailer to entitle the customer to a savings on a specific item at the time of purchase.

Coupon Plan: A continuous program offering a variety of premiums to consumers for collection of coupons, labels, or other tokens from one or more products.

Credit Card Offer: An offer of product or merchandise where payment may be made by credit card. Sometimes used as a method of payment for "self-liquidating" premiums.

Cross-Ruff: A coupon or assortment of coupons good for one or more products printed on or inserted in a different product package.

Dead Net Pricing: That price to the trade which is based on the maximum quantity discount when the off-invoice, merchandising allowance, and/or price pack value has been applied to the trade cost. It is typically expressed per single unit of product.

Deal: A temporary promotional offer to sell goods under terms that vary from the customary terms in a manner that favors the buyer (see allowance).

Dealer Incentive: A reward given to a retailer (dealer) in return for special quantities of purchase or special services to be supplied by the dealer.

Dealer Listing: A listing of local dealers (retailers) added to an advertisement used over a large geographical area. Such a listing can be varied by state, metropolis, or region when an advertisement is run nationally, depending on the publication's capability to produce such local editions.

Dealer Loader: Merchandise and/or travel gifts offered to the trade for purchasing or ordering out of an account's warehouse a quantity of product and giving it special in-store merchandising support, usually a display.

Delivery Time: FTC rule, which requires that mail-in offers for which the consumer has submitted payment must be shipped within the time promised or 30 days if a time is not stated. If shipment cannot be made within the required time, the supplier must notify the consumer of the delay and offer the opportunity to cancel the order.

Direct Mail Advertising: Advertising delivered directly to prospects through the mail.

Direct Marketing: The consummation of a sale of a product by mail or telephone, without the involvement of intermediaries or personal face-to-face selling. Similar to mail order advertising.

Direct Store Delivery: A delivery of merchandise from a manufacturer directly to a retailer rather than via a warehouse or wholesaler. Also drop shipment, store door delivery.

Display: A physically contiguous arrangement of goods for advertising, possibly with decorative material, intended to call attention to and prompt the sale of a product or service. Also used as a verb when referring to the act of erecting a stack of products in a selling area.

Display Advertising: Advertising in print that usually uses illustration(s) as well as type (compare to classified advertising, which is all type).

Display Allowance: A merchandising allowance granted to retailers in return for displaying merchandise, usually in special areas of the store in addition to regular shelf position.

Display Bin: An open bin, usually of heavy paper or cardboard, for the display of merchandise piled inside; usually in special areas of the store in addition to regular shelf position.

Display Card: A printed or hand-lettered sign attached to a store display (see shelf-talker).

Display Loader: A premium that is built into a display and received free by the dealer when the display is taken down (usually related to a consumer self-liquidating premium offer of the same item).

Distribution: 1. The extent to which dealers carry a retail item; usually measured by either the percentage of all dealers who carry the item (store count basis), or by the percentage of the total volume of business done by those who carry the item (ACV or All Commodity Volume basis). 2. The means by which a manufactured product reaches the customer including storage, transportation, sales, etc., and the way these elements are organized.

Distribution Allowance: A discount made by a manufacturer to a wholesaler or store chain to cover the cost of distributing a product, especially for the first time. Care must be exercised to prevent price discrimination, a violation of the Robinson-Patman Act.

Door-to-Door Sampling: Delivery of a sample to the door of a potential consumer to insure trial with a minimal amount of effort on the consumer's part.

Door-Opener: A relatively inexpensive premium item given by a door-to-door salesperson to persuade a prospect to listen to a sales presentation.

Drive Period: A limited time period scheduled by a manufacturer or wholesaler sales organization for presenting deal and promotional terms to retail sales prospects and consumers. Also promotion drive period, promotion period, canvass period.

Drop Shipment: Merchandise that is shipped directly from a manufacturer to a retailer, but is invoiced to a wholesaler, who in turn bills the retailer.

Duplication: The percent of offers or messages going to one consumer more than once rather than to separate consumers. Duplications can reduce the total coverage of an offer. Opposite: unduplicated audience.

Effective Distribution: All commodity distribution after deducting out-of-stocks from total distribution. Also, net effective distribution.

End Aisle Display: A special retail store display in which the promoted product is prominently positioned at the end aisle gondola location.

Expiration Date: The last day on which a consumer can use a coupon or place an order for an offer.

Face Value: Actual cash discount value (for the consumer) of a coupon when redeemed at a retail outlet.

Factory Pack: A special pack produced at the factory that requires some change from normal production procedure and occasionally can require different shelf space in the retail store.

Fair Trade: A principle according to which retailers agree to sell an item at no less than the price agreed upon between the manufacturer and other retailers in the area. Until suspended, such practices were often enforced by a state law (fair-trade law).

Feature: 1. A retail item being given special sales attention, especially co-operative advertising of a price reduction. 2. An important characteristic of a product or service. 3. To give a retail item special sales promotion.

Field Activated Promotion: A promotion initiated by a sales representative and a retailer or store manager.

Flag: A "flag" on the front (and often on the sides) of a package refers to the graphic treatment (shape) and corresponding copy that calls attention to a promotional incentive.

Flanker: A new product that is marketed under an existing brand name, but is intended for use in a different (but usually related) product category from the *parent* brand's original product line. Also flanker item.

Floor Stand: A standing bin for the display of retail merchandise.

F.O.B.: These initials stand for "free on board." The expression comes from the fact that goods sold "F.O.B. a certain location" will be loaded aboard a freight car or truck at that point at the expense of the seller. From that point, the buyer must pay all freight and delivery charges.

Focus Group: This is a qualitative form of consumer research that involves inviting 10–12 people to a "group" discussion about certain brand or usage habits. These sessions are moderated by a professional researcher and frequently viewed by client or agency members from behind a two-way mirror so that their presence does not inhibit discussion. Focus groups are most valuable in helping to design questions for quantitative research, or to familiarize copy writers with consumer terminology, or to look for major negatives in copy or promotion ideas; but not for management decision making.

Forced Distribution: Automatic distribution of a product by retailers as a consequence of anticipated or actual customer demand created by advertising or consumer promotion. In test markets, automatic placement of products in panels of cooperating stores.

Form/Certificate: Printed description of a mail-in offer that includes space for the respondent's name and address. Required by most manufacturers for compliance to the offer terms.

Free Goods: Merchandise that is conferred without charge or obligation. Formerly this was a synonym for bonus goods, but this use is discouraged as misleading by the Federal Trade Commission.

Free Mail-In (FMI): A premium consumers may obtain in the mail without charge by sending in proof(s)-of-purchase.

Free Offer: An offer that does not cost any amount of money.

Free-Standing Insert (FSI): A preprinted advertisement in single or multiple page form that is inserted loose into newspapers, particularly Sunday editions and supplements.

Frequency Discount: A reduction in advertising rates based on the number of insertions or commercials in a given time period.

Frontload: To schedule the use of the bulk of a budget for the first part of a planned promotion period; serves to assure that all of a budget is used for its originally designated ends.

Fulfillment: The processing of consumer requests for mail-in (or phone-in) offers such as refunds, premiums, coupons, or samples.

Full Disclosure: Manufacturers of specified products must disclose certain kinds of specific information about them; for example, processed food makers list the nutritional value of their products on labels and in advertisements.

G

Game: A promotional vehicle that includes a number of predetermined, pre-seeded winning tickets in the overall, fixed universe of pieces. Participants may learn immediately if they have won a particular prize category. Sometimes called Instant Winner Sweepstakes.

Generics: A category of unbranded products usually sold in a plain, one-color printed container by a retail account at substantial savings to the consumer compare to national brand items.

Gift Enterprise: Legal term referring to an illegal lottery.

Giveaway: 1. Merchandise or services given away for promotional purposes. 2. A television or radio show where merchandise is given away to contestants or to members of the audience.

Gross Rating Point: A unit of measurement of audience size for television, radio, or outdoor advertising, equal to 1 percent of the total potential audience universe; used to measure the exposure of one or more programs or commercials without regard to multiple exposure of the same advertising to individuals. Also, the product of media reach times exposure frequency. Abbreviated G.R.P.

Group Promotions: A promotion involving several brands from the same or different companies, usually integrated by a theme or mutually shared promotional overlay like a sweepstakes or refund.

Gummed Proofs: Paper "cuts" or pictures supplied to sales representatives for making simple advertising layouts for newspapers or handbills.

H

Handbill: A circular that is intended for distribution by hand either to persons encountered on the street or to homes, offices, etc. Also throwaway, flyer.

Handling Allowance: An allowance from a manufacturer to a distributor or retailer for handling merchandise requiring special attention or display (must be offered to all competing retailers).

Handling/Postage Charge: A charge covering the cost of preparing and mailing a premium or refund.

I

Island Display: A retail store display that is accessible on all sides. Also, island.

Image Related: Promotions that work to enhance a brand's name, use, or perceived quality.

Impulse Purchase: Purchase of consumer goods that had not been planned in advance.

Instant Redeemable Coupon: A coupon placed on the outside surface of the package. The coupon can be removed easily without destroying the package and used as a price reduction on the current purchase.

Instant Winner Promotion: A prize promotion in which the participant knows immediately if he/she has won a prize.

In-Ad Coupon: A coupon placed in a store or chain's own retail advertisement, redeemable on the specified product only at the particular store or chain. Also in-ad.

Incentive: Cash, merchandise, or travel offered to consumers, salespeople, or dealers as a tangible reward for a purchase or sales performance. A premium.

In-House: A term used to describe a company that implements one or more services within the company as opposed to contracting with outside suppliers.

In-Pack Coupon: A redeemable coupon enclosed in a product's package for potential later use by the product's buyer; may be redeemed on a subsequent purchase of the same product, or on a different product (cross coupon).

In-Pack Premium: A premium item enclosed inside a product's package; usually offered with a full measure of product at no extra charge.

Insert: A special page printed by the advertiser and forwarded to a publisher who binds it in the publication. Also, an advertising tabloid placed inside a newspaper (see free-standing insert).

Institutional Advertising: Advertising whose purpose is to create goodwill for a company rather than to advertise goods or services.

Investment Spending: Increased expenditures for advertising or promotion for a product or service, typically funded by temporary reductions in the profit contribution in the expectation of future increases in sales and profits (see business-building test; incremental spending; payout).

Invoice: A bill sent to a customer for merchandise shipped to it. It lists quantities, brands, prices, and date of shipment.

Joint Promotion: A mutually beneficial merchandising event with one or more outside companies promoting under a unifying theme or concept.

Keeper: A premium offered in direct-mail marketing for accepting a free trial of the sale merchandise which is kept by the consumer even if the sale merchandise is returned.

Key Account: 1. A major customer, from the viewpoint of a manufacturer or a distributor. 2. A major client of an advertising agency.

Key Code: To code an advertisement or coupon so that responses can be identified by carrier medium or distribution location. This usually involves putting a code number or letter in a coupon or in the advertiser's address so that the particular advertisement or medium producing an inquiry can be identified. Also sometimes just called a key.

Line Extension: A new product form, flavor, or formulation marketed under an existing brand name, intended for use in the same category as the "parent" brand's original product, or product line, while being designed to draw new users to the brand's franchise from products competitive to the original product; e.g., "dry" and "oily" new shampoo products using the brand name of an existing shampoo are line extensions (see flanker; brand extension).

Logo: The artistic rendition of a brand name on a package. Also used in promotion materials.

Loss Leader: A retail item advertised at an attractively low price, often below cost, in order to attract customers to a store for the purchase of other, more profitable items.

Lottery: A plan categorically illegal in commercial sales promotion, which awards a prize on the basis of chance and requires consideration to enter. Becomes a legal sweepstakes or game when consideration is removed, or a contest when the chance is eliminated. Only governmental units like states may operate legal lotteries in the United States.

M

Mail-in Offer: A promotion requiring the respondent to mail proofs-of-purchase, tear-off sheets, receipts, etc., to receive the item/money being offered.

Makegood: An advertisement run without charge by a medium as an adjustment for error usually because of omission or poor reproduction.

Manufacturing Representative: A sales representative of a manufacturer who may be either a salaried employee or a broker acting as an agent for several manufacturers on commission. Also manufacturer's agent.

Market Area: A geographical section of the United States that becomes a cohesive area for marketing. It tends to have the same distribution patterns, the same supply sources, and frequently, political boundaries.

Market Development Index: The number of units or dollar value of all brands of a product or service category that have been sold per thousand population within an area in a stated period, usually a year. Also category development. Loosely, a product's, service's, or category's degree or rate of usage in markets and market segments to which it is available.

Market Potential: Sales volume for a product or service that is available to or desired by a supplier; influenced by category development and often expressed in terms of share of market.

Market Share: The percentage of a category's sales, in terms of dollars or units, that is accounted for by a brand, line, or company.

Marketing: The act of taking a product and moving it from its place of manufacture to the ultimate user at a profitable price. Includes development, design, packaging, advertising, promotion, pricing, selling, and delivery.

Marketing Concept: A management philosophy that holds that the best means to satisfy corporate objectives is to focus all corporate efforts to find ways to permit customers to satisfy their desires.

Marketing Mix: The levels and interplay of the constituent elements of a product's or service's marketing efforts, including product attributes, pricing, promotion, advertising, merchandising, distribution, and marketing spending, especially as decisions relating to these elements affect sales results.

Marketing Plan: 1. A strategy for marketing a product or service. 2. A comprehensive document containing background, rationale, and supportive detail regarding a marketer's objectives and strategies. Also plan.

Markup: The increase, in either dollars and cents or a percentage, between cost and the selling price.

Match and Win Sweepstakes: A form of sweepstakes in which the consumer must take their symbol/number entry, which appears in print media, to the product or store display to determine if they have won a prize and what it is.

Matte: A printing term for not glossy; without strong highlights; a matte finish. Also mat.

Medium: Any vehicle used to convey an advertising message, such as television, magazines, newspapers, or direct mail. Also, the methods and tools used by an artist, such as a pen and ink, crayon, or photography.

Merchandising: 1. Marketing activities, including sales and promotion, designed to make product available, attractive, and conspicuous in a retail store. 2. Solicitation of salespeople and retailer support for a marketing effort.

Merchandising Committee: A group of executives appointed by a store chain, wholesaler, or the like to decide on the acceptance of new products, manufacturer's promotions, etc. Also buying committee.

Mint Condition: Coupons that appear gang-cut or carefully stacked. Coupons that are not soiled or dirty or even bent, wrinkled, or torn, and unlikely to have been properly redeemed. Redemption of coupons presented either by persons who have not made the purchases the coupons are intended to promote, or by retailers who have not redeemed the coupons in the normal course of business with properly qualified customers.

Motivation Research: Research that attempts to relate behavior to underlying desires, emotions, and intentions, in contrast to research that enumerates behavior or describes a situation; it relies heavily on the use of techniques adapted from psychology and other social sciences.

Multi-Buyer: A person who has purchased more than once from a firm, on different occasions. May be called a repeat buyer.

Merge/Purge: A computer process whereby lists may be "merged" together to facilitate zip code sequencing and testing segments, and "purged" of duplicate names, pander names, and undesirable names or names that are to be saved for later mailing.

N

Near-Pack: A premium item offered free or for a discounted price with the retail purchase of another product, and positioned near to (but not touching) this product at the point-of-sale. Also near-pack premium. A promotion making use of the near-pack premium. Also near-pack event. A container or receptacle used to hold and display near-pack premiums.

New Item Slotting Allowance: An allowance offered by manufacturers to motivate the trade to stock a new item. This allowance is based on absolute total dollars, not a per case rate.

New Product: A product that has been in distribution, available to its ultimate consumer, for less than six months. Also, a product bearing a new brand name, or a newly introduced flanker item or line extension; occasionally used loosely to refer to an improved product of an existing brand, or a new size.

Nielsen Drug (Food) Index: Reports on the market movement and inventory of products, by type and brand, through panels of drug stores and food stores.

Nixie: A piece of mail that is undeliverable.

Objective: A statement of the desired outcome of a promotion containing:

1. Marketing goal.
2. Quantifiable level of achievement.
3. Time and place in which the activity will take place.

Off-Invoice (OI): A deduction from an invoice from a manufacturer or wholesaler to a retailer normally made in exchange for the retailer's promotional efforts. Also off-invoice allowance or deal.

Off Label: A special reduced savings offer marked over the regular label of an item (see price pack). Also, an inferior grade of a brand, which is discount priced and specially labeled.

Offset: The modern application of lithography process printing from a thin metal plate where the reaction of water and greasy ink play the important role. In the process, the plates are sensitized to receive ink on the area desired and not in the remaining area, which is covered with a thin film of water. The main difference in offset vs. direct lithography is that the printing plate is never in contact with the paper but "offsets" its linked image on a rubber blanket roller, which in turn transfers the impression to the paper.

On-Pack: A premium, advertising matter, coupon, etc., attached to or part of the exterior of a product package.

One-Cent Sale: A promotion offer where the consumer purchases one package at the normal price and the second package for one cent.

Organizer: A sheet of paper, usually carried in a binder, which presents pertinent reasons for a dealer to purchase or promote an item. In the presentation, the sales representative "organizes' his talk around the points covered on the sheet and uses the written words to reinforce the spoken.

Out of Stock: Refers to a condition where something that is normally sold is presently not available, especially for retail sale, because of inadequate supply or insufficient distribution support.

Outsert: Printed material attached to the outside of, rather than inserted into, a package. Also, package outsert.

Overlay: In a printing sense, any sheet, image, printed matter, etc., superimposed on an existing design or piece of artwork. Also, can refer to a promotional theme structure lending unity to the elements of a promotion effort.

Overrun: A number of additional copies of a printed piece in excess of those required for general circulation, distribution, or quantity ordered. Also, excessive production of items, creating a manufacturer's overstock.

Package Insert: Advertising material packed with a shipment of a product, usually to advertise a different product.

Packaged Goods: Products wrapped or packaged by the manufacturer, normally of uniform sizes. Items are used broadly and frequently consumed; typically sold through food, drug, and mass merchandiser retail stores.

Payout: A profit return on an investment of marketing expenditures, usually above the ongoing spending rate. Also payback (see investment spending).

Performance Allowance: A rebate of a portion of the purchase price of goods provided to those retailers who agree to perform cooperative merchandising services such as advertising or display; paid after the retailer provides proof of performance.

Pica: A unit of measurement for type or other printed material; six picas equal one inch.

Pilot Test: A preliminary test run on a limited basis to determine if broader testing is warranted.

Planogram: A valuable merchandising tool used by manufacturer's salespeople to present a product category shelf space allocation recommendation to the trade for their stores. Designed to insure that a manufacturer's product is getting a fair share of store space.

Point-of-Purchase: The place at which a customer encounters a retail item that he or she may buy. Also point-of-sale, P-O-P, P-O-S.

P.O.P.A.I.: Point of Purchase Advertising Institute. An association of printers and manufacturers formed to disseminate information on point-of-sale display materials promoting both their use and efficiency.

Pole Piece: A display backcard in a retail store, mounted on a pole for greater visibility. Also, spectacular.

Pop-up: A special die-cut folder made so that when opened part of it rises from the center fold of the publication.

Pop-up Coupon: A tear-off perforated coupon that is stitched into the binding of a periodical as a separate, small space unit.

Position: In marketing strategy, the consumer perception of a product's or service's benefit or benefits, in comparison to its competition, which its manufacturer attempts to create and encourage via advertising, packaging, and/or promotion. Also positioning, product positioning, product position. Also, the placement of an advertisement in a publication in terms of page number, side, etc., or of a commercial in a program. Also positioning.

Premium: 1. Merchandise offered free or at a reduced price as an inducement to buy a different item or items. 2. An extra charge, as for a preferred advertising position or for special treatment of advertisements. Also premium price. 3. Noting or pertaining to a product's pricing level as compared to most competitive products.

Premium Container: A container for a retail product that is reusable after the original contents are gone, hence functions as a premium. Sometimes called a container pack.

Premium Pack: A package of a product offering an item, usually in either in-pack or on-pack form.

Premium Rep: A specialized manufacturer's representative serving premium users; a commissioned salesperson representing several different manufacturers or premium supply sources.

Pre-Pack Display (floorstands, pre-assembled displays, PADs): Displays with merchandise (product and/or premiums) placed inside at the plant and shipped as one unit rather than shipping display pieces, premiums, and product separately. This procedure makes it relatively easy for the retail outlet to display the product.

Preprice: To mark a retail item with its retail price before it is delivered to a retail store.

Preprint: 1. A printing of periodical advertising on separate sheets before actual publication; done by an advertiser for special purposes, e.g., to serve as retail displays or in order to merchandise his advertising support to retailers. 2. A color newspaper advertisement (e.g., spectacular printed on one side of rotogravure stock that is then supplied pretrimmed to the newspaper, which does its own printing on the opposite side.

Price Pack: A specially produced retail package announcing a temporary reduction from the standard retail price, used as a promotional inducement to purchasers. Also price-off pack, cents off.

Private Label: A wholesaler's or retailer's label bearing his brand name.

Prize: Reward given to winner in a contest, sweepstakes, or chance promotion; also sometimes referred to as salespeople's incentive award, and official state lottery awards.

Promotion: 1. A marketing tool that is a temporary effort to create extra interest in the purchase of a product or service by offering values in excess of those customarily afforded by such purchases; includes temporary discounts, allowances, premium offers, coupons, contests, sweepstakes, etc. Also sales promotion. 2. Loosely, any effort to encourage the purchase of a product or service.

Promotion Allowance: A rebate or discount offered by a manufacturer or his agent to a wholesaler or retailer who agrees to promote the product purchased under allowance. Also merchandising allowance.

Promotion Marketing: An element in the marketing mix designed to stimulate consumer actions and/or dealer effectiveness through various incentives.

Promotion Strategy: A statement of how a marketer plans to meet defined, measurable objectives or goals.

Proof Seals: This term usually refers to a specially printed or affixed shape that serves as a proof-of-purchase for a specific rather than an ongoing offer.

Proof-of-Purchase: Evidence that a consumer has purchased a product or service, as a receipt, label, package, or portion thereof, etc.; usually specified by manufacturers as appropriate evidence of product purchase in compliance with the terms of a mail-in offer. Often abbreviated as P-O-Ps.

Purchase-with-Purchase: An offer that allows the consumer to purchase an additional product at an attractive, reduced price. The reduced price is not available if the basic purchase is not made.

Push Money: A special reward given by manufacturers or service sources to agents' or dealers' employees for encouraging the sale of their own goods rather than a competitor's; usually paid on each sale, regardless of whether it is pushed or not. Abbreviated P.M., spiff.

Quantity Discount: A discount from list price for buying greater quantities of merchandise.

Redeem: To fulfill the requirements of a consumer promotional offer, as a coupon or trading stamps, in a prescribed manner resulting in receipt of goods at a reduced price or free. Redemption.

Redemption: 1. The cashing in of coupons when merchandise is purchased, or trading stamps in order to obtain discounts or premiums. 2. The percentage of coupons or trading stamps issued that are eventually cashed in. Also redemption rate.

Redemption Center: A place where premium merchandise is made available in exchange for trading stamps.

Redemption Rate: The actual or expected percentage of coupons, proofs-of-purchase, etc., that have been used by consumers.

Redemption Reserve: Funds put aside by a stamp firm or the user of a coupon plan to pay the cost of merchandise for future redemptions, which may come in several years after stamps or coupons are originally issued. Check IRS regulations.

Redemptions per case (RPC): A number used to indicate how many coupons are redeemed to move a case of product. The figure is calculated by taking the product's volume split of shipments by size over the most recent 12 months, converting cases to physical units and assuming that redemptions fall proportionately across the sizes. Obviously, if a coupon is size-directed, this will have a bearing upon the RPC figure.

Referral Premium: An item that is offered to a satisfied customer who refers the seller to a friend who may purchase a product. Also "use-the-user plan."

Refund: 1. A promotion device that offers purchasers a return of some or all of an amount of money or coupons when they send proofs-of-purchase to the manufacturer. 2. To issue such a return.

Reusable Container Pack: A container for retail product, which is reusable after the original contents are gone, and hence functions as a premium. Sometimes called a container pack.

Rotogravure (Roto): A form of printing where the image is chemically etched upon a copper cylinder. Most Sunday magazine supplements are printed by the rotogravure process on various grades of coated paper. Also refers to special color circulars run by retail accounts to highlight special product savings.

Run-of-Press: The status of an advertisement positioned at the publisher's discretion. Also, run-of-book, run-of-paper. Abbreviated R.O.P.

Salable Sample: A product sample or smaller-than-normal trial size, which is sold at a normal price at retail.

Sales Contest: A competition open to a company's sales personnel or to prospects, structured to reward superior performance or unusually large purchases (see sales incentive).

Sales Incentive: A reward in excess of salary or commission provided to a salesperson in return for achieving or exceeding a stated sales goal (see sales contest).

Sales Promotion: See promotion marketing.

Sampling: Delivery of a product to the consumer with the intent of encouraging trial of the product. The size of the sample will vary depending on consumer behavior and costs.

Satellite Switching: A group of brands that consumers consider to be equal and acceptable for use.

Scratch-and-Sniff: Trademark. A micro-encapsulation process, used to convey a specific scent to readers of print media; such scents are released by scratching a properly treated area of paper or scratching a tape affixed to the printed piece, which breaks the microscopic-sized, plastic "scent bubbles" thus releasing the aroma.

Seasonality Index: A measurement that expresses the variation in sales of goods or services, for a brand or category, from an even distribution throughout the year as influenced by seasonal factors; e.g., suntan lotions have an extremely high summer seasonality index.

Self-Liquidator: A premium having a cost fully covered by the purchase price for which it is offered. Also, a display unit provided by a manufacturer in return for payment by a retailer covering its cost. Self-liquidating.

Share: 1. The percentage of total retail purchases, in terms of dollars or units, for a given category of product that is enjoyed by any one brand in that category. Also share of market, share of retail sales. 2. In a rating survey the percentage of the television or radio audience in a coverage area that is tuned to the program being rated.

Share Point: One percent of the total market or audience.

Shelf: 1. A retail store's physical facility for displaying products above the floor in areas open to customers; usually, a long, narrow series of six or seven horizontal tiers (see rack). 2. In current availability, as off-the-shelf.

Shelf Card: A display card designed to be set up on a shelf in a retail store.

Shelf Extender: A traylike extension that projects outward from a retail store shelf, used for special displays or as a means of increasing the regular shelf display. Also extender.

Shelf Pack: A container for retail items of sufficiently small size to permit the full amount to be placed on a shelf with ordinary clearance height.

Shelf Space: The amount of point-of-purchase space occupied by a type of merchandise in a retail store; measured in terms of square feet, linear feet, or number of facings.

Shelf-Talker: A printed advertising message designed to hang over the edge of a retail store shelf.

Short-Shipped: An order that has been shipped incomplete, usually caused by shortage of stock or warehouse error. Results in out-of-stock at retail level.

Significant Difference: The size of the difference is sufficiently large such that there is less than one chance in 20 that it could have occurred by chance alone when there is not a true difference.

Slick: A proof printed on glossy (coated) paper, clean in appearance and suitable for reproduction. Also enamel proof.

Slippage: 1. Those people who purchase a product with the intent of claiming a promotion reward for such a purchase (e.g., send for a refund, or premium, or redeem a coupon), who fail to fulfill this intent. 2. The ratio between such purchases, and purchases by those people who claim such a reward; usually stated as a percentage of total purchases. Also slippage rate.

Slot: Describes a physical space in a trade warehouse used to store a product or price variation.

Sorry Copy: A printed message, usually on the cardboard backing of certificate pads, that indicates the address for obtaining the offer certificate by mail, or provides details for responding to the offer. This provides the consumer with a way to participate in a mail-in offer when all of the certificates have been removed by previous shoppers.

Space Allocation: The amount of shelf space allotted to a product or group of related products in a retail store.

Special Canvass: An intensive round of sales visits to a chain or group of retail stores intended to obtain support for a new brand or promotion.

Special Purchase Allowance: An allowance granted by a manufacturer or wholesaler to a retailer, made in addition to a basic merchandising allowance for the purchase of goods within a stated period. Abbreviated S.P.A. (must be offered to all competing retailers).

Spending Split: The percentage or dollar amounts allocated by a marketer's plans to each of the three key marketing spending elements, that is, advertising, consumer promotion, and trade promotion.

Spiff: See Push Money.

Spillout: Product shipments that go to retail outlets outside a given marketing/sales area. May also refer to TV messages that go outside of a test area.

Split Run (in periodical printing): A press run that carries two or more different forms of an advertiser's message in different copies or issues, to test the effectiveness of one advertisement against another or to appeal to regional or other specific markets.

Standard Metropolitan Statistical Area: A federally designated urban area consisting of counties that meet certain standards for population, urban character, and economic and social integration with the county or counties serving as the urban center. Abbreviated S.M.S.A.

Storecast: A radiolike presentation of music, advertisements, etc., through a sound system in a retail store.

Store Check: An examination of the merchandise carried by a retail store by persons not on the store's staff, and usually not a salesperson; done as a means of sales or marketing management intelligence gathering.

Store Door Delivery: Delivery of product or materials directly to a store by a manufacturer or his employee.

Sunday Supplement: Any of various non-news sections included with a Sunday newspaper, such as comics, or television schedules, FSIs, and especially general interest magazine sections.

Supermarket: A large, departmentalized self-service food store, often with a large variety of nonfood items; a warehouse supplying the store regularly and a large parking lot for patrons are generally regarded as characteristics of a true supermarket. Some industry sources reserve the term "supermarket" for stores whose annual All Commodity Dollar Volume is $1 million or more.

Sweepstakes: A chance promotion involving the giveaway of products and services of value to a randomly selected group of those who have submitted qualified entries. To prevent infringement of lottery laws, such promotions do not require qualifying entrants to provide a monetary consideration, such as a purchase. The odds of winning depend on the number of entries received.

Swing Buyers: Purchasers who will change their brands to take advantage of a promotion offer.

Target Market: A group of the population believed to hold the greatest sales potential for the product. The advertiser often tries to isolate media that reach the target market and designs messages that communicate with its members.

Tear-Pads: Tear-pads or "take-one" pads consist of several sheets in a pad, designed to communicate the details of a consumer offer at the point-of-purchase (usually affixed to a shelf or used in conjunction with a large piece of display material).

Tearsheet: An unbound page from a periodical showing an article, advertisement, etc., as printed; used as a proof or as an extra copy.

Test Market: A limited geographical area in which a test of an alternate marketing plan variable or new product is conducted (see sales area test).

Test Market Translation: A conversion of a national marketing plan to test market dimensions. Or, conversely, a projection of test market results to a larger geographic area. Also translation.

30-Day Rule: FTC rule, which requires that mail-in offers for which the consumer has submitted payment must be shipped within the time promised or 30 days if a time is not stated. If shipment cannot be made within the required time, the supplier must notify the consumer of the delay and offer the opportunity to cancel the order.

Tie-In Promotion: A single promotion event intended to encourage the sale of more than one product or brand.

Tip-In: A preprinted advertising page or card inserted into a periodical whose regular page size is larger.

Tip-On: A coupon, sample, or reply card glued by one edge to a page of advertising.

Trading Stamp: Any of various stamps offered as premiums with merchandise purchases, the number given being in proportion to the total sale amount; such stamps, in specific numbers, are redeemable for specific types of merchandise.

Traffic Builder: A relatively low-cost premium offered free as an inducement to a consumer to visit a store for a demonstration.

Travel Incentive: A trip, group or individual, offered to salespeople or dealers for meeting specific sales quotas. Often tied in with sales meetings at resort areas.

Trial: A purchase or use of a product or service by a consumer interested in personally evaluating its value, as a step preceding a subsequent purchase or regular use.

Trial Size: A product package of small size and low price, intended or serving to attract product trial.

Twin Pack: A promotion event whereby two product units are sold as one, at a discounted price; usually implemented by packaging, which physically unites the two units and flags the savings offered.

Two-for-One: A promotion that offers consumers two units of product for the price of one.

U

Universal Product Code (UPC): A special code number and striped visual code on the package used by optical scanners at checkout counters to automatically record the brand and its price.

V

Volume Merchandising Allowance: An allowance offered to a retailer for the purchase of large volumes of goods; offered as an encouragement to the retailer to merchandise the goods aggressively. Abbreviated V.M.A. See quantity discount.

Voluntary Chain: A group of independent stores that combine under a common trade name for purchasing and merchandising purposes, often under the sponsorship of a wholesaler. Also voluntary association, voluntary group, voluntary.

Voluntary Store: An independent retailer who is a member of a voluntary chain.

W

Warehouse Inventory Reduction Allowance: A specific payment offered to the trade for case of product moved from the warehouse to retail during a specified period of time. This allowance is measured on a count-recount basis.

Warehouse Store: A retail store, usually of large size, offering discount prices by means of eliminating or reducing such services as carryouts, deliveries, price marking of items, shelf stocking, etc.

When appropriate, The Promotion Marketing Association of America, Inc., will send new glossary additions until the next publication date.

PMAA
322 Eighth Avenue
Suite 1201
New York, NY 1001
212-206-1100
Fax 212-929-1408

INDEX

G

H